TV GENRES

TV GENRES

A
Handbook
and
Reference Guide

Edited by
BRIAN G. ROSE

Robert S. Alley, *Advisory Editor*

Greenwood Press
Westport, Connecticut • London, England

Library of Congress Cataloging in Publication Data
Main entry under title:

TV genres.

Bibliography: p.
Includes index.
1. Television programs—United States—Addresses,
essays, lectures. 2. Television plays—History and
criticism—Addresses, essays, lectures. I. Rose, Brian
Geoffrey. II. Alley, Robert S., 1932– . III. Title:
T.V. genres.
PN1992.3.U5T88 1985 791.45′75′0973 84–22460
ISBN 0-313-23724-7 (lib. bdg.)

Library of Congress Catalog Card Number: 84–22460
ISBN: 0-313-23724-7

First published in 1985

Greenwood Press
A division of Congressional Information Service, Inc.
88 Post Road West, Westport, Connecticut 06881

Printed in the United States of America

10 9 8 7 6 5 4 3 2 1

Contents

Preface

Like most popular entertainments, television thrives on a multiplicity of formats, which all seem to coexist in a happy jumble. The older television gets (the medium is now in its fifth decade of commercially supported existence), the more its once rigid genres blend into one another. Situation comedies are now frequently charged with melodramatic undercurrents; the previously somber instincts of daytime serials are often interrupted with dashes of wild humor; police dramas are laced with aspects of hip comedy; and news programs are sometimes indistinguishable from the talk and variety shows that surround them.

Nevertheless, television formats, like the formats of literature and motion pictures, are still usually guided by a few basic principles that are readily understood by producers and public alike. These principles are at the heart of a genre's appeal and play an important role in keeping a genre alive and popular.

But what are the observances and rules that give television formats their distinctive qualities? What separates the TV situation comedy from earlier comedy forms? How does a television detective differ from his literary or film counterparts? Why is the talk show one of television's few genuinely original genres? What principles have reality-based formats been forced to adopt from the entertainment formats that rub up against them during the course of the broadcast day?

This book is an attempt to answer these questions by systematically examining the central elements in a wide variety of television genres. The nineteen formats selected for this volume reflect the medium's astonishing diversity. With the exception of the Western, every one of these programming formulas still constitutes an active part of the TV schedule.

As is obvious from glancing at the chapter titles, television has not really added a significant number of new formats to the existing body of popular entertainment. What it has done is to alter the terms of existing formulas by reshaping them to its specific demands. The medium's relatively small screen, its lack of visual clarity, its time restrictions, the mighty influence of sponsors, and the sometimes presumed standards of the public have all played important roles in establishing the operating principles of most TV genres. The "Historical Development" section included in every chapter offers a way to study how these forces have helped guide a genre's direction during the decades of its television incarnation; the "Themes and Issues" section explores the specific factors that have been most prominent in making each genre distinctively identifiable. To amplify these points, every chapter concludes with an annotated bibliography to help readers search for additional sources of programming information and a "Videography" that lists the key programs in a format's history.

The wide range of television genres that make up the typical broadcast day testifies to television's programming diversity. This seems especially clear when one considers the mutations and hybrid genres that keep appearing to satisfy what appears to be a new, restless TV viewership. Still, it is possible to classify the varying styles and impulses of most television formats as either fictional or reality-based, and that is the approach used in arranging the chapters of this anthology. Chapters two through nine deal with programming that is clearly fictional. The tenth chapter on docudramas is a transition from the artfully dramatic and imaginary to those formats that depend on some essential relationship with reality (chapters eleven through fifteen). Finally, the last four chapters concern formats that are far broader in concept than the more specific genres discussed earlier. Religious programming, cultural and educational programming, children's programming, and advertising all share an expansive range that can easily accommodate both fictional and nonfictional forms.

It is my hope that this volume will prove useful to everyone who has an interest in the history and central concerns of television's formats. Scholars, I trust, will find it useful as a resource guide; each chapter not only offers a detailed historical survey and an analysis of a specific genre's principal themes and issues, but also a comprehensive bibliography. In addition, each chapter concludes with a "Videography" that cites a dozen or so programs that are of special significance. The "Videography" also provides brief information on a show's network history and its primary stars; readers eager for more detailed casting data are advised to consult Tim Brooks and Earle Marsh's definitive reference work, *The Complete Directory to Prime Time Network TV Shows 1946–Present* (New York: Ballantine Books, 1981).

This book would not have been possible without the help and cooperation of many people. Its impetus came from Marilyn Brownstein of Greenwood Press, who approached me in 1980 to put together a book of scholarly chapters on the relatively uncharted subject of TV genres. In the three years it took to complete this project, Marilyn has been a constant source of encouragement and a trusted editorial advisor. One of her many fruitful suggestions was to contact Robert Alley, whose assistance I have greatly valued in his role as the book's advisory editor. He played a large part in helping me determine structural guidelines and in recommending the names of suitable contributors. My editor at Greenwood,

Cynthia Harris, has been understanding and gracious in guiding me through the many difficulties I encountered in assembling this book.

I would also, of course, like to thank the eighteen contributors whose scholarship made this book possible. Their cooperation, generosity of ideas and time, and willingness to work under what were often strict deadlines helped make my position as editor much more easy and enjoyable. Special thanks are also due to Tom O'Brien of NBC's Programming Analysis Department. Tom provided a wealth of information that I simply could not have found elsewhere, and always did so with great cheerfulness.

Finally, I want to acknowledge the prodigious assistance of Kassie Schwan, who participated in this project as actively as I did. Her clearheadedness, sharp editorial judgment, and unflagging enthusiasm proved to be the most important fuel in helping this volume see the light of day.

Brooklyn, New York
September 1984

TV GENRES

1

Introduction

BRIAN G. ROSE

Television is by far the most popular source of entertainment in America. The medium may not offer the most diverse assemblage of formulas, but it certainly commands the largest audience for its daily mixtures of drama, comedy, romance, and information. Its once mighty competitors in the realm of variety production have lost their hold on loyal patrons in its wake. Hollywood, which formerly attracted great hordes of weekly customers for its offerings of Westerns, mysteries, and melodramas, is now concerned with creating mega-blockbusters for release during peak vacation periods. The film industry's profits may potentially be greater, but the momentum of steady consumption, fostered by the studio system for more than forty years up to the early 1950s, has disappeared. Radio, which used to provide a rich diet of every conceivable type of entertainment, has long since abandoned variety and massive general audiences in favor of strict musical or conversational formats with precise demographic targeting.

A vital factor in television's popularity can be clearly traced to its absorption of radio and Hollywood's central formulas and techniques. The genres that flourished at the movies and on the radio (and in popular literature) were a natural choice for the home screen, since they had already proven their appeal for decades, if not centuries. Television's voracious need for material, especially in its early years when the motion picture industry refused to cooperate, forced the networks to re-create and transform reliable formats in any way they could. Radio was the principal raiding ground, as high rated programs were moved over, or, in some cases, broadcast on both media simultaneously. Radio's scheduling and production traditions were also expropriated. TV shows were originally made in 15 (and later 30) minute blocks that were aired at times of the day when their content and advertising intentions seemed most appropriate.

The most popular programs during television's infancy reflect the debt the new medium owed its electronic predecessor. During the first three years of Nielsen ratings (which cover the 1950 through 1952 seasons), transplanted radio shows (e.g., "The Lone Ranger," "Dragnet," or "Jack Benny") or radio formats (e.g., the variety show, dramatic anthology, or character comedy) dominate the top ten. The genres that radio created (the soap opera, quiz program, and news documentary) or transposed and adopted (the situation comedy and most of its dramatic and musical formulas) would all make the move to television, usually with renewed if not greater popularity.

The necessity to fill the broadcast schedule prompted television programmers and producers to not only continue searching for other workable formats, but also to begin taking into account the distinctive qualities television could bring to entertainment material. While TV shared many similarities with radio in terms of production, personalities, and audience appeals, its visual nature inevitably altered the terms and the experience of an audio-only genre. Obviously, motion picture styles and practices could be used to transform "Dragnet" or "The Lone Ranger" for television, but the medium's formal limitations (its small screen, lack of subtlety in contrast and details) presented new challenges. One solution, reached initially through budgeting and technical restrictions, soon became an aesthetic standard. Since there was little money at first to shoot programs from scenic locations or to utilize elaborate sets, close-ups of performers became a practical way to compensate for what wasn't there behind them (or could barely be seen if it was). Later this concentrated attention on faces and gestures would be celebrated by many critics as one of television's most powerful assets.[1]

The diminished visual qualities of television, in comparison with movies, also helped foster an approach that emphasized intimacy rather than panoramic sweep. Since the TV image lacked depth and shading, foregrounding quickly became the principal stylistic technique. The television camera centered its concern on the drama of personality and how individuals reacted to the conflicts and the issues directly in front of them. The Western and mystery formulas adapted for TV made a point of stressing domestic aspects. The family on the range or the pseudo-family of the police station or office served as the chief playing ground; the difficulties they encountered together guided the action from program to program.

The personal and familiar qualities the medium emphasized were also a reflection of its physical presence in the homes of its viewers. By literally appearing in people's living rooms, characters on TV programs were part of the family environment. The stars and formats that flourished were those which exploited this connection by highlighting friendliness and likability or by strongly reaffirming the conventional codes of domestic morality. Exoticism or passion was not as welcome on the small screen as was an easy manner or an ingratiatingly lovable personality.

Television's intimate focus would inevitably transform most of the genres it touched. Popular radio formats like the variety and musical shows, which had their origin in vaudeville, underwent a shift in emphasis once they arrived on television in the early 1950s. Guest-star appearances and a wide range of entertainment were no longer enough. The medium's demand for sustained visual interest and camera appeal made the role of the program host of central importance, especially since his or her charm and interactive skills were now so visibly apparent. Performers such as Arthur Godfrey and Perry Como, who were already popular in other media, attracted large followings to their TV shows not only because of their talent but also because of their smooth, unforced television presence. Like many television stars, Godfrey and Como possessed an intuitive sense of how to relax in front of the camera and make viewers feel like a member of an extended TV family. Though the variety show traditionally encompassed many diverse elements, its success on television often depended on this type of reassuring, anchoring personality, even if it was embodied in a figure as seemingly moribund as Ed Sullivan.

The situation comedy was another radio format that was remodeled after its move to TV. While domestic concerns were a prime factor in such popular radio comedies as ''Amos and Andy'' and ''The Aldrich Family,'' the situation comedy on television offered a direct feel for the way people lived and acted. Kitchens, living rooms, and offices came to visible life, and viewers could now see how characters fit in with their surroundings. More important, thanks to the TV camera, gestures and mannerisms assumed a role impossible on radio (which could only rely on verbal and vocal style). The television situation comedy was free to concentrate both on physical humor and on unspoken interplay and reaction. Some of the genre's funniest moments occurred when gifted comedians like Jackie Gleason, Lucille Ball, and Art Carney collided with their immediate environment and didn't say a word.

However, despite its physical freedom, the TV situation comedy rarely detoured into total, aimless slapstick. Its family orientation, bolstered by the stability of its setting and cast, week after week, gave most series a firm rooting in a world with which its viewers could feel comfortable. Even a program like ''I Love Lucy,'' which consistently employed the wildest horseplay, was first and foremost a story of marriage and friendship. Regardless of the varying nature of its premise, the TV situation comedy's ability to promote a sense of appealing familiarity and continuity with its characters would prove to be one of its greatest virtues.

The medium's visual possibilities and limitations clearly influenced television's reworking of traditional genres (and its eventual creation of new genres), but there was a much more important factor affecting basic program structure and formatting—the economics of broadcasting. TV genres, like radio genres, movie genres, or the genres of popular literature, are essentially commodities, manufactured for, and utterly dependent on, public consumption and support. While popular culture theorists may argue about the hidden needs and desires genres reflect and fulfill, the formulas that have endured are those which manage to yield a regular profit for their producers.

Unlike movies or books, broadcasting didn't require direct audience revenues from a particular format. It simply demanded that a program reach as many people as possible in order to satisfy the wishes of advertisers who paid the bill.

Radio genres, and later TV genres, were therefore conceived for the broadest of appeals. To facilitate their production, a factory system, initially controlled by advertisers and modeled on Hollywood practices, was introduced by the early 1930s.

Episodic dramatic series soon became a mainstay of the broadcast genre industry because of their popularity and stability. Audiences enjoyed following the adventures of their favorite characters week after week, and the strictness of the standardized formats made the programs relatively easy to produce. Since these continuing shows were designed, as Muriel Cantor has noted, "to consider the commercial break at the end of each 15 minute segment," writers were forced to develop new storytelling techniques for the electronic media.[2] The brief quarter hour dramatic units encouraged broad action and vivid characters at the expense of narrative and emotional complexity. A vital feature of this streamlined plotting was its predictable rise to a point right before climax at the end of the mid-segment "so that the viewer will be drawn back to the show after the commercial break."[3]

The genres that prospered on radio and made the move to TV were those which lent themselves to frequent interruptions, strong personality identification, mass audience involvement, and a conventional moral view unlikely to ruffle the sponsors. This meant that, by and large, broadcast formats rarely strayed from familiar situations and from the entertainment formulas already popularized by literature, theater, and motion pictures. The broadcast production industry, like Hollywood, also favored a certain standardization of its commodities. After all, once a program type had proven its appeal, it was much simpler to continue manufacturing the basic design with small variations than to risk failure with something new and untested.

With the emergence of television in the late 1940s, the demand for formatted entertainment programming increased tremendously. Most of the successful radio genres were able to find new life on the new medium, but television's larger costs played an important role in shaping the nature and types of material available. Once the principal formats of comedy, drama, and variety had established their beachhead on TV, there was very little program experimentation. As Christopher Sterling and John Kittross have observed, "few advertisers wish to risk supporting non-conventional programs" and with the greater expenses now involved in TV production, the creators of TV programming were naturally more cautious.[4] Despite the medium's insatiable appetite for new shows, TV producers and the networks have usually stayed within very narrow limits of familiarity— a condition that not only proves their economic allegiance to formula but also confirms Sterling and Kittross's belief that "a medium that constantly reaches so many people is bound to have a shortage of real talent and new ideas."[5]

The popularity of particular television genres, like the products of other media industries, seems to follow a predictable cycle. Every four or five years, a new format (or more often, an innovative variation on an old format) emerges and, to the frequent surprise of the networks, captures the public's fancy. The immediate response by the Hollywood TV producers is to climb on the bandwagon and hopefully share in the ratings bounty. However, the very flood of imitations and spin-offs invariably yields an overflow, and after a few seasons of Nielsen glory, the format subsides from exhaustion.

In its more than 30 years of programming, television has been affected by many such cycles. A prominent example is the rise and fall of the TV Western. Prior to 1956, no Western had ever appeared among the top 15 rated shows. In the 1956–57 season, one finally did (it was "Gunsmoke," which had premiered that fall and ended up in the number eight spot for the year). In the 1957–58 season, six Westerns were listed among the highest rated shows ("Gunsmoke" was now number one). In the 1958–59 season, Westerns dominated the Nielsen ratings, holding nine of the 15 slots (including the top four programs). Four years later, however, only one Western remained popular ("Gunsmoke" again), and the number would never be more than three in the years that followed. With "Gunsmoke" 's death in 1975, Westerns disappeared from TV all together, and, as of this writing, have yet to return to the Nielsen top ten chart.

The cycle of Westerns that peaked in the late 1950s resembles the ebb and flow of other program trends—the mania for quiz shows in the early to mid-1950s, the vogue for cold war or military oriented programs in the middle 1960s, the infatuation with realistic comedies at the beginning of the 1970s. All of these once profitable formulas ultimately lost their grip on the viewing audience (some forever, others to return in different guises) but oversaturation is not entirely to blame. Program popularity is also the result of a mysterious element that is hard to predict—changing public taste. The very conditions that suddenly boost a genre into the ratings stratosphere will often cause its demise just a few seasons later.

Many TV theorists have been more than willing to speculate about why certain formats achieve Nielsen success at certain times. Erik Barnouw feels that the flood of spy dramas in the mid-1960s was partially a response to the news of clandestine activities of the CIA and helped Americans accept the idea that "if our government had really developed a 'department of dirty tricks' . . . it must have been brought on by dire necessities."[6] Sociologist Todd Gitlin suggests that the wave of "jiggle" shows in the late 1970s was an attempt "to appeal to the prurience of the male audience by keeping the 'girls' free of romance, thus catering to the male (and female) backlash against feminism."[7]

Tempting as these retrospective cultural analyses are, it is difficult to accept the view that the TV genre production process has ever been decisively shaped by the immediate political or social environment. Too many other factors preclude such a direct response. Television's need to satisfy the country's largest advertisers by reaching the largest possible audience makes it imperative that programs stay comfortably behind the times in order to avoid alienating anyone. The public seems to prefer familiarity and predictability in its weekly program fare, which helps account for the fact that once a series wins its way into viewers' hearts, it usually will remain on the air for at least a few seasons before dropping off in popularity.

When TV genres do change, it is more often the result of network programming practices and production techniques than a sudden thematic reaction to new cultural concerns. One of the most important sources of format development has been the intense competition between ABC, CBS, and NBC for the ratings supremacy. In their battle to attract large and loyal audiences, the three commercial networks have introduced a variety of elements into their programs to increase their immediate appeal. Like most genre manufacturers, the chief weapons in the networks' competitive arsenal have usually included the perennially popular spices of violence and sex. ABC was the first to make a systematic challenge against its rivals by counter-programming with strong action and adventure shows. The bullet strewn atmosphere of "The Untouchables" in the early 1960s helped catapult the show into the top ten and, as Erik Barnouw reports, in order to keep it there "a network script supervisor combed through each script to make sure it was active enough."[8]

ABC's success with hard-line physicality was soon embraced by its competitors, and together now "in their order to Hollywood studios, the networks demanded more action. They never—or seldom—said 'violence,' but that is what they got."[9] For the next decade and a half formats that stressed brute force and gunplay would continue to be churned out with the networks' active encouragement. However, by the mid-1970s, with the growing outcry from pressure groups against TV violence, ABC, CBS, and NBC finally retreated from portraying assault and mayhem. The cop and detective genres, which had been the chief vehicles (and beneficiaries) of the networks' passion for action, declined in number; those that remained were often much gentler in character.

Sexual themes and innuendoes were another much used network seasoning to boost the popularity of individual formats. In the early 1960s, then CBS President James Aubrey issued his famous "Aubrey dictum" that called for "broads, bosoms, and fun" in his network's prime time fare.[10] Through the years, practically every TV genre, from variety shows to news documentaries, has been periodically rearranged to include such crowd-pleasing (and Nielsen-snaring) items as scantily clad women and suggestive interplay. With violence severely reduced by the late 1970s, sexual concerns became a prominent feature of various genres. Many situation comedies and detective shows suddenly found themselves overrun with pneumatic blondes and provocative encounters. Nevertheless, this leering tone lasted only a few seasons; by the early 1980s a threatened boycott against TV advertisers by fundamentalist church organizations led to the removal of most "jiggle" programming. Though sex had not been entirely banished, it was now dispensed somewhat more judiciously, as the networks learned to limit, at least for the time being, their penchant for titillation.

While the infusion of violence and sex into programming has played a notorious role in TV genre development, the long term impact has not been crucial. Most formats can still survive perfectly well without excessive hard-nosed action or blatantly risque overtones. A much more decisive factor in recent genre evolution has been the simple fact of program durability. Those series fortunate enough to last for many seasons now frequently take advantage of one of the medium's most distinctive features—the ability to develop and grow over time. Beginning in the 1970s, the basic dramatic formats went through a remarkable change as they began to experiment with evolving characters and themes. Situation comedies in particular abandoned the rigid notion that each episode existed in its own universe with no reference to the past. Pioneering programs like "The Mary Tyler Moore Show," "All in the Family," and "M*A*S*H" presented a gradually shifting landscape during their years on the air, as their characters grew into new jobs, new responsibilities, and new feelings. Viewers could watch Mary Richards, Edith Bunker, and Margaret Houlihan evolve from month to month and share in their development. The innovative police show "Hill Street Blues" went one step further, offering a kaleidoscope of stories that often continued for weeks, mirroring the ongoing activities of its characters, while also reminding us of their history. Like many other popular dramas of the late 1970s and early 1980s, "Hill Street Blues" incorporated the basic structural techniques of the daytime serial to provide nighttime audiences with the satisfactions of intricate plotting and long-range character growth.

Fictional formats were not the only TV genres that underwent great changes during the last decade. News broadcasts have been transformed as a result of new technologies and a new sense of competition, prompted by ABC's success with the faster pace and livelier tone of its "World News Tonight." Sports coverage has become an electronic battleground of special effects that make actually attending an event in person seem pale by comparison. Children's educational programming has been revolutionized by programs like "Sesame Street" and "The Electric Company," which exploited television's power to make learning quick, exciting, and fun. Talk shows have shifted their focus to include just about every style from the openly controversial ("The Phil Donahue Show") to the self-consciously absurd ("Late Night with David Letterman") to a hybrid mixture of news and entertainment popularized by shows such as "Good Morning America" and "Hour Magazine."

The diversity of TV genres over the last 35 years testifies to commercial television's ability to satisfy the changing demands and desires of advertisers and audiences. The medium's enormous need for material—it must provide programming from early in the morning to late at night every day of the week—has led to the creation of a variety of flexible formats with different appeals. The formulas the networks and Hollywood TV production companies employ repeatedly are designed to accommodate sponsor interest in the shifting demographics of the broadcast day. The bubbly news and information shows of early morning are geared to the limited attention span of busy adults getting ready for work. The afternoon soap operas, while still largely for housewives, now include more juvenile romance and stylish action to please the growing viewership among teenagers. Network newscasts are shedding their traditional stodginess to actively court a much younger crowd. The peak prime time viewing hours of 8:00 P.M. to 9:00 P.M. are now, as ever, heavily skewed toward family entertainment, primarily situation comedies; later hours are targeted at various segments of the adult population who favor detective shows or romantic melodramas and made-for-TV movies.

The range of TV genres reflects the medium's varied efforts to reach just about everybody. Though television's mission may change in the future with cable's interest in selective audiences, there is little doubt that the basic TV formats will still endure. The dramatic and nonfiction formulas television adapted from films, literature, theatre, and radio have proven their versatility and electronic appeal for decades. As the most popular source of mass entertainment and one of the most profitable, TV's attachment to the bedrock of its particular crowd-pleasing genres is likely to continue for a long time to come.

NOTES

1. In his influential study of TV genres, *TV: The Most Popular Art* (Garden City, N.Y.: Anchor Press, 1974), Horace Newcomb proclaims that "television is at its best when it offers us faces, reactions, explorations of emotions registered by human beings" (pp. 245–46). David Thorburn, in his provocative essay "TV Melodrama," which appears in the anthology *Understanding Television*, ed. Richard Adler (New York: Praeger, 1981), notes that "the medium's reduced visual scale grants him [the actor] a primacy unavailable in the theater or in the movies, where an amplitude of things and spaces offer competition for the eye's attention" (p. 77).

2. Muriel Cantor, *Prime-Time Television* (Beverly Hills, Calif.: Sage Publications, 1980), p. 29.

3. Ibid., p. 30.

4. Christopher Sterling and John Kittross, *Stay Tuned* (Belmont, Calif.: Wadsworth, 1978), p. 459.

5. Ibid.

6. Erik Barnouw, *Tube of Plenty* (New York: Oxford University Press, 1975), p. 367.

7. Todd Gitlin, "Prime-time Ideology: The Hegemonic Process in Television Entertainment," in *TV: The Critical View*, ed. Horace Newcomb (New York: Oxford University Press, 1982), p. 438.

8. Barnouw, *Tube of Plenty*, p. 263.

9. Ibid.

10. Ibid., p. 264.

2

The Police Show

BROOKS ROBARDS

OVERVIEW

No genre of television programming has been more popular—with the exception of situation comedy—than the police show. And no genre of television programming has been more controversial because of its predilection for portraying violence. This apparent discrepancy in social values and goals—fascination and disapprobation of violence—has provided a profitable area of debate for academics and politicans alike over the last thirty years.

It began when Estes Kefauver's Special Senate Subcommittee on Juvenile Delinquency first put the limelight on television as the nemesis that threatened to turn our children into callous, asocial criminals. The issue still hasn't been laid to rest.

The National Institute of Mental Health issued an update to the 1972 Surgeon General's findings as recently as 1982 reaffirming the presence of causal links between violence as we see it on television and violence in real life.

The irony of the attacks on television's violence, which have been aimed predominantly at police shows and their cousins the detective dramas (Westerns have borne their share of the attack, too), is that these attacks tend to obscure the real nature of police shows. Police shows are obsessed with coming out on top in the eternal struggle between right and wrong. As such, they comprise a deeply conservative genre that works to re-establish over and over again the importance of social order and the need for the elimination of wrongdoing.

Violence in police shows becomes the visual analogue for the re-establishment of the order upon which this action-dominated genre relies. The important element of the car chases, shootouts, and fist fights that we associate with police shows is that they are a way of reducing conflict to its simplest form and of making the statement that conflict can always be resolved, usually on the side of the righteous. John Fiske and John Hartley have analyzed the function of violence on television in semiotic terms and find that it represents "not the dominance of one personality over another, but of one social role over another social role."[1] Television violence, they observe, functions according to artistic convention, and the audience readily distinguishes it from real violence.

The closely related cousin to the police show, the detective drama, depends less on action and more on character, moving in the direction of romance and fantasy where the police show stays grounded in reality. The police show is television's version of telling it like it really is, often with help from real policemen. A little like voyeurs, the audience gets to ride in the back seat of the squad car and experience firsthand the seamy side of life.

Implicit in such vicarious adventurism is the audience's secret wish to explore its own darker impulses. But we always do it in safety, protected by our Vergillian guide, the cop. He is a patriarchal figure who commands respect and authority, a person who remains the legitimate and accomplished representative of our social order. At the same time that he has achieved his position, he has maintained his individuality. He manages to have it both ways.

Police are heroic most often in their feats of physical strength and skill and the clarity of their vision of right and wrong. There is never much question about how bad the bad guy is on a police show or whether he's bad (and even more important, whether we're good), just as there is a minimum of concern for due process of law or any of the other legal mechanisms of justice. All that matters is that the policeman bring in his quarry. Once the crook is caught, order has been restored, and the audience can rest easy, undisturbed by subtleties related to the metaphysical nature of good and evil and how we determine which is which.

The emphasis stays on the process by which society deals with crime and criminals. Although occasionally there have been attempts to mix the police genre with the Western, the genre's locus is invariably urban since the city serves as the metaphor for society in general, as well as being the instigator of its misfits and their misdeeds. The continued power and success of the police genre reside in that strange mix of reality and fiction that is basic to the structure of television and which is particularly compelling in the case of police shows.

HISTORICAL DEVELOPMENT

From the early years of the genre when the cop reigned supreme as a macho authority figure and the distinction between good and evil always remained clear, the police show has evolved into a form in which good and bad have a far more complex relationship. The police force has been integrated by both blacks and women; it is no longer an exclusively male genre. The absolute authority of the police no longer goes unquestioned. Television has humanized the police by making the audience privy to their personal lives. The genre has come of age, attempting at times to explore the intricate, interrelated nature of good and evil.

The roots of the police show lie in the special capacity of television and its predecessor, radio, to give storytelling a sense of the authenticity of real-life experience. Early television producers' sensitivity to the medium's powerful and unique ability to convey the real is demonstrated in some of the unusual gimmicks they came up with in early versions. The 1949 audience for "Chicagoland Mystery Players" had to read the next day's *Chicago Tribune* to find out what finally happened. "Stand By for Crime," the first television program transmitted from Chicago, solicited phone calls from viewers before it revealed the culprit.

Many of the earliest police shows were crossovers: popular radio shows that expanded to television. However, success on radio didn't guarantee it in the new medium. "Dick Tracy" was broadcast on radio from 1935 to 1942 but didn't even last a full season on television. "Mr. District Attorney," probably the most popular crime radio show of the 1940s, because of its realism, was another false start for the television genre.

It took two former radio shows running in an alternate week schedule in 1952 to transform the radio police show into a successful television genre. Both of them used actual cases from police files narrated in a semidocumentary style. One was the radio classic "Gangbusters," and the other was a relatively new radio show called "Dragnet." Both became smash hits overnight in the new medium of television, but for reasons only an NBC archivist could hope to explain, "Gangbusters" was cancelled in December 1952, to allow "Dragnet" to run weekly. It averaged a 45 percent share of the sets in use, and Brooks and Marsh point out it was "probably the highest-rated program ever to be cancelled in the history of television."[2]

Just as "I Love Lucy" provided the prototype for the television situation comedy, "Dragnet" set the standard for police shows. With its creator Jack Webb as the taciturn Joe Friday, who asked for "Just the facts, ma'am," "Dragnet" was an unvarnished moles-and-warts look at police work. In its straightforward, unprepossessing way, it celebrated the cop on the beat and the unglamorous legwork required by the job. That the public ate it up is evidenced by a *TV Guide* article published in 1953 that observed, "Webb has come to represent for the American public the ideal of the regular police detective, as contrasted with the 'private eye,' and with real police methods, as contrasted with fictional melodrama."[3]

Interestingly enough, there was little violence on the show, and *TV Guide* quotes Webb as saying that in a year's worth of programming, only 15 bullets were fired, and all of three fights took place.[4] Audiences learned to recite the lingo of police talk and the show's musical theme became a hit record .

Sergeant Joe Friday's no-nonsense, professional approach to police work might have been chilly without the softer mien of Ben Alexander playing his partner, Detective Frank Smith. But there was never any question about who was in control, both in the partnership and in the arena of crime-fighting. The righteous indignation of Joe Friday was an awesome sight, and the audience knew that with law enforcers like him on the beat, the crooks couldn't get away with much.

The more personality prone detective genre was nearly as popular in the fifties as the police shows, with David Janssen starring as Richard Diamond, Peter Lawford as the "Thin Man," and Lloyd Nolan as Martin Kane. Jack Webb radiated respect rather than charm and kept "Dragnet" at the top of the Nielsen ratings for five years, from 1952 to 1957.

"Dragnet" spawned a crop of semidocumentary-style police shows that touted their use of real cases. "The Lineup" was a CBS copycat; "Police Story," a precursor to the popular seventies show; and "Scotland Yard," a British variation. "Crime Syndicated" boasted as its narrators the former chief counsel and the former chairman of the Senate Crime Investigating Committee.

"Highway Patrol," starring Broderick Crawford and running from 1955 to 1959 as one of the most popular shows in syndication, was probably the first police show that attempted to incorporate elements of the Western, a genre that the police show has flirted with many times since. Set against the backdrop of an unidentified western state, most of "Highway Patrol" took place outside, using patrol cars and motorcycles in place of horses.

In contrast, "Naked City," which aired in 1958 and ran until 1963, was set firmly in a landscape of New York skyscrapers and streets. It took the police show beyond the formulaic tedium of "Dragnet" to a new level. It also helped typecast its star James Franciscus as an urban cop. Premiering a year later, ABC's "The Untouchables" with Robert Stack as Elliot Ness, the Prohibition-era gangbuster, was a sophisticated excursion into the past that raised a storm of protest because of its extreme violence and alleged stereotyping of Italians.

The realism that "Dragnet" had made its trademark was carried through in "The Untouchables" to include the re-creation of authentic thirties sets, shoot-em-ups, costumes and characters, including the likes of Al Capone and Bugsy Moran. In response to picketing by Italian-American organizations, "The Untouchables" eliminated fictional hoodlums with Italian names and promised to emphasize the contributions to American culture made by Italian-Americans. The bloom was off the police show as humble promoter of social justice and the witchhunt against television violence was underway.

Perhaps in response to continued public and Congressional concern—this time from Senator Thomas Dodd of Connecticut—police shows shied away from violence in the sixties. There was enough violence in the streets and on the battlefield, and the public was probably more interested in the romance of the old West and the glamour of detective shows like "Peter Gunn" or "77 Sunset Strip." The police show entries of the early sixties were mainly derivative as producers searched for a format that would capture the public's imagination.

"The Lawless Years" tried to parlay twenties' nostalgia of the sort that worked for Westerns into success, but it was left in the dust by "The Untouchables." A syndicated offering, "Manhunt," pushed itself beyond mediocrity with good acting by Victor Jorey and Patrick McVey paired as a San Diego detective and a veteran police reporter. "Man from Interpol" was precursor to the highly successful international spy format used by "The Man from U.N.C.L.E.," and the "Asphalt Jungle," a spin-off from the movie, used jazzy background music by Duke Ellington in an obvious imitation of the popular "Peter Gunn."

Robert Taylor spent four moderately successful years from 1959 to 1962 in "The Detectives," which experimented with a primarily ensemble cast, allowing the show to spotlight different characters each week. "Dan Raven" in 1960 tried to cash in on the glitter of "77 Sunset Strip," which had started two years earlier, by using a Hollywood locale and celebrities like Buddy Hackett, Paul Anka, and Bobby Darin.

A variation on the glamour angle, which more properly belongs to the detective genre, was Gene Barry's portrayal of a millionaire chief of detectives in "Burke's Law." Also borrowing from the detective genre, "Cain's Hundred" combined the semidocumentary style of "Dragnet" with a greater emphasis on character typical of detective shows by focusing on the exploits of a gangland lawyer turned FBI agent. Electronic gadgetry was the gimmick "The New Breed" used in 1961, but never as successfully as the spy drama, "Mission: Impossible" in the later sixties.

The only "police" show to make it to the top of the Nielsen ratings in the early sixties was a situation comedy, NBC's "Car 54, Where Are You?" which may say something about the public's temporary loss of interest in a genre that makes heroes out of society's moral guardians. It may also have reflected the inability of television producers at the time to find new ways to explore what was by now a maturing genre. The one exception was a show called "Brenner," which first aired in 1959 and ran until 1964. "Brenner" used the format of a father-son police team to explore the theme of generational conflict. A little before its time, it never experienced quite the success of a later police show, "Streets of San Francisco," which used the same format.

By the mid-sixties, television producers had regrouped and introduced four police shows that became major hits. Starring Efrem Zimbalist, Jr., as Inspector Lewis Erskine, ABC's "The F.B.I." drew on the "Dragnet" tradition of cool professionalism and actual case histories. Winning praise from J. Edgar Hoover, himself, it stayed on the air from 1965 until 1974, one of the most tumultuous periods in twentieth century American history. A less popular version of the cop as guide through the gritty real world was "N.Y.P.D.," which was filmed on location in New York City and was duly praised by Mayor John Lindsey.

A number of actors tried to make police shows into star vehicles without much luck during this period of celebrating individualism. Burt Reynolds made a brief appearance in 1966 as an Iroquois Indian turned N.Y.C. cop in "Hawk." William Shatner played an overeager assistant DA in 1965 in "For the People." Howard Duff in "Felony Squad" was the only one to last more than a season, probably because the show explored a father-son theme.

It was perhaps no coincidence that the most popular television cop in the mid-sixties was confined to a wheelchair. Raymond Burr had already established a successful track record as a lawyer in "Perry Mason." He was at the peak of his career when that show went off the air in 1966. "Ironside," which started its eight-year run in 1967, provided the perfect foil for Burr's talents. Its emphasis on character, rather than action and violence, was an antidote for the times. As Fiske and Hartley have pointed out, " 'Ironside's' wheelchair serves not only to identify him, but, more importantly, is an overt sign that he uses non-physical and non-violent methods."[5] The fact that Ironside relied on his superior intelligence and experience allied the police and detective genres more closely and planted the seeds for a host of similar, personality-oriented police dramas in the seventies. Ironside's disability was an evocative symbol of the contemporary disaffection with unquestioned authority, and a number of police and detective shows were to follow, copying the theme of the partially disabled hero.[6] What remained of the traditional police genre was the absolute certainty with which Chief Ironside distinguished between good and bad and tracked the latter down. He compensated for his confinement to a wheelchair by the use of sophisticated equipment, including an elaborately outfitted van that served as his office on wheels. He also acted as a father figure to his two younger assistants and body-guard. Although he was still very much in command, his role in part was to dispense wisdom and guidance to his younger charges, who conveniently included a woman, a black, and a young male. As Horace Newcomb observes, crime was starting to become " . . . the device through which the audience explores interpersonal relationships," although those explorations were still safely contained within a tightly familial context.[7] "Ironside" stayed at the top of the Nielsen ratings from 1968 until 1973. Only one police show surpassed its popularity at the time: "Hawaii Five-O."

"Hawaii Five-O" took from "Dragnet" the distinction of being the longest-running police show in television history. Running continuously from 1968 to 1980, it surpassed "Dragnet" insofar as the older show was off the air from 1959 until 1967, when it resumed for another three less successful years.

"Hawaii Five-O" 's exotic Pacific setting makes it seem like a better candidate for the more romantic fantasies of the detective genre, but Steve McGarrett, played by Jack Lord, stands solidly in the "Sgt. Friday" tradition of no-nonsense, stoical authority figures. The lush Hawaiian background may have been what made this old-style hero not only palatable but appealing. The fact that the villains were often Oriental suggests an underlying racism that never had to be confronted as overtly as the nation's black and white conflicts.

According to Robert Alley, "Hawaii Five-O" has been "more regularly criticized for gratuitous violence than most other action programs on T.V."[8] However, as Alley points out, the show's use of graphic violence may seem unique primarily because, unlike many other police shows, it did not shy away from portraying the consequences of violence. When someone got shot, the audience was not shielded from seeing how it happened.

"Hawaii Five-O" producer Philip Leacock also worked on another popular police drama of the late sixties, "The Mod Squad." Les Brown pointed out as early as 1971 that, " 'The Mod Squad's' claim to fame was not its apparently liberal, counterculture facade, but its underlying law and order conservatism."[9] Still, it was a popular show, making the top twenty-five in three out of its five years on the air between 1968 and 1973. "The Mod Squad" consisted of a special youth squad, recruited to track the always over-thirty crooks who preyed on members of the hippy generation. It was composed of a demographically perfect balance of three young adults with colorful and less than law-abiding histories. Julie Barnes was a runaway and the daughter of a prostitute. Linc Hayes came out of the ghetto, and Pete Cochran was the long-haired black-sheep son of a wealthy family. The crooks had to share the spotlight with the personal and ideological conflicts that this unholy threesome vocalized.

A popular police show that came on the air in 1968 serves as an even better predictor of the swing the country took toward conservatism in the seventies. NBC's "Adam-12" featured two young policemen in uniform and emphasized the day-to-day routine of their work. Who produced it? Jack Webb, of course, who had merely updated his "Dragnet" formula by employing multiple plot techniques, moving the locale closer to the suburbs, and incorporating more human interest. The police genre was about to reach new heights, and (although the traditional, gumshoe cop show has always found a place in the hearts of television viewers) "Adam-12" represents an anachronism in some ways. By spotlighting two policemen, the show contributed to the movement away from single, heroic authority figures.

Along the way to a decade filled with funky, individualistic cops who somehow learned to walk the line between independence and the system, Burt Reynolds tried and failed again to make it as a television cop in "Dan August," which aired on ABC from 1970 to 1971. But the new trend was confirmed by NBC, which was experimenting with a repertory format in which several shows alternated in a single weekly slot. An early entry, "McCloud," set the tone with Dennis Weaver playing a southwesterner come East to plague the New York City police with his unconventional methods. "McCloud" began in 1970 as the first part of four NBC mini-series grouped under the title, "Four-in-One." A year later, it had found a permanent berth in the "NBC Mystery Movie" along with two other highly successful shows, "McMillan and Wife" and "Columbo." It is a credit to the quality of these shows that they survived the confusing rotations of a once-a-month schedule. Comedy was the new ingredient that at first seemed to set these police shows apart and account for their popularity.

Sam McCloud's cowboy clothes and accent made him a natural for the kind of low-key humor that became the show's hallmark. He was the most rural of a series of charming misfits in the seventies with its cult of personality in cop shows. A more urbane approach was taken by "McMillan and Wife," which used Dashiell Hammett's formula from The Thin Man to set up the witty interaction between San Francisco Police Commissioner Stewart McMillan and his beautiful wife Sally. In this seventies version, however, Mrs. McMillan is the one with the unerring instinct for nosing out unusual crimes. Strong acting by Rock Hudson and Susan Saint James, along with supporting stars John Schuck,

Nancy Walker, and, later, Martha Raye, helped keep this show at the top of the Nielsen ratings.

The third entry in the "NBC Mystery Movie" lineup was "Columbo," a show more rightfully belonging to the detective genre. Peter Falk as Lt. Columbo played a self-effacing, apparently bumbling, plainclothes cop replete with rumpled raincoat, who always managed to collar the right culprit through his brilliant powers of deduction. The emphasis on ratiocination reflected the movement of police drama away from pure action toward character development. "Columbo" was the most popular of the "NBC Mystery Movie" series because of its emphasis on personality. Columbo's relationship with his wife was an important element of his life and led, eventually, to a separate detective show for her.[10] Lt. Columbo was almost diametrically opposite from the flinty-eyed, steel-gripping hero of the traditional police show. He relied on ingenuity rather than physical prowess, and he remained a kindly man without being morally soft. His pleasure came from deceiving everyone about his real abilities, and he always nailed his suspect.

Only one police entry in the original "NBC Mystery Movie" series was not a success. "Amy Prentiss" featured a 35–year-old widow as chief of detectives in the San Francisco Police Department. Television audiences were apparently not ready yet to have a woman in charge in such a male-dominated program genre. Producers did not give up trying, however, and put "Laugh-In" regular Teresa Graves into "Get Christie Love," as a black female supercop in 1974. Like most cops of the seventies, Christie Love was all spunky individualist— apparently too much so for viewers. NBC came up with the right combination in "Police Woman," also in 1974, by starring Angie Dickinson as Sgt. Pepper Anderson. Dickinson had appeared the year before in an episode of another NBC cop show, Joseph Wambaugh's Emmy-winning "Police Story." Dominated by her superior Lt. Bill Crowley, Pepper Anderson stayed soft and sexy enough to suit television audiences until the show was cancelled in 1978. She worked as an undercover cop, conveniently masquerading as prostitutes and bad guys' girlfriends in what is hard not to interpret as a reflection of the audience's own ambivalence about the role of women and their moral identity.

Capitalizing on the successful return of the straightforward, documentary-style format used in "Adam-12," which by now was settling into middle age, "Police Woman's" predecessor, "Police Story," is called by Tim Brooks and Earle March "one of the more realistic police stories to be seen on television."[11] It was created by former policeman Joseph Wambaugh, who had written two best-selling police novels. No aspect of police work was too mundane to escape treatment, and using an anthology approach, the show also spent considerable time examining the personal lives of the force. Since no one character appeared week after week, careful plot development and good writing were essential. As with "Dragnet," the emphasis was on authenticity. According to Robert Alley, the producers interviewed real-life Californian policemen and selected suitable plots from the material they collected.[12]

The networks tried and discarded a potpourri of police formats in the early seventies as they cast about for the right combination of what was clearly going to be a winning streak. ABC tried the Elliot Ness approach with "The Silent Force," in which government agents fought organized crime. CBS had slightly better luck with "O'Hara, U.S. Treasury," produced with the help of the Treasury Department and featuring an assortment of customs, IRS, and other cases. NBC juggled police work with courtroom drama in "The D.A." and tried an ensemble approach in "87th Precinct." None of these shows lasted much longer than one season.

Nor did a spate of police shows with exotic locales of one sort or another run for very long. "Cade's Country" featured Glenn Ford as a California county sheriff, while "Nakia" put Robert Forster in a New Mexico town and surrounded him with Indians. Clint Walker roamed the tundra in an Alaskan-based "Kodiak." Two shows that may have been ahead of their time were "Chase" and "Chopper One." The four specialist cops in "Chase" used their skills in dog handling and in piloting helicopters, hotrods, and motorcycles to catch their quarry. Partners Don Burdick and Gil Foley of "Chopper One" concentrated on helicopter missions. The emphasis on vehicular action in both these shows was out of sync with the demand for personality police shows, and the audience hadn't gained enough distance from Vietnam to appreciate the symbolic resonance of helicopters on which later movies like *Apocalypse Now* capitalized.

Two 1972 shows that should have been naturals probably got lost in the shuffle of repertory schedules. Rebel Frank Dain hunted down missing persons in "Jigsaw" but had to share a time slot with two spy dramas as part of ABC's anthology, "The Men." "Madigan" became a casualty of NBC's too-rapid expansion in the face of its success with "McCloud," "Columbo," and "McMillan and Wife" in "The NBC Mystery Movie." Two nights a week of this genre was simply too much crime, and even Richard Widmark playing a loner with a soft streak fell by the wayside after a season, along with detective shows "Banacek," "Cool Million," "Tenafly," and "Faraday and Company"; "The Snoop Sisters" failed the next year.

CBS emerged with a winner in 1973 in "Kojak." Model of the rugged individualist for the seventies, Telly Savalas was his own man but still part of the system. His arrogantly bald head and lollipops were the visual analogues of his personal style: a cop secure enough in his masculinity that he could safely thumb his nose at convention without being written off as a rebel.[13] Robert Alley called "Kojak" in 1977 "the most prominent dramatic personality currently on the TV screen."[14] Certainly audiences seemed to agree and kept the show in the top twenty of the Nielsen ratings for its first three years. It seemed appropriate that among the exponents of the seventies cult of personality cops, "Kojak" should be a CBS offering. CBS, the king of the networks, was described by Les Brown in terms of its elegant, establishmentarian architecture as "cold poetry, all rhythm and no melody."[15]

It also seemed fitting that one of the other leading personality cops, "Baretta," aired on ABC, the youngest of the networks and a spoiler. Robert Blake as undercover Detective Tony Baretta picked up on rebelliousness against the system where Kojak left off. The contrast was as explicit as the difference between Baretta's tee shirt and jeans and Kojak's suit and tie. It was also clear in Tony's penchant for flights of oratory and his unsavory associates, ranging from alcoholic Billy, played by veteran actor Tom Ewell, and an inebriate parrot, to the occasionally eloquent and always flamboyant pimp, Rooster, played by Michael Roberts.

"Baretta" had emerged from the ashes of another police show, "Toma," which had lost its lead actor, Tony Musante. Baretta almost never appeared in the station house but worked out of his seedy hotel digs, donning a variety of ingenious disguises to perform his undercover work. An orphan, he had grown up on the streets he patrolled and served as passionate correlate to Kojak's cooler paternalism. Baretta was a cop who was to use whatever means were necessary to keep the little guys—no matter what side of the law they operated on—from falling victim to the big bad guys.

The moral of the police story had begun to change. No longer were right and wrong so clearly dichotomized; nor was it clear that good always prevailed. Indeed, it sometimes appeared that Tony Baretta condoned petty crime if it meant survival for the denizens of the ghetto. Violence, which imaged the struggle of good and evil, was no longer taboo, despite the attempts of the networks' imposed Family Viewing Hour to segregate it in late-night time slots. Without benefit of "Kojak's" higher quality script writing and laboring under the onus of what Harry Castleman and Walter Podrazik call "a new attempt by the producers of *Toma* to cash in, more gracefully, on the violent cop show trend," "Baretta" was a tour de force of acting by Robert Blake.[16]

The pivotal cop show for the seventies was actually a situation comedy. ABC's "Barney Miller" which ran from 1975 to 1981, took the police genre and gently poked fun at its excesses in the exploration of character. Captain Barney Miller led a posse of self-parodying cops, most memorably: Fish, the ever-ailing, aging, and complaining Jew; Wojo, the sweetly dumb Polack; Yemana, the incoherently inscrutable Oriental; Harris, the half-classy black with a demi-dozen get-rich-quick schemes up his sleeve; and Dietrich, the would-be German expressionist-intellectual. It had been done before. This time, however, the generic transformation of police show into situation comedy emanated not only from excesses in the cult of personality; it also reflected the further maturation of the genre insofar as there was something substantial at which to poke fun. Police shows had come a long way from shoot-outs, car chases, and men of steel. The most successful cop shows of the second half of the seventies mark a decline into pure action and violence without the leavening effect of character analysis. "S.W.A.T.," an acronym for Special Weapons and Tactics, has the dubious distinction of being one of the most violent police shows in the history of television.

Ironically, it grew out of "Police Story," considered by some critics to be the most morally proper of police programs.[17] "S.W.A.T." militarized its team of police officers, all of whom were Vietnam veterans, into a Gestapo-like force of exterminators. The show experienced a brief flurry of popularity at its onset in 1975, rising to sixteenth place in the Nielsen ratings for the year, before disappearing a little over a year later.

"Starsky and Hutch," going easier on the heavy metal, lasted quite a bit longer (it ran from 1975 to 1979 on ABC). Pairing a streetwise Starsky with the more educated Hutch, the show established a better balance between bald-faced violence and personality. A host of other cop shows came and went during the 1975–76 season. Bumper Morgan was Joseph Wambaugh's attempt to extend his winning streak from "Police Story" to "The Blue Knight." Played with a touch of Baretta flair by George Kennedy, Morgan was nevertheless a hard-nosed uniformed cop on the beat. "Caribe" had Stacy Keach patrolling the Caribbean for half a season, while Lloyd Bridges tried to bring color to another patrolman walking his beat in "Joe Forrester." NBC's "Jigsaw John" was a puzzle solver in the "Columbo" tradition, and "Bert D'Angelo/Superstar" got lost in the shuffle between New York and San Francisco, where the lead character had been transferred.

Judd Hirsch lifted "Delvecchio" out of the monotony of independent-minded, big-city cop shows long enough to earn a sinecure on the situation comedy, "Taxi," but even Robert Stack couldn't keep the "Most Wanted" gender-integrated team of police experts in work longer than a year. "Serpico" was an unsuccessful attempt to translate the immensely popular movie starring Al Pacino into a television series.

Of the half dozen entries of 1976, only one was a hit. "Quincy, M.E." extended the genre transformations of "McCloud" and "Barney Miller" by combining cops and doctors. It was introduced in the sixth season of "The NBC Mystery Movie" series but proved so popular that it was given its own time slot. "Night Gallery" and "Odd Couple" veteran Jack Klugman brought a belligerent charm to the medical examiner whose principles wouldn't allow him to let deaths by unnatural causes go unsolved, and the show stayed on the air into the eighties. Although less complex than the character studies of the earlier seventies, Quincy was an amicable mix of individualist, who lived on a boat and hung out at a bar called "Danny's Place," and organization man, who contained himself enough to keep his buffoonish boss Dr. Astin from canning him.

"Quincy" was the exception rather than the rule, and out of nearly a dozen forays during the rest of the decade, only "CHiPs" on NBC was a winner. Action was the ingredient that worked for "CHiPs" and kept Officers Jon Baker and Ponch Poncherella outdoors and highway-bound on their motorcycles. The youth and good looks of these California highway patrolmen turned one of them, Erik Estrada, into a teen-aged idol of sorts. For all its popularity, "CHiPs" registered a decline into decadence in the genre.

High-caliber actors or celebrities could not rescue shows like "Lannigan's

Rabbi,'' in which Art Carney played a small-town police chief with a sleuthing rabbi for a friend; ''Paris'' with James Earl Jones as an overblown intellectual black cop; and ''David Cassidy—Man Undercover,'' the title of which speaks for itself. A handful of other efforts tried to exploit the public's interest in the South generated by the election of Georgian Jimmy Carter to the presidency. ''Eischied's'' chief of detectives was a southerner transplanted to New York City. Country music star Jerry Reed headlined in ''Nashville 99,'' which was filmed on location and used plenty of other country music celebrities. ''Carter Country,'' ''Lobo,'' and ''Enos'' provide examples of depths of bad taste southern slapstick could sink to, matched only in misguidedness by the man-dog team of ''Sam.'' Like ''CHiPs,'' these shows represent a failure to expand the boundaries of the genre in meaningful ways.

Women cops fared almost as poorly as southerners in the late seventies. In ''Dog and Cat,'' plainclothes veteran Jack Ramsey and rookie J. Z. Kane were the contentious partners of the show's title. Brenda Vaccaro unsuccessfully tried to portray some of the more serious difficulties of balancing career with the more traditional female roles in ''Dear Detective'' and vanished after a month. It wasn't until ''Cagney and Lacey'' brought a new twist to the old dilemma of a by-the-book cop working with an individualist by making them both women that it looked as if women had begun to find a niche for themselves in the police genre.

A male version of the individualist-traditionalist format, ''Freebie and the Bean'' spelled disaster and lasted only a month. ''B.A.D. Cates,'' blatantly copying ''CHiPs,'' but using hotrods rather than motorcycles, also had a speedy demise. Lasting only a little longer was a television adaptation of the Buford Pusser vengeance movie, ''Walking Tall.'' ''Stone,'' a futile attempt to provide Dennis Weaver with another police vehicle to follow ''McCloud,'' unabashedly imitated the life of Joseph Wambaugh by making its hero a best-selling novelist. With a busted cop as its lead, ''Riker'' seemed to reflect the general state of the police genre: fallen on hard times. There was one exception.

A program called ''Hill Street Blues,'' which came on the air at midseason in 1981, turned the genre upside down and sent shock waves through all of television programming. It had an unprepossessing start, doing so poorly in the ratings that NBC almost cancelled it until its small but loyal following protested loudly enough. Using an ensemble format, ''Hill Street Blues'' incorporated the many disparate character elements the genre had acquired, from the cheerfully fascist SWAT leader Howard and the mildly bigoted Renko, to Lucy the cop-as-female, Bleker the grimy rebel, Esterhaus the macho rhetorician, Joyce the beauteously liberal and liberated public defender, and, finally Captain Frank Furillo, the resident stoic with a heart. The mix was part gritty police drama, part situation comedy, and part soap opera. The softening influence of sitcom humor balanced the grimmer dimensions of police realism. The sometimes over-explicit delvings into the characters' personal, and in particular, sexual, lives, gave them a depth and fascination that transcended the histrionics of pure soap opera, which had been experiencing a renascence in prime time, and counter-balanced the generic tendency to make forays into excessive violence and hyperactivity.

Plotting acquired a new complexity in "Hill Street Blues." The characters not infrequently revealed their confusion over the distinction between good and evil. They did not always provide pristine role models, nor did they necessarily nail the crooks. If those crooks happened to be a neighborhood street gang, the members of the force might actually end up playing basketball with them in an attempt at détente. "Hill Street Blues" laid down the new assumption that crime did not happen "out there"; it sometimes quite literally erupted within the confines of the station. Nor could it be safely isolated as the "other," capable of permanent, noncontaminating extirpation. The dialectic of right and wrong became suitably metaphysical.

Production techniques themselves addressed the quantum shift in approach. Hand-held cameras, "dirty" sound, and a frame overflowing with people mimicked Electronic News Gathering (ENG) conventions and helped translate the messy, unresolved, and complex world of the Hill Street precinct into an artistic as well as a social statement. Much in the pattern of "All in the Family," "Hill Street Blues" gradually became popular as the audience accustomed itself to what was in fact a radical change in conventions. Even the show's tendency to leave plots hanging for weeks à la soap opera style capitalized on the episodic structure of television and made it into an eloquent statement about the nature of crime.

ABC's "T. J. Hooker," a traditionalist approach to the genre showcasing "Star Trek" celebrity William Shatner, seemed pale next to the brilliance of "Hill Street Blues." Michael Pollan suggests that it was spawned by the programming crisis NBC found itself in after the departure of Fred Silverman and that it reflects some of the traditional directions that network has taken to attract the most profitable segments of the audience.[18] Indeed, "Hill Street Blues" seemed to be spawning a new mode of programming as evidenced by at least one other quality show—this time in the hospital genre—"Saint Elsewhere," and plans for others.

Efforts at bringing back old-style cop shows with tried-and-true performers like Mike Connors in "Today's FBI," Robert Stack in "Strike Force," and James Arness in "McClain's Law" didn't work. Even "Shannon" misfired, in which "Kojak" veteran Kevin Dobson, worried about impotence as well as arson, played a widowered cop with a ten-year-old son. While the emphasis on personal life in "Shannon" was in the new style of police shows, the focus on one cop and the single-parent format lifted from sixties situation comedy was tired and tiresome. Still, even flops like "Shannon" demonstrated that police shows had come a long way from the cardboard-charactered, leaden-plotted prototypes of the early fifties. The genre had grown along with the medium itself, learning how to exploit television's intrinsic structure to create more complex heroes and develop story lines with subtletly as well as action.

THEMES AND ISSUES

Ulysses may have had to wander the four corners of the earth and Achilles may have had to fight the Trojan War to establish themselves as heroes. Today's heroes face different challenges. The police show is television's heroic genre, and the arbitration of right and wrong for society has become the function of the television cop. It might seem that his role is more simply that of an avenger, one who seeks out wrongdoers, tracks them down, and restores social order. This is the primary pattern of action used in police shows, and certainly the heroic qualities of television cops consist of either exceptional physical or mental skills—if not both. What must not be overlooked, however, is the television cop's more genuinely heroic capacity to distinguish clearly between right and wrong. He/she has an unerring instinct for determining what is wrong and dis-covering who the bad guy is. As such, cops stand head and shoulders above the rest of society and at the same time relieve us of our need to question the complexity of our moral system or to confront our ambivalences about it.

The police's clarity of moral vision gives them license to exact vengeance from the guilty without fear of retribution and without contamination. Because of the importance of the social role the police play, we give them permission to use means not condoned for ordinary citizens. They can employ violence, in-timidation—even lying and blackmail—in the course of duty and not lose our respect. They have developed into an art form the elements of pursuit, which Siegfried Kracauer argues are intrinsically cinematic, but which just as rightfully belong to the medium of television.[19]

In addition to their exceptional mental or physical talents, another important characteristic of television cops is the role they play as mediators between the individual and society. At times they function as loners, alienated from or an-tagonistic toward society and unencumbered by family or other responsibilities, maintaining only the most tenuous connections to society through the police organization of which they are a part. At other times they have taken a more cooperative stance, joining forces with partners or teams of cops to work col-lectively and articulate concerns that extend beyond the immediate arena of their jobs into their private lives. Their function as mediators is frequently defined in terms of generational conflict. In this case the cop serves as either the parental figure who attempts to guide younger charges or as the youthful challenger who tries to accommodate and assimilate the old-fashioned ways of elders.

The implicit progression of television cops is toward the tragic. Castleman and Podrazik point out that "in the seventies, the easily understood and clearly identified molesters and crime czars of the past had been replaced in the public's mind by more amorphous, but equally frightening forces."[20] As evil becomes pervasive and undefined, cops are left exposed, no longer impenetrable. The more human and humane they become, the more vulnerable they are to moral flaw, and the simplistic, larger-than-life qualities of the heroic begin to mimic the more complex colorings of an Oedipus or Othello.

It might be argued that it is the detective who had the potential to ascend to tragic stature.[21] However, the detective's isolation from society and lack of contamination by what John Cawelti calls "the ordinary concepts of success and respectability" push the balance in that genre too far in the direction of independence and individualism.[22] The detective genre, relying on a romantic or fantasy mode, celebrates the potency of the individual and his freedom to investigate moral conduct. The cop maintains his identity as a legitimate representative of society as well as a loner, and as crime becomes increasingly complex and unsolvable, his task of reconciling personal motive and private ambition with social order and public justice becomes increasingly impossible.

In his discussion of the police genre in the related medium of film, Julian Petley locates an underlying tragedy for the cop in his rejection of sexuality. Petley describes the film genre as "dominated by images of men fleeing from women in search of an elusive masculine El Dorado where violence often becomes a substitute for erotic sexuality."[23] While women are not excluded from the police genre on television to the extent that they are in film, it remains a male-centered genre and one in which an underlying repression of sexuality necessarily corrupts the cops more than the robbers, who are frequently involved in sexual exploitation or degradation. Certainly it is never far from the cop as regulator of moral codes to the cop as sexual censor. The potentially tragic nature of the TV cop is primarily inclination—the manifestation of subtlety and nuance in character—rather than actuality. Certainly, the moral authority of the police remains too important a component of the genre to be compromised in the end. Besides, as Robert Warshow suggests, "the sense of tragedy is a luxury of aristocratic societies, where the fate of the individual is not conceived of as having a direct and legitimate political importance, being determined by a fixed and supra-political—that is, noncontroversial—moral order or fate."[24]

The more democratic mien of the television cop, which prevents his transcendence into the truly tragic, also accounts for attempts to establish a documentary-like realism in the genre. Authenticity is a highly praised and problematic attribute of the police genre on television. It capitalizes on the unique capacity of the medium to mix fiction and reality in unorthodox ways. The ordinariness, however, of a Joe Friday, a Mike Stone, a Baretta, or a Kojak is illusory. At the same time that television exploits their actuality, it also transforms them into heroes of the people.

The mythical underpinnings of the genre are also clear in its presumption of an urban landscape and the notion that the city must provide the context for crime. The recurrent concern of sociologists that television distorts the actual statistics of crime, emphasizing murder over domestic disputes and throwing blame on the businessman and the corporation, betrays the misguided aim of many to see television act solely as a mirror and example of social progress. The television cop—little guy and hero, superman and man of the streets—remains an artifice.

His weekly re-emergence on our television screens requires of him a genuineness and naturalness that often elude literary and cinematic cops. The reductive scale of the television screen makes him one of us, sustaining the battle against crime in the city week after week, without failure, but also without lasting success. He is our talisman, an arbiter of good and evil, who is both braver and wiser than we while remaining an ordinary guy. The violence that he employs may be seen on occasion as a displacement of sexual energy or more frequently as the symbolic representation of conflict in general. It is never simply an antisocial act or a measurable instigator of further violence. Television frees the cop to act, clearly and decisively, and the imaginary world in which he/she operates, closely as it may approximate our own, becomes the arena for a symbolic dialogue between good and evil. With the wisdom of Socrates, television cops always stay on the right side of the argument.

NOTES

1. John Fiske and John Hartley, *Reading Television* (New York: Methuen, 1978), p. 35.

2. Tim Brooks and Earl Marsh, *The Complete Directory to Prime Time Network TV Shows, 1946–Present*, rev. ed. (New York: Ballantine Books, 1981), p. 275.

3. "Dragnet Catches 38 Million Viewers," in *TV Guide: The First 25 Years*, ed. Jay S. Harris (New York: New American Library, 1978), p. 20.

4. Ibid., p. 21.

5. Fiske and Hartley, *Reading Television*, p. 175.

6. The most obvious example was a detective show, "Longstreet," starring James Franciscus as a blind insurance-company investigator.

7. Horace Newcomb, *TV: The Most Popular Art* (Garden City, N.Y.: Anchor Press, 1974), p. 103.

8. Robert Alley, "Television Drama," in *Television: The Critical View*, 3d ed., ed. Horace Newcomb (New York: Oxford University Press, 1982), p. 105.

9. Les Brown, *Televi$ion: The Business behind the Box* (New York: Harcourt Brace Jovanovich, 1971), p. 100.

10. It was variously called "Kate Columbo," "Kate the Detective," and "Kate Loves a Mystery" and ran from February through December 1979.

11. Brooks and Marsh, *The Complete Directory*, p. 60.

12. Alley, "Television Drama," p. 96.

13. In fact, Savalas has or had a full head of hair, according to a 1973 *TV Guide* story, and he shaves his head daily. See Al Stump, "Tales of Telly," in *TV Guide: The First 25 Years*, p. 216.

14. Alley, "Television Drama," p. 108.

15. Brown, *TV*, p. 6.

16. Harry Castleman and Walter Podrazik, *Watching TV: Four Decades of American Television* (New York: McGraw-Hill Book Company, 1982), p. 260.

17. For example, Robert Alley.

18. Michael Pollan, "Can 'Hill Street Blues' Rescue NBC?" *Channels*, March–April 1983, p. 32.

19. Siegfried Kracauer, *Theory of Film* (New York: Oxford University Press, 1960), p. 42.

20. Castleman and Podrazik, *Watching TV*, p. 246.

21. Indeed, Robert Warshow has claimed that title for the movie gangster, and Horace Newcomb makes an appeal for the hero of the Western as capable of a certain transcendence.

22. John G. Cawelti, *Adventure, Mystery and Romance* (Chicago: University of Chicago Press, 1976), p. 144.

23. Julian Petley, "Rough Justice," *Focus on Film*, October 1980, p. 36.

24. Robert Warshow, "The Gangster as Tragic Hero," in *The Immediate Experience* (New York: Atheneum, 1970), p. 127.

BIBLIOGRAPHICAL SURVEY

The starting point for an examination of the police genre should be John Cawelti's book, *Adventure, Mystery and Romance*. Although Cawelti's focus is popular literature and the detective, among other genres, he provides the necessary foundation for an understanding of the origins of all types of crime narratives in the nineteenth century. Robert Warshow's early but important essay, "The Gangster as Tragic Hero," from his book, *The Immediate Experience*, also lays important groundwork.

As with most television programming, there is little criticism of the police genre beyond the historical-descriptive mode. John Fiske and John Hartley, operating from a semiotic perspective, offer the most sophisticated analysis of the police genre in their comparison of "Ironside" with a British cop show in *Reading Television*. Geoffrey Hurd's essay "The Television Presentation of the Police" sheds further light on semiotic concerns in exclusively British police shows. Horace Newcomb includes a chapter entitled "Mystery: Order and Authority" in his book, *TV: The Most Popular Art*, which tends to blur the distinctions between police, detective, and other crime genres but still has interesting comments to make.

The best historical overview comes out of Harry Castleman and Walter Podrazik's book, *Watching TV: Four Decades of American Television*, but the reader has to pore through the entire book, or else sift for comments on individual shows. Also helpful are Christopher H. Sterling and John M. Kittross's general broadcast history, *Stay Tuned*, and Larry James Gianakos's three-volume series, *Television Drama Series Programming: A Comprehensive Chronicle*.

Les Brown looks at individual shows from a corporate and economic perspective that is often illuminating. A sampling of reviews of early shows like "Dragnet," "The Untouchables," and "Kojak" is available in *TV Guide: The First 25 Years*. For a look at the genre as it appears in film, the reader might start with Siegfried Kracauer's *Theory of Film* for its discussion of cinematic affinities, including the chase. For analyses that concentrate on the police genre itself in film, Julian Petley's "Rough Justice" in *Focus on Film* and Philip French's "Cops" in *Sight and Sound* are both worthwhile. Although the cinematic genre is a little different, many aspects complement those found in the television cop show.

The best of the social impact studies of the genre is Robert S. Alley's essay "Television Drama," available in the anthology, *Television: The Critical View*, but his analysis is limited by the assumption of a clear relationship between televised and real-life violence. A sampling of the range of commentary on television violence and the genre can be found in Walter Goodman's "Bang-Bang! You're Dead!" in *The New Republic*, Jerome Ellison's "Television: Stimulant to Violence" in *The Nation*, Arons and Katsh's "How TV Cops Flout the Law" in the *Saturday Review*, and "Who Breaks the Law on TV?" by Richard Lacayo in the *New York Times*. A rather spotty pop sociology attempt to analyze the genre in terms of the social background of television producers appears in Ben Stein's book, *The View from Sunset Boulevard*.

Reviews and features on individual shows can be found in *TV Guide*, although most libraries don't keep back issues. *The Reader's Guide to Periodical Literature* provides an index under the heading of "Television Program Reviews" to articles in more accessible popular magazines. Brooks and Marsh's *The Complete Directory to Prime Time Network TV Shows, 1946–Present* is an invaluable and compact reference tool. Two articles are worth singling out on "Hill Street Blues" since that program appears to reflect future directions the genre will take. They are "Can 'Hill Street Blues' Rescue NBC?" by Michael Pollan in *Channels* and "Make It Look Messy" by Todd Gitlin in *American Film*.

BOOKS AND ARTICLES

Alley, Robert S. "Television Drama." In *Television: The Critical View*, edited by Horace Newcomb. 3d ed. New York: Oxford University Press, 1982.

Arons, Stephen, and Ethan Katsh. "How TV Cops Flout the Law." *Saturday Review*, March 19, 1977, pp. 11–18.

Brooks, Tim, and Earle Marsh. *The Complete Directory to Prime Time Network TV Shows, 1946–Present*. Rev. ed. New York: Ballantine Books, 1981.

Brown, Les. *Televi$ion: The Business behind the Box*. New York: Harcourt Brace Jovanovich, 1971.

Castleman, Harry, and Walter J. Podrazik. *Watching TV: Four Decades of American Television*. New York: McGraw-Hill Book Company, 1982.

Cawelti, John G. *Adventure, Mystery, and Romance*. Chicago: University of Chicago Press, 1976.

Ellison, Philip. "Television; Stimulant to Violence." *The Nation*, December 21, 1963.

Ferkiss, Victor C. "Cops, Robbers, and Citizens." *Commonweal*, June 10, 1955.

Fiske, John, and John Hartley. *Reading Television*. New York: Methuen, 1978.

French, Philip. "Cops." *Sight and Sound*, Spring 1974.

Gianakos, Larry James. *Television Drama Series Programming: A Comprehensive Chronicle, 1947–1959*. Metuchen, N.J.: The Scarecrow Press, 1980.

Gitlin, Todd. "Make It Look Messy." *American Film*, September 1981.

Goodman, Walter. "Bang-Bang! You're Dead!" *New Republic*, November 1, 1954.

Harris, Jay S., ed. *TV Guide: The First 25 Years*. New York: New American Library, 1978.

Hurd, Geoffrey. "The Television Presentation of the Police." In *Popular Television and Film*, edited by Tony Bennet, Susan Boyd Bowman, Colin Mercer, and Janet Woollacott. London: British Film Institute Publishing, 1981.

Kracauer, Siegfried. *Theory of Film: The Redemption of Physical Reality*. New York: Oxford University Press, 1960.

Lacayo, Richard. "Who Breaks the Law on TV?" *New York Times*, March 6, 1983, Section 2, pp. 25, 34.

Newcomb, Horace. *TV: The Most Popular Art*. Garden City, N.Y.: Anchor Press, 1974.

Petley, Julian. "Rough Justice." *Focus on Film*, October 1980.

Pollan, Michael. "Can 'Hill Street Blues' Rescue NBC?" *Channels*, March–April 1983.

Stein, Ben. *The View from Sunset Boulevard: America as Brought to You by the People Who Make Television*. Garden City, N.Y.: Anchor Press, 1980.

Sterling, Christopher H., and John M. Kittross. *Stay Tuned: A Concise History of American Broadcasting*. Belmont, Calif.: Wadsworth Publishing Company, 1978.

Warshow, Robert. *The Immediate Experience: Movies, Comics, Theatre and Other Aspects of Popular Culture*. New York: Atheneum, 1970.

VIDEOGRAPHY

"Dragnet"
  NBC, various prime times
  Premiere: January 3, 1952
  Stars: Jack Webb, Ben Alexander (1953–1959), Harry Morgan (1967–1970)
  Last Program: September 10, 1970

"Highway Patrol"
  Syndicated
  Premiere: September 1955
  Star: Broderick Crawford
  Last Program: Spring 1959

"Naked City"
  ABC, various prime times
  Premiere: September 30, 1958
  Stars: James Franciscus (1958–1959), John McIntire (1958–1959), Horace McMahon (1959–1963), Paul Burke (1960–1963)
  Last Program: September 11, 1963

"The Untouchables"
  ABC, various prime times
  Premiere: October 15, 1959
  Star: Robert Stack
  Last Program: September 10, 1963

"The F.B.I."
  ABC, various prime times
  Premiere: September 19, 1965
  Star: Efrem Zimbalist, Jr.
  Last Program: September 8, 1974

"Ironside"
  NBC, various prime times
  Premiere: September 14, 1967
  Star: Raymond Burr
  Last Program: January 16, 1975

"Adam-12"
  NBC, various prime times
  Premiere: September 21, 1968
  Stars: Martin Milner, Kurt McCord
  Last Program: August 26, 1975

"The Mod Squad"
  ABC, various prime times
  Premiere: September 24, 1968
  Stars: Michael Cole, Clarence Williams III, Peggy Lipton
  Last Program: August 23, 1973

"Hawaii Five-O"
  CBS, various prime times
  Premiere: September 26, 1968
  Stars: Jack Lord, James MacArthur (1968–1979)
  Last Program: April 26, 1980

"McCloud"
  NBC, various prime times
  Premiere: September 16, 1970
  Star: Dennis Weaver
  Last Program: August 28, 1977

"Columbo"
  NBC, various prime times
  Premiere: September 15, 1971
  Star: Peter Falk
  Last Program: September 4, 1977

"McMillan and Wife"
  NBC, various prime times
  Premiere: September 29, 1971
  Stars: Rock Hudson, Susan St. James
  Last Program: August 21, 1977

"The Rookies"
  ABC, various prime times
  Premiere: September 11, 1972
  Stars: G. Sanford Brown, Michael Ontkean, Kate Jackson
  Last Program: June 29, 1976

"The Streets of San Francisco"
  ABC, various prime times
  Premiere: September 16, 1972
  Stars: Karl Malden, Michael Douglas (1972–1976), Richard Hatch (1976–1977)
  Last Program: June 23, 1977

"Police Story"
  NBC, various prime times
  Premiere: September 25, 1973
  Stars: Anthology
  Last Program: August 23, 1977

"Kojak"
  CBS, various prime times
  Premiere: October 24, 1973
  Stars: Telly Savalas, Kevin Dobson
  Last Program: April 15, 1978

"Police Woman"
  NBC, various prime times
  Premiere: September 13, 1974
  Stars: Angie Dickinson, Earl Holliman
  Last Program: August 30, 1978

"Baretta"
  ABC, various prime times
  Premiere: January 17, 1975
  Star: Robert Blake
  Last Program: June 1, 1978

"S.W.A.T."
  ABC, various prime times
  Premiere: February 24, 1975
  Stars: Steve Forrest, Robert Urich
  Last Program: June 24, 1976

"Starsky and Hutch"
  ABC, various prime times
  Premiere: September 3, 1975
  Stars: Paul Michael Glaser, David Soul
  Last Program: August 21, 1979

"Quincy, M.E."
  NBC, various prime times
  Premiere: October 3, 1976
  Star: Jack Klugman
  Last Program: September 5, 1983

"Hill Street Blues"
  NBC, Thursday, 10:00–11:00 P.M.
  Premiere: January 15, 1981
  Stars: Daniel Travanti, Michael Conrad, Veronica Hamel

3

The Detective Show

MARTIN F. NORDEN

OVERVIEW

One of the most durable genres in the history of narrative television is the detective show. Well over one hundred programs have focused on the activities of private investigators and police detectives, and the network interest in such programs has shown no signs of abating.

Several reasons suggest themselves for the genre's enduring popularity. With their emphasis on three intriguing "Cs"—crime, cerebration, and chases—detective shows can trace their popularity to likeminded novels, radio plays, and movies that have proliferated throughout this century. Indeed, many of these works have served as the basis for TV detective shows, including Frederic Dannay and Manfred Bennington Lee's Ellery Queen mystery novels, which began appearing in 1929 (and which also inspired an Ellery Queen series on CBS radio in 1939), and Earl Derr Biggers's novels featuring popular sleuth Charlie Chan, who eventually moved to radio, films, and television after his original literary appearance in 1925. Even comic strips have influenced the TV gumshoe program, as reflected by the short-lived "Dick Tracy" and "Fearless Fosdick" shows.

In addition to having a ready-made audience for detective shows, TV producers have discovered that such programs could be, and frequently are, relatively easy to create. Unlike their fantasy and science-fiction relatives, gumshoe programs require few if any elaborate special effects. And, unlike Westerns and other period programs, they are usually set in contemporary times and do not require special settings and costumes.

Otherwise, the detective genre has shared a number of similarities with its Western counterpart. In their initial TV forms, both genres frequently featured self-reliant heroes who took on assorted villains with pistols, fists, and strong moral convictions. The TV detective is also similar to the Western hero "in his aversion to violence on principle but constant indulgence of it in practice," as suggested by Edward Stasheff and Rudy Bretz.[1] The detective genre has matched if not passed the Western as the most popular dramatic programming on network television. Stasheff and Bretz wrote in 1973 that the detective had reached folk hero status and had given the Western hero serious competition as the most popular character on TV.[2] Given the decline of the Western during the 1970s and early 1980s and the continuing rise of the detective show, it is reasonable to conclude that the gumshoe has indeed surpassed the Westerner in popularity.

The detective genre overlaps considerably with a number of others: most notably, cop shows, spy shows, lawyer shows, and even newspaper shows. All have relied to some degree on aspects of detection work. To keep this chapter to a manageable length, however, it will concentrate only on those programs in which detection is the *key* element: namely, private eye and police detective shows.

HISTORICAL DEVELOPMENT

The detective drama has played a significant role in television ever since the medium began, thanks largely to an accident of history; the birth of network television coincided with a time when Hollywood filmmakers were exploring a new kind of cinema, labeled "film noir" by French film critics. Alternately considered a genre and a visual style, film noir generally referred to American movies of the immediate post–World War II period that focused on hardboiled detectives and other cynical loners who probed the corrupt underbelly of society amid urban environments. Film noir provided a fertile bed in which the new visual medium could spawn, and the result was an early and enduring interest in detective shows.

It is worth noting at this juncture that the detective story, regardless of medium, has always strongly encouraged audience participation. Indeed, a number of TV shows have gone out of their way to elicit an active audience role. At the conclusion of every episode of the 1975 video version of "Ellery Queen," for example, the title character, played by Jim Hutton, would turn to the camera and ask the audience if it had guessed the murderer's identity.

This tendency was most pronounced during the earliest TV antecedents of the video gumshoe genre: programs that combined elements of criminal dramas and game shows. Such programs included "Public Prosecutor," a half-hour series in which host John Howard presented a filmed mystery to a trio of contestants who had to figure out the identity of the culprit, and "They Stand Accused," a courtroom drama first telecast by Chicago's WGN-TV in early 1948. In this latter program, which CBS carried during the first half of 1949 before the DuMont network acquired and ran it for five years, actors improvised their lines during a trial before real-life judges and lawyers, while a studio audience acted as a jury. The actors based their "testimony" on a very basic scenario designed by Illinois Asst. Atty. Gen. William Wines.

The short-lived series "Barney Blake, Police Reporter" was another predecessor of the detective genre on television. Though the series was cancelled by its sponsor after only 13 weeks, it along with the drama/game shows cleared the way for the first great wave of true detective programs in 1949, when nine such series burst onto the TV screen.

Appearing in January of that year, "Stand By for Crime" has the distinction of being the first program transmitted to East Coast audiences from Chicago. This half-hour ABC series, which lasted for about eight months, featured what became a standard murder mystery format: a police inspector collecting and evaluating clues. Yet the show also manifested a legacy from the game-shows by inviting viewers and occasional guest celebrities to guess the identity of the guilty party. "Armchair Detective," CBS's answer to "Stand By for Crime," which appeared for three months in the middle of 1949, stressed the type of viewer participation that has been associated with the genre ever since. Each week the show's producers would present two 15-minute whodunit plays replete with clues for the audience to follow. The show did not have a detective per se, but a member of the California State Legislature would discuss the solutions at the end of each installment.

By September of 1949 all four networks had placed detection programs into their lineups. The most famous was the NBC live offering that ran until 1954: "Martin Kane, Private Eye." During the show's lifespan, the title character was played by four actors who, on the surface, were completely different: hounddog-faced William Gargan, hardboiled tough guy Lloyd Nolan, pipe-chomping Lee Tracy, and suave and handsome Mark Stevens. At first, the incorruptible and tenacious Kane worked closely with the police, but he eventually evolved into a more cynical loner.

The show's sponsor, the U.S. Tobacco Co., played a major role in shaping several of the program's elements. Kane always used a nearby tobacco shop as headquarters, and audiences frequently saw the first two Kanes (Gargan and Nolan) puffing away on Sano cigarettes, a U.S. Tobacco product. When Lee Tracy took over the role in 1952, Kane suddenly became a pipe smoker, since U.S. Tobacco became interested in promoting its Old Briar pipe tobacco. When the show was revamped as "The New Adventures of Martin Kane" the following year, Mark Stevens, the fourth "Kane," was seen smoking Sanos once again.

September also saw the appearance of TV's first laid-back detective, Police Inspector Hannibal Cobb (Chuck Webster) of ABC's "photocrime" mystery show, produced in association with *Look* magazine. The show failed to catch on, however, and the network cancelled it within three months. Audiences weren't ready for Cobb's low-key approach to solving crimes; they preferred tough-guy detective shows such as the long-running "Man Against Crime," which CBS launched in October 1949. The program featured Ralph Bellamy as Mike Barnett, a private eye who relied on his fists to see him through his predicaments. Like "Kane," the show was set in New York City, produced live, and ran until 1954 (NBC's attempt to revive the show during the summer of 1956 with Frank Lovejoy in the main role failed). Yet its producers quickly changed its "live" status to film so that they could stage its many chases and fight scenes more realistically.

Also appearing that month was DuMont's "The Plainclothesman," a police detection show that borrowed heavily from the techniques that Robert Montgomery employed in his innovative 1946 film treatment of Raymond Chandler's *The Lady in the Lake*. The show, which featured a nameless police lieutenant who never appeared on screen (Ken Lynch) working on various murder cases, presented the details of its stories exactly as the lieutenant saw them. If he got punched in the face, the image would go fuzzy and wobbly, and the screen would go black before the camera refocused on its subject from the ground level. Like Robert Montgomery's Philip Marlowe, Lynch's nameless detective never appeared on screen, unless he passed by a mirror. One might think the technique would grow old fast, but the popular "Plainclothesman" remained a staple of DuMont's lineup for five years.

Not satisfied with presenting only one detective show, DuMont quickly launched another, which became the network's most popular dramatic serial. "Rocky King, Inside Detective," which the network began delivering to its affiliates, aired in January 1950. Roscoe Karns played the title character, a New York City police detective occasionally prone to pugilism. While Rocky King was no Sherlock Holmes, he did have a special tenacity and common sense, which, combined with his sense of humor, made him a hard-working detective in this realistic program that was produced live.

The year 1950 also saw the first of the TV treatments of that durable mystery-writer turned sleuth, Ellery Queen. Queen was so proficient at solving crimes that his father, homicide Inspector Richard Queen of the New York City police, frequently turned to him for help. As produced live by DuMont, the show starred John Hart in the title role. Following Hart's untimely death several months after the series began, he was replaced by Lee Bowman, who remained with the series through its move to ABC in late 1951 until the latter network cancelled it a year later.

The detective genre continued to prove popular with the networks in 1951 with three new programs appearing that year. ABC brought together the familial aspects of detective work as demonstrated in "Ellery Queen" to create "Crime With Father." This show, which lasted half a year, featured a police detective whose teenaged daughter frequently obstructed and then helped solve his homicide cases. The same year also witnessed DuMont's "The Gallery of Mme. Lui Tsong," sharring Anna May Wong as the beautiful owner of a string of art galleries who, in the tradition of Dr. Yat Fu in "Mysteries of Chinatown," was a detective on the side. Mme Lui Tsong did not fare nearly as well as the intrepid Dr. Fu, however, and was shanghaied off the airwaves after less than three months.

The most important detective show to appear that year was "Mark Saber." Initially titled "Mystery Theater," "Mark Saber" starred debonair actor Tom Conway as a refined and thoroughly British homicide expert working with the

New York City police force. Elegant in speech and appearance, Mark Saber was the quintessential British sleuth who solved murder cases with incredible powers of deduction. After ABC had dropped the series after three years, it rejuvenated it a year and a half later under the title "The Vise." The show had undergone more than just a nominal change. Donald Gray had replaced Tom Conway as Mark Saber, the show's producers had changed the settings to various locations only in Europe, and Saber now had only one arm. "The Vise" ran for one and a half years on ABC before NBC picked it up in September 1957 and ran it for another three years. "Mark Saber" has the distinction of undergoing more name changes than any other program in television history; it has been variously called "Mystery Theater," "Mark Saber Mystery Theater," "Mark Saber," "Inspector Mark Saber—Homicide Squad," "Homicide Squad," "The Vise," "Saber of London," "Uncovered," and "Detective's Diary."

Approximately ten detective shows were on the air each year from 1949 through 1952. This four-year period marked the first peak of the TV shamus genre, but it declined over the next four years. It reached a low in popularity during 1955 and 1956 as comedy shows, game shows, and dramatic anthologies attained dominance on the networks. CBS's "The Tell-Tale Clue," a 1954 summer replacement that stressed scientific detective methods, was one of the exceedingly few new sleuth shows to appear on the networks during this time.

Producers of syndicated programming picked up the slack left by the networks and created several detective shows of reasonably high quality during those lean years. Among them was the "The Lone Wolf," featuring Louis Hayward as international detective Michael Lanyard, a character introduced by novelist Louis Joseph Vance in 1914. Originally a gentleman jewel thief, Lanyard was transformed into a dedicated sleuth in both his film and TV manifestations.

Far more noteworthy was the first television version of Sir Arthur Conan Doyle's legendary sleuth, "Sherlock Holmes." This brief series, filmed in Paris, featured a major change in the medium's portrayal of the detective. Instead of the brawling tough-guy older sleuth so common up to that point, series producer Sheldon Reynolds cast the youthful and sensitive-looking Ronald Howard as Holmes, who underplayed his role to the delight of critics of the time. This series, along with "Mark Saber," paved the way for several other shows that featured cerebral British sleuths employing scientific detection methods. They included ABC's 1957 "Scotland Yard," an anthology based on actual Scotland Yard cases, and 1958's "Colonel March of Scotland Yard," with film star Boris Karloff playing the one-eyed title character of that series.

If the pickings were slim from 1953 to 1956, the genre made a strong comeback in 1957, with a wide range of sleuth shows represented. In addition to "Scotland Yard," "M Squad" first appeared that year, starring Lee Marvin as tough-guy Lt. Frank Ballinger, one of several plainclothes police detectives who worked alone. "Meet McGraw," another detective show, starred Frank Lovejoy (who had worked briefly as Mike Barnett in "The Man Against Crime" the year before) as a detective *sans* first name, gun, and official license. A mercenary and archetypal loner, McGraw frequently deserted women to pursue yet another profitable situation involving detection work.

Also that year, David Janssen starred as the title character of "Richard Diamond, Private Detective," a television remake of a popular radio series starring Dick Powell. Diamond was a private eye who had once been a New York City cop and who often used his connections with the police department to gain information and assistance. Late in the series, after its producers had changed the locale to southern California, the producers added a woman known only as "Sam," who worked at an answering service that Diamond used. "Sam," shown only from the waist down, was briefly played by a young model named Mary Tyler Moore.

Several famous film detectives made the transition to the small screen in 1957. The celebrated Chinese sleuth Charlie Chan made his first appearance as a TV detective in a series of the same name, featuring a miscast J. Carroll Naish as the wise, humble, and aphoristic Chan. Also that year American audiences were introduced to the video versions of Nick and Nora Charles, the lead characters of the durable and delightful "Thin Man" series of theatrical films produced from 1934 to 1947. As a TV show "The Thin Man" starred Peter Lawford and Phyllis Kirk in the roles that William Powell and Myrna Loy had made famous in the films. Based on a story by Dashiell Hammett, the film series and the TV program had the same premise: two happily married, well-to-do New Yorkers and their dog Asta combined their talents to pursue their unusual hobby of solving crimes. The show expertly blended sophisticated comedy with detection work.

Acknowledgment should also be made of the appearance of "Perry Mason" that year. Though Mason (Raymond Burr) was a lawyer and not a detective, he did have a gumshoe on retainer, the intrepid Paul Drake (William Hopper). Mason relied on Drake to obtain information for his cases, and Drake often obliged by bringing key clues or witnesses into the courtroom during climactic moments—a tendency that became his trademark.

The upswing in detective shows continued in 1958. NBC rejuvenated the "Ellery Queen" series, which ran for a year and starred George Nader and later Lee Philips in the title role, while several syndicated shamus shows flickered across the small screen for the first time. They included "Mike Hammer," which starred Darren McGavin as Mickey Spillane's hard-hitting private eye, and "Official Detective," a series headed by Everett Sloane that dramatized real criminal cases.

Nineteen fifty-eight will also be remembered as the year in which the detective genre entered the "hip age," when sleuths seemed "cooler" and more debonair and their exploits were often accompanied by a jazz (or at least a finger-snapping) score. Led by "The Investigator," an NBC summer series in which a hip young private eye often solved mysteries with the aid of his ex-reporter father, two shows figured prominently in the new era of the TV detective: "Peter Gunn" and "77 Sunset Strip."

"Peter Gunn" featured Craig Stevens as a young swinger who also happened to be a very proficient detective. The handsome Gunn, who certainly had a way with the ladies, often relied on the help of Lieutenant Jacoby (Hershel Bernardi) to see him through his professional entanglements. The show was similar to "The Investigator," but with one difference: NBC chose this time to change the familial connection. Though audiences never saw any of Gunn's relatives, he did spend of lot of his spare time at a jazz nightclub called "Mother's," run by a woman known only by that name.

Another long-running sleuth show was "77 Sunset Strip," an early Warner Brothers production for ABC. It was an important show in the genre; as Tim Brooks and Earle Marsh have suggested, the program "was the prototype for a rash of glamorous private-detective teams in the late 1950s and early 1960s."[3] This globe-trotting team consisted of Stu Bailey (Efrem Zimbalist, Jr.), an urbane former college professor who had worked for the Office of Strategic Services during World War II, and Jeff Spencer (Roger Smith), who had put in time as a government agent before turning to a career as a private investigator. They were frequently assisted by Gerald Lloyd Kookson, III, better remembered as "Kookie" (Edward Byrnes), a jive-talking young man who parked cars for a living at the restaurant next to their Hollywood agency. At the behest of Ed Byrnes (who had walked out on the show after demanding a bigger role in the series), Kookie eventually became a full-fledged member of the detective agency.

As a host of new shamus shows began complementing the already existing ones, "77 Sunset Strip" led the gumshoe genre to another peak in 1959. Warner Brothers attempted to capitalize on its success with "77 Sunset Strip" by turning out a number of imitators, including "Bourbon Street Beat," set in New Orleans. Like its predecessor, "Bourbon Street Beat" had two established private eyes, a young hopeful trying to join the agency, and a distinctive setting. When the show folded in a year, a major character of "BSB," Rex Randolph (Richard Long), briefly became a partner of the detective agency on Sunset Strip, while "Kookie" surrogate Kenny Madison (Van Williams) became the star of yet another Warner Brothers detective show, "Surfside Six," in 1960. Set in Miami, "Surfside Six" hewed to the formula of its predecessors and lasted about two years.

"Hawaiian Eye," another Warner Brothers entry debuting in 1959 on ABC, also followed closely the pattern established by "77 Sunset Strip." As with the other WB programs, it featured two hip detectives surrounded by kooky helpers and beautiful women in an exotic setting. The team this time consisted of Tom Lopaka and Tracy Steele (Robert Conrad and Anthony Eisley), who were often assisted by Cricket (Connie Stevens), a cute, somewhat scatter-brained young woman who sang for a living at the hotel where Lopaka and Steele had their offices, and Kazuo Kim (Poncie Ponce), a seemingly demented cab driver with a pronounced affection for ukuleles and bad jokes.

Warner Brothers took the format of its four ABC detective shows a step further by having characters from one series appear on another as guest stars. For example, Stu Bailey of "77 Sunset Strip" appeared in the eighth episode of

"Hawaiian Eye" to help the latter program's ratings. Writing on ABC's program strategies in a 1959 M.A. thesis, future programming wiz Fred Silverman was intrigued by the technique, called "cross-plugging." When he became CBS program head year later, he reintroduced the technique using the popular shamus shows "Cannon" and "Barnaby Jones."[4]

It is also worth noting that Raymond Chandler's famous gumshoe Philip Marlowe first appeared on the small screen in 1959. As played by craggy-faced Philip Carey, Marlowe was considerably toned down from his manifestations in Chandler's novels. Though still a cyncial loner, Carey's Marlowe was much less aggressive, conforming to the blander contours of the television medium.

The detective genre continued strong into 1960, with more than 15 programs in each year (1959 and 1960) focusing primarily on detection work. Among the new programs were "Michael Shayne," featuring Richard Denning as yet another debonair, womanizing private eye, and Eric Ambler's original work for TV, "Checkmate."

The next few years began seeing some slippage in the popularity of the genre, with only three new detective shows appearing in 1961 and none the following year. The most interesting of the three new programs (all of which succumbed within a year) was the first detective/Western hybrid: NBC's "Whispering Smith," staring World War II hero Audie Murphy as an 1870s Denver detective who applied analytical methods of detection to his cases.

The eroding strength of the detective genre during the early and mid 1960s may be interpreted as an indirect response to the Cold War, then heating up. In the wake of the hugely successful James Bond movies and their imitators, the networks began shifting their emphasis from detective to spy programs, throwing the gumshoe genre into a temporary tailspin. An example of this trend is one of the few detective shows to materialize during those years, "Burke's Law." Amos Burke (Gene Barry) was a wealthy, womanizing chief of detectives in Los Angeles when the series began in 1963. Yet the program's network, ABC, could not ignore the growing popularity of spy movies and TV shows and in 1965 changed Burke into an international spy working for the U.S. government. The program's altered title reflected the transformation: "Amos Burke—Secret Agent."

A 1965 ABC spin-off of the revamped Burke program featured Anne Francis in the title role of "Honey West," and it too reflected the network's new interests. Honey West was a private eye, but with her martial arts talent and penchant for using fancy weaponry, she resembled a female counterpart of James Bond more than a typical sleuth.

Yet the genre did not stay down for too many years. Amid many new police dramas, the detective program made something of a comeback in the late 1960s. NBC's long-running "Ironside," first telecast in 1967, told the story of San Francisco Chief of Detectives Robert Ironside (Raymond Burr), who became paralyzed from the waist down after an assassin firing a high-powered rifle struck his spine. Forced to resign his position, Ironside convinced the police commissioner to let him stay on as a special consultant. Accompanied by a police detective (Don Galloway), a black personal aide (Don Mitchell), and a police-woman (first Barbara Anderson, then Elizabeth Baur), the wheelchair-bound Ironside proved most effective at solving crimes.

Other police detective shows appearing during that time included ABC's "N.Y.P.D." Highly regarded for its realism, "N.Y.P.D." featured an integrated group of plainclothes detectives working on a wide variety of cases all over the island of Manhattan. Police detectives also covered other island territory begin-ning in the late 1960s—the Hawaiian Islands—in the redoubtable CBS police drama filmed on location, "Hawaii Five-O." This group of state police detec-tives, led by Steve McGarrett and Danny Williams (Jack Lord and James MacArthur), frequently matched wits with various underworld bosses.

Despite Lord's wooden acting and the predictable scripting (the phrase "Book him, Danno" became a staple of virtually every episode, for example), "Hawaii Five-O" has been the longest-running police detective show as of this writing, lasting from 1968 to 1980.

"Mannix," a CBS detective show whose tenure on the tube coincided almost exactly with that of "Ironside," resembled a reaction to the spy shows that had enjoyed considerable popularity. At first Joe Mannix (Mike Connors) worked for an agency that employed the most sophisticated of detection equipment, including computers, but as Tim Brooks and Earle Marsh have suggested, "Man-nix seemed happiest with no implements other than his own intuition and fists."[5] By the series' second year, the macho Mannix had quit the company, become a self-employed gumshoe, and hired Peggy Fair (Gail Fisher), the widow of a police friend, as his secretary. "Mannix" was the brainchild of Bruce Geller, who also produced the hugely successful "Mission: Impossible" and who cor-rectly read the shifts in audience interest away from spy shows during the late 1960s to create this vehicle for Mike Connors. "Mannix," one of the most violent of detective shows, was an obvious throwback to the tough-guy type of shamus program so popular during the late 1940s and early 1950s.

Otherwise, the new detective programs of the late 1960s through 1970 were undistinguished, highly derivative, and snuffed out within a year. One of these, "Dan August," starred soon-to-be movie star Burt Reynolds as a no-nonsense police detective in southern California, but the show received lukewarm ratings. It lasted until 1971, when it was cancelled, fittingly, in August.

By 1971, however, the networks apparently believed that audiences had had their fill of spy shows and embraced the detective genre once again. They introduced a wide range of gumshoe shows, two of which—"Cannon" and "Columbo"—became long-running hits. Ironically, these two programs emerged as a reaction to the handsome, macho types of detectives exemplified by Joe Mannix and Steve McGarrett. During the early 1970s the networks had, in the words of industry-watcher Sally Bedell, "overloaded their schedules with mo-notonous copies" of such shows as "Hawaii Five-O" and "The F.B.I." and had "glutted the airwaves with more than two dozen of these series, starring law-and-order characters of every stripe."[6] CBS programming chief Fred Silverman began looking for an "antihero antidote" to the rugged, handsome detective and discovered one in the form of rotund, balding actor William Conrad, whom he had seen and liked in a TV-movie. Silverman approached Quinn Martin, an expert action-show producer, to build a shamus series around Conrad, and the result was "Cannon."

Frank Cannon was a middle-aged private detective who loved the finer things in life, as his ample girth and flashy Continental clearly reflected. Unlike many other TV detectives who combined youthful good looks with a well-developed ability to handle a gun or a fist, Cannon scrupulously avoided violence wherever possible, preferring instead to rely on brainpower to see him through. Though the show featured a rather dumpy lead character (and no regular supporting cast), "Cannon" exploded into a quick success and appealed to a wide audience. William Conrad explained the program's popularity this way: "Kids seem to like the show because they think Cannon is honest. Middle-aged people see him as one of their own making it—not some stereotyped Hollywood god, but the guy they see on the street."[7]

Dumpiness was an even stronger hallmark of Lieutenant Columbo of the Los Angeles Police Department, whose overly polite behavior and rumpled appearance—an effect created mainly by his famous ancient raincoat—masked an incredibly sharp and analytical mind. "Columbo" producers Richard Levinson and William Link originally wanted Bing Crosby to play the lead role in the series. After the 67–year-old singer rejected their offer, they hired the relatively unknown Peter Falk, who put the indelible stamp of his own personality on the role. As portrayed by Falk in this program (which NBC originally rotated with "McMillan and Wife" and "McCloud"), the stogie-chomping Columbo appeared hopelessly incompetent to the wealthy suspects of the intricately plotted crime that began each episode (and which was usually the episode's only violent act). Yet he always managed to unravel the crime and identify the criminal by episode's end, to the utter amazement of all involved in the case. Since audiences knew very little about Columbo's background, they derived most of their satisfaction from his disheveled charm and adroit verbal fencing with the criminal, which became a cherished ritual of the show.

The early to mid-1970s saw a renewed interest in presenting ethnically diverse detectives—a tradition begun years before but limited largely to Chinese gumshoes such as Charlie Chan, Mme Lui Tsong, and Khan. Among the newest of the ethnic gumshoe shows were NBC's "Banacek," starring George Peppard as Polish-American Thomas Banacek, a successful investigator for insurance companies, and a trio of CBS entries: "Shaft," based on the highly successful series of films starring Richard Roundtree (who also starred in the show) as a streetwise black detective in New York; "Bronk," featuring movie villain Jack Palance as Alex Bronkov, a police lieutenant hired by a southern California mayor to investigate the corrupt conditions of his town; and "Kojak," starring Telly Savalas as a lollypop-sucking cop of Eastern European descent.

In addition, a kind of "gray liberation" occurred during this time, as a number of senior citizens found themselves playing detectives. In 1972 CBS chief of programming Fred Silverman was interested in placing another nontraditional detective show into the network's lineup as quickly as possible, and once again turned to veteran producer Quinn Martin for help. Martin obliged by creating "Barnaby Jones," which went on the air in January 1973. The slow-paced but durable "Barnaby Jones" presented Buddy Ebsen as a former private eye lured out of retirement after his son, who had taken over the agency, was murdered while conducting an investigation. After he and his son's widow Betty (Lee Meriwether) successfully tracked down the killer, Jones elected to keep his agency in business. Jones's appearance and demeanor, like that of Columbo, often led his suspects to believe that he would be incapable of (or at least slow at) solving the crime, yet he too proved them wrong. To help give the show an early edge in the ratings, Silverman employed the "cross-plugging" technique he had first discovered while writing his M.A. thesis of ABC's programming years before and had William Conrad as Frank Cannon appear in the show's first episode.

Another show following the exploits of a geriatric gumshoe, ABC's brief 1973 series "Griff," starred erstwhile "Bonanza" patriarch Lorne Greene as Wade Griffin, a 30-year police captain who resigned from the force to create his own investigation agency. Finally, ABC's "The Snoop Sisters" featured the venerable actresses Helen Hayes and Mildred Natwick as two elderly mystery writers who lived up to their name by frequently becoming entangled in real crimes. They were assisted in this short-lived 1973–1974 series by their chauffeur and their nephew, who just happened to be a police lieutenant.

The mid-1970s also continued to see the emergence of private eyes with singular characteristics. For example, the unusual quality of gumshoe Harry Tenafly (of NBC's "Tenafly") was the fact that he was black, happily married, spent considerable time with his family, and regarded his work as a private eye as only a job, not an obsession. Another rarity of the time was Amy Prentiss of the NBC show of the same name, a young widow who became the first woman to become chief of detectives in San Francisco. Both shows were quickly cancelled, but NBC hit paydirt with another "oddball"—an easy-going fellow who had served time in prison before turning to a life of sleuthing. He became perhaps the most popular TV detective of all time: Jim Rockford of "The Rockford Files." He had been incarcerated for a crime he didn't commit, and on his release he turned to the life of a shamus with a special interest in taking on closed cases. Working out of a trailer, Rockford (James Garner) was frequently assisted by his father "Rocky" Rockford (Noah Beery), an ex-con friend (Stuart Margolin), and a young detective whose boyish charm fooled many criminals, Richie Brockelman (Dennis Dugan). Dugan had his own detective show in 1978 for five months. Rockford's exploits often landed him on the other side of the law; whenever that happened, his attorney girlfriend Beth Davenport (Gretchen Corbett) always managed to spring him from jail.

"The Rockford Files" was blessed by witty writing and fine acting, particularly by Garner, whose seemingly effortless style won him an Emmy in 1977. After the show scored high in the ratings during its first season, CBS tried to take down Rockford's shingle by counter-programming its megahit "Hawaii Five-O" against the series. Fearing the worst, NBC executives wanted to jettison the show's humor and low-key approach in favor of matching "Hawaii Five-O's" heavy action, but Garner, whose company produced the show, refused to cooperate. NBC eventually gave in and allowed the show to continue in its original format, which resulted in a mixed blessing. CBS pulled "Hawaii Five-O" out of its new slot after only two months as "The Rockford Files" grew even stronger, but thereafter "Rockford" began losing ground and never attained the heights of popularity it had once reached.

Matching Jim Rockford in the casual lifestyle department was Harry Orwell of ABC's "Harry O." Harry (David Janssen, who had also starred in "Richard Diamond, Private Detective") lived in a cottage on a San Diego beach and often rode the city bus to get around town. As a police officer, he had been shot in the back and was forced to resign. To supplement his meager disability payments, Harry—still carrying the bullet in his back—became a private eye taking on cases that intrigued him.

Several detectives made famous in other media made the journey to the small screen but with decidedly uneven results. Based on novels by Donald Hamilton and movies starring Dean Martin, "Matt Helm" ran for only half a season in 1975, audiences having apparently tired of the spy character who had been transformed into a globe-trotting detective for TV. Even more disastrous was the television version of Ross MacDonald's famous detective in "Archer." The veteran actor Brian Keith gave generally realistic performances as Lew Archer, but his work could not save the show, which lasted only about six weeks. Faring somewhat better was the second revival of "Ellery Queen," starring Jim Hutton in the title role and David Wayne as his father. This time around, NBC set the show during the 1940s, but this gimmick was not enough to save the show after one year.

If for no other reason, 1976 will be remembered as the year when TV audiences were introduced to three beautiful but vacuous young women who worked for a detective agency headed by an unseen fellow named Charlie Townsend. "Charlie's Angels" sprung from the fevered brows of Aaron Spelling and Leonard Goldberg, who in 1974 proposed a show to ABC tentatively titled "The Alley Cats," about three beautiful female detectives. The network was cool to the idea, however, until Fred Silverman stepped on board as ABC's entertainment head. No doubt aware of the growing popularity of NBC's sexy "Police Woman" series, Silverman eagerly embraced the Spelling-Goldberg series, by now renamed "Charlie's Angels." The producers hired Ivan Goff and Ben Roberts, who had scored heavily with "Mannix," to rewrite the pilot script, and the project was now off the ground.

The original cast included Kate Jackson as Sabrina Duncan, the supposed leader of the women, Jaclyn Smith as Kelly Garrett, a former show girl, and Farrah Fawcett-Majors as Jill Munroe, the one with the flowing blonde mane and pearly white choppers. They took their orders from an unseen private eye (the voice was supplied by John Forsythe) and were shepherded by Charlie's assistant Bosley (David Doyle).

Despite extensive research, the resulting series featured weak scripts and acting to match.[8] Nevertheless, the show was an instant success. As co-producer Goldberg noted, "It was then that the *Charlie's Angels* phenomenon began and it was as startling to us as the Farrah Phenomenon that grew out of it. We thought it was a nice little show, nothing more, and we were totally unprepared for what happened. It was a hit from the start."[9] The show's success was largely due to its glamorous trio of detectives and the various states of undress in which they found themselves (all in the line of duty, of course). It was primarily a prime-time version of soft-core porn masquerading as a detective show, a point supported by the program's most famous member, Farrah Fawcett-Majors, who stated: "When the show was No. 3, I figured it was our acting. When we got to be No. 1, I decided it could only be because none of us wears a bra."[10]

Farrah Fawcett-Majors was relatively unknown when the series began; her major claims to fame prior to "Charlie's Angels" were her appearances in shampoo and toothpaste commercials and her roles as David Janssen's neighbor in "Harry O" and Raquel Welch's bedmate in the movie *Myra Breckinridge*. Yet she quickly eclipsed the erstwhile star of the show, Kate Jackson, thanks largely to her appearance and a carefully mounted promotional campaign that swept the country. Believing she had a viable career as a film actress, Fawcett-Majors resigned from the show the following year, to be replaced by Cheryl Ladd as Jill's younger sister Kris. As the series progressed, Jackson dropped out and was replaced by model Shelley Hack. The producers blamed the show's faltering ratings on Hack and fired her a year later, replacing her with Tanya Roberts. The sultry Roberts could not improve the ratings, however, and the show was eventually cancelled. She and the others associated with the program never overcame its fundamental problems: bad dialogue, flat characterizations (the women's roles were interchangeable for all intents and purposes), mediocre acting, an undue reliance on "skin," and boring stories resolved by the most coincidental of circumstances.

The year 1976 might also be considered as the year of the police detective drama, with five such programs debuting. Four of them—"Jigsaw John," "Serpico," "Delvecchio," and "Holmes and Yoyo"—were all short-lived affairs. The fifth, NBC's "Quincy, M.E.," set in Los Angeles, remained a durable entry into the genre. This program was an oddity among police detective shows in that Quincy (Jack Klugman) was not officially a detective but often behaved like one. As a medical examiner for the county coroner's office, Quincy often believed that some deaths that the police had officially labeled as accidental were actually murders. He and his lab assistant Sam Fujiyama (Robert Ito) spend much of their time gathering clues and other evidence to prove his suspicions, much to the consternation of their boss and the police officers assigned to the cases. Qunicy's rather grisly job as a pathologist never stood in the way of the program's popularity.

Early 1977 saw the premiere of a pair of intertwined shows featuring youthful amateur detectives. The first of these, "The Hardy Boys Mysteries," was a contemporary video version of Edward L. Stratemeyer's popular books and starred teenage heartthrobs Shaun Cassidy and Parker Stevenson as Joe and Frank Hardy, respectively. The sons of a famous private investigator, they frequently found themselves in various nonviolent mystery situations but always had time for girls and performing pop music. The show originally alternated with ·"The Nancy Drew Mysteries," with Pamela Sue Martin as the title character. Within a year the producers were cross-plugging the Hardys and Nancy Drew into each others' programs, and by early 1978 ABC merged the programs into the entitled "Hardy Boys/Nancy Drew Mysteries," in which all three young stars appeared simultaneously. The entire program folded in 1979.

NBC's "The Eddie Capra Mysteries" and CBS's "Kaz" were two detective/ lawyer shows appearing in 1978 that stressed the unconventionality of its lead characters. Both Eddie Capra (Vincent Baggetta) and Martin "Kaz" Kazinsky (Ron Leibman) were young and approached their work in nonconformist ways while working for very conventional law firms. Audiences cared little for the accent on upstart detectives, however, and Capra and Kaz along with youthful Rockford protégé Richie Brockelman were quickly ejected from the network lineups.

Faring much better that year was a new show that presented the adventures of a private detective working in the desert city of slot machines and gaming tables: ABC's "Vega$." Robert Urich starred as Dan Tanna, the latest in a long line of good-looking, quick-witted shamuses often surrounded by glamorous women. Bedecked in blue jeans and leather vest, Tanna matched wits with the most corrupt criminals Las Vegas had to offer, often at the request of Bernie Roth (Tony Curtis), a wealthy casino owner who kept Tanna on retainer.

Five new detective shows appeared during 1979, but only one of them became an unqualified hit. The losers were CBS's "Paris" and "Big Shamus, Little Shamus," NBC's "Whodunit," and ABC's "Detective School."

The year's winner was ABC's "Hart to Hart." Jonathan and Jennifer Hart were played by Robert Wagner and Stephanie Powers, two veterans of the TV detective genre whose roles were fashioned after the sophisticated and loving husband-wife team of Nick and Nora Charles of "The Thin Man" fame. Though the premises of many of the episodes were highly improbable (every week, a friend would be murdered or accused of murder, or Jennifer would be kidnapped), the obvious chemistry of its two stars made the show sparkle and enjoyable for years.

As we entered the 1980s, the detective genre continued to intrigue networks and audiences alike, despite the relatively quick cancellation of two highly promising gumshoe shows, ABC's "Tenspeed and Brownshoe" and NBC's "Nero Wolfe."

A quality detective program that had the additional good fortune of becoming both a critical and ratings success was "Magnum, P.I." Set in Hawaii, the show was originally designed to exploit the good looks of former model Tom Selleck (whose previous claim to stardom was playing a tuxedoed cowboy in TV commercials for a cologne company), but Selleck along with producers Glen Larson and Donald Bellisario turned "Magnum, P.I." into a detective show with well-developed characters and interesting situations. The major characters included Magnum himself, an athletic Vietnam vet turned private eye who lived on an estate of a perpetually absent millionaire writer; Jonathan Higgins, the estate's eminently proper manager, played with precision by John Hillerman; T.C. (Roger E. Moseley), a helicopter pilot; and Rick (Larry Manetti), a local innkeeper. Their interplay has been one of the show's highlights; they have made deals among themselves, suckered one another, bailed each other out of tight situations, and tried to outwit one another—all accomplished in a playful, affectionate spirit. "Magnum, P.I.," a truly charming show, is unlike a number of other recent detective programs in that the lead character does not accidently but conveniently come across solutions; Magnum works hard at his craft, which lends a strong air of believability to the situations he is investigating.

CBS continued to have good fortune with the detective genre during the 1981 season with the debut of "Simon & Simon." A throwback to the 1960 sibling shamus series "The Brothers Brannagan," this new show focused on the activities of two young San Diego-based private eyes who also happen to be distinctly different brothers: A.J. (Jameson Parker), a city dandy whose boyish good looks belie a sharp mind, and Rick (Gerald McRaney), his rough-and-tumble country counterpart. A common plot ploy is to have the Simons begin a simple investigation that quickly escalates into an unanticipated situation of major proportions. In one episode, the Simons' probing into a kidnapping case lands them in hot water with wildcatters. In another, they wind up in the middle of a battle between a gunrunner and the F.B.I. while attempting to track down graduates for a class reunion. "Simon & Simon" normally follows CBS's popular "Magnum, P.I." series on Thursday evenings, though the network often pre-empted the newer show for specials and movies. Despite such treatment "Simon & Simon" proved popular enough for CBS to renew it. In an attempt to bolster the show's ratings at the onset of its second season, CBS cross-plugged Thomas Magnum and the Simons into each other's shows as the sleuths ironically worked *against* each other on a case that extended from one program into the other.

The detective genre was alive and well on television during the 1982 season, with four new gumshoe shows making their appearance that year. Two shows, "The Devlin Connection" and the whimsical supernatural detective program "Tucker's Witch," quickly bit the dust, but "Matt Houston" and "Remington Steele" remained relatively durable.

The title character of "Matt Houston" is a wealthy, womanizing young Texan who runs a private investigation agency in Los Angeles on the side, mainly for the benefit of his friends, who are constantly getting into trouble. As for "Remington Steele," it proved to be the highlight of the new entries of 1982. Laura Holt (Stephanie Zimbalist) was a hard-working private investigator whose company teetered on the brink of bankruptcy because no one wanted to hire a female shamus. The situation changed considerably after she concocted a fictional character with a thoroughly masculine name (which she created by suturing the names of an electric razor and an NFL football team) who would be her "boss" and receive the credit for the investigative work that she performed. The ruse worked perfectly until a nameless narcissistic swindler distinctly resembling a young Cary Grant (Pierce Brosnan) showed up at her door and threatened to expose her charade unless she hired him to play Steele. She reluctantly agreed, and the new Steele, though a bit of a bumbler, caught on quickly to the intricacies of detective work and has naturally taken full credit for every case they solve.

THEMES AND ISSUES

The TV detective show inherited from its literary, film, and radio forebears a pronounced tendency to encourage strong audience participation. The first video manifestations of the detective programs, which combined mystery and game-show formats, amply demonstrated this quality. As the genre matured, it encouraged audiences to participate in more traditional ways. They were asked to discover the clues along with the protagonist or to see how the hero would arrive at the conclusion they already knew, having learned the identity of the criminal early in the episode.

Unfortunately, certain other requisites have dominated the detective genre, creating a sameness among many of its shows. As Edward Stasheff and Rudy Bretz have sarcastically suggested, "whether we know 'who dunit' from the very beginning or derive a large part of our viewing pleasure in trying to figure out who the culprit must have been, the guns must blaze and the cops must scream around corners, or the ratings drop. Whether the programs run for thirty minutes or sixty, the culprits must run for four or five minutes at the very least and meet their end with a shoot out in a darkened warehouse!"[11]

Producers of detective dramas may have succumbed to these temptations too frequently, but they also have recognized the necessity of distinguishing their shows from other ones, precisely because of the considerable overlap among programs in the genre. With its exotic settings for ABC, the Warner Brothers company pioneered a major technique for setting apart detective programs. During TV's first decade, gumshoe shows were almost always set in New York City or Chicago, but Warner Brothers changed that by setting its programs in Hollywood, Hawaii, New Orleans, and Miami. Though the Big Apple and the Windy City continue to serve as backdrops for many detective shows, the interest in using other environments has continued strong, with Hawaii and San Francisco emerging as particular favorites.

Another context-related technique that producers have used (if infrequently) to differentiate their gumshoe programs from others is the period setting. In addition to the 1870s Denver locale of "Whispering Smith," producers perhaps intrigued by the movie *Chinatown* used 1930s settings for a handful of shamus programs telecast during the mid-1790s. Though short-lived as a strategy, the period setting matched its exotic-setting counterpart in the strong sense of place that it provided.

Producers have realized, however, that creating a unique hero is a less extravagant means of distinguishing a detective show from others, and it remains the clear key to such a program's prosperity. As Arthur Asa Berger has noted, "The problem of identity is critical in detective dramas, for if a program is to be successful, the hero must stand out in some way, must be distinctive. Otherwise he will be lost in the clutter of other heroes, an anonymous figure with no claim to fame."[12]

The easiest way for producers to make their gumshoes stand out is to give them a gimmick or a trademark—something even the most jaded observer will notice and remember. Ironside is distinguished by his wheelchair, while Columbo is known for his sloppy raincoat. The races of John Shaft and Charlie Chan distinguish them, just as Thomas Banacek's ethnic heritage distinguishes him. Other gimmicks have included age, both young (the Hardy Boys) and old (Barnaby Jones, the Snoop sisters); sex and glamor (Honey West, Charlie's Angels); even pudginess (Frank Cannon, Nero Wolfe).

Yet detective-show producers have learned to differentiate among detectives without relying exclusively on such devices, which are often rather crude and prone to stereotyping. Producers have frequently made audiences aware of their detectives' distinctive qualities through the characters' regular interactions with other "team members," an important consideration since many recent gumshoe programs have emphasized the necessity of teamwork. Modern shamuses have seldom followed the example set by such early TV private eyes as Martin Kane and Rocky King, who often worked alone; indeed, the collective hero has supplanted the loner, though the group—often a diverse group—is almost always dominated by one person around whom the series revolves. Magnum has frequently relied on his island buddies to help him crack a case, yet he has remained the central personality of the series. In the case of "Ironside," the crew consisted of a paraplegic, a WASPy male, a black, and a woman, yet Ironside clearly controlled the proceedings.

Despite producers' attempts to differentiate their gumshoe programs, the main characters tend to fall into a handful of basic categories that transcend the medium but are unique to the genre. In their article "Past the Visceral Sleuth," William Borrows and Marlene Simon develop a basic classification system for the many detectives that have appeared in literature.[13] Their typology easily covers the programs discussed in this chapter.

The first category is the *cerebral sleuth*. The cerebral sleuth is almost always refined and upper class, occasionally British, and never goes searching for crimes; they always seem to fall into his or her lap. Sherlock Holmes is the most obvious member within this category, but there are certainly others: the various manifestations of Ellery Queen, Nick and Nora Charles, and, more recently, Jonathan and Jennifer Hart. Though the recurring characters may have interesting personalities, the focus of cerebral sleuth shows tends to be on plot. More specifically, they concentrate on the method by which the criminal commits the crime. The cerebral sleuth's eventual solutions are often unexpected but always accurate.

The second category is the *transcendental sleuth*. The archetypal hard-boiled loner, the transcendental sleuth is often a cynical private eye who knows that society is beyond repair but believes that a moral victory is more important than money or achieving a suitable punishment for the criminal. Transcendental sleuth programs stress character over plot; indeed, the latter often becomes so convoluted that it's nearly impossible to follow. Violence and aggression are also frequent hallmarks of this type of gumshoe show. Philip Marlowe and Michael Shayne are clearly in this category, but a number of others are, too, including such early heavyweights as Martin Kane and Rocky King. With his cynical ways and preference for working alone whenever possible, Jim Rockford might be regarded as a more recent manifestation of the transcendental sleuth.

The third type of detective is the *visceral sleuth*. The visceral sleuth is often a bachelor who lives in a fancy apartment, drives an expensive car, and generally enjoys the trappings of the upper middle class. The visceral sleuth exhibits little of the cynicism so characteristic of the transcendental sleuth; instead, he goes his mercenary way, usually treating the detective work only as a job. Mike Hammer is an obvious member of this group, but so are Lew Archer, Thomas Magnum, Frank Cannon, John Shaft, and Dan Tanna.

Borrows and Simon's final category is the *organizational sleuth*. This category is perhaps the broadest, since all police detectives fall under this heading. The organizational sleuth frequently has to put up with bureaucratic rules and must occasionally bend them to accomplish some task. Police detection procedures are the usual highlights of such programs.

Jack Shaheen, who has fruitfully applied Borrows and Simon's typology to film detctives, has arrived at a fifth category, the *amateur sleuth*, in which an ordinary person is thrust into the role of a detective.[14] Akin to the cerebral sleuth, the amateur sleuth as represented on TV is usually very young, such as the Hardy Boys and Nancy Drew, or very old, such as the nosy Snoop sisters.

Several TV producers have created singular detectives by twisting the conventions of one of these types, combining them with those of another, or both. While Columbo's nonviolent ways and skill at unraveling a crime equal those of any classic cerebral sleuth, he also resembles that type turned inside out; far from being smooth, wealthy, and elegant, he is rumpled, cheap, and seemingly doltish (indeed, the guest stars of "Columbo" come far closer to matching the cerebral sleuth in outward appearances and wealth). In addition, Columbo as a police lieutenant shares the organizational sleuth's policy-following behavior. Other hybrids include Qunicy, who combines traits of the organizational and amateur sleuths, and Matt Houston, who merges aspects of the cerebral and visceral sleuths.

Regardless of the type or combination of types they follow, TV detectives have proven a durable lot. Whether we derive our satisfaction from matching wits with them, marveling at their deductive powers (and/or physical appearances), or simply basking in their weekly assurances in word and violent deed that "crime does not pay," TV detectives have entertained us for more than a generation. It would take no Ellery Queen to deduce that small-screen shamuses will continue their sleuthing ways for a long time to come.

NOTES

1. Edward Stasheff and Rudy Bretz, "Program Formats," in *Coping with Television*, ed. Joseph Fletcher Littell (Evanston, Ill.: McDougal, Littell & Co., 1973), p. 82.

2. Ibid.

3. Tim Brooks and Earle Marsh, *The Complete Directory to Prime Time Network TV Shows, 1946–Present* (New York: Ballantine Books, 1979), p. 555.

4. See Sally Bedell, *Up the Tube: Prime-Time TV and the Silverman Years* (New York: Viking Press, 1981), p. 10.

5. Brooks and Marsh, *Complete Directory*, p. 378.

6. Bedell, *Up the Tube*, p. 55.

7. Quoted in Richard Meyers, *TV Detectives* (San Diego: A. S. Barnes & Co., 1981), p. 162.

8. See Bedell, *Up the Tube*, pp. 134–39.

9. Quoted in Bill Davidson, "The Farrah Phenomenon," in *TV Guide: The First 25 Years*, ed. Jay S. Harris in association with the editors of *TV Guide* (New York: New American Library, 1980), p. 262.

10. Ibid., p. 263.

11. Stasheff and Bretz, "Program Formats," pp. 82–83.

12. Arthur Asa Berger, *The TV-Guided American* (New York: Walker & Co., 1976), p. 102.

13. William Borrows and Marlene Simon, "Past the Visceral Sleuth: Reflections on the Symbolic Representation of Deviance," *Studies in Public Communication* 4 (Autumn 1962), pp. 75–76.

14. Jack G. Shaheen, "The Detective Film in Transition," *Journal of the University Film Association* 27 (1975), pp. 36–38, 45.

BIBLIOGRAPHICAL SURVEY

As is the case with most other television genres, the detective show has received minimal attention from critics and scholars. One of the few major works to appear is Richard Meyers's appropriately titled *TV Detectives*. Though hardly scholarly (indeed, many of his observations are as flat-footed as some of the characters discussed), Meyers's book examines the television detective genre up to 1981 in a near-comprehensive way and provides a gold mine of information. In his obvious enthusiasm for the genre, however, Meyers unfortunately devoted considerable coverage to programs only remotely related to the classic gumshoe drama, such as "Lou Grant," "The Man from U.N.C.L.E.," and "CHiPs." The author is also guilty of sidetracking himself into areas with little or no relevance to the topic, as when, for example, he inexplicably observes that some people thought Neil Armstrong's 1969 moon walk was faked. These tendencies, along with occasional factual errors and Meyers's annoying habit of including the most banal of trivia, seriously weaken the book. (Who really cares what the police badge numbers were on "Adam-12"?) The chief values of this work are that it does act as a fine memory jog and represents a good place to begin further research.

Aside from *TV Detectives*, most of the other critical and historical writings on the genre are scattered throughout a range of books, magazines, and journals. Sally Bedell's *Up the Tube* offers a number of useful comments on "Charlie's Angels," "The Rockford Files," and "Columbo" within the context of network decision making. Particularly interesting is her six-page study of the birth and development of "Charlie's Angels," which includes the ABC research department's eight-point report on how to improve the then-unaired program. Also related to "Charlie's Angels" is Bill Davidson's brief examination of the "Farrah Phenomenon," initially published in *TV Guide* and reprinted in a 1980 anthology of *TV Guide* articles.

Several books contain sections that deal specifically with the TV gumshoe program. Arthur Asa Berger's *The TV-Guided American* contains a provocative chapter on "Ironside," the highlight of which is a modest Oedipal reading of that long-running series, while Horace Newcomb's *TV: The Most Popular Art* presents an insightful chapter on mystery programs and their traditional attraction for audiences.

Siegfried Kracauer's *Theory of Film* contains a number of remarks concerning the appropriateness of "sleuthing" to the film medium, and his comments on the topic have clear applicability to television. Also worth noting is David Bowman's "Detective Melodrama on TV," the lone television article in a special 1975 issue of the *Journal of the University Film Association* devoted to the detective genre in film.

Finally, several general TV programming reference guides have proven invaluable for discovering the basic plot summaries, air dates, casts, and networks of a wide range of genres appearing on TV. These works include Tim Brooks and Earle Marsh's now inaccurately titled *The Complete Directory to Prime Time Network TV Shows* and Larry Gianakos's *Television Drama Series Programming*. They played significant roles in the research for this chapter.

BOOKS AND ARTICLES

Bedell, Sally. *Up the Tube: Prime-Time TV and the Silverman Years*. New York: Viking Press, 1981.

Berger, Arthur Asa. *The TV-Guided American*. New York: Walker & Co., 1976. See in particular "Ironside; or, The Secret of the Wheelchair," pp. 101–9.

Borrows, William, and Marlene Simon. "Past the Visceral Sleuth: Reflections on the Symbolic Representation of Deviance." *Studies in Public Communication* 4 (Autumn 1962).

Bowman, David. "Detective Melodrama on TV." *Journal of the University Film Association* 27 (1975).

Brooks, Tim, and Earle Marsh. *The Complete Directory to Prime Time TV Shows, 1946–Present*. New York: Ballantine Books, 1979.

Cocks, Jay. "Lunks, Hunks and Artifacts." *Time*, November 15, 1982.

Davidson, Bill. "The Farrah Phenomenon." In *TV Guide: The First 25 Years*, edited by Jay S. Harris in association with the editors of *TV Guide*. New York: New American Library, 1980.

Gianakos, Larry James. *Television Drama Series Programming: A Comprehensive Chronicle, 1959–1975*. Metuchen, N.J.: Scarecrow Press, 1978.

Higgins, George V. "The Private Eye as Illegal Hero." *Esquire*, December 1972.

Kracauer, Siegfried. *Theory of Film: The Redemption of Physical Reality*. New York: Oxford University Press, 1960.

Meyers, Richard. *TV Detectives*. San Diego: A. S. Barnes & Co., 1981.

Newcomb, Horace. *TV: The Most Popular Art*. Garden City, N.Y.: Anchor Books, 1974. See in particular "Mysteries: Order and Authority," pp. 83–109.

Rothenberg, Fred. "New Detective Shows Are Certainly No 'Dragnet.' " *Hampshire Gazette*, October 12, 1982. An Associated Press article.

Stasheff, Edward, and Rudy Bretz. "Program Formats." In *Coping with Television*, edited by Joseph Fletcher Littell. Evanston, Ill: McDougal, Littell & Co., 1973.

VIDEOGRAPHY

"Martin Kane, Private Eye"
  NBC, Thursday, 10:00–10:30 P.M.
  Premiere: September 1, 1949
  Stars: William Gargan (1949–1951), Lloyd Nolan (1951–1952), Lee Tracy (1952–1953), Mark Stevens (1953–1954)
  Last Program: June 17, 1954

"The Plainclothesman"
  DuMont, various prime times
  Premiere: October 12, 1949
  Stars: Ken Lynch, Jack Orrison
  Last Program: September 19, 1954

"Rocky King, Inside Detective"
  DuMont, various prime times
  Premiere: January 14, 1950
  Stars: Roscoe Karns, Grace Carney
  Last Program: December 26, 1954

"Mark Saber"
  ABC, NBC, various prime times

Premiere: October 5, 1951
Stars: Tom Conway (1951–1954), Donald Gray (1955–1960)
Last Program: May 15, 1960

"77 Sunset Strip"
ABC, various prime times
Premiere: October 10, 1958
Stars: Efrem Zimbalist, Jr., Roger Smith
Last Program: September 9, 1964

"Hawaiian Eye"
ABC, various prime times
Premiere: October 7, 1959
Stars: Bob Conrad, Connie Stevens
Last Program: September 10, 1963

"Ironside"
NBC, various prime times
Premiere: September 14, 1967
Stars: Raymond Burr, Don Galloway
Last Program: January 16, 1975

"Mannix"
CBS, various prime times
Premiere: September 16, 1967
Stars: Mike Connors, Robert Reed (1969–1975)
Last Program: August 27, 1975

"Hawaii Five-O"
CBS, various prime times
Premiere: September 26, 1968
Stars: Jack Lord, James MacArthur (1968–1979)
Last Program: April 26, 1980

"Cannon"
CBS, various prime times
Premiere: September 14, 1971
Star: William Conrad
Last Program: September 19, 1976

"Columbo"
NBC, various prime times
Premiere: September 15, 1971
Star: Peter Falk
Last Program: September 4, 1977

"Barnaby Jones"
CBS, various prime times
Premiere: January 28, 1973
Stars: Buddy Ebsen, Lee Meriwether
Last Program: September 4, 1980

"The Rockford Files"
NBC, various prime times

Premiere: September 13, 1974
Stars: James Garner, Noah Beery
Last Program: December 21, 1979

"Charlie's Angels"
ABC, various prime times
Premiere: September 22, 1976
Stars: Farrah Fawcett Majors (1976–1977), Kate Jackson (1976–1979),
Jaclyn Smith
Last Program: September 24, 1981

"Quincy, M.E."
NBC, various prime times
Premiere: October 3, 1976
Star: Jack Klugman
Last Program: September 5, 1983

"Hart to Hart"
ABC, various prime times
Premiere: September 22, 1979
Stars: Robert Wagner, Stephanie Powers

"Magnum, P.I."
CBS, Thursday, 8:00–9:00 P.M.
Premiere: December 11, 1980
Stars: Tom Selleck, John Hillerman

"Remington Steele"
NBC, various prime times
Premiere: September 24, 1982
Stars: Stephanie Zimbalist, Pierce Brosnan

4

The TV Western

MICHAEL BARSON

OVERVIEW

Of all the genres that flourished during television's first two decades, none has suffered a more precipitous decline than the Western. Where the talk show, the variety show, the original drama and the situation comedy all have survived and flourished into the 1980s, the Western has been riding off into the sunset since Watergate meant no more than an expensive hotel in Washington, D.C.

Looking at the kinds of action series that predominate today, one explanation for the general apathy toward Westerns immediately suggests itself. Westerns are an archaic form that makes use of dramatic situations and conflicts better expressed in contemporary, urban settings. Thus, cop shows, private detective series, and para-military extravaganzas such as NBC's "The A-Team" would seem the logical heirs to the popularity once enjoyed by the Western. What this theory fails to take into consideration, however, is that cops and private eyes were television prime-time staples even *before* the Western came into its own in the mid-fifties. Nevertheless, for a period of almost twenty years, the Western more than held its own against all other genre shows. But when America's love affair with the Western was over—and this holds true not only for the television Western, but also for media such as film, pulp and slick magazines, paperback novels, comic books and newspaper comic strips—it was over, never to burn again. It is axiomatic that all things are cyclical in the mass media, but one wonders, after the many failed attempts to rejuvenate the genre over the past ten years, whether the Western could ever again capture the imagination of the American public. Certainly not to the extent that it did in its heyday, circa 1960, when Western movies, television shows, tie-in games, and toys and comic books were seemingly everywhere at once. The probability of a comeback for the Western is particularly unlikely via television, as success on television is meas-ured in the tens of millions of viewers, where movies require, say, one-tenth of those numbers for the same relative degree of success, and books but a tenth of that.

Thus in talking about the Western, one is put in the position of the paleon-tologist who may not know *why* the brontosaurus disappeared from the face of the earth, but who is nevertheless quite certain of one thing: it is not very likely to ever return.

HISTORICAL DEVELOPMENT

The television Western, like the other kinds of shows that were aired during television's first decade, took its form from the movies, reshaping itself when constraints of budget and time dictated. Indeed, the very first television Westerns were no more than old "B" features and serials chopped up to fit into 30- and 60-minute slots. The first Western film star to cross over into the new medium of television was Gene Autry, "The Singing Cowboy," in 1947. A year later William Boyd—better known in his incarnation of Hopalong Cassidy—followed, bringing along the hundreds of hours of "B" films he made in the late 1930s and early 1940s. Boyd had the uncanny foresight to purchase the rights to these films long before anyone realized how hungry this new television medium would be for programming material.[1] Both Autry and Boyd were quick to recognize the possibilities television offered to the Western. In effect, each home could be turned into a Saturday matinee, with one inexpensively produced or recycled Western following another for hours on end. Autry would in short order develop four other Western series, which were offered, like his own show, as syndicated features that local stations could purchase and show in the time slot of their choice: "Range Rider" (which gave new life to the career of Western stuntman Jock Mahoney, who now held down the lead role), "Buffalo Bill, Jr.," "Annie Oakley," and "The Adventures of Champion." The last was a tribute to Gene's own horse. Boyd also parlayed his popularity into an empire; by 1951 his show was on 63 television stations, in addition to 152 radio stations, and 155 news-papers carried his comic strip. Both Autry and Boyd (as "Hoppy") also had licensed their own monthly comic books, which generally featured color portraits of each star on the front and back covers.[2]

The third major mass-media star to cross over in the late 1940s was a character who had gained his initial popularity not from films, but from radio. By the time "The Lone Ranger" debuted as a television series in 1948, he had already conquered the all-important supporting media of newspaper comics, comic books, Big Little Books, toys, and games. Thus, a pre-existing demand was being served by bringing the Lone Ranger into weekly-series format. His adventures would require some 130 episodes, which ran as new features until 1961 and then lived again as reruns for many years thereafter. Clayton Moore, a minor actor in his Hollywood days, achieved cult status when he took over the role in the series' second year, the first case of a Western star generated from a television series. He would not be the last. Television very quickly demonstrated the capability of creating its own stars. For every former film star such as Gabby Hayes and Roy Rogers who was awarded his own series (in 1950 and 1952, respectively), there was a Duncan Renaldo, unknown until his syndicated series "The Cisco Kid" (debut: 1951) transformed him into a media hero.

So enthusiastic was America's response to these first Western series that local stations around the country began to produce their own, very low budget oaters. The first such production was Philadelphia's "Action in the Afternoon," which was broadcast live five afternoons each week from a converted lot outside the city that was optimistically passed off as Tombstone, Dodge City, or Death Valley, as the occasion demanded. Someone named Jack Valentine was the show's star; unfortunately, archives of such local features are virtually nonextant, making it a matter of speculation exactly what Mr. Valentine did on the air five days weekly. But the mid-afternoon time slot indicates clearly that the show was targeted toward children just home from school. Other cities that produced similar shows were Dayton, Ohio, with "Lucky 13 Ranch House"; Salt Lake City, with "Sheriff Jim's Sagebrush Play"; Louisville, with "The Old Sheriff"; and Boston, with "Boom Town." This last, hosted by "Rex Trailer," offered a mix of live comedy and audience participation interspersed with old serials and "B" movie segments.[3]

During these early days of the television Western, the networks were conservative about putting Westerns into production for prime-time display to meet the challenge of the syndicated product. Their hesitation made perfect sense, as the syndicated adventure series were slanted toward a juvenile audience, and prime-time programming depended in large measure upon adult interest. NBC, CBS, and ABC knew that the sight of a paunchy Gene Autry riding after a bunch of hapless outlaws on a tired Champion was not likely to hold the attention of most Americans over the age of 13. Still, a craze for Westerns *was* sweeping the country—Disney's 1954 made-for-TV movie *Davy Crockett* had confirmed that fact, and on prime time, to boot, and the networks wanted to cut themselves in on the action. But "B" movies with patently fake fistfights and endless horse chases were not the answer. What was, then?

The answer was obvious. Produce Westerns that could appeal to adults, who, after all, comprised the bulk of the audience for prime-time programming. The road had been paved by Hollywood during the past ten years, with adult Western fare such as *My Darling Clementine* (1946), *She Wore a Yellow Ribbon* (1949), *Broken Arrow* (1950), *The Gunfighter* (1950), *Arrowhead* (1953), and *Apache* (1954) slowly displacing the "B"-rated films, as mature stars such as Henry Fonda, Jimmy Stewart, Gregory Peck, Charlton Heston, and Burt Lancaster moved into the territory formerly homesteaded by Gene Autry, Roy Rogers, Gabby Hayes, and Tim Holt. (John Wayne was virtually the only Western "B" star who made the transition into adult fare successfully with his two 1948 films, *Red River* and *Fort Apache*, directed, respectively, by Howard Hawks and John Ford.)

Thus it was that all three networks were prepared in the fall of 1955 with at least one adult Western series—"adult," again, being used as a relative term in comparison to previous television Westerns. CBS had the simplest job, mounting a production of "Gunsmoke," which had for the past several years been a radio success. The network's fortuitous choice of towering James Arness to replace the golden-voiced but portly William Conrad as Matt Dillon had much to do with the show lasting long after the Western boom had faded into memory. ABC countered with "The Life and Legend of Wyatt Earp," a genuinely innovative series in that its format was dynamic rather than static, following Earp's career in a relatively accurate manner as he moved about the West, from Ellsworth, to Dodge City, to Tombstone. Guest appearances by historical characters such as Bat Masterson, Doc Holliday, and Ned Buntline were carefully coordinated over a period of years to coincide with Earp's actual involvement with them.[4] (NBC inherited Bat four years later for his own weekly series, "Bat Masterson.") Hugh O'Brian portrayed Earp as a flower-vested, double-Buntlined, town-tamer, whose string tie and polished boots belied his ethical toughness. As one critic noted, "in adult Westerns they shot to kill."[5]

ABC debuted a second adult series in 1955. Unlike Wyatt Earp, Cheyenne Bodie, the protagonist of the rotating series "Cheyenne," did not uphold the formalized law of a town and in fact rarely set down in a town for more than a few hours. Cheyenne was a frontier scout, thus foregoing the dapper trimmings enjoyed by the television Earp. But, as portrayed by 6' 7'' Clint Walker, Cheyenne seemed something of a primal force, somehow bigger than both the town-bound Dillon and Earp put together. Ironically, actor Walker proved to be as tough as his character. When his studio, Warner Bros., wouldn't share the profits of "Cheyenne" more equitably, he elected to sit out the 1958 season, returning the following year.

NBC's primary entry in these adult Western sweepstakes was an anthology series entitled "Frontier." A few months earlier, in the summer of 1955, ABC had experimented with an anthology series entitled "Pall Mall Playhouse." The ratings had not been high enough to inspire renewal in the autumn, but NBC elected to try the format anyway. "Frontier" was narrated by Walter Coy, who also acted in some of the episodes, after the format of radio's long-running "Death Valley Days." A year later Dick Powell used the same format for his CBS series, "Dick Powell's Zane Grey Theater," in which he narrated all the episodes and acted in certain ones. "Frontier" lasted only that one season, but Powell's show—thanks perhaps to Powell's familiarity and a higher-powered list of guest stars—lasted into 1962. Even so, anthology series without regularly featured protagonists did not seem to serve the Western as well as series that offered charismatic stars week in and week out.

This lesson was not lost upon the networks, who in 1957 codified the formulas into near-perfect states. NBC's "Wagon Train" solved the problem of audience loyalty posited by "Frontier" by installing Ward Bond and Robert Horton as Major Seth Adams and his chief scout, Chris Hale. Each week the wagon train would proceed westward, focusing on a different group of travelers and a different set of problems, anchored by Major Adams's Mary Worth-like wisdom and Chris Hale's form-fitting buckskin and Elvis Presley haircut. The show was so popular that even the death of Ward Bond (veteran of dozens of John Ford films) in 1961 and Robert Horton's departure for greener pastures (which predictably turned out to be arid) could not terminate that endless journey. John McIntire replaced Bond, and Robert Fuller, Horton for the 1961 season. In 1962 the series moved to ABC, where it lasted into 1965. (The "Wagon Train" format was adaptable to genres other than the Western, and in fact was the basic structure of "Star Trek," which appeared just as "Wagon Train" was put into dry dock.) The 60-minute format allowed dramas of a more complex nature to be developed than "Frontier's" 30 minutes had, and numerous guest stars from movies gave a glamour to the proceedings that indicated the network's approach to the show as a flagship.

ABC employed a different, but equally innovative approach to the adult Western in 1957 with "Maverick," a tongue-in-cheek, cleverly written show that depended heavily upon the chemistry between stars James Garner and Jack Kelly, who played the affable Southern con men, Bret and Bart Maverick. The series flourished for three seasons, at which point Garner pulled a Clint Walker and went on strike for a sweeter deal. Once again Warner Bros. had to find a replacement, which for "Maverick" in the 1960 season turned out to be Roger Moore (now the incumbent James Bond, but then a virtual unknown), who was written in as Cousin Beauregard. He couldn't fill Garner's shoes, but Warners this time refused to capitulate, and instead of Garner returning for the 1961 season, another newcomer, Robert Colbert, was brought in as yet another Maverick relation, Brent. This didn't work either, and the series was cancelled in the summer of 1962. "Maverick's" contributions to the genre were primarily parodic; "Gunsmoke" was the target one week, "Dragnet" and "Bonanza" at other points of the run.[6] But, while parody might signal the end of a genre's ability to be taken seriously, the popularity of "Maverick" did not signal the end of the cycle. "The Wild, Wild West" probably holds that honor.

The other important adult Western that debuted in 1957 was the CBS series, "Have Gun Will Travel." One of the most peculiar Westerns ever aired, it was also one of the most popular and arguably the most "adult." Paladin—no first name was ever proferred—was the first genteel gunslinger (just as Wyatt Earp was the first dandified sheriff), a West Point-educated troubleshooter who fancied fine wines, gourmet food, and well-cut clothes and who was as likely to toss off a quote from *Hamlet* as to draw his pistol. His name was derived from the white chess knight—the paladin—that he used as his symbol on his business cards, which advertised, "Have Gun, Will Travel . . . Wire Paladin, San Francisco." (The Hotel Carlton was his between-assignments pied-à-terre.) As portrayed by actor Richard Boone, Paladin was a study in contradictions, a man with a personal code of ethics who used his gun to make a living; an erudite, civilized man who used force to effect change. America responded to this black-garbed figure who smoked 58-cent cigars while pondering the meaning of life between gunfights: "Have Gun Will Travel" was the number-three rated program on television from 1958 to 1961, trailing only two other adult Westerns, "Gunsmoke" and "Wagon Train."[7] The show lasted into the 1963 season, long enough to spawn a top forty recording of the theme song by guitarist Duane Eddy. (In 1972, Boone returned to the West as "Hec Ramsey," a rotating series about a gunfighter with a scientific bent, which lasted three seasons.)

The television season of 1957 ended fittingly with the Emmy award for best dramatic series going to "Gunsmoke." The next year the Western would be segregated in a separate category, and "Maverick" would be the first—and only—winner of the "Best Western Series" Emmy; after the 1958/59 season, the category was eliminated, marking the last major nonacting award a Western would win.[8]

Nineteen fifty-seven also marked the first year that the Western was widely accepted by the prime-time viewing audience. No Western ever finished in the top fifteen for the year prior to 1956, and "Gunsmoke," at number 8 was the lone representative for the 1956/57 season. But the 1957/58 season found no fewer than six Westerns among the top fifteen shows of the year: "Gunsmoke" was number 1; "Tales of Wells Fargo" number 3; "Have Gun Will Travel," number 4; "The Life and Legend of Wyatt Earp," number 6; "The Restless Gun," number 8; and "Cheyenne" was number 13. Additionally, in this first year of extending the list to include the top 25 shows, "Dick Powell's Zane Grey Theater" placed 21st; "Wagon Train" was number 23; and "Sugarfoot," one of the series that rotated with "Cheyenne," was number 24.[9] In this first bloom of the adult Western, then, a happy balance existed between artistic innovation and mass acceptance—a confluence that happens rarely in the popular arts, particularly on TV, one of the most conservative mass media. In all, some 16 Westerns aired in prime time during the 1957/58 season. Among the series that finished out of the money that year: "Broken Arrow," spun off from the 1950 movie; "Tombstone Territory"; "Adventures of Jim Bowie"; "Colt .45"; and "Trackdown." Also, there were a number of series that were on the borderline between Westerns and other categories, including "The Adventures of Rin Tin Tin," "Zorro," and "Sgt. Preston of the Yukon."

The next two years marked the peak of popularity for the television Western. Amazingly, six of the top seven shows of 1958/59 were Westerns, with another six scattered between the tenth and twenty-first positions. Only "The Danny Thomas Show," in fifth position, interrupted the skein of Westerns holding the number 1 through number 7 positions. In order, they were: "Gunsmoke" (which finished first for the second of four consecutive years); "Wagon Train," "Have Gun Will Travel," "The Rifleman," "Maverick," and "Tales of Wells Fargo." Other top-25 finishers were "Wyatt Earp" at number 10, "Zane Grey Theater" at number 13, "The Texan" at number 15, "Wanted: Dead or Alive" at number 16, "Cheyenne" at number 18, and "Sugarfoot" at number 21.[10] Of this group, the most significant new entries were ABC's "The Rifleman," the first Western with an emphasis upon father-son relations, and "Wanted," which had as its hero a bounty hunter, the ultimate anti-hero for a series. Chuck Connors and Johnny Crawford played the father and son in "The Rifleman," which ran for six seasons, though this first season was its only appearance in the year's top ten. "Wanted: Dead or Alive" (CBS) introduced Steve McQueen, who in short order deserted the small screen for the silver one. The series ended in 1960.

The 1959/60 season showed Westerns to be nearly as dominant as in the previous year. The same series finished one, two, three, and eight others placed between the 9th and 23d spots.[11] Among the many newcomers that year was a show that did not finish among the top 25, although for the next twelve years it would—often in the number 1 spot. "Bonanza" was only a moderate success for its first two seasons, when NBC broadcast it at 7:30 P.M. on Saturday night. But it was moved to the 9:00 P.M. Sunday slot at the start of the 1961 season, where it stayed for the next 12 years. During that time it finished in the top ten all but in the 1971/72 season, when it began showing signs of age. A year later it was gone. But its tenure was one of the most remarkable in television history. What "Bonanza" did was posit the last of the important Western formats. Taking a tip from the success of "The Rifleman," "Bonanza" extended the saga of a father and his son to a father and his *three* sons (beating Fred MacMurray's sitcom by a full year), played out against the backdrop of the United States's largest spread, the Ponderosa. That this was also the first *color* Western undoubtedly has much to do with its success. But just as certainly, Americans took to it because of its explicit concern with tensions among family members whose love for one another enables them to surmount the problems, internal as well as external, that confront them. On this level, the fact that "Bonanza" was set in the West a century earlier became almost irrelevant; this was a show about a family, watched at the peak family viewing time of Sunday night. The Cartwrights were able to survive more than a decade's worth of divisiveness and struggle, just as America itself did. During the peak years of Vietnam, "Bonanza" could never be found far from the number one spot, where it finished from 1964 through 1966. Even the desertion of Adam Cartwright—actor Pernell Roberts left at the end of the 1964/65 season—could be accepted by an audience, which had seen so many of its own sons leave for alien lands. More damaging to the show's survival was the death of Dan Blocker just before the 1972/73 season was to begin production. That left just Michael Landon and Lorne Greene as members of the original family unit, and by January of 1973 "Bonanza's" long run was over. Only "Gunsmoke," which lasted through the summer of 1975, enjoyed more success than "Bonanza." And what was "Gunsmoke," if not a drama about a symbolic family, the residents of Dodge City—Matt Dillon, Chester, Kitty, Doc, Festus, and the rest?

Thus, by 1960 the Western had achieved all of its incarnations, which critic Douglas Brode has enumerated as three distinct types: 1) the *historical hero*, embodied by such shows as "Wyatt Earp," "Bat Masterson," and "Jim Bowie"; 2) The *roving adult hero,* embodied by "Cheyenne" and its rotating brother shows, "Bronco" and "Sugarfoot," along with "Restless Gun," "Gunslinger," and "Have Gun Will Travel"; 3) the *fictional hero in a fixed locale*, as typified by such series as "Lawman," "Tombstone Territory," and "Gunsmoke."[12] As far as they go, Brode's archetypes are fine, but surely there should be a fourth category, *the family unit*, to take care of shows such as "Bonanza" and "The Big Valley." And what of such series as "Rawhide," which debuted the same year as "Bonanza," in 1959, and which ran until January of 1966 on CBS? Perhaps a fifth category—*the team*—would be useful for "Rawhide" and its ilk: "Laramie" (NBC, 1959–1963), "Overland Trail" (NBC, February–September 1960), and "Laredo" (NBC, 1965–1967). The point is, all of these story structures had been introduced by 1960; everything that followed was inevitably little more than a gussied-up package for the same old brands of oats. Roving gunslingers came and went until the only way to distinguish them was by their guns ("Colt .45," "Yancy Derringer," "Shotgun Slade"). New patches held for a season or two, then let out the air: "Tate," a 1960 summer series featuring a hero with one arm in a black sling; "Hotel de Paree," which from 1959 to 1960 offered Earl Holliman as Sundance, whose silver-studded hat blinded his foes whenever one drew on him (until a cloudy day finished him, one might assume); "A Man Called Shenandoah," which for the 1965/66 season featured Robert Horton, late of "Wagon Train," as an amnesiac wandering through the West, searching for his identity. And so on and on.

But this is simply the history of the television series: invention becomes codified, and what remains is convention. The adult Western *did* offer something new for a few years, but it could not *continue* to invent after its substance had been absorbed into the mainstream. Even the actors began to recycle themselves—Robert Horton moving from "Wagon Train" to "Shenandoah;" Chuck Connors, from "The Rifleman" to "Branded"; Robert Fuller, from "Laramie" to "Wagon Train"; Doug McClure, from "Overland Trail" to "The Virginian"; Peter Breck, from "Black Saddle" to "The Big Valley"; Jock Mahoney, from "Range Rider" to "Yancy Derringer"—it was enough to send audiences stampeding back to "The Ed Sullivan Show," where at least Ed was the same every week.

Of course, Westerns sinned in this regard no worse than other genres, such as the spy shows of the mid-sixties and the cop shows of the mid-seventies, to name but two cycles that played themselves out in short order—indeed, far shorter order than the Western, which despite its dearth of innovation after 1959 continued to offer good entertainment values on shows such as "Gunsmoke," "Rawhide," and "The Virginian" well into the sixties. The debut of "The Wild, Wild West" (CBS, 1965–1970) did make it hard to view the Western with a straight face, with its broad intermarriage of the spy and Western genres, but the writing had been on the wall for some time. After the entry of "Rawhide" to the top 25 list for the 1959/60 season, no new Westerns registered on that final tally until "The Virginian" scored in 1963. For the remainder of the decade, only three other new Westerns registered even a blip on the list: Chuck Connors' "Branded" in 1964/65 at number 14, "The Wild, Wild West" in 1965/66 at number 23, and "Daniel Boone" in 1966/67 and 1968/69 at number 25 and number 21 respectively.[13] Two of those three shows don't even qualify as adult Westerns, which basically leaves "The Virginian" (and its latter-day incarnation, "The Men from Shiloh") as the lone Western to have debuted after 1959 and made any kind of an impact in the 1960s. But even "The Virginian" did not truly represent an influx of new blood; as Douglas Brode points out, "The Virginian" was "an apotheosis of every TV western that preceded it . . . render[ing] all other shows obsolete."[14]

However, the Western was not quite done as the 1970s dawned. No sooner did Michael Landon find himself out of work as "Bonanza's" Little Joe than he set about developing a new series that could parlay his 14 years of experience as a family member in the Old West into another television standard. Amazingly, he succeeded on his first try. In the capacity of executive producer, Landon cast himself as Charles Ingalls in the town of Walnut Grove, Minnesota, in the late 1870s. Not exactly Dodge City, but by any definition "Little House on the Prairie" qualifies as a Western, albeit a heavily domestic one. Debuting in the fall of 1974 on NBC, "Little House," based on the books by Laura Ingalls Wilder, took over where "Gunsmoke" had left off the previous year, finishing number 13 for 1974/75. For some reason it did not place in the top 25 the following year, but it was number 16 in the 1976/77 season, number 7 the following year, and by the end of the decade had hit the number 1 position, making it the first Western to do so since "Bonanza" in 1966/67.[15] Under the circumstances—that is, the flagging popularity of the Western since the mid-sixties—Landon's accomplishment certainly qualified him as a latter-day Orson Welles, donning as he did the different hats of director, writer, actor, and producer on the series at various times. The series ended after a very healthy ten-year run.

"Little House," though the only full-fledged success the Western could claim for this period, did not stand alone as a representative of its genre. Perhaps the most innovative series of the 1970s was "Kung Fu," a blend of the American West and Chinese East that star David Carradine somehow made believable and engrossing. It limped along from 1972 through 1975, preventing ABC's executives from cancelling it for a surprising length of time. ABC had a moderate success with "How the West Was Won," which brought monolith James Arness back to the screen as a mountainman. Stunning scenery and Arness were enough to vault this adaptation of the 1963 John Ford film into the 11th spot on the year's-end list of the 1977/78 top shows.

In 1981, NBC tried to recapture the glory of 24 years previous by bringing James Garner back in his original role in "Bret Maverick." The abject failure of the series, despite Garner's immense popularity, which carried over from his previous series, "The Rockford Files," was a clear message that the Western could not expect to survive in the 1980s on the basis of nostalgia. The series was cancelled before the end of the season.

As new Westerns are developed for the 1980s, it would appear that the best chance of success lies not in tired parodies or ancient formulas, but rather in an imaginative blending of the Western's particular themes and settings with a currently palatable story structure, as Landon achieved by integrating the family drama with the 1870s West in "Little House." Whether this approach can again succeed remains to be seen; the possibility exists that the American public simply is no longer interested in viewing Westerns other than as pleasant curiosities from a quarter century past. The failure of the Western to attract an audience in recent films such as *The Long Riders* and *Tom Horn* and the diminishing audience for Western literature suggest that television is not likely to reverse this trend in the immediate future.

THEMES AND ISSUES

In his seminal study of the Western, *The Six-Gun Mystique*, John Cawelti argues that

in analyzing a popular form like the Western, we are *not* primarily concerned with an individual work, such as a single episode of *Gunsmoke* or a particular novel by Zane Grey, but with the cultural significance of the Western as a type of artistic construction .... The culturally significant phenomenon is not the individual work, but the formula or recipe by which more or less anonymous producers turn out individual novels or films. The individual works are ephemeral, but the formula lingers on, evolving and changing with time, yet still basically recognizable.... A popular form, like the Western, may encompass a number of standard plots.[16]

The subject matters that Cawelti finds recurring in Western films are instructive in this regard. They are: the building of the railroad, outlaws, Injuns, comedies and parodies, the cavalry, the modern west, musicals, the marshal (sheriff), cowboys and cattle kings, gunmen, pioneers and settlers, and serials.[17] Except for the categories of musicals and serials, TV Westerns have made use of all of the above, sometimes in combination, as their basic premise. Thus, for the category of the building of the railroad, we have the ABC series "Iron Horse," which ran for a season and a half from 1966 to 1968; for outlaws, ABC's "The Legend of Jesse James" (1965/66) and NBC's "The Outlaws" (1969–1962), which in its first season showed each week's drama from the point of view of the outlaws being chased by the regulars, a marshal and his two deputies; for injuns, "Broken Arrow" (ABC, 1956–1960) and "Law of the Plainsman" (NBC, 1959/60); for comedies and parodies, ABC's "Maverick" and CBS's "Wild, Wild West" (although lumping these shows together seems somehow unclean); for the cavalry, "Boots and Saddles"; for the modern west, NBC's "Redigo" (1963) and (in its earlier incarnation) "Empire" (1962/63); the marshal in vast numbers, including "Gunsmoke," CBS's "Johnny Ringo" (1959/60), "The Life and Legend of Wyatt Earp," and NBC's "The Deputy" (1959–1961); cowboys and cattle kings in such series as ABC's "Big Valley" (1965–

1969), "Rawhide," and "The Virginian"; gunmen—perhaps the most popular genre—represented by "Have Gun Will Travel," "Wanted—Dead or Alive," and "The Restless Gun," among many others; and pioneers and settlers, another particularly popular TV category, illustrated by "Wagon Train," "Little House on the Prairie," and ABC's "The Monroes" (1966/67).

Cawelti's categories are virtually all-inclusive, failing only to cover such aberrations as "Kung Fu" and, perhaps, "The Rifleman," which could be seen as a gunman-turned-settler show; an extended "Shane," as it were. Of course, the particular episode that might appear on a given week of a series could itself draw from any of the above-named categories so that "Little House" might one week draw its drama from the appearance in town of a gunman, while "Bonanza" might offer a story concerned with the plight of an injun. And, as noted earlier, a show such as "Maverick" was prone to parody the formulas represented by "Gunsmoke" and "Bonanza."

Beyond these descriptive categories, however, a Western was likely to draw its conflicts from the range of human drama found across the spectrum of ancient myths up to and including contemporary issues. A father unable to communicate with his son; a mob unwilling to tolerate different kinds of people and beliefs; a wife who no longer loves her husband; a boy, eager to be recognized as a man; an outsider, eager to become part of a community—any one of these story premises might one week be the basis for an episode of a Western, the next the basis for a cop show, a family drama, or an episode of "Star Trek." During the sixties, when hippies were in full flower, "Bonanza" had an episode entitled "The Weary Willies," which concerned a group of lazy peaceniks who roam from town to town, searching for who-knows-what. These long-haired Civil War veterans are shown to disadvantage compared to the hard-working, proud Cartwrights, much as an episode of the 1960s version of "Dragnet" might have centered on the fecklessness of hippies and the danger they represented to society.[18] (And, in fact, "Star Trek" offered at least two episodes that in allegorical fashion dealt with the hippies and the peace movement.)

Even the characterization of the protagonist of a Western has little that is endemic to that genre alone. Paladin, of "Have Gun Will Travel" sells his services for a fee, just as Jim Rockford of "The Rockford Files" does; both are forces for good, however, and cannot be bought off merely for money. The mercenary premise to their characterization, then, is something of a sham. By the same token, Eric Fleming's character of trail-boss Gil Favor and Ward Bond's Major Seth Adams on "Rawhide" and "Wagon Train," respectively, served the same function—that of the implacable, humane leader—as did William Shatner's Capt. James T. Kirk on "Star Trek" and as does Daniel Travanti's police captain Furillo on "Hill Street Blues." One may be in the Old West, another in outer space, and another on the streets of the Bronx, but they are all aspects of the same man—just as the issues they are called upon to deal with are aspects of the same conflicts that have been troubling mankind for a decade, a century, a millennium.

In the end, then, what finally doomed the Western—at least as far as television audiences are concerned—is this plastic, flexible quality to all the elements of the show other than setting. True, a story concerning an Indian is far more likely to appear on "Gunsmoke" than on, say, "Hill Street Blues," but "Hill Street" offers mini-dramas concerning many dispossessed minorities, all of which function in approximately the same manner as do the Indian stories on a Western. In short, a Western does not and did not offer anything truly different on a dramatic level than several other television genres did. As these dramas began appearing on "Kojak" and "CHiPs," audiences, for whatever reason, decided that they preferred to see those stories in a contemporary, urban setting to the setting of the West a hundred years ago. But already "Kojak" and "CHiPs" are off the air, and the stories have shifted to new formats, new containers. It is even conceivable that the preference for Westerns will again come into vogue. Shows such as "Gunsmoke" and "Bonanza" succeeded not because their characters wore six-shooters and rode horses, but because they dealt with recognizable human emotions, problems, and issues. At the moment, other kinds of shows are performing that function. The Western has been put out to pasture; it grazes, waiting for the next call to action. It's a call that may never come, but the history of television always will remember seasons such as 1959 and 1960, when one could watch a Western from the beginning of prime time to the end almost every day of the week, simply by turning a dial. That's a claim that few other TV genres can make.

NOTES

1. Rita Parks, *The Western Hero in Film and Television* (Ann Arbor: UMI Research Press, 1982), p. 127.

2. Ibid., pp. 126–27.

3. Ralph Brauer with Donna Brauer, *The Horse, the Gun and the Piece of Property: Changing Images of the TV Western* (Bowling Green, Ohio: Popular Press, 1975), p. 31.

4. Douglas Brode, "They Went Thataway," *Television Quarterly* (Summer 1982), p. 34.

5. Arthur Shulman, *How Sweet It Was* (New York: Bonanza, 1966), p. 302.

6. Tim Brooks and Earle Marsh, *The Complete Directory to Prime Time Network TV Shows, 1946–Present*, rev. ed. (New York: Ballantine Books, 1981), p. 390.

7. Ibid., pp. 252–53.

8. Ibid., pp. 775–76.

9. Ibid., p. 804.

10. Ibid.

11. Ibid., pp. 805–8.

12. Brode, "They Went Thataway," pp. 34–36.

13. Brooks and Marsh, *Complete Directory*, pp. 805–8.

14. Brode, "They Went Thataway," p. 39.

15. Brooks and Marsh, *Complete Directory*, pp. 807–10.

16. John Cawelti, *The Six-Gun Mystique* (Bowling Green, Ohio: Popular Press, 1970), p. 25.

17. Ibid., pp. 113–17.
18. Brauer, *The Horse*, pp. 193–94.

BIBLIOGRAPHICAL SURVEY

For a genre that seems to be nearing extinction, to judge by the constantly decreasing number of Western films, television shows, and paperback novels, it is surprising to find so much first-rate criticism readily available. Perhaps it is this very lack of life to the genre that attracts critics who otherwise might have to tackle much more unwieldy territory.

Any discussion of the Western properly should begin with John Cawelti's *The Six-Gun Mystique*, which so clearly establishes the archetypal patterns that we recognize as forming the boundaries of the Western. Cawelti's theory of formula—a mixture of the conventional and the inventional elements of storytelling—provides a framework both malleable and expansive into which a Western novel from 1924, a Western film from 1939, and a Western television show from 1957 all fit with equal ease. If the book has a weakness, it is Cawelti's preoccupation with literature and film to the exclusion of the contributions made by television.

Douglas Brode's "They Went Thataway" directly addresses the television Western in concise, but consistently provocative terms. While his theoretical framework differs slightly from the one offered by Cawelti, Brode does provide tools that can be applied to good effect by even newcomers to the television Western.

The Western Hero in Film and Television by Rita Parks is something of a problem. Her insistence on dealing with the television Western as a transformation of the myth from epic to pastoral fences her in to a debilitating degree. Some of the statistics she offers are also suspect—a number of shows, for instance, are assigned an erroneous debut date—but nevertheless, this is one of the better full-length studies available.

On the other hand, Ralph Brauer's *The Horse, the Gun and the Piece of Property* is as awkward as its cumbersome title might suggest. Brauer approaches the history of the television Western from a personal viewpoint, which results in a mixture of information, theory, and Brauer's intimate remembrances of TV shows and politics past. To his credit, Brauer is one of the few critics who took the time to delve into the particulars of individual episodes that plug in quite neatly to the theories preferred by Cawelti and Brode. Alas, Brauer himself seems to have no theories, only memories of these electronic madeleines.

For a book that does not pretend to have academic credentials, Tim Brooks and Earle Marsh's *The Complete Directory to Prime Time Television* offers a surprising amount of pungent commentary. Arranged in alphabetical format, the volume requires some jumping around on the part of the reader; nevertheless, a more complete picture of the particulars of the television Western simply does not exist. Especially useful is Brooks and Marsh's meticulous attention to cast changes and contract squabbles, which often determine the shape a show might take for an entire season.

Other useful surveys of the TV Western can be found in Christopher Sterling and John Kittross's *Stay Tuned* and Erik Barnouw's history *Tube of Plenty*.

BOOKS AND ARTICLES

Barnouw, Erik. *Tube of Plenty*. New York: Oxford University Press, 1983.

Brauer, Ralph, with Donna Brauer. *The Horse, the Gun and the Piece of Property: Changing Images of the TV Western*. Bowling Green: Popular Press, 1975.

Brode, Douglas. "They Went Thataway." *Television Quarterly*, Summer 1982.

Brooks, Tim, and Earle Marsh. *The Complete Directory to Prime Time Network TV Shows: 1946–Present*. Rev. ed. New York: Ballantine Books, 1981.

Cawelti, John. *The Six-Gun Mystique*. Bowling Green, Ohio: The Popular Press, 1970.

Parks, Rita. *The Western Hero in Film and Television*. Ann Arbor: UMI Research Press, 1982.

Shulman, Arthur. *How Sweet It Was*. New York: Bonanza, 1966.

Sterling, Christopher, and John Kittross. *Stay Tuned: A Concise History of American Broadcasting*. Belmont, Calif.: Wadsworth Publishing, 1978.

VIDEOGRAPHY

"The Life and Legend of Wyatt Earp"
  ABC, Tuesdays, 8:30–9:00 P.M.
  Premiere: September 6, 1955
  Star: Hugh O'Brien
  Last Program: September 26, 1961

"Gunsmoke"
  CBS, various prime times
  Premiere: September 10, 1955
  Stars: James Arness, Amanda Blake
  Last Program: September 1, 1975

"Have Gun Will Travel"
  CBS, Saturdays, 9:30–10:30 P.M.
  Premiere: September 14, 1957
  Star: Richard Boone
  Last Program: September 21, 1963

"Wagon Train"
  NBC (1957–1962), Wednesdays 7:30–8:30 P.M.
  ABC (1962–1965), various prime times
  Premiere: September 18, 1957
  Stars: Ward Bond, Robert Horton
  Last Program: September 5, 1965

"Maverick"
  ABC, Sundays, various prime times
  Premiere: September 22, 1957

Stars: James Garner, Jack Kelly
Last Program: July 8, 1962

"The Rifleman"
ABC, various prime times
Premiere: September 30, 1958
Stars: Chuck Connors, Johnny Crawford
Last Program: July 1, 1963

"Rawhide"
CBS, various prime times
Premiere: January 9, 1959
Star: Clint Eastwood
Last Program: January 4, 1966

"Bonanza"
NBC, various prime times
Premiere: September 12, 1959
Stars: Lorne Greene, Michael Landon, Dan Blocker, Pernell Roberts
Last Program: January 16, 1973

"Kung Fu"
ABC, various prime times
Premiere: October 14, 1972
Stars: David Carradine, Keye Luke
Last Program: June 18, 1975

"Little House on the Prairie"
NBC, various prime times
Premiere: September 11, 1974
Stars: Michael Landon, Karen Grassle, Melissa Gilbert
Last Program: September 5, 1983

5

Medical Melodrama

ROBERT S. ALLEY

OVERVIEW

Unlike almost any other major television genre, medical melodrama can be examined with a reasonable degree of thoroughness in short compass. This is possible because of the rather small number of medical series that have been a part of prime-time viewing since 1954.

The "doctor" shows that will be addressed here have themes that are particularly bound both to traditional cultural patterns *and* changing scientific understandings. Hence the nostalgia so prevalent in family series of the fifties and sixties was necessarily tempered by modern developments in medicine. The context was a post-World War II America described by historian Eric Goldman as lacking a sense of humor. His reference was to the fifties, when citizens were preoccupied with the bomb and communist witch-hunts. In general, scientists were viewed with awe by a public just experiencing an economic recovery that made new technology available to large portions of the population. This idealizing of the scientist was in large measure a result of a public ignorance that made science a mystery. And medicine was the profession most closely allied to the popular culture of those that imbibed the heady knowledge of science. Added to an already existing belief in the moral rectitude of doctors, there emerged an idealization of physicians and particularly surgeons bordering upon worship. New discoveries contributed to an image of invincible doctors battling death and winning remarkable victories. Personal, and as knowing and caring as the best clergyman, the doctor could do battle with the powers of evil on earth aided by a science beyond the ken of most humans.

In contrast, today the family physician has become the exception; "miracle drugs" have been proven fallible; the cost of medical care has created anger while doctors' salaries are regularly viewed as excessive, and often as a social inequity. The doctor has been humanized. Concurrently, the unbridled enthusiasm over science has cooled. Space travel has become commonplace; pollution is perceived as a by-product of scientific failure and greed; chemical waste is a scandal; insecticides haunt us from our recent past; nuclear power is no longer a panacea.

Yet, even as science has been tarnished, the medical profesion has retained a unique, emotionally charged ingredient: It still does battle with death. In this engagement heroes are still possible, even for a culture jaded by political corruption, social discord, Three Mile Island, Love Canal, computer warfare, and dehumanizing technology. The television representations of doctors, while reflecting an altered public image of the profession, continue to reinforce that vestigial respect for the practitioners of the healing arts.

HISTORICAL DEVELOPMENT

During the fifties medicine was a growth industry, a science, a pioneering profession seeking to provide better health and longer life. The adversary was disease and/or ignorance. Thus the first doctor series, "Medic," atempted to convey information on the serious subjects of alcoholism, civil defense, birth, cancer. Richard Boone, who began his TV career with this series, introduced each episode with a description of the doctor as "guardian of birth, healer of the sick, and comforter of the aged."[1] "Medic" was shot at hospitals and clinics, often including real doctors and nurses in the cast. Boone, as Dr. Konrad Styner, participated in a number of the cases, while narrating all the episodes.

Unlikely as it may seem today, "Medic" was fashioned by NBC "to put a big dent in the top rating of CBS's 'I Love Lucy'."[2] Understood in that light, a description of the first episode is revealing.

The opening show was starkly simple in plot: after seven years of marriage, a woman finally becomes pregnant only to learn that she must die of leukemia, perhaps even before the baby is born. Blunt-featured Richard Boone carried authority as the doctor who fights to keep the mother alive until childbirth, and the delivery-room scenes were as sensational and convincing as anything yet seen on TV.[3]

While the hoped-for upset of "Lucy" was not forthcoming, by February 1955, "Medic" was receiving so many letters from viewers with real or imagined ills that the Los Angeles County Medical Association agreed to forward the letters to appropriate medical associations in the states from which the correspondents came. From its inception the program's content was controlled by the LACMA, which served both as censor and prod to the producers. A newsmagazine noted: "A show dealing with homosexuality was 'tabled' by the doctors, but they have lifted some TV taboos, e.g., in a film about an unwed mother, NBC balked when the doctor—as he normally would—asked the girl when her last period had occurred. LACMA insisted that the word stay in."[4]

The Medical Association was convinced that the series gave good press to the profession.

A lot of people have been propagandized by this or that group advocating socialized medicine or compulsory health insurance. . . . But when "Medic" pictures medicine as it is actually practiced and Mrs. Jones looks at it on her TV set, it is not hard for her to believe that medicine is pretty fine and that doctors, by and large, are rendering good medical care to the American people.[5]

"Medic" was TV realism as no viewers had experienced it in previous series. Reviewing the show after two months on the air, Jack Gould remarked that "the hysterics, the sensationalism, marred the program in part,"[6] and a year later *Time* wrote that the show "is ordinarily more interested in shock value than in therapy."[7] But Gould as well as other critics found much in the series to commend; its "seriousness and high mindedness" were seen as models, and one 1955 episode was commended by the *New York Times* because it "avoided scientific mumbo-jumbo and shabby melo-dramatic incidents."[8]

By 1956 even the friendliest critics were uneasy about the tone of some segments. In an episode entitled "The Glorious Red Gallagher" the *Times* suggested that the depiction of a Caesarian section was "too stark" and "too realistic."[9] In its April 23, 1956, issue *Time* agreed:

This week one of Helffrich's [NBC director of continuity acceptance] more tactful decisions probably went unnoticed by the millions whose viewing was affected by it. Without any outside pressure, he eliminated 90 seconds from NBC's "Medic." The shocker of a sequence was shot in a hospital operating room and showed a Caesarian section, including the incision and birth of the baby. "Pointless realism," said Helffrich, "that was calculated to horrify."[10]

While the *Time* article may have perceived no "outside pressure," the evidence is clear that Father T. J. Flynn, Director of Media and TV of the Roman Catholic Archdiocese of New York, had protested the program in early March, stating that the episode "was not the proper subject for an entertainment show." He argued that the role of sex educator belonged to the church and the home.[11] And during the first week in April, prior to the *Time* report, the Los Angeles County Medical Association withdrew its endorsement of the show. (In 1972 the LACMA inaugurated a syndicated documentary, "Medix," that appeared on some 75 stations and received an Emmy award for community service.)

It is uncertain whether "Medic" would have returned to the fall schedule of NBC in any circumstances, but this clear effort to censor, one that prompted cancellation of sponsorship by General Electric and Procter and Gamble, undoubtedly brought about its demise in May of 1956.[12]

During its brief stay on the air, it appears that "Medic" affected network programmers who offered "March of Medicine," a documentary that was sponsored by the AMA, on NBC in the summer of 1955. The first program covered live the removal of a tumor from a woman's breast.[13] ABC broadcast "Medical Horizons," another documentary that appeared in prime time during the 1955–56 season.

Five years elapsed before two medical series were developed for airing in 1961—"Dr. Kildare" on NBC and "Ben Casey" on ABC. In the strict sense, these were the first medical melodramas. Of course, "Medic" was fiction, but it employed real doctors, nurses, and operating rooms. It may well have been the first genuine docudrama. It was all business, focusing upon the discipline of medicine. Both new series created plots in search of diseases.

While it cannot be verified, it is tempting to suggest that the presidency of John F. Kennedy provided a context for a new perspective on the healing arts, one that favored a moral crusade against illness. While Richard Chamberlain and Vincent Edwards were cast in the heroic mold of the traditional surgeon, they created characters whose dedication and youth sparkled as they struggled against bureaucracy, caution, and tradition.

Of course, the series had their elder statesmen, Dr. Gillespie and Dr. Zorba, tempering youthful passion, but with understanding and moral support for their younger associates. One observes this same style in "Trapper John, M.D." when Dr. McIntyre tells Dr. Gates it would be unwise for him to become involved in a hospital administrative conflict. However, McIntyre further advises that, if Gates persists, he should at least not get *caught* stealing evidence. This passing of the torch is not unique to doctor shows, but it works in a particular way in such stories just because in popular wisdom doctors have been clothed with rectitude. Thus the elder becomes nearly a god figure not only for the younger surgeon, but for the audience as well. The reasoned caution and suggested compromise of the older generation, contrasted with the idealism of young surgeons anxious to champion unpopular causes, is never allowed to detract from the sense of common cause that justifies the rash outbursts and moral indignation of the new generation.

Monday night belonged to "Ben Casey" beginning October 2, 1961. Dr. Casey was jarring, aggressive, a believer in justice. He was angry most of the time, perhaps because Edwards had difficulty acting "nice," or perhaps because the show was produced by James Moser, the man who created "Medic."[14] Whatever the reason, the series was constructed around a personality, featuring a no-nonsense surgeon with very little humor. His sense of justice transcended the protocol of his profession. He was impatient. He even dared draw comparisons between the long, underpaid hours of his hospital staff and the lucrative private practice of physicians who passed through County General. Above all, Ben Casey was dedicated to principle, no matter the cost—an appealing character in the year 1963, when America's youth was enthralled with the Peace Corps and the vigor of President Kennedy.

NBC's Thursday night medical series cast Dr. Kildare as cultured and refined.[15] Premiering just a few days before "Casey," "Dr. Kildare" presented the audience with a community of medicine drawn from a popular film series of the forties. Kildare, whose education showed, was, at least on the surface, more respectful of authority than Casey. There was just a touch of piety in his demeanor, contrasting sharply with the abrupt righteousness of his ABC counterpart. Yet Kildare often discovered just causes that were more important than protocol, and on those occasions he was prepared to challenge authority.

The producers had created Ben Casey as a young but established resident neurosurgeon, and this tended to present him as somewhat static, without any ambition for advancement. In contrast, Kildare began as an intern, becoming a resident only in his third season. This device permitted growth in the course of the series. Indeed, executive producer David Victor offered NBC a sixth year in which Kildare would go into private practice, but the network was not interested in a nonhospital setting. Victor returned to prime time with "Marcus Welby, M.D." in 1969, a show he described as "taking up a Dr. Kildare figure in the later years."[16]

Casey and Kildare did not, as had "Medic," focus upon the discipline of medicine. The two young surgeons practiced medicine in dramatic settings in which they became heroic as they battled death and ignorance. The surgeon's struggles in O.R. were impersonal, without human conflict. And just because of this fact, as Kildare or Casey triumphed over disease, as he combatted evil, nonhuman threats to life, he developed a pristine reputation. Armed with this status as invincible knight, the doctor would invariably enter human conflicts with audience support. The viewer identified the surgeon's unquestioned expertise through the use of technical jargon, effective "medical music," and masked faces with knowing glances. Seen struggling against hospital red tape and administrative narrow vision, the surgeon's victory was always a righteous triumph.

In neither series was much effort made to impart understanding about illness and disease. The patient's role was passive. Medical ethics was usually reduced to simplistic issues such as whether to inform a terminal patient of his or her condition. Those issues that might have unmasked the profession and offered a realistic portrait of human frailty in medicine were largely ignored. Plots involving medical incompetence, excessive fees, medical school quotas, birth control, abortion, euthanasia, death with dignity, medical insurance, socialized medicine, unnecessary operations, and the doctors' "fraternity" seldom surfaced. The presumption of the need to encourage trust by the public in the profession of medicine outweighed other considerations, and there is little doubt that the ready cooperation of the AMA in advising producers militated against controversial story lines.[17] In the case of Kildare, the nature of the series was set by the character of its gentle, idealistic executive producer, David Victor.

Two of the awards I most cherish were the only ones I think the American Medical Association ever gave to a layman. I got two, one for "Dr. Kildare" and one for "Marcus Welby, M.D." I helped the positive image of medicine. I don't apologize for that. It's a matter of philosophy. I could do a show like "Medical Story" and you know you're afraid to cross the threshold of a hospital from that point on. I'm not stupid. I know there are abuses and, like in any profession, there are bad apples. I prefer in the long-lived series to concentrate on the good people and their business. People do want assurance, and at ten o'clock at night, before the news and after all the other things, there's a little assurance in the fact that maybe somebody cares.[18]

Victor believes that his work "made a definite impact on the image of medicine," and he intended that influence to be positive. In conversations with him, it it easy to believe in his sincerity. His stories mirror his personality.

There is a quiet sense about Victor's stories, even when they conclude in frustration or tragedy. There is the feeling that problems will be solved with emotional responses as much as with physical action, with individual attention as well as through the efforts of official representatives of authority. Even the dispensation of actual information, the actual cure of the disease . . . is secondary to the assistance given by one human being concerned for another.[19]

Kildare, the lawyer Owen Marshall, and Marcus Welby are not representatives of professional care as it is, but as it should be.

In the case of James Kildare, as with Ben Casey, it was not that doctors were portrayed as holy and incapable of error. Rather, cast in melodramatic form, their heroic natures took center stage because they coincided with a public sense that doctors should be motivated by human service and unselfish ideals. But the popularity of such figures declined in the bitter years after 1965 when Vietnam melted idealism, assassinations eroded optimism, and social inequalities indicated a flawed system of justice. In this environment it became more difficult to create simple heroes. Both series disappeared in 1966, leaving the American viewer without medical attention for three years.

What Michael Real describes as "the cruder dimension of the medical genre" appeared in 1962 under the title "The Nurses." It survived on CBS for three seasons. Unlike its contemporaries, there seemed to be little interest in medical accuracy. Indeed the executive producer, Herbert Brodkin, defended the dramatic devices: "A nurse's job is to prevent dramatic episodes from happening so the climactic situations are in a sense artificial. But without these dramatics we wouldn't have a show."[20] It was unfortunate that this series did not reflect the same degree of care for detail as the two doctor shows had, since it was the first effort to highlight women in the profession. It may have been appropriate for "The Nurses" that it became a daytime serial from 1965 to 1967, following its prime-time run.

In the fall of 1969 NBC introduced "The Bold Ones," a quartet of "relevant" dramas focused on the law, politics, the police, and medicine. The scripts combined social issues with the heroic professional style anticipated in the title. The medical segment, longest-lived of the four (1969–1973), focused not only upon medical practice, but on research as well. David Hartman, who portrayed Dr. Paul Hunter, one of the "New Doctors" at the David Craig Institute of New Medicine, spoke with pride about the series. According to him the show had had medical credibility, dealt with substantive issues in medicine, and was presented with "great objectivity." He insisted that on those occasions when an episode addressed "issues" there were "no shots at anyone." Hartman himself did a great deal of research into medical procedures. He saw the show as having a specific objective, encouraging people to get the best quality of medicine available. In what may have been a forecast of his later position with "Good Morning, America," he insisted that we should "use television to educate and inform while we entertain."[21] He was particularly proud of an episode ("Quality of Fear") dealing with the psychological treatment of cancer patients, which he believed achieved those goals.

"The New Doctors" brought humor to television medicine, seeking to humanize the surgeons in the cast. The wry wit of Dr. Craig, played by E. G. Marshall, was neatly balanced with the banter between Dr. Hunter and Dr. Ted Stuart.

Barely ten days after the premiere of "The New Doctors," David Victor returned his brand of medicine to the air with "Marcus Welby, M.D." One day later CBS unveiled its first medical drama, "Medical Center."

Victor's second major success in TV medicine was a significant departure from previous efforts in the genre in that it examined the careers of two family physicians who worked out of a well-equipped suite of offices in Marcus Welby's home. Welby, an aging Kildare, was a compassionate elder statesman who practiced general medicine. His patients were surburban, well-to-do, with the normal upper-middle-class ills and complaints. Victor readily admits that Welby was "fictionalized, over-sentimentalized," but he insists that "there are some Welbys."[22]

In a twist on the themes generated in earlier series, Welby's young colleague, Dr. Steven Kiley, was portrayed as cautious, going by the book, frequently shocked and disturbed by Welby's unorthodox methods. This approach suggested the limits often restraining young scholars, limits artificially imposed by the nature of modern graduate studies.

"Marcus Welby," the most successful medical series in history according to Nielsen,[23] was the first to move from a hospital setting, allowing Victor to "do all the things that touch people at the hot points of their lives—births, illnesses, weddings, deaths."[24] Welby was a family doctor, to be sure, cut from a fabric of some age, but offering an ideal that clearly struck a positive note with the audience. It has been suggested, without clear proof, that the very concern and attention exhibited by Dr. Welby caused an increase in medical malpractice suits as viewers turned patients received less satisfactory treatment from their own physicians and surgeons.

Medical series are first of all vehicles for dramatic art, entertainment good or poor. Producers who have chosen to use medicine as that vehicle have regularly emphasized the hero rather than the antihero, thus creating what some critics have described as the "deification of Medicine."[25] But the critics may have underestimated the near sacral character assigned to the medical profession in America, a fact that militates against "realistic" representation of the profession even in 1984. Viewers are not in court rooms nor in police stations on a regular basis, but either as patients or friends, most viewers know the pulse of hospitals. Courts and precincts tend to be life threatening, doctors life preserving. The emotions of hope and trust permeate the average American's sentiments concerning doctors. Hence, it is reasonable to assume that such viewers do not demand nor want a realism that tears at their image, whether it be mythic or not. And David Victor is probably correct that most persons have known a Marcus Welby somewhere in their past, a dedicated human being who makes house calls, checks on patients, spends precious minutes in small talk with them as the waiting room fills, attends funerals with the families, and is remarkably talented as a diagnostician. Welby may be as inaccurate in reflecting the true level of medical care in one direction as the story of Serpico, in the other extreme, is in depicting the average police officer, but even the most recent efforts in TV medicine suggest that viewers find it satisfying.

"Medical Center" added the dimension of the matinee idol to the central character. Dr. Joe Gannon had a range of medical and surgical knowledge that boggled the mind. He was moralistic and cool, to use the popular phrase of the early seventies. Gannon championed causes in the name of openness, of letting people "have their space." His was a "plea for tolerance of any deviation one can come up with."[26] Like all his predecessors, Gannon was associated with an elder statesman, Dr. Paul Lochner, who was primarily a counsellor for Gannon.

Frank Glicksman, who along with his partner Don Brinkley, created "Medical Center" and the currently popular "Trapper John, M.D.," said the original purpose of the series was to "explore every area of our society" as a public service.[27] Glicksman illustrated his point by citing incidents when the program had been helpful to people. And he noted that he "looks for subjects that are important, that have something to say."

As one listens to Glicksman and Brinkley and Victor, the startling truth emerges—since 1954 there have been some 40 seasons of dramatic medical shows aired and 30 of that number, over 75 percent, were created and produced by three executives, Moser, Glicksman/Brinkley, and Victor.[28] Even more revealing is the fact that only those three producers have had medical series in the top 25. "The New Doctors" was moderately successful but never achieved public notice. "St. Elsewhere" has become news because it reflects the approach used by "Hill Street Blues," was produced by MTM, and was well received by the critics.

"Medical Center" and "Marcus Welby" ended their runs simultaneously in 1976, even as they had begun, emulating the 1961–66 stints of Kildare and Casey. As these two highly successful ventures wound down, NBC moved two competitors into the prime hours in the fall of 1975. Both "Medical Story" and "Doctors' Hospital" were immediate casualties of ratings, and the last episode of each appeared in the first week of January 1976. The former requires some attention because it alone of all the medical efforts on TV has attempted to remove the mystery and awe surrounding the profession. Reminiscent of "The Hospital," Paddy Chayefsky's 1972 satire, the first episode addressed malpractice and professional incompetence. The young doctor, Ducker, who had the courage to challenge an established, but incompetent surgeon, had the following exchange with the hospital's chief surgeon.

Chief: The Board is not going to renew your contract. It would cause too many tensions. . . . We are going to give you letters of recommendation. . . . This is an organization like anything else. Some things have to be sacrificed for larger things.

Ducker: What if I go to the papers? . . . the accrediting committee?

Chief: I wouldn't do that. You need your letters of recommendation. You'll find there is a tendency to close ranks within the medical profession. If you haven't learned anything else from this episode you should have learned that.

Ducker: I learned that.

Chief: . . . you can't win.

Ducker: All right. I'm fired, but I'm still going to be a doctor.[29]

The marked difference between the TV series and the film "The Hospital" lay in the fact that the heroic, if perplexed and suicidal, surgeon played by George C. Scott determined to remain on the scene at the metropolitan hospital in order to fight for those principles in which he believed. "Medical Story," an anthology, did not offer that continuing figure who just might make things better.

"Medical Story" investigated death with dignity, patient experimentation, abortion, industrial poisoning, malpractice, and sterilization in its brief run. The heroes who appeared did not frequently beat the system or even maintain a "point of order." One piece of nostalgia was present when a doctor, played by Vincent Edwards, was arrested for performing an illegal abortion. The story was not resolved, and in a particularly daring twist a priest was portrayed as the heavy. Such writing led Cleveland Amory to comment: "Imagine a doctor show without a pat or happy ending. We tell you it's a medical millennium."[30]

"Medical Story" was well written, acted, and directed. It caught the flavor of some of the earlier anthologies and maintained a high standard of quality throughout its brief history. But again, as entertainment it failed to appreciate the particular emotional tags associated with doctors by the vast majority of viewers. Its unrelenting quest for realism did not translate into audience acceptance. If "Hill Street" and "St. Elsewhere" are to be compared with the earlier venture, it is important to note that in each of the new shows there is a continuing cast of characters who fulfill the heroic roles while the guest stars offer the seamy side. The question the viewer might pose, "Do I want to go to that hospital?" could be answered in the affirmative for St. Elsewhere.

"Trapper John, M.D." is a spin-off of the popular comedy "M*A*S*H" to the extent that the lead character in the former was one of the two leads in the latter. In this 1979 melodrama, doctor series had their first full injection of humor. In a collection of loosely connected story lines, half the time each week is devoted to light and ludicrous situations. These generally revolve around Dr. Stanley Riverside, son of the most powerful board member of San Francisco Memorial. The emphasis in this series shifts to the emergency room over which Riverside presides. Dr. Gates, something of a protégé of John McIntyre (Trapper), is constructed on the premise that the younger doctor is more daring and more "with it" than his older friend, but that their medical competence is equal and usually infallible. They do lose patients, but to disease not to lack of knowledge.

This sense of assurance is nicely played against the backdrop of a hospital staff that at times borders on the bizarre. Intern pranks and personal problems plaguing Nurse Brancusi consume much time in the halls. Often patients are presented as difficult, and the frustrations of the staff are regularly in evidence. Dr. Gates combines the role of a surgeon with the personality of a concerned country doctor, coursing through the streets of San Francisco to aid and assist his charges. But even as the viewer is drawn to the dramatic characters as entertaining personalities, Glicksman and Brinkley are working their brand of education, instructing the audience in appropriate patient response to the medical profession. As this series plowed familiar ground, it also became the first successful medical series to integrate humor into plots and to highlight human frailty and compassion over medical background.

"St. Elsewhere" requires attention because it appears to combine the frankness of "Medical Story" with continuing characters who reflect a high degree of medical knowledge and human concern. These doctors, staffing what is considered a poor hospital, struggle against that image, bureaucracy, and government interference. The series makes political statements. In one episode the chief of surgery resists the efforts of military officials to make St. Eligius a test site for a simulated nuclear disaster. The doctor makes the case effectively—in the event of such a catastrophe no prior plans will help, indeed to plan is to give a false sense of hope to the public. In the 1983–84 season the series experienced low ratings, and even critical acclaim and comparisons with its sister MTM show, "Hill Street Blues" did not seem enough to salvage this innovative effort. However, NBC sensed a growing support for "St. Elsewhere" and continued it on the schedule, where its rating rose to a respectable level by the fall of 1984.

Of course, there remain the afternoon soaps, those extremely popular serials that use hospitals and medicine as backdrops for explorations of every conceivable human misery and malaise. "General Hospital," a particular favorite among college students in the eighties, does attempt a modicum of accuracy in depicting hospital conditions, but the overpowering influence of human carnage and depravity make the medical setting little more than a backdrop.

The series "Emergency" deserves a brief notice here. Its five-year stay (1972–1977) on NBC at 8:00 P.M. on Saturday was an attraction for younger viewers who saw the work of the Los Angeles County Paramedical Rescue Service dramatized. Jack Webb produced the series with the same staccato style he employed in "Dragnet." As a background for the emergency team, the show depicted a hospital with a medical staff responding to calls from the field, advising, and then handling the incoming emergencies. Dr. Kelly Brackett was all business, knowledgeable, and finally quite human as he ran the gamut of accidental disasters and sudden coronaries.

While this chapter is devoted to considering prime-time drama, two documentaries are worthy of mention. In 1977 CBS inaugurated a series of specials entitled "The Body Human." It received high critical acclaim and an Emmy award in 1979. In September 1978 NBC placed "Lifeline" on its evening schedule (10 to 11 P.M. first on Thursday and then on Sunday). Produced by the same persons who did "The Body Human," the series focused on a different city each week, with a particular real doctor featured. "To produce the program a camera crew followed each doctor for several months, filming him with his family and at work, including actual operating room and emergency room scenes where lives often hung in the balance."[31] The quality of the documentary was of the highest order, but in spite of excellent advertising and critical support, "Lifeline" was not accepted by the viewing public. A hard look at the medical profession, it may have proved too jarring to succeed on a weekly basis.

Finally, since the early seventies there has been a rash of half-hour comedies centered around the medical profession. "M*A*S*H" is in a class by itself, a genuine television classic. Alan Alda was quite emphatic in asserting that the characters were "not just a bunch of cutups at the front."[32] They were trying to convey ideas in the series, but it is fair to say that the chief purpose was not to inform viewers about medical procedures. Medicine was the stage for this antiwar satire, and as such care was taken to be accurate in representing procedures. But if anything, "M*A*S*H" offered super-heroic surgeons, struggling not only against the irrational character of illness and death, but the unfair outrages of war as well. Trapper, Hawkeye, and B.J. lost patients, but never from a lack of dedication or knowledge. One could imagine Ben Casey or Dr. Kildare assuming similar roles in the Vietnam War.

In 1972 "Temperatures Rising" made a brief appearance as did Brian Keith's "Little People," a series about a father/daughter pediatric team in Hawaii. A more successful effort was "The Bob Newhart Show," in which comic characters played various medical roles including a urologist, Dr. Bernie Tupperman, and Dr. Jerry Robinson, a dentist. In that same year Norman Lear introduced Dr. Arthur Harmon as the neighbor in "Maude." Harmon reflected all the social and political conservatism associated with the medical profession in the public mind. Much humor was drawn from Arthur's easy schedule and high fees, but he was represented as a thoroughly competent surgeon and good friend to his patients. He was a caring physician.

Other series of short-lived duration included "Doc" in 1975 and "The Practice" in 1976. Bernard Hughes and Danny Thomas were unable to sustain these efforts. "House Calls" arrived in 1979, and in its short life it took an entire hospital as its arena of humor. Early efforts to make Dr. Amos Weatherby a doddering, incompetent fool (similar to the characterization offered by Art Carney in the film) quickly gave way to a character whose age removed him from surgery, but whose wisdom was much appreciated by the medical staff at Kensington General. In this comedy, as in several of the dramas about hospitals, the administrator was represented as repressive, constantly undermining proper medical care. "AfterM*A*S*H" followed this same style, as it traded upon the three continuing characters from the earlier series.

And finally, there was Quincy of "Quincy, M.E.," the crusading coroner who turned every episode into a moral lesson. It is difficult to get a fix on the medical profession from this series because Jack Klugman, as Dr. Quincy, so dominated every scene that everyone appeared slightly ineffective in comparison. There were times when serious questions were posed about medical ethics, but Klugman's intensity tended to stereotype other cast members, often blunting the effect intended.

THEMES AND ISSUES

The one glaring flaw in nearly all these dramas was their neat, elegant, traditional, middle-class settings. Richard Levinson once commented that "people who make TV only know upper-middle-class." The surgeons and doctors were from the outset and remained white, and mostly males. When, as in the Casey series, there was a female physician, she was conscious of the "place" among her colleagues. In one episode she tells a female patient who wants to help her husband, "Let him make the decisions. Let him decide who your friends are." When the patient observes that such a position will change her whole life, Dr. Maggie Graham says, "Isn't that what getting married means?"[33] In none of the other successful series with continuing characters did a female doctor assume a significant role until "St. Elsewhere." There was in evidence an overwhelming predominance of white male doctors and young, white, female nurses.[34] This sex distinction remained nearly an absolute even as new series appeared in the eighties. As far as race was concerned, there were neither black doctors nor nurses until "Trapper John, M.D." made a black chief nurse a continuing character in 1980. (The exception of course is the 1967 half-hour comedy "Julia.")

The medical profession continues to be well served by the television representations of doctors and nurses. The limited number of producers who have entered this particular field all seem to hold the practice of medicine in highest esteem. David Victor commented that he was very proud that his grandson wanted to be a doctor and that he, himself, would like to have gone to medical school. There is nothing inherently wrong with this condition, but it does militate against a serious critical analysis of the business of medicine. The economics and ethics of medicine are seldom held up to scrutiny. (Hospital administrators do come in for indictment fairly often. But such figures, if they are doctors, are portrayed as having forsaken the high road of medicine.) The alternatives of socialized medicine and government medical insurance are generally ignored. These series have presented a system of values and points of view regarding the medical profession. Like all drama on television, these shows say something.

In an excellent treatment of Marcus Welby, Horace Newcomb wrote in 1974:

The tough problems solved by Welby are the problems of those who must care for the socially, mentally, and physically handicapped. How does one accept a handicapped child? How does one live with one's failures as a parent? How does one accept death? When our counselors and confessors help their fictional characters solve these problems, as they always do, they are again directing advice toward the audience.

Such advice embodies traditional American values, and in structuring these shows television is openly and explicitly didactic. If our society, our culture, offers only a relativistic morality, then we can turn on the television set to see problems worked out for us in terms of a simpler set of shared values.[35]

As observed earlier, the American population of 1984 seems quite capable of accepting the dethroning of heroes in all professions except medicine. It may be that only the doctor can pass muster as a genuine hero in this decade. While excessive fees, malpractice, corporate abuse of drugs, and the like have created a growing skepticism among many, the majority still seem to believe in the heroic doctor. And in a world where science has lost its lustre in the wake of pollution and potential atomic disasters, modern medical science remains in the popular culture as a bulwark against such dangers.[36]

NOTES

1. Tim Brooks and Earle Marsh, *The Complete Directory to Prime Time Network TV Shows, 1946–Present*, rev. ed. (New York: Ballantine Books, 1981), p. 486. Since 1954 there have been several syndicated medical programs offered to local channels. A Canadian produced effort, "Dr. Simon Locke" (1971–74), was the most widely distributed. Daytime serials abounded. This current study addresses only prime-time network programming.

2. *Time*, September 20, 1954, p. 97.

3. Ibid.

4. *Time*, February 21, 1955, p. 65.

5. LACMA's Executive Assistant Jerry Pettis as quoted in ibid.

6. *New York Times*, December 24, 1954, 18:4.

7. *Time*, Decmember 19, 1955, p. 49.

8. See *New York Times*, September 15, 1954, 3:48; Feburary 18, 1955, 3:28; December 27, 1955, 3:47.

9. *New York Times*, March 11, 1956, 5:84.

10. *Time*, April 23, 1956, p. 69.

11. *New York Times*, March 11, 1956, 5:84.

12. *New York Times*, May 25, 1956, 5:47. See also *Time* for June 4, 1956, p. 70. "NBC's 'Medic,' started a year and a half ago in an attempt to knock CBS's 'I Love Lucy' from the No. 1 position in the ratings, will fold up its scalpels and silently steal away in August. The last Nielsen ratings found 'Lucy' still No. 1, 'Medic' No. 81. Both sponsors failed to renew their options."

13. *Time*, June 20, 1955, p. 88.

14. Commenting on Casey's character, *Time* observed: "Neurosurgeon Ben Casey is so bright that his giant brain is already grappling with the most advanced encephalo-pathological problems of 1975. Meanwhile, he is a first-class, 1961-style son of a bitch. Handling several cases on an ABC-hour, his kindest words for his fellow physicians is: 'What the hell do you use for brains?' Rabid women bite him. But, for all his foaming at the mouth, Casey is a marvelous character in a show that accurately captures the feeling of sleepless intensity in a metropolitan hospital." October 20, 1961, p. 79.

15. After "Doctor Kildare's" premiere *Time* complained: "Intern Kildare, as played by Richard Chamberlain, suggests nothing so much as an oversized white rabbit with a stethoscope instead of a watch." October 20, 1961, p. 79.

16. Interview with David Victor held by the author in July of 1975.

17. But this is an oversimplification since there were numerous occasions when "issues" were addressed on Kildare, albeit usually issues touching upon the medical profession as a whole, not a part of it. Richard Levinson and William Link wrote one of their first social dramas for "Dr. Kildare" in 1963 in which they pointed to the outrageous practices in the funeral business. The episode was controversial enough that ABC never reran it.

18. Interview with David Victor by the author, July 30, 1979.

19. Horace Newcomb and Robert S. Alley, *The Producer's Medium* (New York: Oxford University Press, 1983), p. 78.

20. Michael Real, *Mass-Mediated Culture* (Englewood Cliffs, N.J.: Prentice Hall, 1977), p. 124. Real went on to point out that, "Many real-life nurses wrote letters complaining of the ineptness of the student nurse in the program, failure to show her in a student role, overly dramatic presentations of hospital life and the nurse's role, and portrayal of nurses as alcoholics, reactionaries, and neurotics."

21. This, and other remarks by David Hartman, are drawn from two 1975 interviews by the author.

22. Confidential letter to author.

23. In 1969–70 "Welby" ranked 8th; in 1970–71, 1st; in 1971–72, 3d; in 1972–73, 13th. In comparison, "Medical Center," which had the same TV life span, ranked 8th in 1970–71; 13th in 1971–72; 21st in 1972–73.

24. Interview with David Victor by the author, July 30, 1979.

25. Peter Schrag, "The Great American Swashbucklers," *More*, November 1975.

26. Interview with Frank Glicksman, executive producer of "Medical Center," held by the author on July 11, 1975.

27. Ibid.

28. Further, David Hartman, who appeared in the "Bold Ones" for four seasons, was a close personal friend of Victor. Victor fashioned the role of "Lucas Tanner" especially for Hartman.

29. Robert S. Alley, "Media Medicine and Morality," *Television as a Cultural Force*, ed. Richard Adler and Douglass Cater (New York: Praeger, 1976).

30. Cleveland Amory, "Review," *TV Guide* 23, no. 44, November 1, 1975, p. 20.

31. Brooks and Marsh, *The Complete Directory*, p. 434.

32. Interview with Alan Alda by the author, July 1975.

33. Alley, "Media Medicine and Morality," p. 103.

34. James M. McLaughlin, "Characteristics and Symbolic Functions of Fictional Televised Medical Professionals and Their Effect on Children," (M.A. thesis, The An-

nenberg School of Communications, 1975). It is worth noting that when the 1962 series "The Nurses" incorporated doctors into the cast, they were all males. Once again, in 1982, "Nurse" portrayed the life of a veteran nurse against the backdrop of all male physicians.

35. Horace Newcomb, *TV: The Most Popular Art* (New York: Anchor, 1974), p. 133.

36. Television medical drama and comedy continues to reflect this sentiment in its latest offerings. (See "The Return of Marcus Welby, M.D." a two-hour TV movie with Robert Young in May 1984.)

BIBLIOGRAPHICAL SURVEY

Practically the only available material on the subject, apart from the scripts and tapes of actual programs, rests in several chapters of books on the general subject of television. Horace Newcomb wrote an excellent introducton to "Dr. Kildare" in *TV: The Most Popular Art*. Michael Real has some interesting observations on Marcus Welby in a chapter devoted to health in *Mass-Mediated Culture*. In a chapter entitled "Media Medicine and Morality" Robert Alley has addressed the medical genre through 1976 in a book, *Television: Ethics for Hire?* Newcomb and Alley have an extensive interview with David Victor in *The Producer's Medium*.

The Journal of Communication has some excellent articles that address in whole or part the genre of medicine on television. James McLaughlin did a serious examination of professionals as portrayed on TV which served as an M.A. thesis at the Annenberg School. *TV Guide* supplies useful information concerning the popular stars of the various series. The archives of UCLA offer a limited range of old programs available for viewing. The files of *Time*, *Newsweek*, and the *New York Times* provide a sketchy history of medical dramas in cultural and political contexts.

This current chapter is dependent for much information upon personal interviews with David Victor, Frank Glicksman, David Hartman, and Don Brinkley. The simple, time-consuming task of reading scripts also provided insights for this chapter.

BOOKS AND ARTICLES

Adler, Richard, and Douglass Cater, eds. *Television as a Cultural Force*. New York: Praeger, 1976.

Alley, Robert S. *Television: Ethics for Hire?* Nashville: Abingdon Press, 1977.

Brooks, Tim, and Earle Marsh. *The Complete Directory to Prime Time Network TV Shows, 1946–Present*. Rev. ed. New York: Ballantine Books, 1981.

McLaughlin, James M. "Characteristics and Symbolic Functions of Fictional Televised Medical Professionals and Their Effect on Children." M.A. thesis, The Annenberg School of Communications, 1975.

Newcomb, Horace. *TV: The Most Popular Art*. New York: Anchor, 1974.

——— and Robert S. Alley. *The Producer's Medium: Conversations with Creators of American TV*. New York: Oxford University Press, 1983.

Real, Michael. *Mass-Mediated Culture*. Englewood Cliffs, N.J.: Prentice Hall, 1977.
Schrag, Peter. "The Great American Swashbucklers." *More*, November 1975.

VIDEOGRAPHY

"Medic"
  NBC; Mondays, 9:00–9:30 P.M.
  Premiere: September 13, 1954
  Star: Richard Boone
  Last Program: November 19, 1956

"Doctor Kildare"
  NBC, various prime times
  Premiere: September 28, 1961
  Stars: Richard Chamberlain, Raymond Massey
  Last Program: August 30, 1966

"Ben Casey"
  ABC, various prime times
  Premiere: October 2, 1961
  Stars: Vince Edwards, Sam Jaffe
  Last Program: March 21, 1966

"The New Doctors" (segment of "The Bold Ones")
  NBC, various prime times
  Premiere: September 14, 1969
  Stars: E.G. Marshall, David Hartman
  Last Program: June 23, 1973

"Marcus Welby, M.D."
  ABC, Tuesdays, 10:00–11:00 P.M.
  Premiere: September 23, 1969
  Stars: Robert Young, James Brolin
  Last Program: May 11, 1976

"Medical Center"
  CBS, various prime times
  Premiere: September 24, 1969
  Star: Chad Everett
  Last Program: September 6, 1976

"Emergency"
  NBC, Saturdays, 8:00–9:00 P.M.
  Premiere: January 22, 1972
  Stars: Robert Fuller, Bobby Troup
  Last Program: September 3, 1977

"Medical Story"
  NBC, Thursdays, 10:00–11:00 P.M.
  Premiere: September 4, 1975
  Anthology series
  Last Program: January 8, 1976

"Quincy, M.E."
  NBC, various prime times
  Premiere: October 3, 1976
  Star: Jack Klugman
  Last Program: March 16, 1983

"Lifeline"
  NBC, various prime times
  Premiere: September 9, 1978
  Documentary series
  Last Program: December 30, 1978

"Trapper John, M.D."
  CBS, Sundays, 10:00–11:00 P.M.
  Premiere: September 23, 1979
  Stars: Gregory Harrison, Pernell Roberts

"St. Elsewhere"
  NBC, various prime times
  Premiere: October 19, 1982
  Stars: Ed Flanders, Ed Begley, Jr.

6

Science Fiction and Fantasy TV

MARK SIEGEL

OVERVIEW

Science-fiction and fantasy programs have been prominent on television since the beginning of national broadcasting, yet it is not easy to define either the genre itself or the particular ends that it accomplishes that might differentiate it from other programming. There is a general consensus that some few shows are definitely science fiction—"Star Trek" and "Battlestar Galactica," for instance—but many that might be considered in the genre, such as "Mork and Mindy" and "The Invaders," are often listed as sitcoms or adventure-dramas. This is probably because science fiction and fantasy have no particular plot formulas of their own, but borrow from other sources, especially action-adventure, sitcom, mystery ("Dr. Who"), police ("Future Cop," "Holmes and Yoyo"), gothic ("Night Gallery"), and Western ("Space: 1999") genres. The genre is generally distinguished by the involvement of supernatural powers or as yet undeveloped technology or by its being set in either the future or an unearthly locale. Yet, even given this definition, it is not clear whether or not it is really helpful to our understanding of programs to label such shows as "Mr. Ed" or "McDuff the Talking Dog" science fiction or fantasy. There is an entire subgenre of programs, often identified by the appearance of "supervillains," such as "The Wild, Wild West," "Get Smart," and "The Man from U.N.C.L.E.," that sometimes employ elements of fantasy and science fiction, although these elements are not central to their particular concept.[1] Does considering them as science fiction help us to understand them? Finally, nearly every animated program necessarily involves some element of fantasy—talking animals or even human beings that defy normal anatomical laws. These categories at least we ought to drop from our consideration in order to avoid confusing the issue of the genre even further.

By examining the history of television programming and the kinds of themes and issues that this programming, or the best of it, raises, we may hope to come to a fuller understanding of the particular nature of science fiction and fantasy television. While the history of any television genre may seem more like a record of abused audience expectations and failed potentialities, the trends in science fiction programming may at least explain why this is particularly true in this case.

HISTORICAL DEVELOPMENT

Commercial television was born at virtually the same time science fiction was reborn. The interest in science, rocketry, and atomic power generated by World War II helped bring American science-fiction literature off of the back burner, where it had been simmering quite happily for over twenty years, and also launched the first real wave of science fiction films. In 1949, the same year that *Destination Moon* surprised the film industry at the box office, "Captain Video and His Video Rangers" began a six-year run during which it dominated television ratings in its prime-time slot (7:00–7:30 P.M.) five days a week. Even in these early days of the medium, "Captain Video" boasted an audience of over 3,500,000, presumably children and adolescents, and it clearly established the conventions for juvenile science fiction that followed. "Tom Corbett, Space Cadet" (October 1950–September 1952), "Buck Rogers" (April 1950–January 1951), "Johnny Jupiter" (March 1953–May 1954), "Space Patrol" (June 1951–June 1952), "Rod Brown of the Rocket Rangers" (April 1953–May 1954), "Atom Squad" (July 1953–January 1954), "Flash Gordon" (syndicated for 39 episodes in 1953–1957), and other juvenile science fiction programs were all somewhat less successful than "Captain Video," but the proliferation of this program's basic tenets indicates the incredible impact it had on early television. There was no bloodshed, despite "Captain Video's" adventure format. The good guys were so good at their job of policing the galaxy that, with the help of their superscience gadgets, they were able to overcome the enemies of peace without physical violence. Their superweapons included a cosmic ray vibrator that shook people into submission, an atomic rifle that enervated rather than disintegrated its victims, a thermal ejector that made it too hot for the bad guys, an electronic straitjacket with invisible retainers, and an electronic force-field that could be used as a portable prison. The captain's remote carrier beam allowed him to tune in on the past (where he could watch *real* cowboys and Indians performing the same rituals that were so popular on his program), his "opticon scillometer" allowed him to see through anything, and a "discotron" and a radio "scillograph" allowed him to see and hear anything that was happening anywhere. The emphasis on advanced wonders of communication science seemed to be a reflection of its audience's response to the marvel of television, which magically allowed them to see and hear everywhere in time and space. The audience's self-consciousness about the new medium undoubtedly helped it identify more fully with the Video Rangers.

"Captain Video" was clearly a program about personal, social, and political behavior, and not about the real issues of scientific achievement. Interior shots of the X-9 sometimes showed close-ups of instrument panels, but how the technology of the future functioned was a mystery to the audience. Nor was it clear from the behavior of the Video Rangers and their guest villains how human nature had been affected in any way by technological advancement, except for broadening the scope of the game of cowboys and Indians that was being played on other channels and in backyards across America. In fact, the psychology of all the characters was simplistic and usually went unexamined; the most common shot employed, because of the economies of early television and the relative immobility of the camera, was a middle-distance shot better suited to fight sequences and brawling action than to studying the psychological reactions on the faces of characters. Like fairy tales, to which television in general and science fiction in particular have been compared as socializing mechanisms for young children, science fiction television, especially juvenile programs but more adult programming as well, has continued to be morally didactic and insistently unambiguous about what consititutes good and evil behavior.[2]

"The Adventures of Superman," which premiered in July of 1951 and ran until November of 1957, is probably the best known of television's early science fiction programs. Like "Captain Video," it inspired a host of imitations, although, since superheroes already existed in the comic-book medium from which "Superman" had come, it is difficult to assess the responsibility of "Superman" for programs that have followed in its mold, like "Wonder Woman," "The Man from Atlantis," "Bat Man," "The Amazing Spiderman," and, most recently, "The Greatest American Hero." In any event, it seems that television producers like to imitate successes, and "The Adventures of Superman" succeeded for 143 syndicated episodes. (The failure of similar imitations, such as "Bigfoot and Wildboy," "Isis," "Future Cop," "The Gemini Man," "Mr. Terrific," and "Captain America" suggests that imitation isn't enough, of course.) Like "Captain Video," "Superman" was essentially a juvenile program, pitting unambiguous good against equally unambiguous evil. Often Superman explained the moral of the program to young Jimmy Olsen, a more human and therefore sometimes confused character.

Because of the notorious success of these two programs, it is often assumed that early science fiction had only a juvenile side, and in fact there is some merit to the observation that this TV genre had to wait for its audience to grow up before it could follow suit. However, as early as 1951, ABC aired a nonserial program entitled "Tales of Tomorrow" that was considerably more adult, foreshadowing such later programs as "The Outer Limits" (ABC, 1963) and "Twilight Zone" (CBS, 1959). With the syndicated program "Science Fiction Theater," which ran for 78 episodes between 1955 and 1957, these adult science-fiction anthologies were the only real successes, artistic or commercial, in their genre on television—and precisely at a time when more mature science fiction was disappearing from movie theaters. All of them featured weekly episodes that tended to lean heavily on at least the characters and formats developed in gothic and horror fiction, but frequently updated the stories and added a technological backdrop. Perhaps the reason for their early success was that they had an audience—readers of gothic and horror fiction—already in existence in some number.

By the mid-1960s, a merger between the juvenile, action science-fiction program and the more mature study of human nature often represented in the gothic program began to take place. "Voyage to the Bottom of the Sea" (ABC, 1964) employed the action-adventure format in a technological setting, an advanced nuclear submarine that could go where no sailor had gone before. It often presented situations in which strong or weak men were pitted against nature in a test of human nature. In these ways at least, "Voyage to the Bottom of the Sea" can be seen as a predecessor to the successful programs that soon followed, such as "Lost In Space" (CBS, 1965), "Star Trek" (NBC, 1966), "The Invaders" (ABC, 1967), and "Land of the Giants" (ABC, 1968). It is with these programs, and with "Star Trek" in particular, that adult science fiction arrived on television. "Lost in Space," because it often focused on the maturation and socialization of its two child stars rather than on the actions of the adults, is often ranked among the juvenilia, but even this program about a ship-wrecked family struggling to survive and return to their own world was a much more intelligent treatment of social and personal behavior than were the juvenile spin-offs of "Captain Video."

The impact of "Star Trek" on science-fiction television and on the science-fiction genre in general continues to be enormous, if only because it is the one program that even non-science-fiction fans can identify. "Star Trek" reflects a consistent set of values that are typically American, and it is possible to guess the extent and limitations of the impact of culture and contemporary history on television from looking closely at this show.[3] The spaceship in "Star Trek," the Enterprise, has been charged with exploring the unknown reaches of the galaxy, "to boldly go where no man has gone before," suggesting a challenge to Americans that has existed since our first wanderings to investigate the inexhaustible unknown. The universe of "Star Trek" is an existential one; Captain Kirk and his crew are constantly confronted with situations that they could not have imagined before hand, and with which they can have no preestablished plans to deal. While the crew has a well-defined morality involving the primacy of loyalty to their mission, their ship, and to each other and a set of values emphasizing love, compassion, and playing hunches over logic, they are occasionally driven to violate even the few "Federation Directives" (primary rules) of which we are informed when those rules run counter to their morality and values. The humans frequently encounter races that are technologically superior to themselves, but they prove victorious because their values are well adapted to life on the frontier. Like their American pioneer forebearers, they are scrappy, persistent, resourceful, and quick to adapt. While the crew is a mixture of races, its character is obviously American; the racial mixture at best represents the melting pot of American culture under the WASPish control of Captain Kirk.

Historically, it is tempting to suggest that "Star Trek" reflects not merely the general precepts of American culture, but also the particular issues that predominated in the last four years of the 1960s when it originally ran. The most obvious issue concerns the confrontation of human dignity and technological unemployment. "Star Trek" reassured the working American that, however much he might fear the encroachment of technology on his home and his workplace, man would always triumph because of his particularly human qualities.

"Star Trek" dealt overtly with other issues of the day as well—hippies, communism, facism, racism—but the technological issue may have been its most pervasive concern. More recent imitations of "Star Trek," "Battlestar Galactica" (ABC, 1978) and "Buck Rogers in the Twenty-fifth Century" (NBC, 1979), both echoed these qualities. "Battlestar Galactica" in particular made inhumane technology its primary evil, in the incarnation of a civilization of robots that has broken a peace pact with the human race and has attacked and almost obliterated it. Apparently the few remnants of humanity are fleeing through space toward a planet known as Earth, pursued relentlessly by the technological bad guys.

"The Six Million Dollar Man" (ABC, 1973), and its spin-off "The Bionic Woman" (ABC, 1976), provided some counterweight to this trend, since they both involved people who had become superheroes when provided with technological body parts. However, science-fiction television in general ran off in different directions after the cancellation of "Star Trek" in 1969. Beginning in 1970, the long-running BBC program "Dr. Who" started syndication in America. ("Dr. Who" continues to hold the longevity record for science-fiction television productions, which is now over twenty years.) The doctor, a superior being who can travel in time and space, zips about in four or five half-hour episodes solving problems in many cultures much like the British civil servant of old. "Night Gallery" (NBC, 1970), Rod Serling's attempt to recapture his great success with "Twilight Zone," was a similar anthology program with a somewhat greater emphasis on gothic horror elements. "Kolchak: The Night Stalker" (NBC, 1974) was a horror series that, like "Night Gallery," often included a few humorous elements, but the program seemed doomed from the start to a short run because of its limited plot structure, in which an intrepid reporter constantly uncovers monsters in his city's nightlife, only to have his editor squash the stories in disbelief or fright. "Space: 1999" (syndicated from 1975 to 1977), was an exploratory action-adventure series in the fashion of "Star Trek," in which a lunar fragment has been torn out of orbit and flung out into space, subjecting the surviving colonists to one unforeseen and unguided adventure after another. "Wonder Woman" (ABC, 1976; CBS, 1977) attempted to repeat the success of another campy superhero of a decade before, "Batman" (ABC, 1966); the Amazonian comic-book heroine maintained the thin thread of parodistic science-fiction television that has run into the 1980s with "The Greatest American Hero" (CBS, 1981), a story about a school teacher who has trouble mastering the superpowers with which he has been entrusted and continually flies into walls. "The Incredible Hulk" (CBS, 1978), while also a comic-book crossover, treated its story of a scientist who loses control of his super-powerful animal self in a serious, straightforward way. "Fantasy Island" (ABC, 1978) employs the multiple plot format used so successfully in television and films by shows like "The Loveboat" and *Airport* to show weekly visitors to an enchanted island that having their fantasies fulfilled is not always what it's cracked up to be. "Mork and Mindy" (ABC, 1978) was the most successful of all science-fiction sitcoms, surpassing even the program that it most resembled, "My Favorite Martian" (NBC, 1963), because of the popularity of Robin Williams, who played an investigator from the planet Ork trying to understand the strange ways of earth people.

There are a number of theories that account for the evolution of genre formulas from a period of formation, to a classical period, to a self-conscious and often parodistic stage, and finally into decline and extinction or re-evolution. Some argument might be made that the juvenile-oriented programs of the early 1950s marked the establishment of an SF formula, that the mid-1960s, with "Star Trek" and "The Invaders" marked a classical period, and the most recent appearance of self-conscious and sometimes self-mocking SF shows indicates a further stage. However, as was pointed out earlier, science fiction has no single formula, no ritual dance of events and icons of its own but borrows those of other genres. Since these other genres must be at various phases of their existence, it is unlikely that science fiction would decribe a steady progression of form inherent in its own formulaic structure. Furthermore, it is difficult to see how "Star Trek" was more "classical" in its form than "Battlestar Galactica," which appeared more than ten years later.

Rather, science-fiction television seems more responsive to events outside of itself, to social and political trends as well as to trends within the rest of the entertainment industry. The mid-1950s, which also saw the degeneration of the science fiction film back into monster movies and the failure of interest in space sciences, was not a fertile ground for the genre. Following the resurgence of the space program under Kennedy, public interest began to increase, and by the time we landed a man on the moon science-fiction television was booming again. While I suggested earlier that science-fiction and fantasy television were important for metaphorical rather than extrapolative reasons (and this might suggest that a real interest in space should have nothing at all to do with the popularity of space as metaphor), it seems to be that we choose our metaphors *only* because they already occupy important positions in our consciousness. A more important objection to this purely historical interpretation of the cycle of science-fiction television programming is that it is at best a partial explanation, since it does not account for the enormous resurgence in such programming that has continued since the mid-1970s vis-à-vis its rather slow recovery in the early 1960s, after the "space race" had alredy been declared. Perhaps the most obvious additional cause of the popularity of science fiction in both film and television in the 1970s has been the technological revolution in the video arts. The enormous appeal of films like *Star Wars, The Empire Strikes Back*, and their various imitators that reversed production wisdom about the bankability of science-fiction films was at least in part due to the visual marvels made possible by technological innovation within the video arts that were increasingly showcased in science-fiction films since Stanley Kubrick's *2001: A Space Odyssey* in 1966. Science fiction provides a perfect format for what contemporary innovative video technology can do and at least a little of this technology is also applicable to television. This fact should be evident from the number of television programs that were spin-offs of science-fiction films in the early 1970s—"Planet of the Apes," "Logan's Run," "Fantastic Journey"—or conceived in conjunction with films— "Buck Rogers" and "Battlestar Galactica." While the failure of "Battlestar Galactica" may prove that it is impossible to transfer big screen visuals effectively to the small screen of television, many of these visual effects have been translated; John Dykstra, the producer of "Battlestar Galactica," had been the special effects coordinator for *Star Wars* and was sued because of the similarities of certain designs that appeared in the two works. On the other hand, most successful contemporary television programming focuses on human interaction rather than spectacular visuals, and the most important impact of recent science-fiction film on television is probably its attraction of a huge audience that is now ready to accept the metaphors for science fiction in the other visual medium. The film version of *Buck Rogers in the Twenty-Fifth Century*, for instance, which was used to launch the television series in 1979, relied to at least some extent on visual effects patterned after *Star Wars*, but when the series premiered on TV it had a very different look, emphasizing apartment interiors rather than deep space and close-ups of actors rather than huge battle scenes in space. It did carry over the actors and other human interest points from the film version, however, maximizing the possibility of continued audience identification during the transition.

The history of science-fiction film, then, seems to reflect both developments in American culture at large and within the entertainment industry in particular. While science-fiction television cannot capitalize on the recent innovations in film technology to any great extent, it can benefit to a great deal from the audiences being generated by film.

THEMES AND ISSUES

While the success of science fiction on television might be attributed to its attractiveness to those concerned with the future or with the problems of technology or its potential as the ultimate escape for those who prefer fantasy, these notions seem highly unlikely. Television science fiction is not technologically or scientifically oriented, does not project the future in any reasonable or even slightly believable way, and probably does not offer any greater escape from reality than do sitcoms like "Green Acres" or action-adventure shows like "The A Team." Science-fiction literature, which does sometimes attempt more plausible extrapolations of our technological and social futures, has never had, and probably never will have, half the audience of science-fiction films and television. Even in the field of science-fiction literary criticism, where two points of view, one seeking to define the genre as primarily metaphorical and the other as extrapolative, have done battle. Science fiction is almost always considered these days purely from the metaphorical standpoint.

Most American science-fiction television seems to be highly reflective of the culture in which it was produced. The show "The Incredible Hulk," for instance, is typical of the "Christ-with-a-gun," preaching social responsibility and non-violence while destroying anyone who disagrees, seen in so many popular American formulas. Perhaps one reason why science fiction has been so successful on television is that it provides superheroes who can afford to preach pacifism because they are the most capable practitioners of violence. The archetypes of our science fiction are typically American and apparent in any other genre, but the acceptance of a science-fiction setting and treatment of these archetypes is a fairly recent phenomenon. Superman, with his Milquetoast everyday identity as Clark Kent, symbolizes every American's sense that secretly he himself is something very special and powerful. While the Western was, for many years, the dominant genre in treating the anxieties generated by the paradoxical American values of individualism, social order, and a penchant for violence, science fiction, from its early days on television, has been steadily co-opting this function. While the metaphors of the Western spoke loudest to a generation that had grown up with juvenile Westerns and a sense of geographical imperialism and growth, the metaphors of science fiction probably seem more appropriate to a generation that grew up with an awareness that economic and technological imperialism are the new order.

The history of science fiction on television is not merely the history of the steady growth of the genre in its acquisition of the audience of the Western nor of the transition from juvenile to adult programming. Using metaphorical disguises, science fiction programming has always reflected contemporary American issues, as in "Captain Video," as well as more timeless psychological and cultural themes, as in "Superman." This emphasis on the metaphorical significance of science fiction clarifies the position of fantasy and horror programming in relationship to the genre as a whole. Since the appearance of the more adult "Tales of Tomorrow" in August of 1951, science fiction has frequently been mixed in its presentation and in the minds of its audience with tales of the supernatural. (This excellent series mixed such presentations as "The Last Man on Earth," featuring Cloris Leachman, and "Black Planet," with Leslie Nielsen, with Lon Chaney, Jr.'s "Frankenstein" and Boris Karloff's "Momento.") Many science-fiction literary critics insist, for various reasons, on a strict demarcation between "science fiction," which they claim must be based on scientific possibility, and "fantasy," which they note violates one or more accepted scientific laws on a consistent and profound basis.[4] However, on television this distinction seems relatively unimportant, because reality's relationship to either science-

fiction or fantasy programs is strictly metaphorical and almost never extrapolative. Even in a more traditional science-fiction program such as "Star Trek,"
there is no attempt made to show either how the advanced technology (phasers,
faster-than-light drive) works or how it has changed the lives of the human beings
of the future who live with it.[5] While it is clear that the values of the citizens
of the Middle Ages were significantly different from those of people who lived
during the Industrial Revolution, the people of the space age reflect the values
of people alive today. No attempt is really made to understand the future. Science-
fiction television—like fantasy and horror television—reflects only the present
in a metaphorical manner. Whether the metaphor involves a high-tech blaster,
x-ray vision, or a satanic curse, it is the effect and not the form of the metaphor
that is important. This is as apparent in science-fiction sitcoms ("My Favorite
Martian," "Mork and Mindy") and fantasy sitcoms ("Bewitched," "I Dream
of Jeannie") as it is in programs that are less easy to differentiate as belonging
to one subgenre or another ("The Twilight Zone," "Outer Limits"). Therefore,
while programs like "Night Gallery" and "The Inner Sanctum" are closer to
the gothic genre than to science fiction, there will be little difficulty in discussing
their importance under the general category of science fiction.

Most television programs do not strive overtly to promote particular values,
but values are inherent in dramatic situations. "My Favorite Martian," for
instance, had a very similar dramatic base as "Mork and Mindy." Both programs
involved an alien who by virtue of his being stranded on Earth had to learn about
our "strange" ways. This is a perfect vantage point from which to evaluate
cultural norms and traditions, virtually an invitation to social criticism. However,
"My Favorite Martian" evaded this opportunity at every turn, focusing as much
of the time as possible on the eccentricities of the Martian visitor rather than on
our own behavior. It is tempting to see this as a reflection of our ethnocentrism,
now so obvious when looking back on 1965 and the escalation of our involvement
in Southeast Asia. "Mork and Mindy" seems to have reflected the nuances of
the years in which it ran; at first the program considered a number of American
social problems from racism to ageism, as well as simple human problems, such
as learning to express one's feelings, all under the guise of Mork investigating
human society for his leader back on Ork. However, the show gradually lost
this vantage point, becoming more involved in the silly business of a situation
comedy, at the same time that Mork himself became more and more American-
ized and less speculative and self-conscious. The show's producers literally seem
to have made the choice to avoid social introspection in the latter years of the
growing conservatism.

A recent example of adventure-oriented science fiction suggests similar reflections on our cultural trends. "The Greatest American Hero," though spoofing
science-fiction superheroism in its portrayal of the difficulties that even an intelligent and dedicated individual has in mastering such skills as flying, is generally serious and self-conscious in its message. The show's basic premise, that
alien space creatures have knowingly joined two apparently incompatible but

morally sincere men from opposite ends of our social spectrum (or at least from opposite sides of the middle of the road, which is about as far as television ever really goes), suggests that, if America is to survive and progress in solving its problems in the years ahead, we must unite without abandoning our individuality but by learning to understand and appreciate other points of view. Ralph, the liberal and idealistic young schoolteacher who wears the supersuit, comes to appreciate the good qualities of his FBI partner Bill despite the latter's propensity to spout right-wing slogans and blindly support tradition and the establishment. In the two years that the program survived, the characters continued to grow by learning from each other, suggesting the only way that the disparate but well-meaning factions of American society can reorganize themselves to their mutual benefit. Ralph and Bill not only talked about their philosophical differences, but displayed both those differences and ways to resolve them in the action elements of the program.

Science-fiction programs are not usually as aware of their metaphorical structure as was "The Greatest American Hero." More often, series such as "The Incredible Hulk" or "Buck Rogers in the Twenty-Fifth Century" serve as interesting, if not often unconscious, reflections of current contradictions in American society. "Buck Rogers," for instance, was a program dedicated to proving that contemporary twentieth-century American culture would always be the standard against which all other cultures would have to be measured—and that they would be found lacking. The hamburger, rock and roll, our styles of loving and fighting—everything that Buck brings with him into the future tends to be praised and adopted by those around him, since his superiority is so immediately evident. Not only is this point historically absurd and anthropologically implausible, but touting the superiority of our culture in this particular future is dangerously myopic, since we are also told that we managed to start a nuclear war. While Buck is eager to employ physical violence and lives in a wonderful apartment, his material wealth has been made possible partly by the drastic reduction of human population from the war. New Chicago is domed-in from the environment devastated by those who first shared and promoted Buck's value system.

Science fiction in literature has always thought itself to be intellectually avant garde, it not renegade, and while this may be more of a self-deception than an accurate self-appraisal, since any popular literature must generally be supportive of the existing values of its readership, it has dutifully provided us with "alternate realities," cultural scenarios that are at least something of a divergence from contemporary mainstream social thought.[6] Science-fiction television has been considerably more conservative, probably because of the economics of the medium. While a book that sells 100,000 copies is a wild success, a television program that is watched by 100 times that many people will probably be considered a disaster—and in financial terms at least, a much bigger disaster than an unsold novel. Therefore, television tries harder to please a broader audience. Not offending anyone seems to be the prime directive for most television programs, pre-empting every other point of logic about program development. It is highly unlikely that, given the goal of not offending anyone's pre-established tastes, television can offer alternatives to what is already being presented.[7]

Of the science-fiction and fantasy programs airing in prime time as of this writing, ABC's "Fantasy Island" is so ambiguous and inconsistent about what the rules of its fantasy world really are that it can be totally hypocritical in its value judgments. It does not allow us to understand the structure of its symbolic reality or, metaphorically, what it assumes the structure of our reality to be, but insists on the viewer's submission to the authority figure of the program, "wise" old Mr. Roarke. There are limits to the miraculous powers of Mr. Roarke, but the audience can never be sure what they are, since they seem to vary from moment to moment—or at least that is how he justifies his behavior to his dwarf assistant, Tattoo. He is a spokesman for some higher moral authority, but that authority is as vague as are the sources of American values to most contemporary Americans. While he sometimes chooses to teach a lesson rather than to right a wrong, he often seems simply unable to dispense justice himself. His personal code of conduct and that which he seems to expect from others is aggravatingly inconsistent. His powers may be representative of God or of nature, but we can neither know that for sure nor test the significance of that assumption.

On a subliminal level "Fantasy Island" is a metaphor for the American Dreamland, a place where our fantasies and our nightmares surface and are resolved. Unfortunately, most of the fantasies on this program are materialistic and possessive, and their rightness is not only not questioned but is jubilantly affirmed. Except for a few of the guest stars and Tattoo—people on the island are uniformly young and beautiful and apparently wealthy. The fantasies of the guests are often consumer oriented or may involve winning a mate or a contest that they are unequipped to win. The American fantasies that love can be "caught" and that anyone can be successful if they just try hard enough—or wish hard enough—are heavily reinforced, and each week viewers travel the same psychological circuit as the guest stars. "Fantasy Island" offers viewers escape from the dull routine of their lives, while heavily reinforcing consumption-oriented middle-class values.

Certainly not all prime-time television is as materialistic and shallow as "Fantasy Island," but a program does not have to be intellectually serious to provide metaphorical structures that can assist our understanding, even on a subliminal level, or our lives and times. CBS's short-lived 1983 program "Wizards and Warriors," was a complete tongue-in-cheek fantasy about a good kingdom with moral, kind, and loving wizards and warriors trying to preserve itself from an evil kingdom with immoral, power-hungry, cruel, and unscrupulous wizards and warriors. The abilities and characteristics of each of the characters was, however, treated consistently, and the good guys were appealing not simply because they seemed to have power and authority on their side (they often didn't seem to), but because they really were better human beings. That they constantly reminded themselves and their viewers that they were the good guys was cute but unnecessary; unlike in "Fantasy Island," we can see that they were.

Science fiction is likely to hold its own on television as long as the metaphors provided by the genre seem appropriate to the American public. It is not likely that science fiction will ever be a radical force on television or that it will promote values significantly different from those already held in general in our society. However, at its best, science-fiction and fantasy television can offer dramatic and exciting metaphorical structures that will help us to see ourselves and our world in a fresh and constructive way.

NOTES

1. Vincent Miranda discusses this problem at some length in his article on science-fiction film, "The Fantastic Cinema," in *The Science Fiction Reference Book*, ed. Marshall Tymn (San Bernardino, Calif.: Borgo Press, 1981), p. 59.

2. Most of the science-fiction film criticism written by Andrew Gordon, which has appeared in *Literature/Film Quarterly* and *Science-Fiction Studies* takes this approach. The most influential work on fairy tales in this regard is Bruno Bettelheim's *The Uses of Enchantment* (New York: Knopf, 1976).

3. See Gary Grossman, *Superman—Serial to Cereal* (New York: Popular Library, 1977).

4. The best known scholarly works in this area are Darko Suvin's *The Metamorphosis of Science Fiction* (New Haven: Yale University Press, 1979), and Robert Scholes's *Structural Fabulation* (Notre Dame: University of Notre Dame Press, 1975). Countless science-fiction writers have debated the subject for years; Ursula LeGuin, in her introduction to *The Left Hand of Darkness* and her essays in *The Language of the Night*, and James Gunn, in his commentaries and introductions to his four volume set, *The Road to Science Fiction*, are well worth reading.

5. Karin Blair's *Meaning in Star Trek* (Chambersburg, Pa.: Anima Books, 1977) is but one of a number of elaborate and thoughtful analyses of "Star Trek" that have appeared in the last ten years.

6. See Charles Elkins's "An Approach to the Social Functions of American SF," *Science-Fiction Studies* 4 (1977), p. 228.

7. Gaye Tuchman's *The TV Establishment: Programming for Power and Profit* (Englewood Cliffs, N.J.: Prentice-Hall, Inc., 1974) contains a series of essays written from this point of view. Another useful source is David Sallach's article, "Class Domination and Ideological Hegemony," in *Sociological Quarterly* 15 (Winter 1974), pp. 38–45.

BIBLIOGRAPHICAL SURVEY

Despite the great flood of attention received by science-fiction literature and, to a slightly lesser extent, science-fiction films in the past ten years, science-fiction television has received little serious attention. I have authored a number of articles on the subject myself, but most discussions of science-fiction television focus on single programs: Tim Heald's *The Making of Space: 1999*, Gene Roddenberry and Stephen Whitefield's *The Making of Star Trek*, Jean-Marc Lofficier's two-volume *The Doctor Who Programme Guide*, and Mark Scott Zicree's *The Twilight Zone Companion* are typical examples. "Star Trek" has inspired many academic pieces, from Karin Blair's *Meaning in Star Trek* to articles in *Science-Fiction Studies, Extrapolation, The Journal of Popular Culture,* and *The Journal of American Culture,* to essay collections (*The Best of Trek*). Nearly all of these offer some insights into the philosophical implications of "Star Trek," but the very proliferation of explanations implies that the program was open to a wide range of philosophical interpretations.

Broader, theoretical treatments of science-fiction television are hard to find. Don Fabun wrote an interesting early article (1953), "Science Fiction in Motion Pictures, Radio, and Television," that displays a good deal of professional knowledge. Horace Newcomb discusses science fiction briefly in his generally excellent book, *TV: The Most Popular Art,* but seems less familiar with this genre than with most others. Outside of academe, Harlan Ellison, who wrote for a number of science-fiction TV shows, has published two volumes of essays viciously attacking the medium, *The Glass Teat* and *The Other Glass Teat.* *Starlog Magazine* has become a monthly source of information on this subject for the fan and general reader, but, like Gary Gerani and Paul Schulman's pictoral history, *Fantastic Television,* it is not particularly insightful or analytical. These works tend toward critical astigmatism, flaunting favorite shows and ignoring the existence of almost everything else ever shown on television.

BOOKS AND ARTICLES

Blair, Karin. *Meaning in Star Trek.* Chambersburg, Pa.: Anima Books, 1977.

Brooks, Tim, and Earle Marsh. *The Complete Directory of Prime Time Network TV Shows, 1946–Present.* Rev. ed. New York: Ballantine Books, 1981.

Ellison, Harlan. *The Glass Teat.* New York: Pyramid Books, 1975.

———. *The Other Glass Teat.* New York: Pyramid Books, 1975.

Fabun, Don. "Science Fiction in Motion Pictures, Radio, and Television." In *Modern Science Fiction: Its Meaning and Its Future,* edited by Reginald Bretnor. New York: Coward-McCann, Inc., 1953.

Gerani, Gary, and Paul Schulman. *Fantastic Television.* New York: Harmony Books, 1977.

Grossman, Gary. *Superman—Serial to Cereal.* New York: Popular Library, 1977.

Hark, Ina Rae. "*Star Trek* and Television's Moral Universe." *Extrapolation* 20, No. 1 (Spring 1979), 20–37.

Heald, Tim. *The Making of Space: 1999.* New York: Ballantine, 1976.

Irwin, Walter, and G. B. Love, eds. *The Best of Trek,* Vol. 1. New York: Signet Books, 1978.

———. *The Best of Trek,* Vol. 2. New York: Signet, 1980.

———. *The Best of Trek,* Vol. 3. New York: Signet, 1980.

———. *The Best of Trek,* Vol. 4. New York: Signet, 1981.

———. *The Best of Trek,* Vol. 5. New York: Signet, 1982.

Lofficier, Jean-Marc. *The "Doctor Who" Programme Guide,* vols. 1 and 2. London: Target Books, 1981.

McNeil, Alex. *Total Television.* New York: Penguin Books, 1980.

Newcomb, Horace. *TV: The Most Popular Art.* Garden City, N.Y.: Anchor Press, 1974.

Siegel, Mark. "Fantastic Television: A Subversive Art?" *Fantasy Newsletter*, January
     1983.
———. "Science Fiction Characterization and TV's Battle for the Stars." *Science-Fiction
     Studies* 7 (Winter 1980).
———. "SF TV: A Chinese Box." In *Alternate Realities*, edited by Vincent Miranda.
     Westport, Conn.: Greenwood Press, 1984.
———. "Toward an Aesthetics of Science Fiction Television." TBP by *Extrapolation*.
Whitefield, Stephen, and Gene Roddenberry. *The Making of Star Trek*. New York: Signet,
     1976.
Zicree, Marc Scott. *The Twilight Zone Companion*. Boston: Palmer House, 1982.

VIDEOGRAPHY

"Captain Video and His Video Rangers"
  DuMont/Syndicated
  Premiere: June 27, 1949.
  Stars: Richard Coogan (1949), Al Hodge
  Last Program: April 1, 1955

"Superman"
  Syndicated, 143 episodes
  Premiere: 1951
  Star: George Reeves
  Last Program: 1957

"Tales of Tomorrow"
  ABC, Fridays, 9:30–10:00 P.M.
  Premiere: August 3, 1951
  Anthology format
  Last Program: June 12, 1953

"Science Fiction Theater"
  Syndicated, 78 episodes
  Premiere: 1955
  Anthology format
  Last Program: 1957

"The Twilight Zone"
  CBS, various prime times
  Premiere: October 2, 1959
  Host: Rod Serling (anthology format)
  Last Program: September 18, 1964

"The Outer Limits"
  ABC, various prime times
  Premiere: September 16, 1963
  Anthology format
  Last Program: January 16, 1965

"Voyage to the Bottom of the Sea"
  ABC, various prime times
  Premiere: September 14, 1964

Star: Richard Basehart
Last Program: September 15, 1968

"Lost in Space"
CBS, various prime times
Premiere: September 15, 1965
Stars: Guy Williams, June Lockhart
Last Program: September 11, 1968

"Batman"
ABC, various prime times
Premiere: January 12, 1966
Stars: Adam West, Burt Ward
Last Program: March 14, 1968

"Star Trek"
NBC, various prime times
Premiere: September 8, 1966
Stars: William Shatner, Leonard Nemoy
Last Program: September 2, 1969

"The Invaders"
ABC, various prime times
Premiere: January 10, 1967
Star: Roy Thinnes
Last Program: September 17, 1968

"Land of the Giants"
ABC, various prime times
Premiere: September 22, 1968
Star: Gary Conway
Last Program: September 6, 1970

"Doctor Who"
Syndicated
Became available in the U.S. in 1970; made in the U.K. by BBC Productions since 1963
Stars: Peter Cushing (briefly), Jon Pertwee, Tom Baker
Last Program: still running

"Night Gallery"
NBC, various prime times
Premiere: December 16, 1970
Host: Rod Serling (anthology format)
Last Program: January 14, 1973

"The Six Million Dollar Man"
ABC, various prime times
Premiere: October 10, 1973 (as monthly feature in "The ABC Suspense Movie");
became a weekly series in January, 1974
Star: Lee Majors
Last Program: March 6, 1978

"Kolchak: The Night Stalker"

ABC, various prime times
Premiere: September 13, 1974
Star: Darren McGavin
Last Program: August 30, 1975

"Space: 1999"
Syndicated, 48 episodes
Premiere: 1975
Stars: Martin Landau, Barbara Bain
Last Program: 1977

"Wonder Woman"
ABC/CBS, various prime times
Premiere: December 18, 1976
Star: Lynda Carter
Last Program: September 11, 1979

"Fantasy Island"
ABC, various prime times
Premiere: January 28, 1978
Star: Ricardo Montalban

"The Incredible Hulk"
CBS, various prime times
Premiere: March 10, 1978
Star: Bill Bixby
Last Program: September 6, 1982

"Mork and Mindy"
ABC, various prime times
Premiere: September 14, 1978
Star: Robin Williams
Last Program: September 6, 1982

"Battlestar Galactica"
ABC, various prime times
Premiere: September 17, 1978
Star: Lorne Greene
Last Program: August 4, 1979; reappeared for the following year as "Galactica 1980"

"Buck Rogers in the Twenty-Fifth Century"
NBC, various prime times
Premiere: September 27, 1979
Star: Gil Gerard
Last Program: September 6, 1981

"The Greatest American Hero"
ABC, various prime times
Premiere: March 14, 1981
Stars: William Katt, Robert Culp
Last Program: February 3, 1983

7

Situation Comedy

LAWRENCE E. MINTZ

OVERVIEW

Situation comedy, or sitcom as it is widely termed, is at the center of prime-time network programming. Jeff Greenfield reports that sitcom is viewed by network executives as "the bedrock of a successful schedule," and "as the thing we look to first."[1] Ben Stein calls the sitcoms "far and away the dominant mode of top-twenty shows."[2] Harry Ackerman records that in 1964 sitcom accounted for 43 percent of regularly scheduled programming, and that "in every year except one since 1956, the average rating for situation comedies has been higher than that for the average program."[3] In good times, that is, when the genre is at the peak of its popular appeal, it can virtually drive other types of shows from the schedule. Arthur Asa Berger notes that "in 1974 there were 15 sitcoms on network television and 10 of them were in the Nielsen's top 20 programs."[4] More recently Jennings Bryant and Dan Brown note that "in 1978–79 comedy shows filled nine of the top ten positions on television," and as of May 1983 there were five comedies in the top ten, five in the second ten.[5]

Even when the genre is experiencing a relative *prime-time* doldrums—such as at present in the early eighties, with failing new series, cancellations of old standbys, and very little to excite either critic or audience—sitcom reigns supreme in the syndication market and as an exportable commodity.

David Marc contends that "the weekly series in stripped syndication is television's most potent oracle," and that "the situation comedy has proved to be the most durable of all commercial television genres."[6] The audience for situation comedy is enormous. David Grote employs some complicated figures to compare the film and television audiences, presenting a figure for an average night of "Laverne and Shirley" of 50 million viewers against an estimate of between 32 and 38 million total audience for *Star Wars*.[7] Jennings Bryant and Dan Brown provide a still more astounding and impressive statistical claim of a total of 500 *billion* viewings of television comedy in an average week![8] If television is, to borrow Horace Newcomb's title, "the most popular art," surely situation comedy is its most popular genre, and therefore the modern world's most familiar art form.

HISTORICAL DEVELOPMENT

The first sitcoms were inherited from radio for the most part:[9] "The Goldbergs," "The Life of Riley," "The Aldrich Family," "Amos 'n' Andy," "The George Burns and Gracie Allen Show," and a few others pioneered the transition to the new medium during the first few seasons (1949–1951).[10] The basic formula was already established, and these early offerings made little or no important contribution to the genre. "The Goldbergs" and "Amos 'n' Andy" are of interest, if at all, as an example of ethnic/racial humor, while "The Burns and Allen Show" introduced Hollywood and show business as a possible premise for sitcom. Much has been written about the ideological implications of "Amos 'n' Andy" and to a lesser extent about "The Goldbergs." For the times in which they were produced, they were rather tame comedies (compared with similar comedy in the popular theater) with their emphasis on dilemma resolution as much as on caricature or stereotyping. The audience seems to have found them funny and entertaining rather than provocative, though surely they had the potential to offend, then and now.

The 1951–1952 season saw "Mr. Peepers" establish the schoolteacher premise (to be followed by "Our Miss Brooks" the next year) and "My Little Margie," a show which could be linked by an imaginative genealogist to the more modern "single girl as heroine" premise. But the significant program was "I Love Lucy," surely the most important and possibly the best situation comedy ever made. Structurally "Lucy" was a typical sitcom; the normal domestic harmony of the Ricardos was threatened, usually by some scheme of Lucy's intended to improve their situation. At the end, after Lucy had dug herself deeper and deeper into a hole, she was rescued fortuitously and/or forgiven by her exasperated but understanding, loving husband. The scatterbrained wife and the ineffectual tyrant husband are stock comedy characters. The Cuban-American marriage angle was sufficiently different to make the network people uncomfortable, but other than references to Ricky's temper and the type of music played by his band, the difference had no function worth noting. The decision to film "Lucy" in advance and distribute an edited copy taken from three cameras was aesthetically important, but the real significance of "I Love Lucy" was the contrast between her zany behavior and the directions taken by her incredible energy and the normalcy of 1950s domestic America. There was an absurdist comedy in "Lucy," an Ionesco-like juxtaposition of the commonplace and the mad (cf. *The Bald Soprano*). As Michael Kernan remembers,

It always started so logically. A normal, average American family made a normal, average American decision. You went along with this: the same thing could have happened to you.

And then, without warning, you turned an invisible corner and you were in this other dimension. The logic, unchecked, out of control, pursued itself right out the window. The dialogue got left behind and people started doing amazing things, wild things.[11]

Lucy was funny the same way Jerry Lewis is funny—by contrasting normal appearance, normal situation, and moments of calm with bursts of insane energy, childish abandon, and unbridled enthusiasm. The rules of sitcom (and of 1950s America) dictate that this bird must be perpetually shot down, healed, and caged, but phoenix-like, she soared again in the next installment. "I Love Lucy" had less of an impact on the genre than we might expect simply because it could rarely be matched or duplicated; there are few Lucille Balls in every generation. But the show was a monument to the claim that a popular art could also be brilliant.

Though "Lucy" was clearly a situation comedy rather than a domestic comedy by Newcomb's criteria, it seems that the people in the industry failed to understand the distinction. They followed "Lucy" 's success with a string of domestic comedies—"Ozzie and Harriet," "Make Room for Daddy," "The Life of Riley," "Father Knows Best," among others—which had none of the "Lucy" dadaism but all of the domestic-harmony-as-paradise message. But family situation comedy, like the domestic humor of the comic strips, has a sizable and enthusiastic audience. It presents an idealized version of a "typical" American family surviving momentary mini-crises and a portrait of imperfect, nonheroic folk who are nonetheless good people, good neighbors. The formula has considerable emotional and ideological currency in American society. Perhaps it is unfair to dismiss William Bendix's Chester Riley and Eve Arden's Miss Brooks so abruptly. A lot more can (and will) be said about the importance of domestic comedy, but it is hard for the contemporary critic to generate too much enthusiasm for these relics except as nostalgia, as "camp," or as socio-cultural documents.

Nineteen fifty-five brought two highlights: "The Honeymooners" and "You'll Never Get Rich"/"Phil Silvers"/"Sergeant Bilko." "The Honeymooners" transcended domestic sitcom (it is a good example of why the terms domestic comedy and sitcom are not always separating ones) because, like "Lucy," it had a star of great talent (Jackie Gleason as Ralph Kramden) as well as an excellent supporting cast—particularly Art Carney as Norton and Audrey Meadows as Alice. Like Lucy, Ralph expended enormous energy trying to break out of his confined status, in his case socio-economic rather than sex-role-determined. The show had a believable blue-collar ethos (the first and probably last sitcom to do so) and an element of pathos in Alice's weary but acquiescent subjugation and Ralph's deflated bluster, helpless anger, constant frustration, and sad plea for forgiveness. R.A.L.P.H.—The Royal Association for the Longevity and Preservation of "The Honeymooners"—has 3,500 members and has drawn as many as 2,300 people to its convention; a rare case of pop culture fan-aticism that is warranted by the object.

Silvers's Bilko is the con-man figure, an old and effective American comic persona (cf. the medicine show pitchman, for instance). But again it is because of his manic energy, a willingness to defy logic with such confidence, that the viewer suspends disbelief entirely, and the quality of the characterizations elevate the show above the ordinary. Bilko knocked "Mr. Television," Milton Berle, off the air, suggesting that a great sitcom will beat a great variety show and that even well-established viewing habits are vulnerable to a new show that the audience finds attractive.

The late fifties marked time with more domestic comedy—"Leave It to Beaver," "Bachelor Father," "The Donna Reed Show," and child-oriented shows like "The Many Loves of Dobie Gillis." The new decade showed a little life in 1960–61 with Andy Griffith's low-key hillbilly comedy, and "The Dick Van Dyke Show," a program simply better written than most. In 1963 "The Beverly Hillbillies" came along to the delight of the audience and to the horror of the critics. "The Hillbillies" was well done, but its popularity was probably due to characterization—classic American wise-fools, common-sense philosophers, scoundrels, snobs, and other local versions of universal types—and to the prem-ise's simple dramatization of popular American beliefs, such as simple folk are as good or better than the rich and educated, money isn't everything and it can bring problems and unhappiness, but it's also fun to have, innocence will triumph over corruption, and so forth. Like the domestic comedy, the show had a mor-alism made palatable by parable, and it was also amusing.

In 1964 fantasy had a big year with "The Addams Family," "The Munsters," and "Bewitched," but only 1965's "Get Smart" added much worthy of historical mention. "Get Smart" was well written, but it is notable because it is a rare example of parody, or spoof actually, succeeding on network television. The rest of the sixties was hardly an innovative period; one might single out a "Julia" for its self-consciousness on the matter of racial imagery, an "I Dream of Jeannie" because of Barbara Eden, a "That Girl" to give equal time to a different female image, a "The Brady Bunch" for being almost defiantly bad, but unless one wanted to do a close show-by-show analysis of the underlying significance of these programs and their popularity, there would not be much to say about them.[12]

It is rare that decades cooperate with the social historian to form periods in neat ten-year blocks, but it is not difficult to term the 1970s the decade of the situation comedy revolution, and to mark 1970–71 as the season that ushered in the change. The "new wave" in sitcom is often attributed to Norman Lear, auteur of "All in the Family," but some cite MTM and "The Mary Tyler Moore Show" for that honor.[13] Lear's show and its spinoffs and grandchildren, "San-ford and Son" (1972), "Maude" (1972), "Good Times" (1974), "The Jeffer-sons" (1975), and a half dozen less successful cousins were greeted as revolutionary by critics and by people in the business, and when after a slow

start "All in the Family" became a huge success, it seemed to some a sign that
the larger social revolution of the late 60s was also succeeding and using television to spread its good or evil. Arthur Berger cites West Coast critic Dwight
Newton for an example of this rhetoric: "In one smashing, revolutionary opening
half-hour (January 1971), they destroyed old taboos and liberated television
comedy writing."[14]

The object of this praise and alarm was an American copy of a British comedy,
"Till Death Do Us Part," revolving around a blue-collar worker in an urban
neighborhood. Archie Bunker, the American protagonist, is a bigot and a negative
fool—that is, one who exemplifies rather than exposes the traits to be criticized.
He spouts malapropisms and narrow-minded, antagonistic, cynical yet jingoish,
essentially right-wing opinions at his family. Archie is ignored by his wife and
daughter, for whom he is a harmless, petty domestic tyrant, but challenged by
his son-in-law, a liberal college student whose own rhetoric is as empty as that
of his father-in-law. Except for the racist, ethnocentric, sexist, and politically
topical dialogue, the early "All in the Family" does not differ that markedly
from a traditional sitcom. The arguments, however heated, however "relevant"
to tensions in the contemporary society, are much like jokes or "shtick," added
for effect, but not functional. Eventually "All in the Family" begins to deal
with issues. Lear and his admirers enjoy the roll call of issues that were for the
first time mentioned in a prime-time series—abortion, homosexuality, impotence,
menopause, and a host of others.

There is a plethora of critical commentary devoted to the questions of just
how radical "All in the Family" should be judged and whether the program and
the others in Lear's stable are good or bad, harmful or helpful.[15] The first wave
of praise that assumed that bigotry was being lampooned tested popular reaction
and found that many viewers liked Archie Bunker and agreed with his racist and
right-wing sentiments.[16] To be sure, as the show evolved Archie became increasingly a round, ambiguous character whose rhetoric was undercut by his
democratic hero status, the traditions of wise-fool humor that often elevate fools
to naifs and common-sense philosophers, and by his role as victim and loser,
who, despite his bluster, ends up with the bills, the aches and pains, and the
sense of frustration with a world he cannot understand, influence, or fully appreciate for all his hard work and illusory self-image as a success. One can
criticize Bunker's opinions (or, of course, applaud them), but it is hard to avoid
some affection or at least sympathy for the man as an American "everyman"
(cf. George Babbitt, Willy Loman, Ralph Kramden).

Other critics complain that the show "pulled punches"; that is, it dealt with
issues ambivalently, ambiguously, superficially, and sensationally rather than in
any thorough, consistent manner. There is often an illusion of confronting issues
squarely when they are actually sidestepped. For instance, an episode that deals
with homosexuality, a very hard topic to confront anywhere in American culture,
much less in prime-time TV, seems to be radical because Archie's criticism of
one of Mike's friends is clearly out of line; the friend is "straight," but one of

Archie's macho drinking buddies is in fact a homosexual. After all is said and done, though, the message here is only that "you can't judge a book by its cover." Effeminate men might be heterosexual and seemingly masculine types can be gay. This is perhaps a lesson that some in America might have needed in the early 1970s (if it did not just result in increased paranoia and suspicion) but hardly a statement about homosexuality. Indirectly, of course, any public discussion of such a topic can be useful. It brings it out in the open for discussion, consideration, and it makes it easier for others to go even further in presenting it. But from the vantage point of nearly a decade after the fact, the revolution seems to have been more show than substance (even more so on television than it was in actuality). Lear made good situation comedies, but they were good in the ways that other sitcoms are good; they offer characters who hold our attention and affection, well-written scripts, and a creative use of the formula and conventions of the genre.

The same might be said for "The Mary Tyler Moore Show." In its conception it is no more radical than one might expect from a veteran of "The Dick Van Dyke Show." Mary Richards is an intrepid, young, single, career girl who struggles to maintain her position, that is, a "gofer" in a television newsroom. The show's theme song, "You're Going to Make It After All" means she will survive each episode's tests, not that she is going to be a model of female success in any meaningful way. That she is not a virgin, not entirely vapid, and not permanently intimidated by her boss are concessions to modernity, but the show's value is not in its dealing with the issues but in the quality of the characterizations and the scripts. In short, the revolution of the seventies produced better shows; not better than the very best predecessors, perhaps, but better than the majority and much, much better than the worst of the sixties entries. Harry Waters reports that the new sitcoms were termed "hard" by people in the industry, presumably because they employed rougher language, less syrupy sentiment, and more controversial subjects than the earlier shows, but in a sense they are even "softer"; that is, they rely upon well-developed, round characters and sober, serious plotlines rather than the sharp lines of problem-as-situation plus humor/shtick.[17]

The 1972–73 season saw another new, important development in the history of situation comedy, the debut of "M*A*S*H," a Larry Gelbart creation based upon the Robert Altman film (and, of course, a forgettable novel before that). "M*A*S*H" departed significantly from several sitcom traditions and formulas, beginning with its use of film, the elimination of audience involvement, and the elaboration of setting and movement. The show does not *look* like a sitcom. Alan Alda, the actor whose portrayal of the central character, Hawkeye, became more and more the dominant feature of the program, goes so far as to declare outright, "this is not a sitcom."[18] The program's premise, revolving around the activities of the doctors and nurses in an army hospital during the Korean War, insured that many of the situations would be more serious and less cheerfully resolved than one expects in the world of situation comedy. Some critics even called "M*A*S*H" "black humor" (a misleading term easily replaced by "absurd" or grotesque humor), emphasizing the episodes that do not end happily, the theme song ("Suicide Is Painless"), the irony of army doctors patching up what their fellow soldiers keep tearing apart, and the cynicism often expressed by leading characters. But the world of "M*A*S*H" is not really "absurd," certainly not in the sense of much of our modern literary comedy (cf. Barth, Pynchon, Reed, Barthelme). The heroes have a clear sense of purpose, of right and wrong, and a basically positive, healthy attitude. Their frustrations and anger is not directed at a meaningless universe but at the stupidity of various villians from the unspecified "they" who wage war to the more immediate examples of bullies, cowards, boors, snobs, fools, and other stock comic characters.

"M*A*S*H" became more and more moralistic over the years, more melodramatic, more conscious of its "humanistic" potential (largely at Alda's insistence, but this is a sitcom tendency shared by other shows such as "Happy Days," which were less obviously "preachy"). A 1979 episode, for instance, finds Colonel Potter giving his beloved horse to an old Korean cavalry officer so that the latter can regain his shattered dignity. The end of this tearjerker is perfect sitcom; the old man dies happily and Potter has his horse back and a sense of satisfaction in having done the right thing. A lesson of racial tolerance and understanding has been received at no extra cost.

The characters of "M*A*S*H" are superb examples of the process of evolution from flat to round characters over the life of a situation comedy. Hawkeye grows from a smark-aleck, trickster/con-man (whose immorality was generally more verbal than actual, as some critics are quick to point out) to a commonsense philosopher, much in the same way that our nineteenth-century literary wise-fools developed. Margaret "Hotlips" Houlihan progresses from a sexist caricature to a complex woman learning how to juggle being a woman, a military officer, a nurse, and a human being. Even the secondary characters, Klinger, Radar, Father Mulcahey, and the others, are given an opportunity to transcend the stereotypes and comic archetypes in which they were cast. In this sense one might well wish to elevate "M*A*S*H" to a higher status than mere sitcom, but it is essentially just a very good sitcom that developed beyond the limitations of a strict adherence to the formula.

In 1974 "Happy Days" began a string of hits for Garry Marshall. The program, a nostalgic early sixties-like teenager/domestic comedy (cf. "Henry Aldrich," "Ozzie and Harriet," "Dobie Gillis," among others), was designed almost as an alternative to Lear, MTM, and "M*A*S*H." A minor character, Fonzie, played by Henry Winkler, stole the show and caused cultural analysts problems trying to explain why a fifties-style juvenile delinquent was a national hero for kids. The Fonz was, first of all, cool. Tough, confident, independent, arrogant, and above all, *free*, dominated by no one, Fonz was also likeable and not a real threat. As the show developed, he was consciously transformed into a more vulnerable, family-oriented, sensitive sitcom hero, and the show settled around its original premise, that the problems of the "happy days" were not political, public issues, or adult self-knowledge and re-evaluation; they were problems of growing up and of surviving simple dilemmas and minor disruptions.

The success of "Happy Days" led to what might be viewed as a two-stream coexistence among sitcoms for the rest of the decade. There were adult or real-problem-oriented sitcoms such as those of Norman Lear, "M*A*S*H," MTM versus "Laverne and Shirley," and other spin-offs from "Happy Days"; and similarly reactionary fare such as "Welcome Back Kotter," "Different Strokes," and "jiggle-coms" like "Three's Company," which were adult-oriented in their sexual emphasis (sophomoric, immature perhaps, but dealing with alleged adults), but more like the family-oriented shows in tone and in their traditional conventions. There are fine programs in both streams. "One Day at a Time," a sensitive, thought-provoking sitcom, is Lear at his best. "Mork and Mindy" introduced Robin Williams, who at his best operated within the sitcom formula in the same manic way as Lucille Ball and Jackie Gleason. Programs like "Barney Miller," "Alice," "Taxi," and "Cheers" were able to cross the streams or perhaps to mingle them. At their best, they provided episodes that were as ritually satisfying as the sitcoms with which we are all familiar and at the same time gave an interesting look at contemporary themes and values. The 1978–79 season saw between five and eight of the top ten shows in the sitcom genre, with "Happy Days," "Three's Company," and "Laverne and Shirley" often the top three shows. The 1980s so far have seen some slipping in popularity, the cancelling of several old favorites, and not much that suggests new directions or new life. The 1983–84 season offered fourteen sitcoms, two of which are slated for cancellation ("Happy Days," "One Day at a Time"), one of which will be overhauled ("Three's Company" to "Three's a Crowd"), and only two or three for which the critics have any respect ("Cheers," "Kate and Allie," "The Duck Factory," which was cancelled before the end of the season.) The season saw seven new shows fail. [19] But sitcom fans need not fear; the old favorites will reappear again and again, in syndication and in new clothing, and there will be new directions from time to time within the boundaries of the genre with which so many television viewers are so comfortable.

THEMES AND ISSUES

Because, as Newcomb and others persuasively argue, the formula is the key element in understanding television *content* (as distinct from the contexts of production-distribution-consumption, a separate and perhaps more than equal concern), it is important that we spend some time defining and describing the situation-comedy genre. [20] Though exceptions can be uncovered for just about all the rules of sitcom production, the rules of formula or structure are far more important—perhaps more so for sitcom analysis than for any other popular culture inquiry. Beyond the formula of the genre, we encounter important differences of premise, of characterization, of theme, and of humorous activity, but structure is the inevitable point of departure. A sitcom is a half-hour series focused on episodes involving recurring characters within the same premise. That is, each week we encounter the same people in essentially the same setting. The episodes are finite; what happens in a given episode is generally closed off, explained, reconciled, solved at the end of the half hour (the exceptions, again, might be significant individually, but they have not altered the formula in any substantial or permanent way). Sitcoms are generally performed before live audiences, whether broadcast live (in the old days) or filmed or taped, and they usually have an element that might be almost metadrama in the sense that since the laughter is recorded (sometimes even augmented), the audience is aware of watching a play, a performance, a comedy incorporating comic activity.[21]

The most important feature of sitcom structure is the cyclical nature of the normalcy of the premise undergoing stress or threat of change and becoming restored. Sitcoms open up with "situation normal status quo," flirt with alteration of the group/individual serenity of cast member(s), and provide what Newcomb refers to as "the return to normalcy": "I would suggest that the more fundamental appeal of the situation comedy is found precisely in the fact that everything always comes out all right."[22] This faculty for the "happy ending" is, of course, one of the staples of comedy, according to most comic theory. Comedy involves confusion, disruption, and reconciliation. For this reason most sitcom scholars begin by acknowledging the genre's connection with comedy-drama of the past, usually from Roman theater through commedia dell'arte, and the popular theater, to comedy film and radio broadcasting. Newcomb's description is typical: "Its roots go deep, of course, to farce, slapstick, to the confused comedies of the eighteenth century stage, to the raucous silent films, even to Punch and Judy."[23] Anyone familiar with the history of humor would be inclined to agree, particularly as evidence of recycled characters, plots, jokes, and "shtick" is presented.

David Grote, however, insists that sitcom differs in important ways from the comedy-drama of the past:

The sit-com on television is in fact something new. It is a powerful and popular form of entertainment. It has developed much by accident, growing from small ideas and encouraged by the unique economic conditions of American broadcasting. Most of us have watched it all our lives, and for the most part we have simply taken it for granted as the most available and least demanding of the many forms of comedy.

Although the content of any series or episode may reflect the tastes of a given time, the sit-com is more than just a matter of taste. So many features are shared by all the sit-coms, no matter what the kind of humor or the tastes of their audience, that the situation comedy must be seen for what it is; a new kind of comedy. In less than thirty years it has appeared, tested some variations, settled on its basic rules, and perfected its form. In the process, it has overturned more than two thousand years of comic traditions and established an entirely new and unique form of comedy.[24]

Grote argues that audiences familiar with classical comedy would be shocked by and uncomfortable with our sitcoms. He maintains that while traditional comedy builds or develops a plot, starting from a void and ending in something that has been constructed—however convolutedly—along the way, sitcom starts with the entire edifice and ends with it unchanged despite the flirtations in the middle, which he considers to be the "situations" of situation comedy:

The basic plot of television situation comedy is a circle rather than a line. In traditional basic comedy plot, some characters, usually a boy and a girl, start at point A and want to get somewhere else, usually in bed together at point B. No matter how many twists and turns, no matter what the confusions, at the end of the play the characters have moved from A to B. In the usual situation comedy, however, the character is at point A and does not want to get anywhere else, no matter how much he protests that he does not like where he is.[25]

The sitcom afficionado is drawn to dispute this, remembering the ambitions of Lucy Richards, the schemes of Bilko and Kramden, and all of the other Sisyphean efforts of sitcom heroes and heroines. But Grote is right essentially; they all end up where they started out, and they are usually pleased with that result, even if it means a prison camp as in "Hogan's Heroes," Gilligan's deserted island, Kotter's hated classroom, or Mel's crummy diner. The difference is that on television, the *series*, not the play, is the "thing." As David Marc states (perhaps overstates), "no single episode of a sitcom is likely to be of much interest; it may not even be intelligible. The attraction of an episode is the strength of its contribution to the broader cosmology of the series."[26] The implications of this radical difference in structure will be interpreted and discussed later in this section; it is raised here to justify an emphasis on structure and premise as the crucial elements for understanding the genre.

The boundaries of sitcom's premises are as flexible as its structure is rigid. Almost all studies of the genre include a classification system for subgenres and program types.[27] Perhaps the most important distinction is Horace Newcomb's subdivision of comedy-drama into two clearly separate categories: situation and domestic comedy. Newcomb sees domestic comedy as markedly different from sitcom. Domestic comedy is based upon the static home setting but more importantly upon differences in tone. While sitcom is more oriented toward humor, domestic comedy has "more warmth and a deeper sense of humanity."[28] Other critics see the difference more as one of degree than kind, noting that domestic comedy is clearly a separate subtype, but still structurally the same. Since all domestic comedies follow the structural rules for sitcom, and since all sitcom is "domestic" or family-oriented if we expand the definition of family to non-blood-related groups that function as families, it is probably better not to overstate the differences.

Indeed while just about all classification systems single out domestic comedy, many break even that group down to "single-parent comedies," "male-single-parent comedies," and even "smart" or "dumb" male-female domestic comedies. John Bryant provides us with a motif scale that designates eleven program types: domestic, man-woman, parent-child, single man, single woman, professional/military, ethnic, hick, fantasy, town hall (neighborhood, community focus), and parodies.[29] Rick Mitz gives us only seven basic categories—"domcoms," "kidcoms," "couplecoms," "SciFicoms," "corncoms," "ethnicoms," and "careercoms," but he makes up for it by offering a list of sixty-seven recurring premises and/or stock characters including the "cantankerous old geezer," the "sassy secretary," the "dizzy wife," and such.[30] One reason for such clustering of premise and character type is the imitative characteristic of television programming. Whatever has been successful will be imitated and repeated. Writers and producers are acutely sensitive to the traditions of their craft, to formulas and conventions, and to "track records." Indeed, one can also subdivide sitcoms by the production companies—Lear, MTM, Marshall—and trace the careers of writers as they move from one production lot to another and adapt to their new creative environments.[31] According to no less prominent a figure than Carl Reiner, "situation comedy depends largely upon the general approach you find on a given production lot."[32]

Much of the appeal of a situation comedy rests in characterization. The character types are familiar; many of them do go back to the commedia dell'arte and other forms of popular humor (wise-fools, braggarts, cowards, out-of-it pedants, con men, tricksters, termagant wives, bullies, and so forth). But in sitcom we get to know them well over a period of time often many years in length, and they rarely remain flat characters for very long. In many of the better shows their evolution is a complex and fascinating process, but even in the simpler shows it is important that the audience be comfortable with the characters as human beings, develop at least enough concern for them that their struggles are of interest and their "return to normalcy" brings some satisfaction or comfort. The character's personality traits may provide laughs and even the opportunity for approval and disapproval, but they must be integrated to the premise and with the other characters. This has the effect of making sitcom characters generally warm, friendly, and likeable, even if their point of departure is less admirable.

The same might be said for sitcom *humor*. Humor is injected into a program in the form of jokes or "shtick," in varying degrees according to the program's tone, the skills of the writers and actors, and the dictates of the particular episode. In some cases—for example "I Love Lucy" or Robin Williams as Mork—whole shows can be built around humor-activity. Jack Benny, Burns and Allen, Freddie Prinze, Gabe Kaplan, and other stand-up comedians have the opportunity to perform comedy routines within the sitcom frame. But usually humor, like characterization, is a servant of structure and premise rather than its master. A sitcom can have a very funny star and still be a failure, or it can be not very funny and a success. It can also be funny and successful if it is "warm." As Carl Reiner puts it, "warm is an important word. You laugh easier when funny things are happening to nice people."[33] Not all characters are lovable, of course, and not all sitcom humor is benign or restrained, but once again, in sitcom all is subordinate to the ambience of the series, and that ambience is generated by the well-being of the recurring characters and the sanctity of the premise.

Surely one of the major issues in sitcom studies is the question of the meaning of its format: why is this form of popular drama so appealing, so satisfying for the television audience? As suggested here on several occasions, the simplest answer is that witnessing everything "coming out okay" for a group of characters with whom we are familiar, comfortable, and perhaps with whom, to some degree we can "identify" is emotionally desirable, and if we add funny jokes and entertaining "shtick" the experience is enjoyable and pleasing. But there are social implications in the theme that the return to the status quo is always good. Roger Rollin provides one of the best analyses of the meaning of the situation comedy formula, arguing that it reverses the traditional "liberal" functions of comedy.[34] Rollin cites Northrop Frye and other critics of comic literature to maintain that comedy, quoting Frye, "implicitly urges the necessity and value of social change."[35] But Rollin further notes that

the values of society expressed in comedy, values which can be almost as conservative as those of traditional comedy's Old Society, are in effect reasserted and reinforced rather than rejected. The values center upon the nuclear family itself. In an age in which the nuclear family is said to be deteriorating both as a reality and as a social concept, it exhibits in its several television versions surprisingly strong vital signs. . . . One can only conclude that television comedy must gratify deeply felt needs or desires, needs and desires of which neither its audience, its creators, or its sponsors may be fully aware.[36]

John Bryant describes a similar appeal, emphasizing that one set of values, the pursuit of serenity, overrides another, the quest for success, vertical mobility:

In each case the individual's attempt to change roles creates a sense of embarrassment that threatens to disrupt the program's balanced group. The needs of family, friends, and associates are stronger than the glamor of any proposed change in the character's normal lifestyle. The character's own recognition that such a change will create disharmony relieves us from the embarrassing situation. The sitcom is, then, a subtle mode of socialization calling for a balance between personal ability and the group's limitations and demands.[37]

This does not mean that the success of the formula proves that Americans have given up valuing success or vertical mobility in the public realm. Rather, it implies that a significant portion of the population needs some exposure to images that reinforce the idea that personal happiness is more important than public achievement. The sitcom gives them this message in a palatable form. Ordinary people, flawed people, are expected to strive for growth, accomplishment, even greatness. Along the way there will be problems, interruptions, embarrassments, and failures, but we will survive them, and with the help of our family and friends, all will end well. The American Dream is of the yeoman's subsistence farm as much as it is for the hero's achievement. It is therefore not surprising that "trivial entertainment" with so powerful an implication is strong enough to dominate the television market.

The ideological implications of situation comedy are by no means limited, however, to the message in the format. Every premise has its meaning, every characterization, every episode's theme, even every joke and comic "bit of business" has its messages. Sometimes the communication is overt or manifest. Garry Marshall has been outspoken about the teaching, acculturating function of his shows: "We tried to be useful. We did shows about mental health, about diabetes, about death, blindness, epilepsy. Tolerance. That's what we tried to teach. Be nice to each other."[38] He is proud of the fact that the 200th episode of "Happy Days" was written into the *Congressional Record* in recognition of the program's "wholesomeness."[39] Harry Waters reports that a "Laverne and Shirley" episode won an award from the National Association for Retarded Citizens for an episode in which a retarded girl was portrayed sensitively and "constructively," and the people in the industry are quick to cite cases such as the 500 percent increase in public-library-card applications that followed the Fonz's similar application.[40]

The early domestic comedies were clearly conscious of the moral of their stories. Right and wrong and good and bad were as obvious as if there were a tag titled "moral: honesty is the best policy" on the end of each show. Garry Marshall updates that silent film convention: "the most clear-cut comments are Mork's soliloquy at the end, which was designed for just that reason, to say it head-on. It scared the network. They don't understand the ice cream theory. If you give them ice cream, they'll listen."[41]

One is grateful that Marshall has not yet used the "candy corollary"—if you give them candy they'll follow you anywhere! But Marshall is neither alone nor representative of a new, post-Lear sitcom tendency. Sheldon Leonard, one of the old-school producers, has noted that "we can, within a framework of good showmanship, advance valid social comments, valid ethical concepts, valid generalizations about the human condition which have meaning for the audience."[42]

The adult sitcoms of the 1970s were even more loaded with overt social commentary, from Lear's handling of ethnic and racial conflict and sexual issues to Mary Tyler Moore's confronting the role of women in contemporary society, to "M*A*S*H's" sometimes intolerably saccharine preaching on the subject of human understanding and decency. Every critic has his favorite example of an episode in which an important national issue or cultural concern was dealt with by the situation comedy engage, but as was suggested, the issues were often dealt with superficially and deliberately ambiguously. As Nathan Huggins acerbically asserts, "situation comedy will trivialize anything. Intermarriage in "The Jeffersons" is reduced to mere idiocy."[43] Todd Gitlin provides a superb analysis of how sitcom ideology is carefully shaped to please the majority and offend as few people as possible, even when it appears to be controversial and provocative. "TV entertainment takes its design from social and psychological fissures: that is the deep unspoken reason why writers always look for conflict at the heart of the tale. If the messages are susceptible to divergent interpretations, that is no failure for television."[44]

But the ambiguity, ambivalences, and superficiality are themselves instructive and perhaps reflective of the current social climate. A case in point is the controversy over the significance of the treatment of bigotry and narrow-mindedness in "All in the Family." Critics have pored over the evidence that suggests that Lear's intention of lampooning and criticizing Archie Bunker's view of the world was either missed or ignored by a significant portion of the viewing audience.[45] Did the program backfire, create a fascist hero instead of a villain? If so, does this imply that the creator has no control over the functions of the artistic image, that the "reader" or the audience makes the meaning in a work of art, as has been suggested by the reader-response school of literary criticism? In any case, it is clear that the ideological motive or intention does not account for the range of reactions potentially generated. Lear's position is "liberal-establishment," but the cultural milieu of the creative process, as well as the diversity and complexity of the audience, complicates the matter. Our reaction to Archie is ambivalent because he is an ambiguous character and because we, as a culture, are ambivalent concerning much of what he represents, despite our official public policies. We demand, to use Douglas Kellner's terms, *both* "emancipatory" and "conciliatory" ideology in our popular culture.[46] Moreover, Gary Alan Fine has noted that there is a considerable gap between the ideological premises of media humor and those of humor in the public domain (i.e., folk humor, popularly told jokes, joking). He notes a need for more research into "the interface between humour in the media and humour in natural settings. To what extent do scriptwriters, comedians, and jokebook authors employ humour that is already in popular circulation? When they alter it for their particular purposes, do they do this in any systematic way?"[47]

One interesting result of this ideological complexity is the relationship between overt, intended themes and covert, or more subtle, even unintentional implications. In many cases, for instance, the development of the plot carries a different, even antithetical message to the overtly delivered statement. A "Mork and Mindy," for instance, dealt with the problem of the role of the elderly in American society by having Mork cheer up a depressed Mindy's grandmother by his simulating advanced age and courting her. His attentions make her think young and her problem is solved. His concluding report to Orson is a straight castigation of modern American society for its inability to conceive of valid roles for senior citizens, but the only such role demonstrated by the show itself is the denial of the legitimacy of aging and the argument that only perpetually youthful behavior can bring happiness.

In another case, Ann Romano ("One Day at a Time") has to give advice to her daughter on the subject of premarital sex. She takes the modern position that such activity is neither desirable nor taboo; it must be judged only by its motives and results. In other words, sex is permissible if it's what you really want to do, but it should not be connected with ulterior motives. But the subsequent plot development demonstrates that moral judgments about commitment are implied if not stated: the boyfriend's rejection of her operates as "proof" that the decision concerning sexual activity is connected with the socially demanded "meaningful relationships."

In a "Taxi" episode it is made clear that excessive drug use has addled the brain of the Reverend Jim. One would think that the message is virtually the same as the public service spot that says, "don't use drugs," but his spiking of the dispatcher's coffee not only leads to his own employment, it makes the usually unpleasant and unhappy Louie mellow and delightful. The covert message is diametrically opposed to the overt one.

In an episode of "Different Strokes," an attractive, apparently normal teenage girl fears that she has become pregnant. Her problem leads to rather typical sitcom complications and embarrassments; she is afraid to tell her father, and a series of misunderstandings increase the tension before she is rescued, both by her father, who turns out (ideally) to be understanding and rational, and by the writers, who turn her dilemma into just another misapprehension. The overt messages of the show are "honesty is the best policy" and in turn, for parents, calm and helpful responses to children's problems are the proper, acceptable behavior. The covert message is never mentioned, but it is clear that "nice girls do" (or else there would have been no situation for this comedy). The young girl's sexual activity is never questioned or condemned.

Every situation comedy has several covert themes as well as overt ones. A *Newsweek* special issue devoted to television's lessons for kids notes a half-dozen messages bound to the premises of popular shows including, among others, "innocence conquers all," "ethnics have class," and "dumb is cool."[48] It is important that we accept the fact that the clear, obvious social statements made by the adult, issue-oriented comedies of the seventies represent only a tiny fraction of the cultural, social communication going on daily in the world of television situation comedy.

Sitcom analysis should begin with the contexts of production, distribution, and consumption. Some industry analysis is available, mostly biographical studies of the people who make the shows (see the bibliographic survey), and some demographic information is accessible, but there are almost no ethnographic studies of the sitcom audience and how they watch and how they feel about what they watch.[49] Analysis of the text must include an awareness of the meaning of formula, convention, premise, episode-theme, characterization, and both verbal and visual imagery. Sitcom may be simplistic fare, but studies of it must not be, if they are to have any value.

NOTES

1. Jeff Greenfield, "Situation Comedies: Are They Getting Better—or Worse," *TV Guide*, May 24, 1980, p. 4.

2. Ben Stein, *The View from Sunset Boulevard: America as Brought to You by the People Who Make Television*, (New York: Basic Books, 1979), p. 7.

3. Harry Ackerman, "Program Poker: The Half-Hour Form," *Television Quarterly* 6, no. 4 (Fall 1976), pp. 63–64.

4. Arthur Asa Berger, *The TV Guided American*, (New York: Walker, 1976), p. 72.

5. Dan Brown and Jennings Bryant, "Humor in the Mass Media," in *Handbook of Humor Research*, vol. 2, ed. Paul McGhee and Jeffrey Goldstein, (New York: Springer Verlag, 1983), p. 147.

6. David Marc, *Demographic Vistas: Television in American Culture*, (Philadelphia. University of Pennsylvania, 1984), pp. 5–11.

7. David Grote, *The End of Comedy: The Sit-com and the Comedic Tradition*, (Hamden, Conn.: Archon Books, 1983), pp. 130–131.

8. Brown, "Humor," p. 143.

9. See Arthur Wertheim's fine book, *Radio Comedy* (New York: Oxford Press, 1972).

10. Rick Mitz provides basic historical data in readable form in *The Great Sitcom Book* (New York: Perigree Books, 1983).

11. Michael Kernan, "Still in Love with Lucy," *Washington Post*, May 4, 1984, p. B-15.

12. John Bryant's manuscript dealing with the sitcoms of the sixties ("Situation Comedy of the Sixties: The Evolution of a Popular Genre," 1984) will soon make an important contribution to the literature dealing with the genre in that period. Bryant does find a lot to say about sixties sitcoms.

13. For example, Horace Newcomb and Robert S. Alley, *The Producer's Medium: Conversation with Creators of American TV* (New York: Oxford, 1983), p. 197.

14. Berger, *TV-Guided*, p. 11.

15. Note the collection of material in *All in the Family*, edited by Richard P. Adler, (New York: Praeger, 1979).

16. For example, Charles Husband, "The Mass Media and the Functions of Ethnic Humor in a Racist Society," in *It's a Funny Thing, Humour*, ed. Antony Chapman and Hugh Foot (London: Pergamon, 1977) and essays in Adler's *All in the Family* anthology.

17. Harry F. Waters, "TV Comedy: What It's Teaching the Kids," *Newsweek*, May 7, 1979, p. 63.

18. PBS television special, "The Making of M*A*S*H," broadcast January 21, 1981.

19. Walt Belcher, "Sitcoms Can't Keep America Laughing," Tampa *Tribune-Times*, April 22, 1984.

20. Horace Newcomb's *TV: The Most Popular Art* (Garden City, N.Y.: Anchor Books, 1974) is the best place to start reading about the format of the genre. David Grote's *The End of Comedy* and David Marc's *Demographic Vistas* are essential, and the less available but no less useful thinking on the subject by Roger Rollin (see n. 34) and Charles Wolfe ("Bilko's Plots and the Bilko Plots: Toward a Structural Definition of Television Situation Comedy," paper presented at the Popular Culture Association meeting, 1973) are recommended.

21. Perhaps so many sitcoms seem like plays within plays and comedies about comedians or about playing comedy because of the close historical relationship between skits as a part of larger variety shows and the development of the situation comedy genre as such. It is interesting to speculate concerning the effect of this aspect of the genre on the audience's response.

22. Newcomb, *TV*, p. 40.

23. Ibid., pp. 26–27.

24. Grote, *The End of Comedy*, pp. 11–12.

25. Ibid., p. 67.

26. Marc, *Demographic Vistas*, p. 12.

27. I am grateful to a class handout prepared by my colleague at the University of Maryland-Baltimore County, Warren Belasco, for a good summary of the most prominent subcategories available in the critical literature and for many other good tips for TV and sitcom study.

28. Newcomb, *TV*, p. 43.

29. John Bryant, "A Checklist of American Situation Comedy," *American Humor: An Interdisciplinary Newsletter* 5, no. 2 (Fall 1978), pp. 14–31.

30. Mitz, *The Great TV Sitcom Book*.

31. Horace Newcomb and Robert Alley make the case persuasively for the producer as TV's auteur (at least most of the time) in their *The Producer's Medium*.

32. Sheldon Leonard and Carl Reiner, "Comedy on Television: A Dialogue," *Television Quarterly*, Summer 1963, reprinted in A. W. Bluen, ed, *Television, the Creative Experience*, (New York: Hastings House, 1967), p. 95.

33. Larry Wilde, *How the Great Comedy Writers Create Laughter*, (Chicago: Nelson-Hall, 1976), p. 234.

34. Roger B. Rollin, "In the Family: Television's Re-Formation of Comedy," *The Psychocultural Review* 2, no. 4 (Fall 1978).

35. Ibid., p. 175.

36. Ibid., pp. 262–63. The subject of comedy as radical and/or conservative is too complicated to be treated here. Some introduction to humor theory is presented in the bibliography section, and Douglas Kellner's article on TV Ideology in Horace Newcomb's anthology *TV: The Critical View* (New York: Oxford, 1982) is very helpful. An interesting approach to comedy as *entropic* versus *transformative* (disruptive-destructive/creative) is provided by Arlen Hansen's "Entropy and Transformation: Two Types of American Humor," *American Scholar* 43, no. 3 (Summer 1974), pp. 405–21.

37. John Bryant, "Emma, Lucy, and the American Situation Comedy of Manners," *Journal of Popular Culture* 13, no. 2 (Fall 1979), p. 250.

38. Garry Marshall, "Our Happy Days Together," *TV Guide*, April 28, 1984, p. 5.

39. Ibid., p. 9.

40. Greenfield, "Situation Comedies," p. 6.

41. Newcomb and Alley, *The Producer's Medium,* p. 248.

42. Leonard and Reiner, "Comedy," p. 100.

43. Nathan Irving Huggins, "Opportunities for Minorities in Television and Movies: Facade of Humor Can Obscure Substance of Subject," *Washington Post*, April 13, 1978, p. MD 13.

44. Todd Gitlin, *Inside Prime Time*, (New York: Pantheon, 1983), p. 217.

45. See the essays in Adler's anthology *All in the Family* and Husband's "The Mass Media."

46. Douglas Kellner, "TV, Ideology, and Emancipatory Popular Culture," in Newcomb's *TV: The Critical View.*

47. Gary Alan Fine, "Humour and Communication: Discussion," in *It's a Funny Thing, Humour*, ed. Chapman and Foot, p. 333.

48. Waters, "TV Comedy," pp. 64–72.

49. Cf. Janice Radway's forthcoming study of the readers of romance novels. More

of this kind of work is needed in popular culture studies (and less theoretical argument concerning whether or not it is the only valid approach).

BIBLIOGRAPHICAL SURVEY

The study of situation comedy properly begins with background reading in popular culture theory, communications theory, and the study of television as an industry and as a communications medium. It also requires at least some consideration of humor, though reading humor theory is a difficult and not immediately rewarding enterprise. The recent *Handbook of Humor Research* edited by Paul McGhee and Jeffrey Goldstein is a useful reference because it includes both general works and more specific studies. The chapters in volume two of McGhee and Goldstein by Dan Brown, Jennings Bryant, and the author of this chapter are most immediately pertinent. The *Handbook* will lead to surveys of the leading humor theories and to empirical studies with important implications for the study of situation comedy. An earlier volume edited by Anthony Chapman and Hugh Foot, *Its a Funny Thing, Humour*, is also recommended.

The only history of the genre is Rick Mitz's *The Great TV Sitcom Book*, a work aimed at afficionados and trivia buffs rather than scholars but indispensable nonetheless and interesting reading. A scholarly history, preferably one grounded in American cultural studies comparable to Arthur Wertheim's *Radio Comedy*, is badly needed and probably in preparation right now somewhere (the need is too obvious to have been completely overlooked).

David Grote's *The End of Comedy* and the chapters on sitcom in David Marc's *Demographic Vistas* are very valuable recent contributions to understanding the genre, supplementing Horace Newcomb's chapters in *TV: The Most Popular Art*. Roger Rollin's article, "In the Family: Television's Re-Formation of Comedy" is also important for an appreciation of the formula. John Bryant's published work on sitcom and the one unpublished manuscript cited in the bibliography suggest that he is a scholar with significant things to say on the subject.

Among useful specific studies are Robert Sklar's essays in *Prime Time America*, Arthur Asa Berger's *The TV-Guided American*, and articles by Mick Eaton, Todd Gitlin, Douglas Kellner, and Harry Waters, cited in the bibliography. Ben Stein, Larry Wilde, Horace Newcomb, and Robert Alley have provided us with interesting insights concerning the people who make the programs. Much of the work on sitcom is very good; the genre has provoked some spirited popular criticism, some amusing appreciation, and finally some stimulating intellectual inquiry. Much more is called for including the good comprehensive history already mentioned, studies of the major premises and program-types, close studies of particular shows and of periods in sitcom history, and analyses of the messages of the programs and their social and cultural implications.

BOOKS AND ARTICLES

Ackerman, Harry. "Program Poker: The Half-Hour Form." *Television Quarterly* 6, no. 4 (Fall 1976), pp. 63–66.

Adler, Richard P., ed. *All in the Family: A Critical Appraisal*. New York: Praeger, 1979.

Alley, Robert S. *Television: Ethics for Hire*. Nashville: Abington, 1977.

Andrews, Bart. *Lucy and Ricky and Fred and Ethel*. New York: Dutton, 1976.

Arlen, Michael J. "The Media Dramas of Norman Lear." Reprinted in Horace Newcomb, *Television: The Critical View*. New York, Oxford, 1976.

Ball, Lucille. "Lucille Ball: A Seminar Interview," *AFI Dialogue on Film* 3, no. 6 (May–June 1974).

Belcher, Walt. "Sitcoms Can't Keep America Laughing," Tampa *Tribune-Times*, April 22, 1984.

Berger, Arthur Asa. *The TV-Guided American*. New York: Walker, 1976.

Bluen, A. W., ed. *Television, the Creative Experience*. New York: Hastings House, 1967.

Brown, Dan, and Jennings Bryant. "Humor in the Mass Media." In *Handbook of Humor Research*, vol. 2, edited by Paul McGhee and Jeffrey Goldstein. New York: Springer Verlag, 1983.

Bryant, John. "A Checklist of American Situation Comedy." *American Humor: An Interdisciplinary Newsletter* 5, no. 2 (Fall 1978), pp. 14–31.

———. "Emma, Lucy, and the American Situation Comedy of Manners." *Journal of Popular Culture* 13, no. 2 (Fall 1979), pp. 248–56.

———. "Situation Comedy of the Sixties: The Evolution of a Popular Genre." Forthcoming in *American Humor: An Interdisciplinary Newsletter*, Summer 1985.

Cady, Barbara, and Norman Lear. "Playboy Interview: Norman Lear," *Playboy* 23 (March 1976), pp. 53–69.

Cantor, Joanne. "Humor on Television: A Content Analysis." *Journal of Broadcasting* 20 (Fall 1976), pp. 501–10.

———. "Tendentious Humour in the Mass Media." In *It's a Funny Thing, Humour*, edited by Antony Chapman and Hugh Foot. London: Pergamon, 1977, pp. 303–310.

Cantor, Muriel. *The Hollywood TV Producer*. New York: Basic Books, 1971.

Cater, Douglas, and Richard Adler, ed. *Television as a Cultural Force*. New York: Praeger, 1976.

———. *Television as a Social Force*. New York: Praeger, 1975.

Chesbro, James W. "Communication, Values, and Popular Television Series—a Four-Year Assessment." Reprinted, in Horace Newcomb, *Television: The Critical View*. New York: Oxford, 1982, pp. 8–46.

Corliss, Richard. "Happy Days Are Here Again." Reprinted in Horace Newcomb, *Television: The Critical View*. New York: Oxford, 1982, pp. 64–76.

Eaton, Mick. "Television Situation Comedy." In *Popular Film and Television*, edited by Tony Bennett et al. London: British Film Institute, 1981, pp. 26–52.

Fass, Paula S. "Television as a Cultural Document: Promises and Problems." Reprinted in *Television as a Cultural Force*, edited by Douglas Cater and Richard Adler. New York: Praeger, 1976, pp. 37–57.

Fine, Gary Alan. "Humour and Communication: Discussion," In *It's a Funny Thing, Humour*, edited by Antony Chapman and Hugh Foot. London: Pergamon, 1977.

Flamini, Roland. "Television and the Magoo Factor," *American Film* 1, no. 7 (May 1976), pp. 50–53.

Gladden, Jack. "Archie Bunker Meets Mr. Spoopendyke: Nineteenth Century Prototypes for Domestic Situation Comedy." *Journal of Popular Culture* 10, no. 1 (Summer 1976), pp. 167–80.

Gitlin, Todd. *Inside Prime Time*. New York: Pantheon, 1983. See especially "The Turn toward *Relevance*," chapter 10.

Goodlad, Sinclair. "On the Social Significance of Television Comedy." In *Approaches to Popular Culture*, edited by C.W.E. Bigsby. Bowling Green, Ohio: Popular Press, 1976.

Greenfield, Jeff. "Situation Comedies: Are They Getting Better—or Worse." *TV Guide*, part 1, May 24, 1980, 4–8; part 2, May 5, 1980, pp. 30–32.

Grote, David. *The End of Comedy: The Sit-com and the Comedic Tradition*. Hamden, Conn.: Archon Books, 1983.

Hansen, Arlen J. "Entropy and Transformation: Two Types of American Humor." *American Scholar* 43, no. 3 (Summer 1974), pp. 405–21.

Heffner, Richard D. "Television: The Subtle Persuader." *TV Guide*, September 15, 1973, pp. 25–26.

Hough, Arthur. "Trials and Tribulations—30 Years of Sitcoms." In *Understanding Television*, edited by Richard Adler. New York: Praeger, 1981.

Huggins, Nathan Irving. "Opportunities for Minorities in Television and Movies: Facade of Humor Can Obscure Substance of Subject." *Washington Post*, April 13, 1978, p. MD 13.

Husband, Charles. "The Mass Media and the Functions of Ethnic Humour in a Racist Society." In *It's a Funny Thing, Humour*, edited by Antony Chapman and Hugh Foot. London: Pergamon, 1977.

Joslyn, James, and John Pendleton. "The Adventures of Ozzie and Harriet." *Journal of Popular Culture* 7 (Summer 1973), pp. 23–41.

Kellner, Douglas. "TV, Ideology, and Emancipatory Popular Culture." In Horace Newcomb, *Television: The Critical View*. New York, Oxford, 1982, pp. 382–421.

Kernan, Michael. "Still in Love with Lucy," *Washington Post*, April 4, 1984, pp. B1, B-15.

Kirkpatrick, John T. "Homes and Homemakers on American TV." In *The American Dimension: Cultural Myths and Social Realities*, edited by W. Arens and Susan P. Montague. Port Washington, N.Y.: Alfred, 1976, pp. 69–79.

Leonard, Sheldon, and Carl Reiner. "Comedy on Television: A Dialogue," *Television Quarterly*, Summer 1963; reprinted in Bluen, ed., *Television, the Creative Experience*, pp. 93–103.

Leonard, Sheldon. "Why Do You Laugh?" In *Television: A Selection of Readings from TV Guide Magazine*, edited by Barry G. Cole. Free Press, 1970.

McGhee, Paul, and Jeffrey Goldstein, eds. *Handbook of Humor Research*. Volume II. New York: Springer Verlag, 1983.

McNeil, Alex. *Total Television: A Comprehensive Guide to Programming from 1948–1980*. New York: Penguin, 1980.

Malone, Michael. "And Gracie Begat Lucy Who Begat Laverne . . . " *Channels of Communication*, October 1981.

Marshall, Garry. "Our Happy Days Together," *TV Guide*, April 28, 1984, pp. 4–9.

Marc, David. *Demographic Vistas: Television in American Culture*. Philadelphia: University of Pennsylvania, 1984.

Merrill, Sam. "The Hollywood Laugh Track," *New Times*, January 9, 1978, 27–37, pp. 84–90.

Mintz, Lawrence E. "Humor and Popular Culture." In *Handbook of Humor Research*, vol. II, edited by Paul McGhee and Jeffrey Goldstein. New York: Springer Verlag, 1983, pp. 129–42.

Mitz, Rick. *The Great TV Sitcom Book*. NY: Perigree Books, 1983.

Moss, Sylvia. "The New Comedy." *Television Quarterly* 4, no. 1 (Winter 1965), pp. 42–45.

Newcomb, Horace. "The Television Artistry of Norman Lear." *Prospects*, vol. 2. New York: Burt Franklin, 1976, pp. 109–26.

———. *Television: The Critical View*. New York: Oxford, 1st edition, 1976; 2d edition, 1979; 3d edition, 1982. (All three editions have material useful for situation comedy study).

———. *TV: The Most Popular Art*. Garden City, N.Y.: Anchor, 1974.

———, and Robert S. Alley. *The Producer's Medium: Conversations with Creators of American TV*. New York: Oxford, 1983.

Norback, C. T., and P. G. Norback, eds. *TV Guide Almanac*, New York: Ballantine, 1980.

Palmore, E. "Attitudes toward Aging as Shown by Humor." *Gerontologist* 11 (1971), pp. 181–86.

Podhoretz, Norman. "Our Changing Ideals as Seen on TV." *Commentary* 16 (December 1953), pp. 534–40.

Primeau, Ronald. *The Rhetoric of Television*. New York: Longman, 1979.

Rabinowitz, Dorothy. "Watching the Sitcoms." Reprinted in Horace Newcomb, *Television: The Critical View*. New York: Oxford, 1979, pp. 55–64.

Rollin, Roger B. "In the Family: Television's Re-Formation of Comedy." *The Psychocultural Review* 2, no. 4 (Fall 1978).

Shales, Tom. "The Last of the Really Funny People, with the Only Kind of Humor That Will Endure," *Washington Post*, January 20, 1977, pp. F1, F8.

Sklar, Robert. *Prime Time America: Life on and behind the Television Screen*. New York: Oxford, 1980.

Stein, Ben. *The View from Sunset Boulevard: America as Brought to You by the People Who Make Television*. New York: Basic Books, 1979.

Taylor, Paul. "Laughter and Joking—The Structural Axis." In *It's a Funny Thing, Humour*, edited by Antony Chapman and Hugh Foot. London: Pergamon, 1977, pp. 385–90.

Vidmar, Neil, and Milton Rokeach. "Archie Bunker's Bigotry: A Study in Selective Perception and Exposure." *Journal of Communication* 24 (Winter 1974).

Wander, Phillip. "Counters in the Social Drama: Some Notes on 'All in the Family.' " In Horace Newcomb, *Television: The Critical View*. New York: Oxford, 1976, pp. 35–43.

Waters, Harry F. "TV Comedy: What It's Teaching the Kids." *Newsweek*, May 7, 1979, pp. 64–72.

———. "TV: Laughing All the Way," *Newsweek*, January 21, 1974, pp. 62–69.

Wertheim, Arthur Frank. *Radio Comedy*. New York: Oxford, 1979.

Wilde, Larry. *How the Great Comedy Writers Create Laughter*. Chicago: Nelson-Hall, 1976.

Williams, Carolyn Traynor. "It's Not So Much, 'You've Come a Long Way Baby'— as 'You're Gonna Make It after All.' " In Horace Newcomb, *Television: The Critical View*. New York: Oxford, 1979, pp. 64–74.

Williams, Martin. *TV: The Casual Art*. New York: Oxford, 1982.

Williams, Raymond. *Television, Technology, and Cultural Form*. New York: Schocken, 1974.

Wolfe, Charles K. "Bilko's Plots and the *Bilko* Plots: Toward a Structural Definition of Television Situation Comedy." Paper presented at the Popular Culture Association Meeting, 1973.

Yanok, George, and Suzanne Helms Yanok. "What's Funny?" *Mainliner*, 1977, pp. 35–37.

Zillmann, Dolf. "Humour and Communication: Introduction to Symposium." In *It's a Funny Thing, Humour*, edited by Antony Chapman and Hugh Foot. London: Pergamon Press, 1977.

VIDEOGRAPHY

"The Goldbergs"
 CBS, NBC, Dumont, various prime times
 Premiere: January 10, 1949
 Stars: Gertrude Berg
 Last Program: October 19, 1954

"Amos 'n' Andy"
 CBS, Thursdays, 8:30–9:00 P.M.
 Premiere: June 28, 1951
 Stars: Alvin Childress, Spencer Williams
 Last Program: June 11, 1953

"The Adventures of Ozzie and Harriet"
 ABC, various prime times
 Premiere: October 3, 1951
 Stars: Ozzie Nelson, Harriet Nelson
 Last Program: September 3, 1956

"I Love Lucy"
 CBS, various prime times
 Premiere: October 15, 1951
 Stars: Lucille Ball, Desi Arnaz
 Last Program: September 24, 1961

"Father Knows Best"
 CBS, NBC, various prime times
 Premiere: October 3, 1954
 Stars: Robert Young, Jane Wyatt
 Last Program: September 17, 1962

"The Honeymooners"
 CBS, various prime times
 Premiere: October 1, 1955
 Stars: Jackie Gleason, Art Carney
 Last Program: May 9, 1971

"Leave It to Beaver"
 CBS, ABC, various prime times

Premiere: October 4, 1957
Stars: Tony Dow, Jerry Mathers
Last Program: September 12, 1963

"The Dick Van Dyke Show"
CBS, various prime times
Premiere: October 3, 1961
Stars: Dick Van Dyke, Mary Tyler Moore
Last Program: September 7, 1966

"The Beverly Hillbillies"
CBS, various prime times
Premiere: September 26, 1962
Stars: Buddy Ebsen, Irene Ryan
Last Program: September 7, 1971

"The Mary Tyler Moore Show"
CBS, Saturdays, various prime times
Premiere: September 19, 1970
Stars: Mary Tyler Moore, Ed Asner
Last Program: September 3, 1977

"All in the Family"
CBS, various prime times
Premiere: January 12, 1971
Stars: Carroll O'Connor, Jean Stapleton
Last Program: September 16, 1979

"M*A*S*H"
CBS, various prime times
Premiere: September 17, 1972
Stars: Alan Alda, Loretta Swit
Last Program: September 19, 1983

"Happy Days"
ABC, Tuesdays, 8:00-8:30 P.M.
Premiere: January 15, 1974
Stars: Ron Howard, Henry Winkler
Last Program: July 19, 1984

"Taxi"
ABC, NBC, various prime times
Premiere: September 12, 1978
Stars: Judd Hirsch, Danny De Vito
Last Program: July 27, 1983

8

The Soap Opera

MARY B. CASSATA

OVERVIEW

Almost from its beginnings, the American soap opera posed an enigma to the broadcasting industry. Despite the fact that no other genre on radio or television could approach its overall record of longevity (some programs are now well into their third or fourth decades), audience loyalty, and earned revenues, the soap opera, unlike any other genre, was to remain at the center of a storm of controversy over its mission, its content, and its impact. Castigated by critics, shunned by elitists, attacked by pressure groups, and virtually ignored by scholars and researchers, the soap opera imposed upon its creative/technical staff the burden of second-class citizenry. The taint extended to the audience, many of whom understandably appeared reticent about admitting any fascination or, indeed, addiction, to the form. "Closet" listeners developed into "closet" viewers. That is until a remarkable transition appeared to take place, when overnight, the American soap opera seemingly achieved its legitimacy. There was an explosion of interest by virtually every group that previously had shunned it; the audience grew larger, more heterogeneous, and younger; and suddenly the form seemed good enough for prime time to copy.

It is within the attributes and conventions of the soap opera form that its unique power to intrigue and to emotionally involve the audience is achieved. A well-known "hooking" strategy is employed as characters are carefully drawn; they grow, develop, and change, as they are born, become socialized, marry, have children, grow old, and die. In the process, the characters become as real as family, good friends, and neighbors, and the audience learns to track their every mood, share their thoughts, dream their dreams, and weep their disappointments. And also in the process, the audience feels better for having purged itself of worry over its own concerns in the face of the unrelenting problems and traumas in the soap-opera world. The fact that the soap opera has been able to adjust to the interests and moods of its audience underscores its organic nature, and it appears that the soap opera of the eighties is merely catching its second wind.

HISTORICAL DEVELOPMENT

While the question of identifying the particular serial that might legitimately lay claim to being the first American soap opera to be aired might preoccupy some students of the form, others prefer to turn their attention to the roots of the continuing story, which are buried deep within history. This group would trace the soap opera's ancestry to such cultural milestones as Greek and Roman mythology; tribal man's spinning his tales of magic around the camp fire; or Scherherezade's saving her head through telling the story that never ended; to the installment stories of Charles Dickens, Henry James, or Anthony Trollope; the domestic novels; and the spine-tingling Saturday matinee serials at the Bijou. The jump to radio—nighttime first, then daytime—and from daytime radio to daytime television seemed to be the serials' ultimate destination until the prime-time serial surfaced, beginning with "Peyton Place" and "Dallas" in the seventies to the likes of "Dynasty," "Knots Landing," "Falcon Crest," "Bare Essence," and, some would claim, "Hill Street Blues" and "St. Elsewhere" in the early eighties. But, as history has shown, when a new medium—for example, cable—comes into prominence, the content of the old becomes the content of the new. And so we find cable experimenting with the serial format, massaging it and moving it into new uncharted territories. While the ultimate picture still remains to be filled in of cable's impact on the network soap-opera industry, it is clear that some impact will be felt, but that network soap operas will adjust to that impact. In other words, there will be some changes, but they will be within the limits of what the broad general public is willing to tolerate.

One of the most fascinating aspects of broadcasting is the fact that there are many people living today who have shared in its early history. Specifically, in the area of the radio soap opera, it would not be too difficult to find those who not only remember but who can speak with authority about the popular serials that debuted in the thirties: "Just Plain Bill," "The Romance of Helen Trent," "Ma Perkins," "Backstage Wife," "Guiding Light," "Our Gal Sunday," "The Road of Life," "Lorenzo Jones," "Joyce Jordan," "Young Dr. Malone," "Life Can Be Beautiful," and "The Right to Happiness," to name but a few. With great relish and accuracy, they will recall intriguing nuggets of information, as, for example, the epigraph of "Just Plain Bill": 'The real life story of a man who might be your next door neighbor . . . a story of people we all know . . . "[1] Or of Helen Trent, "who, when life mocks her, breaks her hopes, dashes her against the rocks of despair, fights back bravely, successfully, to prove what so many women long to prove, that because a woman is thirty-five, or more, romance in life need not be over, that romance can begin at thirty-five."[2] Or, the question raised in the epigraph of "Our Gal Sunday": "Can this girl from a mining town in the West find happiness as the wife of a wealthy and titled Englishman?"[3] It should also be mentioned that the 1937–38 season was memorable for marking what Professor George Wiley termed as "the most ambitious system of duplication ever undertaken: no less than ten of the serials were repeated at a different hour on a different network and often with a different product being advertised."[4] The forties, which began with its best years (1941 and 1942) sporting 60 serials on the air daily, introduced such popular newcomers as "Portia Faces Life," "The Second Mrs. Burton," "Perry Mason," "This Is Nora Drake," "The Brighter Day," and "Front Page Farrell." But by 1950, the number of serials on the air daily diminished by nearly 50 percent; yet although several new serials debuted in that decade, none of the additions were to survive beyond more than accruing a few years of air time. During the fifties, the numbers of serials steadily grew less until finally, the last organ chord for the radio soap opera serial was played out on Friday, November 25, 1960, when brave Ma Perkins bid her loyal audience, "Goodbye, and may God bless you."[5] Other serials that also saw their last broadcast on that day were "The Right to Happiness," "Young Dr. Malone," and "The Second Mrs. Burton."

However, before we move from radio to television, there are several radio milestones that should be reviewed, one of the most important being the concept of block programming, introduced by CBS in the fall of 1933.[6] Prior to this, the broadcast of serials was scattered throughout the broadcast day. Soon, however, there were enough of them to constitute a serial block, and it became obvious that the technique of lumping several of the serials together would appeal to the serial audience. This concept, of course, has persisted until today and must be appropriately recognized for its role in sustaining the record of success achieved by this particular genre.

But no history of the soap opera is complete without touching upon its early sponsors and writers, the concept of the serials (formula), and the structure of the episodic broadcast.

The earliest writers of soap operas were not that different from those of the present day. Frank and Anne Hummert, who have been credited with actually inventing the soap-opera form, for example, stressed spectacle and glamour over the mundane; they deliberately fed to the fantasies and dreams of adult women in much the same way as they hypothesized that comic strips feed to the fantasy needs of children. Initially writing their serials through the Blackett-Sample-Hummert Advertising Agency in Chicago, they soon established Air Features, their own production company, which some critics disdained as a "writing factory." Not totally unlike the way it is today, the Hummerts, as head writers and creators of a serial, wrote the long story. Then, after writing the first two episodes, they turned over the day-to-day writing of the story to dialoguers who today are called "associate writers." Business people, the Hummerts imposed rigid rules for their help to adhere to and dictated that the original concepts of their serials not be tampered with. Their successes included the most popular soap operas of the day, among them "Ma Perkins," "Just Plain Bill," "Stella Dallas," "Front Page Farrell," "The Romance of Helen Trent," and many more.

The antithesis of the Hummerts was Irna Phillips, perhaps the most influential force of all time in the industry. A pragmatist, Phillips built her stories upon character, and to counteract the dream-wish fantasies of the Hummert characters, hers were closer to reality. She created the model for the present day doctor/ nurses/lawyer dominated soap opera; she emphasized marriage, love, and family; she invented the amnesia convention of soap operas, which pumped new life, when needed, into tired plots; it was she who suggested the bold innovation that the quarter-hour serial be expanded to a half hour. Among her successes after her initial creation, "Painted Dreams," were "Right to Happiness," "The Guiding Light," and "Road of Life." When the indomitable writer followed the serials' shift to television, she created "As the World Turns," "Another World," and "Days of Our Lives," which, of course, with "Guiding Light," remain among the mainstays of the television daytime serial menu.

A third writer whose name must be included along with those of the Hummerts and Phillips is Elaine Sterne Carrington. Her creations included "Pepper Young's Family," "When a Girl Marries," and "Rosemary." Moreover, due to her business acumen, she wisely retained ownership of her serials, and her name became one of the few names of writers to be readily recognizable to radio listeners. It was announced at both the beginning and end of each day's episode. Carrington introduced such innovations into her serials as humor, youthful characters, and current slang.

Although the daytime serials were reportedly dubbed "soap operas" because they were sponsored by one soap company or another, cosmetic and food products companies were also included among their sponsors. Thus, the names of such companies as Procter and Gamble, Colgate-Palmolive-Peet, Lever Brothers, General Mills, and American Home Products have been associated with the form. Procter and Gamble, however, is the company most often associated with the soap-opera business, apart from the three commercial networks. Procter and Gamble not only advertised their products on many of the most popular serials throughout the years, but today they continue to own many of the daytime serials outright. These include "Another World," "As the World Turns," "The Edge of Night," "Guiding Light," "Search for Tomorrow," and the recently defunct "Texas."

James Thurber's classic definition of a soap opera, which he wrote in 1948, except for a few obvious caveats and modifications, might be said to be just as appropriate today as it was then. He wrote:

A soap opera is a kind of sandwich, whose recipe is simple enough, although it took years to compound. Between thick slices of advertising spread twelve minutes of dialogue, female suffering, in equal measure, throw in a dash of nobility, sprinkle with tears, season with organ music, cover with rich announcer sauce, and serve five times a week.[7]

Less poetically than Thurber, Sterling and Kittross described the format of the radio soap opera as being "wonderfully simple," with "a brief musical introduction played on the studio organ, a narrator opening the day's episode with a recap of what had happened before, two segments of action separated by a commercial break, and a closing word from the narrator suggesting the problems ahead."[8] The story was deliberately paced to progress slowly, a mechanism which accomplished two purposes: It allowed for the development of character and permitted the listener to occasionally miss an episode without losing the storyline. It was soon apparent that the soap-opera audience was unique in broadcasting: it was characterized by a fierce loyalty, brought about by its emotional involvement in the lives of the characters.

At this point a review of the elements of the soap-opera formula that, according to one critic, remain a good fit for the daytime serial drama of today, would possibly go a long way toward understanding the soap opera's special lure.[9] The formula was articulated by Hubbell Robinson, Jr., in 1933, affiliated at that time with Young and Rubicam, one of the major advertising agencies handling the Procter and Gamble soap-opera accounts.[10] Astutely recognizing that the radio soap opera was developed for the female audience and therefore revolved around the female perspective, Robinson identified the four cornerstones of the soap opera as follows: simple characterization, understandable predicament, centrality of female characters, and philosophical relevance.

The first cornerstone, simple characterization, might be anchored to a study of the social stratification schema of radio soapland reported by Thurber in which six "highly specialized groups" might be identified.[11] These were: (1) homey philosophers (decent and courageous Ma Perkins and Just Plain Bill); (2) Cinderellas (Stella Dallas's daughter Lolly and Hamburger Katie's Nana, who were beautiful and talented, but poor); (3) doctors and nurses (Young Doctor Malone and Joyce Jordan, who represented a group of professionals who seemed to be more in evidence than their patients); (4) young (unattached) women (Helen Trent and Portia Blake Manning, who actively avoided marriage, although they had numerous suitors constantly pursuing them); (5) men with flexible schedules (a factor that was the key to equalizing the numbers of males and females in the soap-opera world); and finally (6) the clean-living good people of both sexes, who subscribed closely to soap opera's morality code. Within many of these categories, of course, were to be found the strong and the weak, the victims, and the victimizers; but if one generalization were to be drawn, so polarized were these characterizations, that there was little confusion in the minds of the audience as to how they would behave. Arguing that despite the multidimensionality of the characters who populate television's soap operas of today, the simple characterization cornerstone of the soap-opera world remains in evidence, with the sophistication of the audience, shored up by the use of soap opera conventions providing the key to understanding the characters, Cassata developed a schema of daytime television serial archetypes of both sexes.[12] These included romantic heroines and heroes; their rivals and antagonists (usually villainesses and villains); benevolent tentpole characters (solid family types); meddlesome, villainous parents and grandparents; professional men and women; and finally the newly emphasized group—children, from toddlers to teenagers.

The second cornerstone, understandable predicament, was anchored squarely within the problems and triumphs of the family. The emphasis in the radio soap opera was placed upon the ordinary happenings of everyday life, buttressed by such familiar signposts as the use of domestic settings, placed in the present time frame, with an emphasis on talk rather than events. Although television's soap operas today sport a slick look, that look has been attained without doing much violence to the domestic settings/present time frame/talk dimensions. The content, within these dimensions, is substantially the same—mainly focusing on personal problems and trauma. A brace of content analyses of soap operas, for example, as carried out by Stedman, Katzman, and Cassata, Skill, and Boadu, dealt with the elements of crime, sickness, and death.[13] Stedman's study explored the criminal elements in the 26 soap operas on the air in 1952 and found 15 cases of serious crimes or matters under litigation as the content of 50 percent of these programs. Katzman's study of TV soap operas, published in 1972, identified 85 cases of "realistic" problems ranging from shady business deals to marital infidelity. And Cassata, Skill, and Boadu identified 191 cases of soap-opera violence, accidents, disease entities and symptomatologies in the 13 soap operas on the air in 1979.

The third cornerstone, centrality of the female characters, remains as the sine qua non of the daytime serial drama. From 1932 to 1939, for example, of the 89 soap operas that debuted during that period, half of them revealed this bias in their titles. "Ma Perkins," "Stella Dallas," "Joyce Jordan," "Big Sister," "Girl Alone," and "Backstage Wife" were but a few of them. Perhaps the more telltale statistic is the fact that fewer than 10 percent of the soap operas of this period bore the names of male leads in their titles. While the television soap opera of today does not reflect the name of either female or male lead in their titles (only one bears the name of a family in its title: "Ryan's Hope"), there is no indication that any shift at all has occurred in the pivotal role played by women, who have come to symbolize "strength" in the serials. During the Great Depression, a triumvirate of elderly widows (being female and elderly are seen as deficits in the media today), Mrs. Moynihan ("Painted Dreams"), Mrs. Moran ("Today's Children"), and Ma Perkins, inspired their legions of listeners to cope with the grave problems that the economy dealt to American families then. Today, with large-scale unemployment facing our nation, some media critics have drawn parallels between the soaps of today and the soaps of this earlier era in terms of their serving to preoccupy the attention of the unemployed.

But women have been celebrated in the soaps for other achievements. From the very beginning, the soap-opera genre portrayed women as professional people: doctors, nurses, lawyers, journalists, business executives; yet, only recently have women professionals been shown as capable jugglers of career and family. Where formerly such women were portrayed as villainesses in radio and early television soaps, they are portrayed more sympathetically today. And one has only to look at the "equalization" factor of the sexes in soap operas in terms of their numbers as reflecting their true numbers in our society to realize how well the soap-opera genre treats women compared to their treatment in prime time. James Thurber, writing in 1948, reflected on the portrayal of the genders. The typical portrayal of soap-opera males as paralyzed from the waist down and confined to their wheel chairs was interpreted by him as the "symbol of the American male's subordination to the female and his dependence on her greater strength of heart and soul."[14] In her analysis of the role of soap-opera women through 50 years of broadcasting, Cassata concluded that "soap-opera women have managed to remain the dominant figures."[15]

The fourth cornerstone of the soap opera genre, philosophical relevance, refers to the conceptual frame of soap operas in general to reflect the basic social concerns prevalent at particular periods of time. Thus, soap operas have reflected such basic truths as "the meek shall inherit the earth" or "virtue is its own reward," hypothesized as being reflective of the moral tone of earlier years as compared to the more self-seeking, egocentric philosophies of later years. Despite such shifts, however, the soap opera has faithfully adhered to ritualizing the family icon within the framework of today's social community. Writes Goethals:

Because of the daily dramatization the shows can encompass not just one but a number of interrelated families. This leads to a complicated interweaving of births, marriages, sicknesses, divorces, lawsuits, infidelities, and reconciliations. The family environment alone cannot accommodate this rich fabric of human experience. To represent the intricacies and multiplicity of families in crisis, it is necessary to include larger communal areas.... These communal spaces, into which all family crises overflow, eventually provide viewers with images of the entire community in which the families reside.[16]

The fact that the emphasis in early vintage soap opera has shifted somewhat to today's daytime serial drama merely reflects the evolutionary perspective of society and its mirror.

While 1960 signalled the demise of the soap opera on radio, it should not be assumed that the introduction of soap operas in television waited until that time. The entry of soap operas into television began in 1951 with "Search for Tomorrow," which still survives today as television's oldest soap opera. In 1951, there were 27 serials on radio. The following year, in fact, saw an increase in the absolute number of radio soaps to 35, but this was to be the radio serials' last infusion of new life. Thereafter, the radio serials began their final journey into oblivion. Television soap operas, on the other hand, shot up from a lone entry in the 1951 season to 17 serials by 1955. In Katzman's landmark study of the television serial, he describes the decade from 1955 to 1964 as one in which a stabilization of the number of soap operas broadcast per day had occurred.[17] However, the 1963–64 season proved to be memorable for two reasons: many of the serials expanded from the 15-minute to 30-minute episode and during that time, a core of eight soap operas were introduced, marking one of the most remarkable groups of serials to emerge on television and signaling them as a mainstay through the next decade, with most surviving into the eighties. (This core of programs included "As the World Turns," "The Doctors," "Edge of Night," "General Hospital," "Guiding Light," "Love of Life," "Search for Tomorrow," and "Secret Storm.") In addition to Katzman's "core" of programs, others introduced during the 1960s were "Another World," "Days of Our Lives," and "One Life to Live," all of which, of course, still survive today. But among the many programs introduced in the 1960s, few of which survived more than a year or two, "Dark Shadows" should be noted. It was unlike any other soap opera in terms of concept. "Dark Shadows" was a campy show, shot through with thrills and chills. Set in a ghostly mansion, with an ingenious plot that revolved around a vampire, the story moved in and out of previous time periods, sometimes making it difficult for the audience to follow the storyline and even more difficult for the producers to sustain creatively. But its following proved to be legion, as "Dark Shadows" cults diffused through the land. By the time the decade of the sixties was to end, the last three 15-minute serials ("Love of Life," "Search for Tomorrow," and "Guiding Light") expanded to half-hour programs, with a record of 17 soap operas being broadcast for 510 minutes daily as the 1970s began. At this point, according to Katzman, every adult in the United States might be said to be viewing two hours of soap operas on the average every week, or to state it more precisely, "Nearly fifty million viewer hours are spent with these programs every day of every week."[18]

The decade of the seventies proved to be one of the most important in the history of soap operas. According to Cassata and Skill, it was to be the decade that would mark the greatest change and the greatest advances in the history of the form; and in a sense, it would prove to be the period in which soap operas were to achieve their legitimacy at last in terms of public critical recognition.[19]

Overall this period had an inauspicious beginning, with numbers of daily serials on the air and the total number of minutes broadcast in decline. Its lowest point—of 390 minutes per day—was reached during the 1973–74 season. Struck down were some of the brighter promises of the daytime airwaves, including, "Bright Promise," "Dark Shadows," "Where the Heart Is," "Love Is a Many Splendored Thing," "A World Apart," and "Secret Storm." Soap operas also spawned other soap operas: "Another World" begat "Somerset," and "Lovers and Friends" became "For Richer, for Poorer," but their potential never materialized. Yet, three of the most successful in today's serial menu were introduced during this decade: "All My Children" has been praised by the critics as being consistently the most excellent soap opera; "The Young and the Restless" achieved almost instant popularity by combining the "new look" of beautiful, young people with the old-fashioned look of vintage soap opera; and "Ryan's Hope" was noteworthy for stressing reality in characters and setting. In the prime-time and late-night line-ups, such "soap operas" as "Mary Hartman, Mary Hartman" (1976), "All That Glitters" (1977), and "Dallas" (1978) were launched. Each of these serials was uniquely different from what has come to be accepted as standard soap opera fare. "Mary Hartman, Mary Hartman," a funny, satirical, sometimes outrageous program that was more soap opera than comedy, for the first time demonstrated that a syndicated program was capable of becoming the "most talked about series on television."[20] Norman Lear's "All That Glitters" was a spoof on role reversals that did not catch on, and "Dallas" achieved its success by making its hero, J. R., a villain who grew meaner by the second.

The decade of the seventies cannot be dismissed without recognizing that this was a decade of experimentation and tremendous change. Program length went from a half-hour format, to 45 minutes, to one hour, with "Another World" even attempting a 90-minutes-per-episode length. There was also much schedule hopping as serials attempted to find the best time slot in a more concentrated programming block. But perhaps the most significant change of all was in audience composition. The daytime serial audience, which heretofore might aptly have been described as "homogeneous," was beginning to look more heterogeneous. Not only was the audience undergoing a shift in gender (79 percent female, 21 percent male), but the audience was definitely becoming younger, better educated, and more diversified in terms of employment and interests. There was, moreover, the emergence of new patterns of viewing: group viewing was taking place in college dormitory lounges, bars, social clubs, senior citizen centers, and the like. There also emerged a category identified as the second generation of soap opera viewers—that is, employed women, who having acquired the habit of watching soap operas while in college, today videotape their favorites while they are in the marketplace, absorbing them during their leisure hours in the evening. Whereas the largest proportion of soap-opera viewers has continued to reside in the south and northeast as before, with but subtle shifts occurring in other regions, the most dramatic change in the viewership has occurred in the area of income. By the time the decade of the seventies was drawing to a close, more than half of the soap-opera audience was reporting an income of over $15,000, a figure in line with that reported by approximately the same proportion of the general public. As Cassata and Skill reported in their analysis of the soap-opera audience from 1970 to 1980: "It would appear during the last 10 years, serial viewing has begun to equalize itself in a demographic sense. Across regions, locales, and income levels, the serial household is beginning to reflect general households across the U.S."[21]

By the time the decade of the eighties began, soap operas were wearing an entirely new face. Not only were they attracting an increasingly broader and more divergent viewing audience, but they were attracting the attention of all of the media, which were eager to report their phenomenal success. It was a case of the media covering the media, obviously something the media like to do. In addition, critics and scholars appeared eager, as never before, to examine more thoroughly the many facets of the soap-opera phenomenon. For it was clear that there was more here than was apparently meeting the eye. With its sweep of the ratings, "General Hospital," for example, was earning more money than its strongest prime-time competitor, "Dallas." Young people all over the country were taking to soaps and the soaps were taking to young people. Older characters and standard plots were being relegated to the back burners; the issues of the soaps of the seventies were out; fantasy was in. A few soaps died: two old ("The Doctors" and "The Edge of Night") and one relatively new ("Texas," another spin-off of "Another World"), as networks were clearing their schedules for more lucrative soap opera ventures. Beginning with the premiere of John Conboy's new soap, "Capitol," a story of power and politics set in Washington, D.C., on the CBS network on March 29, 1982, both ABC and NBC followed suit with new soap operas of their own. On June 27, 1983, ABC launched its first new soap opera in eight years with "Loving," co-created by Agnes Nixon and Douglas Marland. Aiming for a younger audience, their serial was set in the mythical town of Corinth, home of Adelphi University, and although it was initially conceived as primarily a town and gown story, it was not long before the role of the university had been substantially de-emphasized. The latest of the network soaps, "Santa Barbara," was introduced during the time of the Olympic games by NBC on July 30, 1984. Like "Capitol" and "Ryan's Hope," this soap is set in a specific, identifiable community—the California coastal city of Santa Barbara. Although departing somewhat from vintage soap opera by giving high visibility to several Mexican-American characters, it is essentially a story of the interactions of two powerful feuding families.

THEMES AND ISSUES

Soap operas deal with a multiplicity of themes and issues, some conscientiously and carefully constructed and carried out and others, not. However, the essence of soap operas has always resided in the matter of human relationships. Within this framework, soap operas have exercised virtually every theme within the boundaries of what the serial audience and the network overseers have been willing to allow. There is no question that the daytime serial drama has been deliberately pitched to the interests of women, a factor in keeping with the composition of its audience. But as the audience changed and grew in sophistication within the perspective of that of the adult female, and within more recent years, as it embraced larger segments of the adult male audience, as well as notably younger groups of both genders, the themes and issues of the daytime serial have come to reflect these trends and changes. Thus, although some of the conventions of vintage soap opera are employed from time to time (e.g., themes centering about amnesia, temporary blindness, the newly found "lost" parent, etc.), today's soap operas appear to blend realism with contemporary treatments of fantasy topics.

The theme of personal problems is an all-pervasive one for this genre and constitutes a good beginning point for discussion. In their update of the Katzman study, Cassata and Skill compared the problems and events found in the soap opera world in 1970 with the problems found in 1980.[22] Both studies compared one week's worth of soap operas, the Katzman study analyzing fourteen serials and Cassata and Skill, nine. The 85 problems that Katzman found and the 146 problems identified in the 1980 study by Cassata and Skill were categorized into four main strands as follows:

Events	1979	1980
Criminal	14%	16%
Social	26	25
Medical	24	12
Romantic, Marital	36	47
Totals	100%	100%

While the criminal and social events strands showed minor overall differences over the two decades, there was a 50 percent decrease in the area of medical events and over a 25 percent increase in romantic, marital events in 1980 as compared to 1970. In the area of medicine, mental disease, psychosomatic illnesses, physical disability, pregnancies, as well as successful medical treatments and notable medical research were topics common to both time periods; however, they were more frequently treated in 1980. One important qualitative difference appeared to emerge in the 1980 period—that is, systemic diseases, including heart attacks, began appearing, suggesting that more realistic tendencies were beginning to surface even amidst the more conventional soap-opera traumas. In 1970, as in 1980, romantic, marital events occurred more frequently than any others.

While the proportions of criminal and social events in 1970 and 1980 showed minor differences overall, a close examination of the data reveals some interesting and dramatic departures. In 1980, for instance, in the criminal activity arena, there were three times as many threats of violence and four times as many cases of blackmail compared to 1970. In fact of all criminal activity monitored, crimes in 1980 compared to 1970 were of the more sophisticated, cloak-and-dagger, high-adventure type. Similarly, in the category of social problems, the Cassata and Skill analysis revealed a wider range of problems in 1980 than in 1970: black-market adoptions, religious cults, deceptions, friendships in trouble, and prostitution. It appeared that the social problems in 1970 were more closely linked to family: illegitimate children, family estrangements, children in trouble.

The unique quality of audience involvement has inspired soap-opera writers to incorporate specific social issues into the storyline. Aware that the bottom line is profits, these writers never deviated, however, from the entertainment aspect of their stories—they carefully interwove into them socially responsible information campaigns that would appear to emerge quite naturally from storyline and character development. Among the social issues presented have been child and wife abuse, obesity, alcoholism, drug abuse, rape, and mastectomies. Serial drama has dealt seriously with these issues, choosing to stress therapeutic aspects over sensationalism. Therefore, when "One Life to Live" dealt with a drug-abuse storyline, its writers chose to emphasize the rehabilitation aspect, taping scenes at New York City's Odyssey House, a rehabilitation center. Real addicts participated in the discussion resulting in excellent viewer response as well as an overwhelmingly successful information campaign leading a number of people to seek help at Odyssey House.

"The Young and the Restless" and "All My Children" are examples of two soap operas that have dealt responsibly with social issues. "The Young and the Restless's" handling of obesity resulted in the involvement of viewers in the storyline, with some actually losing weight along with that serial's heroine. Another time, the storyline dealt with runaways, and the Chicago National Runaway Crisis Center's toll-free telephone number was projected on the screen as the story progressed. The message being communicated within an arresting storyline was that crisis centers located in numerous cities across the country were there to help youthful runaways by providing food and shelter, clothing, jobs, and counseling. Their message, however, was one of noninterference in terms of contacting family members, unless they were specifically requested to do so by the runaway.

Also, this program's portrayal of victims of mastectomies or rape stressed rehabilitative aspects. Women were given positive, constructive information in both situations to help them to get on with their lives.

Agnes Nixon's reputation for assuming an active stance to instruct the viewer in coping strategies to meet the assaults of life is well deserved. Her soap operas, especially "All My Children," have dealt with such social problems as wife abuse, rape, uterine cancer, teenage alcoholism, and prostitution. Other soap operas have dealt with the right-to-die issue ("Ryan's Hope," "Search for Tomorrow," "One Life to Live," "The Doctors," and "The Young and the Restless"), interracial romance ("Days of Our Lives"), and prison conditions ("Love of Life"). The number of social issues handled by soap operas is impressive.

In their research on the content of soap operas, Cassata and Skill have explored the portrayal and image of older people, the role of family, the portrayal of lifestyles, power roles of the genders, intimate and other interpersonal behaviors, and the role of women.[23] Stereotypical portrayals, the portrayals of minorities, the question of morality, and the portrayal of professional people, especially doctors and nurses, are aspects of the soap-opera genre that have been explored by various researchers.

Unquestionably, the American soap opera has made significant gains in the last few years toward overcoming substantial image problems both among its programming competition and in terms of its acceptance by the broad television audience. Despite the fact that the soap opera may never attain the stature some think it deserves, its place in American society is indisputable. For more than any genre in broadcasting its longevity and pervasiveness have earned it the undisputed title of being part of Americana.

NOTES

1. Manuela Soares, *The Soap Opera Book* (New York: Harmony Books, 1978), p. 174.

2. Robert LaGuardia, *From Mary Perkins to Mary Hartman: The Illustrated History of Soap Operas* (New York: Ballantine Books, 1977), p. 7.

3. Ibid, p. 10.

4. George A. Willey, "End of an Era: The Daytime Radio Serial," *Journal of Broadcasting* 5 (Spring 1961), pp. 97–115.

5. Ibid, p. 97.

6. Raymond W. Stedman, *The Serials: Suspense and Drama by Installment,* 2d. ed. (Norman: University of Oklahoma, 1977), p. 256.

7. I. Settel, *A Pictorial History of Radio* (New York: Grosset & Dunlap, 1960), p. 116.

8. Christopher H. Sterling and John M. Kittross, *Stay Tuned: A Concise History of American Broadcasting* (Belmont, Calif.: Wadsworth, 1978), p. 166.

9. Mary Cassata, "The More Things Change, the More They Are the Same: An Analysis of Soap Operas from Radio to Television," in *Life on Daytime Television: Tuning-In American Serial Drama,* ed.M. Cassata and T. Skill (Norwood, N.J.: Ablex Publishing Corp., 1983), pp. 85–100.

10. Ibid.

11. James Thurber, *The Beast in Me and Other Animals* (New York: Harcourt Brace Jovanovich, 1948).

12. Cassata, "The More Things Change," pp. 90–91.

13. Stedman, *The Serials,* pp. 44–47; Natan I. Katzman, "Television Soap Operas: What's Been Going On, Anyway?" *Public Opinion Quarterly* 36 (Summer), p. 207. Mary B. Cassata, Thomas D. Skill, and Samuel Osei Boadu, "In Sickness and in Health" *Journal of Communication* 29, no. 4, (August 1979), pp. 73–80.

14. Thurber, *The Beast in Me and Other Animals,* p. 220.

15. Cassata, "The More Things Change," p. 98.

16. Gregor T. Goethals, *The TV Ritual: Worship at the Video Altar* (Boston, Mass.: Beacon Press, 1981), pp. 56–57.

17. Katzman, "Television Soap Operas," p. 201.

18. Ibid. p. 202.

19. Mary Cassata and Thomas Skill, " 'Television Soap Operas: What's Been Going On Anyway?'—Revisited," in *Life on Daytime Television: Tuning-In American Serial Drama,* ed. M. Cassata and T. Skill (Norwood, N.J.: Ablex Publishing Corp., 1983), pp. 157–69.

20. Harry Castleman and Walter J. Podrazik, *Watching TV: Four Decades of American Television* (New York: McGraw-Hill, 1982), p. 277.

21. Cassata and Skill, " 'Television Soap Operas," p. 163.

22. Ibid., p. 164.

23. Cassata and Skill, *Life on Daytime Television.*

BIBLIOGRAPHICAL SURVEY

As appears to be the general rule for locating any serious literature on television, the scholarly literature on soap operas demands a determined search.
There is no one subject abstract or index that appears to be more useful than
any other; therefore all the old standbys should be consulted. In addition, a
wealth of information may be discovered from the popular literature of the
daytime serial drama, about this subject, some of which would not be found
anywhere else. Therefore, it is strongly recommended that some of the more
enduring fan-type magazines for this genre be checked such as *Soap Opera
Digest, Daytime TV,* and *Afternoon TV. TV Guide, People Magazine,* as well
as the Sunday newspaper TV guide sections should not be overlooked for their
regular coverage on soap opera storylines and personalities. The bibliography
contains some of the more scholarly works on this subject, although whenever
it was determined that significant analysis of the daytime serial was found even
in the popular press, those citations were also included. For an up-to-date selected
bibliography of popular works, the Cassata and Skill book should be consulted.

BOOKS AND CHAPTERS

Arnheim, R. "World of the Daytime Serial." In *Radio Research, 1942–43,* pp. 34–107.
    Edited by P. F. Lazarfeld and F. H. Stanton. New York: Duell, Sloan and Pearce,
    1944.
Cassata, M., and T. Skill, eds. *Life on Daytime Television: Tuning-In American Serial
    Drama.* Norwood, N.J.: Ablex Publishing Corp., 1983.
Comstock, G. et al. *Television and Human Behavior.* New York: Columbia University
    Press, 1978.
Edmondson, M., and D. Rounds. *From Mary Noble to Mary Hartman: The Complete
    Soap Opera Book.* New York: Stein and Day, 1976.
Gilbert, A. *All My Afternoons: The Heart and Soul of the TV Soap Opera.* New York:
    A&W Visual Library, 1979.
Goethals, G. T. *The TV Ritual: Worship at the Video Altar.* Boston: Beacon Press, 1981.
Goldsen, R. K. "Desensitization and Resensitization: Erosion of Family Feelings." In
    The Show and Tell Machine: How Television Works and Works You Over, pp.
    16–27. Edited by R. K. Goldsen. New York: Dial Press, 1977.
Herzog, H. "What Do We Really Know About Daytime Serial Listeners?" In *Radio
    Research, 1942–43,* pp. 3–33. Edited by P. F. Lazarfeld and F. N. Stanton. New
    York: Duell, Sloan and Pearce, 1944.
———. "Psychological Gratifications in Daytime Radio Listening." In *Readings in
    Social Psychology,* pp. 561–66. Edited by T. Newcomb and E. Hartley. New
    York: Holt and Company, 1947.
———. "Motivations and Gratifications of Daily Serial Listeners." In *The Process and
    Effects of Mass Communication,* pp. 50–55. Edited by W. Schramm. Urbana,
    Illinois: University of Illinois Press. 1965.
Kaufman, H. J. "The Appeal of Specific Daytime Serials." In *Radio Research, 1942–*

43, pp. 86–107. Edited by P. F. Lazarfeld and F. N. Stanton. New York: Duell, Sloan and Pearce, 1944.

Kutler, J., and P. Kearney. *Super Soaps: The Complete Book of Daytime Dramas*. New York: Grosset & Dunlap, 1977.

LaGuardia, R. *From Ma Perkins to Mary Hartman*. New York: Ballantine Books, 1977.

———. *The Wonderful World of TV Soap Operas*. Revised Edition. New York: Ballantine Books, 1977.

Lazarfeld, P. F., and H. Dinerman. "Research for Action." In *Communications Research, 1948–1949*, pp. 73–108. Edited by P. F. Lazarfeld and F. N. Stanton. New York: Harper, 1949.

Lemay, H. *Eight Years in Another World: The Inside Story of a Soap Opera*. New York: Atheneum, 1981.

MacDonald, F. "Soap Operas as a Social Force." In *Don't Touch That Dial*, pp. 231–79. Edited by F. MacDonald. Chicago: Nelson-Hall, 1979.

McQuail, D., J. G. Blumler, and J. R. Brown, "The Television Audience: A Revised Perspective." In *Sociology of Mass Communications*, pp. 135–65. Edited by D. McQuail. Middlesex, England: Penguin Books Ltd., 1972.

Newcomb, H. "Soap Opera: Approaching the Real World." In *TV: The Most Popular Art*, pp. 161–82. Edited by H. Newcomb. Garden City, N.Y.: Anchor, 1974.

Primeau, R. "From Radio Drama to Daytime Stardom: The Rise of the Soaps." In *The Rhetoric of Television*, pp. 188–206. Edited by R. Primeau. New York: Longman, 1979.

Soares, Manuela. *The Soap Opera Book*. New York: Harmony Books, 1978.

Stedman, R. *The Serials: Suspense and Drama by Installment*. Norman, Oklahoma: University of Oklahoma Press, 1971.

Thurber, J. "Soapland," In *The Beast in Me and Other Animals*, pp. 191–260. New York: Harcourt, Brace and Company, 1948.

Wakefield, D. *All Her Children*. New York: Avon Books, 1976.

ARTICLES

Adler, R. "Afternoon Television: Unhappiness Enough and Time." *The New Yorker* 47 (February 12, 1972): 79–82.

Aldrich, P. G. "Defoe, D. —Father of the Soap Opera." *Journal of Popular Culture* 8, (Spring 1975): 767–74.

Astrachan, A. "Life Can Be Beautiful/Relevant: Social Problems and Soap Operas." *New York Times Magazine*, March 23, 1975, pp. 12–13, 54–64.

Buerkel-Rothfuss, N. L., and S. Mayes. "Soap Opera Viewing: The Cultivation Effect." *Journal of Communication* 31 (Summer 1981): 108–15.

Cantor, M. G. "Our Days and Nights on TV." *Journal of Communication* 29 (Autumn 1979): 66–74.

Cassata, M. B., P. Anderson, and T. D. Skill. "The Older Adult in Daytime Serial Drama." *Journal of Communication* 30 (Winter 1980): 48–49.

Cassata, M. B., T. D. Skill, and S. O. Boadu, "In Sickness and in Health." *Journal of Communication* 29 (Autumn 1979): 73–80.

Compesi, R. J. "Gratifications of Daytime TV Serial Viewers." *Journalism Quarterly* 57 (Spring 1980): 155–58.

Downing, M. "Heroine of the Daytime Serial." *Journal of Communication* 24 (Spring 1974): 130–37.

Falk-Kessler, J., and K. M. Froschauer. "The Soap Opera: A Dynamic Group Approach for Psychiatric Patients." *American Journal of Occupational Therapy* 32 (May-June 1978): 317–19.

Fellman, A. C. "Teaching with Tears: Soap Opera as a Tool in Teaching Women Studies." *Signs* 3 (Summer 1978): 909–11.

Fine, M. G. "Soap Opera Conversations: The Talk That Binds." *Journal of Communication* 31 (Summer 1981): 97–107.

Gade, E. M. "Representation of the World of Work in Daytime Television Serials." *Journal of Employment Counseling* 8 (March 1971): 37–42.

Goldsen, R. K. "Throwaway Husbands, Wives, Lovers (Soap Opera Relationships)." *Human Behavior* 4 (December 1975): 64–69.

Greenberg, B. S., R. Abelman, and K. Neuendorf, "Sex on the Soap Operas: Afternoon Delight." *Journal of Communication* 31 (Summer 1981): 83–89.

Gutcheon, B. "There Isn't Anything Wishy-Washy about Soaps." *Ms.,* August 1974, pp. 42, 43, 79–81.

Hardaway, F. "Language of Popular Culture—Daytime Television as a Transmitter of Values." *College English* 40 (January 1979): 517–21.

Johnson, R. E., Jr. "Television Serials Dialogue, and Novelty and Repetition: Structure in 'All My Children.' " *Journal of Popular Culture* 10 (Winter 1976): 560–70.

Kaplan, F. I. "Intimacy and Conformity in American Soap Opera." *Journal of Popular Culture* 9 (Winter 1975): 622–25.

Katzman, N. "Television Soap Operas: What's Been Going On Anyway?" *Public Opinion Quarterly* 36 (Summer 1972): 200–212.

Kilguss, A. F. "Using Soap Operas as a Therapeutic Tool." *Social Casework* 55 (November 1974): 525–30.

———."Therapeutic Use of a Soap Opera Discussion Group with Psychiatric In-Patients." *Clinical Social Work Journal* 5 (Spring 1977): 58–65.

Kinzer, N. S. "Soapy Sin in the Afternoon." *Psychology Today* 7 (August 1973): 46–48.

LaPota, M., and B. LaPota. "The Soap Opera: Literature to Be Seen and Not Read." *English Journal* 62 (April 1973): 556–63.

Lazarus, H. R., and D. K. Bienlein. "Soap Opera Therapy." *International Journal of Group Psychotherapy* 17 (April 1967): 252–56.

Levinson, R. M. "Soap Opera Game: Teaching Aid for Sociology of the Family." *Teaching Sociology* 7 (January 1980): 181–90.

Lopate, C. "Daytime Television: You'll Never Want to Leave Home." *Radical America* 11 (January–February 1977): 33–51. Also in *Feminist Studies* 3 (Spring–Summer 1976): 69–82.

Lowery, S. A. "Soap and Booze in the Afternoon: An Analysis of Alcohol Use in Daytime Serials." *Journal of Studies on Alcohol* 41 (September 1980 : 829–38.

Lowry, D. T., G. Love, and M. Kirby. "Sex on the Soap Operas: Patterns of Intimacy." *Journal of Communication* 31 (Summer 1981): 90-96.

McAdow, R. "Experience of a Soap Opera." *Journal of Popular Culture* 7 (Spring 1974): 955–65.

Maykovich, M. K. "Comparison of Soap Opera Families in Japan and United States." *International Journal of Sociology of the Family* 5 (Autumn 1975): 135–49.

Meehan, T. "Soaps Fade But Do Not Die." *New York Times Magazine,* December 4, 1960, pp. 27–28, 111–12.

Mendelshohn, H., T. Espie, and G. M. Rogers. "Operation Stop-Gap." *Television Quarterly* 8 (Summer 1968): 39–52.

Miyazaki, T. "Housewives and Daytime Serials in Japan: A Uses and Gratifications Perspective." *Communication Research* 8 (July 1981): 323–41.

Nixon, A.E. "In Daytime TV, the Golden Age Is Now." *Television Quarterly* 10 (Fall 1972): 49–54.

———. "Coming of Age in Sudsville," *Televison Quarterly* 9 (Fall 1970): 61–70.

Porter, D. "Soap Time: Thoughts on a Commodity Art Form." *College English* 38 (April 1977): 782–88.

Ramsdell, M. L. "The Trauma of TV's Troubled Soap Families." *Family Coordinator* 22 (July 1973): 299–304.

Rose, B. "Thickening the Plot." *Journal of Communication* 29 (Autumn 1979): 81–84.

Schreiber, E. S. "The Effect of Age and Sex on the Perception of TV Characters: An Inter-Age Comparison." *Journal of Broadcasting* 23 (Winter 1979): 81–93.

"Sex and Suffering in the Afternoon." *Time* 107, no. 2, January 12, 1976, pp. 46–53.

Sullivan, M. F. "Soap Opera in the Classroom." *Educational Leadership* 37 (October 1979): 78–80.

Turow, J. "Advising and Ordering: Daytime, Prime Time." *Journal of Communication* 24 (Spring 1974): 138–41.

Wander, P. "The Angst of the Upper Class." *Journal of Communication* 29 (Autumn 1979): 85–88.

Warner, W. L., and Henry, W. E. "The Radio Day Time Serial: A Symbolic Analysis." *Genetic Psychology Monographs* 37 (1948): 3–71.

Waters, H. F., with J. Huck, G. Hackett, and E. Gelman. "Television's Hottest Show." *Newsweek,* September 28, 1981, pp. 60–66.

Whan, F. L. "Special Report: Daytime Use of TV by Iowa Housewives." *Journal of Broadcasting* 2 (Spring 1958): 142–48.

Willey, G. A. "End of an Era: The Daytime Radio Serial." *Journal of Broadcasting* 5 (Spring1961): 97–115.

Willey, G. "The Soap Operas and the War." *Journal of Broadcasting* 7 (Fall 1963): 339–52.

Willis, F. "Falling in Love with Celebrities." *Sexual Behavior* 2 (1972): 2–8.

DISSERTATIONS

Adams, M. "An American Soap Opera: 'As the World Turns,' 1956–1978." Ph.D. dissertation, University of Michigan, 1980.

Bond, M. D. "Soap Operas and Liberal Education Values." Ph.D. dissertation, University of North Carolina at Greensboro, 1980.

Compesi, R. J. "Gratifications of Daytime Television Serial Viewers: An Analysis of Fans of the Program 'All My Children.' " Ph.D. dissertation, University of Oregon, 1976.

Downing, M. "The World of the Daytime Serial Drama." Ph.D. dissertation, University of Pennsylvania, 1975.

Fine, M. G. "A Conversation and Content Analysis of Interpersonal Relationships in

Selected Television Soap Operas.'' Ph.D. dissertation, University of Massachusetts, 1980.

Lowery, S. A. "Soap and Booze in the Afternoon: An Analysis of the Portrayals of Alcohol Use in the Daytime Serials." Ph.D. dissertation, Washington State University, Pullman, 1979.

Modleski, T. "Popular Feminine Narratives: A Study of Romances, Gothics, and Soap Operas." Ph.D. dissertation, Stanford University, 1980.

Sari, T. "The Relationship between Daytime Serials and Their Viewers." Ph.D. dissertation, University of Pennsylvania, 1977.

Schreiber, E. S. "Comparative Assessments of Characters of Different Ages in Four Daytime Television Serials by Viewers of Varying Ages." Ph.D. dissertation, Pennsylvania State University, 1977.

Sirota, D. R. "An Ethnographical, Ethnomethodological Study of Soap Opera Writing." Ph.D. dissertation, Ohio State University, 1976.

Stedman, R. "A History of the Broadcasting of Daytime Serial Drama in the United States." Ph.D. dissertation, University of Southern California, 1959.

Timberg, B. M. "Daytime Television: Rhetoric and Ritual." Ph.D. dissertation, University of Texas at Austin, 1979.

Tucker, D. E. "A Multivariate Analysis of Soap Opera Viewing." Ph.D. dissertation, Bowling Green University, 1977.

MISCELLANEOUS

Breen, M. P., and J. T. Powell. "Why College Students Watch Soap Operas," Paper presented at the Annual Meeting of the Broadcast Education Association, Las Vegas, 1980. ERIC Document: ED 185627.

Finz, S. D., and J. Waters. "An Analysis of Sex-Role Stereotyping in Daytime Television Serials." Paper presented at the Annual Meeting of the American Psychological Association, Washington, D. C., 1965. ERIC Document: ED137652.

Johnson, F. L. et al. "Familial Relationships, Topics and Conversation Styles in Family Interaction on Television in the U.S.A." Paper presented at the World Congress of Sociology, Uppsala, Sweden, 1978. ERIC Document: ED159897.

Summers, L. P. *Daytime Serials and Iowa Women*. Des Moines, Iowa: Radio Station WHO, 1943.

VIDEOGRAPHY

"Search for Tomorrow"
  CBS, NBC, various day times
  Premiere: September 3, 1951
  Created by: Roy Winsor

"Guiding Light"
  CBS, various day times
  Premiere: June 30, 1951
  Created by: Irna Phillips

"The Secret Storm"

CBS, various day times
Premiere: February 1, 1954
Created by: Roy Winsor
Last Program: February 15, 1974

"The Edge of Night"
ABC, 4:00–4:30 P.M.
Premiere: April 2, 1956
Created by: Irving Vendig

"General Hospital"
ABC, various day times
Premiere: April 1, 1963
Created by: Frank and Doris Hurley

"Another World"
NBC, various day times
Premiere: May 4, 1964
Created by: Irna Phillips

"Dark Shadows"
ABC, various day times
Premiere: June 27, 1966
Created by: Dan Curtis
Last Program: April 2, 1971

"All My Children"
ABC, various day times
Premiere: January 5, 1970
Created by: Agnes Nixon

"The Young and the Restless"
CBS, various day times
Premiere: March 26, 1973
Created by: William J. Bell and Lee Phillip Bell

"Ryan's Hope"
ABC, 12:30–1:00 P.M.
Premiere: July 7, 1975
Created by: Claire Labine and Paul Avila Mayer

9

The American Made-for-TV Movie

GARY EDGERTON

OVERVIEW

There is an often stated misconception that the American made-for-TV movie is today's "B" picture. The implication, of course, is that the telefeature is an inferior product modeled on the Hollywood paradigm. In fact, this supposition is an oversimplication of the generic origin and nature of the TV movie. Primarily, this film genre is derivative of both the traditional Hollywood feature movie and the live dramatic TV anthologies of the 1950s, although other secondary progenitors are certainly traceable in the aesthetics, technology, economics, and culture of American society during the past century. All the same, the made-for-TV movie fits comfortably into the developing narrative tradition that is at present inextricably linked to commerce and industry in the United States.

Telefilms now cost millions of dollars to make and are channeled throughout the world by a number of old and new distribution technologies. Very few TV movies garner the astronomical income of a Hollywood blockbuster; still, the substantial majority of "vidpics" return a profit in contrast to only 20 to 25 percent of their more prestigious counterparts. In addition, a successful made-for-TV movie can attract approximately 40 to over 70 million viewers at any one time, while only 20 million people attend *all* the theatrical movies in America in any given week. Obviously, the commercial influence of the telefilm is immense, as this type of picture has been a consistently productive programming source for over twenty years at the three networks. Paradoxically, however, the aesthetic and socio-cultural significance of this genre is usually dismissed. The American telefeature is underrated; and for the most part, it still labors under a critical reputation as Hollywood's "stepchild" or second-class citizen. Nevertheless, the made-for TV movie, albeit young, is a rich and varied genre, encompassing its own unique formal, stylistic, and topical strategies on which the process of definition and evaluation can continue to develop.

As with any genre, determining the parameters of the telefilm remains its foremost challenge. Since 1964, well over 1,500 examples have appeared on network television in the United States, varying in length from 74-minute offerings fitting into 90-minute time slots to a 26.5-hour mini-series. Overall, this aggregation can be divided into three manageable categories: the telefeature, the docudrama, and the mini-series. In addition, all three of these subgenres can be either original creations or story adaptations from a previous source. First, the telefeature refers to a fictional narrative produced for TV that is a discrete entity occupying at least 90 "commercial" minutes but not exceeding one evening of programming. Next, the docudrama is a story film designed to recreate actual persons, places, and events. Moreover, this form is purported to blend essential aspects of both the fictional and the documentary film modes, although the narrative form has usually dominated in its subsequent execution on American television to date. Thirdly, the mini-series is an extended telefeature or docudrama that is broadcast in multiple segments over two or more nights. As a final note, these three short explanations are meant to be working definitions, and each will be elaborated on in more detail.

From a critical standpoint, movies made-for-television have historically struggled to adapt and eventually merge their roots in the classical cinematic style of Hollywood with the inherent contingencies of the television medium. In the beginning, the grammar and story types of the theatrical feature took precedence,while the basic method of storytelling and characterization indigenous to TV drama eventually surfaced as well to better balance the aesthetic form that is today characteristic of the television movie. What resulted is a media hybrid with a variation of its own rules governing technique and plot structure, an audio-visual dialect, a star system, and particular thematic emphases and concerns. In other words, the usual telefilm is a "high-concept" picture, that borrows from the intrinsic topicality of the TV medium itself. Likewise, this concept can be a controversial theme, a historical recreation, or a spin-off from an already popular book, play, theatrical feature, or cultural trend. The important point here is that there is a previously established familiarity between the American viewing public and the subject matter at hand. Additionally, the TV movie's inherent aesthetic strategy is to provide a personal dramatization of this theme or topical issue, while always remaining within the bounds of "good taste" and network proprieties. In this way, the feature-length film form is filtered through the domesticity, "living-room" intimacy, and social relevancy of the television environment. In turn, this union suggests a new and evolving generic type, mixed in origin, but essentially unique as the ultimate offspring arising out of the respective traditions of Hollywood in the 1930s and 1940s and the golden age of TV drama during the 1950s.

HISTORICAL DEVELOPMENT

The idea of any "golden age"—be it Hollywood in the 1930s and 1940s or television drama during the 1950s—is best taken by all with a grain of salt. This observation is meant in no way to demean the high points of either of these eras; still, it is far more probable that the golden label applied to both film and TV springs more from feelings of nostalgia than a rigorous critical view. As film historian Gerald Mast recounts: "Although Hollywood produced some 7,500 feature films between 1930 and 1945, only some two dozen directors and two hundred films maintain their original power and entertainment value (as opposed to their "camp" value) today."[1] The same can certainly be said for television's live dramatic anthologies from 1947 through 1961. Indeed, TV's golden reputation stands today in spite of the fact that most of these original broadcasts are lost forever. In fact, less than 100 are available for critical appraisal at the Museum of Broadcasting in New York; and, of course, this contingent contains many of the most celebrated and, no doubt, best possible examples from this particular genre and era. On one level, the media historian can evidently investigate most of the more influential representatives on kinescope recordings or videotape. In another way, however, judging an era by its best, rather than its median level, is far more likely to result in a less tempered, more inflated estimation of worth.

In contrast, there exists no similar inclination to champion a golden age of movies made-for-television. In America this genre is like the TV medium itself— forever available in prime time and syndication, as well as clearly accessible to mass understanding. There is a critical pretension that dies hard, even in mass communication studies, which assumes that if an art object is easily obtained and understood, odds are it is insubstantial and maybe frivolous. In retrospect, however, the American made-for-TV movie is not really the bastard son of Hollywood and television. On the contrary, the telefilm is the rightful generic heir to this lineage, which, if not golden in hindsight, is appropriately rich and provocative in form, style and content.

Hollywood's two peak years for attendance were 1930 and 1946, when approximately 90 million people attended the movies each week. Like television after it, the film industry during this era provided America with a commercial product that was moderate, often times bland, and essentially family oriented. The movie colony's ultimate target was always the majority consumer, and this mass focus did not waver at all until the networks began usurping this audience much against Hollywood's will in the late 1940s. In 1947, there existed a split structure between film and television production; Hollywood, of course, was the home of the feature-length film, while TV programming was clearly centered in New York City. Within ten short years, though, this structure would be incessantly linked together by its shared relations in economics, technology, and most obviously, talent and storytelling.

On May 7, 1947, the live dramatic anthology format was introduced to TV with the premiere of the "Kraft Television Theatre." Over the next fifteen years, dozens of other similar programs appeared with varying degrees of success, including the "Philco-Goodyear Playhouse," "Omnibus," the "Hallmark Hall of Fame," the "U.S. Steel Hour," and the "Armstrong Circle Theater." Most of these offerings were one hour in length, although a few also filled a 30- or even a 90-minute time slot. One of these longer weekly series was "Playhouse 90," "the most ambitious and . . . the standard against which all the others are judged."[2] As a genre, however, television drama clearly prefigured the made-for-TV movies as "an effective barometer of contemporary attitudes and values. In fact, television's original plays, those which [were] indigenous to the new electronic medium of communication, [had] assumed the major responsibility for exploring the social reality and domestic problems of a majority of Americans."[3]

The dramatic formula underlying these weekly anthologies was first explored in 1948 at "Studio One" by its producer, Worthington Miner. In adapting this show from radio to TV, "his concern was with the visual impact of the stories" rather than sole emphasis on the written word, as "Miner's major contribution to television drama was more in his experimentation with camera techniques and other innovations in what the viewer saw . . . than in what was heard."[4] In turn, the visual emphasis evident in these live television dramas was clearly of a different nature than that which was then standard in Hollywood. The informal, personal, and private depiction of everyday characters in an assortment of medium shots and close-ups was the forte of these teleplays. Characterization became the crucial generic element, as plot structure and setting were both scaled down as a means of better shaping these conventions to the shorter length and segmentation of prime time and the lower definition and smaller aspect ratio for the TV screen. As writer-producer Rod Serling remembered, "the key to television drama is intimacy. The facial study on a small screen carries with it a meaning and power far beyond its usage in motion pictures."[5]

Film grammar, on the other hand, was evolving in a totally different direction during the 1950s. Ambitious productions touting wide-screen, color, and larger-than-life story-types and protagonists were the norm of the day. In addition, the amount of on-location shooting also increased with the imminent demise of the studio system. By the mid-1950s, Hollywood and television were already experiencing a symbiosis of programming content on two levels. First, several smaller movies companies, most notably MCA's Revue, Columbia's Screen Gems, and United Artist's Ziv, began filming prime-time series for the networks in 1951; and more importantly, the major studios also became involved in series TV between 1955 and 1957. Hollywood next flooded the television market with most of its pre-1948 features and shorts in the 1956–57 season.[6] However, these movies were only broadcast on network schedules for 1956 and 1957 because of both the cost factor and the mistaken assumption by the networks that feature films would not attract large audiences, since many people had already seen these pictures in movie theaters. It wasn't long before this inexperienced prognosis was proven false as the Hollywood movie reappeared in earnest on prime time in the early 1960s.

On September 23, 1961, NBC introduced its new series, "Saturday Night at the Movies," featuring Marilyn Monroe, Lauren Bacall and Betty Grable in

"How to Marry a Millionaire." This broadcast was an astounding success and pointed to Hollywood's growing inclination to release its post-1948 movies to television. Seven more series representing all three networks and every night of the week appeared over the next five years. The culmination of this trend was an ABC Sunday telecast of "The Bridge on the River Kwai" in September 1966. "An estimated 60 million viewers in 25 million homes sat down to watch one movie" for which ABC had "paid Columbia Pictures $2,000,000."[7] Even at the price, the American Broadcasting Network was understandably delighted, as the television viewing public clamored to consume big-budget, star-studded, color extravaganzas from Hollywood in the privacy of well over 95 percent of the homes in the United States. The only drawbacks, of course, were that these feature pictures were still over four years old on the average; and more critically, Hollywood's supply was quickly being depleted by prime-time TV. Consequently, ABC's video stage was appropriately set for the successful nurturing of the American made-for-TV movie.

The precise birth date of the telefilm is arguable, although only a handful of contenders exist prior to 1961. Claims range from Ron Amateau's 60-minute Western, "The Bushwackers," which appeared on CBS in 1951, to Disney's "Davey Crockett, King of the Wild Frontier," which was broadcast as three separate segments during the 1954–55 debut season of "The Wonderful World of Disney."[8] Also, it was not uncommon during the late 1950s for TV's dramatic anthologies to present some of their teleplays on either film or videotape. Three shows especially, "Desilu Playhouse," "Kraft Theatre," and "The Bob Hope Show," filmed a number of their one-hour offerings, while a few of these presentations were even expanded into a second hour airing the following week as a finale of a two-parter.[9] Still, these haphazard examples have really more to do with trivia than historical precedent, as the man primarily responsible for pioneering the formal properties of the telefeature is Jennings Lang, a New York lawyer who became programming chief for MCA's Revue in the late 1950s.

Lang had been promoting a longer form beyond the television series as early as 1957. "He began his experiments with anthology shows like 'The Alfred Hitchcock Hour' and 'The Chrysler Theater,' in the one-hour format, and he had a big hand in the first 90-minute regularly scheduled series, 'The Virginian,' " which premiered on NBC in 1962.[10] Nineteen sixty-two was also the year that the powerful talent agency, the Music Corporation of America (MCA), purchased Universal Pictures. As a result, this operation absorbed and merged with Revue, which, in turn, considerably extended the operational purview of Jennings Lang and his subsequent television ventures. Lang, now of Universal Television, foresaw "the era of the TV epic, when an entire evening [would] be given over to a single spectacular, made for the occasion."[11] In fact, the term "event programming" had not even been coined yet, although each network would be exploring this strategic avenue in their own separate ways by 1966.

As mentioned earlier, the fall of 1966 was when ABC first decided to begin telecasting a number of Hollywood "blockbuster" films, including "The Bridge on the River Kwai'' and later "The Robe.'' CBS, on the other hand, strove for prestige programming to counterbalance its lineup of popular, though pedestrian situation comedies, such as "The Beverly Hillbillies,'' "Green Acres,'' "Petticoat Junction,'' the "Andy Griffith Show,'' and "Gomer Pyle, U.S.M.C.'' These specials were composed mostly of important American plays, like "Death of a Salesman" and "The Glass Menagerie,'' which actually pulled moderate, though respectable ratings for a time. Most important, however, Lang was first able to interest NBC in financially promoting the made-for-TV form in the spring of 1964. By 1966, it was apparent to both Universal TV and NBC that they had gambled themselves into developing a television genre of enormous potential, as economic dividends were realized almost immediately from this feature-length hybrid. In contrast, however, much of the aesthetic and socio-cultural possibilities inherent in the telefilm would lie dormant for another five years.

NBC and MCA, Inc., inaugurated 1964 by creating "Project 120,'' a never fully actualized weekly film anthology whose very name echoed the live dramatic series of the 1950s. NBC allotted $250,000 for the first telefeature, as MCA-Universal hired Hollywood journeyman Don Siegel to direct " 'Johnny North,' " an adaptation of Ernest Hemingway's short story, 'The Killers,' " starring John Cassavetes, Lee Marvin, Angie Dickinson, and Ronald Reagan in his last role.[12] The movie that resulted eventually cost over $900,000 and was deemed by the network "too spicy, expensive, and violent for TV screens.''[13] Clearly, it was evident to both NBC and MCA from the outset that the budgetary constraints and the dictates of content would be different for the telefilm from what was previously expected for the usual theatrical picture. As a result, "Johnny North" was retitled "The Killers,'' and the film was subsequently released to movie theaters nationwide. Mort Werner, NBC-TV vice president in charge of programming at the time, reflected upon this experience: "We've learned to control the budget. Two new 'movies' will get started soon, and the series probably will show up on television in 1965.''[14]

Actually, the very first made-for-TV movie, "See How They Run,'' premiered on October 17, 1964, a few months sooner than expected. This Universal production is a mediocre crime melodrama that was quickly followed six weeks later by the broadcast of Don Siegel's next excursion into the telefilm genre, "The Hanged Man.'' Like "The Killers" before it, Siegel's second assignment for NBC-MCA is another remake of a classic film noir, "Ride the Pink Horse.'' Without a doubt, this movie along with the only telefeature to appear during the 1965–66 season, a Western pilot for Dale Robertson entitled, "Scalplock,'' both point to the fact that the early TV movie was more derivative of Hollywood for source material than any other dramatic avenue. In fact, the telefilm had not yet produced its own crop of production talent. In the late 1960s, this genre harkened most to Hollywood's least "respectable" genres for story ideas and themes: the Western, the melodrama, the spy thriller, and the horror/supernatural tale. Therefore, in retrospect, it is obviously no surprise that the trade publications and movie critics alike were immediately inclined to christen this new form—the rebirth of Hollywood's B-movie; indeed, it would take the made-for-TV film genre a dozen more years to outgrow this benign, though ultimately disparaging label.

Still, all three networks were alerted to the windfall potential inherent in the TV movie by the end of the 1966–67 season. During Thanksgiving weekend in 1966, NBC hyped its two-hour pilot "Fame Is the Name of the Game" as a "World Premiere" on its "Saturday Night at the Movies." To the pleasant surprise of NBC's programming department, this rather predictable remake of Alan Ladd's 1949 investigative mystery, "Chicago Deadline," now starring Tony Franciosa, Jill St. John and Susan Saint James, garnered a 44.4 percent share for its timeslot. Corporate wisdom had already concluded that, although a semi-frequent series of telefilms was evidently a resurrection of the anthology format, it would none the less be better not to remind prospective audiences that stars and story types would not recur on a regular basis. Instead, pretesting implied that the network should exploit the fact that this was the first public presentation ever of these movies; and NBC could not argue with the subsequent results.

NBC's next "World Premiere" was Rod Serling's thriller and character piece, "The Doomsday Flight." This telefeature aired exactly three weeks after "Fame Is the Name of the Game," and did even better in the ratings. In response, ABC and even CBS began gearing up for additional TV movie production. Actually, eight of the eleven telefilms broadcast during 1966–67 were Universal-NBC products. A staggering figure about these "World Premieres" is that each had a Nielsen rating over 20; and, additionally, "they had, on the average, an audience of 20 percent more people than the average of all other movies shown on the networks."[15] In retrospect, "both 'Fame Is the Name of the Game' and 'Doomsday Flight' turned up among the ten most popular films on TV that season," while MCA-Universal was also becoming a major supplier of prime-time programming in America.[16] The 1967–68 season would be an even greater source of optimism for the telefeature, as this form went on to average 42.2 percent of the available audience for the year; in comparison, theatrical films claimed only 32 percent.[17]

The next major innovation in the TV movie category was the inauguration of "The ABC Movie of the Week" in the fall of 1969. Programming trends already suggested that the American viewing public would be receptive to a movies made-for-television anthology that would be available on a regular weekly basis. "In 1960 there were 76 series on the three networks; in 1967–68, the total (had) dropped by one-fourth."[18] Clearly, specials and feature films of all kinds were now competing successfully with variety shows, half-hour comedies, and hour dramas for the available space on prime time. Barry Diller, the young and newly promoted head of prime-time programming at ABC, is the man most responsible for conceptualizing the TV movie of the week at this network. Diller and his boss, Leonard Goldberg, the vice-president in charge of programming, negotiated a deal with Universal Television that would enable the telefeature to become more prominent and widespread than ever before. "It was an innovative twenty-six-week series of original, ninety-minute 'world premiere' movies specially produced (at an average cost of $375,000 per movie) for television, and it became a roaring success"[19] So much so, in fact, that "in the first five years of MOW [Movie of the Week], Diller managed to place 20 films on the list of 25 all-time top-rated made-for-TV movies."[20]

Experience gained during the first few years of producing "The ABC Movie of the Week" refined those practical and essential characteristics of the genre that were first explored by Jennings Lang, before he transferred over to Universal's theatrical film division in the early 1970s. Lang and his replacement, Sid Sheinberg, along with Diller and Goldberg codified that the usual telefeature would evidently have a tight budget, a short shooting schedule, a high-concept storyline, and use as much in house talent and publicity as possible. By the end of the 1969–70 schedule, both ABC and NBC were experimenting with a handful of new plot and thematic directions that expanded the TV movie beyond traditional Hollywood formulas. Small, personal dramas, somewhat more reminiscent of the live television anthologies of the 1950s than theatrical feature films, approached such relevant subjects as Vietnam ("The Ballad of Andy Crocker"), marital infidelity ("Silent Night, Lonely Night"), race relations ("My Sweet Charlie"), and environmentalism ("A Clear and Present Danger"). In addition, the made-for-TV movie secured its first Emmy awards on June 7, 1970, as Richard Levinson and William Link (scriptwriting) and Patty Duke (acting) all won recognition for their work on "My Sweet Charlie," an "NBC World Premiere Movie." This was an important indicator showing the inevitable acceptance of the telefilm by the National Academy of Television Arts and Sciences. Within two more years, "Brian's Song" would not only be awarded the Emmy, but also the coveted Peabody Award for dramatic excellence, ensuring a growing recognition of the added quality and subsequent status now being accorded the TV movie genre.

These institutional acknowledgments were more a sign of approaching sophistication than any public admission that a new and mature aesthetic and sociocultural film form had arrived. Several of the aforementioned telefeatures are certainly dated today, while a handful of their contemporaries that won fewer or no awards at the time—including "Stranger on the Run," "Prescription: Murder," "Deadlock," "Then Came Bronson," "Tribes," "Jane Eyre," "Thief," "Duel," "The Night Stalker," "Goodnight My Love," "That Certain Summer," and "The Marcus-Nelson Murders"—are all equally interesting studies in the development of the telefilm genre. Still, the TV movie again demonstrated a pattern that previously manifested itself in both Hollywood and series television: the tendency for creative talent to flourish despite the presence of commercial restraints, once the generic form is defined and understood. In this way, the faint beginning of the mini-series and the telefilm version of the docudrama were slowly emerging as movies of the week by 1973.

In 1971, the cost of the usual telefeature had risen slightly to $400,000 when

NBC decided to invest $2.1 million for "Vanished," a four-hour two-parter, based on the Fletcher Knebel best seller.[21] This novel-to- television aired on two succeeding nights in March 1971 and received a respectable share of the audience, as well as two Emmy nominations for Richard Widmark's and Robert Young's acting. In January 1973, a two-part adaptation of "Frankenstein" appeared on ABC's late night "Wide World of Mystery" series, while NBC countered eleven months later with its own version, "Frankenstein: The True Story." Still, none of these productions quite had the impact of Lorimar and Lee Rich's "The Blue Knight," a four-hour mini-series that was broadcast in one-hour nightly segments between November 13 and 16, 1983. This gripping drama starring William Holden was both a critical and ratings success and marked the first major triumph for an American mini-series on network television.

The formal roots of the developing mini-series in the United States are directly traceable to innovations explored during the previous decade by the British Broadcasting Corporation. Americans had their first taste of the longer format when NET (National Educational Television) ran the 26-part, BBC-produced "Forsyte Saga" on a weekly basis beginning in October 1969. This adaptation of John Galsworthy's novels was one of public television's few hits that year. Next, in the fall of 1970, the newly formed Public Broadcasting System brought the British mini-series here to stay when it first telecast "Masterpiece Theater." Subsequent offerings, such as "Upstairs, Downstairs," would later strongly influence the style and content of what was to come from American producers.

The first domestic production to approach the cost and dramatic scope of the British mini-series was Screen Gems and ABC's six-hour, $2.5 million novel-to-television, "QB VII." Essentially a courtroom melodrama, this two part presentation attracted over 40 million people nightly on March 29 and 30, 1974, and ended up receiving thirteen Emmy Award nominations. Nevertheless, it was Universal and ABC's 12-hour, "Rich Man, Poor Man," that finally established the mini-series on network television. Broadcast as six, two-hour segments over a seven-week time period, this adaptation of Irwin Shaw's best-seller held the American viewing public in rapt attention between February and March of 1976. More importantly, however, "Rich Man, Poor Man" was the most successful U.S. mini-series yet to translate the aesthetic strategy of the British long-form— presenting a prime-time soap opera that clearly evokes socio-historical themes— to a plot structure, setting, and characters that were more appropriate to American culture and audience sensibilities. In fact, the success of "Rich Man, Poor Man" spurred ABC to proceed with its plans to finance additional mini-series, including an even more ambitious undertaking based on Alex Haley's "Roots."

The docudrama, on the other hand, has a long and provocative history in literature, theatre, film, radio, and even several live dramatic TV anthologies, most notably in occasional segments of the "Hallmark Hall of Fame," the "Armstrong Circle Theater, " and also "Profiles in Courage." In all these various media, however, the crucial dilemma with the docudrama is destined to remain the inveterate tension between history and fiction that is embodied in the very name of this subgenre. Is reality being distorted under the guise of poetic license? Are not all stories based in one way or another on "fact"? Obviously, there are no simple answers to these questions, and the controversy surrounding the docudrama in all media is sure to continue; all the same, discussion concerning the made-for-TV docudrama is destined to be more heated than most, simply because of the power and pervasiveness of the television medium.

The first docudrama presented in telefilm form was "The Weekend Nun," a December 1972 broadcast. This small and intimate melodrama was based on the life of a young sister caught between her vocation and her job as a juvenile probation officer. Overall, this film had little influence, since the next made-for-television docudrama would not appear for another fifteen months. In March 1974, though, some of the best talent in the TV movie genre teamed up to produce "The Execution of Private Slovik." Writers Richard Levinson and William Link and director Lamont Johnson, who had previously created two other controversial telefeatures together, "My Sweet Charlie" (race relations) and "That Certain Summer" (homosexuality), again tackled a delicate portrayal that explored the story of the only American soldier executed for desertion in World War II. This film was both widely acclaimed and commercially successful. At this time, docudrama production also began to show subsequent signs of life at the three networks.

In the spring of 1975, David Wolper presented his first docudrama of note, "I Will Fight No More Forever," a touching dramatization of the 1877 rebellion of Chief Joseph and the Nez Perce Indians. This was another of only five made-for-TV docudramas aired during the first ten years of the telefilm. Nevertheless, the 1975–76 season would be the turning point for this subgenre, as 24 of 72 TV movies that season were based on real people, places, and events.

In brief review, on October 2, 1975, Lamont Johnson directed George C. Scott, William Devane, and Lois Nettleton, in an involving teleplay by David Rintels entitled "Fear on Trial," which recounted the blacklisting era of the 1950s. Three days later, the thin line between fact and fiction was distorted and abused as Sissy Spacek starred as "Katherine," a rich girl turned revolutionary in a TV movie that apparently exploited the Patty Hearst affair. On January 11 and 12, 1976, the four-hour, "Eleanor and Franklin" aired as the first docudrama mini-series. This superb production was recognized with nine Emmys, including "Outstanding Special," and best director for Daniel Petrie. Next, Lorimar's "Helter Skelter" became the most watched docudrama in television history on April 1 and 2, 1976. This CBS presentation, based on the Charles Manson "family" and the trial involving the Tate-LaBianca murders, pulled a successive 57 and 60 share of the prime-time audience, respectively. In turn, the docudrama was now firmly established as a made-for-TV staple by the spring of 1976.

The short shooting schedule characteristic of the TV movie genre provides for an extremely brief turnaround time, beginning when a news event occurs to when it can be subsequently depicted as a docudrama. The most famous case in point is the July 4, 1976, Israeli raid on the airport at Entebbe, Uganda, in order to rescue a planeload of hostages. On December 13, 1976, David Wolper premiered "Victory at Entebbe," a big-budgeted extravaganza starring Kirk Douglas, Richard Dreyfuss, Helen Hayes, Burt Lancaster, and Elizabeth Taylor. Not to be outdone, producer Edgar Scherick countered with Charles Bronson, Peter Finch, Martin Balsam, Sylvia Sidney, and Jack Warden in "Raid on Entebbe" on January 9, 1977. Although this second offering is a better-than-average telefilm, both the speed of production and the star-studded approach of each of these docudramas indicate merely two of many important reasons why the license of fiction usually overrides the historicity of narrative when this subgenre becomes a movie of the week.

As for the telefeature, it embarked on its second decade as a subgenre of considerable creative force and escalating prestige. Even a mainstream periodical like *Time* heralded: "it may be that 1974 will enter such television annals as there are as the year made-for-TV movies came of age."[22] This enthusiasm is small wonder since within the previous four months the American viewing public had the opportunity to see nearly a dozen gripping social and humanistic melodramas, including the aforementioned "Private Slovik," "A Case of Rape," "The Morning After" (alcoholism), Tom Gries's "The Migrants," and John Korty's "The Autobiography of Miss Jane Pittman" (slavery in America). It was clearly evident that the writing, acting, and directing characteristic of the usual American telefilm had made a quantum leap forward to the point where even an occasional movie critic was finally acknowledging the genre's improvement. In fact, one month after Richard Schickel's comment appeared in *Time*, *The Saturday Evening Post* proclaimed: "it is obvious that the entire future of movies as mass cultural events lies with movies made for television."[23]

By the mid-1970s, ABC was the avowed leader in both experimenting with the widest range of possible story and subject ideas and expanding the conventions of the TV movie genre. NBC was obviously second, while CBS had not undertaken full-scale telefeature production until 1972 and consequently lagged far behind in third place. Still, CBS would soon be advancing itself in this area, as all three networks joined in record outputs by the end of the decade. In fact, 32 percent of all the feature films shown on television during the 1975–76 season were made-for-TV movies. By 1978–79, this figure would be up to 57 percent and rising, as the telefilm was now the undisputed champion on network television in America.[24]

The telefeature would also flourish by becoming ever more relevant during the rest of the 1970s and the beginning of the 1980s. Although an occasional TV movie could yet evoke the traditions of a classic Hollywood genre, by and large, most telefilms further refined an aesthetic strategy that was now inseparable from the form of reality programming. In this way, both the telefeature and the docudrama spent most of the decade capitalizing on an assortment of sociocultural angles, such as teen-age sex, venereal disease, handicaps, death, middle-age pregnancy, sexism, alcoholism, war, racism, drug abuse, child molesting, ecology, cancer, and unemployment, to name only a few. Moreover, a sampling of the more accomplished offerings since the mid-1970s includes "Larry" (mental institutions), "Tell Me Where It Hurts" (a disenchanted housewife's search for meaning), "The Law" (lawyers and the courts), "Queen of the Stardust Ballroom" (loneliness and alienation), "Hustling" (prostitution), "Sybil" (mental illness), "The War between the Tates" (marital infidelity), "Breaking Up" (divorce and a search for personal meaning), "The Storyteller" (television violence), "See How She Runs" (a middle-aged housewife's self-assertion), "Siege" (harassment of senior citizens), "First You Cry" (mastectomy), "Too Far to Go" (a dissolution of a marriage), "Fast Friends" (a working mother/behind-the-scenes at a television network), "Friendly Fire" (Vietnam and the loss of a son), "Strangers: The Story of a Mother and Daughter" (familial estrangement), "The Jericho Mile" (prison life and running), "Guyana Tragedy: The Story of Jim Jones" (cults), "Gideon's Trumpet" (the court and the prison systems), "Off the Minnesota Strip" (teen-age runaways), "Skokie" (neo-Nazism and anti-Semitism), and "Playing for Time" (the Holocaust). Certainly, this listing can only begin to cite a fraction of over 1,500 shows that aired. A distinguished minority of this total deals with their subjects with honesty, integrity, and human sensitivity. A number of the 1,500 TV movies also fall toward the other end of the spectrum, where issues are reduced to mere formula and topics are ultimately exploited in either naive or condescending ways.

On February 11, 1979, ABC's telefilm "Elvis" actually outrated two Hollywood blockbusters, "Gone with the Wind" and "One Flew over the Cuckoo's Nest," following a head-on-head confrontation during a "sweeps week." After this ratings milestone for the TV movie, network executives no longer underestimated the potential of this genre as a viable and dominating source of "event programming." Of course, the subgenre that is most responsible for this attitude is the mini-series, and the first and most celebrated display of grabbing the undivided attention of over 70 million American viewers every night for more than one week belongs to ABC's "Roots."

David Wolper's production of "Roots" ran on eight consecutive evenings from Sunday, January 23, through Sunday, January 30, 1977. In reporting this media happening, *Variety* aptly surmised several days later, *"Roots Remakes TV World in Eight Nights!"*[25] This mini-series was a dramatization of Alex Haley's family history, covering two hundred years and a number of generations. "Roots" so completely captured the imagination of middle America, that seven of the eight segments placed on the top-ten list of most viewed television programs of all time, while the one remaining portion also reached thirteenth at the time. Overall, "the A.C. Nielsen Co. recorded an average 66 share of the audience—130 million people [tuned into "Roots" at one time or another]—more than had ever watched anything, anytime, anywhere."[26] Quite simply, "Roots" proved to be the supreme example of "event programming," as ABC not only profited from this mini-series itself, but in addition, its entire prime-time schedule was promoted by the increased exposure and enthusiastic attention.

Over the next three years, ABC and NBC especially tried to reconstruct the success of "Roots" with several more attempts at budgeting and producing telefilms in the long form. These results were generally mixed until the 1980s, as only NBC's four-part, 9½-hour, "Holocaust," which aired in mid-April 1978, even approached the widespread popularity and appeal of "Roots." In fact, a handful of mini-series were outright disasters, especially ABC's "The French Atlantic Affair" and NBC's "King." In these cases, the respective networks had no choice but to suffer low ratings and a nightly humiliation until the multi-part telefilm in question simply came to the end of its run.

ABC, NBC, and CBS learned very quickly that the key to a successful mini-series is to create the idea that it is "special" in the "collective mind" of the American viewing public. In turn, this strategy fosters a commitment on the part of the spectator to keep coming back as the story unfolds nightly. The majority of mini-series are now profitable in the 1980s; and more importantly, they embody the quality and prestige necessary to attract viewers back to the networks from the rapidly growing cable audience in the United States.[27] The three most notable and stupendous successes in recent years have been NBC's five-part, 12-hour "Shogun," in September 1980; ABC's seven-part $40 million "The Winds of War" in February 1983; and ABC's four-part "The Thorn Birds," in April 1983, which ended up passing both "The Winds of War" and "Roots," to become the most watched mini-series of all time. According to the final A.C. Nielsen ratings, 140 million Americans saw at least some portion of this steamy melodrama.

As a final note, a new production source for the telefilm has already appeared in the form of pay-television. As is evident to everyone involved in or watching the movie, broadcasting and/or cable industries, television has entered a period of rapid transition during the past decade. As a result, the TV movie genre is not immune to these larger developments in the mass communication and entertainment industries in general. Specifically, HBO premiered its first made-for-pay-TV movie, "The Terry Fox Story," in May 1983. This docudrama starring Eric Fryer and Robert Duvall garnered strong reviews. For the 1983–1984 season, HBO presented a half-dozen more of its own made-for-pay TV movies, including its first mini-series costing $12 million, "The Far Pavilions"; in turn, this pay TV network continued its plans to diversify its programming agenda in 1984–1985 by further expanding into telefeature production.[28] In addition, Showtime, The Movie Channel, and The Disney Channel all followed suit in this new move towards premiering originally produced telefilms during 1984 with a number of their own offerings as well.[29]

As for the future of the made-for-TV movie at the three networks, expectations couldn't be brighter. NBC and ABC are both planning to increase their already substantive output of two-hour telefilms and mini-series for the 1983–1984 season. Also, CBS Entertainment TV finally plans to balance its network-leading number of telefeature and docudrama productions with an added emphasis on the long form for the first time. Clearly, since the growth of pay-television, the made-for-TV movie is the "bread and butter" of network TV, at least as far as feature films are concerned.

As the theatrical movie became the favorite of pay outlets like HBO, Showtime, and The Movie Channel in the late 1970s, all three networks set out to fill the product shortage and progressively higher rental fees, by aggressively producing more movies on their own. In turn, more films are made for television each year than are presently being released to movie theatres nationwide by Hollywood's six major studios. Also, more talent than ever before is now working in the TV movie genre, and the average cost per film has risen to just above $2 million. In conclusion, the business prognosis for the telefeature, the docudrama,as well as the mini-series, is bullish, while a simultaneous development and growth in generic form, style, and content has seemingly benefited from this commercial explosion of the telefilm during the past five years. Optimistically, this trend should continue, at least, for the near future.

THEMES AND ISSUES

A rather curious and ultimately telling remark accompanied a number of the reviews for the theatrical features "Kramer v. Kramer" (1979) and "Ordinary People" (1980). In referring to the interpersonal focus of these films, an opinion was presented that each one resembles movies made-for-television, or "seem as nicely suited to the small screen as to the large."[30] The implication of these statements, of course, travels far beyond the particulars of these two films; it also suggests that these critics and their readerships alike know how telefilms are different from the theatrical variety. In addition, this knowledge, at present, probably also lingers in a kind of instinctual grey area caused by watching hours of these TV films but not really thinking all that much about them. In other words, a critical view for the made-for-TV movie is yet to be developed, although the process of defining, analyzing, and better understanding this relatively new albeit hybrid form is clearly imminent. Consequently, this section will address three questions. First, how does the TV movie constitute a genre? Second, how do the conventions of this genre work as both a constraint and catalyst for the artists and producers in the industry? And third, how does this genre invoke a context for audience participation and response?

To begin with, generalizations can be offered about the form, style, and content of the telefilm genre, even though exceptions are inevitably evident when referring to specific TV movies. Nevertheless, the form of the made-for-TV movie is shaped by particular rules governing plot structure and idiom. Like all products of commercial television, there are very definite structural contingencies to the telefilm both internally and externally. Internally, every TV movie has precise time constrictions because of advertising requirements. In this way, the story is segmented by "act breaks" every ten to fifteen minutes to provide time for approximately two minutes of commercials. These sequences, therefore, affect the cause-effect relations in the narrative whereby climaxes of increasing intensity are usually accomplished as the drama proceeds along toward its denouement. As a result, scriptwriters and directors working in the telefilm are confronted with an exact formal imperative, just as if they were writing a sonnet, or composing a rondo.

External structure is where the made-for-TV movie is most obviously a hybrid. Clearly, the 90-minute and two-hour telefilms resemble the overall duration of a theatrical picture, although the TV movie must be strict about fitting into its time-slot. On the other hand, pilots and mini-series are also connected to the format of series television. Pilots introduce a prospective prime-time concept in a feature-length contour, while mini-series actually expand the format one step further by employing a serial formula. In this manner, the external structure of the mini-series attains a middle ground between a one-shot movie and a continuing series.

Characteristically, the speech form or idiom of the TV movie, and most of what is on television for that matter, is melodrama. David Thorburn most aptly points this out in his seminal article, "Television Melodrama." Still, what are the grammatical obligations of melodrama? Overall, this idiom is composed of five basic ingredients: a predictable fictional world, the display of exaggerated emotions, stereotyped characters, distinct poles of good and evil with justice usually prevailing, and resolution through action. Thorburn argues that contemporary audiences intuitively understand the conventions of melodrama so completely that attention can be shifted from the "formula-story" to the performers who "display themselves so intensely and energetically."[31] In other words, characterization usually dominates plot on TV, and the inherent intimacy of the medium is best fulfilled by an aesthetic of performance. Consistently, most telefilms emphasize this strategy as themes are generally played out by no more than a handful of protagonists on a very personal level. The audience closely identifies with the relevant issue being dramatized, and thus responds in an equally confidential way in the privacy of their homes.

The form of the made-for-TV movie also is complemented by its generic style. Stylistics, of course, refer to the repetition of specific filmic and video techniques into an identifiable look and sound. The aesthetics of the TV movie, as with any genre, are codified by usage and tradition. Time allows for the trial-and-error process of exploring the most appropriate methods of realizing the aesthetic of performance by the artists and producers and the corresponding sense of closeness elicited from the viewers. Technically, then, the typical telefilm emphasizes new and intimate shot types, usually favoring the medium shot, the close-up, and the extreme close-up; a shallow depth-of-field and higher key lighting strategies because of the low definition of the TV picture; very simple and confined settings; uncomplicated editing, characteristically in continuity style; and a straightforward and functional use of sound.

The great teleplays of the 1950s are where a reliance on many of these techniques began. Without a doubt, close shot types allow for the psychological revelation of facial studies. This approach can even be successfully practiced to the near exclusion of the long shot. For example, not only is the drama of the three-hour "The Missiles of October" largely dependent on faces and expressions, it is infrequent that more than one actor is occupying the frame at any one time. The performances are gripping, as these characterizations supersede, as well as find a way to complement, the story of the Cuban missile crisis, which has ultimately been oversimplified in this docudrama. In other words, the acting which is highlighted and magnified by the intimate shot selection carries the film off, not the plot line. This physiognomic stress and its resulting camera style is not all that uncommon for the TV movie in general.

There is less room for experimentation with other visual and audio techniques associated with movies made for television than is comparatively possible with a theatrical feature. Two major problems are the smaller budgets and the shorter shooting schedules employed in the usual telefilm which, of course, restrict the amount of technical improvisation that is possible. The emphasis in telefeature production is then grounded on simply getting the job done on time and for the projected expense, while the stylistic challenge, if at all possible, is to make a $2 million made-for-TV movie look and sound like it cost two or three times that much money. Many talented filmmakers—such as Daniel Petrie, David Greene, Delbert Mann, John Korty, Steven Spielberg, Lamont Johnson, Richard Pearce, John Badham, and Joseph Sargent, just to name a few—have done just that by expanding the techniques used in the telefilm through their respective works. The TV film genre embodies a number of other aesthetic imperatives that are better understood and acknowledged than ignored and pointlessly mishandled. Both the relatively small video screen, with its limited definition, and the lack of adequate sound reproduction (which is subsequently the result of the mediocre speakers that are inside the average television receiver) are two major restrictions that, at least for the time being, are part of the technology of making movies for this medium.

Even an exercise in pure filmmaking like Steven Spielberg's "Duel" is a case in point. Essentially, this telefeature is a chase thriller involving a protagonist in a car being pursued by an unseen antagonist in a trailer truck. All the high tension sequences are edited in a rapid and uneven montage style that is very effective. Spielberg consistently keeps the camera firmly transfixed on various medium shots and close-ups of the automobile, its driver played by Dennis Weaver, and the ominous black transporter, although each combatant spends most of the story hurtling down an interstate through such wide-open spaces as a desert and a mountain range. In contrast, a theatrical film would characteristically use longer shot types and would manipulate the multiple planes of compositon—foreground, midground, and background—in order to highlight movement within the frame and thus externalize the conflict as much as possible. In "Duel," however, tight shots are customarily restricted to one plane at a time, as Spielberg emphasizes inner complexity and characterization over physical action alone. In this way, the limited texture of the television picture is turned from a liability to an asset because the point-of-view is placed squarely on the face of Weaver and his internal conflict. Similarly, Spielberg uses as much audio flexibility as is presently available to him. He frequently fluctuates the volume as a means of exciting and sometimes jarring the viewer. Nevertheless, the subtleties of pitch, tone, and multi-track recording are, by and large, lost in the process of telecasting this film.

A similar problem arises with lighting for TV movies. Maintaining the appropriate clarity of the televised image usually demands high-key and middle-high-contrast lighting strategies as opposed to the harsh shadows thrown in a low-key setup. For example, Peter Hyams's entertaining telefilm parody of film noir entitled "Goodnight My Love" couldn't quite capture the appropriate dark and gloomy look of this Hollywood style from the 1940s and early 1950s. Part of the difficulty here was that this movie made for television was originally shot on videotape, which immediately sacrifices a significant degree of picture quality and visual flexibility. Still, a filmed version would have ultimately lost much of its definition and contrast as well, for it too would have had to have been broadcast over a characteristic home television monitor. As Pauline Kael has so perceptively pointed out: "we almost never think of calling a television show 'beautiful,' or even complaining about the absence of beauty, because we take it for granted that television operates without beauty."[32]

Beauty, in and of itself, is not really missed either. The style of the telefilm, like the medium itself, hardly needs to be aesthetically transcendent. Instead, it tends toward a new kind of video realism that is simultaneously intimate and personal in design. The made-for-TV-movie genre is more commonplace than beautiful, and its technical potential is aimed at transmitting the everyday, however imperfectly. Overall, the well-crafted television film is effective, pervasive, immediate, and alarmingly contemporary. For lack of a better name, the style of the TV movie is generally referred to as "reality programming."

This inclination toward "telerealism" also suggests the content priorities of the made-for-TV movie. As alluded to earlier in this chapter, telefilms are now issue-oriented in nature, and they consistently use occurrences derived from the day-to-day happenings in America's cities and heartland as common references on which to build their plots, characters, and themes. Certainly, "television programs . . . don't 'reflect' American society in any precise sense, but to be popular they do need to express, in their various conventional stylized ways, some of the real feelings and concerns of their audience."[33] Put another way, made-for-TV films are the "televisionization" of contemporary American interests, affectations, and obsessions. In a very real sense, when a socio-cultural issue becomes subject matter for a movie of the week, it is a fairly reliable indicator that middle America is about to begin addressing this idea, although subsequent assimilation in the national character is ultimately a much longer and complicated process involving every American institution.

The telefilm also has an evolving production network, complete with its own collection of procedural constraints and catalysts. These codes of operation developed rapidly; and overall, they were highly derivative of Hollywood's old studio system. The early days of the made-for-television movie revived the contract player, as the established film companies continued to expand their TV operations. Above-the-line personnel of all sorts became regularly employed in making films for TV, especially by Universal. This company, in fact, was so stimulated by the TV movie that it "turned out 80 feature films in 1972, breaking an industry record set back in 1927."[34] Of this number, however, 55 were telefilms, as more film than ever was now being shot in Hollywood, but for release to both the theatrical and television windows combined.

In this process, the TV movie industry also successfully developed its own star system. In the beginning, only feature film stars who were past their prime were attracted to work in telefilms. Occasionally an actor of the stature of Henry Fonda would appear, but, by and large, limited budgets and prestige forced TV movie companies to look elsewhere for onscreen as well as offscreen talent. Ultimately this constraint turned into a catalyst, as a wholly new cadre of "home grown" actors, some borrowed from prime-time series television, began to populate the TV movie. A partial listing of the featured players and character types who emerged during the first decade of telefilm production includes Patty Duke Astin, Diane Baker, Gene Barry, Ted Bessell, Gary Busey, Robert Conrad, Richard Crenna, Barbara Eden, Barbara Feldon, Sally Field, James Franciscus, Larry Hagman, Hal Holbrook, Cloris Leachman, Elizabeth Montgomery, Stephanie Powers, Lee Remick, Martin Sheen, Lindsay Wagner, Robert Wagner, Dennis Weaver, and William Windom. Clearly, this catalogue of names varies according to degrees of expertise and charisma, as would a comparable grouping of the top theatrical movie stars. Still, the TV movie business learned when Elizabeth Taylor and Richard Burton "bombed out in 'Divorce His/Divorce Hers' " in 1973, that popularity in the theatrical film world did not necessarily translate into success on television.[35] In contrast, most of the aforementioned TV movie stars would usually guarantee solid ratings by their presence in a telefilm.

The process of realizing this made-for-TV movie production system resulted in at least five significant developments that unequivocally separated the respective emphases of the TV and theatrical film industries. First of all, the TV movie genre created many more leading and supporting roles for women than its older and more established counterpart, especially during the 1967–76 decade. The previous listing of telefilm stars suggests this pattern somewhat. Second, and to a lesser degree, the made-for-TV movie provided more work for blacks and other minorities. Unquestionably, nonwhites are still underrepresented in television movies. On the other hand, opportunities for blacks in the theatrical film culture have been close to nonexistent since 1973, after a small but vital renaissance between 1968 and 1972.

Third, there has always been a crossover in talent between movies made for television and films produced for theaters. In fact, one of the major justifications for the misconception that the made-for-TV movie is today's "B" movie is the assertion that the telefilm is really a training ground on which the better talents can learn their trade, and eventually "graduate" to theatrical feature filmmaking. Some of the more glamorous examples are those directors who have made this transition, including John Badham, Michael Ritchie, and, of course, Steven Spielberg, and these men are subsequently cited as proof positive for the "B" movie "farm system" theory. Contrary to this popular belief, however, most above- and below-the-line talent that work in telefilms choose to stay within this form for most of their careers. Furthermore, during the past decade there has actually been far more crossover from the theatrical side to TV movies than vice versa; there are a number of crucial reasons why the flow has been stronger in this particular direction.

The drawbacks in producing movies made for television are well known and publicized. Budgets have been generally five times smaller than the average theatrical film ever since 1972. As a result, there is little time for rehearsal, shooting schedules are approximately four times shorter, while the comparable shooting ratio is about half as much footage.[36] All in all, these limitations can be a source of persistent consternation to workers who are used to the greater resources available in movies made for theaters.

As an alternative, however, TV movies also offer three attractive inducements for Hollywood talent. First, and most practically, the job market in the telefilm industry is now bullish. Indeed, steady work and substantial salaries can be a bright incentive for employees who are used to the mercurial and fickle nature of the entertainment industry in general. Next, as scriptwriter Fay Kanin explains, the prospects of reaching a group with the size of a potential television audience is both exciting and an incentive: "when we did 'Hustling,' which had an audience of about forty-eight or fifty million, and when we did 'Friendly Fire' and we had sixty million, I got the full impact. There is something about the way television can relate very personally to vast numbers of people that I must say is extremely heady. And extremely awesome."[37] Lastly, the approach of TV movies is much different than the big-budget, high-tech blockbusters that are now characteristic of Hollywood. In turn, some creative people do prefer the smaller scaled-down movies made for television that specialize in "people, relationships," and "strong subjects."[38] Obviously, working in either the television or the theatrical film mode is a trade-off to some extent. Nevertheless, it is no longer valid to think of the made-for-TV movie as the contemporary "B" picture. Instead, it has emerged with an identity all its own; today, the telefilm is unique unto itself.

The fourth development that distinguishes movies made for television from the Hollywood feature film is its reliance on "high-concept" subject matter. In other words, "for the TV-movie, there is no word of mouth. Execution is irrelevant. You have only one shot at the audience. The title has to grab them."[39] In comparison, where the average advertising and marketing outlay for a theatrical picture today is nearly $7 million, the networks can only count on "a strong story premise and a promotable hook—something that can be summed up in one line in *TV Guide*.''[40] Consequently, it is imperative that telefilm topics already have a strong recognition factor with the American viewing public. The downside of this, of course, is that both the names of TV movies and the initial exposition of storyline and characters—approximately the first 10 to 15 minutes of the picture—are designed both to grab an audience and make sure that it doesn't change the channel. Therefore, titles and opening sequences can often pander to the lowest common denominator by employing gratuitous sexual and violent innuendo. An alternate ploy is to be overly sentimental, as in the handicap telefilm subgenre, which is sometimes critically and rightfully referred to as the "disease of the week." Nonetheless, these constraints of content have often been transcended by very talented filmmakers. For example, since only a small portion or the most superficial trappings of the telefilm are those parts that usually end up being the most formulaic and/or exploitative, many moviemakers have used the rest of the film's structure, style, and content to create innovative and breakout concepts and offbeat approaches. Again, compromise is inherent in the commercial sponsorship of the form, while the emergence of the made-for-pay-TV movie should go a long way toward easing the more hysterical aspects common to the worst in network telefilms. More importantly, though, a strong and vivid identity based on topicality and "telerealism" now enlightens the American TV movie genre, despite these occasional excesses.

Fifth, the characteristic made-for-TV movie audience is demographically more flexible than the usual attendees of theatrical feature films. Most movie theater-goers are between 12 and 35, and fall into a pyramid shaped distribution, where the widest rung—the base of the structure—is formed by the youngest viewers. As the audience members get older, the pyramid in turn narrows progressively to its point. The median moviegoer is a teenager, between 17 and 19 years old. The most popular theatrical movies typically reflect the age and maturity of this target audience. In contrast, the composition of telefilm audiences varies widely. Actually, each night of the week is programmed for a different age, sexual, racial, educational, geographical, and socio-economic make-up. Overall, though, the characteristic TV movie viewer is older than the customary movie theater attender. The broadcast standards department acknowledges this fact and allows more flexibility in topics and approaches in movies made for television when compared to prime-time series. Adult themes and messages are today more common on the small screen than even in movie theaters. Certainly, a major part of this is due to the demands, needs, and expectations of the respective television movie audiences. Nevertheless, as the average American gets older, she or he opts to see more and more movies on TV, and an increasing and substantial number of these pictures also tends to be telefilms.

Movie theaters and wide screens are scarcely on the verge of extinction. Still, it is hardly rash to pose that the future of the movies is far more intertwined with television than with any other distribution-exhibition medium now available. Growth and expansion of the TV film genre was an inevitable step, once television production moved to the West Coast for good in the mid-1950s. In this way, it was only a matter of time before the Hollywood studios began doing for TV what they have always done best, namely produce feature films. In the interim, movies made for television have also become an "event," outgrowing their usual ninety-minute to two-hour length and spilling over into multiple evenings attracting tens of millions of viewers. Like the medium of television itself, the TV movie is a great legitimizer of trends, fads, and social issues. It also helps set the standard for exactly who and what are important, at least for the moment, to the American viewing public. Network executives busily try to gauge popularity through their research departments, which provide them with "Q scores" and "comp makeups" in a corporate exercise that is, for the most part, irrelevant to those more than eighty million families watching in the intimacy of their own private television environments.[41] Over the last two decades, the made-for-TV movie has found success by gearing itself more and more toward the domesticity of this setting, as the telefilm genre has taken hold and flourished by touching the average American viewer with entertainment, insights, and emotions that ultimately find their deepest expression at home.

NOTES

1. Gerald Mast, *A Short History of the Movies* (New York: Bobbs Merrill-Pegasus, 1971), p. 274.

2. Tim Brooks and Earle Marsh, *The Complete Directory to Prime Time Network TV Shows; 1946–Present*, rev. ed. (New York: Ballantine Books, 1981), p. 605.

3. William I. Kaufman, ed., *Great Television Plays*, with an introduction by Ned E. Hoopes (New York: Dell Publishing, 1969), p. 9.

4. Brooks and Marsh, *The Complete Directory to Prime Time Network TV Shows*, p. 723.

5. Kaufman, *Great Television Plays*, p. 10.

6. The reason that post-1948 movies were not released to television at this time is because films made after August 1948 were bound by contractual agreement whereby performers had to be paid additional income for subsequent TV showings.

7. Charles Champlin, "Can TV Save the Films?" *Saturday Review*, December 24, 1966, p. 11.

8. Darrell Y. Hamamoto, "Interview with Television Producer Rod Amateau of 'Dukes of Hazzard,' " *The Journal of Popular Film and Television* (Winter 1982), p. 166. Alvin H. Marill, *Movies Made for Television* (New York: Da Capo Press, 1980), p. 10.

9. Douglas Brode, "The Made-for-TV Movie: Emergence of an Art Form," *Television Quarterly* (Fall 1981), p. 55.

10. Bill Davidson, "Every Night at the Movies," *Saturday Evening Post*, October 7, 1967, p. 32.

11. Henry Ehrlich, "Every Night at the Movies," *Look*, September 7, 1971, p. 62.

12. "Johnny North," *TV Guide*, May 2, 1964, p. 8.

13. Henry Harding, "First Attempts at Making Movies for TV," *TV Guide*, July 4, 1964, p. 14.

14. "Johnny North," p. 9.

15. Davidson, "Every Night at the Movies," p. 32.

16. Harry Castleman and Walter J. Podrazik, *Watching TV: Four Decades of American Television* (New York: McGraw-Hill, 1982), p. 191.

17. Judith Crist, "Tailored for Television," *TV Guide*, August 30, 1969, p. 7.

18. Davidson, "Every Night at the Movies," p. 31.

19. Patrick McGilligan, "Movies Are Better Than Ever—on Television," *American Film* (March 1980), p. 52.

20. Dwight Whitney, "The Boom in Made-for-TV Movies: Cinema's Stepchild Grows Up," *TV Guide*, July 20, 1974, p. 23.

21. Ehrlich, "Every Night at the Movies," p. 62.

22. Richard Schickel, "The New B Movies," *Time*, April 1, 1974, p. 51.

23. Benjamin Stein, "Hooked on Television Movies," *Saturday Evening Post*, May 1974, p. 34.

24. Cobbett Steinberg, *Reel Facts: The Movie Book of Records*, rev. ed. (New York: Vintage Books, Random House, 1982), p. 30.

25. Castleman and Podrazik, *Watching TV*, p. 275.

26. Dwight Whitney, "When Miniseries Become Megaflops," *TV Guide*, July 19, 1980, p. 3.

27. Stuart Bykofsky, "The Miniseries Come of Age," *The Blade*, Toledo, Ohio, January 9, 1983, p. TV1.

28. Harry F. Waters with George Hackett and Don Shirley, "Can HBO Change the Show?" *Newsweek*, May 23, 1983, p. 81.

29. Tom Girard, "Indie Product for Disney Channel," *Daily Variety*, April 21, 1983, p. 1.

30. Peter J. Boyer, "Made-from-TV Executives," *American Film* (July-August 1983), p. 16.

31. David Thorburn, "Television Melodrama," in *Television: The Critical View*, 3d ed., ed. Horace Newcomb (New York: Oxford, 1982), p. 536.

32. Pauline Kael, *Kiss Kiss Bang Bang* (New York: Bantam Books, 1971), p. 277.

33. Robert Sklar, "The Fonz, Laverne, Shirley, and the Great American Class Struggle," in *Television: The Critical View*, 3d ed., ed. Horace Newcomb (New York: Oxford, 1982), p. 82.

34. Thomas W. Bohn and Richard L. Stromgren with Daniel H. Johnson, *Light and Shadows: A History of Motion Pictures*, 2d ed. (Sherman Oaks, Calif.: Alfred Publishing, 1978), p. 387.

35. Whitney, "The Boom in Made-for-TV Movies," p. 26.

36. A shooting ratio refers to the percentage of footage shot during the entire production period to the actual amount of film remaining in the print that is released to movie theaters and television. In this way, the typical shooting ratio for a telefilm is characteristically between 3:1 and 4:1.

37. Fay Kanin, "Dialogue on Film," *American Film* (March 1980), p. 58.

38. Ibid., p. 58.

39. Benjamin Stein, "Words that Sell in TV-Movie Titles," *TV Guide*, July 25, 1981, p. 34.

40. "Movies on the Tube," *Newsweek*, April 10, 1972, p. 87.

41. Q scores are measurements of a TV star's popularity. Comp makeups are a statistical designation of a television show's demographic appeal.

BIBLIOGRAPHICAL SURVEY

A historical-critical view of the American made-for-TV movie is just beginning; and consequently, most of the sources now available on the subject are either available in popular journals, like *TV Guide, Time,* and *Newsweek,* or in the various trade publications, such as *Daily Variety, Variety, The Hollywood Reporter,* and *Broadcasting.*

In addition, there are also a handful of very useful reference books. Alvin Marill's *Movies Made for Television* and Christopher Wicking and Tise Vahimagi's *The American Vein: Directors and Directions in Television* are both extremely helpful as overviews of the telefilm in particular, while Tim Brooks and Earle Marsh's *The Complete Directory to Prime Time Network TV Shows, 1946–Present,* rev. ed., and Harry Castleman and Walter J. Podrazik's *Watching TV: Four Decades of American Television* are excellent directories of prime-time programming in general.

Lastly, Richard Levinson and William Link's *Stay Tuned: An Inside Look at the Making of Prime-Time Television,* Douglas Brode's "The Made-for-TV Movie: Emergence of an Art Form," and Patrick McGilligan's, "Movies Are Better Than Ever—On Television" all include a more comprehensive critique of the TV movie, and are therefore good places to start a subsequent investigation of this genre. This selected bibliography is a guide for further readings.

BOOKS AND ARTICLES

Adler, Dick. "Where Do New Series Come From?" *TV Guide,* August 28, 1971, pp. 5–8.

————, and Joseph Finnigan. "The Year America Stayed Home for the Movies," *TV Guide,* May 20, 1972, pp. 6–12.

Allen, Tom. "The Semi-Precious Age of TV Movies." *Film Comment,* July-August 1979, pp. 21–23.

Arlen, Michael J. "Upriver in Samurai Country," "Surprised in Iowa, Surprised in Nam," and "Adrift in Docu-Drama." *The Camera Age: Essays on Television.* New York: Penguin Books, 1982, pp. 81–91, 96–105, 276–84.

Auster, Albert. "If You Can't Get 'Em into the Tent, You'll Never Have a Circus: An Inteview with Len Hill." *The Journal of Popular Film and Television,* Winter 1981, pp. 10–17.

Barnouw, Erik. *The Image Empire: A History of Broadcasting in the United States.* Vol. 3 from 1953. New York: Oxford, 1970.

Bart, Peter, and Dorothy Bart. "TV and Movies: A Trial Marriage." *TV Guide,* June 11, 1966, pp. 8–11.

Boyer, Peter J. "Made-from-TV Executives." *American Film,* July-August 1983, pp. 16–18, 59.

Brode, Douglas. "The Made-for-TV Movie: Emergence of an Art Form." *Television Quarterly,* Fall 1981, pp. 53–78.

Brooks, Tim, and Earle Marsh. *The Complete Directory to Prime Time Network TV Shows, 1946–Present.* Rev. Ed. New York: Ballantine Books, 1981.

Cantor, Muriel G. *Prime-Time Television: Content and Control.* Beverly Hills, Calif. Sage, 1980.

Castleman, Harry, and Walter J. Podrazik. *Watching TV: Four Decades of American Television.* New York: McGraw-Hill, 1982.

Champlin, Charles. "Can TV Save the Films?" *Saturday Review,* December 24, 1966, pp. 11–13.

Clift, III, Charles, and Archie Greer, eds. *Broadcast Programming: The Current Perspective.* 7th ed. Washington, D.C.: University Press of America, 1981.

Crist, Judith, "Tailored for Television." *TV Guide,* August 30, 1969, pp. 6–9.

———. "The Ten Best TV-Movies of 1979." *TV Guide,* December 29, 1979, pp. 2–6.

———. "The Ten Best TV-Movies of 1980." *TV Guide,* January 10, 1981, pp. 12–14.

———. "1981 in Review: The 10 Best TV-Movies." *TV Guide,* January 2, 1982, pp. 4–8.

———. "1982 in Review: The 10 Best TV-Movies." *TV Guide,* January 8, 1983, pp. 4–8.

Davidson, Bill. "Every Night at the Movies." *Saturday Evening Post,* October 7, 1967, pp. 30–33.

Denny, Jon S. "Lee Rich, TV's High Roller." *American Family,* May 1981, pp. 26–33.

Ehrlich, Henry. "Every Night at the Movies." *Look,* September 7, 1971, pp. 62–63.

Gold, Herbert. "Television's Little Dramas." *Harper's,* March 1977, pp. 88–93.

Hamamoto, Darrell Y. "Interview with Television Producer Rod Amateau of 'Dukes of Hazzard.' " *The Journal of Popular Film and Television,* Winter 1982, pp. 166–70.

Hoffer, Thomas W., and Richard Alan Nelson. "Evolution of Docudrama on American Television Networks: A Content Analysis, 1966–1978." *Southern Speech Communication Journal,* Winter 1980, pp. 149–63.

Kanin, Fay. "Dialogue on Film." *American Film,* March 1980, pp. 57–64.

Kaufman, William I., ed. *Great Television Plays,* with an introduction by Ned E. Hoopes. New York: Dell Publishing, 1969.

Kerbel, Michael. "The Golden Age of TV Drama." *Film Comment,* July-August 1979, pp. 12–19.

Lafferty, Perry. "Dialogue on Film." *American Film,* April 1981, pp. 57–63.

Levinson, Richard, and William Link. *Stay Tuned: An Inside Look at the Making of Prime-Time Television.* New York: Ace Books-St. Martin's Press, 1981.

Marill, Alvin H. *Movies Made for Television.* New York: Da Capo Press, 1980.

McGilligan, Patrick. "Movies Are Better Than Ever—on Television." *American Film,* March 1980, pp. 50–54.

"Movies on the Tube." *Newsweek,* April 10, 1972, pp. 87–88.

Nolan, Tom. "From Headlines to Hollywood: TV's Scramble for Hot Ideas." *TV Guide,* August 8, 1981, pp. 8–12.

" 'Roots': Eight Points of View." *Television: The Critical View.* 2d ed. Edited by Horace Newcomb. New York: Oxford, 1979, pp. 204–30.

Schickel, Richard. "The New B Movies." *Time,* April 1, 1974, p. 51.

"Special Report: The Golden Age of Television." *American Film,* December 1981, pp. 57–64, 72.

Stein, Benjamin, "Hooked on Television Movies." *Saturday Evening Post*, May 1974, pp. 30–34.

———. "Words that Sell in TV-Movie Titles." *TV Guide*, July 25, 1981, pp. 34–35.

Stone, Douglas, "TV Movies and How They Get That Way: Interviews with TV Movie Makers Frank von Zerneck and Robert Greenwald." *The Journal of Popular Film and Television*, Summer 1979, pp. 146–57.

"TV and Hollywood Sing a New Duet." *Business Week*, April 16, 1966, pp. 107–8.

Wicking, Christopher, and Tise Vahimagi. *The American Vein: Directors and Directions in Television*. New York: E.P. Dutton, 1979.

Whitney, Dwight, "The Boom in Made-for-TV Movies: Cinema's Stepchild Grows Up." *TV Guide*, July 20, 1974, pp. 21–26.

———. "A Pair of TV-Movie Writers with Clout." *TV Guide*, March 9, 1974, pp. 21–26.

———. "When Miniseries Become Megaflops." *TV Guide*, July 19, 1980, pp. 2–8.

VIDEOGRAPHY

Since the number of American made-for-TV movies has now exceeded 1,500 and is rising rapidly, a list of only 33 selections cannot contain all the aesthetically and socio-culturally important telefilms yet produced. The following group is merely some of the many possible significant examples that have already appeared during the twenty-year history of the TV film genre and is meant solely as an introduction. In addition, both Alvin Marill's *Movies Made for Television* and Judith Crist's annual selection of the ''10 Best TV-Movies'' (ever since 1979) are valuable reference catalogues containing listings of individual telefilms.

"My Sweet Charlie"
  Universal, 2 hours
  Network: NBC
  Premiere: January 20, 1970
  Talent: director: Lamont Johnson; scriptwriters: Richard Levinson and William Link; players: Patty Duke and Al Freeman, Jr.

"Duel"
  Universal, 90 minutes
  Network: ABC
  Premiere: November 13, 1971
  Talent: director: Steven Spielberg; player: Dennis Weaver

"Brian's Song"
  Screen Gems/Columbia, 2 hours
  Network: ABC
  Premiere: November 30, 1971
  Talent: director: Buzz Kulik; screenwriter: William Blinn; players: James Caan and Billy Dee Williams

"The Night Stalker"
  ABC, Inc., 2 hours
  Network: ABC

Premiere: January 11, 1972
Talent: producer: Dan Curtis; scriptwriter: Richard Matheson; player: Darren McGavin

"That Certain Summer"
Universal, 90 minutes
Network: ABC
Premiere: November 1, 1972
Talent: director: Lamont Johnson; scriptwriters: Richard Levinson and William Link; players: Hal Holbrook, Martin Sheen, and Scott Jacoby

"The Blue Knight"
Lorimar, 4 hours
Network: NBC
Premiere: November 13–16, 1973
Talent: director: Robert Butter; scriptwriter: E. Jack Neuman; players: William Holden and Lee Remick

"Catholics"
Sidney Glazier Production, 90 minutes
Network: CBS
Premiere: November 29, 1973
Talent: director: Jack Gold; players: Trevor Howard and Martin Sheen

"The Glass Menagerie"
Talent Associates/Norton-Simon, 2 hours
Network: ABC
Premiere: December 16, 1973
Talent: producer: David Susskind; scriptwriter: Tennessee Williams; players: Katherine Hepburn, Sam Waterston, and Michael Moriarty

"The Autobiography of Miss Jane Pittman"
Tomorrow Entertainment, 2 hours
Network: CBS
Premiere: January 31, 1974
Talent: director: John Korty; scriptwriter: Tracy Keenan Wynn; players: Cicely Tyson, Thalmus Rasulala, Rod Perry, and Michael Murphy

"A Case of Rape"
Universal, 2 hours
Network: NBC
Premiere: February 20, 1974
Talent: director: Boris Sagal; scriptwriter: Robert E. Thompson; players: Elizabeth Montgomery and William Daniels.

"The Execution of Private Slovik"
Universal, 2½ hours
Network: NBC
Premiere: March 13, 1974
Talent: director: Lamont Johnson; scriptwriters: Richard Levinson and William Link; players: Martin Sheen, Ned Beatty, and Gary Busey

"Larry"
Tomorrow Entertainment, 90 minutes

Network: CBS
Premiere: April 23, 1974
Talent: director: William A. Graham; player: Frederick Forrest

"The Law"
Universal, 2½ hours
Network: NBC
Premiere: October 22, 1974
Talent: director: John Badham; players: Judd Hirsch and Gary Busey

"Queen of the Stardust Ballroom"
Tomorrow Entertainment, 2 hours
Network: CBS
Premiere: February 13, 1975
Talent: scriptwriter: Jerome Kass; players: Maureen Stapleton and Charles Durning

"Hustling"
Filmways, 2 hours
Network: ABC
Premiere: February 22, 1975
Talent: director: Joseph Sargent; scriptwriter: Fay Kanin; players: Jill Clayburgh and Lee Remick

"I Will Fight No More Forever"
David Wolper Productions, 2 hours
Network: ABC
Premiere: April 14, 1975
Talent: producer: Stan Margulies; scriptwriters: Jeb Rosebrook and Theodore Strauss; players: Ned Romero and James Whitmore

"Fear on Trial"
Alan Landsburg Productions, 2 hours
Network: CBS
Premiere: October 2, 1975
Talent: director: Lamont Johnson; scriptwriter: David W. Rintels; players: George C. Scott, William Devane and Lois Nettleton.

"Eleanor and Franklin"
Talent Associates, 4 hours
Network: CBS
Premiere: January 11–12, 1976
Talent: producer: David Susskind; director: Daniel Petrie; scriptwriter: James Costigan; players: Jane Alexander and Edward Herrmann

"Rich Man, Poor Man"
Universal, 12 hours
Network: ABC
Premiere: February 1, 2, 9, 16, 23, March 1, 8, 15, 1976
Talent: directors: David Greene and Boris Sagal; scriptwriter: Dean Reisner; players: Peter Strauss, Nick Nolte, Susan Blakely, and Edward Asner

"Helter Skelter"
Lorimar, 4 hours
Network: CBS

Premiere: April 1–2, 1976
Talent: producer/director: Tom Gries; player: Steve Railsback

"Sybil"
Lorimar, 4 hours
Network: NBC
Premiere: November 14-15, 1976
Talent: director: Daniel Petrie; scriptwriter: Stewart Stern; players: Sally Field and Joanne Woodward

"Roots"
David L. Wolper Production, 12 hours
Network: ABC
Premiere: January 23-30, 1977
Talent: executive producer: David L. Wolper; producer: Stan Margulies; directors: David Greene, John Erman, Marvin J. Chomsky, and Gilbert Moses; scriptwriters: William Blinn, Ernest Kinoy, James Lee, and M. Charles Cohen; players: LeVar Burton, Cicely Tyson, Edward Asner, Louis Gossett, Jr., Leslie Uggams, Olivia Cole, and Ben Vereen

"The War between the Tates"
Talent Associates, 2 hours
Network: NBC
Premiere: June 13, 1977
Talent: executive producer: David Susskind; scriptwriter: Barbara Turner; players: Elizabeth Ashley, Richard Crenna, and Annette O'Toole

"Breaking Up"
Time-Life, 2 hours
Network: ABC
Premiere: January 2, 1978
Talent: executive producer: David Susskind; director: Delbert Mann; scriptwriter: Lorion Mandel; player: Lee Remick

"Holocaust"
Titus Productions, 9½ hours
Network: NBC
Premiere: April 16–19, 1978
Talent: executive producer: Herbert Brodkin; director: Marvin J. Chomsky; scriptwriter: Gerald Green; players: Rosemary Harris, Michael Moriarty, Meryl Streep, Sam Wanamaker, David Warner, Fritz Weaver, James Wood, and Blanche Baker

"Siege"
Titus Productions, 2 hours
Network: CBS
Premiere: April 26, 1978
Talent: director: Richard Pearce; players: Martin Balsam and Sylvia Sidney

"A Question of Love"
Viacom, 2 hours
Network: ABC
Premiere: November 26, 1978

Talent: scriptwriter: William Blinn; players: Gena Rowlands, Jane Alexander, and Ned Beatty

"Les Miserables"
Norman Rosemont Productions, 3 hours
Network: CBS
Premiere: December 27, 1978
Talent: director: Glenn Jordan; players: Richard Jordan and Anthony Perkins.

"Too Far to Go"
Sea Cliff Productions, 2 hours
Network: NBC
Premiere: March 12, 1979
Talent: director: Fiedler Cook; scriptwriter: William Hanley; players: Michael Moriarty, Blythe Danner, and Glenn Close

"The Jericho Mile"
ABC Circle Film, 2 hours
Network: ABC
Premiere: March 18, 1979
Talent: director: Michael Mann; scriptwriters: Patrick J. Nolan and Michael Mann; player: Peter Strauss

"Fast Friends"
Columbia Pictures TV, 2 hours
Network: NBC
Premiere: March 19, 1979
Talent: scriptwriter: Sandra Harmon; player: Carrie Snodgrass

"Friendly Fire"
Marble Arch Productions, 3 hours
Network: ABC
Premiere: April 22, 1979
Talent: director: David Greene; scriptwriter: Fay Kanin; players: Carol Burnett, Ned Beatty, and Sam Waterston

"Strangers: The Story of a Mother and Daughter"
Chris-Rose Productions, 2 hours
Network: CBS
Premiere: May 13, 1979
Talent: scriptwriter: Michael de Guzman; players: Bette Davis and Gena Rowlands

"Guyana Tragedy: The Story of Jim Jones"
CBS, 4 hours
Premiere: April 15-16, 1980
Talent: players: Powers Booth, Ned Beatty, LeVar Burton, Colleen Dewhurst, James Earl Jones, and Diane Ladd

"Gideon's Trumpet"
CBS, 2 hours
Premiere: April 30, 1980
Talent: players: Henry Fonda, Jose Ferrer, John Houseman, and Fay Wray

"Shogun"

NBC, 12 hours

Premiere: September 15-19, 1980

Talent: director: Jerry London; players: Richard Chamberlain, Yoko Shimada, and Toshiro Mifune

"Skokie"

CBS, 2 1/2 hours

Premiere: November 17, 1981

Talent: producers: Herbert Brodkin and Robert Berger; director: Herbert Wise; script writer: Ernest Kinoy; players: Danny Kaye, Kim Hunter, Eli Wallach, Carl Reiner, and Ed Flanders

"The Winds of War"

ABC, 18 hours

Premiere: February 6-11, and 13, 1983

Talent: producer and director: Dan Curtis; scriptwriter: Herman Wouk; players: Robert Mitchum, Ali MacGraw, Jan-Michael Vincent, John Houseman, Polly Bergen, and Lisa Eilbacher

"The Thorn Birds"

ABC, 9 hours

Premiere: March 27-30, 1983

Talent: director: Daryl Duke; scriptwriter: Carmen Culver; players: Richard Chamberlain, Rachel Ward, Jean Simmons, Richard Kiley, Barbara Stanwyck, Bryan Brown, Piper Laurie, and Ken Howard

"Adam"

NBC, 2 hours

Premiere: October 10, 1983

Talent: players: Daniel J. Travanti and JoBeth Williams

"The Day After"

ABC, 2 hours and 25 minutes

Premiere: November 20, 1983

Talent: director: Nicholas Meyer; scriptwriter: Edward Hume; players: Jason Robards, JoBeth Williams, Steve Guttenberg, John Cullum, and John Lithgow

"Something about Amelia"

ABC, 2 hours

Premiere: January 9, 1984

Talent: director: Randa Haines; scriptwriter: William Hanley; players: Ted Danson, Glenn Close, and Roxana Zal

10

Docudrama

THOMAS W. HOFFER, ROBERT MUSBURGER, AND RICHARD ALAN NELSON

OVERVIEW

While the number of investigative television documentaries has declined, a mixture of fact and fiction called docudrama has been increasingly featured in the prime-time schedules of commercial TV networks and the public television system. In recent years, however, docudramas have evoked sharp criticism and occasional meritorious acclaim. "Controversial" is a mild way of describing the current condition of this hybrid form, a program type which has never defined itself very clearly. For the journalist community, and some documentary filmmakers, this mixture of fact and fiction is simply incompatible and abrasive to reportorial traditions. The docudrama has been accused more than once of committing the same sins as newspapers and the documentary: sensationalism, sexploitation, the creation of "news stars" (or "news victims"), and the generation of audiences to sell to advertisers. Historians, some from academia, have buttressed their condemnations on particular programs, often with considerable justification, exclaiming distortion or omission. Yet, histories continue to reflect the selective biases of their authors for many of the same reasons.

The combination of documentary and drama in a TV program as a technique and form has experienced a slow but steady, sometimes jaundiced, growth on American TV networks since the early 1970s. Because of the declining audiences for theatrical and TV documentaries and the diminished numbers of TV documentary programs, it would seem appropriate and timely to adjust critical priorities while examining the potential for docudrama beyond entertainment functions and goals.

Raymond Carroll's 1978 dissertation serves as an excellent springboard to the literature discussing the documentary from which docudrama is partially derived. For Carroll and others, "The documentary has been defined as a reconstruction of reality, using real people and events in a socially-meaningful structure, and recorded at the time and place of their occurrence. Its purpose is to inform, perhaps motivate, the audience.''[1] He expanded his definition to include a program that ''deals with actual events and circumstances in a manner that maintains fidelity to fact, and uses the actual geographic locations and participants in the situation, is based on a 'purposive' point of view, conveying 'knowledge about' a situation and is a delayed analysis—recorded on film or video tape—of the circumstance or event.''[2] In our definition of documentary-drama, or docudrama, we would say that docudramas are simply accurate re-creations of events in the lives of actual persons, as in the "pure example," "Missiles of October." This was a 1974 ABC-TV program recreating the buildup to the Cuban missile crisis (October 1962) and depicting events in the lives of President John Kennedy and his key aides. The docudrama was based on articles, diaries, transcripts, and other documentary materials.

Another earlier example of docudrama programming on the commercial networks was "The Armstrong Circle Theatre," which used a format of factually based dramatizations with a newsman as host-narrator. The content was based on contemporary news events using actors speaking dialogue created or paraphrased by dramatic writers. Carroll considered this form to remain documentary despite the element of re-creation embellished with dialogue and actors. We do not agree that "Armstrong Circle Theatre" is an example of the documentary form, but it certainly fits well within our definition of docudrama. In the definition, the key words and phrase are re-creations, events, and lives of actual persons.

Implied in the term re-creation are all the dramatic elements used to factually depict the events. These include film techniques such as constructive editing, as articulated by Vsevolod Illarionovich Pudovkin, in which events are ''re-created'' on the editing bench instead of the time frame of the original photography.[3] Add to such restructuring, even if the picture is thoroughly ''factual,'' a musical theme (which usually superimposes emotional consistency or counterpoint not present in the original photography) and post-recorded sound effects (which establish new continuities not present in the original photography), and new problems in documentary classification arise. The irony in this definitional hair-splitting is the critically acclaimed compilation documentary ''Victory at Sea.'' By going this far, we only hope to parenthetically raise some problems that normally flow from too strict a definition for both documentary and docudrama. Our general definition seems to provide a more logical extension to the variations encountered later. Our definition enables us to separate monologues, event-oriented programs, personality-oriented programs, religious docudramas, fictionalized documentaries, documentarized fictions, partial docudramas, and aberrations, while remaining close to the docudrama ''family.''

HISTORICAL DEVELOPMENT

This hybrid of fact and fiction does not exist in a vacuum but is found in a complicated social, political, and economic environment. Manifestations of the current trend toward re-creating personalities, events, and things include the resurrection on the theatrical stage of celebrated heroes (James Whitmore as Theodore Roosevelt), the songs and lives of dead rock singers (Johnny Harra as Elvis Presley), or replicas of art objects (Nelson Rockefeller's plan). In recent years, the economics of star and event exploitation have pushed the "re-creations" to new heights of nostalgic and commercial activity. Perhaps this activity has conditioned consumers to accept re-creations in all media. Thus, the task of sorting out what event influenced what re-creation, at least recently, is not an easy one.

But the docudrama on American television can clearly locate its roots in theatre, motion pictures, radio, newspapers, and books. The concept of re-creating events for an audience is as old as theatre itself. According to theatre historians, all extant tragedies of the influential golden age of the Greek theatre are based on history or myth, although each playwright rendered his own interpretation. The theatre of the Roman Caesars staged *venationes*, or wild animal fights, which pitted animal against animal, or in some cases, animal against human. Julius Caesar staged the first naumachia, or sea battle, in 46 B.C. Nearly a hundred years later nineteen thousand participants fought in a battle staged on Lake Fucine to celebrate the completion of an aqueduct.[4]

During the late nineteenth century, Theatre Libre in Paris used real properties, such as fresh meat in a butcher shop scene, in an attempt to achieve realism in a staged production. Emile Zola's influential "slice of life" theatre called for a new naturalism in drama that would deal with real people and their struggles.

In the 1930s, the Federal Theatre Project created the Living Newspaper, a series of stage productions that used slides, recordings, actual voices, and actors to bring journalism into the theatre. Much of the dialogue was taken from speeches, newspapers articles, and government documents, but the use of actors removed the program from the documentary form and placed it in the somewhat vague form of fictional re-creation of life.[5]

Following World War II, the German theatre developed the "theatre of fact," which also was known as "docudrama." By the 1960s, this genre used actual events, generally recent, to explore a concern for guilt and responsibility in public affairs and morality. Three of the best-known writers of this form are Rolf Hochhuth, Peter Weiss, and Heinnar Kipphardt.[6]

As the docudrama began to take root in American television, it began to disappear from the German stage. But American theatre felt the influence of theatrical docudrama as manifested in *The Trial of the Catonsville Nine* (1971) and *The Last of Mrs. Lincoln* (1972) or monologues such as *Will Rogers' U.S.A.* (1974) and *Clarence Darrow* (1974).

Halfway through the eighteenth century, the modern novel emerged, " . . . a long story organized toward a significant conclusion and dealing with convincing, though imagined, people in relation with one another."[7] The novelist, placing imagined people in believable settings, while describing characters and relationships, closely parallels the work of the television writer. And, just as the storyteller's selection determines what the reader imagines, the writer of a docu-drama selects what the viewer will accept as part of the televised story.[8] Henry Fielding's eighteenth-century novel *Tom Jones* was written as a fast-paced story of a fictional young man coming of age, but it is a fairly accurate description of what life was like in eighteenth-century England. During the nineteenth century, Sir Walter Scott opened the eyes of British and other Europeans to their own his-tory with his novels, *Ivanhoe* and *Kenilworth*. Neither could be cited for historical exactness, but each provides an overview of the times. Modern novelists such as Mary McCarthy (*The Group*) and Aleksandr Solzhenitzyn (*Ivan Denisovitch*) have created for their readers lives so vivid as to have the appearance of reality.

The motion picture had developed in several forms including drama, docu-mentary, newsreel, and functional or informational film, each contributing to docudrama. As early as 1898, Spanish-American War "actualities" used faked re-creations of battles when cameramen couldn't film the real thing. In these early "newsreels" deception was not the filmmaker's main intent, although fakery and wholesale invention would lead to greater distortion in the newsreel era. At this time, filmmaking was still struggling as a penny-arcade amusement and was not commonly recognized as a journalistic medium. Most of the films before the turn of the twentieth century were simple reproductions of reality. Little more than recording life before the camera seemed enough to sustain audience interest. Raymond Fielding, author of the landmark study about the American newsreel, attributes the first news film in the United States to Thomas Edison and his associates who photographed the prize fight between Leonard and Cushing in 1894.[9]

In contrast, the films of Georges Méliès were pictorial fantasies, mixtures of staged reality and drama. His *L'Affaire Dreyfus* might be considered the first filmed docudrama because the film consisted of the re-creation of an event that took place only days before the filming. Some participants in the actual trial thought that they spotted themselves in the film.[10]

World War I accelerated the mixing of fictional elements with true-life situ-ations, in newsreels as well as dramatic films from the European battlefields. In the Soviet Union, the communist regime recognized the propaganda potential of the film medium, leading to the innovations exemplified by Sergei Eisenstein in *Battleship Potemkin* (1925). Despite the fictional "massacre" on the Odessa steps, the film has a strong documentarylike quality in the depiction of events during the abortive 1905 uprising against the czar.

It was Robert Flaherty's *Nanook of the North* that was considered to be the benchmark for the American documentary. Lewis Jacobs wrote that Flaherty's technique " ... broke with the purely descriptive; it swept away the notion that what the camera recorded was the total reality. Flaherty proved there was another reality which the eye alone could not perceive. . . . ''[11] His interpretation, in-cluding a large dose of romanticism, was what elevated Flaherty's films beyond the travelogues of the day. Moreover, Flaherty used his filmed participants to repeat actions for the convenience of the camera.

By the 1930s, the thrust of the documentary had become more social. John Grierson's films such as *The New Generation* (1932) or *Telephone Workers* (1933) were about injustices in Britain's working class. Through the work of Leni Riefenstahl and her *Triumph of the Will* (1936), the documentary also became a finely tuned propaganda tool. Similarly, *The Plow That Broke the Plains* (1936) is a dramatic account of the Midwest dust bowl and its derivations. In this film, Pare Lorenz used stock footage to create a memorable sequence showing how the overuse of the land in the early World War I years had helped to ruin it. Composer Virgil Thomson worked closely with Lorenz to create music that added strong emotional elements to the story, not too dissimilar in the result obtained with the Robert Russell Bennett scores to the NBC-TV "White Paper" documentaries decades later. These techniques provided a basis for contemporary docudrama production and helped condition audiences for something beyond the mere recording or editing of reality.

Even before regular radio network newscasting became a reality, the idea of dramatizing news by using actors to impersonate headline personalities had been demonstrated on radio in the "March of Time" and its predecessors. This was accomplished with an imposing roster of actors including Orson Welles, Agnes Moorehead, Martin Gabel, and Jeanette Nolan. Some of the regular cast members, like Jack Smart, played a half dozen roles each week, perhaps ranging from an English gentleman to a Chinese peasant. Dwight Weist specialized in playing Hitler, John L. Lewis, and Mayor Fiorello LaGuardia. The programs also used intense narrators, known as the "Voice of Time," read by Harry VonZell, Ted Husing, Edward Everett Sloane, and, perhaps best known for his stentorian quality, Westbrook Van Voorhis. Sound effects cinched the realism quotient in the weekly re-created news dramas, using recordings and mockups. While the program might have been a tad pretentious, there was little, if any, sponsor interference during production. After seven seasons on CBS, the program moved to the NBC blue and red networks and finally ended its thirteenth season on ABC. Toward the end, the format lost its dramatizations of the news in favor of more news actualities, reflecting changes in technology and the increased capability of using shortwave reports from the field.

Dramatizing events, by using actors to reenact key actions, was carried over into the theatrical film version of the documentary series *March of Time*, which began in 1935. The object was not to mislead but to explain controversial issues. Bohn and Lichty note:

The creation of this style emphasized several distinct and unique techniques. The most notable, and at times, controversial was the reenactment of events. This allowed the producers to select and arrange their material in ways best suited to the construction of dramatic narrative. The reconstruction of reality in journalism was not new, of course. What ws new, however, was admitting this reconstruction and declaring it valid.[12]

Two following programs may have conditioned critical response against re-creations that perhaps extends to the present day. One was an aberration called

Bill Stern's "Colgate Sports Newsreel." In the seventeen years after its premiere on October 8, 1939, Stern would weave broadcast tales based on hearsay, co-incidence, or completely fabricated from imagination. John Dunning wrote:

He told tales of horse races won by dead jockeys, of limbless baseball players, of any thread-thin influences sport had had on the lives of the great. Stern never let the facts get in the way of a good story—occasionally he told the same story twice (allowing for a decent time span between tellings), using conflicting facts and passing off both versions as true.[13]

But the most notable example illustrating listener vulnerability and production technique carefully couched in realism was contained in Orson Welles's legendary "War of the Worlds," aired by CBS in October 1938. A month after the Munich crisis, the Mercury Theatre opened the Sunday evening broadcast with a simple announcement, followed with a dramatic introduction by Welles, setting the stage for a considerably revised version of the H. G. Wells tale. This version was "modernized" for the radio medium, right down to interrupting news bulletins, studio orchestras, and simulated confusion, cleverly woven into an unfolding sound mosaic that slowly enveloped many listeners as the suspense mounted. The newscast simulations were intensified, building on the same techniques used by the radio networks weeks earlier as bona fide newscasts reported changing events from Europe. Some dial-twisters, who missed the qualifying announcement at the beginning of the Mercury Theatre broadcast when they tuned in late, heard a news reporter giving a simulated actuality report from a mythical Grover's Mill, New Jersey. He was tensely talking about a cylinder of unknown origin hitting earth with the force of an earthquake and followed with a description of something coming out of that cylinder. As the program elapsed, the news reports were shortened, sometimes frantic, interspersed with dramatic action and dialogue, almost too fast and with few disclaimers included. While the entire country did not panic—far from it—enough confusion, accidents, and panic occurred to stimulate sociologist Hadley Cantril to survey part of the affected population. His conclusions concerning the hysteria among some listeners involved a growing fear with some about impending war in Europe, heightened by radio broadcasts just one month before.

Radio also served as the breeding ground for more reality-based programs such as "Gangbusters" (1935–40, NBC; 1940–48, Blue/ABC; 1948–55, CBS; 1955–57, Mutual), "Dragnet" (1949–56, NBC), and many others, most of which were transplanted to television with varying degrees of success. These programs often relied on police or government case files.

"The Big Story" (1947–55 NBC radio; 1949–55, NBC-TV) is among the more interesting "file-based" docudramas in that it represented the beginning of "checkbook journalism." Reporters were paid for stories based on their experiences, and the producers used actual persons and locales when possible. What differentiates the television version of a program like "The Big Story" from later docudramas is important to note. Crude by today's standards and hampered by low budgets, weekly serialization, and a 39–week production commitment, the producers exhibited the tendency to overlook factual details and to fictionalize when necessary to insure an upbeat conclusion.

An aberrant example in radio is "You Are There" (CBS, 1947–50), identified by Erik Barnouw as "punctiliously researched," while reporting great events in history.[14] Well-known newscasters including John Daly, Don Hollenback, and Richard C. Hottelet took radio audiences to the settings of the events, such as the U.S. Senate for the impeachment of Justice Samuel Chase, the battlefield at Gettysburg, the last days at Pompeii, or the assassination of Julius Caesar. While the radio version stopped in 1950, the television episodes of "You Are There" persisted from 1953 to 1957 with a very brief revival in the early 1970s. Reporters, omniscient interviewers with one foot in the present time frame of the listener and the other foot squarely in the middle of the depicted event, would query the main historical character about the event or his own status in it. No effort was made to mask this dual time-frame and orientation; it was as if a simulation were unfolding, complete with all the conversational nuances and reporter techniques. Indeed, even the central historical characters would answer the reporter's questions unmindful of the unfolding crisis for but a moment. Given such discontinuities, leaping from reporter intrusion to a depiction of the actual event, the aberration distracted the presentation. Such interruptions did provide, however, for a number of "what if" challenges to central historical figures, so that new viewpoints or interpretations might be presented to such characters for testing or to obtain their reaction. To this day, many of the television episodes still remain in educational film libraries for use in secondary schools.

In the 1930s, as network radio emerged, film audiences were becoming accustomed to re-creations of stories torn from the front pages of contemporary newspapers. Warner Brothers successfully exploited a gangster cycle with such films as *Little Caesar* (1930), *The Public Enemy* (1931), and their later imitators. Warners also followed with a line of distinguished biographical films such as *The Story of Louis Pasteur* (1936), *The Life of Emile Zola* (1937), and *Juarez* (1939). Other movements such as the Film and Photo League produced politically motivated "social documentaries" during the depression years. These often re-created key incidents in anticapitalist labor struggles and also formed part of the docudrama tradition. Certainly the postwar "street films" of the Italian neo-realist movement and the Noir films of the 1940s such as *House on 92nd Street* (1945) and *Naked City* (1948) contributed to television docudrama.

The March of Time moved to theatrical screens four years after its introduction on network radio. Following the February 1, 1935, premiere of the first issue, the *New York Times* reported that it was " . . . an interesting, well-made supplement to the newsreel standing in about the same relationship to it as the weekly interpretative news magazine bears to the daily newspaper."[15]

The man chosen by Time, Inc., to develop this new film series was Louis de

Rochemont, who had started as a stringer for newsreel companies in New England. While still in high school, de Rochemont attracted national attention with his coverage of a German saboteur charged with destroying a bridge in Maine. None of the newsreel cinematographers arrived in time to film the capture and arrest. De Rochemont waited until the reporters and others had left; he then asked the county sheriff to bring the prisoner out of his cell and restage the capture and arrest. The obliging sheriff and prisoner pantomimed the seizing, handcuffing, and jailing for the young man's camera. While his competitors sharply criticized him, de Rochemont argued that the film reenactment was no different than having an editor rewrite the words of a reporter. He also felt that reenactments provided an opportunity to produce a sharper and more detailed view of the actual occurrence.[16]

At the age of thirty, de Rochemont had become head of short subjects at Fox Movietone News, as well as producer of the travelogue series *Magic Carpet* and the *Adventures of a Newsreel Cameraman*. He also produced for Columbia Pictures a series called *March of Years*, which recreated important news items of the past using professional actors.[17] As producer of the *March of Time*, de Rochemont combined file film and additional material shot especially for a story, re-creating the event if necessary. In the second year, *March of Time* film crews discovered that the persons actually involved in the story being filmed could be photographed redoing, or restaging what was reported on more easily and efficiently than restaging the event using actors.[18] As discussed earlier, even Robert Flaherty restaged some of this documentary footage.

With the beginning of World War II, American documentary filmmaking for theatrical release received a stimulus with U.S. Government funding, as many agencies produced films to help unite the country behind the war effort. One series of war propaganda films, under the supervision of Major Frank Capra, was *Why We Fight*, designed to explain to the U.S. fighting man the reasons behind the allied war efforts and American involvement. In these films, Capra incorporated animation, multiple narrators, re-creations, and juxtaposed editorial constructions using segments of Leni Riefenstahl's 1936 film of the sixth Nazi party congress, *Triumph of the Will* and other materials. Capra's reconstructions of the party congress films, imposed an anti-Nazi construction on films originally designed to glorify the 1936 Nazi party, a classic example illustrating the power of editing in propaganda work. Moreover, the blare of trumpets heralding the master race and other sound effects were embellished in Capra's versions in deliberate counterpoint to the authoritative narration or selective images of the soldiers and Adolf Hitler. Hitler's highly animated speeches were excerpted in the Capra counter-propaganda, removing them entirely from the Reifenstahl context. This made it appear as if the Fuhrer were completely irrational, perhaps crazed with power. In fact, a viewing of the entire speech-making sequences provides a completely different meaning and presents a more orderly rationale for Hitler's appeal to the party members and ultimately many outside of the Nazi party.

With the end of the war came the end of the cause that had united those in documentary filmmaking, and of course, government funding for this type of film. But the documentary had projected some influence on the postwar fiction film, with notable examples including *The House on 92nd Street* (1946), *Boomerang* (1947), and *Naked City* (1948), the latter produced by Louis de Rochemont. *Boomerang*, also produced by de Rochemont, was based on a true story, using a narrator to provide background explanations throughout the film—a technique borrowed from the documentary and the newsreel. In *Naked City* cinematographer William Daniels used a hidden camera to capture candid viewpoints, and he won an academy award for his work on this picture. This picture was the root to a TV series of the same name ten years later but the visual documentary-style in the TV version was a pale comparison to the theatrical film. *The House on 92nd Street* used exteriors in New York City, emulating the documentary-fiction found in Roberto Rossellini's *Open City* (1945), photographed in wartime Italy simply because there were no studios that escaped damage. *Open City* established what historians would later call the "neorealist" movement in theatrical films. All depended upon location shooting, incorporating natural settings, which sometimes eliminated expensive set construction, but introduced new production problems such as location sound recording and logistics. The improving technology of lighter cameras, innovation of magnetic sound recording in films, and faster film emulsions would enhance such location work, providing a more credible, realistic look to theatrical features. But such technology would also enable directors to escape the expensive confines of the film studio. By 1948, another set of forces would alter the organization of the American film business, resulting in a slow breakup of the studio system and opening up American screens to independent films from domestic and foreign sources.

Alan Casty in his *Development of Film* credits director William Dieterle as one of the leaders in adding documentary elements in several theatrical films prior to and following World War II. In the Warner Brothers' commercially successful biographical-historical dramas, Dieterle was able to juggle politically oriented scripts, historical details, and specific issues of the day. *The Story of Louis Pasteur* (1936), *Juarez* (1939), *Dr. Erlich's Magic Bullet* (1940), and *The Searching Wind* (1946) are relevant examples. The last effort attracted little notice but illustrates the use of a fictional character moving through historical events of the 1920s and 1930s, in the same way that the Navy Captain Pug Henry did in the 1982 TV miniseries, "The Winds of War."[19]

Early American commercial television naturally drew from the foregoing experiences and models, but from 1948 to about 1969, the pure mixture of documentary and drama, usually in the form of historical or biographical "prestige" presentations, was not a major program type on the commercial networks.

Like radio, early television was live and dependent upon the type of programming that could be done in a controlled environment in real time. Sports provided the bulk of programming in the earliest days of television. The capacity to report events as they happened was expanded beyond the staged athletic contests to the reporting of national news events such as the opening of Congress (January 1947). But the "live" mode of TV production was the only efficient method possible, prohibiting directors from extensive manipulation of space and time except in the time frame of the actual telecast. Thus, the manipulations similar to Frank Capra's use of film from Riefenstahl's *Triumph of the Will*, for example, were very difficult to achieve in live television and seldom attempted until film or videotape permitted such juxtapositions in a more efficient, high-quality manner. There were the usual lists of "firsts" in the medium, however, occasioned by taking the bulky TV equipment to various remote locations for sporting and special events. By the 1947 and 1948 TV seasons, some radio formats and personalities began to appear on the expanding TV networks, but until 1950 or so, the audiences for network television were limited. In 1950, about 9 percent of all homes were equipped with TV sets. By 1955, that had mushroomed to 65 percent, representing a phenomenal growth and diffusion of a new technology.[20] A number of comedy-variety programs increasingly appeared on the networks, some retreading successful runs on the radio networks. Television networks expanded service into the morning hours with news, variety, talk, and audience-participation shows and daytime serial drama, most done live.

"Armstrong Circle Theatre," beginning in February 1955, is generally recognized as the first continuing 60-minute series to utilize the pure docudrama form. Unlike conventional fiction dramas, which utilized well-known actors, "Circle Theatre's" fact-based dramatizations focused on the story itself, as the "star" of the program.[21] Executive producer David Susskind and producer Robert Costello set the guidelines for this unique format. Costello later discussed what they had in mind:

We aim to combine fact and drama—to arouse interest, even controversy, on important and topical subjects. . . . We support them with authoritative statements by recognized leaders in specified fields. . . . We can't use an idea only or a news story only, we must also be able to present some potential solution, some hope for your citizens to consider, to think about.[22]

Despite the earlier radio and film influence on docudrama, the form did not immediately realize its full potential for public affairs, probably for these reasons. First, it has always been easier and cheaper to present fictional entertainment under the guise of realism instead of attempting a meticulously factual recreation. "Highway Patrol" (1955, syndicated), and the later "The Untouchables" (1959–63, ABC-TV) are police-style programs originally based on real-life occurrences, utilizing a narrative format and other documentary elements. As they grew from their basic core stories, it was necessary to invent new fictional plots, or as in the case of "Dragnet" (1952–59, 1967–70, NBC-TV), "change the names to protect the innocent." From a legal standpoint, "Dragnet's" change of names minimized lawsuits for invasion of privacy.

For children, an interesting combination of drama and history was found in

Worthington Miner's "Mr. I. Magination" (1949–52, CBS), using a series of musical fantasies that dramatized historical events.

Unlike the earlier documentaries for theaters, television documentaries were, at least initially, too easily controlled by advertiser-sponsors or subject to the subtleties of network concerns about controversy and a reluctance to alienate any part of the growing mass audience. But there were three exceptions, "See It Now," "Project Twenty," and "CBS Reports." By the early 1950s, even the "March of Time," now transplanted to television, lost its verve and rigor for controversial subjects, a condition that also characterized the postwar years of the theatrical version. Some argue that the Federal Communication Commission's fairness doctrine, which required broadcasters to program public affairs material tuned to the needs of their broadcasting service areas, acted as a brake on controversial subjects. The doctrine also required that opposing points of view be presented at a reasonable opportunity to respond to the initial broadcast of controversial matter. Providing another party response time could be costly to the broadcaster and interrupt previous scheduled time for profitable, episodic entertainment series programs. The result for many stations was simply to do as little public affairs broadcasting as possible, and when it was done, various points of view were larded into the broadcast, turning the program into a bland, rudderless statement without a point of view. To a degree, the doctrine is claimed to function in the same way at the present time, undoubtedly affecting the docudrama treatment of some personalities or controversial situations of a contemporary nature.

For many, "See It Now" was a milestone in television journalism. Edward R. Murrow and Fred Friendly used an interview technique that had always been available but was seldom used, the crosscut interview. Lengthy, detailed interviews would be filmed, but in editing, they would be cut up, using short segments throughout the program. A. William Bluem, in *Documentary in American Television* concluded that this process permitted "not only arresting and rapid flow of visual interest but a bold juxtaposition of different points of view in short and emphatic bursts."[23] The method could, under careless circumstances, contribute to sensationalized interpretations taken out of context. While much has been written about the emphasis of reporting in "See It Now," the program brought back elements of the screen magazine and occasionally the photo essay that had preceded television documentaries.

"Project Twenty" (1954–62, NBC) initially concentrated on compilation reconstructions from twentieth-century history, characterized by "Nightmare in Red" (the rise of communism), "The Twisted Cross" (Adolf Hitler), and "The Jazz Age" (the 1920s in America). In 1959, under the leadership of Donald B. Hyatt, the theme documentary reached back into history for a better grasp of religious, political, and cultural influences on American life, to events that antedated the motion picture. Using a "stills-in-motion" technique by moving the camera over still photographs or paintings combined with period music and narration, new reconstructions were made in "Meet Mr. Lincoln," "Mark Twain's

America," and "The Real West." In underscoring the importance of dramatic elements and re-creation in the theme documentary, Donald Hyatt said, "The mood, history, feeling of the past can only be captured by going to original source materials—the photographs, sketches, music, words of an era—and weaving them together in a dramatic form, attempting to capture the real flavor of bygone times."[24] From the standpoint of manipulation, there would not appear to be a great distinction between animating still photographs, setting them to music, and the use of actors reciting dialogue based on documentary evidence. In fact, all of these devices are manipulative, serving to re-create events in the lives of actual persons, but to varying degrees. Richard Hanser, part of the "Project Twenty" team, described how narration can be written to exploit the reconstructions between image and spoken word.

The basic peculiarity is, of course, that the words have to be tailored to footage—a bastard form of composition that obtains in no other field, the stop-watch method imposed by the nature of the medium.

Another basic factor is compression and placement. The right sentence with the right choice of words, planted at the right place, can, when combined with the right pictures, suggest whole areas of information and emotion in one quick stroke.[25]

"CBS Reports" (1959–present) evolved biographical treatments of important newsmakers, usually exploiting the interview or compilation. In more controversial programs, the reporter-interviewer would be cut out, and the interviewee's "arguments" or quotations would be edited together, building a rhythm sometimes synchronized to appropriate visuals beyond pictures of the interviewee.

By this point in the history of the docudrama, its antecedents, including more recently the documentary film, the newsreel, feature films, radio, and live television, had provided four distinct methods of re-creating an event for an audience. The first is the use of reenactment, either by actors or the actual participants in the event. Second, there are the various methods of editing picture and sound of the actual event, potentially constructing viewpoints while creating the appearance of reality. Third, the stills-in-motion animation technique can re-create the past, especially if embellished with sound effects, narration, dialogue, and music. Finally, there is the possibility of combining any of the previous approaches, and indeed, by the 1970s a number of docudramas would exhibit sophisticated combinations, especially integration of newsfilms. These include "Ike" (1979), "Winds of War" (1982), "Holocaust" (1978), and "G. I. Diary" (1978, syndicated).

The 1950s were not notable for much controversial or contemporary programming despite the well-remembered confrontation between Edward R. Murrow and Senator Joseph McCarthy. Television was still a novelty, largely consisting of transplanted radio content and formats. The documentary had far less access to theatrical screens, and through the networks, new variations grew on television. The form received a major stimulus in the era following the payola and quiz scandals at the end of the decade.

Through the 1950s and 1960s, there were a few docudrama series including "Profiles in Courage" (1964–65) and "You Are There," an aberrant form (1953–57, 1971–72). Other programs that had individual episodes utilizing docudrama approaches included the series of specials, "Hallmark Hall of Fame" and "Saga of Western Man," produced by Helen Jean Rogers and John Secondari. The Secondari-Rogers team incorporated the moving camera, drawn from the experience of cinema verite, together with first person narration of "characters" introduced in the re-created story. Those stories and themes focused upon historical figures and events.

By the 1970s, however, the docudrama would acquire new life, this time based on contemporary history and newsmakers. Columnist Les Brown claimed that the program forms which would indirectly influence such revived programming were slowly incubating in public television.[26]

In the mid-1960s, public television had little influence due to an elitist image, lack of network interconnection, and an absence of regular funding. Following the uncertainties of funding and a history of political manipulation by the Nixon administration, public TV now has a modified form of regular interconnection and has become a rich source of docudrama programming.

"NET Playhouse" telecast the four part mini-series "Victoria Regina" (1966), "A Choice of Kings" (1967), and "A Celebration of William Jennings Bryan" (1968). Public TV stations have had more flexible scheduling in contrast to their commercial counterparts since the programs are not aimed at generating audiences for advertisers on a national basis. For over twenty years, many of the docudramas on American public television were imported from Great Britain, as the British had experimented with this form on TV much earlier. "The Forsyte Saga" was a 26-episode British series produced in 1967. The TV movie and the mini-series were important changes in TV programming and had direct implications for the docudrama offerings on the American commercial networks by the mid-1970s.

In the United States, made-for-TV movies emerged to replace the dwindling supply of theatrical films available to free television at a reasonable cost. Although the made-for-TV movie form and the docudrama did not merge until "Brian's Song" (1971), the long format has been used for many notable docudramas including "The Longest Night" (1972), "The Marcus-Nelson Murders" (1973), "Babe" (1975), and "A Circle of Children" (1977).

In the world of newspapers and magazines, the "new journalism" was creating interest and controversy with its mix of literary form and reporting. According to Richard Kallan, one of the major premises of "new journalism" is that there are not necessarily two equal sides to each story.[27] Other terms have described this characteristic: saturation reporting, advocacy journalism, and participatory journalism.[28] The technique of presenting the facts but from a personal perspective is at the heart of many docudramas, including "Kill Me If You Can" (1977), "Skokie" (1981), and "Bitter Harvest" (1981).

The 1977 TV season on public television brought forward another "pure form" of drama, a fact that elegantly illustrated the potential of docudrama for public affairs. "Eyewitness" was a mini-series of four, one-hour news magazine programs taking contemporary issues and dramatizing them for a fuller analysis impossible with a strictly documentary presentation. Like "Armstrong Circle Theatre," "Eyewitness" deemphasized the role of actors to provide a clear, analytical thrust. Explored were such contemporary matters as the motives of four would-be or accused assassins (Lee Harvey Oswald, Arthur Bremer, Sara Jane Moore, and Sirhan Sirhan), an investigation of recent germ and drug experiments conducted by agencies of the U.S. government, and a second-by-second recreation of a descending aircraft before it crashed, killing 71 persons. In the latter segment, viewers heard dramatized dialogue of the pilots and control tower personnel while they watched actors reenact the cockpit scene. A split screen, with one portion showing a radar-like profile of the descending aircraft against the hilly ground, provided a new perspective for understanding the pilots' behavior as they fast approached the ground. This series of four programs, entirely based on transcripts, personal journals, and other authenticated materials, was tied together with a narrator who provided a frame of reference. The producer, Thomas McCann, argued that daily news stories are often covered inadequately. In other cases, news media are either not able to record the event or are barred from coverage. Some stories involve issues and actions that are too complex for treatment in two minutes or less on the typical daily newscast, and thus, McCann concluded, TV news is often just a cut above a news bulletin service. In the case of Karen Quinlan, the story is complicated by moral, religious, ethical, legal, and medical issues, rendering a 45-second treatment of it nearly useless. In "Eyewitness," about forty minutes was devoted to the Quinlan case, potentially increasing public understanding of the issues involved. But one continuing problem in docudramas involves reducing the personalities to stereotypes. Dialogue writers are sometimes more motivated to create "colorful" action than follow historical fact. McCann and his partner, Webster Lithgow, combined fact and fiction in 1974 when they produced "The White House Transcripts," reducing 1,300 pages of raw material into a ninety-minute special. One year later, they produced "The Watergate Coverup Trial," at least bringing inaccessible transcripts to life for millions of Americans who might otherwise never have known their contents. One argument aften advanced to justify the docudrama is the assertion that television has become the main source of news for most people and consequently it has the responsibility to do more to enhance public understanding of contemporary events. Docudramas are one possible mechanism to fulfill this need.

The difference between the "pure form" of docudrama and the potential it has for dramatizing and analyzing public issues can be illustrated by comparing the two broadcast versions of the Karen Ann Quinlin case. In addition to the "Eyewitness" version, a docudrama special on NBC-TV, ("In The Matter of Karen Ann Quinlin," September 1977) starred Brian Keith and Piper Laurie as Joseph and Julia Quinlin, distraught parents of the 23-year-old girl in a coma since 1975. In the "Eyewitness" version, the emphasis was on the issues, such as the question as to removing Karen from the respirator. In the NBC-TV version, laced with star personalities, an entirely new dimension was projected, dealing more with the parent's and family's reaction to the dilemma and their emotional struggle with moral and civil problems. Certainly, the perspective in both programs was valuable. But in terms of public affairs, the "Eyewitness" approach was a more objective handling of those matters because it downplayed the emotionalism.

The season concept was transplanted from radio to the emerging TV networks and by the late 1960s, the "second season" had been invented. As in network radio in the 1940s, early TV seasons began about mid-September each year and continued for 39 weeks. If a program was sold to advertisers for another full season, the summer break would either feature reruns or perhaps a summer replacement. As the cost of TV programming increased, the 39 weeks of original episodes were drastically revised downward, with planned reruns beginning as early as February or March. Later, specials or one-time-only programs would preempt a regular series episode. Now, only a handful of episodes for a new series are produced for each fall premiere in order to minimize risk in the event that the program does not obtain an audience of sufficient worth to sell to advertisers. By the 1970s, the failure of many first-season TV series ushered in a "second season," or new prime-time offerings beginning as early as mid-January. In search of a solution to remain competitive through the spring and summer months, network programmers began to orchestrate a "third season" of reruns, pilot films, and specials from mid-March through June. This "window" in the network schedules allowed some docudramas to get access to mass audiences.

Some made-for-TV movies (such as "The Execution of Private Slovik," March 1974) and mini-series of thirteen episodes or less achieved impressive ratings while defying traditional programming strategies. The introduction of the third season concept, however, was the final condition that opened up prime-time schedules for the new docudrama form. With the bicentennial celebration approaching and the Watergate scandals fully exposed, both historical and newsmaker personalities achieved new currency in the media marketplace. The private and public lives of newsmakers were retold and synthesized in the news, magazine features, and eventually book-length versions of their celebrated status. Consider, for example, *Melvin and Howard*, a theatrical film about Howard Hughes and a Utah gas station attendant. John Dean's "Blind Ambition" aired in May 1979 and was produced by David Susskind, who was also executive producer for the "Armstrong Circle Theatre."

The increasing public appetite for news and the desire of programmers to satisfy that perceived demand points out two factors important to the revival of docudrama in the 1970s and 1980s. First, the demand for news conditioned the audience to become accustomed to reality as well as the sense that, because television covers all events, all the events covered are therefore important.[29]

More importantly this also stimulated new programming strategies that included the pseudo-events described by Daniel Boorstin. These are not spontaneous events, but planned ones, whose purpose is to be reported, remain ambiguous, and in the end become self-fulfilling prophecies.[30] The simplest and most common among them is the news conference. In entertainment programming, the pseudo-event was visible in such programs as "Real People," "That's Incredible," and "The People's Court." The events re-created or presented are real, of course, but the program is the only reason they have been created.

In the early 1970s, the reality syndrome began to hover over comedy and dramatic shows. With "All in the Family" (1971–80) leading the way, new situation comedy programs featured topical themes with characters tinged in shades of realism, at least to the degree that they reflected social issues through humorous attacks on stereotypes. "The Mary Tyler Moore Show" (1970–77), "M*A*S*H" (1972–83), "Bob Newhart" (1972–78), and "Barney Miller" (1975–81) are prime examples. Other entertainment programs with reality connections were "The Waltons" (1972–82), "Kojak" (1973–78), and "Baretta" (1975–78) but none were docudramas as defined in this chapter. Many of these popular series, such as "Kojak," "The Waltons," and "Baretta," began as made-for-TV movies.

The interest in the inner workings—and often the corruption—of high levels of government is reflected in a wide range of docudramas of the 1970s, repeating the cycle of some theatrical films in the depression years that exploited news personalities, crooks, and crime. The most obvious were docudramas that dealt with Watergate including the documentarized fiction "Washington: Behind Closed Doors" (1977) and "Blind Ambition" (1979). On public TV there was "The Impeachment of Andrew Johnson" (1974) clearly outlining the impeachment process for the country at a time when Congress was still in the middle of its inquiry into the Nixon White House. Other docudramas provided new windows to view well-known events such as "The Missiles of October" (1974) and "Backstairs at the White House" (1979). "Fear on Trial" (1975) dealt with McCarthy and the blacklisting era and was based on John Henry Faulk's memoir.

While TV programming ignored the Vietnam War until recent years, "The Andersonville Trial" (1973) on public television had obvious parallels to the perspective of accountability and war crimes such as those examined in "The Court Martial of Lt. Calley" (1975). "The Execution of Private Slovik" (1974) and "Farewell to Manzanar" (1976) were docudramas that examined injustices in World War II. "Pueblo" (1974) examined individual responsibility in an organizationally troubled system of military decision making. Monologues such as "Clarence Darrow" (1974) and "Paul Robeson" (1979) were attempts to create profiles of famous persons with occasional insights into their lives and highly selected perspectives. A fictitious character traced her life through the struggle of blacks for civil rights in "The Autobiography of Miss Jane Pittman" (1974), which created a portrait of a woman who turned social disadvantages into personal triumphs. Four years after hostilities ended in Vietnam network TV boldly released "Friendly Fire" (1979).

As the bicentennial approached, historical and biographical docudramas were appropriately scheduled, including the mini-series from public television, "The Adams Chronicles" (1975). Other American heroes and heroines were represented in "Harry Truman Plain Speaking" (1976), "Patrick Henry: Give Me Liberty or Give Me Death" (1976), "Eleanor and Franklin" (1976), and "Sandburg's Lincoln" (1975). "Roots" (1977) represented a fictionalized documentary where actual persons' lives were re-created, but the events were telescoped and sometimes fictionalized, while cast against a historical mosaic that was based on fact.

Programs exploiting the background stories of historical events continued, including "Raid on Entebbe" (1977), "Rumor of War" (1980), "Kent State" (1981), and "Lois Gibbs and the Love Canal" (1982).

Unresolved problems in American life and history led to aberrations providing "what if" speculations on historical events, such as "The Trial of Lee Harvey Oswald" (1977) and "The Court-martial of George Armstrong Custer" (1977). In the 1980s, fictional programs took a few steps more to provide simulations such as "The Day After" (1983) or "World War III" (1984). While these programs have allowed writers and producers to explore the probative value of current evidence and thus raised informed speculations and sometimes provided a better perspective on fictional event, these aberrations have brought gaming to American mass audiences. Through "The Day After " (1983) and "Special Bulletin" (1983) audiences have been presented behavioral models in defined social and political contexts. Followup broadcasts about the programs further illuminate issues or provide perspective to various outcomes dramatized in the aberrations. In "Special Bulletin," a city is held hostage by nuclear terrorists; in "The Day After," the United States is destroyed in a nuclear attack from the Soviet Union. In each simulation, the dramatization overwhelms the factual context, aided greatly by documentary techniques and special effects evolved from film, radio, and television. Some argue such gaming merely conditions the mass audience to accept as inevitable the programmed outcome in the storyline. Others argue that the simulation allows the audience to ponder and rationalize the pathways toward such ends, perhaps enhancing public understanding and action. In "Adam" (1983) we find the most recent instance of how a docudrama can spur widespread public attention on a pressing social problem. Whether the more sensationalized simulations might prevent world atomic devastation is mere speculation at this point, but such models might help the public grasp an emergency with control, not panic, or provoke the political process.

The docudrama form has become an important factor in contemporary programming strategy. Its emergence was tied to increasing interest in news, the country's bicentennial, and a public infatuation with news personalities or "stars." Long-standing loyalties and patterns in the industry were weakened by ABC's rise to the number one network spot. The docudrama was created, in part, by the networks' attempts to lure youth and new audiences through "stunting"— the practice of placing many specials and mini-series in the lineup. The door for this genre has remained open on all the commercial networks for increasing experimentation while maintaining audience flow just before and during prime time.

For years, the staple of the industry has been the series with self-contained episodes revolving around continuing characters. In the early 1970s, younger viewers were not as committed to the program formats or even TV viewing as were their parents. Thus, in 1977, ABC experimented with the so-called third season. Their willingness to cancel weak programs opened up the window for the docudrama in the form of the made-for-TV movie or a mini-series. The TV movie, typically scheduled on one night, potentially serves to preserve audience flow from the beginning of prime time to the end. The mini-series, typically continued night to night or week to week, helps the flow of audience from day to day.

According to Sally Bedell, the big breakthrough came in 1976 when ABC scored high ratings with the fictional mini-series "Rich Man, Poor Man."[31] The idea of scheduling a mini-series over eight consecutive nights as a followup to that success was considered risky. Yet, on the final episode, "Roots" achieved a 51.1 rating and a 71 share. What followed the ratings success of both the fictional "Rich Man, Poor Man" and the "Roots" mini-series was a succession of programs, many of which were docudramas. Among them were "Washington: Behind Closed Doors" (1977), "Holocaust" (1978), "Pearl" (1978), "King" (1978), "Backstairs at the White House" (1979), "Roots: The Next Generation" (1979), "Ike" (1979), "Blind Ambition" (1979), and "Shogun" (1980).

In recent years, the docudrama has obtained a closer association with contemporary history and news events. ABC telecast the British docudrama "Invasion," a reenactment of the 1968 Soviet invasion of Czechoslovakia and then followed that evening with a report on Soviet-Polish relations on "Nightline." "The Saving of the President" was a reenactment produced for George Washington University Hospital by Holly and Paul Fine (WJLA-TV, Washington, D.C.) and telecast on ABC-TV's "Twenty-Twenty" (1982) one year after the assassination attempt on President Reagan. Unlike the documentaries that characterized earlier assassination attempts, this one achieved a riveting, high level of tension and involvement, to paraphrase some of the rave reviews. The nurses and doctors who attended the president reenacted their roles with actor Donald Williams, who played the stricken Reagan, from the reconstructed action in front of the Washington, D.C., Hilton Hotel to the conclusion of the surgery, and an appearance by the president at a White House checkup. What is especially appealing about this videotape is the rich, detailed activity revealed for the first time, while the news-hungry public was only getting periodic updates through press spokespersons of the actual happening. A number of other docudramas have also modeled individual behavior in adversity, perhaps providing an important social benefit while exploiting the personality. These include "The Patricia Neal Story" (1981), which portrayed her comeback from a mind-crippling stroke; "Bill" (1981), Mickey Rooney's sensitive performance of a mentally retarded worker coping in the world of work; "Anatomy of an Illness" (1984), Norman Cousins's bold strategy to tackle and conquer serious disease; "Who Will Love My Children" (1983), a dying mother making plans to place her children in new homes; and "The Killing of Randy Webster" (1981), which dealt with how some Houston policemen shot a young man, covered it up, and the parent's anguish in exposing the crime, while forced eventually to accept the fact of their son's death. All have strong elements of drama; some are perhaps too pretentious and melodramatic. Other docudramas have exploited star names for their own audience-generating potential or sex themes with little social value. Critics and consumers usually recognize that under the purview of free speech and general use of broadcast frequencies, producers of television programming are not under any stricture, ethic, or code to be responsible. The marketplace determines what ideas for programs will have currency and which will not. As a form, docudrama has won public acceptance, but not all docudramas would strive for respectability. Docudramas have strong appeals to several constituencies. Writers can use them to espouse controversial ideas in safe historical formats. Producers are drawn to the format because many contemporary docudramas are already pre-sold by heavy news coverage. For advertisers, the bottom line is the demonstration that the program will generate the right kind of audience at the most efficient cost, consistent with all the other needs of the advertiser.

THEMES AND ISSUES

Television is a creative field that functions under specific government regulations and offers the opportunity for extremely high financial return. The effects on the audience in viewing programming have been discussed widely and, though not agreed upon generally, some impact is rarely denied.[32] This impact, and the controversies engendered by past problems, raises ethical and legal issues. The concern operates on two levels. First, there has been the complaint that in an effort to attract mass audiences, the docudrama writers and producer will tamper with the facts. Second, there is the concern that the audience, conditioned to the reality of television as a medium of reportage, will not be able to distinguish between reality and "dramatic truth."

With respect to the issues involving distortions and manipulations, docudramas in the last decade have garnered a large number of complaints. A former member of the Marine Corps fighter squadron VMF 214, in his analysis of "Baa Baa Black Sheep" (1976–78, NBC), presented *TV Guide* with a "fact versus fiction" list, concluding that the series was as phony as a three dollar bill.[33] In "Collision Course" (1976, ABC) Patrick Buchanan argued that MacArthur's alleged snub of Truman at Wake Island never happened.[34] In "Judge Horton and the Scottsboro Boys" (1976, NBC), scriptwriter John McGreevy admitted to inventing dialogue.[35] There is some small comfort in recognizing that such charges are not new to documentary filmmaking nor electronic journalism. This does not excuse deliberate falsification, but there are some justifications for altering setting or telescoping events, given the limited time frame in which such re-creations must be depicted provided, of course, that such changes do not materially distort the analysis or deliberately mislead the viewers.

Selection, modification, and interpretation of elements in a dramatized event or life of a person seem to be the bases of much criticism about docudramas, with distortion going far beyond those three areas. Assessing just what the limits or parameters of any event are, following analysis, is a continuing problem for historians who try to reach, with their work, beyond description. For the film-maker or TV producer, the list of manipulatable variables that can impinge on the authenticity of the event is long and complex. In documentary film, for Richard Blumenberg, the list begins with the choice of subject matter and includes the camera manipulations, editing, and sound.[36] The problem is determining when selection, modification, or interpretation "ranges" exceed the shape of the observed and recorded event, thereby introducing distortion and fabrication. A few examples will show how some docudrama production persons are approaching their ethical responsibilities of the form.

John Blassingame, black history specialist and Yale graduate, was hired by the producers of "Beulah Land" (1980), a docudrama about the South after the Civil War. As the six-hour mini-series applied to one plantation in Georgia, the program was judged historically accurate, but Blassingame concluded that the film was not an accurate reflection of the South in that period.

Ostensibly based on a book by Noah Dietrich, top executive in the Hughes empire for 32 years, and Bob Thomas, "The Amazing Howard Hughes" (1977) drew from other sources, some of whom offered contradictory information about the recluse millionaire's final days. In the face of contradictions, and with no way to verify the stories, the producers "selected" the version that seemed most plausible and dramatized it in the mini-series.

Sometimes the accusations of bias or distortion are not identified but the clamor creates more attention to the broadcast, as in the case of "Death of a Princess" on "World" (1980), a series of infrequent specials on public television. The special traced the search of reporter-producer Antony Thomas for the facts behind the death of a Saudi Arabian princess found guilty of adultery in 1977. Thomas decided to present his research in the docudrama form because many of his interviewees would not appear on camera for documentary interviews.[37] The princess was shot and her lover was beheaded, following Islamic law. But the Saudi Arabian government complained first to the British government when the two-hour film aired there, alleging inaccuracies (but not identifying any) and calling the program a grossly distorted and biased image of Saudi Arabia, its religion, and traditions. After the British telecast, the furor moved to the United States, but the Public Broadcasting Service distributed the program anyway to surprising overnight ratings in many cities. A panel discussion followed the telecast and in four markets measured, most of the audiences remained to watch the discussion. With the panel of experts, some "balance wheel" effect was potentially possible, but there was no further indication of damage to "World," but the program received renewed life for another season.

Interpretations of events have been a continuing dilemma for producers of documentary films and docudramas for as long as there have been films exhibited to audiences. In "Playing for Time" (1980), playwright Arthur Miller, concentrating on the torment of Nazi victims, describes the plight of Auschwitz survivor Fania Fenelon. But the organized protests against the program were aimed at Vanessa Redgrave, who is an outspoken supporter of the Palestine Liberation Organization yet starred as a Jewish survivor of a death camp. This seemed incongruous for some in the American Jewish community, including Fania Fenelon herself. In a strange twist, Miss Redgrave would have been denied the part because of her political beliefs, not her acting ability. The casting might have had some implication for the interpretation of the role, but protestors only agreed that it was in bad taste. One compared casting Ms. Redgrave as Ms. Fenelon to selecting J. Edgar Hoover to portray Martin Luther King. In the final result, while strongly organized, the nationwide protest had no impact on the ratings of the telecast, and Ms. Redgrave earned critical acclaim for her performance.

"Washington behind Closed Doors" (1977) was criticized because it presented a fictional story against a national publicity campaign reminding audiences of the connections to the Watergate affair. Adapted from John Ehrlichman's novel, *The Company*, the mini-series was a dramatization of President Richard Monckton and his aides as they rise to and fall from power. While the program had its defenders, Michael Arlen was skeptical of the mix of real-world events with the make-believe world of television fiction. While he conceded that the audience would probably accept the program as Ehrlichman's interpretation of what had happened, certain events in the novel's adaptation to TV might be misleading. For example, the docudrama tells of Monckton's plan to have the Twenty-second Amendment repealed so he could run for president a third time—perhaps confusing the viewer into thinking that these were the actions of former President Nixon. The interpretation was toying with the audience's perception of what was factual and introducing distortion.[38]

Because docudramas must often fit complex historical detail into a suitable dramatic context, the practice of modifying some facts is often used. Telescoping events or creating composite characters are two typical devices that often lend docudramas to intense criticism. In "Skokie" (1981) a new ending was advocated by early reviewers, perhaps adding the march itself. The docudrama was a highly charged story of a Jewish community's response to a planned Nazi march, but the march never occurred. While the lead character was fictitious, the program ended as the events had happened—without the march. In the story of the internment of Japanese-Americans during World War II, "Farewell to Manzanar" (1976), modifications were made. Some were made for dramatic reasons, according to John Korty, collaborator on the adaptation of the docudrama from a book by Jeanne Wakatsuki Houston and her husband James D. Houston. Korty's credits include "The Autobiography of Miss Jane Pittman" (1974). For example, Toyo Miyatake smuggled his camera equipment into Manzanar, and the script called for him to lug it around disguised as a lunch pail, but that did not happen, he recalled. One collaborator asked to have his name removed from the credits due to several complaints about the adaptation, in part because the issue of white racism in concentration camps had not been treated. Another reviewer complained that the opening of the made-for-TV movie, with an integrated party, distorted the fact that Japanese-Americans were not well accepted.

In 1977, the now defunct National News Council urged the networks to go beyond routine disclaimers, usually placed at the beginning of each program, and to do something more to assure a proper regard for factual and historical accuracy. The advice found no takers. Two years later, the Academy of Television Arts and Sciences staged a docudrama symposium consisting of historians, writers, producers, and others associated with the controversial form. Most of the recommendations made at that meeting were directly related to ethical concerns. A new name for the form was urged. Better and more intensive use of professional historian's expertise in the production process was advocated. The suggestion was made that more public information, with alternative sources about each upcoming docudrama, should be released well in advance of a telecast.

The legal considerations for producers of docudrama programming involve three major areas: privacy, defamation, and copyright. At the outset, it is obvious that consultation with a lawyer or a law library, especially the database systems WESTLAW or LEXIS, is mandatory to remain up-to-date in this very dynamic area. In cities with law schools, occasional access to these databases is possible. These databases are by far the best sources for current information. Thus, our discussion here will merely describe the legal issues and not attempt a summary of the legal status of the three topics.

Privacy has been a continuing problem for filmmakers. Case histories vary from state to state.[39] The law for "public persons" may serve to protect program producers but the problem becomes more complex if the only notoriety a person has acquired is from a docudrama. This raises the issue of how a person reaches the status of being a "public person" and imposes the requirement of malice or recklessness on the part of the producer—a very difficult issue for the plaintiff to prove.

Privacy is actually five torts: appropriation, intrusion, public disclosure of private facts, false light in the public mind, and the right of publicity. Docudramas have the highest potential for abuse in cases about public disclosure of private facts, false light, and rights of publicity. Appropriation cases involve the plaintiff's right of recovery when the defendant has used plaintiff's likeness, name, or picture for some business purpose. Intrusion is an invasion of privacy resulting from the defendant's intruding into the plaintiff's home or other quarters, but includes eavesdropping on private conversations or wire tapping, window peeking or persistently telephoning the plaintiff. When there has been no defamation, a plaintiff might sue for public disclosure of private facts, provided the disclosure is highly objectionable. Past decisions in successful lawsuits include recovery for publicity given the plaintiff's debts, release of medical pictures of intimate anatomy, or embarrassing details about a woman's masculine characteristics. Persons formerly in the public eye have argued that the passage of time vitiates the publicity, and they accordingly regain their right of privacy after several years. Historical events that are recounted in the present are generally protected. That is, a plaintiff with a criminal record could not recover damages against a docudrama producer should the program recount the criminal activity. But if there appears to be some purpose in embarrassing the plaintiff because of past conduct, the outcome is not so clear. Another type of legal action might be appropriate if the publicity places the plaintiff in a false light. Publicly attributing to the plaintiff some opinion that he has not, in fact, given, unauthorized use of a name on a petition, or entering someone in an embarrassing public contest are examples of this tort. Here no defamation is required, although such an action may also lie. But the test is whether such disclosure would be objectionable to a reasonable person. An example would be associating a named individual with a crime ring in a docudrama when he would not otherwise be associated with that group. The right of publicity involves the plaintiff's right to control commercial exploitation of his or her name or likeness. Not all jurisdictions, however, recognize this ancilliary right in privacy law, and the case law is not rich in a consistent line of decisions. In most states, the right of publicity ends with death, but in other instances the right might be passed on to heirs, confusing the situation in a series of contradictory decisions. Generally speaking, the right continues after death if the deceased also exploited that right in their lifetimes, especially in the instances of prominent persons. But, there are other decisions which conclude with the opposite result: no recovery against defendants who use a deceased's likeness or story even if the deceased did exploit his or her name during a lifetime.

Defamation is more a problem in journalism than in the production of a docudrama because the law is more uniform across jurisdictions, and the previous decisions provide far more certainty than the common law in privacy. Moreover, docudrama research, writing, and production are not subject to the beat of daily deadlines common to news reporting. A short definition of this tort is simply any communication that holds up a person to ridicule, contempt, hatred, or scorn, that may lower one's reputation in the community, or cause others not to associate with one. There are some statements or assertions that have obvious defamatory meaning. These include any statement that suggests or states a person has been accused of a crime when they have not. Statements or suggestions about an individual's sexual deviations, abnormalities, honesty, liquor consumption, diseases, or mental illness can be sensitive. Of course, truth is a complete defense in a defamation action, but sometimes proving this is a difficult task. There are some privileged communications that may further relieve a defendant of liability for defamation. Absolute and qualified privilege cover a variety of forums where statements are made and may be reported without fear of legal action from an angry plaintiff. These include speeches in legislative and judicial forums—which many contemporary docudramas depict in trials where the dialogue is edited from court transcripts. Official communications by executives in government also qualify for the privilege. When the privilege is qualified there is no absolute immunity, but it is conditional on the fairness, accuracy, or summary of the action cited. Generally, in matters of defamation, if a person depicted in a TV production is a public figure, as is often the case with docudramas, the plaintiff must plead and prove that the program was defamatory and produced with the knowledge of falsification, exhibited reckless disregard for the truth, or actually intended malice in the publication of the defamation. This is difficult to prove in the case of the public person, but the definition of such a status is not altogether uniform across all the states.

Copyright is a property right that confers upon the owner the exclusive right to reproduce the copyrighted work in any form for any reason. Before a copyrighted work may be reproduced in any form, the consent of the copyright owners must be obtained. Their monopoly extends only to original works of authorship fixed in any tangible medium of expression. Thus copyright extends to anything that may be reproduced, but certainly includes magazine articles, books, motion picture films and videotapes, advertisements, personal letters, and newspaper articles. The right of publicity, appropriation (privacy law), or common law copyright may likely protect spontaneous speech-making or improvised performances not otherwise fixed in a tangible medium of expression.

Only "original" works may be copyrighted. Thus, docudramas based exclusively on court transcripts are not original works. But a scenario reorganizing such transcript excerpts as part of a new work would be copyrighted, as long as such original contributions were beyond trivial or minor contributions to the work. With regard to "news" of an event, specific versions incorporating an identified literary style or quality are protected by copyright. The "event" is not copyright because facts by themselves are not copyright. Indeed, under recent holdings, even the research to obtain those facts is not protected by copyright, although the manner of presentation or style is protected.

Privacy and defamation areas of the law have the most inhibiting effect on the writing and production of docudramas. Avoidance of legal claims may cause extensive rewriting, perhaps greater fictionalization, and a kind of distortion now conditioned by the law, which serves to protect the makers of the hybrid mixture of truth and fiction. In copyright, the concept of "fair use" permits a form of legalized copying of the original works of others so long as it is limited. But the law of copyright provides an exception in regard to factual events, which belong to everyone and are not to be brought into the central domain of copyright owners. Thus writers of history and public affairs are given considerable latitude to exploit what is now known about our past.

NOTES

1. Raymond L. Carroll, "Factual Television in America: An Analysis of Network Television Documentary Programs, 1948–1975" (Ph.D. diss., University of Wisconsin, Madison), p. 4.

2. Carroll, "Factual Television," p. 4.

3. Karel Reisz and Gavin Miller, *The Technique of Film Editing* (Boston: Focal, 1982), pp. 15–39; V. I. Pudovkin, *Film Technique and Film Acting* (New York: Grove Press, 1976).

4. Oscar G. Brockett, *History of the Theatre* (Boston: Allyn and Bacon, Inc., 1977), pp. 19, 60.

5. William A. Bluem, *Documentary in American Television: Form, Function, Method* (New York: Hastings House, 1977), p. 74.

6. Brockett, *History of the Theatre*, pp. 76–77.

7. Rewey Belle Inglis and Josephine Spear, *Adventures in English Literature* (New York: Harcourt, Brace and Co., 1958), p. 343.

8. Roger Shattuck, "Fact in Film and Literature," *Partisan Review* 44 (1977), p. 547.

9. Raymond Fielding, *The American Newsreel: 1911–1967* (Norman, Oklahoma:)klahoma Press, 1972), p. 9.

10. Shattuck, "Fact in Film," p. 548.

11. Lewis Jacobs, ed., *The Documentary Tradition* (New York W. W. Norton and Co., 1979), pp. 7–8.

12. Thomas W. Bohn and Lawrence W. Lichty, " 'The March of Time': News Drama," *Journal of Popular Film* (Fall 1973), pp. 373–87.

13. John Dunning, *Tune In Yesterday* (Englewood Cliffs, N.J.: Prentice-Hall, Inc., 1976), p. 140.

14. Erik Barnouw, *The Golden Web: A History of Broadcasting in the United States, 1933 to 1953* (New York: Oxford University Press, 1968), p. 238.

15. "The Screen: Pictorial Journalism," *New York Times*, February 2, 1935, p. 10.

16. Ray Fielding, *The March of Time* (New York: Oxford University Press, 1978), pp. 29–30.

17. Fielding, *March of Time*, p. 20.

18. Ibid., pp. 136–37.

19. Alan Casty, *Development of Film: An Interpretive History* (New York: Harcourt Brace Jovanovich, Inc., 1973), pp. 156–57.

20. Lawrence W. Lichty and Malachi C. Topping, eds. *American Broadcasting: A Source Book on the History of Radio and Television* (New York: Hastings House, 1975), p. 522.

21. Myron Berkley Shaw, "A Descriptive Analysis of the Documentary Drama Television Program, 'The Armstrong Circle Theatre' 1955–1961" (Ph.D. diss., University of Michigan, 1962), pp. 47–48. Shaw analyzed over 100 docudramas during the life of the program. He identified "Portrait of America" and "American Inventory," weekly half-hour programs, as among the first docudrama series.

22. Shaw, "A Descriptive Analysis," p. 64.

23. Bluem, *Documentary in America*, p. 99.

24. Ibid., p. 159, citing Clifford L. Jordon, Jr., "The World of Donald Hyatt," *Dartmouth Alumni Magazine*, (January 1961).

25. Ibid., pp. 150–51. From remarks delivered at the 1957 University of Denver Seminar Workshop in Documentary. "Anatomy of a Documentary," *Journal of the University Film Producers Association* (Winter 1962), pp. 5–7, 20–21.

26. Les Brown, "Public Broadcasting Serves as Incubator for Commercial Networks," *New York Times*, March 29, 1977, p. 62.

27. Richard A. Kallan, "Entrance," in *New Journalism*, ed. Marshall Fishwick (Bowling Green: Bowling Green University Press, 1975), p. 9.

28. Ronald Weber, "Some Sort of Artistic Excitement," in *The Reporter As Artist: A Look at the New Journalism Controversy*, ed. Ronald Weber (New York: Hastings House, 1974), p. 14.

29. David L. Altheide, *Creating Reality* (Beverly Hills: Sage Publications, 1976), p. 12.

30. Daniel J. Boorstin, *The Image: A Guide to Pseudo-Events in America* (New York: Atheneum, 1975), pp. 11–12.

31. Sally Bedell, *Up the Tube: Prime-Time TV and the Silverman Years* (New York: Viking Press, 1981), pp. 131–40.

32. George Comstock et al., *Television and Human Behavior* (New York: Columbia University Press, 1978), pp. 1–18; Williams Rivers et al., *Responsibility in Mass Communication* (New York: Harper and Row, 1980); Frank Mankiewicz and Joel Swerdlow, *Remote Control: Television and the Manipulation of American Life* (New York: Times Books, 1978).

33. Frank E. Walton, " 'Baa Baa Black Sheep' Is Pulling the Wool over Our Eyes," *TV Guide*, April 23, 1977, pp. 15–20.

34. Patrick Buchanan, "How History Was Distorted in TV Drama," *TV Guide*, January 13, 1976, pp. A5–6.

35. "Scottsboro Dialogue Invented," *Tallahassee Democrat*, July 9, 1977; "Scottsboro Film Libel Suit Against NBC Is Dismissed," *New York Times*, July 13, 1977.

36. Richard M. Blumenberg, "Documentary Films and the Problem of 'Truth,' " *Journal of the University Film Association* 29, no. 4 (Fall 1977), p. 20.

37. Simon Applebaum, "Death of a Princess Brings Life to World," *Watch Magazine* (June 1980), p. 48.

38. Michael J. Arlen, "The Air: Getting the Goods on President Monckton," *New Yorker*, October 3, 1977, pp. 119–23.

39. Peter L. Felcher and Edward L. Rubin, "Privacy, Publicity and the Portrayal of Real People by the Media," *Yale Law Journal* 88, no. 8 (1979), p. 1578.

BIBLIOGRAPHICAL SURVEY

There are no books devoted exclusively to the subject of docudramas, although a few academic dissertations have examined some facets of the program form. The literature of this hybrid is buried in a number of existing works, as identified in this brief essay and the bibliography, along with other published materials that are deemed important for perspective.

An overview of broadcasting and new technologies, in what is probably the best volume on this subject, is contained in Sydney Head's *Broadcasting in America: A Survey of Television, Radio, and New Technologies*. Because docudrama owes a debt to the documentary tradition, several volumes in that defined genre are also appropriate. From the standpoint of editing, we would recommend Karel Reisz and Gavin Millar's *The Techniques of Film Editing* for a summary of the early editing approaches from which docudrama techniques have evolved. Erik Barnouw's *Documentary: A History of the Non-Fiction Film* and A. William Bluem's *Documentary in American Television: Form, Function, Method* are very necessary. Charles Hammond's *The Image Decade: Television Documentary, 1965–1975* fills a critical need for the present but gives only slight notice to the docudrama form in one year (1974), as if that were the only year the form was used. Ray Fielding's two books, *The March of Time: 1935–1951* and *The American Newsreel: 1911–1967* are also mandatory for an understanding of film beginnings of theatrical newsreels and the *March of Time* theatrical series. The "company histories," *Time, Inc.*, and *The World of Time, Inc.*, by Robert Elson, are also useful for the newsreel era.

In recent years, several volumes have chronicled television programming in considerable detail. Harry Castleman and Walter J. Podrazik have written *Watching TV: Four Decades of American Television*, which contains a long narrative on program trends along with detailed schedules beginning in 1944.

Four volumes in very recent years have provided insight into network decision making, particularly as it related to the "reality syndrome," docudramas and other specials, and changing content. Sally Bedell's *Up the Tube: Prime Time TV and the Silverman Years* has the narrower focus of the two books, following the career of Fred Silverman from ABC to CBS to NBC. She attributes many of her quotations to those who have recently passed through the revolving doors of the network hierarchies. Todd Gitlin's *Inside Prime Time* takes a very critical view of docudrama movies-for-TV in his ninth chapter, but his book outlines some conditions for this status including the marketing function. The work rambles but contains interesting anecdotes about program decision making. In a sometimes opinionated and complaining style, Gitlin does write about network and producer biases that have just as much to do with what does not get produced as what does, pointing out that reality programming may be conceived in an environment of chance, and perhaps too much tempered by marketing considerations, and the catering to the mass audience, " . . . the guy who's used to walking around and getting a beer." (p. 188) The producing team of Richard Levinson and William Link wrote *Stay Tuned: An Inside Look at the Making of Prime-Time Television*, which discusses the production of "Columbo," "My Sweet Charlie," and "The Execution of Private Slovik." More critical of the corporate view is Frank Reel's *The Networks: How They Stole the Show*. His argument explains how the networks have robbed television of much of its creative potential while protecting their own private interests and profits.

In *Deciding What's News*, sociologist Herbert J. Gans conducted a twelve-year study of the news gathering operations at the networks and news magazines. His interest was the news-gathering process and the factors that affected the choices journalists made in their work. Older, but complementary to Gans is Daniel J. Boorstin's *The Image: A Guide to Pseudo-Events in America*, establishing the thesis that much of our news is manipulated or staged. One common thread in the Gans and Boorstin books is the view that what is considered news has varying degrees of truth or reality, except for the rare spontaneous event.

BOOKS AND ARTICLES

"The Anatomy of a Documentary." *Journal of the University Film Producers Association* 14, no. 2 (Winter 1962), pp. 5–7, 20–21.

Applebaum, Simon. "Death of a Princess Brings Life to 'World.' " *Watch Magazine*, June 1980, pp. 48–49.

Arlen, Michael J. "The Air: Getting the Goods on Pres. Monckton." *New Yorker*, October 3, 1977, pp. 115–25.

Barnouw, Erik. *Documentary: A History of the Non-Fiction Film.* New York: Oxford University Press, 1974.

————.*The Golden Web: A History of Broadcasting in the United States, 1933–1953.* New York: Oxford University Press, 1968.

Barsam, Richard Meran. *Nonfiction Film: A Critical History.* New York: E. P. Dutton & Co., 1973.

Bedell, Sally. *Up the Tube: Prime-Time TV and the Silverman Years.* New York: Viking Press, 1981.

Bluem, A. William. *Documentary in American Television: Form, Function, Method.* New York: Hastings House, 1977.

Blumenberg, Richard M. "Documentary Films and the Problem of 'Truth'." *Journal of the University Film Association* 29, no. 4 (Fall 1977), p. 19–22.

Bohn, Thomas W., and Lawrence W. Lichty. "*The March of Time*: News Drama." *Journal of Popular Film* 2, no. 4 (Fall 1973), pp. 373–87.

Boorstin, Daniel J. *The Image: A Guide to Pseudo-Events in America.* New York: Atheneum, 1975.

Breitbart, E. "From the Panorama to the Docudrama—Notes on the Visualization of History." *Radical History Review* 25 (1981), pp. 114–25.

Brockett, Oscar G. *History of the Theatre.* Boston: Allyn and Bacon, Inc., 1977.

Brode, Douglas. "The Made-for-TV Movie: Emergence of an Art Form." *Television Quarterly* 18, no. 3 (Fall 1981), pp. 53–78.

Brown, Les. "Public Broadcasting Serves as Incubator for Commercial Networks." *New York Times*, March 29, 1977, p. 62.

Buchanan, Patrick. "How History Was Distorted in TV Drama." *TV Guide*, January 13, 1976, pp. A5–A6.

Carroll, Raymond L. "Factual Television in America: An Analysis of Network Television Documentary Programs, 1948–1975." Ph.D. dissertation, University of Wisconsin, Madison, 1978.

Castleman, Harry, and Walter J. Podrazik. *Watching TV: Four Decades of American Television.* New York: McGraw-Hill, 1982.

Casty, Alan. *Development of Film: An Interpretive History.* New York: Harcourt Brace Jovanovich, Inc., 1973.

Caughie, John. "Progressive Television and Documentary Drama." *Screen* 21, no. 3 (1980), pp. 9–35; and London Documentary Drama Group, "A Response to John Caughie." *Screen* 22, no. 1 (1981), pp. 101–5.

Comstock, George, et al. *Television and Human Behavior*. New York: Columbia University Press, 1978.

Dunning, John. *Tune in Yesterday: The Ultimate Encyclopedia of Old-Time Radio, 1925–1976*. Englewood Cliffs, N.J.: Prentice-Hall, Inc., 1976.

Elson, Robert T. *Time, Inc.: The Intimate History of a Publishing Enterprise, 1923–1941*. New York: Atheneum, 1968.

———.*The World of Time, Inc.: The Intimate History of a Publishing Enterprise, 1941–1960*. New York: Atheneum, 1973.

Felcher, Peter L., and Edward L. Rubin. "Privacy, Publicity, and the Portrayal of Real People by the Media." *Yale Law Journal* 88, no. 8 (July 1979), pp. 1577–1622.

Fielding, Raymond. *The American Newsreel: 1911–1967*. Norman: University of Oklahoma Press, 1972.

———.*The March of Time: 1935–1951*. New York: Oxford University Press, 1978.

Gans, Herbert J. *Deciding What's News: A Study of CBS Evening News, NBC Nightly News, Newsweek, and Time*. New York: Pantheon Books, 1979.

Gitlin, Todd. *Inside Prime Time*. New York: Pantheon Books, 1983.

Hammond, Charles M. *The Image Decade: Television Documentary, 1965–1975*. New York: Hastings House, 1981.

Head, Sydney W., with Christopher H. Sterling. *Broadcasting in America: A Survey of Television, Radio, and New Technologies*. 4th ed. Boston: Houghton Mifflin Co., 1982.

Inglis, Rewey Belle, and Josephine Spear. *Adventures in English Literature*. New York: Harcourt, Brace and Co., 1958.

Jacobs, Lewis, ed. *The Documentary Tradition*. 2d ed. New York: W. W. Norton and Company, 1979.

Jordon, Clifford L., Jr. "The World of Donald Hyatt." *Dartmouth Alumni Magazine*, January 1961.

Kaid, L. L., W. M. Towers, and S. L. Meyers. "Television Docudrama and Political Cynicism: A Study of *Washington: Behind Closed Doors*." *Social Science Quarterly* 62, no. 1 (1981), pp. 161–68.

Kallan, Richard A. "Entrance." In *New Journalism*, edited by Marshall Fishwick, pp. 8–15. Bowling Green, Ohio: Bowling Green University Popular Press, 1975.

Levinson, Richard, and William Link. *Stay Tuned: An Inside Look at the Making of Prime-Time Television*. New York: St. Martin's Press, 1981.

Lichty, Lawrence W., and Malachi C. Topping, eds. *American Broadcasting: A Source Book on the History of Radio and Television*. New York: Hastings House, 1975.

Mankiewicz, Frank, and Joel Swerdlow. *Remote Control: Television and the Manipulation of American Life*. New York: Times Books, 1978.

McArthur, Colin. *Television and History*. Television Monograph no. 8. London: British Film Institute, 1978.

McKerns, Joseph P. "Television Docudramas: The Image as History." *Journalism History* 7, no. 1 (1980), pp. 24–25, 40.

Pudovkin, Vsevolod Illarionovich. *Film Technique and Film Acting*. New York: Grove Press, 1976.

Reel, Frank. *The Networks: How They Stole the Show*. New York: Scribner's, 1979.

Reisz, Karel, and Gavin Miller. *The Technique of Film Editing*. 2d enlarged ed. London and Boston: Focal, 1982.

Rivers, William L., Wilbur Schramm, and Clifford G. Christians. *Responsibility in Mass Communication.* 3d ed. New York: Harper and Row, 1980.

"*Scottsboro* Dialogue Invented." *Tallahassee Democrat,* July 9, 1977.

"*Scottsboro* Film Libel Suit Against NBC Is Dismissed." *New York Times,* July 13, 1977, p. A8.

"The Screen; Pictorial Journalism." *New York Times,* February 2, 1935, p. 10.

Shattuck, Roger. "Fact in Film and Literature." *Partisan Review* 44, no. 4 (1977), pp. 539–50.

Shaw, Myron Berkley. "A Descriptive Analysis of the Documentary Drama Television Program 'Armstrong Circle Theatre,' 1955–1961." Ph.D. dissertation, University of Michigan, 1962.

Walton, Frank E. "*Baa Baa Black Sheep* Is Pulling the Wool over Our Eyes." *TV Guide,* April 23, 1977, pp. 15–20.

Weber, Ronald, ed. *The Reporter as Artist: A Look at the New Journalism Controversy.* New York: Hastings House, 1974.

VIDEOGRAPHY

"Profiles in Courage"
  NBC
  Premiere: November 8, 1964
  Executive Producer: Robert Saudek
  Last Program: May 9, 1965

"The Missiles of October"
  ABC, December 18, 1974
  Stars: William Devane, Martin Sheen
  Executive Producer: Irv Wilson
  Writer: Stanley Greenberg

"Eleanor and Franklin"
  ABC, January 11–12, 1976
  Stars: Jane Alexander, Edward Herrmann
  Executive Producer: David Susskind
  Writer: James Costigan

"Roots"
  ABC
  Premiere: January 23, 1977
  Stars: Ben Vereen, LeVar Burton
  Executive Producer: David Wolper
  Last Program; January 30, 1977

"Playing for Time"
  CBS, September 30, 1980
  Star: Vanessa Redgrave
  Writer: Arthur Miller

"Invasion"
  ABC, January 1, 1981
  Writer: David Boulton

"Hall of Fame: Mister Lincoln"
  PBS, February 9, 1981
  Star: Roy Dotrice
  Executive Producer: David Susskind
  Writer: Herbert Mitgang

"Bitter Harvest"
  NBC, May 18, 1981
  Star: Ron Howard
  Executive Producer: Charles Fries
  Writer: Richard Friedenberg

"Skokie"
  CBS, November 17, 1981
  Star: Danny Kaye
  Executive Producer: Herbert Brodkin
  Writer: Ernest Kinoy

"20/20: Saving of the President"
  ABC, April 1, 1982
  Producer: Holly and Paul Fine and George Washington University

11

Television News

RAYMOND L. CARROLL

OVERVIEW

When viewers say they "watch the news," they probably mean a network program, although more people watch local than nationally broadcast news. Even when we establish which, the program watched can make a difference. Viewers don't necessarily get a single version of an event from reports presented by the three traditional networks or, in an increasing number of homes, Cable News Network (CNN) or Satellite News Channels. Differences in these and other televised news sources include length of time devoted to a given story, thoroughness of the report, subtle interpretations by correspondents, and any number of other potential nuances in story treatment. Few newspaper readers would assume that a report on a news event provided by the *New York Times* is the same as one published in the *Chicago Tribune*. Similarly, viewers should not assume that ABC-TV's version of the "World News Tonight" will be the same as CBS's interpretation of "the way it is." Still, there are a great many similarities. The differences are better examined by scholars who employ rigorous news analysis techniques.[1]

We are interested here in the more general aspects of television news programs and what determines their characteristics. "Local news" and "network news," while similar in many respects, have structures and content orientations that are dictated by their origin. Network television news, especially, has a tradition that exerts considerable influence on its nature.

An important attribute of news is controversy. "The news," by general convention, is often unpleasant, and viewers sometimes react negatively. Many no doubt wish much of the material that comprises television news would "all go away"; that is, that the catastrophes they see reported each evening would be replaced with nonthreatening "good news."

From another perspective, though, people watch television news programs because they want to feel they are aware. Within a short period of time, the interested viewer is provided a visual survey of the major events of the day. But while consumers want to know as quickly as they can, it is not feasible for them to spend their days in front of the newswire machines, nor do they have the time to gather the information first hand. They must rely on specialists who work in the news media to do the job for them.

Those who practice the craft of television journalism follow a credo of service to the public. Former NBC journalist (now with ABC-TV) David Brinkley has described the role of broadcast news as well as anyone:

I think of it to a great extent as a service industry, in some ways similar to a bakery. You can bake your own bread, but it's easier to buy it—most people don't have time to do it. We do the public a service that they're not really equipped to do for themselves— by keeping track of what happens around the world and telling them about it at 6:30 or 11:30 or whatever.[2]

HISTORICAL DEVELOPMENT

Television news didn't "just begin." Neither it nor other television program forms were created in a vacuum. Radio news and documentary and cinema newsreel contributed much. In fact, radio was the medium in which the reputation of one of television's most important journalists was established.

Edward R. Murrow's early contribution to the development of television net-work news was that he hired many of the radio reporters who became prominent correspondents on the CBS news team. Some of "Murrow's boys," as they were called during World War II, went on to establish great careers in television: Eric Sevareid, Howard K. Smith, and Charles Collingwood successfully made the transition after the war, and their careers have spanned the history of television news. Walter Cronkite, whose name is synonymous with television news, was a United Press news service reporter during World War II and did not sign on with CBS until 1951.

Murrow's considerable reputation developed as a result of his news broadcasts during the war, particularly those from the rooftops of London during German bomb attacks.[3] His career in television began in 1951 when he and Fred W. Friendly co-produced the most important early documentary series, "See It Now." This weekly program made a particular impact on standards for broadcast journalism that are still followed, particularly at the network level. Chapter 12, "Television Documentary," deals more extensively with Murrow's contribution and "See It Now."

A number of important early programs were the basis for the development of television news programs. The first nightly network news program began in June 1947 on the now-defunct DuMont network, but it was to last only 11 months. A program that enjoyed considerably greater success, NBC's weekly "Meet the

Press," was brought over from radio a few months later, in November 1947. It has had the longest run of any TV news program and is still on the air. The importance of "Meet the Press" and its imitators on the other networks is not the size of their audiences, but in the forums they provide for public figures. Guests are often quoted in newspapers and their statements seen on the nightly network newscasts. CBS began a news-interview program, "Face the Nation," in 1954. ABC's "Issues and Answers," which began in 1960, was replaced by "This Week with David Brinkley" in November 1981. "This Week" included interviews but had a broader range of subjects and guests than the traditional news-interview format. "This Week" made inroads on the audience of "Face the Nation," and CBS announced it would be replaced in 1983 by a news program with a different format.

Actually, the format of news-interview programs was not new with television. The basic difference between the radio and television versions was the pictures of the guests and their interrogators. In a return to an era before the development and adoption of videotape equipment, network and local station news programs have begun using live interviews. The introduction of sophisticated electronic equipment has made it commonplace for anchorpersons to turn to television monitors on their sets to interview reporters in the field or to ask questions of newsworthy persons who respond from separate studios during the broadcast.

In earlier times, however, live telecasting was commonplace because it was necessary. Videotape had not yet been introduced, and the news departments did not even have their own news film crews. That quickly changed, though, and a priority was placed on having someone who could introduce the recorded reports and summarize events when film was unavailable. The first network TV news program to have a regular anchorman to perform this function was the "CBS TV News" in 1948. Douglas Edwards, who is still with CBS News, anchored the nightly broadcast until he was replaced by Walter Cronkite in 1962.

Anchormen, introducing the filmed reports and tying the whole program together, became an established part of television news. It was the original producer of the CBS TV news program, Don Hewitt (who later became executive producer of the highly-rated "60 Minutes"), and Edwards who established that a "star" in the form of the anchorperson would be the single consistent personality in creating an identity for each network's news program.

NBC's answer to Edwards's program was the "Camel News Caravan," anchored by John Cameron Swayze (he is no longer associated with television news, but can still be seen in watch commercials). Swayze's stint began in 1949 and lasted until 1956, when he was succeeded by the team of Chet Huntley and David Brinkley. Swayze was known more for his good looks and the boutonniere in his lapel than his journalistic qualifications. Each evening he would enthusiastically say, "Now let's go hopscotching the world for headlines," to introduce a series of unrelated items that ended the "News Caravan" broadcast.[4]

The sober style espoused by Douglas Edwards became the standard for network anchormen and correspondents in their delivery of news stories. John Cameron

Swayze, on the other hand, was a forerunner of what came to be described as local news "happy talk." His enthusiasm and breezy style were not to have lasting influence on network news. In fact, it was his lack of journalistic depth, added to his program's declining ratings, that caused his dismissal from NBC.

The ABC television network was at a disadvantage in news competition from its very start. ABC was not established until 1943, when NBC was forced to sell one of its two radio networks. Naturally, the weakest was spun off. The new network was in a poor financial position, so the transition to television was difficult. ABC did not have a radio news tradition on which to build a strong television program; thus, when ABC moved forward, it was only after hiring individuals from CBS and NBC.

These limitations prevented the network from establishing a continuing nightly television news broadcast until 1953. ABC TV news, playing catch up to the other networks, struggled along. It was not until the late 1960s that the right combination of elements made it truly competitive.

From the earliest days, an important service of network departments has been coverage of special news events. Audiences have seldom been large, but a great deal of attention has usually been given to these telecasts. Early broadcasts also made important contributions to the tradition that established the networks' obligation to cover such events as the Senate hearings on the Vietnam War in 1965 and the 1972 Senate Watergate investigation.

Earlier coverage had also been significant. A major television event in 1951 was the Senate hearings on organized crime. ABC carried the hearings in full; the network had nothing to lose, since its regular daily schedule did not begin until 2:00 P.M. The most important thing about the coverage was not the subject, but the demonstration of television power's to catapult a public official to national prominence. Largely because of the exposure he received as chairman of the Senate crime committee, Senator Estes Kefauver of Tennessee secured the Democratic Party's nomination as its vice presidential candidate in 1952. A parallel came 20 years later, during the Senate Select Committee's hearings on Watergate. Senator Sam Ervin of North Carolina became well known across the country when he chaired that investigation before the television cameras. Ervin, in the twilight of his career, obtained no particular political advantage. The clearest beneficiary was Senator Howard Baker of Tennessee, whose performance as the ranking Republican member of the committee earned him the admiration of many viewers and helped him secure the support needed to become the GOP's Senate leader. Later, in 1980, Baker entered the race for the Republican nomination for the presidency.

Political conventions have traditionally provided a showcase for network reportorial talent, establishing a number of correspondents as stars. While Douglas Edwards continued as CBS's evening news anchor, Walter Cronkite gained prominence as the CBS convention coverage anchor and by hosting other CBS news programs.

NBC used the 1956 conventions to introduce viewers to a new anchor team of Chet Huntley and David Brinkley. Their performance was so successful that later in that year the "Huntley-Brinkley Report" made its debut as NBC's nightly news program. The days of the announcer-as-anchorman on network news programs were numbered. John Cameron Swayze, the early ratings leader in the CBS-NBC ratings race, had been overtaken by "Douglas Edwards with the News." When Huntley and Brinkley began to gain viewer popularity, the ratings for Edwards's CBS news program began to slip. His replacement, Walter Cronkite, went on to become the nation's premiere news anchor, introducing stories that reported on a turbulent era in modern America. Television had become an important source of news for the public. The high standards that are part of the tradition of network television news reporting, however, were begun earlier.

Following World War II, a political movement fueled by fear of communism and charges that its agents had infiltrated high levels of government spread through the United States. Joseph R. McCarthy's name became synomous with the era, but he simply took advantage of the prevailing attitudes. McCarthy was able to make accusations without substantiating his charges because he had the protection of the United States Senate.

In a series of reports on "See It Now," Edward R. Murrow examined the issue of freedom of expression and the activities of McCarthy and other anti-Communist crusaders. The culmination came in a broadcast that showed statements made by McCarthy in his public speeches. To say the least, it generated great controversy and is credited for opening the way for the televised Army-McCarthy hearings that gave the American public an extended view of the senator's personality and tactics. It was these telecasts that clearly contributed to McCarthy's downfall, but Edward R. Murrow is remembered for having the courage to examine the issues and the senator's tactics when few were speaking out.

If McCarthy was the loser when television finally began to scrutinize his activities, the winner was ABC, which, along with the DuMont network, telecast the hearings live each day while CBS and NBC broadcast filmed summaries during the evenings. Thanks to the public interest generated by the hearings, the ABC television network became much more competitive. It would still be a number of years, however, before ABC news achieved parity with CBS or NBC.

Public affairs and documentary programs enhanced network prestige and may have had more impact on viewers than the evening news programs. Certainly, the kinds of programs included in the "See It Now" series and special events coverage generated controversy and attention. (It was said, for instance, that television news came of age with the Murrow-McCarthy broadcasts.) As the United States entered the 1960s, yet another special broadcast drew attention to television and its news service. It has often been observed that an important, if not a decisive, factor in the 1960 presidential election was the series of televised debates between Richard Nixon and John Kennedy. These telecasts gave viewers a window through which to form impressions of both candidates. Kennedy, a young, fairly obscure senator from Massachusetts, more than held his own against the two-term vice president of the United States. That first debate, on September 26, 1960, helped establish him as a strong candidate. Once again, coverage of a special news event demonstrated television's capacity to provide information and influence viewers.[5]

Kennedy, who recognized the power of television, was the first president to permit live telecasts of his press conferences. Perhaps as telling of his appreciation of the political importance of television news, Kennedy agreed to be interviewed when the networks expanded their nightly news programs. CBS's regular 30–minute broadcasts commenced September 2, 1963, and NBC followed on September 9. ABC did not expand its nightly news from 15 minutes until 1967.

Only a few months later, on November 22, 1963, President Kennedy was killed by an assassin in Dallas. Network coverage of his murder and funeral did much to unite the nation during this period of shock and grief. As with other special events coverage, television provided an immediacy and perspective not possible through any other medium.[6]

The Kennedy assassination marked the beginning of an era of turmoil and rapid change in American life. It was a period of racial unrest and demonstrations for civil rights, a time when the United States became embroiled in a war in Southeast Asia, and a time of dissaffection among many of the youth of the country. Due to these and other societal changes, television news came into its own. By the mid-1960s, CBS and NBC had not only expanded their news programs but were airing weekend broadcasts as well.

During this period, the networks provided extensive coverage of "the living room war"—so-called because so many Americans saw reports about Vietnam on their television sets. As the U.S. military presence in South Vietnam increased, so did each network's news staff. For a time, Saigon had the largest network news bureaus anywhere outside the United States.

It was television's first war. Radio still predominated during the Korean conflict, but television soon became the primary mass medium in the United States and an important source for news. News coverage of the war in Southeast Asia was extensive and was presented over a long period of time.

Another continuing story that no doubt contributed to viewer interest in late-breaking news on television was the civil rights movement that began in the 1950s and escalated through the 1960s. Television news can be credited with drawing viewer attention to the tumultuous events in the South, including marches and demonstrations in various southern cities. Television news was not, in itself, responsible for turning the situation around. As with the Vietnam War, news coverage of the civil rights movement added tremendous impact to events also being described in newspapers, magazines, and on the radio.

It was a particularly trying time for the establishment. Television was helping to violate the sanctity of traditional leadership as the evening news reported protests on college campuses and in the cities.

The new Nixon administration sensed a current of resentment against television news coverage and capitalized on it. Less than a year after taking office, Vice

President Spiro Agnew dropped a bombshell when he accused network television news of undue influence and a lack of objectivity and fairness. News decisions, the vice president, said, were made by a tiny handful of men. Their liberal vision, he charged, was limited to thinking typical only of those native to the East Coast. Ironically, this November 3, 1969, speech was carried by all three networks.

Agnew's remarks drew a tremendous response from the "silent majority"— people weary of the coverage of criticism of the establishment and the parade of protestors seen on the nightly news. Among Agnew's objections were network correspondents' assessments of presidential speeches, which he labeled "instant analyses." Despite the common practice of providing copies of the speeches to members of the news corps hours before their delivery and even though the analysts were seasoned reporters familiar with the issues and apprised of the possible consequencs of presidential policies, many affiliates announced they would no longer carry post-speech analyses.[7]

Eventually, the stigma associated with "instant analysis" was lifted. The networks resumed a bolder stance in their news coverage, but it took a major government scandal, Watergate, to stimulate this more resolute attitude.

In the meantime, television news at the local level had been increasing in importance. In earlier days, news departments were expensive to maintain and did not generate much interest or revenue. Management was in a quandary since their stations, licensed by the federal government, were obligated to provide such public services as news programs. Happily, the problem evaporated, as it became apparent that news programs were about their only distinguishing characteristic. Along with the utility of providing local market identity, managers discovered that audiences for news programs had begun to grow; thus, stations became more competitive in their news offerings.

Local news programs in most markets have expanded to the point where, in many cities, viewers can watch two hours of news during the early part of the evening, followed later that night by another half hour of local news. In most cases, though, much of the content is repeated from earlier broadcasts during the day.[8]

While these developments were occurring at the local level, two networks, CBS and NBC, were highly competitive while ABC languished in third place. In 1969, ABC finally made its bid for prominence in the evening news race. In the revolving ABC anchor chair, Peter Jennings had been replaced by Frank Reynolds and then by the tandem of Reynolds and former CBS news correspondent Howard K. Smith. Later, CBS correspondent Harry Reasoner was lured over to ABC, where he replaced Reynolds as co-anchor in December 1970. The Reasoner-Smith team continued for five years, and ABC's "Evening News" began to draw respectable ratings.

Meanwhile, controversy over television news continued, including heavy criticism of CBS following its broadcast of "The Selling of the Pentagon" on February 23, 1971. The program was not a part of the nightly news, but it is a good example of another network news activity that contributed to growing allegations that all network news programs were biased. The documentary, sharply critical of the publicity efforts of the U.S. military, was panned by the Pentagon, the White House, and various members of Congress, who charged distortion and half-truths in the CBS presentation.

The House of Representatives Commerce Committee subpoenaed outtakes (portions of film not used in the broadcast). An attempt to obtain a contempt of Congress citation against CBS President Frank Stanton was rejected, ending the issue except for the bitter aftertaste created by the documentary among its critics.[9]

Controversy, which was associated with television news throughout the Nixon administration, heated up when revelations of the Watergate break-in were being published and broadcast. President Nixon, who had never had a particularly cordial relationship with the press, became increasingly acrimonious—particularly when television news reporters pressed him on the Watergate matter. This was apparent during televised press conferences and especially when CBS White House correspondent Dan Rather rose to question the president.

Shortly after Nixon resigned the presidency, many concluded that earlier administration efforts to remove Rather from his White House beat had finally been achieved when he was appointed as the first permanent CBS documentary correspondent since Edward R. Murrow. While Rather asserted that the move was a compliment and a promotion, the boost to his career really came when he was assigned as a regular correspondent on "60 Minutes." This role was instrumental in keeping him in the public eye yet allowing a period of time to diminish the hostility associated with his position as a White House correspondent. Eventually, Rather was selected to replace the nation's premiere news anchorman, Walter Cronkite.[10]

Meanwhile, other anchorperson moves were taking place. Harry Reasoner was joined as co-anchor on the ABC Nightly News by Barbara Walters on October 6, 1976. She had received a five-year contract worth one million dollars a year to leave NBC and the "Today" show. No one ever said Walters was not good, but there was considerable consternation over the huge salary she had received. Many in television news were sure that entertainment priorities were going to dominate journalistic considerations from that point on. That did not happen, but she and Reasoner did not remain partners for long.

In July 1978, "World News Tonight" and a new ABC news format was unveiled. Frank Reynolds anchored part of the news from Washington, D.C., instead of a traditional New York studio location. From Chicago, Max Robinson, the first black network nightly news anchorperson, presented a portion of the program. In London, Peter Jennings reported world news. Reynolds emerged as the "most equal" in the trio until his unexpected death in July 1983. Soon thereafter, Jennings was appointed the sole anchor and Robinson was assigned other duties.

Part of the "World News Tonight" format was the "whip-around," where some stories were introduced from the field, passing directly from a correspondent reporting from one location to another reporter somewhere else, tying all stories on a similar theme together without going back to the anchorperson in the studio. These changes drew some criticism, of course, but that eventually subsided and ABC news gained greater respectability, if not top ratings.

Television news' involvement in foreign affairs had begun before satellite interconnection of major cities around the world, but with the increasing speed in getting dramatic news reports on viewers' screens in the United States, world affairs were influenced even more by television coverage. ABC's Barbara Walters managed to get a live television interview with Egyptian President Anwar Sadat and Israel's Prime Minister Menachem Begin, each appearing from his own capital. Walters scooped CBS's Walter Cronkite and John Chancellor of NBC by several hours. While it is not clear who should be credited with starting the initiative that prompted Begin to invite Sadat to make his historic visit to Israel, television diplomacy was clearly in the middle of it all.[11]

Television news again demonstrated its influence on public opinion during the summer of 1982 when Israel invaded Lebanon to eradicate Palestine Liberation Organization strongholds. As the military campaign began, public sentiment seemed clearly on the side of the Israelis; but when television cameras recorded the devastation of the city of Beirut by Israeli mortars and the uprooting of natives ostensibly being liberated by the Israeli army, that attitude changed. The invasion had no significant effect on Americans, but there was great concern in the United States over the damage being inflicted with American-supplied firepower.[12]

Just as television news had played a role in Egyptian-Israeli negotiations, it was important during the takeover of the U.S. embassy in Iran where, for over 14 months, more than 50 American citizens were held captive. A satellite transmission station in Tehran made it possible to send out immediate reports. Americans thus became accustomed to seeing chanting mobs in front of the U.S. embassy on the evening news. There were frequent appearances by Iranian leaders, who played to television audiences in the States. The Iranians, who clearly were aware of the power of television, permitted or denied news reports of interest to American news audiences to leave their country at will.

ABC news seized the initiative in airing late night reports on the hostage crisis. Their series "The Iran Crisis: America Held Hostage" was the forerunner of a regularly scheduled late-evening news program, "Nightline," that started in March 1980. It was the first of several late-evening and early-morning network programs to serve as alternatives or extensions of the traditional nightly news formats. Eventually, ABC added a late-late night program that dealt with current affairs topics in interviews and viewer's call-in questions. "Nightline's" success prompted ABC to expand the program to 60 minutes in April 1983. "NBC News Overnight," which began at 1:30 P.M., provided insomniac viewers with late news from June 1982 through December 1983.[13] CBS began a similar program, "Newswatch," in October 1982.

The networks did not neglect the early morning either. The competition had virtually conceded the morning news audience to the "Today" show until ABC introduced "AM America" in January 1974. That program struggled and was revamped in October 1975. By 1980, "Good Morning America" had overtaken "Today" in audience ratings. Meanwhile, the CBS morning news hour languished in third place. In September 1981, CBS lengthened the program to 90 minutes and changed anchors in an attempt to attract a larger share of the audience.[14]

The networks also expanded news service by appending their morning news programs. In July 1982, ABC and NBC added half-hour early news programs that preceded "Good Morning America" and "Today".

A noncommercial alternative to the network nightly news, available since January 1976, is PBS's "MacNeil-Lehrer Report." Broadcast live each evening (although taped and broadcast at various times by PBS affiliates), it was expanded from 30 minutes to an hour on September 5, 1983, becoming the first hour-long nightly network news program to be broadcast during the early evening.

Expansion of the commercial networks' nightly news programs from 15 to 30 minutes back in 1963 was resisted by affiliates, who had to give up revenues from commercials during progrms they scheduled during that time period. More recent efforts have been successfully opposed. There is little likelihood of an expansion during the time of day that the greatest number of viewers are available to watch television news. The revenue potential to local stations is just too compelling for them to give that time over to their networks.[15]

Even without a longer time period, the jockeying for news program audience ratings has continued among the networks, who place a great reliance on the effectiveness of their anchorpersons to attract an audience. When David Brinkley gave up his co-anchor position on the "NBC Nightly News," speculation was fueled that John Chancellor would soon quit or be replaced. He continued until January 1982, when Tom Brokaw and Roger Mudd assumed the NBC anchor positions. ABC news and sports president Roone Arledge's maneuvering may have precipitated that decision, since ABC was interested in Brokaw as a possible "steal" from NBC. In the meantime, CBS announced that Dan Rather would take over from Walter Cronkite, which he did in March 1981. That caused Mudd's defection to NBC because he was passed over at CBS. At NBC, Mudd shared anchoring responsibilities from Washington, D.C., where he had been a congressional correspondent for CBS.[16]

When Rather took the helm at CBS, it was generally thought that the other networks could make inroads in CBS's evening news audience supremacy. More than two years later, however, Rather and the "CBS Evening News" were still in the lead.

The greatest changes may be yet to come, as alternative news services crop up. Cable News Network (CNN) began its transmission via satellite in June 1980, offering 24-hour news to cable television subscribers.[17] Independent stations (not affiliated with the ABC, CBS, or NBC television networks) can now obtain a satellite-distributed national news program from Independent Network News. Perhaps seeing the future, ABC went into partnership with Westinghouse

Broadcasting to create Satellite News Channels, an alternative to CNN. This resulted in the establishment of CNN2, a headlines service available to any television station or cable system.

The list of news and information services will probably grow. Where that will leave traditional network and local television news programs can only be speculated. Clearly, though, technology is influencing the content, form, and choices of televised news.

The number of programs has increased, but their style of presentation has remained fairly consistent. The nature of the news is influenced by traditions that persevere.

THEMES AND ISSUES

While certainly a legitimate journalistic form, television news is still a "show" as all television programs are "shows." News programs have formats as predictable as any regularly scheduled dramatic series. They take on the values of entertainment programs because they are set in an entertainment medium and their outlets (television stations) strive to attract the largest audiences possible. These viewers are no more nor any less important to program sponsors than any group of purchasers of antiperspirants, soft drinks, or headache remedies.

Inevitably, the commercial motive causes conflicts between the traditions of television journalism and the purposes for attracting and maintaining the largest possible audiences. As William Kuhns has pointed out, there is a tension between accuracy and the need to entertain; between depth reporting and the need for strong visual content; between accurate reporting of events and the tendency to create events by the presence of cameras at the scene.[18]

News programs bring prestige to their networks. In much the same way that electronic and print news-gathering organizations look to the *New York Times*, the *Washington Post*, and a few other newspapers for a standard of excellence in journalism, local broadcast news professionals often look to the network news departments as standard-bearers for broadcast journalism. Part of this is because many local television journalists aspire to network positions, and occasionally someone who has established his or her reputation at one of the network news organizations takes a position at a local station.

Though it isn't a salable commodity, prestige is very useful as a counter to criticism of less-acclaimed but considerably more profitable entertainment fare. In fact, both stations and their networks find it useful to ballyhoo their news and public affairs program awards and occasionally point out that the profits from the other programs make such quality broadcasts possible.

Prestige is a consideration at local stations, but profits are clearly more important. Stations have found an increased revenue potential in their news programs, which has given rise to the news consultant.

Consulting firms service their client stations by surveying audience interests, analyzing audition tapes of news personalities, and reviewing news program structure as a basis for recommending changes that might attract larger audiences. Inevitably, critics have come to associate such advice with a change from a journalistic to an entertainment orientation.[19]

Consultant's recommendations have resulted in a striking similarity in news programs seen in cities across the country. Not only are station managers and news directors advised on who should read the news (often a tandem of a mature man with a young, handsome, energetic woman), but on the program introduction (e.g., "eyewitness news," "news alive" or "action news"), the colors used in the news set, shape of the anchor desk, kind of clothing the principals wear, and their hair styles.

These are cosmetic changes. The real concern comes from suggestions (often labeled by news directors as tampering) by consultants on the length and emphasis of news stories. A frequent recommendation has urged emphasis on "news you can use"—consumer reports that feature advice from pharmacists, physicians, and even veterinarians and reviews of current movies. Such "soft" news, it is charged, replaces less entertaining but more vital information.

Network news programs have also increased their quotas of "soft news," but not nearly to the extent of local news programs. One reason for the difference is the critical scorn that can be heaped on network news organizations. Another, which is closely linked, is the well-established professional tradition embraced by most network news executives and correspondents.

Whether entertainment or information is the motive, the viewer must choose among the available channels. What is the real distinction between, say, Channels 5, 8, and 12 in a particular television market? To most viewers, very little, except for the distinctive sets of news personalities. In the parlance of the marketing analyst, these are elements that help "position" stations and programs in the minds of viewers. Therefore, a real value of television news is in helping stations and networks establish their identities. At the local level, though, there is a particular focus on the anchorpersons at the expense of building strong staffs of reporters to enhance the reputation of the program. Network anchors are given the greatest attention in promoting their news programs, but the professionalism and experience of correspondents in the field also get considerable attention. Nevertheless, when an anchor cannot draw a sufficiently large audience, he or she is likely to be replaced. A case in point is Roger Mudd, who co-anchored the "NBC Nightly News" for only a few months before being abruptly removed in 1983. Although generally considered one of the best reporters in Washington, D.C., the NBC news department management apparently decided he did not have the right stuff to attract viewers in the ratings war with ABC and CBS.

The anchor's persona can be compared with that of the action-adventure program hero. The anchor must exude authority, certainty, and wisdom. Like the hero of the drama, the anchor must appear to be ahead of the story and on top of the action, organizing it effectively.[20]

As this description implies, the anchor must not only convey knowledgeability but friendliness and "likeability." Similar to a variety show host, the anchor is the glue that bonds the disparate elements of the program, as he or she introduces reports and other participants, who provide most of the details. As a part of the format, anchorpersons may interview correspondents in the field to elicit follow-up information of interest or importance to the audience. Importantly, this information comes through the anchorperson's efforts rather than directly from the correspondent.

There are few personalities in network news who do not convey maturity, seriousness, and a generally reserved outlook. The few exceptions include "hip" reporters like Geraldo Rivera of ABC, and CBS sports reporter Heywood Hale Broun, who is virtually the only network reporter to affect loud plaid sports jackets.

Such oddities in personality type are rare at the networks, either as correspondents or anchorpersons. The tradition of network news seems to dictate that the anchorperson, especially, be a dignified individual. One of the best known local news anchor personalities, Tom Snyder, has never been given a position as anchor of a network nightly news program. (He was with NBC News as host of "Tomorrow" and anchored its magazine news program, "Prime Time Saturday.") His ability to attract an audience seems clear, but network news executives consider him a potential embarrassment and have therefore denied what is reported to be his ambition to anchor the nightly news.[21]

At the station level, extremes in personality are much more likely to be found among other members of the station's "news team" than in the anchorpersons. Sports and weather reporters, who are important secondary members of the anchor team, are more likely to be the "characters." This is not to say that anchors are bland, but certainly, they would never be called "zany,"as weather reporters may be.

Network news programs do not place much emphasis on weather personalities and weather information since conditions vary so widely across the country. Exceptions are Willard Scott on NBC's "Today" show and John Coleman on "Good Morning America." These individuals made the step from local stations, bringing distinctive personalities to their network programs.

At local stations, weather personalities vary widely. Many stations treat the weather segment seriously, employing highly qualified reporters who may hold master's or Ph.D. degrees in meteorology. Generally, such weathercasters are straightforward and factual. The majority of the local station weather reporters, however, are less qualified to interpret conditions and make predictions. Many are performers who rely on a jovial manner or an ability to draw cartoons or arrows that help illustrate weather conditions.

In recent years, visual interest has been added to weather reports with computer-based graphics and color radar patterns. While they can be impressive visual shows, graphics may add little actual information. Sometimes such devices are included because the station management wants to have the latest gimmick before the competition gets it.

At the local level, television news has a history of overkill in adopting new technology. For instance, when "ENG" (electronic cameras and video tape technology) was introduced, stations initially embracing the technology overused it, as if to justify the expenditure. One station even presented a live telecast of a Volkswagen-stuffing contest from a local bar during its late-evening news program. This event was broadcast, one must presume, because "it was there" and the equipment was capable of presenting it—not because viewers needed to know and see how many bodies could be crammed into the car.

Live mini-cam reports that preempt entertainment programs diminished in popularity after news personnel acknowledged that, while convenience and speed are improved, the news occurring in most communities seldom justifies cancelling commercially sponsored programs—particularly since station managers are sensitive to the effect of preemptions on profits. A solution to that dilemma is live reports during the broadcast of the news program. Many local news programs schedule "standuppers" by their street reporters to coincide with a particular time slot during the broadcast. Again, these appear to be motivated more by the fact that they are possible than the timeliness of the reports.

Virtually all stations now use ENG equipment. Another current trendy item is the helicopter. One or more stations in most major markets use them, ostensibly to increase their news coverage of the area. Their real function is often promotion, however, with little actual use in news coverage.

Gimmicks have not been limited to equipment. A few years ago, ABC owned and operated stations in New York, Chicago, and Los Angeles introduced their news program audiences to "happy talk," a successful ploy to attract more viewers.

Happy talk struck a chord among audiences weary of hearing how things were going wrong in the world. Its premise was not to limit the program to good news but to present the news in a friendly manner. The joviality, in its excesses, included jokes and banal banter following accounts of tragedies. These were sometimes insensitive, if not in downright bad taste. Still, many stations, seeking higher ratings, used the happy talk idea, encouraging a sense of familiarity between viewers and those gathered at the anchor desk.

Aside from the question of taste, anchorperson interchanges reduced the amount of time that could be devoted to reviewing the news of the day. At worst, the tone of many news programs changed from a straightforward and serious account of the day's events to an emphasis on "soft" news. That move is, of course, more congruent with entertainment, the environment in which news programs are scheduled.

Death and violence are, in a curious way, forms of entertainment. Witness, for instance, the number of onlookers at the site of an auto accident. Many local news programs have provided such diversions. Their excesses are known in the business as "blood 'n guts news." Stations using this approach present story after story of violent tragedy: fires, murders, automobile wrecks, and the like.

Such coverage illustrates the influences on some news programs in their quest for larger audiences. Their structure is generally influenced by these same considerations. The news has a structure that is as ritualistic as any entertainment program. The typical major market (and most secondary market) programs open with a fast-paced, carefully edited montage of scenes of the area being served. A device often used to denote action is a shot of a jet airliner's nose as it taxies up to the terminal. If the station has a helicopter, viewers are sure to see it in flight over the city's skyline.

It is exciting visual material, denoting vibrance and action. But it is also the stuff of most entertainment programs. What makes the news unique is that it is presented as a survey of the important events of the day. Viewers believe they are being informed, even if their recall of content is sketchy. A part of the superficiality is due to viewer inattention, but also because the news programs—especially at the local level—embrace content that appeals to the entertainment desires of the television audience. As important, the length of most news programs does not permit much depth in coverage or analysis of events being reported.

Limited time, coupled with the competitive motivation to make the program as interesting and attractive as possible to somewhat inattentive viewers, has prompted local and network producers to try various visual communication techniques. When network news programs experiment with visual presentations, they can be subject to a great deal more criticism than local stations. Witness, for instance, the reaction by critics when CBS news anchor Dan Rather began wearing a sweater under his suit jacket in an effort to heighten his audience appeal. And when some innovative graphics were introduced on the ABC evening news program they also drew comment because they broke with the studied seriousness of network news.

The presentation of news in an entertaining package in a limited amount of time requires simplification through symbolism. Another demand is for "action," which comes at the expense of the depth of the information that can be provided. The worst kind of television news programs is radio with pictures, where viewers simply see the news reporter reading the report. Talking heads are to be avoided when possible, which results in news reports that may be full of visualization but short on explanation. Local anchorpersons and reporters are coached by news program consultants to gesture, which is important in the attempt to show subjects *doing* something—anything except standing motionless while talking to the camera.

Television relies on symbols. With so little time available in the half hour and hour forms, the audience for a TV drama must quickly recognize the good guys and villians. There is little time to dig up examples to illustrate a story and not enough time to show all that could be found. Neither local nor network television news organizations have reporting staffs sufficient to provide detailed coverage of all the news. Instead, representatives or symbols are used to illustrate. For example, a story on the cost of living is easily visualized and made more interesting by its human interest factor when it focuses on a "typical" family. A popular news icon is the supermarket meat counter, which has the advantage of immediate recognition (meat is a traditionally costly item in household budgets). Thus, the reporter's narrative is supported by a symbol of the cost of living in the same way a network news correspondent reports on the activity of the president in a standupper that shows the White House in the background.

Whether the subject of a report is sufficiently explained may be secondary to maintaining entertainment values. The actions of the zoning commission or the police chief probably have a more direct effect on the average viewer than all the accidental deaths, fires, and stabbings ever reported, but stories about meetings do not make for very interesting television.[22] Little can be shown except somber ladies and gentlemen silently listening to the debate. Such reports usually include an obligatory pan of the room and a quick jump to the hallway or exterior of the building where the reporter summarizes the action taken in the meeting in a standupper that has some symbol like the city hall in the background.

Reports of this kind reflect influences on television news that we have described. The difference between one program and another may be in whether an attempt is made to live up to the traditions of television reporting and the extent to which program producers and reporters acquiesce to the entertainment values attached to all television programming.

This is not to say that television news programs are not worthwhile—they are. Some are a travesty of the journalistic craft, but most provide a highly useful service to their audiences. The thoughtful viewer, however, recognizes the limitations and the demands on the form.

NOTES

1. Readers interested in analysis of television news should see William Adams and Fay Schreibman, eds., *Television Network News: Issues in Content Research* (Washington, D.C.: George Washington University, 1978).

2. David Brinkley, in "The View from the Trenches," *Broadcasting*, November 15, 1982, p. 99.

3. Biographies of Murrow include R. Franklin Smith, *Edward R. Murrow: The War Years* (Kalamazoo, Mich.: New Issues Press, 1978); Fred W. Friendly, *Due to Circumstances Beyond Our Control* . . . (New York: Vintage Books, 1967); and Alexander Kendrick, *Prime Time: The Life of Edward R. Murrow* (New York: Avon Books, 1969).

4. Erik Barnouw, *Tube of Plenty: The Evolution of American Television* (New York: Oxford University Press, 1975), pp. 102–5; and Gary Paul Gates, *Air Time: The Inside Story of CBS News* (New York: Harper & Row, 1978), pp. 50–81.

5. Readers interested in the debates should see Sidney Kraus, ed., *The Great Debates* (Bloomington, Ind.: Indiana University Press, 1962); and Theodore H. White, *The Making of the President, 1960* (New York: Pocket Books, 1961), pp. 335–54.

6. Wilbur Schramm, "Communication in Crisis," in *The Process and Effects of Mass Communication*, rev. ed., ed. Wilbur Schramm and Donald F. Roberts (Urbana, Ill.: University of Illinois Press, 1971), pp. 528–53.

7. Two sources of the transcript of Vice President Agnew's remarks and the network reactions are Marvin Barrett, ed., *Survey of Broadcast Journalism, 1969–1970* (New York: Grossett & Dunlap, 1970), pp. 131–39; and Michael C. Emery and Ted Curtis

Smythe, eds., *Readings in Mass Communication* (Dubuque, Iowa: Wm. C. Brown, 1972), pp. 309–46.

8. Marvin Barrett, "TV Diplomacy and Other Broadcast Quandaries," *Columbia Journalism Review* (May/June 1979), pp. 74–75; Marvin Barrett and Zachary Sklar, eds., *The Eye of the Storm* (New York: Lippincott & Crowell, 1980), pp. 58–72.

9. The transcript of CBS's "The Selling of the Pentagon," as broadcast February 23, 1971, is reprinted in Marvin Barrett, ed., *Survey of Broadcast Journalism 1970–1971* (New York: Grosset & Dunlap, 1971), pp. 151–71. CBS President Stanton's remarks to a special subcommittee of the House of Representatives Interstate and Foreign Commerce Committee on June 24, 1971, are reprinted in Emery and Smythe, eds., *Readings in Mass Communication*, pp. 99–105.

10. For an overview of Rather's career, see Norman King, *Dan Rather* (New York: Leisure Books, 1981). Much of this account can also be found in Gates, *Air Time*.

11. Barrett, "TV Diplomacy," pp. 69–70.

12. Edward Cody and Pnina Ramati, "Covering the Invasion of Lebanon," *Washington Journalism Review* (September 1982), pp. 18–21; and Roger Morris, "Beirut—and the Press—Under Siege," *Columbia Journalism Review* (November/December 1982), pp. 23–33.

13. "New News in the News," *Broadcasting*, July 5, 1982, pp. 71–73; Richard Zoglin, "News in the Night: The Networks Race for Unclaimed Territory," *Washington Journalism Review* (September 1982), pp. 22–25; and Michael Hammerschlag, "TV's Night Owl News Shows," *Columbia Journalism Review* (July/August 1983), pp. 46–49.

14. Michael D. Mosettig, "Breakfast for Bonzo," *Washington Journalism Review* (June 1982), pp. 49–51.

15. Marvin Barrett, "The Sixty-Minute Hour," *Rich News, Poor News*, ed. Marvin Barrett (New York: Thomas Y. Crowell, 1978), pp. 24–38.

16. Dennis Holder, "Television News Enters the Redi-Whip Era," *Washington Journalism Review* (January/February 1982), pp. 20–24.

17. James Traub, "The Nonstop News Network," *Columbia Journalism Review* (July/August 1981), pp. 58–61; and Marvin Barrett, "The Cable Revolution," in *Broadcast Journalism, 1979–1981*, ed. Marvin Barrett (New York: Dodd, Mead & Co., 1982), pp. 80–97.

18. William Kuhns, *Why We Watch Them: Interpreting TV Shows* (New York: Benziger, 1970), p. 50.

19. Three useful summaries are " 'The Trojan Horse': News Consultants," in *Moments of Truth?* ed. Marvin Barrett (New York: Thomas Y. Crowell, 1975), pp. 89–112; Leslie Fuller, "News Doctors: Taking Over TV Journalism?" *Broadcasting*, September 9, 1974, pp. 21–28; and Ralph Renick, "The Cumulative Impact of News Consultants after Ten Years in the Field," in *Broadcast Journalism, 1979–1981*, ed. Marvin Barrett (New York: Dodd, Mead & Co., 1982), pp. 195–203.

20. Joyce Nelson, "TV Formulas: Prime Time Glue," *In Search* (Fall 1979), p. 26.

21. Bill Barol, "Tom Snyder", *Washington Journalism Review* (January/February 1983), pp. 27–31.

22. Quite aside from the "interestingness" of such reports, Ben H. Bagdikian makes the point that there are so many significant public bodies such as school boards, public works commissions, etc., in television markets (which are defined not by civic boundaries but by merchandising territories) as to make their routine coverage virtually impossible in *The Information Machines* (New York: Harper Colophon Books, 1971), pp. 81–86.

BIBLIOGRAPHICAL SURVEY

An important on-going series of reviews edited by Marvin Barrett is based on national Alfred I. duPont/Columbia University surveys. They not only describe the status of broadcast journalism and delineate current issues in covering the news but collectively serve as a recent history of news programs.

The way network news organizations gather, assimilate, refine, and finally report "the news" is described in Edward Jay Epstein's *News from Nowhere*. It is a hallmark in illustrating the values and demands that are a part of the process that shapes the kind of stories seen on network nightly news. While Epstein limited his observations to NBC's New York operation, it serves as a description of what one could expect to find at any network. He reviews the attitudes of editors, producers, and correspondents and how they affect the product that is aired.

Another analysis of network news organization is *Deciding What's News* by Herbert Gans. This study of the CBS and NBC evening news programs and *Newsweek* and *Time* magazines is based on analysis of their content and on observations made over several months at each of the organizations. Like Epstein, Gans assesses the value systems and the pressures that determine what will be included in news programs.

From a much different perspective, Ron Powers describes the nature of television news in *The Newscasters*. He lambasts local news personalities, consultants, and the practices of news operations. It serves as a useful description of excesses committed in the name of local news and includes some swipes at network-level practices also. The assessment is almost entirely critical, so the reader should be prepared to look elsewhere for descriptions about how local news, at least, does it right.

An excellent analysis is made by Paul H. Weaver in "Newspaper News and Television News," where he describes differences and similarities in how news is presented in these mediums.

Some useful descriptions of the television news process are gathered in *What's News*, edited by a former NBC correspondent and dean of the Columbia School of Journalism, Elie Abel. "The Selection of Reality," by Edward Jay Epstein, reemphasizes points made in his already mentioned book. A review of criteria for television news programs is given by William A. Henry, III, in "News as Entertainment." Among the beliefs he says are held by television news people are that events are better stories than ideas or trends; stories must be essentially new—on-going stories are to be avoided unless they have high interest appeals like sex, violence, and scandal—dramatic unity is important in each story; and programming should reflect the values of the community in local news or of the nation in network stories. Political news coverage is analyzed by Michael Jay Robinson in "A Statesman Is A Dead Politician," where network coverage of the 1980 campaign is assessed. This is but one of many sources for studies of television news in the political process.

Political campaigns and other issues in television news are discussed in Adams and Schreibman's *Television Network News*. This primer for analyzing news content describes how research should be done, posits standards, and recommends approaches for advancing research.

An insider's description of individuals who were and are CBS news has been written by Gary Paul Gates, a former writer at CBS news. *Air Time* provides insight into the personalities of executives and correspondents that made up the CBS-news organization. This is one explanation of how and why decisions were made there.

In an era when network news correspondents have achieved star quality, it is inevitable that biographies and autobiographies would appear. In addition to works like Gates's, we can find an account of Dan Rather's career, as told by Norman King. Rather and co-author Mickey Herskowitz also recount his career in *The Camera Never Blinks*. Later, with Gates's help, Rather described his experiences as the CBS White House correspondent during the Nixon presidency in *The Palace Guard*.

Two former CBS news people who now pursue other journalistic endeavors have written their stories. Sally Quinn, the *CBS Morning News* program's ill-fated answer to Barbara Walters, described her experience in *We're Going to Make You a Star*. Daniel Schorr was suspended and later resigned from CBS news after leaking a congressional committee report on its investigation of the CIA to *The Village Voice*. His opus, *Clearing the Air*, serves as his version of that incident, but the book also describes his reporting on Watergate and the CIA. More recently, autobiographies have been written by NBC correspondent Judy Woodruff (now with the "MacNeil-Lehrer NewsHour") and anchorwoman Jessica Savitch.

BOOKS AND ARTICLES

Abel, Elie, ed. *What's News: The Media in American Society*. San Francisco: Institute for Contemporary Affairs, 1981.

Adams, William C., and Fay Schreibman, eds. *Television Network News: Issues in Content Research*. Washington, D.C.: George Washington University, 1978.

Barrett, Marvin. "Broadcast Journalism since Watergate." *Columbia Journalism Review*, March/April 1976, pp. 73–83.

———. "TV Diplomacy and Other Broadcast Quandaries." *Columbia Journalism Review*, May/June 1979, pp. 69–80.

———, ed. *Survey of Broadcast Journalism: 1968–1969*. New York: Grossett & Dunlap, 1969.

———, ed. *Year of Challenge, Year of Crisis*. New York: Grosset & Dunlap, 1970.

———, ed. *A State of Siege*. New York: Grosset & Dunlap, 1971.

———, ed. *The Politics of Broadcasting*. New York: Thomas Y. Crowell, 1973.

———, ed. *Moments of Truth?* New York: Thomas Y., Crowell, 1975.

———, ed. *Rich News, Poor News*. New York: Thomas Y. Crowell, 1978

———, ed. *Broadcast Journalism, 1979–1981*. New York: Dodd, Mead & Co., 1982.

Barrett, Marvin, and Zachary Sklar. *The Eye of the Storm*. New York: Lippincott & Crowell, 1980.

Epstein, Edward Jay. *News from Nowhere: Television and the News*. New York: Random House, 1973.

Gans, Herbert J. *Deciding What's News: A Study of CBS Evening News, NBC Nightly News, Newsweek and Time*. New York: Vintage Books, 1980.

Gates, Gary Paul. *Air Time: The Inside Story of CBS News*. New York: Harper & Row, 1978.

King, Norman. *Dan Rather*. New York: Leisure Books, 1981.

Powers, Ron. *The Newscasters: The News Business as Show Business*. New York: St. Martin's Press, 1977.

Quinn, Sally. *We're Going to Make You a Star*. New York: Simon and Schuster, 1975.

Rather, Dan, and Gary Paul Gates. *The Palace Guard*. New York: Harper & Row, 1974.

Rather, Dan, with Mickey Herskowitz. *The Camera Never Blinks*. New York: William Morrow, 1977.

Savitch, Jessica. *Anchorwoman*. New York: G.P. Putnam's Sons, 1982.

Schorr, Daniel. *Clearing the Air*. Boston: Houghton Mifflin, 1977.

Weaver, Paul H. "Newspaper News and Television News." In *Television as a Social Force*, pp. 81–94. Edited by Douglass Cater and Richard Adler. New York: Praeger, 1975.

Woodruff, Judy. *This Is Judy Woodruff at the White House*. Reading, Mass.: Addison-Wesley, 1982.

VIDEOGAPHY

"Meet the Press"
   NBC, Sunday, various afternoon and prime times
   Premiere: November 6, 1947
   Moderator: Martha Rountree, November 6, 1947–November 3, 1953
   Ned Brooks, January 3, 1954–December 26, 1965
   Lawrence E. Spivak, January 1, 1966–November 9, 1975
   Bill Monroe, November 16, 1975

"CBS Evening News"
   Daily, various early evening and prime times
   Premiere: May 3, 1948
   Anchor: Douglas Edwards, May 3, 1948–April 13, 1962
   Walter Cronkite, April 16, 1962–March 9, 1981
   Dan Rather, March 11, 1981

"NBC Nightly News"
   Daily, various early evening and prime times
   Premiere: February 14, 1949
   Anchor: John Cameron Swayze, February 14, 1949–October 26, 1956
   Chet Huntley (co-anchor), October 29, 1956–July 31, 1970
   David Brinkley (co-anchor), October 29, 1956–August 13, 1971; June 1976–October 8, 1979.
   John Chancellor (co-anchor), August 3, 1970–April 2, 1982
   Frank McGee (co-anchor), August 3, 1970–August 13, 1971

Roger Mudd (co-anchor), April 5, 1982–September 2, 1983.

Tom Brokaw (co-anchor), April 5, 1982

"Today"

NBC, Weekdays, 7:00–9:00 A.M.

Premiere: January 14, 1952

Hosts: Dave Garroway, January 14, 1952–July 14, 1961

John Chancellor, July 17, 1961–September 7, 1962

Hugh Downs, September 10, 1962–October 11, 1971

Frank McGee, October 12, 1971–April 10, 1974

Jim Hartz (co-host), July 29, 1974–June 4, 1976

Barbara Walters (co-host) April 22, 1974–June 4, 1976

Tom Brokaw, August 30, 1976–December 18, 1981

Jane Pauley (co-host), October 11, 1976

Bryant Gumble (co-host), January 4, 1982

"ABC Evening News"

Daily, various early evening and prime times

Premiere: October 12, 1953

Anchor: John Daly, October 12, 1953–December 16, 1960

Don Goddard, (7:15–7:30 P.M. September 15, 1958–May 1959)

Bill Shadel, December 16, 1960–March 23, 1962

Ron Cochran, March 26, 1962–January 29, 1965

Bob Young, January 1, 1968–May 24, 1968

Frank Reynolds, May 27, 1968–December 4, 1970; (co-anchor), July 10, 1978–April 20, 1983

Howard K. Smith (co-anchor), May 26, 1969–September 12, 1975

Harry Reasoner, December 7, 1970–July 9, 1978

Barbara Walters (co-anchor), October 4, 1976–July 9, 1978

Max Robinson (co-anchor), July 10, 1978–September 2, 1983

Peter Jennings, February 1, 1965–December 29, 1967; (co-anchor), July 10, 1978–September 2, 1983; Anchor, September 5, 1983

"Issues and Answers"

ABC, various Sunday afternoon times

Premiere: November 27, 1960

Last Program: November 8, 1981

"CBS Morning News"

CBS, weekdays, 7:00–7:30 A.M.;

March 21, 1969: 7:00–8:00 A.M.;

September 28, 1981: 7:30–9:00 A.M.

Premiere: September 2, 1963

Anchor: Mike Wallace, September 2, 1963–August 26, 1966

Joseph Benti, August 29, 1966–August 28, 1970

John Hart, August 31, 1970–February 11, 1972

Nelson Benton, February 14, 1972–August 3, 1973

Hughes Rudd, August 6, 1973–February 7, 1975

Sally Quinn (co-host), August 6,1973–December 7, 1973

Bruce Morton, July 1975–September 1977

Richard Threlkeld (co-anchor), October 1977–January 26, 1979

Leslie Stahl (co-anchor), October 1977–January 26, 1979
Bob Scheiffer, January 29, 1979–September 26, 1980
Morton Dean, September 29, 1980–October 24, 1980
Charles Kuralt, October 27, 1980–March 12, 1982
Diane Sawyer (co-anchor), September 28, 1981
Bill Kurtis (co-anchor), March 15, 1982

"Face the Nation"
CBS, various Sunday morning and afternoon times
Premiere: November 7, 1954–April 20, 1961
Revived: September 15, 1963
Moderator: Ted Koop, November 7, 1954–August 1955
Stuart Novins, August 1955–December 1959; October 2, 1960–April 6, 1961
Paul Niven, October 1963–July 1965
Martin Agronsky, July 1965–December 1968
George Herman, January 1969

"MacNeil-Lehrer Report"
PBS, daily, various times
Premiere: January 5, 1975
Anchors: Robert MacNeil, January 5, 1975
Jim Lehrer (co-anchor), October 1976
changed to "MacNeil-Lehrer News Hour"
Premiere: September 5, 1983 (hour version)

"A.M. America"
ABC, weekdays, 7:00–9:00 A.M.
Premiere: January 6, 1975
Host: Bill Beutel
Stephanie Edwards (co-host), January 6, 1975–May 1975
Nancy Dussault (co-host), May 1975–October 31, 1975
Last Program: October 31, 1975

"Good Morning America"
ABC, 7:00–9:00 A.M.
Premiere: November 3, 1975
Host: David Hartman
Nancy Dussault (co-host), November 3, 1975–April 22, 1977
Sandy Hill (co-host), April 25, 1977–August 1980
Joan Lunden (co-host) August 1980

"Sunday Morning"
CBS, 9:00–10:30 A.M.
Premiere: January 28, 1979
Anchor: Charles Kuralt

"Iran Crisis: America Held Hostage"
ABC, weeknights, 11:30–11:50 P.M.
Premiere: November 8, 1979
Anchor: Frank Reynolds, November 8, 1979–February 8, 1980
Ted Koppel, February 11, 1980–March 21, 1980
Last Program: March 21, 1980

"Nightline"
   ABC, weeknights, 11:30 P.M.–12:00 A.M.
   April 25, 1983: 11:30 P.M.–12:30 A.M.
   Premiere: March 24, 1980
   Anchor: Ted Koppel

"This Week with David Brinkley"
   ABC, Sunday, 12:30–1:30 P.M.
   Premiere: November 15, 1981
   Host: David Brinkley

"PBS Late Night"
   PBS, weeknights, 11:30 P.M.–12:30 A.M.
   Premiere: January 4, 1982
   Host: Dennis Wholey

"This Morning"
   ABC, weekdays, 6:00–7:00 A.M.
   Premiere: July 5, 1982
   Anchors: Steve Bell and Kathleen Sullivan

"Early Today"
   NBC, weekdays, 6:00–6:30 A.M.
   Premiere: July 5, 1982
   Anchor: Jane Pauley and Bryant Gumbel, July 5, 1982–July 29, 1983

"NBC Sunrise"
   NBC, weekdays, 6:30–7:00 A.M.
   Premiere: August 1, 1983
   Anchor: Connie Chung

"Overnight"
   NBC, weeknights, 1:30–2:30: A.M.
   Premiere: July 6, 1982
   Anchor: Lloyd Dobyns (co-anchor), July 6, 1982–November 12, 1982
   Linda Ellerbee (co-anchor), July 6, 1982
   William Schechner (co-anchor)
   Last Program: December 2, 1983

"Early Morning News"
   CBS, weekdays, 6:00–6:30 A.M.
   Premiere: October 4, 1982
   Anchors: Diane Sawyer and Bill Kurtis

"Nightwatch"
   CBS, weeknights, 2:00–6:00 A.M.
   Premiere: October 4, 1982
   Anchor: Harold Dow, Christopher Glenn, Felicia Jeter, Karen Stone, Mary Jo West

"The Last Word"
   ABC, weeknights 12:00 P.M.–1:00 A.M.
   Premiere: October 26, 1982
   Host: Greg Jackson
   Last Program: April 21, 1983

"One on One"
    ABC, weeknights, 12:30–1:00 A.M.
    Premiere: April 25, 1983
    Host: Greg Jackson
    Last Program: July 29, 1983

12

Television Documentary

RAYMOND L. CARROLL

Perhaps no program form has brought so much praise and controversy to the television medium as the documentary. Over the years, documentaries have been the "flagship" programs of network news departments, where their traditions are very deeply rooted. They have carried the banner of prestige for their networks. Their serious and thoughtful treatment have garnered accolades from critics, if not wide attendance from viewers.

"Documentary," by implication and tradition, means factual exposition—the antithesis of fabrication or fantasy. Topics treated are usually of some significance in terms of their historical, political, scientific, or economic subject matter. Some have indulged in examination of the trivial, but most documentary topics are of informational utility, even if their topics appear to have little social significance.[1]

Informational appeal is not the most compelling to most viewers, as evidenced by the low ratings of most documentary broadcasts. Yet some documentaries have gathered reasonably large audiences because they can take viewers to places or show them things they would otherwise never experience. Nature subjects and some scientific topics, such as space exploration, have successfully attracted viewers. Other documentaries have proven interesting to a large number of viewers because their subjects are of wide interest and not altogether "serious"— at least in most people's minds. For example, an "ABC News Closeup" documentary, "Sex for Sale: The Urban Battleground," broadcast April 22, 1977, drew a large audience (a very respectable 37 percent of all those watching TV at the time).[2] Most other subjects—no more seriously approached—have not attracted nearly so many viewers.

Some treatments are simply tedious. The problem is partially due to the difficulty in visualizing issues. "Talking heads" do not automatically make for dull television, but the documentary that relies too heavily on excerpts from interviews and shows the viewer little that is tangible is virtually doomed to the ratings basement. Yet another factor is the need to fill out standard television program increments. Thirty to 60 minutes can be more time than necessary to develop a subject satisfactorily.

The effective documentary (whether widely viewed or given scant attention by viewers) tells a story; thus, it includes exposition, development, and climax, focusing on a few examples to illustrate its points. The documentary has not so much evolved as its premise has been adapted in other program forms. Trends in its development and the introduction of variations are all a part of the history of the television documentary.

HISTORICAL DEVELOPMENT

The television documentary evolved from traditions and concepts developed earlier by cinema newsreels, especially the work of "March of Time" producer Louis de Rochemont; still photographers, including Dorothea Lange, Walker Evans, and Margaret Bourke-White; the cinema documentary work of such notables as Frank Capra (better known for his Hollywood movies), Pare Lorentz, and Robert Flaherty; and radio documentary.[3]

In 1946, during the predawn of the television age, the CBS Radio Network created its first documentary unit. Development was limited, however, until audio tape became available. The alternative was the rather crude wire recorder.

The first significant use of audio tape did not occur in radio but in the creation of a series of three phonograph albums entitled "I Can Hear It Now." These historical reviews, released in 1949, formed the earliest association between Fred W. Friendly and Edward R. Murrow. Their partnership continued with a CBS radio documentary series, "Hear It Now," broadcast during the 1950–51 season. "Hear It Now" was important in establishing the working relationship between Friendly and Murrow that carried over to the new medium of television.[4]

The radio documentary began to be seriously developed only shortly before television began its rapid expansion, taking radio's place as the dominant mass medium in the United States. This coincided with a decline in other outlets. Television news usurped the newsreels' function, and TV was partially responsible for changes in the movie attendance habits of the American public. The elimination of short subjects in theaters removed an opportunity for documentary exhibition, as theaters began scheduling double features in an effort to attract customers. It is not surprising, given these developments, that television became the natural outlet for the documentary.

None of the early documentary series broadcast on the ABC, CBS, and NBC television networks came close to the importance of "See It Now." At the start of the first broadcast in that series, on November 18, 1951, an off-camera announcer introduced it as " 'See It Now,' a documentary for television." It was the first time the term "documentary" had been associated with any television program.

The beginnings were inauspicious. They were, as Murrow said in the premiere program, "an old team trying to learn a new trade." During its first two seasons, producers Murrow and Friendly were apparently feeling their way toward establishing a production style.[5] Early programs used a magazine-style format, with as many as five topics treated in a half-hour broadcast. Their subjects were similar to those of current magazine programs. Examples include interviews with General Omar Bradley and Vice President Alben Barkley, a live underwater broadcast aboard a U.S. Navy submarine, peacetime uses of atomic energy, the story of the Brooklyn Dodgers after their winter lay-off, and coverage of the Missouri flood of April 1952. It was not until the 1953–54 season that ''See It Now's'' format really emerged, with emphasis on a single subject.

''See It Now'' was the first television documentary series of any consequence to attempt to deal with current issues.[6] This journalistic approach to the documentary was important in a number of precedent-setting ways, including being the first regularly scheduled program to shoot film for specific purposes instead of using existing footage. And unlike other documentaries, ''See It Now'' sent its camera crews out without a prepared script. Actors were never used; participants never rehearsed.[7]

''See It Now'' was the real beginning for the news documentary. It marked the first network commitment to a documentary series employing a production team—producers, writers, field producers, reporters, and film crews—devoted to a weekly journalistic series. It was also the first documentary series to broach contemporary and controversial topics. Other programs of the era remained in safer territory, avoiding either attribute.

While ''See It Now'' was developing, the first documentary series to have much of an impact was a compilation series about World War II. ''Victory at Sea,'' an authoritative record of the U.S. Naval campaign, took two years to produce. During its initial run on NBC, it received resounding critical acclaim and a considerable audience. A two-hour version was distributed in motion picture theatres; there were three phonograph recordings of the musical score and a book version of the series. Its success has continued to the present day, as the 26-program series is still broadcast occasionally.[8]

The ''Victory at Sea'' success made opportunities for other compilation documentaries that would also achieve notable critical and audience acclaim.[9] Where ''See It Now'' made its contribution as the first journalistic documentary, ''Victory at Sea'' established the cultural documentary as a popular form. An outgrowth of that experience was the establishment of the ''Project 20'' unit at NBC. It specialized in compilation documentaries, where existing film footage and still pictures were used to document some event or era. The content is of existing materials drawn together to form historical account, using original narration and musical scores. In addition to compilation films, ''Project 20'' initiated a ''stills-in-motion'' technique of camera movements on photographs and paintings.[10]

Meanwhile, Murrow and Friendly were biding their time before broaching controversial subjects. It was an era when attention was focused on accusations that the federal government was infiltrated with Communists and their sympathizers. A series of broadcasts on "See It Now" examined threats to liberty made by organizations purporting to protect society from communism's threat. Included was a program entitled "A Report on Senator Joseph R. McCarthy," broadcast on March 9, 1954. With little commentary, Murrow introduced excerpts from films of the senator as he pursued his crusade against persons he believed to be disloyal. Reaction to the broadcast was highly charged, with considerable criticism by McCarthy's supporters.

In spite of the credit given Murrow and "See It Now," the program was not really responsible for McCarthy's downfall. Murrow himself acknowledged that his broadcast came late in the game. The impact of television, propelled by Murrow's prestige, no doubt dealt the senator a blow, but it only added to criticism building in newspapers and the growing alienation of McCarthy's political support.

The televising of the Army-McCarthy hearings in April 1954 was of greater importance in ending McCarthy's influence. Viewers who saw the blustering senator browbeating witnesses could also observe the dignified refutation of his tactics by Joseph Welch, the Army's special counsel. Not long after the hearings concluded, McCarthy was censured by the Senate and faded into obscurity.

The McCarthy era effectively ended. Whether Murrow's broadcast was instrumental, as some have said, is not so important as that it took place at all. No one doubts the courage it took to speak out when little was being said publicly against the demagogism of the time. Murrow's work stands as a shining moment in the history of television journalism, when a network, a program, and a reporter stood up and were counted.[11]

Precedents set by "See It Now" were followed in NBC's "Background," a news documentary series broadcast during 1954 and 1955. This program, which seems to have been NBC's "answer" to "See It Now," used a different decision-making process. Where Murrow and Friendly had editorial control over the content (Murrow is said to have once asserted "News is what I say it is"), "Background" had an editorial board. Eventually, the committee process was used for most documentary series. Typically, when proposals for topics were approved, the production would proceed under supervision. Contemporary documentaries require the final approval of the executives in charge of documentaries and perhaps those responsible for the entire news operation.

Rising profitability of television programming and increasing reluctance to endure unfavorable reaction led to the cancellation of "See It Now" in July 1958.[12] Importantly, Edward R. Murrow had lost his access to the heads of the CBS corporate structure, William S. Paley and Frank Stanton, which considerably lessened his ability to overide objections to the topics and content of "See It Now." Few individuals in any network news organization have had Murrow's freedom to decide which topics were worthy of treatment.

Soon thereafter, allegations of fraud in the conduct of television quiz programs climaxed with Charles Van Doren's confession that he had been provided answers to questions while a contestant on a popular television quiz show. The networks' response to the outcry from legislative and governmental officials was to broadcast more public affairs, educational, and cultural programming during prime time.[13]

An important part of the networks' effort to temper the unfavorable publicity was to present more documentaries. The greatest number ever broadcast during a single period came during the 1961–62 season.[14]

Scandals and the ensuing criticism do not alone account for the considerable increase in documentary programs between 1959 and 1967. This was also an era of intense network news rivalry. In 1959, CBS started a "prestige documentary" series, "CBS Reports," and named Fred Friendly as its executive producer. NBC initiated the "White Paper" series, and ABC countered with "Bell & Howell Close-Up." Moreover, in 1960, ABC contracted with Robert Drew Associates to produce documentaries. This is one of the few instances where a network has gone to an outside production agency for public affairs programs. (The next major instance also involved ABC, when it again broke with tradition in 1978.[15])

Robert Drew's 1960s documentaries and those broadcast later by ABC used the cinema verité approach. The more typical network documentary was narrated by a news correspondent. In cinema verité, "natural sound" recorded during filming takes precedence over narration. Most such films rely on the voices of participants to tell the story. Instead of carefully planned filming sessions, cameras attempt to capture a sense of spontaneity in viewer involvement.

A particular kind of television documentary, prominent since the 1958–59 season, is the "instant special." These special reports, broadcast on short notice, combine straight news reports, analysis, and archival footage. They have become the electronic equivalent of the newspaper's "extra" edition.[16]

NBC created a special unit in 1960 and secured a regular sponsor for news specials that were broadcast as events warranted. CBS took another approach, scheduling a weekly report on the top story of the week. "Eyewitness to History" (later "Eyewitness") was broadcast each Friday evening between September 1960 and April 1963. After that, each network relied on irregularly scheduled special broadcasts.

The 1979 Iranian hostage crisis motivated another regularly scheduled "instant special" series. "The Iran Crisis: America Held Hostage" was broadcast on week nights at 11:30 P.M. by ABC.

The success of these special reports prompted ABC to schedule a regular late-night news program. "Nightline," which premiered on March 21, 1980, was similar to the earlier CBS "Eyewitness" in that each broadcast was usually limited to a single topic. (When the program expanded to an hour on April 25, 1983, several topical news items were treated in each broadcast.)

An earlier ABC weekly news program dealt with current events in yet another deviation in documentary form. As with "See It Now" and "Bell & Howell Close-Up," the sponsor of "Howard K. Smith News and Comment" did not interfere in the program's content. Host Smith was sharply critical of both John

Kennedy's presidential administration and the Congress, but his most widely publicized broadcast, "The Political Obituary of Richard M. Nixon," elicited the angriest response because it included a film clip of Alger Hiss. Interestingly, the comparatively harsher assessments of JFK caused much less reaction. In each program, Smith assessed a situation, offered background and evidence to support a point of view, and submitted solutions to problems.[17] It was an instance where the principal journalist was allowed to determine what was important enough for the focus of his weekly program. Smith's program was in the tradition of "See It Now" and "Bell & Howell Close-Up." The sponsor did not interfere or withdraw support because there was harsh reaction to some of the broadcasts.

In addition to "actuality documentaries," many documentary-style dramatizations have been broadcast. CBS news produced "You Are There" between 1953 and 1957 and revived the series as a children's program from 1971 to 1973. It was a carry-over from radio that imaginatively placed news correspondents in the time when historic events had occurred.[18] A long-running series that started on NBC in 1955 and shifted to CBS in 1957 was "Armstrong Circle Theatre." The original host, news anchorman John Cameron Swayze, was replaced by Douglas Edwards when the series went to CBS. Edwards was removed, though, because CBS felt a non-news program could affect his credibility as its news anchor. He was replaced by former ABC news reporter Ron Cochran.[19]

Such series preceded "docudramas" such as "The Missiles of October," a reenactment of the Kennedy administration's Cuban crisis. There have been few instances where network news productions have used dramatization. Network news is clearly oriented to reality reporting, but more importantly, there are frequent questions about docudramas' fidelity to fact.[20] Some dramatic license must be taken in embellishing stories and filling in gaps. The news organizations concentrated on actuality documentaries that dealt with current events, especially as the United States became involved in a remote war in Southeast Asia.

During the Kennedy administration, documentaries reporting on the conflict in Indochina increased with American involvement there. Indeed, documentaries after 1964 reflected its status as a "television war." Vietnam is the most frequent topic of all documentaries that have been produced by the network news organizations. Virtually every aspect of the war was examined, from its effect on U.S. GIs and the natives of Vietnam, to the nature of the enemy (the North Vietnamese).[21]

An important development in documentary presentation came in the 1968–69 season with the premiere of CBS's "60 Minutes" and NBC's "First Tuesday." The magazine format (which had its roots in commercial television documentaries as far back as "See It Now") owes a real debt to the 1967 series, "PBL," National Educational Television's Public Broadcasting Laboratory. Magazine programs permit flexibility in scheduling documentary reports on topics not otherwise used in traditional documentaries. That is, most magazine segment subjects are rather narrow aspects of larger topics. Where the full-fledged documentary most often provides "the big picture," giving a background on the subject and examining its major current aspects, the magazine typically deals with a "little story." For example, where the traditional documentary might examine the United States' military preparedness, a magazine segment would more likely focus on a single aspect such as the mechanical reliability of U.S. Army tanks.

Where earlier magazine programs followed a traditional news documentary approach, NBC's "Weekend" extended the concept beyond conventional news department treatment, injecting topical humor and satire while not deviating from a journalistic foundation. Critic Lawrence Laurent described the show as " . . . cheeky or impudent or cynical (depending on whether it amuses you or wounds you)."[22] In addition to more traditional news documentary pieces, "Weekend" included brief animated films with social commentary and "title cards" shown between segments and before station breaks that carried such slogans as "Vote for Jimmy Carter or he'll get even" and "Caution: I Brake for Fish." The emphasis in "Weekend" segments was visual rather than verbal—a philosophy somewhat contradictory to the Murrow-Friendly approach.[23]

With the ratings success of CBS's "60 Minutes," NBC scheduled "Weekend" during prime time during the fall, 1978 season. But the program fared badly in audience ratings and was cancelled in April 1979.

"Weekend's" successor was "Prime Time Sunday," hosted by NBC news personality Tom Snyder. A notable difference between "Prime Time" and other magazine series was a live interview in which Snyder talked with two or more guests brought together electronically from remote locations. Scheduling problems and meaningful content apparently could not be satisfactorily controlled, as "Prime Time" slipped into a more conventional format, where all segments were prerecorded.

The ratings succcss of "60 Minutes" and the flexibility of the magazine format were instrumental in CBS's decision to schedule "Who's Who," a prime-time program that specialized in personality profiles. It failed to establish a clear identity with the television audience, but the networks planned more series.[24]

NBC brought back Lloyd Dobyns, who had hosted "Weekend," in another prime-time magazine series, "Monitor." A ratings failure, it was revised as "First Camera" and scheduled opposite "60 Minutes," where it fared no better in attracting viewers.

ABC's response to the lure of prestige and audience ratings was "20/20," which made its debut to universally unfavorable reviews on June 6, 1978.[25] After immediate retooling, including the replacement of the original hosts with veteran Hugh Downs, "20/20" quality improved considerably. The format is a mixture of investigative reports (some of which border on the sensational), consumer-interest segments, and features on popular entertainers and fads. "20/20" has enjoyed a following that is respectable, if not as large as that of "60 Minutes."

Where the magazine format has enjoyed unparalleled popularity, the traditional documentary has languished due to budget cutbacks and low audience attendance.

A major change in documentary policy came with the purchase of independently produced programs by ABC for use in its "Close-Up" series. These have achieved considerable critical acclaim, thus holding up to question the long tradition, held especially by CBS and NBC, that news documentaries should be produced under the direct control of their news divisions.

The Edward R. Murrow tradition at CBS continued with Dan Rather's appointment as the first permanent correspondent for CBS documentary broadcasts since Murrow. Rather left this assignment for "60 Minutes," where he was a correspondent until he was named anchor of the "CBS Evening News." When Rather left his documentary post, he was succeeded by Bill Moyers, who had established a considerable reputation in public television as a thoughtful and thorough documentary reporter. Moyers left CBS because he could not get a commitment for a regularly scheduled program. He was lured back, though, and embarked on yet another variation in the documentary form.

There have been many half-hour documentary series over the history of network television, but the first in some years came with the summer 1983 debut of "Our Times with Bill Moyers." Some critics were concerned that the shorter 15-20 minute treatments in magazine programs and in Moyers's latest 30-minute vehicle would spell the demise of the traditional hour-long documentary.[26]

There is little agreement on the future of the documentary. The magazine form has flexibility and an audience appeal that is very functional. Moyers's 1983 series demonstrated that a half-hour is sufficient time to probe many important questions. Still, there seems little likelihood that the hour form has gone the way of live television drama. There will always be important topics that are too complex to be adequately handled in less time. Perhaps as important, a news tradition carried on by the networks for over 30 years is not likely to die quickly.

THEMES AND ISSUES

In contrast with reports broadcast as part of the nightly news programs, documentaries are detached from the demands of the clock and the calendar. (An exception is the "instant special.")

The basis for the documentary is recorded actualities, edited in such a way to present a story or make a point. The documentary producer assembles materials and weaves them into a coherent story line, rather than taking content directly from an event without juxtaposition or editing. Broadcasts of discussions, interviews, and other events as they unfold are not within the definition of documentary. Recorded excerpts, however, could be included, just as a scholar might quote from various works in support of his thesis.

Dramatized depictions and live coverage occur under some circumstances, but these are exceptions to the actuality recordings and analytical orientation of the television documentary.

Documentaries can be classified as "news," "social issues," "historical," "cultural," "human interest," and "nature." There is some overlapping in this scheme, but most fit into one category or another fairly clearly.

The news documentary deals with current topics and includes a summary of the issues and developments. The accounting is straightforward. Opinion may be included, but it is generally balanced with other points of view. When these broadcasts arouse reaction it is usually because the issue is controversial rather than because the documentary's conclusions are at issue.

Social issues documentaries provide network news departments with their greatest source of pride and the most headaches. While journalistic integrity and objectivity are inherent, social documentaries differ because they take a point of view on subjects that are a part of the social fabric. The Murrow tradition, begun in the 1950s, is followed: " . . . they report not only what is happening but also *what was wrong with what was happening.*"[27] They also follow the Murrow dictate that "news is what I say it is" in focusing on social ills and issues that viewers should be aware of and, presumably, do something about.

One of the best such documentaries, narrated by Murrow, was "Harvest of Shame," broadcast at Thanksgiving time in 1960. It followed migrant farm workers as they harvested the crops that would appear on the tables of well-fed Americans. The program documented the cycle of poverty that most workers were unable to escape. A sequel, broadcast by NBC in 1970, showed that the conditions reported ten years earlier had not changed since Murrow's program was broadcast. And ten years later, in 1980, yet another sequel was broadcast on NBC.

Each of the broadcasts received considerable negative reaction from farmers' groups and producers of crops harvested at sites shown on the programs. Coca-Cola, on whose land some of the filming for the 1970 version was done, boycotted NBC television advertising for a time. Such controversial economic sanctions, along with politically based criticism, is the kind of reaction the networks have learned to dread when their documentaries tread on the wrong toes.

Another kind of social documentary emphasizes consumer protection. An "ABC Close-Up," "Fire," reported the lack of attention given fire risks in consumer products by manufacturers and government officials. The report included a section about the flammability of infant clothing and bedding. A lawsuit filed by a crib manufacturer prevented the inclusion of a scene showing a burning mattress, which illustrates the extent of the reaction by concerned parties, even before a broadcast.

Television is a business that is highly profit-oriented. It also has great dependence on public favor and political support, since broadcasting is a regulated medium. It is not good business to rile consumers or advertisers (the indirect and direct sources of revenue) or elected officials who might impose sanctions on the operation. Consequently, network management has generally looked with disfavor on programming that engenders controversy. Upsetting any or all of the groups noted here generally has a disquieting effect on business as usual.

Still, the tradition inspired by Edward R. Murrow has been kept alive at all three commercial networks. Each occasionally presents a documentary examination of a topic that causes considerable ire in an affected group. Such programs are the work of well-intentioned television journalists who adhere to the notion that the documentary should expose problems, shortcomings, and malfeasance. The most prominent social documentaries examine sensitive military, political, or economic policies that can affect people with vested interests. Two cases in point are "The Selling of the Pentagon" and "The Uncounted Enemy: A Vietnam Deception."

"The Selling of the Pentagon," which examined the promotional efforts of the U.S. military, prompted an attempt in Congress to cite CBS President Frank Stanton for contempt. The motion was defeated, but the offense to promilitary members of Congress and to the presidential administration was strongly registered at considerable expense to CBS.

More recently, CBS news has been criticized for "The Uncounted Enemy: A Vietnam Deception." The documentary accused General William Westmoreland of deceptive reports on the progress of the war. Westmoreland promptly filed a lawsuit against CBS news that is still in litigation. At the least, a cost to CBS has been the publicity that raises questions about the professionalism and credibility of its news operation. The CBS news division conducted an internal investigation and concluded that they were on solid journalistic ground. That did not dissuade Westmoreland in pressing his suit, nor has it cleared the air regarding the editorial judgment made in producing the documentary.

By comparison, historical documentaries are relatively isolated from controversy. Topics are either not controversial or their level of sensitivity has diminished over time. Most historical treatments are compilations of existing film assembled to illustrate the documentary's point. The most significant such series during recent times is the 13-part "Vietnam: A Television History" broadcast on PBS beginning in October 1983. It was a six-year effort that included contributions from British and French television, with primary production responsibility by WGBH-TV, Boston. The assessment made in the programs would have been hotly controversial a few years earlier. Some critics were quick to refute the series' version of what happened during American conduct of the war.[28]

The cultural documentary may be historical or devoted to a contemporary topic. But in either case, it delves into noncontroversial areas such as art and culture, museums, and performing artists. Another kind of cultural documentary examines some way of life that is either part of the contemporary scene or that may have, somehow, avoided its influence. In any case, the topic, while worth examining, is not "newsworthy" as that concept is generally accepted. Like motherhood and apple pie, the subject would be unlikely to generate negative reaction. In many ways, the cultural documentary is approached much like the "human interest" treatment.

Human interest documentaries deal with interesting topics, but they would not be counted among the burning issues of the day. Profiles of famous, great, and otherwise interesting individuals, places, and things are typical. Andy Rooney, whose puckish essays have been a regular feature on "60 Minutes" during recent seasons, was teamed with Harry Reasoner in 1972 to produce "A Bird's Eye View of California" (from the vantage point of a helicopter). Rooney also wrote and produced documentary essays on doors and bridges. NBC's medical series, "Lifeline," is another example. Each program featured a medical doctor seen working with several patients. For some, the doctor's efforts were in vain, but in most of the cases shown, medical science and dedication triumphed.

Nature documentaries are closely allied with human interest. Their appeal is in showing viewers the drama of nature, and many are very compelling studies. "The Undersea World of Jacques Cousteau" series combined Cousteau's research with interesting looks at inhabitants of the deep. One of the best producers of animal documentaries, Survival Anglia, Ltd., has turned out some excellent studies. "The Year of the Wildebeeste," for example, chronicled the cross-country migration of the herds of animals. It was a spectacle, documenting an instinctive ritual in a dramatic demonstration of nature's law of the survival of the fittest. An especially sensitive study, "Gorilla," was a look at the much-misunderstood animal. It followed these large but shy creatures as they roamed their natural habitat, providing viewers an entirely different perspective from the fictional King Kong stereotype.

The increased scheduling of magazine programs by the networks has occurred for several reasons. First, "60 Minutes" and "20/20" have demonstrated that they can attract audiences. Moreover, a number of separate segments within a single program has several advantages. The format's flexibility accommodates treatments of varying length, typically 15-20 minutes. The time is sufficient to examine many topics, but if more is required, longer treatments can be accommodated within the program. Magazine programs have included segments as long as 40 minutes, which still leaves time for other, unrelated items. And there have been occasional broadcasts in which each of the separate segments dealt with the same topic.

Such flexibility makes it easy to include not only investigative treatments, but other segments that are more likely to attract audiences. ABC's "20/20" has employed this tactic with some success. Typically, a consumer-interest piece (reporting a hazard or fraud), an investigative news report, and a profile of a popular recording artist or other celebrity have been grouped in a single broadcast. A similar formula is used by "60 Minutes." Its approach may be a little more "highbrow," focusing on opera stars instead of rock performers, but generally includes human interest features that balance out the investigations for which it has become known.

What's more, magazine programs seem able to examine important and controversial subjects without causing anywhere near the stir that a full documentary treatment might. Perhaps it is because the examination is limited to about 20 minutes, but it may be that such reports are tempered by "softer" segments that usually surround it.[29]

Two derivations in documentary form take advantage of the appeal of human interest in approaches that are similar to the legitimate documentary. Unlike the magazine form, which deviates by clustering shorter, unrelated segments in a single program, docudrama and "info-tainment" broadcasts raise the possibility that stretching the truth or trivializing information will then diminish credibility of legitimate documentary.

Stories based on facts have always been a part of literature and drama. Television versions, known as docudrama, purport to depict the way events actually occurred. While dramatized accounts may be generally accurate, they must inevitably resort to "poetic license" to maintain dramatic apeal in the production. It is not possible to know everything about the events being described, yet viewers are shown conjectured exchanges between principal figures in dramatized recountings. Some docudramas have attempted to surmise what these individuals were thinking—conclusions that are speculative, at best. Viewers may thus be misled into thinking the events they have seen depicted were the unvarnished truth when, in fact, they may have included dramatic fabrications.

A second derivative program type presents brief profiles of unusual and interesting people. "That's Incredible" and "Real People" are two such programs. One fairly typical segment was a report about a young man who described how he had begun passage to the beyond when hovering near death. Viewers were shown a reenactment of the events following the attack that nearly killed him, including a depiction of his spiritual elevation from his body. Other segments have included a profile of the elderly "disco king" of Fort Wayne, Indiana, and a report on a dog that enjoys flying in his master's ultra-light airplane. Whether the treatment calls for a warm chuckle or a "gee whiz" reaction from the program hosts, it is enthusiastically presented in the context of serious information.

This is entertainment masquerading as information. "Info-tainment" programs are to television news magazine programs what *People* magazine is to *Time* or *Newsweek*. The former is a shallow source of information. It makes no attempt to contribute to the understanding of issues and events that may affect audiences' lives.

There is nothing wrong with entertainment, nor with information on matters that are more interesting than crucial. But viewers may come to demand information that is encased in an entertaining format. If entertainment values override informational considerations, the seriousness of subjects and the depth to which they could be explored might be severely limited.

Conflict, whether fictional or factual, is a compelling appeal to television audiences. Both "60 Minutes" and "20/20" have discovered this, and it has helped attract viewers to these programs. But it brings up frequent criticism of magazine programs. If they must constantly seek out villains to be exposed, credibility may be stretched for the sake of a good story. The seemingly "bad guys" may be victimized by those in white hats seeking to expose wrongdoing. The consequences can be news mountains from factual molehills. When indignation over apparent misconduct is not clearly substantiated, it lessens a program's credibility when presenting more important reports.

Another difference between magazines and regular documentaries is the magazine's penchant for telling the "little story." In the relatively brief time allotted for each segment, the subject is generally limited to rather specific instances or personal profiles. This approach is often adequate, but it does not permit an exposition that includes much background—the broader perspective cannot be provided for viewers. This limitation of time may also be contributing to the trivialization of important issues, since the magazine format does not accommodate long, thoughtful examination.

The truly great documentaries have usually broached topics that resulted in controversy. This is because they identify important social issues and express a point of view. When attention is directed to matters that affect influential groups or persons, there is a possibility that the medium will be accused of misleading implication, misrepresentation of fact, or false conclusions. But for documentaries that have made their point in a memorable fashion, such reactions go with the territory.

Other programs provide enlightenment on a more neutral basis. Like their more controversial counterparts, they will be remembered because they have been especially captivating and sensitive in the presentation of the drama of reality.

NOTES

1. Perhaps the most comprehensive discussion of the television documentary form and its antecedents is in A. William Bluem, *Documentary in American Television* (New York: Hastings House, 1965).

2. Kevin Phillips, "News Watch: Documentaries Discover Cure for Low Ratings: Sex," *TV Guide*, May 28, 1977 (North Alabama ed.), pp. A3–4.

3. Bluem, *Documentary in American Television*, pp. 13–72.

4. See Fred Friendly, *Due to Circumstances Beyond Our Control...* (New York: Random House, 1967); and Alexander Kendrick, *Prime Time: The Life of Edward R. Murrow* (New York: Avon Books, 1969) for detailed accounts of the album series and subsequent Murrow-Friendly projects.

5. Kendrick, *Prime Time*, p. 384; and Erik Barnouw, *Documentary: A History of the Non-Fiction Film* (New York: Oxford University Press, 1974), p. 223.

6. Thomas Whiteside, "The One-Ton Pencil," *The New Yorker*, February 17, 1962, p. 78.

7. Kendrick, *Prime Time*, p. 384.

8. John Horn, "TV's Durables," *New York Herald Tribune*, December 20, 1964, television section, p. 38.

9. Museum of Modern Art Film Library, *Television U.S.A.: 13 Seasons* (Garden City, N.Y.: Doubleday, 1962), p. 25.

10. The two most extensive analyses of the "Project 20" series are Philip J. Lane, Jr., "NBC's Project XX: An Analysis of the Art of the Still-in-Motion Film in Television"

(Ph.D. diss., Northwestern University, 1969); and Albert J. Abady, "Project Twenty: An NBC Television Network Series" (M.A. thesis, Pennsylvania State University, 1965). Also, see Bluem, *Documentary in American Television*, pp. 146–63, for his review of the "Victory at Sea" and "Project 20" series.

11. Broadcast historian Erik Barnouw offers a similar perspective on the series in *Tube of Plenty* (New York: Oxford University Press, 1975), pp. 172–84.

12. See Friendly, *Due to Circumstances*, for an insider's account of the demise of "See It Now."

13. Meyer Weinberg, *TV in America: The Morality of Hard Cash* (New York: Ballantine Books, 1962).

14. Raymond L. Carroll, "Factual Television in America: An Analysis of Network Television Documentary Programs, 1948–1975" (Ph.D. diss., University of Wisconsin-Madison, 1978), pp. 210–17.

15. In 1978, ABC purchased broadcast rights to "The Police Tapes," a 90-minute documentary that originally aired on WNET, New York, and about 20 other public television stations. A 60–minute version was broadcast by ABC as part of its "ABC News Close-Up" series on August 17, 1978. See "ABC Buys Docu Aired on WNET," *Variety*, August 9, 1978, p. 40.

16. Neil Hickey, "They're Off and Running," *TV Guide*, June 15, 1974, p. 31; and Chet Hagen, "TV Instant Specials," *The Quill* 49 (March 1961), pp. 12–13.

17. A good analysis of the series is made by Barbara Jane Selph, "A Descriptive Analysis of the Network Television News Commentary Program 'Howard K. Smith, News and Comment' " (M.A. thesis, Ohio State University, 1963).

18. Bluem, *Documentary in American Television*, pp. 164–65.

19. Myron Berkley Shaw, "A Descriptive Analysis of the Documentary Drama Television Program, The *Armstrong Circle Theatre*, 1955–1961" (Ph.D. diss., University of Michigan, 1962).

20. For a more extensive overview of the dramatized documentary form, see Thomas W. Hoffer and Richard Alan Nelson, "Docudrama on American Television," *Journal of the American Film Association* 30 (Spring 1978), pp. 21–27; and idem, "Evolution of Docudrama on American Television Networks: A Content Analysis, 1966–1978," *Southern Speech Communication Journal* 45 (Winter 1980), pp. 149–63.

21. Carroll, "Factual Television," pp. 218–25, 288–93.

22. Lawrence Laurent, "Strong Weekend," *Milwaukee Journal*, September 7, 1975, *TV Screen* magazine, p. 25.

23. Frank Gell, "Look Here," *TV Guide*, February 18, 1978, pp. 36–39.

24. Most observers feel the success of "60 Minutes" influenced the trial of "Who's Who" and prompted ABC and NBC to develop magazine programs for broadcast during prime time. See John J. O'Conner, "TV's Mike and Morley Show," *Milwaukee Journal*, February 25, 1973, *TV Screen* magazine, p. 3; "Salant Senses Public Mandate for More Ambitious News Efforts," *Broadcasting*, May 10, 1976, p. 22; "As We See It," *TV Guide*, February 26, 1977 (Wisconsin ed.), p. A4; Tony Schwartz with Ann Ray Martin, "Sons of '60 Minutes,' " *Newsweek*, May 16, 1977, p. 107; and "Chasing '60 Minutes,' " *Broadcasting*, November 21, 1977, p. 39.

25. Typical reviews include Betsy Carter, "Trash News," *Newsweek*, June 19, 1978, p. 68; and " '20/20' Gets Both Eyes Blackened," *Broadcasting*, June 12, 1978, p. 46.

26. The questionable status of the "long form" or traditional news documentary is

discussed by Bill Carter, "Whatever Happened to TV Documentaries?" *Washington Journalism Review* (June 1983), pp. 43–46.

27. Charles Montgomery Hammond, Jr., *The Image Decade: Television Documentary, 1965–1975* (New York: Hastings House, 1981), p. 40.

28. Conflicting reactions have already been expressed regarding its interpretation of events. See, for instance, Jean Callahan, "War Stories," *American Film* (October 1983), pp. 10–11.

29. At least one critic agrees. See Steve Knoll, "Sponsor Aversion Main Roadblock on TV Documentary's Comeback Trail," *Variety*, December 24, 1969, p. 24.

BIBLIOGRAPHICAL SURVEY

Comprehensive and concentrated analyses of American television documentary are sparse. To date, only two such analyses have been published. The most important, A. William Bluem's *Documentary in American Television*, reviews the development of the form and the contributions of newsreels, still photography, cinema, and radio documentary. Its early publication date limits its attention to more contemporary broadcasts, but the major drawback of the book is its selectivity. As in most overviews, it ignores many series and individual documentaries that were important in the development of television documentary. But it is, nevertheless, a good base on which to build the body of literature on the topic.

A sequel, Charles Hammond's *The Image Decade*, concentrates on the ten-year period following Bluem's analysis. Its merit is that it is the only such work to appear since Bluem's contribution, but the reader should be cautious about errors in dates, program titles, and so forth that can be found throughout the text.

Broadcast historian Erik Barnouw has, in *Tube of Plenty*, demonstrated considerable interest in the television documentary. But this work, like others by Barnouw, is of such a scope that little attention is given to any single item. No aspect of documentary, therefore, is treated in any great depth. Still, Barnouw's work is the only cohesive history of television in print that devotes particular attention to documentary broadcasts.

In *Documentary: A History of the Non-Fiction Film*, Barnouw provides a useful overview of the development of film documentary and television's assimilation of the form. The limitations are those already mentioned. The narrative moves rapidly without dealing thoroughly with any aspect pertinent to television. Like the previously cited work, though, *Documentary* provides a perspective for better understanding of the development of the television documentary and the influences of its antecedent forms.

Two related books provide a great deal of information on the career of Edward R. Murrow and his associates at CBS. Fred Friendly, Murrow's co-producer on "See It Now," has written *Due to Circumstances Beyond Our Control . . .*, an account of events that affected the status of documentary presentation at the CBS television network. It is a first-hand account of the life of "See It Now" and

"CBS Reports" up to the time of Friendly's resignation. An excellent companion book is Alexander Kendrick's *Prime Time*, which provides further perspective on events and personalities—especially Murrow's—that were important in the development and status of documentaries at CBS. This remains the single best biography of Murrow.

A biography of an important NBC documentary producer is *Special: Fred Freed and the Television Documentary*. Author David Yellin reviews Freed's contributions and has annotated a listing of his documentaries.

Interested readers can find transcripts of some broadcasts in three books: Edward Bliss, Jr., has edited a compilation of Edward R. Murrow's broadcasts, including some of his television documentaries. The portions quoted are usually the most succinct statements from the program but do not allow the reader complete access or understanding of the total broadcast. A book edited by Murrow and Friendly, *See It Now*, includes both complete and partial transcripts of some of the programs in that series. Finally, transcripts for the segments broadcast during the 1979–80 season were published in *60 Minutes Verbatim*. The real shame is that there is no published source for transcripts of all the broadcasts in this or any other important documentary series.

BOOKS AND ARTICLES

Barnouw, Erik. *Tube of Plenty: The Evolution of American Television*. New York: Oxford University Press, 1975.

———. *Documentary: A History of the Non-Fiction Film*. New York: Oxford University Press, 1974.

Bliss, Edward, Jr., ed. *In Search of Light: The Broadcasts of Edward R. Murrow, 1938–1961*. New York: Alfred A. Knopf, 1967.

Bluem, A. William. *Documentary in American Television*. New York: Hastings House, 1965.

CBS News. *60 Minutes Verbatim*. New York: Arno Press, 1980.

Friendly, Fred W. *Due to Circumstances Beyond Our Control . . . .* New York: Random House, 1967.

Hammond, Charles Montgomery, Jr. *The Image Decade: Television Documentary, 1965–1975*. New York: Hastings House, 1981.

Kendrick, Alexander. *Prime Time: The Life of Edward R. Murrow*. New York: Avon Books, 1969.

Murrow, Edward R., and Fred W. Friendly, eds. *See It Now*. New York: Simon and Schuster, 1955.

Yellin, David G. *Special: Fred Freed and the Television Documentary*. New York: Macmillan, 1972.

VIDEOGRAPHY

"See It Now"
    CBS, Weekly, 1951–May 15, 1956, approximately monthly thereafter

Premiere: November 18, 1951
Co-producers: Edward R. Murrow and Fred W. Friendly
Anchor: Edward R. Murrow
Last Program: July 7, 1958

"Victory at Sea"
NBC, Sunday, 3:00–3:30 P.M.
Premiere: November 30, 1952
Producer: Henry Salomon
Narrator: Leonard Graves
Last Program: May 3, 1953

"You Are There"
CBS, weekly
Premiere: February 1, 1953
Producer: William Dozier
Narrator: Walter Cronkite
Last Program: October 13, 1957
Children's Version
Premiere: September 8, 1971
Narrator: Walter Cronkite
Last Program: May 6, 1973

"Background"
NBC, Monday, 8:30–9:00 P.M.
Premiere: August 16, 1954
Producer: Ted Mills, August 16, 1954–April 3, 1955; Rueven Frank, May 1, 1955–
June 26, 1955
Anchor: Joseph C. Harsch
Last Program: June 26, 1955

"Project 20"
NBC, approximately monthly
Premiere: September 13, 1954
Producer: Henry Salomon, September 13, 1954–September 28, 1958
Donald B. Hyatt, February 11, 1959–December 31, 1971
Narrator: various
Last Program: December 31, 1971

"Armstrong Circle Theatre"
Production: Talent Associates
NBC, September 9, 1955–June 25, 1957
Premiere: September 9, 1955
Producer: David Susskind
Narrator: John Cameron Swayze
CBS, October 2, 1957–August 28, 1963
Narrator: Douglas Edwards, October 2, 1957–September 13, 1961
Ron Cochran, November 11, 1961–December 6, 1962
Henry Hamilton, December 19, 1962–August 28, 1963
Last Program: August 28, 1963

"Eyewitness to History"
  CBS, Fridays, 10:30–11:00 P.M.
  Premiere: August 27, 1959
  Producer: Paul Levitan, August 27, 1959–June 24, 1960
  Leslie Midgley, September 23, 1960–August 2, 1960
  Anchor: Walter Cronkite, August 27, 1959–June 24, 1960; January 27, 1961–April 13, 1962
  Charles Kuralt, September 23, 1960–January 20, 1961
  Charles Collingwood, April 20, 1962–August 2, 1963
  Last Program: August 2, 1963

"CBS Reports"
  CBS, various prime times
  Premiere: November 11, 1959
  Executive Producer: Fred W. Friendly, various others
  Anchor: various CBS News correspondents

"Bell & Howell Close-Up"
  ABC, various prime times
  Premiere: September 27, 1960
  Executive Producer: various
  Anchor: various ABC News correspondents
  Last Program: July 7, 1963

"NBC White Paper"
  NBC, various prime times
  Premiere: November 29, 1960
  Executive Producer: Irving Gitlin, various others
  Anchor: various NBC News correspondents

"Howard K. Smith, News and Comment"
  ABC, prime time
  Premiere: February 14, 1962
  Producer: Bill Kobin
  Anchor: Howard K. Smith
  Last Program: June 16, 1963

"PBL (Public Broadcasting Laboratory)"
  NET, two hours bi-weekly, 1967–68; weekly 1968–69 season
  Premiere: November 5, 1967
  Producer: Av Westin
  Anchor: Edward P. Morgan
  Last Program: May 25, 1969

"60 Minutes"
  CBS
  Premiere: September 24, 1968
  Executive Producer: Don Hewitt
  Anchors: Mike Wallace, Harry Reasoner, Morley Safer, Dan Rather, Ed Bradley

"First Tuesday"
  NBC
  Premiere: January 7, 1969
  Executive Producer: Eliot Frankel

Anchor: Sander Vanocur, January 7, 1969–April 6, 1971
Garrick Utley, May 4, 1971–August 7, 1973
Last Program: August 7, 1973

"ABC News Close-Up"
ABC
Premiere: October 18, 1973
Executive Producer: Av Westin, October 18, 1973–January 5, 1976
Pamela Hill, January, 1978
Anchor: various ABC News correspondents

"Weekend"
NBC, monthly, Saturday, 11:30 P.M.–1:00 A.M.
Premiere: October 19, 1974
Executive Producer: Rueven Frank
Anchor: Lloyd Dobyns
Sunday, 10:00–11:00P.M.
September 10, 1978–April 22, 1979
Anchors: Lloyd Dobyns and Linda Ellerbee
Last Late-Night Program: June 3, 1978

"Who's Who"
CBS
Premiere: January 4, 1977
Executive Producer: Don Hewitt, January 4–March 8, 1977
John Sharnik, March 15–June 26, 1977
Anchor: Dan Rather
Last Program: June 26, 1977

"20/20"
ABC, Thursday, 10:00–11:00 P.M.
Premiere: June 6, 1978
Executive Producer: Bob Shanks, June 6–August 29, 1978
Various, including Jeff Gralnick, Jan Rifkinson, and Al Ittleson, September 1978–
August 1980
Av Westin, August 14, 1980
Anchor: Harold Hayes and Robert Hughes (June 6, 1978)
Hugh Downs, June 13, 1978

"Lifeline"
NBC
Production: Tomorrow Entertainment, Inc.
Premiere: September 7, 1978
Executive Producers: Thomas W. Moore and Robert E. Fuisz, M.D.
Narrator: Jackson Beck
Last Program: September 6, 1979

"Prime Time Sunday"
NBC, Sunday, 10:00–11:00 P.M. through September 23, 1979
Saturday, 10:00–11:00 P.M. beginning December 29, 1978
Premiere: June 24, 1979
Executive Producer: Paul Friedman

Anchor: Tom Snyder
Last Program: July 5, 1980

"Monitor"
NBC, Saturday, 10:00–11:00 P.M.
Premiere: March 12, 1983
Executive Producer: Sy Pearlman
Anchor: Lloyd Dobyns
Last Program: August 13, 1983

"Our Times"
CBS, Tuesday, 8:30–9:00 P.M.
Premiere: June 26, 1983
Executive Producer: Andrew Lack
Anchor: Bill Moyers
Last Program: August 23, 1983

"First Camera"
NBC, Sunday, 7:00–8:00 P.M.
Premiere: September 18, 1983
Executive Producer: Sy Pearlman
Anchor: Lloyd Dobyns
Last Program: April 1, 1984

"Vietnam: A Television History"
PBS, Tuesday, 9:00–10:00 P.M.
Production: WGBH-TV
Premiere: October 4, 1983
Executive Producer: Richard Ellison
Narrator: Will Lyman
Last Program: December 20, 1983

13

Sports Telecasting

GARY EDGERTON AND DAVID OSTROFF

OVERVIEW

Sports in America are a source of high drama; they involve ceremony and public ritual, intense displays of emotion by both players and spectators, and resolution through action. The rules of each sport usually dictate a predictable storyline, although the improvisational nature of when things will happen and who exactly will enact them is clearly a large part of the attraction of this genre of activity. Sports produce heroes, "chokers," journeymen, old pros, and rookies; two sides always compete according to a scenario that holds both an infinite variety of plot twists and a denouement that clearly establishes winners and losers. Whether the rivalry is directed toward others or the competition is with oneself, the beauty of sport derives from the struggle. These games always provide a potential forum for self and group expression, as well as the fleeting possibility for human transcendence. Sports in America are at once meaningful to the culture and profoundly gripping; they are also more transitory than yesterday's news and non-essential for life and survival. In retrospect, it is small wonder that sports and broadcasting embraced each other from the very beginning. Sports can readily provide plenty of excitement, entertainment, intimacy, spontaneity, and spectacle while almost never violating the proprieties of a network or the sensibilities of the viewing public.

Actually, sports in America have taken on an increasing amount of importance during the last one hundred years. The second half of the nineteenth century in the United States is characterized as a period of rapid national growth spurred by the industrial, economic, urban, transportation, and communications revolutions. Each of these five forces was clearly evident in America after the Civil War, and together they have since worked in concert to transform many aspects of U.S. society and culture, even sports. Baseball became professionalized for the first time during the 1870s, and teams were promoted by major metropolitan centers in the industrialized Northeast and Midwest. Sport personalities had also emerged in boxing and, to a lesser degree, in football, as both amateur and professional gamesmanship became legitimate topics of interest for a new and growing breed of journalist in the United States—the sportswriter. Consequently, by the turn of the century, the print media had long ago delivered the "sports world" to the public's attention, while American thought and culture were already well within the process of imbuing their most popular sports with a rich mythology and symbolic worth that reflected the evolving national character. Indeed, radio during the 1920s and 1930s even accelerated this continuing movement toward institutionalizing the world of sport in the United States. At the same time, however, this medium also prefigured, on a much smaller scale, the awesome symbiotic relationship that would be born between television and sports in 1939.

Today the average American watches over six hours of television a day, and one-fifth of that time is spent watching sports. In fact, the mean level of watching sports fare is even higher for the males in the audience, at over 25 percent of total viewing time. Of course, this statistic hardly escapes American advertisers as sports and the commercial system are linked together on the nation's video screens in a mutually advantageous relationship. Unlike one hundred years ago, television presently saturates over 99 percent of the United States, and the sports profession is a billion dollar industry. The market demands of big business structure the sports world; in turn, television harnesses and transmits sports to millions, while the subsequent drama and characters capture the imagination of sports fans throughout the country. Commerce, mass communication, and culture interplay to provide the American viewing public with hours of entertainment, a subtle means of socialization, as well as an efficient method of ensuring a flow of goods and services on a scale that enriches the interests of nearly everyone involved. Quite simply, TV and sports have successfully grown up together beyond anyone's wildest dream, and their economic and socio-cultural symbiosis is stronger than ever during the 1980s.

HISTORICAL DEVELOPMENT

1939–1958: Trial and Error in Sports Telecasting

A year of many firsts for both television and sports was 1939. On May 1, a broadcast of the opening ceremonies for the New York World's Fair marked the start of a regular daily television schedule by RCA-NBC. During the next twelve months, NBC covered a wide range of on-location events with a mobile unit consisting of "two huge buses; one was a studio crammed with equipment for field use; the other housed the transmitter that relayed the program to the Empire State tower for rebroadcast by the main transmitter."[1] On May 17, 1939, this mobile unit covered the first sports telecast that involved a college baseball game where Princeton beat Columbia two to one at Baker Field in uptown New York. On the following day, the *New York Times* reviewed this event, concluding that it "was pretty well done," although "the players [looked] like white flies running across the 9-by-12 inch screen."[2] By and large, much of the credit for the relative success of this telecast was accorded to announcer Bill Stern, who was already famous for his radio work at the time. Actually, this first sportscast was vague and hard to follow, since only one camera with a fixed lens was used. In addition, the awkwardness of a swish pan was the only means of including the interplay between both the pitcher and the batter. A few days later, another *Times* reporter succinctly analyzed this problem of televising baseball with only limited technology when he wrote: "A single camera anchored at one spot does not see the complete field; it leaves too much to the imagination. Baseball by television calls for three or four cameras, the views of which can be blended as the action calls for it."[3] Incredibly, this sportswriter then goes on to prefigure techniques—such as the employment of portable minicameras to capture intimate reaction shots from both players and fans—that would slowly evolve over the next three decades. He also hints at the inherent difficulties in telecasting some sports more than others, namely baseball. In addition, it is obvious from the above quote that television had almost immediately caught the imagination of the serious sports fan, even if only four hundred sets were then operating in the entire New York metropolitan area.

Throughout that first summer and fall, NBC's mobile unit broadcast a number of other firsts—bicycle racing, boxing, tennis, major league baseball, college football, and professional football—over experimental station W2XBS, which was later to become WNBC-TV. Boxing, which along with baseball were the two most popular games on TV during the first decade of sportscasting, made its debut on June 1 as Lou Nova handed Max Baer a TKO at Yankee Stadium.[4] From the outset, it was apparent to NBC that the specifics of boxing—a small, confined arena with only two participants—lent themselves much better to the technical and aesthetic limitations of early television than the broad field, the wide dispersion of players, and the comparatively fast and unpredictable play of baseball. Still, baseball was already the national pastime, as two cameras, radio personality Red Barber, and NBC inaugurated major league baseball to television with an Ebbets Field doubleheader between the Brooklyn Dodgers and the Cincinnati Reds on August 26. Years later, this program's producer-director, Burke Crotty, reminisced about the hardships and realities surrounding that early, primitive broadcast: "In those days, TV was a foul weed in the garden of entertainment. The public gawked at us as a curiosity. Radio people viewed us as a freak. We had hardly any money and practically no staff. And we had absolutely no prestige at all."[5] Certainly, these words temper any inclination to underestimate the difficult process of commercializing any new viable media technology, even television. Nevertheless, before the year was out, CBS and DuMont were both anxiously following NBC's lead in pioneering the beginnings of sports telecasting in America.

NBC also televised the first college and professional football games in the autumn of 1939, although these early events were hardly portents of the fact that no sport would benefit more intimately from the close interrelationship between TV and sports than football. Again, Bill Stern called the action for this college game between Fordham and Waynesburg on September 30 at Triboro Stadium on Randall's Island in New York City. The camera was actually mounted on a moving cart as it followed the line of scrimmage from the sidelines. Less than one month later, Allen "Skip" Walz called the play-by-play for the first televised professional football game as the Brooklyn Dodgers beat the Phila-delphia Eagles, 23–14. This event occurred at Ebbets Field in Brooklyn on October 22 and clearly indicated from the outset that the relatively narrow dimensions of the field, the close formation of the players, and the frequent natural breaks followed by short, intense segments of action were all ideal game conditions for the evolving craft of sports telecasting.

Three more major sports were introduced in the winter and spring of 1940. The first professional hockey game to be televised was played on February 25 at Madison Square Garden between the New York Rangers and the Montreal Canadians. Hockey is one sport that has never really found an altogether com-fortable home on American TV, especially at the networks. In hindsight, the following critical diagnosis analyzes the reason why: "The only sports that are not entirely satisfactory on TV are baseball, golf and hockey. In each case the ball, or puck, is so small the camera cannot focus on its unpredictable flight over a wide range of action."[6] The extremely long periods and nearly continuous play of hockey would also prove to be a bane to future commercial broadcasters who would need to insert the appropriate number of 30 and 60 second spots.

Still, the experimental station was the leading television entity in those early days, as W2XBS's mobile unit once more returned to Madison Square Garden just 72 hours after the aforementioned pro hockey match for the first telecasting of a college basketball game in which Pittsburgh beat Fordham, 50–37. New York's Madison Square Garden would also be the site for the first college track meet to be televised as 23 schools participated in the 19th Annual American Amateur Athletic Association affair on March 5.[7] Throughout the next 14 months, occasional sports telecasts were conducted primarily in the New York area; however, the war effort ultimately postponed further television experimentation of all kinds for most of the next three years. Consequently, the lion's share of sports broadcasting was accomplished by radio during this period of national emergency. In fact, no significant efforts for the development of TV would be initiated again until the spring of 1944.

In a very real sense, each sport can be considered a subgenre of television sports, emphasizing its own particular rules, dramatic structure, character types, accompanying television aesthetics and style, setting, and socio-cultural themes and significance. In many ways, TV technology and audience predisposition were the two primary factors in determining which sports enjoyed the most popularity on the nation's airwaves in those first dozen years after World War

II. The limited facilities available on the early mobile units of all four networks— NBC, CBS, ABC, and DuMont—clearly favored the restricted setting and the fewer number of necessary participants, which are characteristic to sports like boxing, wrestling, and roller derby. On the other hand, the late 1940s and early 1950s were also a time of severe growing pains for the relationship between television and baseball; and moreover, professional football finally emerged from its second-class status, largely on account of its developing symbiosis with the TV cameras.

The crucial element was added to the equation linking television and sports in the summer of 1944; Madison Avenue and America's advertising industry became interested and attentive to the new medium. On Friday evening, September 29, 1944, "the first successful long lasting commercial network television program premiered, 'The Gillette Cavalcade of Sports.' "[8] That evening, world featherweight champion Willie Pep defeated Chalky Wright in fifteen rounds. The Gillette Razor Company would continue its sponsorship of this successful series for the next sixteen years. Clearly, boxing was very popular in America at the time, and the sport became a fixture on all four networks by 1950, as well as being a major component of local programming. Matches from all weight classes received television exposure during this era, as boxing's greatest names— Rocky Marciano, Sugar Ray Robinson, Archie Moore, and Rocky Graziano— all appeared on prime time. "There were periods in the late 1940s and early 1950s when it was common to have as many as five or six network boxing shows on during consecutive evenings of the same week."[9] Nevertheless, the love affair between this sport and TV slowly began to wane as the decade progressed. By 1964, the ratings had "slumped from 32.9 percent of the potential audience to 11.1 in ten years."[10] Advertisers had already begun to look to other sports as a means of acquiring more prestigious events and better demographics, while all the premier matches—including every heavyweight championship bout—had already opted for the gate potential of closed circuit television by 1959. Indeed, the final knockout punch was the constant criticism and public reaction against Emile Griffith's fatal beating of Benny "Kid" Paret on ABC. At least for a time, the underside of boxing had surfaced as an obsession for America's viewing public; in turn, most advertisers, network executives, and sports fans turned their backs on this sport because of its inherent brutality.

Actually, a similar fate would be in store for big time wrestling and roller derby. In the final analysis, prestige was also the major problem with these events of hype and spectacle that blended elements of both sport and show business. In retrospect, the early response to wrestling and roller derby was ardent and enthusiastic, although neither had the ultimate staying power of boxing's 20-year reign. Still, the personalities and intensity generated on TV by these three sports caught the imagination of the American fan during the late 1940s; in fact, many tavern owners rushed out to acquire television sets as a successful means of attracting customers for these "especially powerful attractions."[11]

Big time wrestling appeared on all three networks, although DuMont's "Wrestling from Park Arena" (or Jamaica Arena) hosted by Dennis James was undoubtedly the sport's most successful offering. James was "equipped with dog biscuits, walnut shells, and pieces of wood, which he would crack into the microphone whenever a wrestler would apply a bone-crushing hold."[12] In turn, characters, like Gorgeous George and "Argentina" Rocca would try to outdo each other before the camera with bold and usually caricatured histrionics and outfits. DuMont succeeded in keeping wrestling on prime time for seven years, from 1948 to 1955, until the network itself ceased functioning as a national entity. By that time, though, big time wrestling was relegated to its present fate and condition as a local offering on weekend afternoons appearing on sporadic independent stations nationwide.

By contrast, roller derby actually disappeared altogether for a time from America's airwaves in the mid-1970s, after scoring a consistently winning share of the audience during its early years on television. Indeed, "Roller Derby" was the most popular program on the ABC schedule as it highlighted three evenings a week for all of 1949 and 1950. This game was "a Chicago product of the Great Depression," and "the hard-knocks sport quickly won over the entire country with its exuberant mix of skilled skating, ferocious elbowing and raucous grandstanding."[13] Stars emerged from both sexes, like Charlie O'Connell and Joan Weston, playing for such colorful teams as the San Francisco Bay Bombers and the Midwest Pioneers. As prime-time network programming became more developed and sophisticated during the early 1950s, however, roller derby also found a home in local syndication, where it continued to pull respectable ratings well into the late 1960s.

Americans, of course, have been lovingly attached to major league baseball for over a century; television would eventually learn to fuel this attraction, if somewhat reluctantly at first. Baseball's World Series was first telecast in 1947, as the New York Yankees battled their across-town rivals, the Brooklyn Dodgers. Red Barber was at the microphone for NBC, which transmitted the games along a four-city network between New York City, Philadelphia, Washington, and Schenectady, New York. During the next season, the major leagues successfully attracted their largest gate up until that time: 26,972,601 paid admissions. Fifteen years later, however, "the figure had dropped to 20,477,465, a slump of 25 percent despite the addition of four teams and a longer schedule."[14] Something was seriously wrong, and industry insiders in both baseball and broadcasting knew it was television.

Baseball first reached the prime-time schedule on ABC in 1951, although the game had already been a regular staple on local telecasts since 1949. Today it is widely known that these regional broadcasts severely hampered baseball's minor leagues, as attendance plummeted from 41,872,762 for 448 teams in 59 leagues in 1949 to 17,031,069 fans supporting 205 teams in only 26 remaining leagues by 1956.[15] A significant amount of baseball's public merely stayed home and watched the big leagues on television rather than venturing out into the "bush" circuits as paying customers.

To a lesser degree, this pattern of shrinking attendance influenced those major league franchises that sold away their telecasting rights. Branch Rickey, who was then president of the Brooklyn Dodgers, prophetically pinpointed this problem in 1949 when he was being criticized by his stockholders and the press for refusing to part with the TV rights for his team at the very generous pre-1950 rate of $150,000. Rickey held fast, and proclaimed, "radio stimulates curiosity, television satisfies it."[16] Three years later, the Boston Braves would be a case in point. In 1948, the Braves concomitantly won the pennant and set a team record for attendance. During the next few months, the management then sold away the next two years of local television rights for a paltry $40,000. By 1952, paid admissions dropped "a disastrous 81 percent. To salvage the team, the Boston Braves moved to Milwaukee and blacked out television coverage in their new home."[17] Slowly, the Braves set about the task of drawing a respectable following from their new base in the Midwest.

Eventually, broadcast revenues throughout the major leagues would accelerate to offset such calamitous losses at the gate. Still, major league baseball and television would be unable to suitably arrange and administer this balance until the 1960s. By then, the relationship would stabilize and turn bullish after these rather shaky beginnings in the early 1950s.

Television also effected a number of other changes in the major leagues as well; in a very real sense, the medium was successful in opening up the west to baseball in two ways. First, broadcasts of the games further deepened fan interest from coast to coast. Second, two New York franchises were moved to California. Prior to the mid-1950s, St. Louis was the only big league team west of the Mississippi. However, in 1958 Walter O'Malley and Horace Stoneham moved the Dodgers and Giants to Los Angeles and San Francisco, respectively. What most perplexed the traditionalists in baseball about this switch was that each of these New York teams represented a very stable business enterprise, especially the Brooklyn Dodgers. Nevertheless, congressional hearings on antitrust matters involving organized professional team sports were also being held in 1958. Both O'Malley and Stoneham were two of many witnesses called before this subcommittee, and their testimony made it evident that the Dodgers, Giants, and Skiatron TV, Inc., were in negotiations over a pay-TV venture that would ultimately furnish the West Coast with baseball on cable.[18] Apparently, this scheme had unlimited potential. In the long run, though, the prospects of pay-cable never materialized, as California voted down the implementation of this plan on a statewide referendum. Fortunately, this setback had only minor repercussions for baseball, as Los Angeles and San Francisco enthusiastically embraced their new teams. The Dodgers, especially, broke attendance records, owing in no small part to Mr. O'Malley's premeditated refusal to sign away his ballclub's local telecasting rights.

In conclusion, by 1958 it was apparent that television was affecting baseball on at least three significant fronts: gate attendance, "switches in franchise location, and changes in the legal environment."[19] Soon, rule alterations and style changes could also be added to this list of effects, although baseball would only be the first of many sports that would shift and mold its structure, operation, setting, schedule, and overall image for the efficacy and convenience of both television and Madison Avenue. In a certain sense, the traditionalism and innocence of American sports was finally coming to an end with the 1950s. In return, TV would provide the nation's most popular games, teams, owners, coaches, and players with unimagined resources, revenues, and influence during the next decade.

1959–1976: The Meteoric Rise of Sports Telecasting

Although New York had lost two of its three major league baseball teams to the West Coast, the city showed no inclination of pining over its misfortune. Instead, New York sports fans quickly turned their attention to other franchises in town, as one old standby in particular caught the imagination of the entire northeast region: the New York Giants. An appropriate starting point for this new and increased level of zeal and enthusiasm came to a head for Giants' fans and the rest of the American viewing public, for that matter, during the 1958 National Football League championship game held on December 28. This contest was the first NFL sudden death overtime match, and although the Giants lost to the Baltimore Colts, 23–17, pro football was now a popular and viable staple throughout the New York metropolitan area.

This development should not be downplayed, since any professional league ultimately needs enthusiastic support from America's major media centers—New York City, Los Angeles, and to a lesser degree, Chicago—to survive in the marketplace. Actually, survival was not a pressing problem for the National Football League during the 1950s; still, college football was probably more popular with the American sports fan, as was major league baseball by a long shot. Professional football, however, was about to make its move, and television exposure was the main reason for its subsequent pervasive and lucrative success.

In 1955, the NFL averaged approximately $100,000 a team in television residuals. By 1960, this income would double, and "by 1965 this figure had skyrocketed to approximately $1,000,000 per team" per year.[20] Pete Rozelle, who became NFL commissioner in 1960, and the owners he represented were all thunderstruck by the dollar amounts they were offered during their negotiations with the networks; later, they would acknowledge that it was beyond their wildest dreams. "In 1963, the combined AFL-NFL football schedule cost $7.6 million. By 1969, it was $34.7 million," and $52 million "in 1975 alone."[21] Overall, the National Football League front office has estimated "that between 1961 and 1975 the NFL collected a whopping $606 million in television rights."[22] The stability and growth potential provided by this amount of capital is indicative of the astronomical rise in popularity experienced by American professional football during the 1960s.

Of course, NBC, CBS, and ABC would not part with this kind of money if, in fact, they were not making the necessary profits themselves. By 1963, four of the top ten rated shows of all time were football events that had only first appeared on TV within the previous two years; and since 1966, the perennial Super Bowl consistently garners a peak share of the television audience. The American Football League was able to subsist over its first five years of existence because of the base monies it was provided from its contract with NBC. Introduced in 1960, the AFL was both clever and lucky enough to secure immediate visibility on a network. The new league's relationship with television afforded it the time to establish itself in the marketplace and even compete for fans and players with the more established NFL. The most publicized and dramatic example of both this competition and the healthy influx of finances coming from TV was the signing of Alabama's star quarterback, Joe Willie Namath, for a reported $427,000 in 1965.

By 1966, NFL Commissioner Pete Rozelle was instrumental in negotiating an AFL-NFL merger, as the new league accomplished its goal of parity in six short years. By no means did the rapidity of this success go unnoticed by the rest of the sports world. Fledgling leagues were spawned in basketball, hockey, tennis, and even football again during the next decade; nevertheless, none of these experiments were able to repeat the marked achievement of the AFL. Certainly timing had something to do with it. Still, the importance of a consistent television contract with a major network cannot be underestimated, as none of these other leagues were able to maintain such a relationship.

As a culmination to its meteoric rise and expansion during the 1960s, professional football produced one last breakthrough with television in 1970. By and large, all sports had been relegated to afternoon and weekend broadcasts since the early 1950s. Although there were sporadic attempts to bring sports to prime time during the late 1950s and 1960s, none of these programs proved successful. In the spring of 1970, however, ABC narrowly secured a contract with the NFL over heated bidding with the Hughes Sports Network and premiered "Monday Night Football" during their upcoming fall lineup. Overall, this show has been a consistent prime-time winner ever since.

The key, of course, is the chemistry generated between the various announcing triads that have populated the broadcast booth on Monday evenings. Howard Cosell, Don Meredith, Frank Gifford, Keith Jackson, Alex Karras, and Fran Tarkenton have all enjoyed some degree of success during these sometimes unorthodox telecasts. Cosell, Meredith, and Karras, especially, have taken liberties in their color commentary that would have been unheard of during the usual weekend style of sportscasting. In fact, football purists have criticized "Monday Night Football" from time to time as fostering a circus-like atmosphere. Roone Arledge, the man behind ABC sports, has subsequently countered these charges by saying, "On Monday nights, we are in the entertainment business, competing against other networks for prime-time ratings. Here we work at pontificating less . . . we also try to document the action in a little more personal manner.''[23] Nevertheless, stylistic changes aside, televised football was more prominent and popular than ever during the 1970s, and major league baseball would be the next game to scale the fortress of prime time.

One side effect of the NFL's growing symbiosis with TV during the 1960s was the persistent argument appearing in the sports press concerning whether or not football was actually supplanting baseball as America's national pastime. The average ratings for football were consistently higher, although admittedly America's seasonal viewing patterns characteristically favor the fall-winter schedule of football rather than the summer months of baseball. Still, many of the problems that plagued the relationship between the major leagues and television were subsequently alleviated during the 1960s and early 1970s as sportscasting technology caught up with the particulars of the game.

Certainly the 12 to 18 cameras employed in each contemporary World Series contest are a far cry from the relatively meager facilities available throughout the 1950s. Today, viewing baseball on TV is an intimate and involving experience due in no small part to modern stadiums that are designed with television in mind; more flexible and powerful camera lenses; and slow motion and instant replay capabilities. As the aesthetics of sports telecasting evolved, the resulting prospects of televising baseball improved. "From 1960 to 1970, network payments for major-league baseball climbed from $3.25 million to $16.6 million.''[24] By 1972, NBC attempted to duplicate the success of ABC's "Monday Night Football" by experimenting with "Monday Night Baseball" as a summer replacement for "NBC Monday Night at the Movies." "Curt Gowdy and Tony Kubek provided coverage of the major game telecast each week, with other sportscasters covering secondary games. After four years on NBC, "Monday Night Baseball" moved to ABC in the spring of 1976.''[25] Again, ABC decided to use an announcing crew of three rather than two; and the subsequent atmosphere was substantially more "colorful" than the NBC prime-time offering had been. Bob Prince, Warner Wolf, Bob Uecker, Al Michaels, Keith Jackson, Don Drysdale, and Howard Cosell have all been in front of the microphones, at one time or another, for nighttime baseball on ABC.

In addition, World Series and All-Star games are also a prime-time fixture today, as ABC and NBC tend to alternate these events. The fourth game of the 1971 World Series between Baltimore and Pittsburgh was the first time that the post-season classic was televised during the evening. Since then, this pattern has escalated to the point where the majority of playoff and series games make their way into prime time. As for major league baseball generally, its future prognosis is very optimistic. On the one hand, gate attendance has been healthy and rising for over a decade. On the other, the major leagues have signed a television contract with both ABC and NBC that will enrich professional baseball by a reported $1 billion for rights that extend from 1983 until 1992.[26] The symbiosis between TV and baseball seems to be as fluid and mature as it is for television and football.

Basketball has also enjoyed a successful relationship with the networks, although the dimensions of this union are modest in comparison to the ones enjoyed by the NFL and major league baseball. "In 1965, the National Basketball Association received $600,000 from ABC to televise league games. In 1974, CBS paid $9 million for them."[27] During this period, the NBA became a big business as both the increased ratings and the subsequent influx of capital expanded team budgets, player's salaries, and the overall number of franchises. The windfall pattern that had beset football and baseball during the 1960s was now beginning to influence basketball in the early 1970s. Television had already had a similar effect on golf in the mid-1960s. Eventually the medium would correspondingly elevate the stakes of both men's and women's tennis when it proceeded to focus more and more attention on that sport after 1973.

It is very easy to determine that the most innovative figure in the history of sports telecasting has been Roone Arledge. In 1960, he went to work at ABC as a producer at a time when college football was the only major game that this network had under contract. Arledge set out to acquire more with less, as he christened television's first sport magazine in 1961 called "ABC's Wide World of Sports." Since Arledge was not in a position to exploit the major, traditional sports, his alternative was to explore new and exciting avenues between sports and television. Ultimately, he accomplished this added symbiosis in three ways. First, Arledge turned to minor games that, for the most part, had been ignored by television; next, he expanded the realm of sports possibilities to include the international forum; and lastly, he pioneered some crucial aesthetic developments in TV sportscasting.

From the beginning, "ABC's Wide World of Sports" offered a very different sports viewing experience to the American public. Not only were gymnastics, track and field, skiing, swimming and diving, rodeo, and automobile racing made available on the nation's airwaves most Saturday and some Sunday afternoons, but also such offbeat competitions as demolition derby, parachute jumping, and the world barrel jumping championships were provided. The results defied logic; ABC had a long running hit from its sports department, and Roone Arledge summarily became the head of sports programming at this network.

In the process, Arledge had successfully equipped "ABC's Wide World of Sports" with a well-trained production crew anchored by Jim McKay. These professionals would learn and perfect their trade during the 1960s and later transcend their craft by their quality coverage of the 1972 and 1976 summer Olympic games. Then as now, the typical "Wide World of Sports" show usually alternated between a number of events that were originating from all over the world. Arledge, however, used this program to change the stress in TV sportscasting from game analysis and strategy to an emphasis on the display of human emotions. As the show's directing force, he made sure that the program's opening promise about "the thrill of victory and the agony of defeat" was visibly apparent to all on the video screen. Arledge accomplished this by turning the cameras toward the spectators and using closer shots of the participants. The personalities are what mattered most at ABC Sports; this overall aesthetic design was ideally suited to the inherent intimacy of the medium.

ABC's sports programming department is what ultimately brought a modicum of prestige to the "third network." The Olympic games had been a part of TV ever since 1956, when selected filmed highlights were broadcast domestically several days after the events occurred. Throughout the 1960s, the winter Olympics characteristically drew humble ratings, while the summer games tended to generate a fair to goodly share of the available audience. By 1972, in Munich, Germany, though, ABC averaged "a 52 percent share . . . on Olympic nights."[28] Much of this accelerated interest centered around a group of Israeli athletes who had been taken prisoner by a band of Palestinian terrorists. The episode ended in disaster, as all the hostages were killed during a violent shootout between the Arabs and the police. The ABC production crew adapted admirably to the emergency, as the subsequent coverage was thorough, thoughtful, dignified, and touching. Four years later, ABC Sports would again demonstrate its expertise at the winter Olympics in Innsbruck, Austria, and the summer games in Montreal. This time, however, each event was a smashing success both aesthetically and financially, as the 49 percent share accomplished for the two weeks in Montreal skyrocketed ABC into the Number 1 network position for the first time in its history.[29] In May 1977, the network rewarded Roone Arledge for his hard work and creativity with an additional executive position to complement his presidency of network sports operations; at this time, he assumed his second post as president of ABC news.[30]

1977–Present: The Future of Sports Telecasting

All facets of television have been dramatically affected by the sudden and rapid diffusion of the new video technologies over the last decade, and sports programming is no different. The commercial potential of both cable and pay television is finally being realized; and so far, movies and sports have proven to be the most popular types of software that are delivered by these modes of distribution. On September 7, 1979, the Entertainment Sports Programming Network, a subsidiary of Getty Oil, commenced service as the first 24-hour total-sports cable network in the world. At the time, Chet Simmons, then president of NBC Sports, assumed the directorship of ESPN. He found the chore of filling 24 hours a day with programming to be a staggering proposition. Slowly but surely, however, ESPN has grown from 1.4 million subscriber homes in 1979 to a projected 40 million by 1985; in addition, the network's overall ratings finally began to show some promise in the spring of 1983.[31]

ESPN has also been instrumental in the appearance and formation of a new football conference, the United States Football League. Chet Simmons left this cable network to become commissioner of the USFL, as another NBC veteran, Scotty Connal, took over the leadership of ESPN. ABC Sports is also involved in the development of the USFL, as cable and television network exposure should be one of the major contingencies determining whether this new league can attain solvency in the sports marketplace. Another organization, the USA Network, is a direct competitor to ESPN and a unique cable franchise that programs both sports and feature-length films. Finally, a number of superstations—or independent TV stations that receive nationwide distribution with the help of satellite and cable transmission—are also important developments from a historical point of view. Ted Turner's WTBS in Atlanta, WGN in Chicago, and WOR from New York City, all deliver professional games originating from their own local environs to millions of cable subscribers all over the country.

Any discussion involving the future prospects of sports telecasting should end where the relationship between TV and sports all began 45 years earlier—with the networks and the local stations. In the 1980s, the whole of broadcast television is substantially committed to sports programming. Today, football, baseball, basketball, tennis, golf, boxing, hockey, and a handful of other games are all firmly entrenched on the nation's airwaves. In 1975, NBC, CBS, and ABC invested a combined $250 million for the production of sporting events.[32] By 1980, this figure grew to $1 billion, and was rising. Indeed, the symbiotic union between sports and television is stronger than ever; and evidently, this partnership has already coalesced into a multi-faceted generic identity that merges aspects of technology, aesthetics, business, economics, and culture to produce a form, style, and content that is both rich and diverse.

THEMES AND ISSUES

The history of television and sports has contained elements of controversy, but the relationship has been significant for all concerned. A number of issues surround the production and distribution of televised sports, and the impact of the marriage of television and sport will continue.

Television's impact on sport has been widespread and, in some cases, immense. Many teams and entire leagues owe their existence to money provided by television, while others have died because television monies were not forthcoming. Similarly, athletic personalities have achieved fame because of television exposure; in some cases the fame exceeded the accomplishments of the athletes, while other athletes have not achieved similar fame because they were not favored by extensive exposure.

Television has affected the way games are played. On a positive note, the opportunity to see demonstrations of superior athletes in action may have improved the technical expertise of younger players. On the other hand, television's needs have led to rule changes, scheduling modifications, and other effects on sports.

Television has altered the expectations of viewers and spectators. Federal law now mandates television coverage of some events, while modern stadiums and arenas now include large TV screens to provide the live spectator with a view as good as that available to the viewer at home.

The relationship has not been one-sided, of course. Television would not carry sporting events if there was no profit. Sports provide large audiences (and, thus, large advertising revenues) for television, and these audiences are told about other nonsports programs on the network. Further, coverage of major events brings prestige to the networks and their affiliates.

Today, greater changes appear on the horizon. New production equipment will provide the viewer with an even better "seat" in the TV stadium. New distribution media, such as cable TV, and communication satellites, may increase the amount of sports available to the viewer with access to them and, therefore, the money available to teams and athletes.

The Economics of Televised Sport

Television's greatest impact on American sports has been economic. The rights to carry games cost networks and stations hundreds of millions of dollars each year; and this doesn't include the cost of actually producing the telecasts.

The three major television networks pay over $1 billion for the rights to cover the NFL, while the NCAA's current contract (which runs until 1987) with ABC, CBS, and the "Turner Broadcasting System" (actually, a station in Atlanta distributed nationally by satellite and cable) totals almost $290 million.[33] Recently, Major League Baseball sold its national rights extending into the next decade (including the World Series, All Star Game, League Championship Series and Games of the Week) to NBC and ABC for more than $1 billion.[34] The contract means each major league baseball team will earn $5 million before the first ticket is sold. Further, each team retains the local rights to broadcasts; this can mean an additional $1 to 3 million per year, with the two New York teams each earning more than $10 million in 1983 for their rights.[35]

Of course, television networks would not pay such astronomical sums without some prospect of return. Sports events often attract large audiences and, particularly important, the audiences are composed of people (male, often young and affluent) attractive to some advertisers. It is to reach this audience particularly that such sports as golf are an important part of the television schedule.[36]

Sporting events are important as direct sources of income to television, but the value can be indirect as well. Sports events can bring prestige to the network and affiliates. For example, an ESPN spokesman admitted his company lost money on its 1983 telecasts of National Basketball Association games, but it was important to the image of the network that it carry major league sports.

ABC makes heavy use of its sports telecasts to promote its entertainment programs. While the most noticeable example is "Monday Night Football," perhaps the most successful effort occurred with the 1976 Olympics. The network, historically third in the ratings, used its late-summer coverage to promote upcoming programs and "accustom" viewers to watching ABC; the network became number one in 1976–77 and has remained out of the bottom spot until the beginning of fall, 1985.[37]

While television has benefited from sports, the money paid has had a greater impact on sports. Not only teams, but entire leagues own their existence to television. NBC's purchase of the rights to American Football League games for a per team sum equivalent to that paid to the established NFL provided the impetus to the merger of the leagues.[38] On the other hand, failure to gain long-term television contracts has helped doom such leagues as the American Basketball Association and World Football League.

Television money affects where teams may be located. While the population base from which to draw spectators is important, the size of the television market has been responsible for such acts as the move of the Braves from Milwaukee to Atlanta[39] and the expansion of the NFL to Tampa, Florida.[40]

Schedules of leagues and teams have been altered to fit the demands of television. World Series games are now played at night (in very low late-October temperatures) or early evening (on the West Coast, to accommodate the start of prime time in the East) because the games attract larger audiences than when they were played in daylight.[41] College football now begins in early September because of its interest in television coverage (creating the irony of some freshman players appearing in games weeks before they even begin attending classes). As the late Alabama coach "Bear" Bryant put it, "We think TV exposure is so important to our program, so important to our university, that we will schedule ourselves to fit the medium. I'll play at midnight if that's what TV wants."[42]

It is not only schedules that have been changed to accommodate television. Rule changes are often made to make the game more suitable for television.

In 1982 many college basketball conferences began to experiment with rules requiring players to shoot every 30 seconds and to allow an extra point for baskets made from longer distances. The impetus for these changes came, in part, because of criticism of a telecast the previous year; in the nationally televised Virginia-North Carolina game, North Carolina successfully employed the strategy of holding the ball for long periods without shooting. The ploy kept the ball from Virginia's All-American center, Ralph Sampson, and resulted in a low-scoring and, to some viewers, dull game.

Professional golf used to follow a format called "match" play, in which golfers competed on a hole-by-hole basis; the number of holes won determined the winner. Since this meant the tournament winner could be determined short of 18 holes, television was unable to plan the time needed for a telecast. Therefore, the tournaments now use "medal" play—total strokes—to determine the winner.

In a relatively few cases, serious manipulations of rules have occurred because of television. The most notorious occurred in the mid-1970s at a college all-star football game. To meet the commercial time demands of the rights-holder, the game's first quarter was shortened (without prior warning to spectators or viewers), while the final quarter was allowed to go beyond the normal 15 minutes. The winning touchdown was actually scored after the game should have ended.

It is noteworthy that many of these examples have been from college, that is, "amateur" sports. One of the apparent effects of television sports has been the "professionalizing" of amateur athletes. For example, leading performers have been paid to run in the annual Boston Marathon.

More troubling to many has been the effect of television money in college football. Traditionally, the National Collegiate Athletic Association has represented all of its members in negotiating contracts with the networks; the contracts prohibit sale of live local coverage by individual teams or conferences. The contracts limit the number of appearances (and, therefore, money) a school can make during the life of the contract. As a result, lesser teams receive some television exposure, and the money is spread wider among football-playing schools.

Many of the largest schools have begun to rebel against this practice. In 1982, the "College Football Association" sold rights to its members' games to NBC. Although the NCAA was able to block the telecasts in court, the U.S. Circuit Court of Appeals has ruled in favor of the Universities of Oklahoma and Georgia and stated that the NCAA actions violate the antitrust laws.[43] It is anticipated the case will eventually be decided by the Supreme Court of the United States. If the large football-playing schools win the right to control the rights to their games, the result will be both proliferation of football telecasts and a threat to the viability of many smaller football programs.[44]

Neither has the money from television been ignored by professional athletes. Escalating salaries, particularly in baseball and basketball, can be partly attributed to the income from television. In the 1950s and 1960s, salaries of $100,000 per year were paid only to such baseball superstars as Stan Musial, Mickey Mantle, and Willie Mays. In 1983, the average salary in major league baseball was almost $90,000, and some players earned more than $1 million a year.

In an interview in the 1983 *Sport Magazine*, Oakland A's President Roy Eisenhardt noted that the high salaries seem to affect players' performance. His team's planning includes the expectation that when a player signs a large contract, the following season will be an "off year."

Television and Status Conferral

A great deal of social science research supports the idea that the media "confer status." Simply by being on television a person seems important. Thus, the effort by some colleges to expand the number of times their football teams appear on television is as important for recruiting new athletes and gaining support from alumni as the direct rights payments. When Major League Baseball sought to have the World Series moved to prime time, Commissioner Bowie Kuhn said, "We're trying to promote baseball to the American public. How are we going to do that by playing these big games on a Wednesday afternoon?"[45]

Television exposure has made some athletes nationally known. Star athletes, such as Babe Ruth, Joe Louis, and Ben Hogan were famous without television, but TV exposure has elevated many lesser athletes to acclaim.

Perhaps the most interesting example of the medium's capacity to create stars occurred in the 1972 Olympics. ABC's coverage of the gymnastics competition centered around the elfin performer Olga Korbut. Although she finished behind some of her teammates from the USSR, she was the most visible performer to viewers. To those at the Olympic site, she was a competent but hardly noteworthy young athlete. In an interview on ESPN, Pete Axthelm related what occurred when he filed a story about the Olympics to his employer, *Newsweek*. The editor called back in a rage, demanding to know why there was nothing on Olga Korbut. The reporter, on the scene in Munich and away from the American television picture, hadn't even heard of the new "darling" of the fans!

Other athletes are negatively affected by the absence of exposure. One example is Henry Aaron, the greatest career home-run hitter in baseball history. Aaron played his entire career in Milwaukee and Atlanta, away from the media spotlights. As a result, Aaron received considerably less attention than his peers, such as Mickey Mantle in New York and Willie Mays in San Francisco and New York.

The fame athletes derive from television has begun to be "recycled." Most telecasts now include at least one "ex-jock" as an analyst or play-by-play announcer. The use of former athletes and coaches is controversial. While many, such as Frank Gifford, Tony Kubek, John Madden, and Al McGuire have proven to be successful announcers, others have been little short of disastrous. While Sandy Koufax and Bob Gibson may have been the most dominant pitchers of their era, they proved less effective when they moved to the announcing booth.

Criticism of the use of former athletes centers around the fact they are used for their name rather than their expertise. Sportswriter Glenn Dickey has noted, "The influx of former athletes into broadcasting has made it almost impossible for the cream to rise to the top. Thus, most of the good announcers in the country are local ones, and many are . . . radio men."[46] Howard Cosell argues, "Writing is a profession, and so is broadcasting. . . . Let the ex-athletes vie in open competition with any young person getting out of college trained in communications and journalism. Then, let the real standards of the profession prevail."[47]

Athletes are also used to promote commercial products. Of course, such endorsements are traditional—in the early 1900s there were even Ty Cobb cigarettes. Recently, entire television advertising campaigns have been built around athletes like Reggie Jackson and Arnold Palmer. Perhaps the most famous example has been the Miller Lite Beer campaign using former athletes.

Television can also make prominent nonathletes as well. Announcers such as Howard Cosell, Jim McKay, and Brent Musberger are often more famous than the athletes whose exploits they describe.

Fans, too, often go to great lengths to share in the glory of television coverage. Viewers are familiar with the costumes, signs, and other devices spectators use to attract the camera.

Perhaps the strangest example of the power to bestow status involves the

"Halftime Highlights" shown on "ABC's Monday Night Football" game. Fans have complained vociferously to the network because the importance of their team's Sunday game wasn't validated by inclusion in the highlights segment.

Since colorful exploits are more likely to attract television coverage to athletes, the result is that such behavior is encouraged, sometimes to the detriment of the game. According to John Underwood, "The object isn't to play to win, the object is to humiliate. Taunt the other guy. Shake the ball in his nose. Wave your fingers as you cross the goal. And when you do, make a big display. Spike the ball. Do the funky chicken. End-zone discotheque is great for the ratings."[48]

Not all of television's lessons are negative. While high school or college coaches may decry the tendency of their athletes to imitate the worst behaviors of professional athletes, others note television has improved the skills of athletes. According to Ray Meyer, long-time basketball coach of DePaul University, "Kids today are much better basketball players than they used to be. TV, not vitamins, should get the credit. Today, every kid who's interested can watch all the games he wants on TV, with the fine points shown him in slow-motion instant replay."[49]

Television can make an athlete or announcer prominent. It also has a voracious appetite. Players and sports go through cycles of popularity and overexposure, just as do the genres of series programming. Boxing is the most prominent example, as it dominated early television, went into an eclipse in the 1960s and early 1970s, and has been returned to prominence in the last decade. However, ratings for recent championship fights have been in decline, and the sport may be suffering again from overexposure.

The demand for televised sports has become so great that the networks have resorted to creating their own events. Such made-for-TV quasi-sports shows as "Celebrity Tennis" and "Battle of the Network Stars" were ratings successes in the 1970s and early 1980s.

With all of the televised sports available, there were fears expressed that Americans would become a nation of spectators. In fact, this has not been the case, as participation in various team and individual sports has increased in recent years. Television coverage of such sports as tennis and gymnastics has created new participants and competitors.[50]

Television, then, has brought prominence to some athletes and some sports. Clearly, the medium has focused the viewer's attention. It has also shaped the way viewers and live spectators perceive sporting events.

Television as the New "Sports Arena"

It has long been a cliché that the television viewer of a sports event has "the best seat in the house." The home viewer has the benefit of close-ups of plays, instant replays, and updated statistics and information about injuries, player performance, and games in other locations. While the color and activity of the spectators may be missing from the television program, some producers, such as ABC's Chuck Howard, attempt to utilize camera shots, interviews with fans, and similar devices to convey to the viewer the feel of the game.[51]

To redress the balance between live spectator and TV viewer, modern arenas and stadiums have become giant living rooms. Large-screen video displays provide close-ups and instant replays of the very plays seen live.

Television is an entertainment medium, and sports teams have tried to make the games more appealing to the viewer. We have previously mentioned some of the rules changes made to accommodate television, but other changes have been effected as well.

For example, since color television has become prevalent, uniforms have replaced the more drab attire suitable for black and white telecasts. Baseball has replaced the traditional "home white, road gray," uniforms with a rainbow of colorful mix and match outfits. In tennis, where only "whites" were to be worn on the court, an explosion of color has appeared to make the game more amenable to television pictures.

Other visual elements have been made to cater to the TV viewer. Even professional teams now have cheerleading squads, despite the fact that none of these lead cheers and are difficult for the stadium spectators to even see. However, they add allure to the telecasts, as they are seen in scantily clad close-ups by the home viewer. The most famous of these professional groups, the Dallas Cowboy Cheerleaders, have even had a made-for-TV movie produced about their made-for-TV exploits.

Television provides an expanded view of the game, allowing the audience to see plays from various angles and perspectives, in slow-motion, and in repeated "instant replays." But in televising sports the medium frames games in its own traditional forms. Drama, conflict, pathos, and humor are emphasized, often overshadowing the athletic performances.[52]

Televised sporting events often become contests between the veteran and the young star. The drama of a traded star returning to the site of former glories is often highlighted. Viewers of the 1983 National Basketball Association playoffs were often led to believe the most important question was not which was the best team, but whether Philadelphia's Julius Erving would finally win a league championship in the twilight of his career.

Many of the dramatic "confrontations" emphasized by television wouldn't exist if it were not for the telecast itself. Perhaps the most absurd situation occurs with football. Commonly the dramatic "plot" is stated as a confrontation between star quarterbacks or star running backs. During pre-game shows highlights of the competitors are shown, and graphics provide statistical background on the players' past accomplishments. Interviews are often included, and during the game updated statistics of the accomplishments of the respective players provide a score-card of the competition.

The fallacy of such a television drama is, of course, that such players as quarterbacks don't compete against each other. Their real competition comes from the opposition defense!

Television relies heavily on violence or potential violence in its programs, and the same is true for televised sports. Replays often emphasize legal and illegal violence. Particularly fierce collisions between football players are often replayed even when the play is relatively insignificant in the game's outcome. During the 1983 NCAA College Basketball Tournament a cheerleader mistakenly thought that a time out had been called; she ran out onto the floor, where she collided with a player running at full speed. Replays of the young woman being bowled over were shown repeatedly during the weekend's sports reports, despite the fact that she was unhurt and the incident in no way affected the outcome of the game.

Videotape replays allow television producers to provide incidents of violence to enliven an otherwise nonviolent program. For example, the 1983 Indianapolis 500 was run without any serious accidents. During its same-day replay of the race, ABC presented a lengthy story on safety measures at the race. Included in the segment were a gratuitous series of replays of major crashes from previous "500s," despite the fact the safety report did not specifically deal with the accidents.

The marriage of sports and television to create entertainment programming is best exemplified by ABC's "Monday Night Football," as well as made-for-TV sports events such as "Battle of the Network Stars" and the "Superstars" competition. On the other hand, television, like Hollywood, has been generally unsuccessful in using a sports motif for dramatic or comedy series. Among the biggest disasters in prime-time programming history have been sports-centered shows like "Waverly Wonders" (with former football star, Joe Namath), and "Ball Four" (written by and starring former major league baseball player Jim Bouton.)

Just as television has altered viewers' perceptions of the games, so, too, it has altered the audience's expectations of telecasts of athletic events. The matter has achieved the status of a public policy issue. The most noteworthy example of the importance of televised sports was the anti-blackout law passed by Congress in 1973; the Senate voted 76 to 6 and the House 336 to 37 to require that professional football games be televised in the home city if the game was a sellout.[53] Only one other activity—politics—has triggered such a constitutionally suspect legal requirement that television programmers must carry a specific type of programming (stations are required to sell time to candidates for federal office and must provide time for a reply to criticisms of candidates or supporters of issues).

Television and sports, then, have had a long, usually profitable relationship. Actually, they have affected each other in a series of both major and insignificant ways. The development of new television production and distribution technologies promises to raise new issues and bring additional changes to this relationship.

Sports and New Video Technologies

New technologies are coming on-line to improve producers' abilities to present sports events. Other technologies, some already well in place, are promising changes in the distribution of sports programming to viewers.

In the case of production capacities, two advances seem most important. These are the development of small minicameras and the increased graphic and alphanumeric technologies available for production.

The early telecasts of sports were accomplished with one or two cameras positioned far away from the action. As cameras have become more portable, the viewer has been taken to the sidelines of a football or basketball game and high above the playing surface in blimps or gondolas. Roving hand-held cameras allow viewers to feel as though they are part of the crowd of live spectators.

New generation cameras, using digital signal processing and solid state components, have been reduced in size to little more than that of movie cameras, and prototypes have been built of video cameras the size of 35-mm still cameras. The resulting portability should afford an even greater variety of pictures from television.

During an auto race in 1983, a minicamera and microphone were placed inside one of the competitor's stock car. The television audience was treated to a running commentary from what proved to be the winning driver and a view of the race previously seen only by the competitors, as they look through the windshield. As cameras become smaller and more rugged, future viewers may see the action (or at least replays) from the perspective of the quarterback, the baseball catcher, or the referee.

Television provides viewers with a larger amount of information and more varied visual perspectives than have been available to the spectator in the stadium. This capacity will increase in the near future. New special effects equipment will allow multi-image replays and improved graphics to show the flight of a ball. Alphanumeric computer displays will provide continually updated statistics, information about other games, and the other data that can make televised sporting events more understandable to the less informed viewer.

As great as the impact of new technologies will be on the production of sports telecasts, the increase in distribution media may be even more significant. Communication satellites, used in direct-to-home systems, and cable TV will be particularly significant, with additional channels becoming available from Low Power TV (LPTV) and Multi-point Distribution Systems (MDS).

These new technologies bring the potential (already realized in many parts of the country) for an increase in programming needs by operators, and sports seem a natural to fill some of the hours of channel time. The technologies are also likely to change the economics of televised sport.

Two national sports-oriented program services, ESPN and USA, are already available to many cable subscribers. ESPN now provides 22 hours a day of live and prerecorded sports events, including such "major league" events as NBA and NCAA basketball and the United States Football League. Thus far, ESPN has faced financial difficulties.[54] It has, however, had the resources to pay a reported $10-11 million for the rights to televise USFL games in 1983 and 1984.[55]

USA, owned primarily by Time, Inc., features sports in the evening. USA televises such events as National Hockey League games and in 1983 was in the final year of a two-year agreement with Major League Baseball to televise a game of the week.[56]

The superstations, WTBS, WGN, and WOR, also provide nationally available major league baseball games through their telecasts of Atlanta Braves, Chicago Cubs, and New York Mets games, respectively. Ted Turner's WTBS has also purchased the rights to a package of NCAA football games for $17.6 million and to such one-time events as the Georgetown-Virginia basketball game of 1982.[57]

Major League Baseball is apparently exploring the creation of a nationally distributed pay cable service to go into operation after its current contract with the networks expire in 1990.[58] Meanwhile, a national pay service Super Sports Channel began in 1983 presenting games for a few teams.[59] However, most of the activity related to the new technologies has been at the regional and local levels.

Half of the major league baseball teams had contracts in 1983 for pay TV telecasts. For example, the New York Yankees are reportedly receiving $5 million for each of the 15 years of its contract with Sportschannel, and the Texas Rangers have a five year contract estimated to be worth $10-15 million.[60]

A number of cable television systems provide coverage of local teams on their own local origination channels. These telecasts can range from play-by-play coverage of Pop Warner league football, to high school sports, to such big-time events as those played by Big Ten universities and even major league professional teams.[61]

The prospect of having games televised on cable or satellite-distributed channels has excited entrepreneurs and athletic officials. These telecasts have brought money and public notice to such heretofore obscure competitors as the college basketball Sunbelt Conference (South Alabama, Old Dominion University, etc.).

The consequences of the new distribution technologies may be great. Already, the demand for broadcast rights has escalated the amounts being paid—to the benefit of the professional and college teams. For example, ESPN bid what it considered a reasonable $8.5 million for the rights to NCAA football. Turner Broadcasting System won the contract with a bid of more than double that.[62]

What remains unknown is who will benefit most from the expanded demand for sports rights. Will this provide an opportunity for smaller colleges and lesser professional sports to achieve television exposure and income? Or will the prospect of televising NFL or Notre Dame football games shut out the Bowling Greens and Fresno States? The outcome of the College Football Association-NCAA dispute will have a profound impact. If the NCAA's ability to restrict telecasts is ended, we can expect proliferation of telecasts of major college football games, to the detriment of smaller schools.

Much of the excitement about the new distribution systems involves the potential for pay television. ESPN, USA, and the various superstations are called "basic" cable services—the cable subscriber receives them as part of the monthly subscription charge. But, as in the case of the various major league baseball teams, much of the action may shift to a system where a viewer must pay an extra fee to watch a game or sporting event.

While this may bring additional income to the teams, it may also deprive many viewers, without the ability to pay, from seeing the games. Sports play an important role in bringing together communities—small towns virtually shut down on Friday nights while everyone attends the local high school football game. More than one million fans of the Philadelphia 76ers lined the parade route to honor their NBA champions in. In 1968, in the midst of racial disturbances in San Francisco, the Giants agreed to televise an important series of baseball games from Candlestick Park. The telecasts kept many people home and off the streets and helped in easing the tensions. These positive functions of televised sport may be reduced or disappear if access is limited only to those with the ability to pay.

Already, however, some members of Congress and some television and sports executives have expressed the opinion that such events as the Super Bowl and World Series would remain on free TV. Although the constitutional implications of legislation mandating such action are fascinating to contemplate, the evidence it provides about the importance of televised sports is impressive.

The relationship between television and sports has been long and often controversial. Observers have criticized the medium's impact, pointing to such aberrations as the distorted length of the quarters of an all-star football game, the circus atmosphere of "Monday Night Football," the threat that we would become a nation of spectators.

In fact, most of the effects of television on sports have been rather trivial. Changing a game time to accommodate television doesn't threaten the integrity of any sport, and the creation of media personalities causes no harm to spectators.

The money television has brought the team owners and athletes is awesome. However, sports is and always has been part of the entertainment business. The income of even superstar athletes pales beside those of superstar musicians or movie actors. Further, the financial prospects of sports television has led to the formulation and expansion of leagues, creating new opportunities for athletes and bringing sports to areas previously deprived of them.

Some people have expressed the fear that television exposure may oversaturate the viewers' interest, diminishing live attendance. While some sports, such as boxing, have suffered, firmly established sports have benefited from television. Major league baseball, pro football, and college basketball have had record attendance in recent years; the personalities created by television attract crowds to the stadiums.

Clearly, the televised sporting event is framed and plotted by producers and announcers. It is possible, however, that TV viewers may need these cues to make sense of the game; TV viewers may be more casual fans than those who make the effort to attend games in person, and television may help them to better enjoy the game. Long-time fans may agree with Glenn Dickey when he says, "I think if I hear the term 'seams of a zone' one more time, I'll go rushing and screaming into the street."[63] The novice fan, however, may appreciate the information.

Sports comprise a major component of the television schedule. While the relationship between the medium and sports may change and new techniques of presentation may evolve, it is unlikely the importance of televised sports will diminish.

NOTES

1. Erik Barnouw, *The Golden Web: A History of Broadcasting in the United States, 1933 to 1953* (New York: Oxford, 1968), p. 127.

2. "First Television of Baseball Seen," *New York Times*, May 19, 1939, p. 29, col. 4.

3. "Collegians Play Ball as Television Mirrors the Game," *New York Times*, May 21, 1939, p. 10x, col. 1.

4. James P. Dawson, "Title Bout Chance at Stake Tonight," *New York Times*, June 1, 1939, p. 33, col. 5.

5. "Sports Coverage, Then and Now: A Far Cry from the Flatbush Safari," *TV Guide*, November 28, 1959, p. 19.

6. Stanley Frank, "The Golden Age of Sports," *TV Guide*, April 4, 1964, p. 18.

7. Patrick Clark, *Sports Firsts* (New York: Facts on File, Inc., 1981), pp. 58, 157.

8. Harry Castleman and Walter J. Podrazik, *Watching TV: Four Decades of American Television* (New York: McGraw-Hill, 1982), p. 15.

9. Tim Brooks and Earle Marsh, *The Complete Directory to Prime Time Network TV Shows; 1946–Present*, rev. ed. (New York: Ballantine Books, 1981), pp. 104–5.

10. "TV Kayo; End of Televised Boxing," *Newsweek*, January 6, 1964, p. 41.

11. Barnouw, *The Golden Web*, p. 244.

12. Arthur Shulman and Roger Youman, *How Sweet It Was* (New York: Bonanza Books, 1966), p. 408.

13. "Can Roller Derby Get Back on Track?" *Newsweek*, April 4, 1983, p. 14.

14. Frank, "The Golden Age of Sports," p. 18.

15. Donald Parente, "A History of Television and Sports" (Ph.D. diss., University of Illinois at Urbana-Champaign, 1974), p. 65.

16. Frank, "The Golden Age of Sports," p. 16.

17. Robert Campbell, *The Golden Years of Broadcasting: A Celebration of the First 50 Years of Radio and TV on NBC* (New York: Charles Scribner's Sons, 1976), p. 90.

18. Parente, "A History of Television and Sports," pp. 66–67.

19. Ibid., p. 74.

20. Ibid., p. 73.

21. Campbell, *The Golden Years of Broadcasting*, p. 84.

22. Ibid.

23. Bruce Berman, "TV Sports Auteurs," *Film Comment*, (March-April 1976), p. 35.

24. Campbell, *The Golden Years of Broadcasting*, p. 84.

25. Brooks and Marsh, *The Complete Directory to Prime Time Network TV Shows*, p. 64.

26. "ABC Sports in Six-Year Deal for Baseball," *Daily Variety*, April 8, 1983, pp. 1, 26.

27. Campbell, *The Golden Years of Broadcasting*, p. 84.

28. Castleman and Podrazik, *Watching TV*, p. 236.

29. Ibid., p. 269.

30. Ibid., p. 292.

31. *ESPN Sports Almanac '83* (Charlotte, N.C.: Total Sports Publications, 1983), p. 6.

32. Don Kowet, "For Better or for Worse?" *TV Guide*, July 1, 1978, p. 2.

33. Carl Levine, "Cable vs. Network Sports," *Videopro* (February 1983), p. 19.

34. Victor Livingston, "Baseball Scouts Pay TV," *Cablevision* April 25, 1983, p. 14.

35. "Baseball 1983," *Broadcasting*, February 28, 1983, p. 56.

36. Don Kowett, "Playing for Blood," in *Television Today: A Close-Up View*, ed. Barry Cole (Oxford: Oxford University Press, 1981), p. 80.

37. William Oscar Johnson, "A Contract with the Kremlin," *Sports Illustrated* February 21, 1977, p. 16.

38. Stanley Frank, "Pro Football's Shotgun Marriage," *TV Guide*, September 3, 1966, pp. 4–7.

39. William Johnson, "TV Made It All a New Game," in *Sport and Society: An Anthology* ed. John T. Talamini and Charles H. Page (Boston: Little, Brown and Company, 1973), p. 471.

40. James Michener, *Sports in America* (New York: Random House, 1976), p. 307.

41. Ironically, television first resisted the idea of prime-time World Series telecasts, fearing the audience would be smaller than for regular series. The change came at baseball's insistence, and the ratings have been so high that even Sunday games are now played at night. See Don Kowett, "For Better or for Worse?" in *Television Today*, ed. Cole, p. 90.

42. Ibid., p. 88.

43. "NCAA Tries Again to Keep Negotiating Rights for Sports," *Broadcasting*, May 23, 1983, pp. 72–73.

44. The decline of baseball's minor leagues, in the face of televised major league games in the 1950s, may prove an accurate foreshadowing of football's fate. John Underwood, *The Death of an American Game* (Boston: Little, Brown and Company, 1979), p. 26, notes many small schools can hardly afford the loss of even a few ticket buyers.

45. Quoted in Kowett, "For Better or for Worse?" p. 90.

46. Glenn Dickey, *The Jock Empire* (Radner, Pa.: Chilton Book Company, 1974), p. 103.

47. Howard Cosell, *Like It Is* (Chicago: Playboy Press, 1974), p. 218.

48. Underwood, *The Death of an American Game*, pp. 24–25.

49. Quoted in Kowett, "For Better or for Worse?" p. 91.

50. Ibid., p. 89.

51. Berman, "TV Sports Auteurs," p. 35.

52. A study of football telecasts has uncovered at least 15 such dramatic elements. Jennings Bryant, Paul Comisky, and Dolf Zillmann, "Drama in Sports Commentary." *Journal of Communication* (Summer 1977), pp. 140–49.

53. Michener, *Sports in America*, pp. 413–14.

54. William Taaffe, "Getting Down to Business," *Sports Illustrated* February 10, 1983, p. 93.

55. "Football Takes a Favorable Bounce for Broadcasters, Cablecasters," *Broadcasting* February 28, 1983, p. 41.

56. "Baseball 1983," p. 54.

57. Levine, "Cable vs. Network Sports," p. 18.

58. Livingston, "Baseball Scouts Pay TV," p. 14.

59. "Baseball 1983," p. 54.

60. Ibid.

61. Jean Bergantini Grillo, "For the Sport of It," *Cablevision* April 18, 1983, pp. 94–102.

62. Levine, "Cable vs. Network Sports," p. 18.

63. Dickey, *The Jock Empire*, p. 100.

BIBLIOGRAPHICAL SURVEY

The published literature about television and sport is rather scattered. No single work provides a comprehensive description or analysis, although many books and periodicals devote some of their pages to the topic.

Donald Parente's Ph.D. dissertation, "A History of Television and Sports" (University of Illinois, 1974) provides a useful starting point for those looking for historical data. Other broadcast histories that include some sports information include Erik Barnouw's *The Golden Web* and *The Image Empire* (Volumes two and three of his three-volume *A History of Broadcasting in the United States*), and Robert Campbell's *Golden Years of Broadcasting*, a pictorial history of the National Broadcasting Company.

By far the leading television sports organization is ABC. The history and philosophies of Roone Arledge and his colleagues are chronicled by Bert Sugar in *"The Thrill of Victory": The Inside Story of ABC Sports*.

Useful sources of information are the autobiographies written by some of the announcers. Howard Cosell, probably the best known contemporary announcer, has written *Cosell*, and *Like It Is*, which describes such matters as Monday Night Football, boxing, and the practice of using former athletes as announcers. Red Barber's *The Broadcasters* relates the experiences and opinions of the man many consider the best baseball announcer of all time.

Commentary about television and sport abounds. One of the better essays appears as a chapter in James A. Michener's *Sports in America*, while Glenn Dickey's *The Jock Empire: Its Rise and Deserved Fall* and John Underwood's *The Death of an American Game: The Crisis in Football* are less than complimentary about the medium's effects on sport.

An amusing and useful examination of the subject is William O. Johnson, Jr.,'s *Super Spectator and the Electric Lilliputians*, although its 1971 publication date makes it more valuable as a historical reference. Johnson's earlier essay, "TV Made It All a New Game" is reprinted in *Society and Sport: An Anthology*, edited by John T. Talamini and Charles H. Page.

Barry Cole's edited volume *Television Today: A Close-Up View* reprints a number of essays from *TV Guide*, including Don Kowett's "Playing for Blood," and "For Better or for Worse" and Melvin Durslag's "From Barrel Jumpers to Belly Floppers." *TV Guide* is a useful source of information about sports. *The TV Guide 25-Year Index* is a good starting point.

Other valuable sources of current comment and information about televised sports, including the new technologies, are *Sports Illustrated* and *The Sporting News*. The latter is a weekly newspaper that features a column on televised sports, currently being written by Jack Craig.

Useful as sources about current economic, programming, and legal aspects of television and sports are the weekly trade publications *Broadcasting* and *Cablevision*. In addition to news stories about events, both publications provide occasional feature stories. Particularly useful are *Broadcasting*'s annual surveys of football (usually in early August) and baseball broadcasting (in late February or early March). These articles include information about financial and advertising matters as well as programming philosophies of the broadcasters and the sports organizations involved.

Finally, some academically oriented journals have provided useful information. Particularly interesting is the summer of 1977 *Journal of Communication*, which contains a series of articles on televised sport, including Donald Parente's "The Interdependence of Sports and Television," and "Drama in Sports Commentary," by Jennings Bryant, Paul Comisky, and Dolf Zillmann. Legal issues are explored in Joe Horowitz's "Market Entrenchment and the Sports Broadcasting Act" in *American Behavioral Scientist* January-February 1978. Bruce Berman's "TV Sports Auteurs," in the March-April 1976 *Film Comment* is probably the best examination of television's imposition of theme and plot line on sporting events.

BOOKS AND ARTICLES

Barber, Red. *The Broadcasters*. New York: The Dial Press, 1970.

Brooks, Tim, and Earle Marsh. *The Complete Directory to Prime Time Network TV Shows, 1946–Present*; rev. ed. New York: Ballantine Books, 1981.

Berman, Bruce. "TV Sports Auteurs," *Film Comment*, March-April 1976, pp. 343–35, 64.

Campbell, Robert. *The Golden Years of Broadcasting: A Celebration of the First 50 Years of Radio and TV on NBC*. New York: Charles Scribner's Sons, 1976.

Castleman, Harry, and Walter J. Podrazik. *Watching TV: Four Decades of American Television*. New York: McGraw-Hill, 1982.

Coakly, Jay J. *Sport in Society: Issues and Controversies*, 2d ed. St. Louis: C.V. Mosby Co., 1982. Includes some discussion of TV sports.

"Conversation with Scotty Connal," *Videography*, November 1982, pp. 56–70.

Cosell, Howard, *Cosell*. Chicago: Playboy Press, 1973.

———. *Like It Is*. Chicago: Playboy Press, 1974.

Dickey, Glenn. *The Jock Empire: Its Rise and Deserved Fall.* Radnor, Pa.: Chilton Book
    Co., 1974.
Grillo, Jean Bergentini. "For the Sport of It," *Cablevision.* April 18, 1983, pp. 93–102.
Horowitz, Ira. "Market Entrenchment and the Sports Broadcasting Act," *American
    Behavioral Scientist.* January/February 1978, pp. 415–30.
Johnson, William O., Jr., *Super Spectator and the Electric Lilliputians.* Boston: Little,
    Brown and Company, 1971.
Levine, Carl. "Cable vs. Network Sports," *Videopro.* February 1983, pp. 18–24; 64–
    68;
Loy, John W., Jr., Gerald S. Kenyon, and Barry D. McPherson, eds. *Sport, Culture,
    and Society: A Reader on the Sociology of Sport.* 2d rev. ed. Philadelphia: Lea
    and Febiger, 1981. Includes Susan Birrell and John W. Loy, Jr. "Media Sport:
    Hot and Cool," pp. 296–37.
Michener, James A. *Sports in America.* New York: Random House, 1976. Includes a
    chapter, "The Media," pp. 285–337.
Parente, Donald. "A History of Television and Sports." Ph.D. dissertation, University
    of Illinois at Urbana-Champaign, 1974.
————, ed. "Symposium on Sports and Television," *Journal of Communication.* Sum-
    mer 1977, pp. 127–70.
Real, Michael R. *Mass-Mediated Culture.* Englewood Cliffs, N.J.: Prentice-Hall, 1977.
Schulian, John. "Personal Foul." *American Film.* Vol. 2, 1977, p. 2.
Snyder, Eldon E., and Elmer A. Spreitzer. *Social Aspects of Sport.* 2d ed. Englewood
    Cliffs, N.J.: Prentice-Hall, 1978.
Sugar, Bert R. *"The Thrill of Victory": The Inside Story of ABC Sports.* New York:
    Hawthorn Books, 1978.
Talamini, John T., and Charles H. Page, eds., *Sport and Society: An Anthology.* Boston:
    Little, Brown and Company, 1973. Includes section, "Sport and Mass Media,"
    pp. 413–72—including "TV Made It All a New Game" by William Johnson
    (pp. 454–72).
Underwood, John. *The Death of an American Game: The Crisis in Football.* Boston:
    Little, Brown and Company, 1979. Includes various comments about television's
    impact on football.

VIDEOGRAPHY

Unlike other TV genres, the bread and butter of sports telecasting does not
necessarily revolve solely around a group of individual prime-time series. Instead, there are literally thousands of memorable games that have usually aired
either on the weekends or during weekday afternoons and evenings. Of course,
most playoffs, championship series, and all-star games are important in team
sports like football, baseball, basketball, and hockey. Major tournaments, like
Wimbledon and the masters, are crucial to individualized sports like tennis and
golf, just as championship bouts are a significant part of boxing and other combat
sports.

Also, unique events may stand out for one reason or another. Reggie Jackson's
three home-run performance during the 1978 World Series on national TV was

a notable achievement, as have been thousands of other examples. The uniqueness and cultural relevancy of the 1973 "Tennis Battle of the Sexes" between Billie Jean King and Bobby Riggs is one event of many that have successfully mixed sports and show business, usually with an obvious emphasis on the hype and spectacle that is a part of all sports telecasting. Lastly, there are those shows that mark a qualitative increase in the symbiotic relationship between sports and television. Scores of incidents like the "Heidi affair" are appropriate here. In this instance, NBC was televising a football game between the New York Jets and the Oakland Raiders on November 17, 1968. With only 50 seconds left in the contest and the Jets leading, 32 to 29, this network cut to a children's made-for-TV movie based on the Heidi tale. To everyone's amazement, the switchboard at NBC was bombarded with complaints for hours. In fact, the whole escapade was further complicated when the fans at home learned that Oakland had scored two touchdowns during these last 50 seconds to pull out an incredible 43 to 32 win. The degree of indignation expressed by the American viewing public signalled loudly to this particular network and to all the rest of the television industry, for that matter, just how important football had become to TV.

It would be impossible to list every key program in sports telecasting history. Therefore, what follows is a selected list of TV sportscasting's most successful series rather than specific contests or memorable games.

"The Gillette Calvalcade of Sports"
    NBC, various prime times on Monday, Tuesday, and Friday evenings
    Premiere: September 1944
    Announcers: Steve Ellis, Bob Stanton, Ray Forrest, and Jimmy Powers
    Last Program: June 1960

Major League Baseball's "World Series"
    NBC and ABC, late September–early October
    Premiere: 1947
    Announcers: Red Barber, Lindsey Nelson, Joe Garagiola, Curt Gowdy, Tony Kubek, and others

The "Summer Olympics" and "Winter Olympics"
    NBC and ABC, late August–early September; and February
    Premiere: 1956, filmed highlights
    Announcers: Jim McKay, Dick Button, Chris Schenkel, Jack Perkins, Keith Jackson, Frank Gifford, and others

"Wide World of Sports"
    ABC, usually 90 minutes on most Saturday and a few Sunday afternoons
    Premiere: April 1961
    Announcers: Jim McKay, Howard Cosell, and others

The NFL's "Super Bowl"
    CBS and NBC, usually during the second week of January
    Premiere: 1966
    Announcers: Curt Gowdy, Brent Musberger, Don Meredith, and others

"Monday Night Football"
  ABC, 9:00 P.M. to conclusion of game
  Premiere: September 1970
  Announcers: Howard Cosell, Keith Jackson, Don Meredith, Frank Gifford, Fred Wil-
    liamson, Alex Karras, and Fran Tarkenton
"Monday Night Baseball"
  NBC and ABC, 8:15 or 8:30 P.M. to conclusion of game
  Premiere: June 1972
  Announcers: Curt Gowdy, Tony Kubek, Howard Cosell, Keith Jackson, Don Drysdale,
    Bob Uecker, and others
The "ESPN SportsCenter"
  ESPN, 2:30–3:30 A.M.; 10:00–11:00 A.M.; 7:30–8:30 P.M.; and 11:00 P.M.–midnight
  Premiere: September 1979, as a half-hour program
  Announcers: George Grande, Bob Ley, Sal Marchiano, Greg Gumble, Sharon Smith,
    Chris Berman, and others

14

The Game Show

RICHARD GOEDKOOP

OVERVIEW

As a genre of American television, game and quiz shows have a long but checkered history. In their earliest conceptions they were viewed as a type of program that could bring information and heighten the public's awareness of the importance of education in society. This idealistic view, which occasionally reappeared in programs like "G.E. College Bowl," was largely discounted when broadcasters became aware that broad-based and immensely profitable audiences could be attracted by making games more interesting and appealing to a lower common denominator. Quiz shows became extremely popular in the 1950s, when certain producers took their packaging of games as far as controlling their outcomes for ratings purposes by giving certain contestants answers beforehand. When this was revealed in 1958–59, quiz shows became forever linked with the word "scandal."

While high-stakes, prime-time quizzes never returned to the air, the genre as a whole was too well suited to be absent from television for long. Programs that emphasized celebrities, witty conversation, and gamelike situations began to take up where the "hard" quiz shows had left off. These and other lower stakes quiz shows, which were profitable for networks and local stations because of their relatively low production costs, were soon to become a staple of daytime and early evening television.

Game shows seem to come in two general forms: programs that tend to emphasize the importance of the contest and the questions, and those that substitute the importance of game-playing for an exploration of relationships and conversation between hosts, contestants, and celebrities. This second kind of game, represented by such older shows as "I've Got a Secret" and "What's My Line?" and more recently by "Hollywood Squares" have all but disappeared.

Its elements and functions are reappearing, though, in present-day talk and information shows.

Game shows are perennially successful in their restricted niches because they use elements of reality by employing average people as players in contests that are often pedestrian imitations of live sporting events. At the same time they combine the fantasy elements of prizes, colorful sets, and masterful hosts who, like Shakespeare's Prospero, command "rough magic." Game shows work on television because the viewers can become involved. They can miss five minutes or a week of the program and still tune back in and be entertained. And these shows offer the vicarious fantasy of "It Could Be You."[1]

HISTORICAL DEVELOPMENT

Although Mark Goodson, co-producer with William Todman of numerous successful game shows, including "What's My Line?" "The Price Is Right," and "Family Feud," called soap operas and game shows "the great indigenous television forms," the real origin of game shows was in the radio era of the 1930s and 1940s, long before television achieved any real commercial success.[2]

The earliest true quiz shows aired on radio during the 1935–36 season. "Professor Quiz" was created by the stereotypically pedantic Craig Earl, who would ask questions of the studio audience and then call up a selected contestant who would first submit to some browbeating by the "professor" (like Groucho Marx). They then got an opportunity to win a cash prize of $5.

Programs of a similar type included the popular "Dr. I.Q." who was played by Lew Valentine. The difference in format between the two shows was that in "Dr. I.Q." a studio assistant would roam the audience in search of a potential contestant. When selected, the contestant was asked a question by the "Dr." If their answer was correct they were paid immediately in silver dollars. While a successful radio program, "Dr. I.Q." didn't work in brief runs on television in 1953 and 1959.

Another popular game show was "Kay Kyser's Kollege of Musical Knowledge." Kyser was a well-known bandleader who combined the elements of musical variety with a comedy quiz show, for which he served as moderator. A popular comic regular on the program was a fellow known as "Ishkabbible," who doubled as Kyser's saxophonist in the band. The show also made the transition to TV. It was seen on NBC irregularly between 1949 and 1954 and was an early showcase for the talents of Mike Douglas and Tennessee Ernie Ford.

Nineteen thirty-eight brought in the first successful game show that relied less on comedy and more on intellect. That program was "Information Please." Developed by independent producer Don Golenpaul and aired on NBC radio for 14 years, "Information Please" solicited questions from listeners who tried to stump a panel made up of a variety of well-known writers, critics, and academics.

Its regular moderator was Clifton Fadiman. "Information Please" made an unsuccessful run on CBS television in the summer of 1952.

Three popular and influential quiz programs made their appearance in 1940. "Quiz Kids" was the first quiz show produced by the prolific Louis G. Cowan. Quizmaster Joe Kelly asked difficult questions of four to five children who were chosen for the game based on their intelligence, grades, and expertise on a particular subject. But they also received assistance prior to the show. On television "Quiz Kids," also hosted by Clifton Fadiman, had a fairly successful four-year-run on NBC. "Take It or Leave It" was influential because it developed the concept (borrowed by the "$64,000 Question" and others) of giving the contestants the option of keeping their prize money or trying another question that doubled the stakes. If the question was answered incorrectly, the previous money was lost. Phil Baker, the host-accordionist of "Take It Or Leave It," originated the phrase "the $64 question" on this show, which ran for 10 years on CBS. Then radio announcer Ralph Edwards conceived of "Truth or Consequences" as a quiz program where guests would have to pay a penalty (consequences) if they could not answer a question (truth). It became apparent after it was on the air for a short while that both guests and audience looked forward most to the "consequences." Edwards was able to make the show go beyond mere pranks, however; frequently contestants were granted their most cherished wishes. "Truth or Consequences" even ran a contest that raised over $1.6 million for the American Heart Fund in 1948.[3] The program later had a long run on network TV and then later in syndication with host Bob Barker.

These and other radio quiz programs were important staples of network programming on NBC Red and Blue, CBS, Mutual, and later on ABC. Their primary competition was from the radio comedians of the era: Bob Hope, Eddie Cantor, Burns and Allen, Jack Benny, and Fred Allen. But after World War II had ended, the fledgling television industry began to take shape and siphon the audience away from radio. In one of the last efforts to bolster radio's sagging ratings "big money" quiz shows were born. None was more popular than Louis G. Cowan's "Stop the Music," hosted by Bert Parks on ABC. Premiering in 1948, this program offered large cash prizes and expensive gifts to members of the home audience who were called at their residence and could name the title of the song that had just been played. "Stop the Music" continued successfully on radio for four years and then switched to television, airing until 1956. It ushered in a short-lived era on radio that included other "big money" programs like "Hit the Jackpot" (1948), "Chance of a Lifetime" (1949), and "Shoot the Moon" (1950). "Stop the Music" put an end to the highly successful NBC "Fred Allen Show." Allen saw his ratings drop to less than half of what they had been in one year's competition with "Stop the Music." He even tried to convince an insurance company to underwrite any listener who lost prizes by not tuning in a quiz program. Unsuccessful and bitter, Fred Allen left radio in 1950.[4]

In time, of course, even the new radio quiz programs could not survive the loss of former listeners who became viewers of television. But there were many quiz programs that made a successful transition to TV in the late 1940s and early 1950s.

Two of these were hosted by the versatile Art Linkletter. "People Are Funny" came to NBC radio in 1942 and made the change to TV in 1954, running in prime time for seven years and thereafter in syndication. The second of Linkletter's programs was "House Party," which debuted on CBS radio in 1944, came to television in 1952, and stayed until 1970. Neither of these programs were pure game shows, but each contained contestants who had to make choices or guesses that led to interviews, hi-jinx, and other diversions between host, guests, and occasional celebrities. The principal elements of "House Party" and "People Are Funny" were imitated in later game shows like "Let's Make a Deal," "Dating Game," and "The Price Is Right."

"Break the Bank" was another radio game show that made the successful transition to TV in 1948. On radio it had several hosts before settling on Bert Parks, who helped make the show a big hit. It was considered a big money program in the early days of television, with prizes over $10,000. Contestants had to choose a category and were then asked a series of increasingly difficult questions on their way to "breaking the bank." In the era of high-stakes TV quiz shows the program was retitled "Break the $250,000 Bank." Again in the 1970s it was brought out of hibernation and syndicated, this time with guest celebrities joining the regular contestants.

Two other game shows of the 1950s had their starts on radio and featured the theme of rewarding people who seemed to be in a great deal of need. The sentimental "Queen for a Day" originated on radio in 1945 and moved to TV in 1955, staying until 1964. "Queen for a Day" featured four "deserving" women contestants who told host Jack Bailey and the audience why they should be chosen "queen." The balance of the show's time was spent in detailed descriptions of the prizes. At the end of the show the audience itself would decide who would be crowned by means of an applause meter.

"Strike It Rich" had a similar premise, except it also allowed men to be contestants and had an actual quiz format to go along with its selection of destitute contestants. Even if the players lost, host Warren Hull might ask viewers to call in and send money on the "Heart Line." The New York City Welfare Department complained about this practice, saying that many poor people were coming to New York in an attempt to get on the show and could not afford the trip home when they were unsuccessful. The situation was even investigated by the New York legislature, but nothing was done.[5] "Strike It Rich" ended its run on CBS in 1955.

If viewers watched "Queen for a Day" and "Strike It Rich" to empathize with the contestants, they tuned into "You Bet Your Life" primarily for the antic wisecracks of host Groucho Marx. "You Bet Your Life" was a tremendous hit on NBC television where it was first seen in 1950. It was consistently in the top ten of the Nielsen ratings, and during the 1953–54 season had a phenomenal 43.6 rating, ranking fourth among all prime-time programs. In 1947 it began as a radio show produced by John Guedel as a vehicle for Marx, who had previously had trouble in getting a radio comedy program to showcase his talents. The secret of "You Bet Your Life" was in letting Marx ad-lib his way through the program, putting down announcer George Fenneman and all of the contestants who had the nerve to appear. The quiz and prizes really played a secondary role in the program. Luckily for Guedel and Marx, as well as for contemporary audiences, "You Bet Your Life" was one of the first programs to be filmed and then edited for viewing, rather than being shown live. The program can still be seen in syndication today as "The Best of Groucho."

The 1950s also ushered in the first wave of game shows designed specifically for television. Two of the more important ones premiered in 1950 and were notable for their emphasis on physical rather than cerebral prowess. "Beat the Clock," another Goodson-Todman production and hosted by Bud Collyer, displayed contestants who were challenged to perform stunts (often requiring props like balloons, whipped cream, and water) within a specified time limit. The attraction of the program was not the prizes or the suspense, but in watching the contestants make fools of themselves. "Pantomime Quiz" showed how visually interesting an old-fashioned game of charades could be if well-known celebrities were the actors. Mike Stokey hosted this perennial summer replacement, which is only one of four programs to appear on all four television networks: ABC, CBS, DuMont, and NBC. Running until 1963, the program is currently being revived for syndication under the title "Mike Stokey's New Pantomime Quiz."

Two other Goodson-Todman productions, "What's My Line?" and "I've Got a Secret," emphasized a more urbane and witty style. "What's My Line?" premiered in 1950 on CBS, and when it finished its run in 1967, it was the longest running game show in the history of prime-time television. Frequently appearing in Nielsen's top 25, "What's My Line?" owed much of its success to the chemistry between its moderator, John Daly, and three of its four regular panelists: Arlene Francis, Dorothy Kilgallen, and Bennett Cerf. The premise of the contest was for the panel to discover, through questioning, the guest's occupation. The highlight of each program was a "mystery guest," a well-known person who would try to stump the then blindfolded panel. "I've Got a Secret" had a similar style built around the panel's attempt to guess a contestant's "secret," which was written on a chalkboard in the studio and thus known to both the in-studio and at-home audience. The interplay of its host, Gary Moore, with the regular panelists—Bill Cullen, Henry Morgan, Faye Emerson, and Jayne Meadows—was again the strength of the program. In addition, it also featured celebrity contestants who appeared bearing ridiculous secrets. Both "I've Got A Secret" and "What's My Line?" were cancelled while still popular in 1967, because of CBS's desire to reach a younger and more demographically profitable audience for advertisers.

Another successful 1950s game show was the musically oriented "Name That Tune." Beginning in 1953 and hosted by George DeWitt, this program had a pair of contestants make a short sprint to a bell when they could identify the title of a popular song. "Name That Tune" is noted for beginning the careers of two personalities: Eddie Hodges, the freckle-faced, redhead who appeared in "The Music Man," and "Hole in the Head"; and Leslie Uggams, the noted actress and singer. Hodges appeared with a then unknown Marine major, John Glenn.

"To Tell the Truth" was one of the last successful 1950s game shows not to emphasise high-stakes competition. It premiered in 1956 from the stable of Goodson-Todman and was hosted by Bud Collyer. Its format was simple. A panel of four tried to guess who of three contestants was the person previously described to them. Two persons were imposters and had been briefed prior to the program on virtually every question they might be asked. "To Tell the Truth" was a successful game show, airing in prime time and in daytime until 1968 and in syndication for another ten years with Garry Moore as host.

The summer of 1955 was a watershed for television game shows. On June 7 the "$64,000 Question" first aired as a summer replacement. Its producer was Louis G. Cowan of "Quiz Kids" and "Stop the Music" fame. It was Cowan's idea to update the old "Take It or Leave It" program by adding a few gimmicks and multiplying the top prize by a thousand-fold. He was able to sell that program vehicle to Charles Revson of Revlon, who was looking for a show to help sell his line of cosmetics. Revson also wanted major control over how the show was produced.[6]

Hosted by Hal March, the program was an instant success parlaying suspense, likeable contestants, and big-money prizes into a number 1 Nielsen rating for the 1955–56 season. That season "$64,000 Question" earned a 47.5 rating, making it the highest rated game show of all time. Given that success, it was not surprising that it spawned its own spin-off "The $64,000 Challenge." Other high-stakes quiz shows also followed: "Twenty-One" (1956) and "The Big Surprise" (1957).

But behind the high ratings, profits and increased sales for advertisers, trouble was brewing. Several of the producers and sponsors of these programs were providing answers to contestants prior to their appearance on the shows. Sponsors wanted "identifiable" contestants for their audiences, and it was good show business to have a player come back week after week. Many contestants became household names and developed their own cult following. Gino Prato, a shoe repairman from the Bronx who appeared on "$64,000 Question," became a celebrity for being an expert on opera. Charles Van Doren, an assistant professor at Columbia University with a Ph.D. in English, became respected and very well known for his appearances on "Twenty-One" in 1957. He won over $100,000 in cash and received a job co-hosting the "Today" program on NBC.[7]

Though rumors of dishonesty had circulated for some time, it wasn't until summer 1958 that an upset and losing contestant on "Dotto" complained that a competitor had received answers prior to the show. After taking a bribe from "Dotto"'s producers, Edward Hilgemeir, Jr., went to the New York State

Attorney General's Office and filed a complaint.[8] In August, Herbert Stempel, who was dethroned by Van Doren, testified before a New York grand jury that the program "Twenty-One" was rigged. In November the grand jury indicted Albert Freedman, producer of "Twenty-One," on a perjury charge.[9] While other quiz shows continued to air on the networks in prime time, most of the big-money games were cancelled by the fall of 1958, ostensibly because of declining ratings.

In mid-1959 the U.S. House of Representatives empowered a special oversight subcommittee to look into the fixing of quiz shows as well as other irregularities in broadcasting, notably payola. In October 1959 the whole truth finally emerged. Testimony indicated that "Twenty-One," "Dotto," "Tic-Tac-Dough," and both the "$64,000 Question" and "$64,000 Challenge" were all rigged. In November Charles Van Doren finally admitted his part in the quiz scandals after denying culpability at other times.

In addition to wholesale cancellations of many game shows on the air, the networks tried to avoid further public blame by taking firm control of program-ming away from advertisers (such as Revlon) and instituting stricter policies and surveillance procedures over all quiz programs that were aired in the future.

After the quiz show scandals, the landscape of prime-time TV had changed. Except for a few respected, ongoing, low-stakes game shows, the genre was never again a permanent fixture on network prime-time schedules. After the demise of CBS's long-running "I've Got a Secret" and "What's My Line?" in 1967, the only game shows to break into anyone's regular prime-time lineup were two Chuck Barris productions: "The Dating Game" and "The Newlywed Game," both on Saturday evenings for ABC. The overwhelming number of game shows would be banished to daytime schedules and to "access time," 7:00–8.00P.M., Eastern Standard Time.

One of the most venerable game shows of this period was "Password." Premiering in 1962 and hosted by Allen Ludden, "Password" paired celebrities with contestants in a game in which one-word clues were given to a partner in an attempt to make them guess the secret word. Airing in various versions on all three major networks until late in the 1970s, "Password" was a game show for people who hated game shows. Some of its upscale appeal can be attributed to host Ludden, who carried with him a serious earnestness from his appearances on "G.E. College Bowl," a Sunday afternoon quiz with college students as contestants.

"Jeopardy" was the most successful daytime game show to appear on NBC. Hosted by Art Fleming and owned by Merv Griffin, "Jeopardy's" premise evolved from an old comedy routine Bill Dana (José Jimenez) used to perform on the "Steve Allen Show."[10] One of the secrets of "Jeopardy's" successful 11–year network run was the wide range of challenging questions that encouraged the home audience to play along with the studio contestants.

During the 1966 television season Americans got to see a companion set of programs developed by producer Chuck Barris: "The Dating Game" and "The

Newlywed Game.'' Each program featured relatively ordinary contestants (although "The Dating Game" players were above average in attractiveness) who bared their thoughts and secrets for viewers. "The Dating Game" featured a single man or woman who questioned an unseen trio of the opposite sex for five minutes and then had to choose one for a weekend date at a romantic location with chaperone. "The Newlywed Game" tried to see how well husbands and wives knew each other. Questions asked of one partner would then be asked of the other (who was previously offstage), points were awarded for correct matches, with a grand prize winner taking home a set of living-room furniture or similar prize. The entertainment value of each program was not the contest itself but the repartee between prospective dates and husbands-wives. On "The Newlywed Game" answers frequently got one spouse in trouble with the other; on both programs the sexual nature of the questions increased as the years went on. Viewers were legally able to become "'peeping-toms" into the dating and married behavior of people who were unknown to them.

Seeing contestants caught off-guard and being portrayed in their most bizarre light was also one of the attractions of "Let's Make a Deal," hosted by Monty Hall. With outrageous dress and noisy behavior, studio contestants vied for the attention of Hall and an opportunity to test their luck in a chancy shell-game played by the emcee. During its 14-year run on the network and afterward in syndication, playing contestants were offered a sure prize or cash for "what's in the box, behind the curtain." Players *might* wind up with a new automobile or vacation home, or $10,000, but there was also a good chance they might win a year's supply of fish food or use of a dairy cow for six months. One of the oddities of "Let's Make a Deal" was that there was absolutely no skill involved in playing the game. Pure intuition was substituted for cognitive skill. That the program works was a tribute to "America's top trader," Monty Hall, and the harmless greed of people willing to make fools of themselves for a chance at big prizes.

While many 60s and 70s game shows deemphasized the importance of celebrities and concentrated on the contestants or the game itself, "Hollywood Squares" clearly was an exception. Technically, two players tried to win a game of tic-tac-toe by confirming or denying the response to a question given by a celebrity occupying a part of the gameboard. In reality the real attraction was the scripted and generally funny responses of the celebrities to the questions posed by host Peter Marshall. Regular "squares" on the program like Paul Lynde, Cliff Arquette, Jonathan Winters, and Rose Marie parlayed their participation to revive declining careers. The "Hollywood Squares" producers were able to stay clear of rules regarding coaching of contestants because only the celebrities received materials before the program.[11]

Between 1967 and 1969 many game shows shown in both prime time and daytime network schedules were cancelled. Although not all quizzes disappeared, many did because of aging demographics, competition from afternoon soap operas, and syndicated situation comedies. One of the reasons for an upswing in the number of game shows on television after 1971 was the adoption by the Federal Communication Commission (FCC) of the prime-time access rule (PTAR). In an attempt to revive competition in the development of programs and to take some power away from the three networks, the FCC limited TV stations in the top 50 markets to 3 hours of network programming per evening except for Sunday.[12] In effect, this opened up the 7:30–8.00 P.M. EST slot and meant that local stations would have to fill that time period with their own programs or shows brought from independent producers or syndicators. Game shows fit the requirements of local stations well, chiefly because of their relatively low costs.

One of the game shows that has fared well in the post-PTAR era is "$10,000 Pyramid." Premiering in 1973 and hosted by Dick Clark and Bill Cullen in syndication, this show paired celebrities with contestants trying, within a time limit, to guess categories from given examples. Categories get more difficult as one gets closer to the apex of the pyramid. Excitement is generated as frenetic celebrities and contestants give rapid clues to try to name the category.

Several other successful game shows appeared during the 1970s. "The New Price Is Right" began its run on CBS in 1972 as a revamped version of the older "The Price Is Right" which aired between 1956 and 1967 with Bill Cullen as host. In its current version, contestants still bid by "pricing" merchandise, but host Bob Barker then goes on to mix a number of additional price estimate games after the initial round played between four players. It is presently one of the few hour-long quiz programs on the air.

In 1976 Chuck Barris introduced the tacky but appealing "Gong Show." The program took the amateur hour format to an extreme with generally untalented performers who were rated or "gonged" by a celebrity panel of three. "The Gong Show" was one of the most notorious programs of the time, and spawned live versions in nightclubs throughout the country as well as a short-lived Chuck Barris spin-off called "The $1.98 Beauty Show" hosted by comedian Rip Taylor.

Probably the most popular and successful game show of the last ten years is Goodson and Todman's "Family Feud," which has appeared in daytime on ABC since 1976 and in syndicated evening versions. "Feud" has at least three elements that contribute to its success. Its host, British-born Richard Dawson, has an appealing personality, which is especially right for game shows' primary audience: women 18–54 years old. His kissing of female contestants on the program has become legendary. Second, the game itself invites vicarious audience participation. People like to guess the most frequent responses to such requests as "name something you do in the morning." Third, there are the families of the contestants themselves. Chosen to be representative of the diverse American culture, they generally show a spirit of wholesome emotion and an attitude of competition under the aegis of "fair play" that is identifiable. In some of its featured weeks and in the evening version, "Feud" has often brought celebrities of former or current television series to play games for charities.

Historically, game shows have been a part of the landscape of American television ever since the medium began in earnest in the late 1940s. While game shows themselves have evolved due to changing social, regulatory, and technical/electronic considerations, most game-show concepts are not new but are continually being reworked for a new audience unfamiliar with its origins. While game shows enjoyed their greatest successes in the 1950s prior to the scandals of 1958–59, they have remained an enduring program form in daytime and early evening access because they combine an interesting combination of fantasy and reality. Americans by nature are generally competitive and also enjoy watching people in intriguing situations. Since game shows combine these elements, they will certainly continue in some form for the foreseeable future.

THEMES AND ISSUES

There reputedly was a sign in Monty Hall's office that said "You can learn more about America by watching a half-hour of 'Let's Make a Deal' than you can from watching Walter Cronkite for a month."[13] Even if we take that maxim at less then face value, game shows do make statements about television and about our culture itself.

While previous discussion has been primarily about game show *programs*, broadcast executives never forget that theirs is a *business* whose goal is to make profits. In broadcasting this is done by maximizing sales of air time. Clearly the most important reason for the success of game shows is that they return a great deal of profit for relatively low investment costs. Daytime game shows cost an estimated $100,000 plus a week for five shows that are usually taped in one day.[14] An average 30-second commercial on the same show costs about $20,000 for a national advertiser. If that figure is multiplied by the six minutes of selling time in each program, the network could assume a profit of $140,000 on the very first program of the week. The rest of the four-day week is pure profit; the typical game show can bring a return of between 600 and 800 percent on investment.[15]

Recently it seems that daytime network programming executives are beginning to bring game shows back to a more important position on their schedules. In the fall of 1982 NBC cancelled two of its soap operas and replaced them with the game shows "Wheel of Fortune" and "Dream House." CBS replaced two sets of situation comedies with "The New $25,000 Pyramid" and "Child's Play," both game shows. And ABC is rumored to be replacing the one hour "Love Boat" reruns with at least one half-hour game show.[16]

While soap operas still hold an advantage over game shows in current daytime network schedules, mornings are back to being dominated by quiz fare. The reasons are primarily economic: development and per episode costs of soaps are very high, game shows are not. So in time periods where audience levels are relatively low, game shows make a lot of economic sense to programmers.

Of course, home audiences are unaware and probably wouldn't even care about the economic factors operating in favor of game shows; for people to watch there must be something else. In the opinion of Bud Grant of CBS, "It's the capacity of the home audience to participate in one fashion or another, in the game. That's vital."[17] And Monty Hall agrees: "You've got to involve the audience to the degree that they're testing themselves on the game to see if they can play it. . . . they're involved because they're identifying with one of the contestants, or because they're emotionally involved, like spectators at a sporting event."[18] At least in some game shows then, audience participation, involvement and identification seems to be a key to success. Of the programs we have examined, "Name That Tune," "To Tell the Truth," the hard-quiz shows of the late 1950s, "Password," "Jeopardy," "$10,000 Pyramid," and "Family Feud" appear to fit into this category. It's not that the contestants or the hosts are unimportant to viewers of these games, but the contest, the stakes, the quiz itself is more important. Audiences since the days of "Professor Quiz" on radio, through "G.E. College Bowl" on television, and up to the "Feud" have been interested in testing their knowledge, ideas, and expertise with that of the contestants. Bill Wine has self-mockingly stated what it means to be a quiz show participant. He spoke specifically about his audition for the now-cancelled show "Knockout" when he said he watched the show

religiously. For the next week my breakfast consisted of juice, toast, coffee, and 'Knockout.' As well as unbridled optimism, fueled by the remarkable set of 'winnings' I compiled each morning at home. True I conceded, those contestants on the air were under a trifle more pressure than I. But not one of them was a match for me. It is obvious, I thought modestly, I was born to compete on this program.[19]

Wine's confession is part of the reason why past, present, and closet-viewers of game shows watch the genre. Competition is fun, especially if the quizzes you are watching make you seem brighter than you really are.

Others complain that the composition of audiences has changed over the years, forcing changes in quiz-oriented game shows. Bob Stewart, a long-time producer says "The American public's quality of intellect, generally speaking, is not the equal to what it was 20 years ago."[20] Game show host Geoff Edwards adds: "As time goes on we're getting a lot more people whose backgrounds are in watching television rather than reading. So you'll find questions like "Who plays Laverne in 'Laverne and Shirley'?" instead of "What are the two cities in *Tale of Two Cities*?"[21]

But there are clear indications that not all of the appeal of the game show is based on questions and answers. Many have entertained audiences and been commercially successful for other reasons. Mark Goodson, of the extraordinary Goodson-Todman production company, feels one of the primary functions of game shows are that "they provide interesting conversation for viewers. The sort of conversation you and I might have at a cocktail party, but not many game-show viewers go to cocktail parties."[22] Without much question shows like "People Are Funny," "You Bet Your Life," "I've Got a Secret," "The Newlywed Game," and "Hollywood Squares" were among a substantial number of game shows that could attribute more of their success to the conversation and humor that evolved between contestants, hosts, and celebrities than to the contest that was supposed to be played. Like Alfred Hitchcock's celebrated "McGuffin" in many of his films, questions and answers were only excuses for bringing interesting people together in a program format that allowed the home audience eavesdropping rights.

But many of the conversation-oriented game shows of the past seem to be in eclipse at the present time. It seems that both radio and television "talk show" formats have taken much of that function away from game shows. But it would not be surprising to see a rebound in this type of game show in the future. After all, programmers at local stations have been playing reruns of "The Best of Groucho" and the syndicated Barris productions "Gong Show" and "$1.98 Beauty Show" in late-night competition against Johnny Carson in recent years.

One element in game shows that does not seem to be changing is the role of the host or quizmaster: "The amiable, attractive, masculine host is as essential a part of the fantasy as the payoff . . . there is no quiz or game show that has successfully installed a female host; [he] is the romantic element common to all of these shows."[23] Not that any of this is very surprising. Sex roles being what they still are and audiences for game shows still being primarily female, game show producers have tended to select warm, attractive, commanding males to host game shows. Arlene Francis, Jacqueline Susann, and Sarah Purcell are among the very few women ever to host or co-host a game show. Even Lin Bolen, female chief of NBC daytime programming in the mid-1970s, went along with the type-casting and installed good-looking younger men (she called them "young studs") into NBC game shows in an attempt to attract a younger female audience for the shows. Bolen was responsible for bringing to TV such hosts as Geoff Edwards, Alex Trebek, and Jim McKrell.[24]

Hosts themselves tend to downplay the role of sex appeal in their jobs. Art Fleming, former host of "Jeopardy," opts for factors of concentration, control, and listening ability as being most important. Bob Barker of "The New Price Is Right" emphasizes listening to contestants and says he tries to treat players as if they were guests in his home. Both he and veteran host Bill Cullen agree that experience from a long career in radio and various announcing jobs are important in preparing the successful game show host. Being able to ad-lib is also a crucial talent.[25]

Even though hosts are important to the success of game shows, they, as well as producer Mark Goodson, agree that "the play's the thing." "The game plays the biggest role . . . the essence of the game show is the central core of the game itself."[26]

And what is the central core of the television game show? The peculiar blend of fantasy and reality seems to be at its heart. "Real people are dropped into a fantasy/crisis environment (where nothing really bad can happen to them save for the failure to win big), surrounded by excitement and glamour, and given the chance at sudden riches."[27] While the game show is a cultivated, technical, artificial facade, its secret has always been its use of ordinary people as an attraction for the audience. Look at the types of people who became "experts" on the "$64,000 Question": a policeman who was an authority on Shakespeare, a psychologist who was an expert on boxing, a grandmother on the Bible, a shoemaker on opera, a marine on cooking.

Today's game shows operate on a similar premise with only a bit more subtlety. The introductions and banter between contestants and host before the game begins does more than occupy time, it functions as identification between the player in the studio and the player at home. "Typical" or "average" contestants are preferred, although there is a recognition by producers that no one type of person or family can represent all of the viewing audience. Witness the wide ethnic background of families on "Family Feud" and the fact that it and other shows even interview contestants on a regional basis to insure that the players maintain a representativeness that cannot be found within a 50-mile radius of Los Angeles.

Of course, the fantasy element is in the game itself. While it's true, as Bob Barker says, that Americans are "game oriented," only in professional sports and on game shows can people actually be paid for playing games successfully.[28] The game show's comparison to sporting events is an interesting one. In the 1950s and 1960s most game shows were televised live, as most sports events still are. The excitement and possibility that events could go somewhat awry within the framework of the game's rules was always an element that induced viewer participation and interest. Now game shows are videotaped, occasionally edited to fit time constraints, and then rebroadcast. But producers still try to maintain the "live" element within the shows (even though most are tightly scripted) by rarely stopping taping for minor errors because, like a live sporting event, part of the essential ingredient of game shows is the contrived suspense that they create. As Bob Stewart says: "We attempt to continue the excitement of the contest and the game play for the live TV audience. We don't want to break the spell or discontinue the buildup of their excitement."[29]

Fantasy elements such as exciting, colorful, movable sets and props abound on current game shows These elements have increased as programs moved out of production in cramped New York quarters to more spacious facilities in Los Angeles. Another fantasy element is the way game-show hosts can command the appearance of cash and prizes from Tiffany's, Dicker and Dicker of Beverly Hills, Nieman-Marcus, and the Spiegel catalogue. It gives them a power that rivals network news anchors summoning live reports from Beirut, Tokyo, and London.

Finally, while most contestants appear to be "everyman" or "everywoman," game-show producers generally test and interview between 100 and 200 people for every player that appears on the air. Wine describes the "ordeal" he went through in finally getting an appearance on "Knockout." Even on the day of taping he sat in a special section of the audience, not knowing for sure whether he would get a chance to compete.[30] While stricter rules brought on by the quiz scandals make much of this necessary, it also places the potential contestant in an ambivalent atmosphere over which he has no control.

But the typical game-show viewer is unaware of all the planning required to portray spontaneity. Game shows are perhaps the purest television representation of William Stephenson's "play theory" of mass communication that says we try to seek out communication "pleasures," which game shows seem to be. While lacking much value beyond their entertainment and diversionary functions, they have "no endings. They go on, and on, and on."[31]

NOTES

1. Title of a 1958–1961 NBC game show hosted by Bill Leyden.

2. Tom Buckley, "Game Shows: TV's Glittering Gold Mine": *New York Times Magazine*, November 18, 1979, p. 180.

3. Maxene Fabe, *TV Game Shows* (Garden City, N.Y.: Dolphin, 1979), p. 117.

4. Erik Barnouw, *The Golden Web* (New York: Oxford University Press, 1968), pp. 286–87.

5. Tim Brooks and Earle Marsh, *The Complete Directory to Prime Time Network TV Shows, 1946–Present* (New York: Ballantine Books, 1979), p. 594.

6. Fabe, *TV Game Shows*, p. 191.

7. Ibid., p. 195.

8. Marsh and Brooks, *The Complete Directory to Prime Time Network TV Shows, 1946–Present*, pp. 169–70.

9. *Broadcasting*, April 27, 1981, p. 101.

10. Fabe, *TV Game Shows*, p. 239.

11. Jeff Greenfield, *Television: The First Fifty Years* (New York: Harry N. Abrams, 1977), p. 199.

12. Sydney Head and Christopher Sterling, *Broadcasting in America*, 4th ed. (Boston: Houghton-Mifflin, 1982), pp. 206–7.

13. Bill Wine, "And Now . . . for $3,000 . . . What's a Polaris?" *Today: The Inquirer Magazine*, February 18, 1979, p. 22.

14. Neil Hickey, "What Do You Mean It's Only a Game?" *TV Guide*, August 10, 1974.

15. Fabe, *TV Game Shows*, pp. 86–87; figures are adjusted for inflation.

16. Dave Potorti, "New Era Game Shows Wash Away Soaps," *Broadcast Week*, December 20, 1982, p. 1.

17. Hickey, "What Do You Mean It's Only a Game?," p. 63.

18. Ibid.

19. Wine, "And Now . . . for $3,000 . . . What's a Polaris?" pp. 22–23.

20. Dave Potorti, "Right Stuff Cuts Odds on Game Shows," *Broadcast Week*, December 27/January 3, 1982, p. 5.

21. Ibid.

22. Buckley, "Game Shows: TV's Glittering Gold Mine," p. 180.

23. Greenfield, *Television: The First Fifty Years*, p. 197.

24. Fabe, *TV Game Shows*, p. 28.

25. Potorti, "Right Stuff Cuts Odds on Game Shows," p. 5.

26. Ibid.
27. Greenfield, *Television: The First Fifty Years*, p. 199.
28. Potorti, "Right Stuff Cuts Odds on Game Shows," p. 5.
29. Ibid.
30. Wine, "And Now . . . for $3,000 . . . What's a Polaris?" pp. 22–23.
31. Buckley, "Game Shows: TV's Glittering Gold Mine," p. 180.

BIBLIOGRAPHICAL SURVEY

The game show is probably the least studied genre of television programming. The only full-scale work on the subject is Maxene Fabe's *TV Game Shows*, a book written by an admitted fan. The work is fairly comprehensive and covers quiz fare from its origins in radio in the mid-1930s through television game shows of the late 1970s. Fabe does analyze programs, but her primary goal is to highlight her favorite and generally the most popular programs on a decade-by-decade basis. There are also sections on the quiz-show scandals and on elements that make up the game programs: contestants, hosts, celebrities, prizes, and so forth. An appendix chronologically lists and gives brief synopses of virtually every game show ever to air on radio or TV. Highly readable, the book's flaws include the lack of an index and bibliography.

Other books devote short chapters or sections to the game show. They include Jeff Greenfield's *Television: The First Fifty Years*, which devotes half of the chapter on "Daytime" to the game show. Greenfield combines rare photographs of old and current game shows with an interesting but brief analysis that suggests the success game shows have had are due to economic factors and their involvement of viewers in a reality/fantasy world. *Don't Touch That Dial* by J. Fred McDonald provides some history and insights into radio quiz shows in his history of radio programming between 1920 and 1960. *How Sweet It Was* by Arthur Shulman and Roger Youman has two chapters, "Next Question" and "While the Dishes Wait," that are interesting pictoral histories of TV game shows through 1966. In Lichty and Topping's *A Source Book on the History of Radio and Television* Howard Blake wrote a piece called "An Apologia from the Man Who Produced the Worst Program in TV History." In it he describes how the program "Queen for a Day" worked and talks about some of its funnier moments. In Max Wilk's *The Golden Age of Television* the chapter "Will You Sign In Mr. . . . ?" is a history of "What's My Line?"

Erik Barnouw's last two volumes of his trilogy on American Broadcasting, *The Golden Web* and *The Image Empire*, provide backstage looks at certain features of early quiz shows and a good survey of the quiz-show scandals. Tim Brooks and Earle Marsh's *The Complete Directory to Prime Time Network TV Shows, 1946–Present* gives brief summaries of game shows that appeared as network evening fare but excludes games that only appeared in daytime. Vincent Terrace's *The Complete Encyclopedia of Television Programs, 1947–1976*, in two volumes, does include daytime game shows as well as some popular programs in Britain. In *The Camera Age* one of TV's foremost critics, Michael Arlen, takes a satirical and critical look at "3's a Crowd" a sexually oriented game show of the early 1980s in the essay "Jim Peck's Cabaret."

Recent magazine articles on the game show include Bill Wine's funny piece in *Today: The Inquirer Magazine* called "And Now . . . for $3,000 . . . What's a Polaris?" Wine describes his short-lived run as a contestant on "Knockout." Also focusing on contestants is the *Esquire* piece by Bob Green, which looks at potential players at a regional tryout in Chicago for "Wheel of Fortune." A Peter Andrews piece for the *Saturday Review* provides a critical look at Chuck Barris's stable of game-show properties. A two-part series by Dave Potorti in *Broadcast Week* looks at the future of game shows and what hosts have contributed to the success of the genre.

Of a more general nature, a *Time* article called "Truth and Consequences" gives a brief look at why game shows are still popular and indicates that games reflect life more clearly than we might believe. A regular contributor to *TV Guide*, Neil Hickey, offers a history and analysis of how games involve viewers in "What Do You Mean It's Only a Game?" *Broadcasting* provides a weekly summary of the industry and is indexed in *Business Periodical Index*. Particularly useful for a history of the quiz-show scandals were *Broadcasting's* April 27, and May 4, 1981, issues, which were part of its 50 year retrospective. Finally, Tom Buckley's piece in the *New York Times Magazine* entitled "Game Shows: TV's Glittering Gold Mine" is an intelligent and comprehensive history of game shows and why they interest audiences and are so profitable to broadcasters.

BOOKS AND ARTICLES

Andrews, Peter. "The Hating Game." *Saturday Review*, March 29, 1980.

Arlen, Michael. "Jim Peck's Cabinet." In his *The Camera Age*. New York: Farrar Straus Giroux, 1981.

Barnouw, Erik. *The Golden Web*. New York: Oxford, 1968.

———. *The Image Empire*. New York: Oxford, 1970.

Blake, Howard. "An Apologia from the Man Who Produced the Worst Program in TV History." In *A Source Book on the History of Radio and Television*, ed. Lawrence Lichty and Malachi Topping. New York: Hastings House, 1975.

Broadcasting. April 27 and May 4, 1981.

Brooks, Tim, and Earle Marsh. *The Complete Directory to Prime Time Network TV Shows, 1946–Present*. New York: Ballantine, 1979.

Buckley, Tom. "Game Shows: TV's Glittering Gold Mine." *New York Times Magazine*, November 18, 1979.

Fabe, Maxene. *TV Game Shows*. Garden City, N.Y.: Dolphin, 1979.

Greene, Bob. "The Fortunate." *Esquire*, July 1982.

Greenfield, Jeff. *Television: The First Fifty Years*. New York: Harry N. Abrams, 1977.

Head, Sydney, and Christopher Sterling. *Broadcasting in America*. 4th ed. Boston: Houghton-Mifflin, 1982.

Hickey, Neil. "What Do You Mean It's Only a Game?" *TV Guide*, August 10, 1974.

McDonald, J. Fred. *Don't Touch That Dial*. Chicago: Nelson-Hall, 1979.

Potorti, Dave. "New Era Game Shows Wash Away Soaps." *Broadcast Week*, December 20, 1982.

———. "Right Stuff Cuts Odds on Game Shows." *Broadcast Week*, December 27/ January 3, 1982.

Shulman, Arthur, and Roger Youman. *How Sweet It Was*. New York: Shorecrest, 1966.

Terrace, Vincent. *The Complete Encyclopedia of Television Programs, 1947–1976*, 2 vols. New York: A.S. Barnes, 1976.

"Truth and Consequences." *Time*, February 18, 1980.

Wilk, Max. *The Golden Age of Television*. New York: Hawthorn, 1974.

Wine, Bill. "And Now . . . for $3,000 . . . What's a Polaris?" *Today: The Inquirer Magazine*, February 18, 1979.

VIDEOGRAPHY

"What's My Line?"
  CBS, prime time, syndication
  Premiere: February 2, 1950
  Hosts: John Daly, Wally Bruner, Larry Blyden
  Last Program: September 3, 1967

"Beat the Clock"
  CBS, ABC, prime time, daytime, syndication
  Premiere: March 23, 1950
  Hosts: Bud Collyer, Jack Narz
  Last Program: April, 1969

"Truth or Consequences"
  CBS, NBC, prime time, daytime, syndication
  Premiere: September 7, 1950
  Hosts: Ralph Edwards, Jack Bailey, Bob Barker
  Last Program: September 25, 1965

"You Bet Your Life"
  NBC, prime time, syndication
  Premiere: October 5, 1950
  Host: Groucho Marx with George Fenneman
  Last Program: September 21, 1961

"I've Got a Secret"
  CBS, prime time, syndication
  Premiere: June 19, 1952
  Hosts: Garry Moore, Bill Cullen
  Last Program: July 5, 1976

"Name That Tune"
  NBC, CBS, prime time, daytime, syndication
  Premiere: June 29, 1953
  Hosts: George DeWitt, Dennis James, Tom Kennedy
  Last Program: January 3, 1975

"Queen for a Day"
  ABC, NBC, daytime, syndication
  Premiere: April 28, 1955
  Hosts: Jack Bailey, Dick Curtis
  Last Program: October 2, 1964

"$64,000 Question"
  CBS, prime time
  Premiere: June 7, 1955
  Host: Hal March
  Last Program: November 2, 1958

"To Tell the Truth"
  CBS, prime time, daytime, syndication
  Premiere: December 18, 1956
  Hosts: Bud Collyer, Garry Moore, Joe Garagiola
  Last Program: August 1979

"The Price Is Right"
  NBC, CBS, ABC, prime time, daytime, syndication
  Premiere: September 23, 1957
  Hosts: Bill Cullen, Dennis James, Bob Barker
  Last Program: September 3, 1965

"Concentration"
  NBC, prime time, daytime, syndication
  Premiere: October 30, 1958
  Hosts: Jack Barry, Hugh Downs, Jack Narz
  Last Program: March 23, 1973

"G.E. College Bowl"
  CBS, NBC, daytime, evening
  Premiere: January 4, 1959
  Hosts: Allen Ludden, Robert Earle
  Last Program: June 14, 1970

"Password"
  CBS, ABC, prime time, daytime
  Premiere: January 2, 1962
  Host: Allen Ludden
  Last Program: February 24, 1975

"Jeopardy"
  NBC, daytime
  Premiere: April 30, 1964
  Host: Art Fleming
  Last Program: January 3, 1975

"Let's Make a Deal"
  NBC, ABC, prime time, daytime, syndication
  Premiere: December 30, 1964
  Host: Monty Hall
  Last Program: August 30, 1971

"The Newlywed Game"
  ABC, prime time, daytime
  Premiere: July 11, 1966
  Host: Bob Eubanks
  Last Program: December 20, 1974

"The Dating Game"
  ABC, prime time, daytime
  Premiere: October 6, 1966
  Host: Jim Lange
  Last Program: July 6, 1973

"Hollywood Squares"
  NBC, daytime, syndication
  Premiere: October 17, 1966
  Host: Peter Marshall
  Last Program: June 20, 1980

"Family Feud"
  ABC, daytime, syndication
  Premiere: July 1976
  Host: Richard Dawson

"Gong Show"
  NBC, daytime, syndicated
  Premiere: September 1976
  Hosts: Gary Marshall, Chuck Barris
  Last Program: July 21, 1978

15

The Variety Show

TIMOTHY SCHEURER

I was within and without, simultaneously enchanted and repelled by the inexhaustible variety of life.

—F. Scott Fitzgerald

OVERVIEW

The history of the TV variety program is marked by people and critics who, like Nick Carraway in Fitzgerald's *The Great Gatsby*, have been drawn and repelled by the form. In the early fifties nearly half the programming was devoted to the variety show, with everyone from Frank Sinatra to Jerry Colonna trying their hand at a series. TV variety, furthermore, insinuated its way into the very fibre of our everyday lives; it gave us a whole new generation of stars, from Julius LaRosa and Pat Boone, to Red Skelton, Jackie Gleason, and John Belushi; it gave us instant history in the form of appearances by Elvis Presley on "Stage Show" on January 28, 1956, and the Beatles on "The Ed Sullivan Show" on February 9, 1964, as well as the simpler joys of catch phrases like "Well, I'll be a dirty bird," or "Bless your pea pickin' heart" or "Sock it to me." In those early days of television it provided an anchor for an audience being exposed to a new medium, and, like vaudeville, through its different formats of "vaudeo" (general variety), musical variety, and comedy variety, it drew on the viewer's past experience to provide entertainment in a new electronic age. Like vaudeville, moreover, it offered audiences grappling with change, of which the technology of television was an important part, a form of entertainment that celebrated human qualities and reaffirmed traditional values. Variety shows are no longer the fashion—they haven't been for nearly ten years—but in isolated pockets like late-night television or specials they continue to influence what happens throughout the medium.

HISTORICAL DEVELOPMENT

The roots of the variety program lie in two distinct but not necessarily separate forms of entertainment: vaudeville and radio. TV's early reliance on vaudeville (and radio by extension) is evident in the ill-fated "Fireball Fun-for-All" (NBC, 1949) starring comedians Olsen and Johnson of *Hellzapoppin'* fame. Slightly more successful was Ed Wynn's early variety show (CBS, Thurs., 9:00–9:30 P.M.) which featured the extraordinary Mr. Wynn and some fine guests stars like Buster Keaton, Lucille Ball, and the Three Stooges; it, however, ran only one season. Radio, similarly, contributed stars like vaudevillians Eddie Cantor, Jimmy Durante, and Bob Hope, but it also contributed formats, and, to a minor degree, that ineffable quality of intimacy. Old radio stars like dance band leaders Paul Whiteman (the "King of Jazz" in the '20s), Vincent Lopez, and Fred Waring, all made easy and, for the most part, successful transitions from radio to TV. TV, in some cases, literally appropriated programs like "The Chesterfield Supper Club," hosted by Perry Como, which was simulcast with few concessions made to the new medium. In time, however, the new medium would stake out its own ground and shake off, ever so tentatively, the remnants of vaudeville and radio.

It is a testimony to the strength and durability of the variety show format that the first hour-long program on network TV was a variety show. "Hour Glass" premiered on May 9, 1946, and represented a major commitment on the part of a network (NBC) and a sponsor (Standard Brands) to "big time" television programming. And a major breakthrough it was; Brooks and Marsh note, "It was the first hour-long entertainment series of any kind produced for network television, the first show to develop its own star [Helen Parrish], the first big variety series, and the most ambitious production by far ever attempted up to its time."[1] The show borrowed a vaudeville bill including comedy sketches, a ballroom dancing sequence, musical numbers, a film about South American dancing, and a long commercial about coffee. The producers and sponsor knew that they had hit on a successful formula, and had the viewing audience been larger, it might have justified continuing the series. As it was, others would have to pick up where "Hour Glass" started; in two years time the audience would be there and so would the creative energies at the networks.

Variety programs produced in the late forties set the standard for the next 30 years. The types, that is comedy, musical, and "vaudeo," came into existence in this period, as well as distinct approaches or, as Jeff Greenfield calls them, "patterns" in presentation. On the one hand there is the pattern reliant on "excitement, on a sense of show business pace that is traceable to the days of vaudeville and the fast-moving, gala Broadway revues"; and on the other there is the pattern characterized by the "relaxed, informal, 'homey' approach which used the television set less as bridge into a glamorous world of show business and more as a harmonious part of the living room itself."[2] The "really big shews," to quote Ed Sullivan, in the late forties were the "Texaco Star Theatre,"

"The Toast of the Town," and "The Admiral Broadway Revue" (to become "Your Show of Shows" the following year), while the intimate format was represented by programs like "Arthur Godfrey and His Friends," "Stud's Place," and "Garroway at Large." These two patterns would thrive, occasionally merge, and dictate the form of the genre.

Debuting in 1948 was a show known today mostly because of the man we now call "Mr. Television." Milton Berle, or Uncle Miltie as he was affectionately labeled, was a mildly successful comic when he assumed the job as temporary emcee for a summer run of the "Texaco Star Theatre Vaudeville Revue" (NBC, Tues., 8:00–9:00P.M.); the producers liked what they saw and asked Berle back on a permanent basis in the fall.[3] Milton Berle can probably be described as one of the first if not the first true TV personality. There was in his comic persona a touch of the anarchic, but he was also a classic vaudevillian who kept people wondering from week to week what he would do next. Berle and "The Texaco Star Theatre" created a successful TV show by not only investing time, energy, and money into showy sets and excellent guests stars, but also by exploiting the visual potential of Berle's own personality and humor.

The other "really big shew" that set standards for future variety programs was, literally, *the* really big shew: "The Toast of the Town" (CBS, Sun., 9:00–10:00 P.M.), later to become "The Ed Sullivan Show." Of all the early shows, "Toast of the Town" probably best deserves the name "vaudeo," although Sullivan himself would have contended that his "shew" transcended the rather mundane parameters of vaudeville. Under the guiding hand of the one-time newspaper columnist with the stiff gestures, clipped delivery, and somewhat dour personality, his shows moved from exotic acrobatic acts, to scenes from recent Broadway musicals, to a stand-up comedy, to perhaps the Bolshoi Ballet. For over 20 years this man controlled Sunday night from 8:00 to 9:00 P.M., showcasing talent like no one else; he could claim the TV debuts of Bob Hope, Lena Horne, Dean Martin and Jerry Lewis, Dinah Shore, and, of course, the Beatles. His was a show of extraordinary range that seemed to know no demographic bounds.

Two other programs deserve brief mention here not so much for their individual achievements but for what they promised for future generations of variety programs. The first was "Calvalcade of Stars" (DuMont, Sat., 9:00–10:00 P.M.), which launched the TV careers of no less than Jack Carter, Larry Storch, Jerry Lester (first of the late-night hosts), and, most importantly, Jackie Gleason. The other program had a short life under its original sponsorship, "The Admiral Broadway Revue," (NBC & DuMont, 1949), but it had two great regulars, Sid Caesar and Imogene Coca, who would go on to make TV history the following year in "Your Show of Shows."

In contrast to the spectacular revue formula was the world of the living room, and by extension, the more relaxed and intimate variety show, dominated by "Arthur Godfrey and His Friends" (CBS, Wed., 8:00–9:00 P.M.). Using a living-room setting, where regulars and guests casually sat around, Arthur Godfrey held forth weekly from 1949 to 1959. Godfrey brought to TV no particular genius or comic or musical talent but he did bring a genuineness, a seeming honesty, which came across in his conversations with his guests and with the audience via commercials. Godfrey was, according to CBS Chairman William S. Paley, "the average guy's wistful projection of what he would like to be."[4] There has not been a show which has utilized the intimate set format that does not owe something to Godfrey's method. Others like Studs Terkel ("Studs' Place," NBC, 1949) and Dave Garroway ("Garroway at Large," NBC, 1949) did some of the same things but not with the same success, although Garroway would do some pioneering of his own as the first host of the "Today" program.

The early fifties saw a refinement of variety show formats and the appearance in 1950 of a program that has almost attained mythical status today: Max Liebman's "Your Show of Shows" (NBC, Sat., 9:00–10:30 P.M.). Featuring a repertory company of Sid Caesar, Imogene Coca, Carl Reiner, and Howard Morris and a staff of writers including Mel Brooks, Larry Gelbart (of "M*A*S*H" fame), Joseph Stein (*Fiddler on the Roof*), Neil Simon, Michael Steward (*Hello Dolly*), and, later, Woody Allen, "Your Show of Shows" literally took the TV world, audiences and critics alike, by storm.[5] Max Wilk notes, "Until 1954 for ninety minutes each week, Caesar and Coca were to ride the top of the Saturday night ratings."[6] Like other variety programs of the day, it offered the gaudy production numbers, but these were also counterbalanced by simpler routines like the Hickenloopers; the mechanical clock of Baverhoff, Bavaria, in which the figures went haywire on the hour; Coca's happy-go-lucky tramp; and, of course, the character, according to Kenneth Tynan, "in which [Mel] Brooks specialized . . . the German Professor, played by Caesar. He appeared under many names—such as Kurt von Stuffer, the dietitian, or Siegfried von Sedativ, the authority on sleep—always pontificating with the same majestic fraudulence in the same bedraggled and ill fitting frock coat."[7] The show mixed spectacle with the sharp edge of satire and a kind of subtle humor one would expect to find in the more intimate settings.[8]

A variety series with great potential for success was the "Colgate Comedy Hour," which debuted in 1950 (NBC, Sun., 8:00–9:00 P.M.). It was a fairly adventuresome series, boasting, as Brooks and Marsh note, numerous TV firsts like being the "first starring vehicle for such names as Eddie Cantor, Fred Allen, Abbott and Costello, Spike Jones, Tony Martin, and Ray Bolger. It was also the first commercial series to originate in Hollywood (September 30, 1951), and it included the first network color telecast, on November 22, 1953."[9] The series, furthermore, experimented with presenting book musicals and with doing remote broadcasts from such "exotic" and legendary entertainment spots as the Coconut Grove and Las Vegas.

In marked contrast to the splashy styles of "Your Show of Shows" and the "Colgate Comedy Hour" were the premieres in 1950 of "The Perry Como Show" (CBS, Mon., Wed., Fri., 7:45–8:00 P.M.) and "The Arthur Murray Party" (ABC and DuMont, Sun., 9:00–10:00 P.M.). Como began in radio on the "Chesterfield Supper Club" and made the transition easily to TV in 1948; in 1950 the program bore his own name and ran for 15 minutes three nights a week, and in 1955 he went to an hour show. He had an easy-going style with guests, much like Arthur Godfrey, and as a singer he pleasantly combined the sound and style of crooners Frank Sinatra and Bing Crosby. One of the show's best loved features was the "We Get Letters" segment where, in response to letters, "Mr. C" sang tunes requested by viewers; Perry Como's series ran until 1963 and thereafter he could be seen in occasional specials and, more recently, as the butt of some "SCTV" sketches.

"The Arthur Murray Party" was a bit more lavish affair than the Como show, but the same "laid back" style was evident. The setting was a party where out of the mingling guests swirled tall, regal Arthur and bubbly, vivacious Kathryn Murray. The show's formula was as smooth as a waltz, with guest stars dancing out gracefully from amongst the assembled partygoers and dance numbers evolving naturally out of the evening's proceedings. For ten years Arthur and Kathyrn danced across TV screens in what one writer called "the longest running commercial in the history of television."[10]

In the early 1950s the world of TV variety was predominantly a man's world, but that was to end in 1951 with the debut of "The Kate Smith Evening Hour" (NBC, Wed., 8:00–9:00 P.M.) and "The Dinah Shore Show" (NBC, Tues., and Thurs., 7:30–7:45 P.M.). Kate Smith's show would last only one season, but Dinah would go on to earn an hour program beginning in October of 1956. A recording star and sometime actress in the 1940s, Dinah brought to TV the essential ingredients for a successful variety series: a winning personality with all the charm of a Southern Belle, and musical numbers and comedy routines tastefully done and utilizing fully the talents of her guests. For 12 years, until 1963, these qualities and her closing where she sang "See the U.S.A. in Your Chevrolet" and then blew her audience a big kiss helped make her the first lady of prime-time television.

The early fifties saw the arrival of two extraordinary TV personalities who helped establish the style for comedy variety programs: Red Skelton and Jackie Gleason. Both men relied upon visual humor and both created characters that gave their sketches variety and continuity. "The Red Skelton Show" (NBC, Sun., 10:00–10:30 P.M.) was a fairly simple affair with Red doing an opening monologue including classic bits like his dialogues between Gertrude and Heathcliff, two gregarious but slightly dopey birds. This was followed by a number of sketches featuring such immortal characters as Freddie the Freeloader, Clem Kadiddlehopper (an archetypal country bumpkin), San Fernando Red (an archetypal loudmouth), and the Mean Widdle Kid (the archetypal brat). Skelton delighted in breaking up himself and his guests, and viewers must have also been delighted as the show reached number four in the ratings in its debut season. From 1955 to 1969 it consistently placed in the top 20 of the Nielsen ratings and usually in the top 15.

Jackie Gleason similarly brought a wealth of comic invention and a unique style to television. Gleason, known primarily as a stand-up comic, was hired as a two week fill-in host for the "Cavalcade of Stars" before he moved to CBS on Saturday evenings from 8:00 to 9:00 P.M. for a long, fruitful relationship. Like Skelton, Gleason created a memorable cast of continuing characters, most notably, Reginald Van Gleason, III, Joe the Bartender, the Poor Soul, and, of course, Ralph Kramden, who would go on to a life of his own in the series "The Honeymooners." Gleason featured leggy girls, risque jokes (as much as they were allowed), large sets, and a range of humor that could be as physical as the oldest vaudeville schtick and, on the other hand, as subtle as a panto-mimist's art (this was particularly true of some of his Poor Soul sketches). In essence, then, Gleason and Skelton, like Ed Wynn, Sid Caesar, and others, created a type of comedy variety format in which the host's personality mattered slightly (and I think it is important to say slightly) less than the characters they created.

A third comedian, who is something of an anomaly in terms of TV genres is Jack Benny. "The Jack Benny Show" (CBS, Sun., 7:30–8:00 P.M.) premiered in 1950 and ran for 15 years. His show was closer in spirit to a situation comedy than a variety show, but his use of occasional small sketches as well as singer Dennis Day and singing group The Four Sportsmen added a touch of variety. He was, in the final analysis, an experimentalist who successfully bridged the gap between variety and situation comedy, but his influence was felt more in the realm of the sitcom.

By the mid-fifties Berle had picked up a new sponsor and a new night and Caesar and Coca had decided to try their hand at separate programs; in spite of the success of "Caesar's Hour," Caesar and Coca's stars were no longer in ascendancy and the networks continued to look for new and not so new faces for new series. Among the new faces who enjoyed middling to no success were Eddie Fisher ("Coke Time with Eddie Fisher," NBC, 1953); Red Buttons, who had a smash hit first season, ending up fourth in the ratings in 1953, and then faded slowly the next season; and Johnny Carson (CBS, 1955). Among the more successful were two shows that debuted in 1954. The first, "The Jimmy Durante Show" (NBC, Sat., 9:30–10:00 P.M.), enjoyed a three-year run; the show was a throwback to vaudeville with Durante re-creating many old routines with his partner Eddie Jackson (of Clayton, Jackson, and Durante). Another highlight was Jimmy's closing where, as he walked to the back of the set under isolated spots, he intoned, "Goodnight Mrs. Calabash, wherever you are." "The George Gobel Show" (NBC, Sat., 10:00–10:30 P.M.), on the other hand, presented viewers with a new face, a face that earned him the Outstanding New Personality Award at the 1954 Emmy Awards. For six years "Lonesome George" entertained TV viewers with his homely catchphrases like "Well, I'll be a dirty bird!" and "You don't hardly get those no more." Gobel brought to the comedy variety format a wry sense of humor and a series of sketches that blended the elements of the variety show and situation comedy.

The late fifties saw a slight decline in production of variety shows, but it also witnessed a renaissance of interest in the musical variety show. In addition to Dinah Shore's hour prime-time "Chevy Show" (NBC, Fri., 10:00–11:00 P.M.)in 1956, viewers saw the debuts of "The Ford Show Starring Tennessee Ernie Ford" (NBC, Thurs., 9:30–10:00 P.M.) in 1956 and "The Pat Boone-Chevy Showroom" (ABC, Thurs., 9:00–9:30 P.M.) in 1957. Tennessee Ernie's Godfrey-like congeniality ("Bless your pea pickin' heart!") and rich baritone voice, which he lent to a pleasant mixture of country tunes and Tin-Pan-Alley standards, earned him a six-year run and a sizeable following. Pat Boone, on the other hand, was partially swept into television because of his cover versions of rock songs like "Ain't That a Shame" and "Tutti Frutti." Boone in many ways was the perfect musical variety host for the late fifties. He was young and handsome— a classic crooner who, in his iconic white bucks, somehow managed to sell rhythm-and-blues to white, middle-class kids and Tin-Pan-Alley standards like "Love Letters in the Sand" (1931) to white, middle-class adults.

Before surveying some of the major shows of the sixties a couple of words need to be said about two extremely talented personalities whose work cannot be confined to any one decade: Steve Allen and Ernie Kovacs. Steve Allen in his long career has had a number of variety shows with the most successful running from 1956 to 1961. Allen carefully assembled routines (such as the now fabled "Man on the Street" segment) for which he selected actors with wit, creativity, and improvisational genius like Louis Nye, Tom Posten, and Don Knotts. A talented musician, Steve Allen seemed interested in and willing to give new performers like Elvis Presley and Jerry Lee Lewis a chance; a Steve Allen show, moreover, was one of the few where audiences might see someone like the controversial Lenny Bruce.[11]

Because of his premature death in an auto accident we can only speculate as to what direction Ernie Kovacs' creative talents would have taken, but it is generally agreed that he was clearly ahead of his time in creating variety shows. As in the best variety programs, Kovacs's shows satirized current fads and foibles in the arts, and like Skelton and Gleason, he created some wonderful characters including the poet Percy Dovetonsils, who combined the worst of Oscar Wilde and the Greenwich Village Beats. Kovacs, moreover, used TV as Melies had used film; a good example of this is the bit in which a lady is merrily taking her bubble bath when suddenly an assortment of people and dogs emerge from the tub, one at a time, while the lady, now somewhat taken aback, can only look on.[12] There has not been a comedian since who has explored so avidly and creatively the comic possibilities of television.

Although fewer variety programs would be produced in the 1960s the genre would flourish and continue to offer viewers some special moments. Where the fifties had been dominated by comedy variety and variety programs, the sixties would be dominated by musical variety, something of a curiosity in an age when musical tastes were undergoing a radical change and, in fact, when the direction of American music would be incontrovertibly altered.

With the Sullivan show dominating Sunday evenings, there was not much activity in the area of general variety. "The Garry Moore Show" (CBS, Tues., 10:00–11:00 P.M.), which premiered in 1958, proved a pleasant surprise and enjoyed a six-year run. The diminutive Mr. Moore, with his ever-present bow tie and crewcut, was aided by the comedic talents of his sidekick Durward Kirby, regular players Carol Burnett, Marion Lorne, and, later, Dorothy Loudon, as well as Allen Funt's "Candid Camera" segments; one of the show's highlights was "That Wonderful Year," which featured musical numbers, comedy routines, and film clips celebrating a selected year. "International Showtime," which debuted in 1961, (NBC, Fri., 7:30–8:30 P.M.), presented circuses, specials from the Ice Capades, magic shows, and various compilations of specialty acts all generating from Europe. The series was hosted by Don Ameche and ran for four years. In a more traditional vein there was "The Hollywood Palace" (ABC, Sat., 9:30–10:30 P.M.), which debuted in 1964. In spite of its successful run of six years, the program never really gained the following that Sullivan or Garry Moore did; Brooks and Marsh feel this is probably because it lacked a central figure as a continuing host.[13] The program, however, was one of the last variety shows, except for Ed Sullivan's, where one could still see with some regularity stars like Bing Crosby, Groucho Marx, Eddie Cantor, and Ed Wynn and acts reminiscent of vaudeville and early television. Finally, "The Jack Paar Program" (NBC, Fri., 10:00–11:00 P.M.). which closely resembled his "Tonight Show" but without the histrionics that made that program such a nationwide sensation, debuted in 1962; it was pretty standard stuff, but he was still able to attract the unusual, as in one show where former vice president Richard Nixon favored the audience with an original composition at the piano. The show left the air in 1965.

With Gleason and Skelton holding sway in the comedy variety category and with musical variety on the rise, few newcomers made their way into the prime-time schedule. "The Jerry Lewis Show," a two-and-a-half-hour extravaganza, premiered with big fanfare and high expectations in September 1963 on ABC but was gone by December. Danny Kaye, on the other hand, was able to assemble a fairly popular series (CBS, Wed., 10:00–11:00 P.M.) mostly on the strength of his comedic talents and his ability to work well with his guests.

Among successful musical variety hours were "The Andy Williams Show" (1962, NBC, Thurs., 10:00–11:00 P.M.), "The Jimmy Dean Show" (1963, ABC, Thurs., 9:00–10:00 P.M.), and "The Dean Martin Show" (1965, NBC Thurs., 10–11:00 P.M.). Having made brief forays into the variety show in 1957 and as a summer replacement in 1958 and 1959, Williams got his own program partly on the strength of his rendition of "Moon River," which would become his biggest hit and theme song. Dressed casually and often sitting on a stool near his audience, Andy Williams proved a worthy successor to the Perry Como style of musical variety show. He stressed informality, easy humor, and a rich sampling of songs that combined the best of Tin Pan Alley and recent tunes such as the movie themes of Henry Mancini. Jimmy Dean, on the other hand, was another country boy like Tennessee Ernie Ford, and his easy affability won him a three-year stay on prime time. His guests included country headliners of the day like Eddy Arnold and Johnny Cash. A regular was Jim Henson's Muppet character Rowlf, who predated the great explosion of Muppet-mania that would overtake America in the 1970s.

Dean Martin's variety hour employed an informal living room setting where he greeted his guests and often performed musical numbers. This informality, however, was counterbalanced by a quasi-Vegas atmosphere; like Jackie Gleason before him, Martin relied on the bevy of leggy, beautiful chorines, in this case called "The Golddiggers," as well as appearances by members of the Vegas entertainment establishment like Frank Sinatra and Sammy Davis, Jr. "The Dean Martin Show" enjoyed a respectable nine-year run, but, in the final analysis, it stands, like "The Hollywood Palace," as symbolic of the passing of a way of life, as Martin was the last crooner to enjoy any sustained popularity on prime-time TV.

The late sixties, however, were not solely a time of exhaustion for the variety show as is evidenced by the appearance of "The Carol Burnett Show," "The Smothers Brothers Comedy Hour," and "Rowan and Martin's Laugh-In," three successful shows which do, however, mark the apotheosis of the form. The first, "The Carol Burnett Show" (CBS, Mon., 10:00–11:00 P.M.), premiered in 1967 and was the most successful variety series of the post-Sullivan-Gleason-Skelton generation (their shows all left the air in the first two years of the 1970s); it ran until 1979. Her program was of the classic comedy variety type. She created unique characters for herself and, like "Your Show of Shows" and, to a lesser extent, her mentor Garry Moore, she assembled a talented and diverse ensemble of players, most notably Harvey Korman and later Tim Conway. The hallmarks of the Burnett show were her classy production numbers and her imaginative and satiric sketches, which offers witty and, at times, uproarious looks at the foibles and follies of our contemporary society.

"The Smothers Brothers Comedy Hour" (CBS, Sun., 9:00–10:00 P.M.) brought to the variety genre not only satire but, occasionally, downright irreverence. The show, definitely a product of the times, was aimed at an audience sympathetic to the new liberalism taking root in the land. The brothers adhered to a fairly traditional variety format, and they featured fine musical guests; in one memorable show Arlo Guthrie and Pete Seeger (representing two generations of musical social commentary) performed "America the Beautiful," making it almost sound like a protest song. The program, however, was riddled with difficulties, primarily from the censors and sensitive CBS executives, and was finally forced to leave CBS in 1969.

Iconoclastic is a term that could also be applied to the final program of the late sixties troika of variety giants, "Rowan and Martin's Laugh-In" (NBC, Mon., 8:00–9:00 P.M.). Frenetic cutting and great blackouts were the hallmark of "Laugh-In." It introduced phrases like "Sock it to me," "You bet your bippy," and "Put that in your Funk and Wagnalls" as well as Artie Johnson's dirty old man, who spoke in poetic terms of his undying lust to Ruth Buzzi's frumpy old prude. Others who got their start with the show were Goldie Hawn, Lily Tomlin, and Eileen Brennan. The show specialized in commentary on the follies of society, wisely using serial routines like the news report, the cocktail party, and the Farkle Family during their five-year run. "Laugh-In" was, indeed, unique. It did, however, spawn a country western imitator in the form of "Hee Haw" (CBS, Sun., 9:00–10:00 P.M.) with hosts Buck Owens and Roy Clark.

In addition to "Hee Haw," viewers witnessed the premieres of four other new musical variety programs in 1969: "The Glen Campbell Goodtime Hour" (CBS, Wed., 7:30–8:30 P.M.), "This Is Tom Jones" (ABC, Thurs., 9:00–10:00 P.M.), "The Johnny Cash Show" (ABC, Sat., 9:30–10:30 P.M.), and "The Jim Nabors Hour" (CBS, Thurs., 8:00–9:00 P.M.). The Campbell and Cash shows were attempts by the networks to capitalize on the growing youth market by featuring singers who could bridge the rock-folk-country gaps. Campbell enjoyed a four-year run, while the Cash show, in spite of occasional guests like Bob Dylan, ran only two years. In a different vein were the Tom Jones and Jim Nabors shows; relying on good looks and more Tin-Pan-Alley-oriented material, their shows tried to lure a female market as well as that intangible silent majority of which President Nixon had spoken.

Throughout the 1970s production of variety shows decreased to a point where now in the eighties the form is practically nonexistent. Significant shows in the seventies can literally be counted on the figures of one hand. The decade opened with the imaginative and successful "Flip Wilson Show" (NBC, Thurs., 7:30–8:30 P.M.). "The Flip Wilson Show" is significant because it was the first major variety show to be hosted by a black entertainer. The show had many fine qualities, not the least of which was the comedic genius of its host. Wilson created some wonderfully eccentric characters like Geraldine ("The devil made me buy that dress!") and the minister of the Church of What's Happenin' Now. For his monologues he used a stage in the round, which gave the show an easy informality. For four years Flip Wilson picked up the mantle of comedy variety in the wake of the departures of Skelton and Gleason, and he proved a worthy successor.

The success of "The Sonny and Cher Comedy Hour" (CBS, Mon., 10:00–11:00 P.M.) and, to a lesser extent, "Donny and Marie" (ABC, Fri., 8:00–9:00 P.M.) are representative of the fate of musical variety in the 1970s. Sonny and Cher began as hippies in the late sixties, communicated messages of love and fidelity during the sexual revolution, and with the dawning of the seventies, found a home on television entertaining an audience who had helped make folk music popular in the late fifties and early sixties. They relied upon the incongruity of their sizes and personalities for a lot of the laughs (Sonny was the smaller and more zany of the two). They were the darlings of prime time, but after their marital and subsequent professional split, they could not generate enough magic individually to carry a show, and a reunion effort in 1976 also bombed. "Donny and Marie," on the other hand, did not run the risk of marital strife. They were perfectly wholesome "kids," relying upon a mixture of mellow rock and Las Vegas panache to earn a following among teenyboppers and adults.

The dramatic decline in the variety show that began in the 1970s has continued into the 1980s with only "Barbara Mandrell and the Mandrell Sisters" enjoying even a modicum of success, and that has been done with a minimum of innovation. There are, however, two programs that debuted in the 1970s which are running strong in the 1980s. Although it is a syndicated program, "The Muppet Show" is a classic variety show with the regular sketches and musical numbers performed by some guest star and Jim Henson's muppets; there is a continuing cast of characters writers can draw on for laughs like Miss Piggy, Kermit the Frog, Fozzie the Bear, and many other creatures, all of whom have captured the affections of viewers, young and old alike. The other program, "NBC's Saturday Night Live" (NBC, Sat., 11:30–1:00 P.M.), has also found success in a non-prime-time slot. It is the most successful variety show to come along since Red Skelton or Ed Sullivan. By mixing the irreverence of the Smothers Brothers with fine ensemble work reminiscent of "Your Show of Shows" and "Carol Burnett," the "Saturday Night Live" cast has produced an innovative, sometimes daring, and always amusing program, and in the process has made stars of the late John Belushi, Chevy Chase, Dan Aykroyd, Gilda Radner, and, more recently, Joe Piscopo and Eddie Murphy. The show catered to a younger crowd as is evidenced by much of the topical humor and political satire, and the musical acts ranging from the Rolling Stones, to the Talking Heads, to Leon Redbone.

With shows like "Saturday Night Live," the networks have attempted to return to their roots to find a suitable formula for the variety shows; things have changed, however, as one could see from a recent appearance on "Saturday Night Live" by that show's spiritual father Sid Caesar. The great comedian's talents were either out of step with the style of humor currently popular among younger audiences or hopelessly squandered in the context of set routines. That night, however, the audience and the cast of the show gave Caesar a thunderous ovation prior to the opening sketch. There was in that act respect, admiration, a shared awareness on the part of both audience and actors of what was and is best in TV variety, and, perhaps, hope that both audience and actors may once again recapture that magic.

THEMES AND ISSUES

When TV was in its infancy, the variety show was the sure-fire formula, and it dominated the airwaves for nearly ten years. The variety show, like vaudeville, to paraphrase Albert McLean, offered to the middle class quite without apology or explanation a means whereby it could be "lured, enthralled, and emotionally satisfied."[14] Variety show producers, like their vaudevillian forebears Tony Pastor and Weber and Fields, relied upon established routines and stars from previous generations to launch their programs, and during a time of transition for TV the variety show kept the accomplishments as well as genuine personalities of actual people, as opposed to fictional characters, in the forefront of TV programming. Just as dramatically, however, within the last ten years the variety show has virtually disappeared. The reasons for its success and decline are, furthermore, coincidental with changes that have taken place in our culture over the nearly 40 years that the medium has been in existence.

For the success, we can look to the very reasons vaudeville and revue were popular throughout the first half of the twentieth century. The variety show—and I am thinking here of "vaudeo" primarily, but it does apply to the other formats as well—in a sense mirrored our American mystique of the melting pot and the American Dream. John DiMeglio notes that "the very nature of vaudeville . . . was representative of the American mystique. The expansiveness of vaudeville, as well, where novelty acts, animal acts, impersonators, acrobats, variety acts, magicians, soloists, monologists, comedy teams, drama sketches, dancers, and even chasers, all got billing and did their separate, highly individual parts, yet all somehow integrating into the whole, served as symbol of Americanism."[15] And so it was with TV variety. On the "Ed Sullivan Show" class distinctions and international ones broke down as audiences watched country western singers, tumblers from Romania, black comedians, and crooners from Las Vegas, all characteristic of the diversity of what we know as America, treated by Ed as though they existed on some intangible plane of excellence. And the only thing asked of the audience was that it be entertained. Richard Dyer has noted the following about entertainment, which can also be applied to the TV variety show: "Two of the taken-for-granted descriptions of entertainment, as 'escape' and as 'wish-fulfillment,' point to its central thrust, namely utopianism. Entertainment offers the image of 'something better' to escape into, or something we want deeply that our day-to-day lives don't provide."[16] The shows provide a metaphor for and testimony to man's creativity and his pursuit of excellence in some area of human activity, be it singing, acting, juggling, and so on. They perpetuate our deepest shared beliefs about the myth of success and the melting pot, and the something better we escape into is ultimately an affirmation of our own humanity.

This affirmation of our own humanity is most evident in how the variety show has allowed Americans to witness first hand the playing out of the myth of success. In any given week someone, reminiscent of Ruby Keeler in the 1933 film *Forty-Second Street*, could go out there a youngster and come back a star. John DiMeglio says the vaudeville headliner "stood as a prime example of what could be achieved in a land of free enterprise."[17] Like their forebears in vaudeville, most variety hosts and stars fit the archetype of the Alger hero, who achieved success only after a lot of hard work, struggle, and some luck and pluck. Milton Berle was a minor stand-up comic before TV; Perry Como was a moderately successful band singer prior to his radio stint and subsequent TV show; and Glen Campbell, as a recent example, was a studio musician for many years before getting a shot on the Smothers Brothers show and then a series of his own. The Alger myth, furthermore, was played out yearly on variety programs as we watched Julius LaRosa, Pat Boone, Carol Burnett, Elvis Presley, and the Beatles all make a grab for glory via their work on TV. In comedy variety series one could find vignettes like Jackie Gleason's "The Honeymooners," where characters like Ralph Kramden were constantly in quest of that elusive brass ring of success. Ralph tried game shows (one reminiscent of "Name That Tune") and other get-rich-quick schemes, and he usually failed; this, however, did not stop him from trying again next week. In his struggles Ralph and the audience were reminded of the importance of friends like Norton (Art Carney) and a good marriage (the sketches done later in the series ended with Ralph hugging Alice and declaring "Baby, you're the greatest"), two further measures of a man's success.

The success of variety series was also dependent on the type of persona the hosts projected and the kind of material they performed on their shows. Jeff Greenfield writes, "Television seems to demand from its variety principals a particular kind of personality: low-key, easygoing, friendly, amiable. A warm personality can survive without talent. So can a personality audiences come to know and trust, even without warmth. Ed Sullivan is a prime example. Talent without that personality cannot succeed."[18] A majority of the variety show hosts have this personality; Arthur Godfrey, for instance, was described by Fred Allen as the "man with the barefoot voice,"[19] while others like Perry Como, George Gobel, and Carol Burnett all were able to communicate a warmth in their shows either through style or through their interaction with guests and/or audience (think especially of the opening of the Burnett shows where she fields questions from her audience). A host like Garry Moore, with his bow tie and crew cut, just does not fulfill one's conception of the show-biz personality; he seems too much like "us." In essence these men and women projected the persona of the average middle-class citizen and/or someone who shared an affinity for that class. It is for this reason that there have been more successful shows hosted by country music performers than crooner Vegas types like Sinatra; their personalities, as well as their music, reflect their roots and the values implicit in those roots— values like honesty, family, home, and country, which are quite in keeping with the values of the average viewer. The variety show host, then, must be an individual with whom the viewer can identify on the one hand and who he can admire and wish to emulate on the other; he is an average guy/girl who has "made it."

The humor and the music in the most successful variety shows similarly mine the experience of the average man to comment on or reinforce middle-class values rather than more idiosyncratic show business or artistically elitist values. Sid Caesar remarks that the "familiar" and the facts of everyday life "were the case word for nearly everything we did [on "Your Show of Shows"]."[20] Indeed, many of the classic routines devised by the cast and writers were inspired by the experience of the average American: the Hickenloopers, the spoofs of the movies; even the satires on professorial knowledge devised by Caesar and Brooks reinforce middle-class norms of behavior and taste. Jackie Gleason constantly portrays in his many sketches and pantomines the "poor soul" struggling with the adversities of everyday life, be it getting on some mode of public transportation or trying to perform a simple task; his Reginald Van Gleason, on the other hand, spoofs the affectations of a supposed suave, sophisticated raconteur. Similarly, Carol Burnett's finest bits were concerned with the experiences of the common man, a case in point being her mini-series centering around Eunice and her Mama, which generally took a bittersweet view of a woman's aspirations and her delusions about herself. Sid Caesar, in describing their work on "Your Show of Shows," has summed up what is probably the unwritten philosophy of the comedy variety shows: "A lot of our humor was a mixture of the sad and the funny. Charlie Chaplin knew that in 1910 and we knew it in 1950. A guy who's in trouble is a very funny guy. A man who's got enough money to pay the rent, there's nothing funny about him. You've got to be involved with or worried about the person you're going to laugh at, or cry at."[21] Variety show sketches, like classic vaudeville routines, reinforce basic notions of good and evil shared by the culture; the satire, furthermore, is never cruel, but instead gently—in a Horatian style. if you will—pokes fun at our foibles and follies. To see Carol Burnett as a harried housewife fighting the encroachments of technology in the kitchen, where, as she tries to unclog the garbage disposal with a broom, that self-same appliance eats the broom, is to see the folly of the reliance upon that machine. At the same time, we are laughing at our fear of that same technology out of control, which is a classic middle-class fear.

Turning to the form of the variety show, we see that it complements the content through that venerable variety-revue technique of the "build," wherein acts and routines are structured to give the show a sense of excitement and drama even though there is no plot. The structure is designed to highlight the individual talents of the star or host, to show how musically or comedically skilled they are, or how astute they are in putting on the show. The build sometimes points to a special act; Ed Sullivan had one blockbuster act per week strategically placed toward the end of the show to keep the audience in their seats. In comedy variety shows the climax was usually an ensemble featuring the entire cast; in "Your Show of Shows" the parodies, like the classic "Strange" (a take-off on *Shane*), were the highlight. The build in musical variety and in some vaudeo led to a stunning production number, a good example being Garry Moore's "That Wonderful Year." Like other genres, the variety show is dependent upon formula. As the show unfolds we see why this talented person is so successful, or we wait for that favorite sketch that reaffirms some commonly held belief or value. Jackie Gleason's show in the early sixties ended with Joe the Bartender, looking like a page out of the Gay 90s, swapping jokes with Frank Fontaine, who also sang some old favorite; the whole routine was a paean to our quest, during a time of social and cultural upheaval, to recapture that which we held dear in the good old days.

From its early dominance of the evening schedule the variety show has reached a nadir from which it may never recover. The decline of the form is, not surprisingly, directly attributable to changes that have taken place in the culture, changes moreover, that have affected the three basic components of the genre: music, humor, and talent. The most successful variety shows were able to appeal to a unified culture, one whose members shared some commonly held beliefs, tastes, and values. The musical product of the "melody years" changed very little since the 1920s; to be sure there were dramatic stylistic changes, as in the case of jazz and swing, but the basic musical product was fairly consistent. One could, for instance, easily hear the 1924 hit "Tea for Two" (complete with the stock soft-shoe dance) in a variety show in 1955. There was a certain continuity in music that the audience could count on and that obviated generational differences in the early days of the medium. However, with the advent of rock music and with the expanded coverage that TV was able to provide of contemporary events, the culture's cherished assumptions about itself began to dissolve. TV responded to the rock phenomenon with homogenized purveyors of the form like Pat Boone, but such attempts were only partially successful. When television finally did begin to recognize rock in the mid-sixties in specialized shows like "Shindig" and "Hullabaloo," the variety show found it couldn't nor did it really seem to care to compete. Kids now had a program where they didn't have to sit through a lot of entertainment targeted primarily for their parents before they got to see the acts intended for them. To further complicate matters for variety show producers, rock music has steadily fragmented over the last 20 years into soft rock, folk rock, country rock, hard rock, heavy metal, punk, and new wave, with black music becoming almost exclusively the music of the black community and itself fragmenting within its own boundaries.

The diversity and confusion in the music industry is reflected in the fact that there have been no successful rock musicians who have hosted variety series. The closest we have come is Sonny and Cher, and their style was hardly representative in those years when Led Zepplin and David Bowie were among the most popular and revered musical acts. It is not surprising that the most successful musical variety hosts within the last 20 years have been drawn from the ranks of country music. The list of successful country hosts, in fact, outstrips similar hosts of the Tin-Pan-Alley variety; we have Tennessee Ernie Ford, Jimmy Dean, Johnny Cash, the Mandrell Sisters, to name the major ones. The decline of the musical variety show is attributable to the fragmentation of America's musical culture over the last 20 years, and it reveals that in spite of its dominance over the last three decades, rock remains the outsider in network television, to be confined, it would seem, to late nights or shows directed specifically at youth, the market traditionally of least interest to prime-time programmers.

In terms of comedy, the variety show has had similar problems. Much of the humor that was the venue of the variety program has been co-opted by situation comedies; relevant satire has been done more thoroughly, and in some cases better, by Norman Lear in series like "All in the Family." Recent variety shows like Richard Pryor's were just too risky for the networks, and stellar comedians like Steve Martin have met with minimal success in their specials; both comedians, in fact, seem to be more interested in film. Moreover, their humor, like so many young comedians' today, is not well suited to television; they require an openness which is more congenial to the nightclub or cable shows like those on HBO where they can swear and refer to drugs without a censor looking over their shoulders. In addition to these factors, the new comedians, with a few exceptions, lack that warmth of which Jeff Greenfield speaks; they have the talent, but they are light years removed from Arthur Godfrey in terms of personableness and that easy-going affability we associate with former stars like George Gobel, Garry Moore, or even Flip Wilson. Much of the humor that is enjoying popularity today is derived from a National Lampoon mentality; it is not Horatian satire, the type one came to expect from Caesar and Coca or Carol Burnett; it is, instead, more Juvenalian, and the attacks on middle-class values, in keeping with the style, have a tendency to shame rather than amuse the viewer. Networks and stars alike have not been able, with the exception of "Saturday Night Live," to parlay this new humor into a successful variety format.

Finally, there is the issue of talent; Perry Lafferty, a programming executive at CBS, has stated, "We don't know where to look for the new talent. . . . It's frightful when I look out my window and think, 'All right, tell me who's ready out there that you're going to put up as a star, to build a comedy variety show around.' "[22] This is not to say that there are not talented people around, but, as has been suggested thus far, that talent is either in quest of a different medium or it cannot speak to the collective tastes of the audience. Another related issue here is recent programming. Within the last ten years a number of programs have cut into what once was the variety market. Thus far, we have mentioned situation comedies as replacements for comedy variety. In terms of music there is now MTV (Music TV) where one can see their favorite rock groups in settings more flattering and interesting than any music variety series or special could produce. Finally, there has been the emergence of shows like "That's Incredible" and "Real People" or the news magazines like "60 Minutes," which deal with the accomplishments (and sometimes the follies) of the common man. In each of these cases talent, although still important, takes equal billing with good writing, flashy film technique, or odd-ball eccentricity.

Albert McLean has written of vaudeville: "As ritual, vaudeville arose in an era of crisis to offer the American people a definitive rhythm, a series of gestures which put man back into the center of his world, a sense of the human community, and an effective emotional release."[23] Much the same could be said of the role of the variety show in the early days of the medium; it did indeed put man at the center of his world through both the personality of the host, someone who was always himself and not a fictional creation, and through the entertainment it offered. Musical numbers and comedy routines reaffirmed our entertainment roots in flashy Broadway-styled production numbers, in great Tin-Pan-Alley standards, and in the little comedy-morality plays that were the heart's blood of both vaudeville and film. Today the variety show no longer addresses the same concerns. The average American, somewhat like Nick Carraway, must be simultaneously drawn and repelled by the mere variety of everything available to him; and with such variety everywhere in the world, the contained world of the TV variety show may, indeed, seem small, or maybe it can no longer speak to our mythic notions of the melting pot, the middle class, and the American Dream.

NOTES

1. Tim Brooks and Earle Marsh, *The Complete Directory to Prime Time Network TV Shows, 1946–Present*, rev. ed. (New York: Ballantine Books, 1981), p. 344.

2. Jeff Greenfield, *Television: The First Fifty Years*, Shortened Version (New York: Crescent Books, 1981), p. 37.

3. This, according to Milton Berle, was the show's original title; later it would just be the "Texaco Star Theatre"; see Linda Gutstein, "Star Talk: Berle on Berle," in *TV Book: The Ultimate Television Book*, ed. Judy Fireman (New York: Workman Publishing Co., 1977), p. 154.

4. William A. Henry, III, "The Man with the Barefoot Voice," *Time*, March 28, 1983, p. 45.

5. There are differing versions as to who actually worked on "Your Show of Shows"; most report the names included here but Sid Caesar in his autobiography, *Where Have I Been?* (New York: Crown Publishers, 1982), states that some of the writers came on during the run of "Caesar's Hour."

6. Max Wilk, *The Golden Age of Television: Notes from the Survivors* (New York: Delacorte Press, 1976), p. 165.

7. Kenneth Tynan, *Show People: Profiles in Entertainment* (New York: Simon and Schuster, 1979), p. 226.

8. Imogene Coca is one cast member who definitely feels that they were doing satire; see *TV Book*, ed. Fireman, p. 171.

9. Brooks and Marsh, *The Complete Directory*, p. 159.

10. Ibid., p. 50.

11. In regard to Allen's treatment of Jerry Lee Lewis, see Nick Tosches's biography of Lewis, *Hellfire: The Jerry Lee Lewis Story* (New York: Delacorte Press, 1982), pp. 127–28, 171.

12. Jerry Bowles, "Remembering Ernie Kovacs," *TV Book*, p. 157.

13. Brooks and Marsh, *The Complete Directory*, p. 337.

14. Albert McLean, *American Vaudeville as Ritual* (Lexington: University of Kentucky Press, 1965), p. 7.

15. John DiMeglio, *Vaudeville U.S.A.* (Bowling Green, Ohio: Bowling Green University Popular Press, 1973), p. 199. For a fuller treatment of this issue see Albert McLean's *American Vaudeville as Ritual*.

16. "Entertainment and Utopia," in *Genre: The Musical*, ed. Rick Altman (London: Routledge and Kegan Paul, 1981), p. 177.

17. DiMeglio, *Vaudeville U.S.A.*, p.199.

18. Greenfield, *Television*, p. 43.

19. Henry, "The Man with the Barefoot Voice," p.45.

20. Caesar, *Where Have I Been?*, p.101.

21. Ibid., pp. 103–4.

22. Wilk, *The Golden Age*, p. 73.
23. McLean, *American Vaudeville as Ritual*, p. 6.

BIBLIOGRAPHICAL SURVEY

Television criticism and scholarship has begun to improve only recently, and writing about the variety show seems to not have improved at all. It is the great neglected genre, except for a few pockets of interest in Sid Caesar, Mel Brooks, and others associated with "Your Show of Shows." Besides these the remainder of the work on variety is of the chatty, gossipy type, concentrating on biographical aspects or historical trivia associated with the various series.

Some books, however, can be mentioned for providing occasional good insights into the subject as well as interesting historical information. Max Wilk's *The Golden Age of Television* is typical Max Wilk: informal, well researched, and blessed by the immediacy of his interviews with different people in the business. In a similar vein, but more comprehensive in scope, is Judy Fireman's anthology of pieces entitled *TV Book: The Ultimate Television Book*. The pieces in her collection do a nice job of capturing the history of medium as well as providing some interesting recollections by stars and critics alike.

On a more serious level, Brooks and Marsh's *TV Directory* is the indispensable guide to the medium. The book is primarily informational, but *what* information, and occasionally they will offer some good historical and cultural insights into various programs. Secondly, there is Jeff Greenfield's *Television: The First Fifty Years*, a lavishly illustrated and extremely readable history of the medium; furthermore, Greenfield makes some interesting and at times profound observations about TV, but he does so without ever sounding stuffy or overtly scholarly. On the other hand, classic studies by the likes of Erik Barnouw and Horace Newcomb were virtually useless in dealing with this subject. Ted Sennett's book on "Your Show of Shows" and Sid Caesar's autobiography are both useful and fine reading for insights into that show's greatness; they also re-create many of the classic bits, giving them further nostalgic value. Finally, if one is interested in the anecdotal, there is Kenneth Whelan's *The Golden Age of Television Turned My Hair to Silver*, which has great material about putting on such variety classics as "The Jackie Gleason Show" and "The Garry Moore Show"; the major problem one has here is sifting through the material to determine what is genuine and what is apocryphal.

Finally, if one wishes to go beyond the merely historical or anecdotal, he will have to look at more generalized studies of the entertainment media. The two most helpful books in illuminating the nature of the variety show were about vaudeville: John DiMeglio's *Vaudeville U.S.A.* and the book from which DiMeglio gleaned a number of insights, Albert McLean's *American Vaudeville as Ritual*. Both books attempt to place the variety form in the context of American values and attitudes and both are, for the most part, successful. Magazine articles that were helpful in this area include the criticism of Goodman Ace, which ran in

Saturday Review; his pieces on the early pioneers are particularly good in light of the variable material generally being written about the medium at that time. Finally, the articles in *TV Guide*, although not usually probing, have been among the few substantive pieces done on various TV programs within the last seven to ten years.

BOOKS AND ARTICLES

Ace, Goodman. "This and That: Popularity of Ed Sullivan's *Toast of the Town*." *Saturday Review*, February 5, 1955, p. 26.

Bowles, Jerry. *A Thousand Sundays: The Story of the Ed Sullivan Show*. New York: G.P. Putnam's Sons, 1980.

Brooks, Tim, and Earle Marsh. *The Complete Directory to Prime Time Network TV Shows, 1946–Present*. rev. ed. New York: Ballantine Books, 1981.

Caesar, Sid, with Bill Davidson. *Where Have I Been?: An Autobiography*. New York: Crown Publishers, Inc., 1982.

DiMeglio, John. *Vaudeville U.S.A.* Bowling Green, Ohio: Bowling Green University Popular Press, 1973.

Greenfield, Jeff. *Television: The First Fifty Years*. Shortened Version. New York: Crescent Books, 1981.

Liebman, Max. "Broadway Revue Every Week." *Theatre Arts*, May, 1953, pp. 74–77.

McLean, Albert, Jr. *American Vaudeville as Ritual*. Lexington: University of Kentucky Press, 1965.

Sennett, Ted. *Your Show of Shows*. New York: MacMillan, 1977.

Thompson, Toby. "How Sweet It Was." *American Film* (November 1982), pp. 38–45, 88–89.

Twenty-Five Year Index to TV Guide. Radnor, Pa.: Triangle Publications, 1979.

Tynan, Kenneth. *Show People: Profiles in Entertainment*. New York: Simon and Schuster, 1979.

Whelan, Kenneth. *How the Golden Age of Television Turned My Hair to Silver*. New York: Walker and Co., 1973.

Wilk, Max. *The Golden Age of Television: Notes from the Survivors*. New York: Delacorte Press, 1976.

VIDEOGRAPHY

"Texaco Star Theatre Starring Milton Berle"
  NBC, Tues. 8:00–9:00 P.M.
  Premiere: June 8, 1948
  Star: Milton Berle
  Last Program: June 1956

"Toast of the Town"
  CBS, various times until 1949, then Sun. 8:00–9:00 P.M.
  Premiere: June 20, 1948
  Star: Ed Sullivan
  Last Program: June 6, 1971

"The Perry Como Show"
  CBS, various prime times
  Premiere: December 24, 1948
  Star: Perry Como
  Last Program: June 12, 1963

"Arthur Godfrey and His Friends"
  CBS, various prime times
  Premiere: January 12, 1949
  Star: Arthur Godfrey
  Last Program: April 28, 1959

"Your Show of Shows"
  NBC, Sat. 9:00–10:00 P.M.
  Premiere: February 25, 1950
  Stars: Sid Caesar, Imogene Coca, Carl Reiner, Howard Morris
  Last Program: June 5, 1954

"The Red Skelton Show"
  NBC, CBS, various prime times
  Premiere: September 30, 1951
  Star: Red Skelton
  Last Program: August 29, 1971

"The Jackie Gleason Show"
  CBS, various prime times, Sat.
  Premiere: September 20, 1952
  Stars: Jackie Gleason, Art Carney
  Last Program: September 12, 1970

"The Dinah Shore Chevy Show"
  NBC, Fri., Sun., various times
  Premiere: October 5, 1956
  Star: Dinah Shore
  Last Program: May 12, 1963

"The Andy Williams Show"
  NBC, various prime times
  Premiere: July 3, 1958
  Stars: Andy Williams, Osmond Brothers
  Last Program: July 17, 1971

"The Dean Martin Show"
  NBC, Thurs. 10:00–11:00 P.M.
  Premiere: September 16, 1965
  Stars: Dean Martin, The Golddiggers
  Last Program: May 24, 1974

"The Smothers Brothers Comedy Hour"
  CBS, Sun. 9:00–10:00 P.M.
  Premiere: February 5, 1967
  Stars: Tom and Dick Smothers, Pat Paulsen
  Last Program: June 1969

"The Carol Burnett Show"
  CBS, various prime times
  Premiere: September 11, 1967
  Stars: Carol Burnett, Harvey Korman, Vicki Lawrence
  Last Program: September 8, 1979

"Rowan and Martin's Laugh-In"
  NBC, Mon. 8:00–9:00 P.M.
  Premiere: January 22, 1968
  Stars: Dan Rowan, Dick Martin
  Last Program: May 14, 1973

"The Flip Wilson Show"
  NBC, Thurs. 7:30–8:30 P.M.; Thurs. 8:00–9:00 P.M.
  Premiere: September 17, 1970
  Star: Flip Wilson
  Last Program: June 27, 1974

"The Sonny and Cher Comedy Hour"
  CBS, various prime times
  Premiere: August 1, 1971
  Stars: Sonny Bono, Cher Bono
  Last Program: May, 1974

"NBC's Saturday Night Live"
  NBC, Sat. 11:30–1:00 P.M.
  Premiere: October 11, 1975
  Stars: John Belushi, Gilda Radner, Eddie Murphy, Joe Piscopo, Martin Short, Harry
  Shearer

16

The Talk Show

BRIAN G. ROSE

OVERVIEW

It is difficult to place one of television's most durable and popular forms, the talk show, into a strict generic classification. Talk shows don't depend on dramatic actions, the imaginary interplay of characters, or the foreseeable working out of formulaic themes. They are, obviously, televised broadcasts of conversation—a definition that would seem to offer little entertainment value in comparison with the thrill of a chase or the release of a situation comedy. But as any viewer can testify, just because talk shows are filled with talk does not mean that they lack excitement, interest, and conflict; nor does it mean that they are not as ordered and purposeful and as efficiently crafted as any other type of popular drama. Talk shows may be based on the principle of the casual and the spontaneous, but a great deal of effort is spent to assure a predictable organization and a steady narrative flow. Though the "plot" of a talk show may not be particularly vivid or provocative, it still offers its audience a chance to experience the pleasures of a clearly defined structure, a variety of character collisions, and a feeling of affirmative resolution.

In the short history of the television talk show, a mere 30 years, millions of viewers have had the opportunity actively to follow the genre's development and share in its growth. What they have seen is the evolution of a type of entertainment uniquely suited to the demands of television. The talk show, at its best, combines some of the principal qualities of other successful dramatic forms—the emotional intimacy of melodrama, the sprightliness of comedy, for instance—while offering a compelling immediacy no work of TV fiction can provide. In some guises, such as "The Today Show" and "Good Morning America," the genre acts as a bridge between entertainment and news, sometimes making news itself when a guest reveals something particularly enticing; in other versions, such as "The Tonight Show" and "The Merv Griffin Show," the genre exists as a supplement to prime time by promoting stars and highlights from current shows and specials. The versatility of the talk show in being able to straddle virtually the whole of television, from journalism to soap operas to sports, makes it an unusually interesting example of how modern generic forms can feed off one another to create new combinations. This lively process of cross-fertilization is found to be a common thread when one begins tracing the talk show's history.

HISTORICAL DEVELOPMENT

During the past 30 years, the television talk show has generally followed one of two approaches. It has usually been dedicated to either light entertainment, complete with comedy, skits, music, and show business guests, or to more serious discussion, in a simple studio, with just an interviewer and an interviewee. The latter format originated in radio, with the many interview programs conducted by the network news departments. The concept of a loose, mostly unscripted program devoted to comedy and casual conversation, however, began with television and would prove to be the formula most popular talk shows would follow. The person responsible for creating this concept was Sylvester "Pat" Weaver.

An extraordinarily inventive, bright, and cheery iconoclast, Pat Weaver joined NBC-TV as a programming executive in 1949, after a successful career in advertising at Young and Rubicam managing the agency's radio programs. At NBC, he quickly shifted his loyalties away from Madison Avenue to a strong belief that television could flourish only if networks wrested control over their programming away from the sponsors.

As a way to increase network control while spurring new advertising interest and participation, Weaver was eager to launch a late-night show to run from 11:30 P.M. to 12:30 A.M. The program, which he described in a memo as "a zany light hearted show on every night at the same time for people in the mood for staying up," was designed to be a blend of the wise-cracking spirit and ensemble comedy interactions of the Fred Allen and Jack Benny radio shows.[1] However, after its premiere on May 29, 1950, Weaver's late-night experiment, now called "Broadway Open House," went through a shaky few weeks trying to find a suitable host who could take a 60-minute unscripted show and transform it into a workable format. Lowbrow comedian Jerry Lester proved to be the answer. Lester, who hosted the show on Tuesday, Thursday, and Friday nights— Morey Amsterdam had Mondays and Wednesdays—was an appealing master of ceremonies who combined inspired improvisation with ancient vaudeville shtick. With his affable crew of supporting players, including orchestra leader Milton DeLugg and the first of TV's shapely "dumb" blondes, Dagmar, he made "Broadway Open House" into the television equivalent of a free-for-all party, complete with audience participation, meandering skits, and horseplay.

The show's popularity continued as long as Jerry Lester controlled (or seemingly controlled) the proceedings. When he left in May 1951, the program tried to replace him with an assortment of comedian/hosts, but with little success. Three months later, on August 24, 1951, "Broadway Open House" went off the air. Yet, even though it lasted for only a year, "Broadway Open House" was an important talk show innovator. It proved that the late-night audience was open to a more casual approach to entertainment and that, in the right hands and with the right cast ensemble, a TV show could succeed by simply emphasizing spontaneity, good cheer, and rambling conversation.

Pat Weaver's next experiment took a somewhat different approach to informal discussion. "Today," which premiered on January 14, 1952, was an attempt to offer an early morning electronic newspaper of the air, complete with live reports and views of headline stories from throughout the country. But despite its jour-nalistic mission, "Today" was a distinctly relaxed, easy going affair, thanks largely to the low-key personality of its host, Dave Garroway. Garroway, whose own network TV show "Garroway at Large" had run from 1949 to 1951, proved to be a comfortable and reassuring guide through the program's varying segments of news, comic skits, and chats with a steady supporting cast and with an endless assortment of authors, politicians, and celebrities. An unlikely addition to the program's company of regulars, the chimp J. Fred Muggs, led "Today" to increased popularity, as a new audience of adults began tuning in to the monkey antics that so delighted their children. "Today" prospered—it had already be-come the most profitable show on television by 1954—and having now conquered the morning hours, Pat Weaver launched another affable talk format in the afternoon, "The Home Show," which premiered on March 1, 1954. With Arlene Francis as mistress of ceremonies, the program offered a variety of individually hosted compartments to meet the needs of its homemaker audience, ranging from decorating, to children's problems, to carpentry. "The Home Show" lasted until August 9, 1957.

Meanwhile, the late-night slot left vacant by the collapse of "Broadway Open House" was being filled on NBC's local New York station by "The Steve Allen Show." Allen had begun his career as a disc jockey whose comic interpolations of commercials and witty ad-libs soon attracted a following. By the late 1940s he was running a successful 11:00 P.M. variety show on Los Angeles radio, which had brought to the fore his two chief talents: madcap improvisation and a gleefully silly rapport with his audience. The flexibility and spiritedness of his approach worked equally well on television. "The Steve Allen Show," which premiered on WNBC-TV on August 27, 1951, established a new style of live TV talk show. Unlike the occasionally creaky vaudeville joints of "Broadway Open House" or the smooth, wisecracking banter of the radio shows hosted by Jack Benny or Fred Allen, "The Steve Allen Show" was a loose and engaging program of Allen's chatty piano playing, breezy banter with a crew of regulars (who often acted in the host's ad-lib routines), audience interaction, and con-versation with a variety of guest stars and common folk. The program's most celebrated feature was its spontaneity. Whether he was creating mayhem in the studio or posing as a traffic cop in one of the show's many remotes on the streets of New York City, Steve Allen brought an inspired sense of controlled lunacy to television. Realizing that at last he had found a workable format for the network's late night schedule, Pat Weaver, now president of NBC, made Allen the first host of "Tonight!" which had its premiere on September 27, 1954.

During his two and a half years with "Tonight!" Allen established many of the foundations that have guided the late night talk show ever since: an opening segment featuring the host in a solo turn at center stage, occasional forays into the audience or streets, a shift to a different platform where the host sits behind a desk flanked by chairs, chats with the orchestra leader and announcer, and, finally, a procession of appearances and discussions with visiting stars and momentary celebrities.

When Steve Allen decided in June 1956 to cut back his appearances to Wednesday through Friday nights in order to devote more time to his new prime-time series, "Tonight!" entered a rocky six-month period that finally led to the show's cancellation on January 24, 1957. Its replacement was an ill-conceived mélange of nightclub remotes from around the country, news reports, and awkward informality called "America after Dark." The program premiered on January 28, 1957, and limped along until June 1957, after losing significant amounts of ad revenues and station clearances. The disaster of "America after Dark" proved that the late-night format of comic host and casual frivolity was an attraction to which viewers had grown accustomed. As a way of recouping their losses, NBC decided to bring back "Tonight!" but with a new name, "The Tonight Show," and a new host, Jack Paar. Paar had come from CBS where he had hosted their breakfast version of "Today" called "The Morning Show" as well as a half-hour afternoon conversation program. With his premiere on "The Tonight Show" on July 29, 1957, the talk show entered a new era, both in terms of popularity and concept.

In contrast to the zany and wittily absurd styles of his late-night predecessors, Jack Paar was engagingly personal and direct. His comic monologues bordered on the homespun and were filled with disarming stories about his wife and daughter. More importantly, he introduced an attitude of emotional honesty that seemed revelatory at the time. He ranted or wept on camera. He got angry and would attack his critics. He would walk off the stage in protest. All of these qualities made him an arresting television personality; for two years in a row, he led the Sindlinger poll of public opinion as the nation's most talked about person.[2]

Jack Paar also opened up the talk show to personal opinion. Assured of his hold on viewers and sponsors—by 1959 "The Tonight Show's" ratings were higher than ever before—Paar vented his beliefs on a wide range of sensitive political topics, including the Cuban revolution and the Bay of Pigs invasion. As a talented and skillful interviewer, he brought on "serious" guests with the confidence that they would interest his late-night audience because they so clearly interested him.

Despite the incandescence of his style and his flair for the revealingly dramatic, Jack Paar did not abandon "The Tonight Show" 's structural legacy. He placed tremendous importance on his opening moments alone with his audience; but since he couldn't play the piano like Steve Allen, he used the time for a comic monologue, which he felt set the crucial mood for what was to follow. When it occasionally fell flat, as Robert Metz reports, Paar "let it cast a pall on the whole evening."[3] His crew of regulars, which included announcer Hugh Downs and orchestra leader Jose Mellis, played parts very similar to Steve Allen's sidekicks Gene Rayburn and Skitch Henderson. Paar also surrounded himself with a cast of occasional performers (such as Cliff Arquette, Pat Harrington, and Florence Henderson) who played in skits and served to sparkle conversation, much like the old "Tonight" 's ensemble of Don Knotts, Louis Nye, Steve Lawrence, and Eydie Gorme. The host's desk was still the center of activity, with each new guest given a seat of privilege to the "king's" right.

Paar's tenure on "The Tonight Show" lasted almost five years (through March 20, 1962) until, like Steve Allen, he abandoned late-night TV for the greener pastures of prime-time television. After six months of substitute hosts, "The Tonight Show" opened its October 2, 1962, program with a new host, Johnny Carson, who, in his more than 20 years with the show, has become more closely associated with the talk show format than anyone else.

Carson was hired by NBC after a successful stint as the sharpwitted host of the ABC daytime game show "Who Do You Trust?" His cool comic style was in sharp contrast to Paar's wayward emotionalism, and under his leadership "The Tonight Show" quickly assumed a brighter and livelier pace. The revealing anecdotes and maudlin reminiscences so characteristic of the Paar days were replaced by a brassier, more contemporary approach. Carson's monologues avoided the personal and the homespun in favor of a sassy mixture of mild topic barbs, one liners, and witty asides lamenting the bad jokes he was forced to deliver.

But Johnny Carson's forte wasn't just in delivering lines; it was also in reacting to them. Like Jack Benny, whose strong influence he readily admits, Carson was a master of the resigned shrug and the quick take when disaster broke out around him. His all-American looks offered a perfect contrast to the naughty glint in his eye, which would appear whenever one of the show's many guest starlets said some innocently provocative remark. As a skilled television performer, Carson possessed what seemed to be an intuitive relationship with the camera. His subtle reactions were ideally suited to the limits of the small screen—a close-up camera was trained on him at all times to capture his expressions—and his comedy often depended on addressing the home audience with the smallest of cracked smiles.

Along with his long-time producer from "Who Do You Trust?" Art Stark, Carson refashioned "The Tonight Show" 's structure to accommodate his more restless temperament.[4] While keeping the format of monologue, desk, skit, and celebrity conversation, the allotted time schedule for each segment was thrown out so that a boring conversation could be easily jettisoned. More extensive pre-interviews, in which prospective guests were prepared for their visit and coached in what to say by the show's staff, were also conducted to help eradicate "dead spots" and smooth the flow.[5] "The Tonight Show" also became the premier showplace for new talent, as talent coordinators scoured the country looking for fresh faces and the oddball guests of whom Carson (like Steve Allen before him) loved to play off.

The specific nature of Johnny Carson's appeal has been the subject of considerable speculation (see the "Bibliographical Survey" with this chapter). Suffice it to say that no one in television has lasted as long as a program's daily host or commanded as durable a popularity. From 1962 through 1977 he performed the unprecedented feat of doubling "The Tonight Show" 's audience.[6] Johnny Carson's crisp style united "The Tonight Show" 's various elements of classical skit comedy, chattiness with announcer Ed McMahon, variety, and conversation into a consistently lively entertainment package. While Carson's cool manner has occasionally frightened some of his guests, his highly polished comic instincts and his unique relationship with his audience has made "The Tonight Show" an institutional emblem of the talk show at its peak form.[7]

Johnny Carson's success on "The Tonight Show" came almost immediately—within four months after his premiere, his ratings were larger than those in the glory days of Jack Paar—and it signalled the fact that by then the talk show had become one of television's most profitable and versatile formats.[8] "The Today Show" still reigned as the early morning talk champion, even though its comedy and skits had been eliminated once the NBC news division took control after Dave Garroway left in June 1961.

Several years earlier, more probing interview talk shows had begun appearing on prime-time television. Programs such as "Person to Person" with Edward R. Murrow and "Mike Wallace Interviews" used their 30 minutes to focus on a single person (or famous married couple) without any of the show business trappings of the Pat Weaver talk concepts. But while they avoided jokes and folksy chattiness, both "Person to Person" and "Mike Wallace Interviews" did use a familiar talk entertainment feature—they were dominated by the dynamic personalities of their hosts and recognized the value of big-name celebrity guests as a way to lure a large viewing audience. Though "Person to Person" ran only through 1961—"Mike Wallace Interviews" was on for only one season in 1958—viewers in many cities could watch local conversation programs clearly modeled on network talk formulas.

Local talk shows had begun appearing with great frequency throughout the 1950's, and they often seemed to be hosted by anyone who could gain access to a camera. For example, in 1959 in New York City, viewers could choose from talk programs with novelist Fannie Hurst, author Ben Hecht, entertainer Gypsy Rose Lee, or Governor Robert Meyner of New Jersey, as well as David Susskind (whose controversial show "Open End" would last for hours, with no fixed time limit, until there was presumably nothing left to say). Audiences in Los Angeles could watch Oscar Levant or Pamela Mason. For stations willing to buy them, there were also syndicated talk shows, with hosts varying in style from Bishop Fulton Sheen to acid raconteur Henry Morgan.

As Pat Weaver had proved at NBC, talk was not only popular, it was cheap. In contrast to the elaborate production demands of dramas and situation comedies, the talk show required only a few chairs, maybe a desk, one glib host, a small staff, and a studio audience (who often clamored to attend for free). This relative lack of expense, combined with the appeal of the form during all parts of the day and night, led to an even greater expansion of the talk show during the 1960s. To counter Johnny Carson's domination of the late-night hours, ABC launched "The Les Crane Show" on November 9, 1964. Crane, a former West Coast disc jockey known for his brashness, tried to offer a more stimulating, controversial discussion show, featuring somewhat more serious interactions with his audience (via a special shotgun microphone) but his efforts met with little success. Four months later he was replaced by the familiar ritual of guest hosts, only to return in June 1965 with a Hollywood-based show (renamed "ABC's Nightlife") that was as entertainment-oriented as his NBC competitor. It lasted until November 12, 1965.

The year 1965 also saw the rise of the syndicated talk show to an important position. The leader in this development was Group W Broadcasting, which offered two programs that turned out to be very popular on hundreds of local stations throughout the country. Their first success, "The Mike Douglas Show," was originally broadcast from their station in Cleveland and was then transferred a few years later to Philadelphia. Douglas was a friendly, handsome, one-time big band singer, whose style was strikingly different from that of the big network talk show hosts. He had little ability to ad-lib, offer witty remarks, or delve into topical issues. What he did possess was a genial personality, which made his guests feel at ease. His program, with its mixture of songs, loose skits, and demonstrations, became a pleasant and undemanding companion for home-bound viewers during the late afternoon hours in which it customarily ran.

Group W's other syndication success was "The Merv Griffin Show." Merv Griffin resembled Mike Douglas in many respects—he was an affable, softly contoured host who also had been a moderately successful singer. Both men were cheery and gracious to their guests and usually conducted their shows like sunny sessions at the country club. But Merv Griffin had more talent for drawing his guests out, and he was not averse to going beyond the traditional show business axis to find personalities from politics or the arts to talk to—a fact which may account for his popularity in early evening hours, when the audience had a bit more time to pay attention. If Merv Griffin was a bit more unctuous than most talk show hosts, he was also, as he once accurately described himself, "a good listener to guests who have something to say."[9] By 1968 his syndicated show could be seen on 170 stations, and a year later he was hired by CBS to tackle Johnny Carson.

"The Tonight Show" was truly the behemoth of talk shows, attracting more than four million viewers by the end of the 1960s and bringing in enormous revenues to NBC. Despite its failures with Les Crane and "Nightlife," ABC continued to try to slow Carson's late night juggernaut. On April 17, 1967, the network premiered another talk show, this time featuring comedian Joey Bishop, who had met with some success as a substitute host on, naturally, "The Tonight Show." During its two and a half years, "The Joey Bishop Show" never found a distinctive character of its own but slavishly imitated its rival. Without Carson's special personality, the structural format "The Joey Bishop Show" so carefully tried to duplicate rarely yielded its magic. The program was finally cancelled on December 26, 1969.

CBS had not had a regularly scheduled late-night program since 1955, but the sweepstakes were now too high not to compete. Though the faltering "Joey Bishop Show" was still on ABC when "The Merv Griffin Show" started on CBS on August 18, 1969, its clear target was NBC's Carson. Unlike his ABC competitor, Merv Griffin at least offered an alternative. His program was more ingratiating and conversationally oriented than "The Tonight Show," though it too had a sidekick (grumpy British actor Arthur Treacher) and a slick orchestra. Where Griffin most differed from Carson was in his absence of sparkle and humor as a host. His appeal was his hominess, a quality that late-night viewers didn't take to as well as Carson's sharp wit. CBS moved the show from new York to Hollywood a year later, hoping to boost the disappointing ratings with the addition of more motion picture stars, but eventually the program was cancelled on February 11, 1972. Griffin returned to syndication a few months later (this time with Metromedia) and continued to produce, with much success, the comfortable, glitzy, low-key talk shows that had been his specialty prior to his network stint.

Carson faced one more challenger of note. With the failure of "The Joey Bishop Show," ABC decided to move a young, sophisticated comedian named Dick Cavett into the 11:30 P.M. battle slot. Cavett, who had previously worked as a comedy writer for Jack Paar and Johnny Carson, had begun his ABC career in March 1968 as the host of a 90-minute daytime show called "This Morning," which, in what would soon be a familiar pattern, won lots of critical acclaim (including an Emmy) but very few viewers. It was cancelled on January 24, 1969. That summer he was given a one-hour 10:00 P.M. prime-time program, which aired Monday, Tuesday, and Friday nights and ended its run in September. Cavett was finally given the late-night position in late December 1969, and for the next six years, he pursued a unique and sprightly approach to the talk show.

Actually, the Cavett approach was already firmly in place with his first morning conversation show in 1968. It consisted of a distinctively alert comic style, which favored ironies, word plays, and urbane witticisms. Though Cavett was steeped in the show business milieu of his predecessors, his interests were wide and mirrored the concerns of the younger audiences networks would soon be so desperately eager to reach. Nothing reflected the bright and lively quality of his shows as much as the range of guests who appeared on them. Cavett was unafraid of intellectuals (perhaps due to his undergraduate days at Yale) and encouraged discussion from his former philosophy professor Paul Weiss, radical journalist I. F. Stone, and Norman Mailer, to name a few. He devoted one-person shows to Ingmar Bergman, Laurence Olivier, Katharine Hepburn, and Marlon Brando. He invited everyone, from controversial rock groups to politicians of every stripe, including segregationist and former governor of Georgia Lester Maddox, who created a flurry by storming off the stage during a heated discussion of civil rights.[10]

Cavett's nimble manner and obvious intelligence offered a refreshing change from the more conventional Hollywood leanings of his competitors. However, "The Dick Cavett Show" was not an entirely radical departure from the traditional formulas of late-night talk. It still observed the proprieties of comic monologue, orchestra, and the steady parade of guest stars with something to promote. But what separated his program from other contemporary talk shows and what made it a landmark was Cavett's eagerness to stretch the boundaries of acceptable TV conversation to include a world much larger than standard show business. Though "The Dick Cavett Show" was certainly not a late-night version of "Meet the Press," it did not instinctively shy away from direct topicality if it was raised; nor did it hesitate to present guests whose accomplishments in intellectual or artistic realms might have made them too somber for talk shows in the past.

Nevertheless, despite its enthusiastic critical notices, its Emmy award, and its feverishly loyal audience, "The Dick Cavett Show" was never very competitive even with CBS's "The Merv Griffin Show," and in January 1973, ABC reduced its run to one three-night week once a month. Two years later it was off the network's schedule entirely. Cavett's style found a more congenial home at PBS in September 1977, when he began a nightly half-hour talk show that dispensed with all commercial trappings. There was no orchestra, no monologue, and, of course, no commercial interruptions. Instead, the PBS Cavett show focused on only one guest (often a serious actor, author, or artist) who rarely, if ever, appeared on a talk show before. This new format permitted Cavett to develop the natural flow of a conversation and to explore matters with less scheduling pressure. But even the oasis afforded by PBS did not prove untroubled, and, due to funding problems and persistent low ratings, "The Dick Cavett Show" was once again cancelled, this time in the summer of 1982.

During most of the 1970s, the talk show was in a boom period, especially in the fertile areas of syndication. Merv Griffin and Mike Douglas continued to flourish. Dinah Shore started a popular afternoon program (based on her NBC afternoon show "Dinah's Place"), which added a domestic twist to the format. It turned the talk show into a celebrity kaffeeklatsch. Unlike the living-room or office-like settings of many talk shows, the set of "Dinah," which began syndication in 1974, was a homey combination of suburban kitchen and solarium. The same Hollywood show business circle that traveled from Johnny—"The Tonight Show" had moved to the West Coast in 1972—to Mike to Merv turned to Dinah to show off their cooking skills and handiwork. If "The Dick Cavett Show" was a chance for stars to discuss what was on their minds and "The

Tonight Show'' was an opportunity to talk about their latest product, "Dinah" was the home stars came to in order to relax and prove that they could be "just folks."

Because they ran during the daytime hours, both "Dinah" and "The Mike Douglas Show" were more oriented toward housewives, which, in television terms, meant that they were softer in content and less harsh in approach than their nighttime counterparts. However, during the early 1970s a new syndicated talk show radically changed the definition of "homemaker" entertainment. "The Phil Donahue Show" started in Dayton, Ohio, and within its first week shattered the mold of complacency and pleasant chitchat that all previous local morning talk programs had religiously upheld. On his opening show on November 6, 1967, Donahue, a former TV newsman, presented, to the shock of his largely conservative audience, atheist Madalyn Murray O'Hare; two days later he featured a film showing the birth of a baby from the obstetrician's point of view, and at the end of the week he displayed an anatomically correct male doll and received hundreds of calls from viewers when he asked them to phone in their opinions.[11]

"The Phil Donahue Show" became a forum for exploring every issue in society, particularly the diversity of sexual lifestyles, in an open manner not previously attempted by any daytime talk show. As a host, Donahue was a probing interviewer who placed great emphasis on letting his studio audience (99 percent of which were women) ask the questions as well. His program broke down the formal barriers of the talk show models of the past, eliminating many of the conventions (such as desk and monologue) that tended to impede the flow of discussion. Guests weren't isolated from the audience; they would often sit in the front of the stage while Donahue roamed through the crowd with a microphone. Local viewers were encouraged to phone in, and, if they were lucky, they might be able to question the guest as well.

Donahue's approach caught on slowly at first, especially as his show was seen on only a few stations in the Midwest, but by the time he moved the program to Chicago in 1973, "The Phil Donahue Show" was becoming a broadcasting phenomenon. It was syndicated to 200 markets, where it usually was the number one program in its time slot. In addition to his Emmys and his lucrative syndication contract, Donahue also became a regular contributor to "The Today Show," which placed him in the unique position of working both independently and for a network at the same time. In the fall of 1982, he switched networks to host a special segment on ABC's late night program, "The Last Word," which remained on the air until April 1983.

The changes Phil Donahue brought to the talk show format had their most direct impact on local morning talk programs throughout the country, which, in order to stay competitive, were now forced to include special segments devoted to women's issues. On night time television, however, "The Phil Donahue Show" 's zest for controversy was not a completely original idea. Not only had ABC experimented with the topicality of "The Les Crane Show," but in the mid-1960s a syndicated late-night talk program from Los Angeles, "The Joe Pyne Show," had offered a volatile example of the rude approach to controversy that was then sweeping radio. Pyne was a combative, edgy host, who, to the shock and delight of his audience, insulted his bizarre assortment of guests whenever he disliked what they said (which was often). His feisty temperament and flair for bad manners was matched by another 1966 syndicated program, "The Alan Burke Show," which also specialized in the theater of indignity. Both shows lasted only a season.

On October 15, 1973, NBC began broadcasting from Los Angeles a late, late night talk show, from 1:00 to 2:00 A.M., which continued a southern California tradition of unorthodox guests and provocative topicality. "The Tomorrow Show" was hosted by Tom Snyder, an aggressive newscaster with a strong interest in whatever seemed off the beaten track. Snyder's style could be brusque, but his program was usually engagingly open and sympathetic to the variety of lifestyles it so eagerly explored. What was distinctive about "The Tomorrow Show" was its ability to successfully mix many of the elements of talk/entertainment programs (like "The Tonight Show") and talk/interview shows (like William F. Buckley's "Firing Line," which began syndication in 1971.) Tom Snyder's compelling presence and his masterful intimacy with the camera, a skill he had developed during his many years as a local news anchorman, made him a forceful interviewer as well as a colorful and lively personality in his own right. However, unlike Les Crane, whose hard-edged approach to controversy had proved strikingly unpopular with viewers in 1964, Snyder's intensity was at heart genial and ingratiating. "The Tomorrow Show" was not just a forum for provocative inquiry, but an entertaining talk show that reflected the affable curiosity of its host. The program remained on the air through January 1982.

During the late 1970s and early 1980s, the traditional talk/entertainment format went through a period of redirection and confusion. Syndicators eager to tap younger viewers launched a series of misbegotten new talk shows, most of which promptly failed. The immediate casualties included "The Toni Tenille Show" (which combined pop singing and awkward conversation on a futuristic stage) and "Everyday" (which featured a cast of eight unknown performer/hosts). Another new entry, "The John Davidson Show," limped along for two years until its cancellation in the spring of 1982. Facing declining audiences, even venerable talk shows such as "Dinah" and "The Mike Douglas Show" tried sprucing up their sets and revamping their approach (the former to include even more guest hosts; the latter to spend more time on the road), but neither rescue mission worked. "Dinah" closed in the spring of 1981; "Mike Douglas" ended its 16-year run in the spring of 1982. The only relative success to emerge from this period of intense talk show activity was a brightly packaged synthesis of local daytime talk features (recipes, medicine, household tips, exercise, and discussion) called "Hour Magazine," which began syndication by Group W in the fall of 1980.

The talk shows remaining on the air by 1982 were those that had proved their strength for many years. Survivors included the morning news/talk programs "Today" and its arch rival, ABC's "Good Morning America"; the still flourishing controversial conversation of "The Phil Donahue Show"; the comfortable Hollywood chatter of "The Merv Griffin Show"; and "The Tonight Show," which had begun to suffer in the ratings after its host, Carson, cut back to an hour in 1980.

An interesting exception in the company of these long running programs was NBC's replacement for its cancelled "Tomorrow Show," entitled "Late Night with David Letterman," which premiered on January 27, 1982. Letterman, whose sly charm and quick wit reminded many observers of a young Johnny Carson, had previously hosted his own notorious daytime talk show on NBC from June 23, 1980, to October 24, 1980. "The David Letterman Show," though well received by the critics, never did well in the ratings, probably because its "Saturday Night Live" satiric tone, its mixture of fake and real celebrity guests, and its carefree sense of mayhem were simply too radical a departure for the typical morning audience of homemakers. (In some ways, the show's anarchistic spirit resembled the 1979 Norman Lear syndicated comedy "Fernwood Tonight" [later called "America Tonight"], which was an entirely bogus talk show, complete with a cloddish announcer, self-centered host, polka-oriented orchestra, and an endless assortment of bizarre guests—with an occasional authentic star mixed in for fun.)

A little more than a year after his morning program failed, NBC decided to give Letterman the slot immediately after "The Tonight Show" realizing that 12:30 A.M. offered a better environment for his talents. His new show, "Late Night with David Letterman" was another playfully self-conscious reflection on the whole idea of talk/entertainment programming. While it used an announcer, it made fun of the tone of most introductions; its band offered a hip commentary on the show business theatrics of "The Tonight Show" orchestra; its set would often fall apart; and its host delighted in lampooning the concept of the self-assured master of ceremonies who can keep everything under control. The program's repeated send ups of talk show artifice, however, were also balanced by the fact that "Late Night" still honored the formula's primary conventions. David Letterman opened each show with a comic monologue; he took part in skits, he talked to his band leader, and he interviewed his guests from behind a desk. For all of its mocking tone and campy irony, "Late Night with David Letterman" was essentially an affectionate salute to the talk show, designed for a generation that had grown up with the genre. It is a testament to Pat Weaver's farsighted programming gifts that, 30 years after "Broadway Open House," the concept of structured conversation still retains its power as one of television's most flexible and durable forms.

THEMES AND ISSUES

Talk shows are the triumph of personality. They don't depend on plot or action; most of the time they don't even provide much in the way of specific content. What they do offer is the opportunity to bask in the atmosphere radiating from a congenial host. The quality of the atmosphere may vary from program to program, but the process is the same. For 60 or 90 minutes, viewers are lured and guided by the style of a central personality (whose name is usually featured in the show's title). Unlike fictional TV genres, the success of a talk show rests on the ability of its star to unify a variety of mostly unscripted segments by the sheer force of his or her "real life" character.

The personalities of TV talk show hosts shape the nature of their programs in a way no narrative-oriented format can observe. Their disposition determines the form; their reactions are the action. The drama of a talk show is in the spontaneous interplay of the star with the many elements of his or her program: how the host meets the audience; how he or she interacts with the company of regulars; and how he or she interacts with a wide range of show business colleagues, new celebrities, and eager authors. Since the talk show has so little actual plot, other than the movement from one segment to the next, hosts are not just a glue to bind things together. They are powerful magnets whose attraction lies in the heightened naturalness of their manner during the course of an hour or more of televised conversation.

Popular talk show hosts embody the traits of ease quick-wittedness and concern so often absent in everyday talk. Though the discussion on most programs rarely rises above a modest level of simple informational exchange, successful talk-masters use the distinctiveness of their own projected style to sustain interest. They represent a new type of realistic actor whose greatest challenge is to create an endlessly appealing and lively character out of themselves. Kenneth Tynan's remark about Johnny Carson applies equally well to his competitors: "There is no place in the other media for the gifts that distinguish him—most specifically, for the gift of reinventing himself, night after night, without rehearsal or repetition."[12]

The talk show host's presentation of self is circumscribed somewhat by the genre's curiously formal attitude of propriety, a custom first noted by Michael Arlen in his essay "Hosts and Guests." In contrast to the rest of America, where social rituals seem to be declining, Arlen observes that television has been eager "from its inception to present itself as a pageant of hospitality."[13] Talk shows, in particular, honor a sense of civility and occasion that is almost courtly. Hosts invariably are amiable agents for both viewers and guests. They introduce each day's participants with a flattering salute to their past achievements; they frequently greet guests with generous gestures of affection; and they politely listen to familiar litanies of self-promotion. No matter how various the temperament of a program's star, from the cuddly affability of Merv Griffin to the detached irony of David Letterman, every talk show offers an essentially polite forum for the gentle conduct of conversation. Hosts who long for durability have no choice but to comply with the agreeable disposition the form demands.

While the personality of the talk show host is a program's chief asset, the supporting cast also plays a valuable role. Beginning with "Broadway Open

House" in 1952, practically every major conversation show has used a company of sidekicks to bolster its star. Announcers such as Hugh Downs and Ed McMahon and band leaders like Skitch Henderson and Doc Severinsen, however, are more than just straightmen and foils for jokes. They comprise a mini-family whose parts are as clearly defined as the host's. Each night their job is to assume a persona complementary to the central performer. The narrow limits of their character give their interplay with the host the quality of an improvised situation comedy. Johnny Carson's jabs with Ed McMahon about his drinking and with Doc Severinsen about his taste in clothes serve the same purpose as Ralph Kramden's threats to his wife on "The Honeymooners" and Archie Bunker's altercations with his son-in-law on "All in the Family." They are entertaining rituals whose very predictability is part of their charm. Talk show sidekicks supply a stabilizing ensemble of personalities to anchor both host and viewers in the midst of the ever-changing parade of featured guests.

In the absence of the dynamic story elements of fictional formats, the talk show stresses the familiarity not only of its characters, but also of its structure. The genre's rigidity, in fact, helps contribute to its appeal. The standard unfolding of programs like "The Tonight Show" offers viewers a satisfying demonstration that form is just as important as content. The endlessly repeatable structure provides orientation as well as a sense of expectation. Conversation with the crew of regulars always follows the monologue; the big guest of the evening always arrives after about 15 minutes; authors always appear last. This predictable progression gives the illusion of dramatic action and movement to a format that is essentially static.

The talk show's durable scaffolding affords one other distinct advantage. Since the audience already knows how the broad pieces of the program's "plot" fit together, the textures of individual segments assume greater importance. Because of the daily repetition of sections such as the monologue and guest interviews, small variations in style become much more apparent. The regimented structure of the form encourages an awareness of the subtle shifts in mood from part to part and also from program to program. Is Merv Griffin more nervous in front of the studio than he is in front of the piano? Is Phil Donahue relaxed only when he is talking with the members of his audience? Is David Letterman sillier in tonight's opening segment than he was in last night's? As long-term viewers discover, skillful talk show performers often test the differing demands of each segment by continually adding new shadings to their delivery and responses. The two-decade popularity of Johnny Carson can be largely explained by Carson's talent for wittily altering the standard material he is expected to present night after night. After 30 years, audiences have grown so familiar with the genre's framework that one of the central attractions of the form now rests in the detection of performer nuance.

Of course, the talk show is more than just the contributions of the host and the subtleties of his or her performance style. It is also a forum for various kinds of conversations with various kinds of celebrities. Discussion subjects seldom vary from a standard routine of current projects and amusing anecdotes, but the ordinariness of the topics is precisely the point. Talk show guests are on the programs to reveal the qualities they share with the millions of viewers at home. They are not there to hide behind their movie or TV roles, but to invite the audience into their "real" lives. Not surprisingly, however, there is often little distinction between on- and off-screen personas. The actors and actresses who parade from show to show are as aware as their hosts are that casual conversation is as demanding a craft as a completely scripted affair, and they recognize that it is their obligation—and important to their careers—to put on a good show. What makes their appearance on talk programs so interesting is the degree to which they are willing to rely on their skills as performers to sustain their new roles as regular folk.

As a participant on a talk show, a celebrity must conform to a general environment of studied cheeriness. For the most part, guests are not invited in order to discuss serious problems or earth-shaking issues. Nor are they expected to wildly overentertain or hog the spotlight. Instead, their principal duty is to be interesting and grateful for the opportunity to appear. The attitude of propriety that Michael Arlen observed in talk show hosts applies also to guests, who, while they may be encouraged to be lively, know that they must never be discourteous.

The disruption caused by flagrant displays of bad manners and the fact that such incidents are deeply etched in viewers' memories testify to the strongly enforced codes of geniality and pleasantry most programs demand.[14] Celebrity guests are expected to engage in the kind of conversations one might overhear from the next table at a country club. As Jeff Greenfield notes, talk shows "act, in fact, as surrogate salons, providing a sense of communal exchange to people who live increasingly atomized lives"; the amiable chats with performers and authors are "designed to make the audience feel that the show is part of their neighborhood, part of their home environment, where interesting people come and talk about the daily events of their lives."[15] Through continued talk show appearances, celebrities become more than just familiar characters from stage, screen, and bookjackets. They become friends whose willingness to discuss openly the details of their ordinary activities gives the genre a close emotional rapport with its viewers.

Nevertheless, the procession of show business personalities that visit Johnny Carson or Merv Griffin, for instance, are not there simply to present themselves as gracious companions or vivid conversationalists. They invariably are in the process of selling their most recent profit-oriented efforts, and, as Gaye Tuchman observed during her backstage experiences with a network talk show, guests "view appearances as a form of advertising."[16] This commercial exchange is understood by everybody—staff producers, host, and audience—and it has become one of the standard features of the genre to acknowledge unabashedly the promotional mission that brought the celebrity to the program. While a few shows have tried to temper their free publicity aspects—"The Tomorrow Show" used to act as if the guest were there simply to chat and would not feature the appropriate book or record cover—other programs, such as "The Merv Griffin Show," have become press agent's dreams, frequently devoting their entire hour to celebrate a star's latest project, complete with adulatory coworkers, numerous excerpts, and a tirelessly congratulatory host.

The business of talk show selling can be tremendously important, especially to an industry like publishing that can't afford the enormous costs regular commercial advertising would entail. The easy chattiness of the talk show provides a perfect environment for certain kinds of authors to discuss certain kinds of books, and, if all goes well, there is an inevitable impact on sales. Producers for "The Phil Donahue Show" estimate that a single appearance of an author on their program will help sell anywhere from 10,000 to 50,000 copies of the book, which may explain why the show is besieged with more than 100 requests a week from publishers.[17] The contracts of nonfiction authors often require that they visit dozens of talk shows throughout the country to publicize their work, and their media itinerary is listed in *Publisher's Weekly* to alert book stores in the areas. Matters have gone so far that, according to *The Washington Post*, "Publishers now routinely screen their writers for mediability, coach them on TV techniques and offer producers video cassettes and audio of the results."[18]

By transforming conversation into a transaction partially founded on commerce, talk shows can be justifiably accused of corrupting the nature of spontaneous conversation. Guests are carefully prepared by staff producers to tell only their most interesting stories, and the host has been thoroughly briefed on what will be said and what questions should be asked. Some critics sense dire consequences. Harry Walters feels that "the peculiar characteristics of talk show babble could well be confusing household onlookers about what casual social conversation is all about. TV talk strains ceaselessly to be chirpily enthused, richly anecdotal and above all, entertaining. It teaches that conversation should rush along at a strong, scintillating pace"; and Arthur Asa Berger warns that "with their super rich diet of strong, assertive celebrities, talk shows are spreading the notion that to be ordinary is to be irrelevant. Without recognizing it, the silent, passive nobodies may be adapting these flashy individuals as role models."[19]

However, it is doubtful if viewers are quite so fooled as Walters and Berger believe. There is no question, certainly, that the talk show attempts to approximate some of the exterior conditions of ordinary conversation. Guests are seated in settings that range from vacation living rooms, to homey dens, to kitchens and libraries. Introductions and pleasantries are handled in much the same way as they would be at a party. The host's job is to make visitors comfortable by a warm embrace and an enthusiastic compliment on their appearance. But, like other television formats, the talk show has its own logic and principles. Though it may be more realistic on the surface than the situation comedy or melodrama, the artificiality of its structure and its formulaic qualities serve as precise dramatic boundaries. Audiences know that the talk show is not a voyeuristic experience— they are not slyly eavesdropping on privileged moments with their favorite stars.

Instead, they are witness to 60 or 90 minutes of jokes and chats calculated to entice pleasantly. The conversations that ensue are governed by the same standards of lively performance that operate in any other area of show business endeavor. To assume that viewers mistake the discussions on talk shows as a strong basis for their own behavior is to assume a similar process takes place in the presence of all commercial entertainment. The talk show's repetitive elements and highly contoured exchanges are constant reminders of the genre's heightened reordering of dialogue and social conduct. Audiences with even the most casual acquaintance with the form can recognize the terms of its mediated environment (e.g., the list of prepared questions in front of every host) and how carefully celebrity conversations are crafted to enhance the commercial elements of on-screen personality.

The talk show's distinctiveness rests on its ability to straddle the breezy spontaneity of an impromptu conversation with the more settled demands of a structured performance. Though the talk show may appear the loosest of genres— after all, it has no specific conflict to develop or story to tell—it does observe a clear progression of situations and segments viewers have come to expect and to which they look forward. The predictability of these features, like the standard attributes of any genre, can become tiresome; but in the hands of a gifted host, the fixed elements can be made continually new through minute variations in approach and manner.

Nevertheless, talk shows generally try to offer the feeling of the unplanned, even if the flow of discussion is judiciously regulated by attentive offstage producers.[20] In between the prearranged questions and the artfully conceived responses there lurk moments where both host and guest let their guard down to reveal protected sides of themselves. Occasionally, the full force of untrammeled reality manages to break through. When this happens (such as the egg fight between Johnny Carson and Dom DeLuise or the evening in the late 1960s when Abby Hoffman wore a shirt made from the American flag on "The Merv Griffin Show" and his entire body was blacked out by the censors) these incidents of abandon become instantly notorious; in the case of "The Tonight Show," they are hauled out once a year in a prime-time special commemorating great accidents of the past.

Still the rarity with which the truly unexpected occurs affirms just how predictable is the course most talk shows willingly follow. Pleasurable familiarity is the key to the form's success and the source of its durability. For 30 years, the talk show has turned casual conversation into an endlessly agreeable and repeatable experience. Without the aid of dramatic conflict or progressive action, this created-for-TV genre has won a large following attracted by the reliability of its formula and the sustained personality emphasis of its orientation.

NOTES

1. Robert Metz, *The Tonight Show* (New York: Summit Books, 1980), p. 34.
2. Ibid., p. 136.

3. Ibid., p. 137.

4. Ibid., p. 211.

5. Gaye Tuchman, "Assembling a Network Talk Show" in *The TV Establishment*, ed. Gaye Tuchman (Englewood Cliffs, N.J: Prentice-Hall, 1975), pp. 123–24.

6. Kenneth Tynan, *Show People* (New York: Simon and Schuster, 1979), p. 135.

7. Ibid., pp. 129–32.

8. Metz, *The Tonight Show*, p. 217.

9. Stanley Frank, "Competition Comes to Carson's Corner," *TV Guide*, October 30, 1965, p. 7.

10. Dick Cavett, *Cavett* (New York: Harcourt, Brace, 1974), pp. 317–18.

11. Phil Donahue, *My Own Story* (New York: Simon and Schuster, 1979), p. 70.

12. Tynan, *Show People*, p. 188.

13. Michael Arlen, *The Camera Age* (New York: Farrar, Straus, Giroux, 1981), p. 310.

14. Tynan, *Show People*, p. 143.

15. Jeff Greenfield, *Television, the First 25 Years* (New York: Harry Abrams, 1977), p. 76.

16. Tuchman, "Assembling a Network Talk Show," p. 125.

17. Curt Suplee, "Selling the Write Show," *Washington Post*, April 28, 1982, p. B-13.

18. Ibid.

19. *Newsweek*, October 29, 1979, p. 78.

20. Tynan, *Show People*, p. 129.

BIBLIOGRAPHICAL SURVEY

The talk show genre is a largely unexamined area, possibly because it does not fit the classical categories inherited from previous media. The books that have appeared on the subject deal mainly with the personalities of talk show hosts. The two most thoroughly researched works are by Robert Metz, *The Today Show* and *The Tonight Show*. Though hardly scholarly in approach, they are informative histories of these two pioneering talk shows, filled with interesting anecdotes and some occasionally penetrating observations about the success of individual formats. Both books are attuned to the importance of personality, especially that of the hosts, in shaping the flavor of each day's program.

The only other books on the field are autobiographies of talk show hosts, some written with collaborators. *Cavett* is a lively and witty look at Dick Cavett's career, told, as is to be expected, with a great deal of flair and containing some incisive views of talk show mechanics and talk show evolution, from Jack Paar to Dick Cavett. Merv Griffin's autobiography, *Merv*, is more straightforward than *Cavett* and a little more show-business oriented; that is, it is overloaded with inside glimpses of Judy Garland, Marilyn Monroe, and Montgomery Clift. Still, *Merv* does a good job of showing the pressures of talk show production; Griffin's recounting of how he was pitted by CBS against Johnny Carson is a fascinating look at the high economic stakes involved in this low budget entertainment form. *Mike Douglas: My Story* is a standard entertainment autobiography, with the usual assortment of pieties, upbeat profiles, and gossip and with very little concrete information on talk show practices. Finally, there is *Donahue: My Own Story*, which, in keeping with Donahue's style, is a relentlessly sober inquiry into the failed marriage, lapsed Catholicism, and personal torment of Phil Donahue. But despite its strained seriousness, *Donahue* does provide an interesting account of how "The Phil Donahue Show" began and what elements its host feels were essential to its astounding success.

Though Johnny Carson has yet to write an autobiography, his career has been explored in dozens of articles (see Metz, *The Tonight Show* for an extensive list) and in a gushy biography by Douglas Covence. The most impressive inquiry into the Carson mystique is an extended profile by Kenneth Tynan in his book *Show People*. Clearly fascinated by the personality of the man he views as the quintessence of American television, Tynan offers an intriguing portrait of how "The Tonight Show" operates and how difficult it is to come to terms with the enigmatic nature of its host. Even in his long interview with Timothy White in *Rolling Stone*, Carson remains strangely elusive.

Carson's contributions as a master of audience complicity and the supreme exemplar of television talk are discussed in an interesting chapter on the talk show in Peter Conrad's *Television: The Medium and Its Manners*. In contrast to other hosts, Johnny Carson is viewed as the only person on television who "derives a special power from his witty acceptance of the medium's alienation effects" (page 61). "The Tonight Show," according to Conrad, is an almost Brechtian exercise in shattering viewer illusions and pointing out the comic artificiality of simulated conversational environments. Interestingly enough, Lewis Grossberger makes the same claims for the man many people feel will be Carson's eventual successor, David Letterman, in a 1982 article in *Rolling Stone*. As Grossberger observes, the talk show in David Letterman's hands has been re-shaped into a format often approaching a giddy sense of absurdity, as every convention in the by now 30-year-old genre is held up to gentle ridicule. Letterman is also the subject of a more conventional background profile by Peter W. Kaplan in *Esquire*.

The nature of the talk show experience, both for guests and for viewers, is examined in two stimulating articles in *Celebrity*, an anthology edited by James Monaco. Peter Schrag, who has appeared on many talk shows, discusses the disposable content and essential "emptiness" of the form in "Heeere's Johnny!" Saul Braun's "Until Joey Bishop, Merv Griffin, and Johnny Carson Do Us Part" is a stream of consciousness memoir of a month spent watching late-night talk shows, which provides a vivid glimpse of the alarming celebrity-oriented universe created by the genre's insatiable need for personable conversation.

TV Guide has published numerous articles on talk show personalities, styles, and formats. A complete listing through 1979 can be found in *TV Guide 25 Year Index*. Among the more useful articles are "Competition Comes to Carson's Corner" by Stanley Frank, "Talk Shows—The Party in Your Living Room" by Harold Clemenko, "The Talk Show—An Endangered Species" by Dwight

Whitney, "Revamping Talk Shows" by Ron Townley, "Late Night Host David Letterman" by Mark Ribowsky, and "Coaches Who Teach How To Be Effective on TV" by Ellen Torgerson Shaw. Other magazine articles featuring informative looks at talk show practices include Harry F. Walter's cover story on Phil Donahue in *Newsweek* and Richard Corliss's ruminations on the world of daytime talk shows in *Film Comment*.

The May/June 1983 issue of *Channels* offers a special section devoted to the talk show. William A. Henry, III's "From the Dawn of Gab" provides a brief history of the genre, concluding with several sharp ruminations on the meaning of television fame and celebrity. Ross Wetzsteon's "Psychochatter" looks at the current trend toward franker sexual conversation on many new talk shows. In Stephen Fenichell's "Talk about Talk: The View from the Sofa," seven authors describe their uneasy experiences selling themselves on a variety of conversation programs.

For an inside view of the mechanics of talk show production Gaye Tuchman's "Assembling a Network Talk Show" is highly recommended. The author, who spent four months behind the scenes of an unidentified talk show, exposes some of the pressures and demands to which producers of the format are routinely subject. Written from a sociology of culture perspective, the article offers provocative insights into how guests are selected, how they are prepared, and what is expected of them in talk show performance.

Finally, there is Michael Arlen's intriguing essay on the nature and function of the talk show, "Hosts and Guests," from his collection of *New Yorker* TV reviews, *The Camera Age*. Though he resembles Peter Conrad in his belief that the talk show is an intricate metaphor for contemporary popular culture, Arlen is not so scathing in his condemnation of the form's commercial premises. Instead, he feels the genre is the last refuge of courtesy and polite ritual in a society that, in its regular activities, seems to have little taste for either.

BOOKS AND ARTICLES

Arlen, Michael. "Hosts and Guests." In *The Camera Age*. New York: Farrar, Straus, Giroux, 1981.

Braun, Saul. "Until Joey Bishop, Merv Griffin, and Johnny Carson Do Us Part." In *Celebrity*, ed. James Monaco. New York: Delta Books, 1978.

Clemenko, Harold. "Talk Shows—the Party in Your Living Room." *TV Guide*, March 20, 1976.

Conrad, Peter. *Television: The Medium and Its Manners*. Boston: Routledge and Kegan Paul, 1982.

Corliss, Richard. "The Talk of Our Town." *Film Comment*, January/February 1981.

Covence, Douglas. *Johnny Carson*. New York: Drake, 1975.

Donahue, Phil. *Donahue: My Own Story*. New York: Simon and Schuster, 1979.

Douglas, Mike. *Mike Douglas: My Story*. New York: Putnam, 1978.

Fenichell, Stephen. "Talk about Talk: The View from the Sofa." *Channels*, May/June 1983.

Frank, Stanley. "Competition Comes to Carson's Corner." *TV Guide*, October 30, 1965.

Griffin, Merv, with Peter Biandosti. *Merv*. New York: Simon and Schuster, 1980.

Grossberger, Lewis. "David Letterman." *Rolling Stone*, June 10, 1982.

Henry, William A., III. "From the Dawn of Gab." *Channels*, May/June 1983.

Kaplan, Peter W. "David Letterman: Vice-President of Comedy." *Esquire*, December 1981.

Metz, Robert. *The Today Show*. Chicago: Playboy Press, 1978.

———. *The Tonight Show*. New York: Summit Books, 1980.

Ribowsky, Mark. "Late Night Host David Letterman." *TV Guide*, October 2, 1982.

Shrag, Peter. "Heeere's Johnny." In *Celebrity*, ed. James Monaco. New York: Delta Books, 1978.

Shaw, Ellen Torgerson. "Coaches Who Teach How to Be Effective on TV." *TV Guide*, October 2, 1982.

Townley, Ron. "Revamping Talk Shows." *TV Guide*, July 5, 1980.

Tuchman, Gaye, "Assembling a Network Talk Show." In *The TV Establishmen: Programming for Profit and Power*. Englewood Cliffs, N.J.: Prentice-Hall, 1974.

TV Guide 25 Year Index. Radnor, Pa.: Triangle Publications, 1979.

Tynan, Kenneth. *Show People*. New York: Simon and Schuster, 1979.

Walters, Harry. "Phil Donahue." *Newsweek*, October 29, 1979.

Wetzsteon, Ross. "Psychochatter." *Channels*, May/June 1983.

White, Timothy. "The Rolling Stone Interview: Johnny Carson." *Rolling Stone*, March 29, 1979.

Whitney, Dwight. "The Talk Show—An Endangered Species." *TV Guide*, July 30, 1977.

VIDEOGRAPHY

"Broadway Open House"
NBC, 11:00 P.M.–12:00 P.M.
Premiere: May 29, 1950
Host: Jerry Lester
Last Program: August 24, 1951

"The Steve Allen Show"
WNBC-TV, 11:15 P.M.–1:00 A.M.
Premiere: August 27, 1951
Host: Steve Allen
Last Program: September 24, 1954

"Today"
NBC, 7:00–9:00 A.M.
Premiere: January 4, 1952
Hosts: David Garroway, January 14, 1952–June 16, 1961
John Chancellor, July 7, 1961–September 7, 1962
Hugh Downs, September 10, 1962–October 11, 1971
Frank McGee, October 11, 1971–April 10, 1974
Barbara Walters (co-host), April 22, 1974–June 4, 1976
Jim Hartz (co-host), July 29, 1974–August 30, 1976
Tom Brokaw, August 30, 1976–December 18, 1981

Jane Pauley (co-host), November 11, 1976–
Chris Wallace (co-host), January 4, 1982–September 24, 1982
Bryant Gumble (co-host), January 4, 1982–

"Person to Person"
CBS, various prime times
Premiere: October 2, 1953
Host: Edward R. Murrow
Last Program: September 1, 1961

"The Home Show"
NBC, various morning hours
Premiere: March 1, 1954
Host: Arlene Francis
Last Program: August 9, 1957

"Tonight!"
NBC, 11:30 P.M.–1:00 A.M.
Premiere: September 27, 1954
Host: Steve Allen
Last Program: January 25, 1957

"Tonight: America after Dark"
NBC, 11:30 P.M.–1:00 A.M.
Premiere: January 28, 1957
Host: Jack Lescoulie (January–June)
Al Collins (June–July)
Last Program: July 26, 1957

"The Tonight Show"
NBC, 11:30 P.M.–1:00 A.M.
Premiere: July 29, 1957
Host: Jack Paar (July 29, 1957–March 20, 1962)
Johnny Carson (October 1, 1962)

"Open End"
WNEW-TV, New York—began syndication a year later, various late-night times
Premiere: October 14, 1958
Host: David Susskind (retitled "The David Susskind Show" 1967)

"The Les Crane Show"
ABC, 11:30 P.M.–1:00 A.M.
Premiere: November 9, 1964
Host: Les Crane
Last Program: November 12, 1965

"The Mike Douglas Show"
Syndicated by Westinghouse Group W, various afternoon and morning times
Premiere: September 1965
Host: Mike Douglas
Last Program: Spring 1981

"The Merv Griffin Show"
Syndicated by Westinghouse Group W, various day and evening times
Premiere: September 1965

Host: Merv Griffin
Last Program: Spring 1969

"Firing Line"
WOR-TV, New York, which offered it in syndication (moved to PBS in May, 1971)
Premiere: April 4, 1966
Host: William F. Buckley

"The Joey Bishop Show"
ABC, 11:30 P.M.–1:00 A.M.
Premiere: April 17, 1967
Host: Joey Bishop
Last Program: December 26, 1969

"The Phil Donahue Show"
Syndicated by Multimedia, various morning and afternoon times
Premiere: November 6, 1967
Host: Phil Donahue

"The Merv Griffin Show"
CBS, 11:30 P.M.–1:00 A.M.
Premiere: August 18, 1969
Host: Merv Griffin
Last Program: February 11, 1972

"The Dick Cavett Show"
ABC, 11:30 P.M.–1:00 A.M.
Premiere: December 1969
Host: Dick Cavett
Last Program: December 29, 1972 (as a five-day-a-week program) January 1, 1975
(as an erratically scheduled program)

"The Tomorrow Show"
NBC, 1:00–2:00 A.M.
Premiere: October 15, 1973
Host: Tom Snyder
Last Program: January 24, 1982

"Dinah"
Syndicated by 20th Century Fox, various morning and afternoon times
Premiere: Fall 1974
Host: Dinah Shore
Last Program: Spring 1981

"Good Morning America"
ABC, 7:00–9:00 A.M.
Premiere: January 6, 1975
Host: David Hartman

"The David Letterman Show"
NBC, 10:00–11:00 A.M.
Premiere: June 23, 1980
Host: David Letterman
Last Program: October 24, 1980

"Late Night with David Letterman"
    NBC, 12:30–1:30 A.M.
    Premiere: January 27, 1982
    Host: David Letterman

17

Children's Programming

KAREN STODDARD

OVERVIEW

Perhaps no other television genre, with the exception of news, has generated as much controversy throughout the history of television as has children's programming. The first generation of children to grow up with television as a constant presence within their environment also happened to be the post-World War II, Benjamin Spock-reared generation, whose parents were socialized to be psychologically correct in their pursuit of well-adjusted offspring. The degree of attention lavished on child-raising in the 1950s meant that any element touching the lives of these children would automatically come under close scrutiny by any number of diverse sources (including psychologists, educators, physicians, and parents), with a resulting array of theories and opinions. Children's television programming, then, is an intriguing blend of entertainment, ideology, and old-fashioned concern for the bottom line that can easily ignite emotionally charged arguments to this day, as the baby-boom generation now struggles to raise its own children.

HISTORICAL DEVELOPMENT

The overwhelming majority of television licensees in the United States developed as network affiliates; consequently, few TV genres developed at other than the network level. Children's programming (along with news and current events/talk shows) marks an exception to this generalization. From the 1940s, local stations filled early morning and late afternoon time slots with locally produced shows that served as lead-ins and lead-outs to network offerings. Indeed, both local and network programmers relegated children's programs to time slots traditionally low in viewership and, consequently, low in revenues; children's programming through the mid-1960s lacked a significant degree of creativity and priority exactly because it was thought to be difficult to make large amounts of money from unemployed children through advertising. All of that, of course, would change.

Most people now in their 30s have fond memories of a local show that they watched religiously during their childhood. The names changed from city to city, but the format was comfortingly consistent. Each show had a host and a scenario—jungle outpost, circus tent, sailboat, monster's castle, mad scientist's laboratory—that set the tone for the filmed portion of the show, usually consisting of cartoons, originally released in movie theatres during the 1930s and 1940s, or thematic movies or serials such as *Flash Gordon, Tarzan,* and countless Westerns. Very often the shows incorporated a studio audience composed of the under-ten crowd or displayed drawings sent in by faithful viewers (becoming, in essence, the video equivalent to mom's refrigerator door). Few affiliates place much emphasis on these shows today; they have discovered (like the networks) that adult audiences can be lured to tune in during time periods formerly written off as fringe. This type of hosted show, however, is still alive on many independent outlets, stations which do not have to worry about delivering adult viewers to the highly profitable local news shows.

The history of network development of children's programming is a checkerboarded story, marked more often by concern for profits than concern for quality. Jeff Greenfield points out that children's programs could rather neatly be divided into two distinct types, "the frenetic, New York show business-based tradition, and the softer, more relaxed, low-pressure approach," two categories that would remain rather consistent over the years.[1] Ironically, even though Nielsen statistics point out that children are the heaviest viewers of television, the networks have traditionally downplayed the amount of programming directed to that audience. When "Captain Kangaroo" was unceremoniously dropped by CBS to make room for early morning news, network television lost the "only network children's show broadcast on a daily basis."[2]

Focusing on a belief (supported by sound evidence) that children have extremely short attention spans, the networks have relied on a consistent dosage of intense, action-packed shows and cartoons to rivet children to the screen. It took the arrival of Fred Silveman at CBS in the mid-1960s to recognize and mine the potential profits waiting for the network in children's programming; whether one sees this as visionary or exploitative is a matter of personal perspective. As Greenfield points out, this audience of people under the age of ten could be isolated rather easily by time and day of the week, so that Saturday morning became a time when the networks could guarantee the advertisers an audience of children, largely unsupervised by their sleeping parents, to receive their assorted sales pitches.

Fringe time periods have not been the only area in which networks were conscious of a young audience. Indeed, early prime time on every night of the week will always deliver a sizeable portion of young viewers. Traditionally, networks provided situation comedies and adventure stories that appealed to the entire family before 9:00 P.M., though the tone of this time period has taken a strong move in the direction of more sophisticated (i.e., with more sexual and violent content) programs during the 1970s. In the mid-1970s, the networks did pioneer a new format for older children in the form of after-school specials, occasional dramatizations exploring issues related to growing up and aimed at the pre-adolescent and early teenage groups. Though a step in the right direction, the inconsistent scheduling of these programs make them a good idea without a permanent time slot, and consequently they have received no permanent commitment from the networks.

By the end of the 1970s, even the federal government (which is traditionally reluctant to exercise a heavy hand in programming matters for fear of accusations of censorship) saw little hope for the commercial networks as a source of viable children's programming. Recognizing that the commercial nature of network programming in the United States effectively precludes any substantial change in current network attitudes toward children's programming, the FCC points to cable TV as the only potential source of new formats for juvenile television viewing (in addition, of course, to current public broadcasting presentaitons).

Perhaps the single greatest force that prompted such minute examination of commercial offerings for children during the 1970s was the unabashedly successful programs developed and aired by PBS. Proving that children's programs could be both educational and entertaining, shows such as "Sesame Street," "The Electric Company," and "Mr. Rogers' Neighborhood" prospered while commercial network shows such as "Captain Kangaroo" struggled to maintain their very existence. Arguably, none of these shows differ dramatically in format from the two programming formats for children developed by network TV; they do, however, exist within a corporate structure that relies neither on ratings nor advertising revenues as priority items in determining program development or evolution.

The late 1970s and early 1980s have also witnessed the beginnings of cable television offerings, led by Warner Communication's Nickelodeon channel, a satellite-delivered service featuring 14 continuous hours of children's TV per day. The public's demonstrated hunger for these alternatives to network children's fare is, perhaps, the most damning commentary on the sad state of commercial children's programming today.

ISSUES

It is difficult to walk a rational path through the volumes of research that have been compiled over the past 35 years regarding children and television. For every study condemning TV as a source of grave social ills such as lower literacy rates and lack of imaginative play patterns among children, one can find equally convincing studies touting television as an ideal adjunct to modern teaching and a source for rapid, common, and standarized socialization. Obviously, the truth must lie at some point in between.

Television networks would like parents to believe that television has no power to affect children; common sense and the networks prove this stance to be decidedly narrow. Indeed, commercial television exists because of the medium's unique capacity to inform consumers of new products and to encourage their ultimate purchase. The networks cannot truly believe that this informative/persuasive process clicks on only during commercials and off during the programs. On the other hand, it is equally difficult to give credibility to anti-TV forces that are all too eager to blame the medium for creating a situation in which Johnny may not be able to read but *can* emulate violent and promiscuous behavior at a moment's notice. Again, common sense and rationality tell a careful observer that television is only one force (though one of considerable magnitude) within a huge and complex society that might affect behavioral patterns on the part of viewers. What we end up with, then, is a position in which television cannot be blamed as a sole variable in measuring social response to it, but neither can television (a powerful and pervasive medium) be regarded as a neutral or ambivalent force within American society.

Concern about television in relationship to young viewers can be discussed within three broad areas, specifically programming content, psychological/developmental effects of viewing, and the appropriateness of directing advertising messages to children. The three areas interact with each other in many ways.

Television has long been considered suspicious because of the immense amounts of time children spend watching it. Nielsen reports that the average American TV household has the set turned on almost seven hours each day; households with preschool children, however, average even more. Many people, seeing that this totals more hours than children spend in school or at church during the week, are concerned that television has replaced these traditional sources of socialization. This may well be true, but whether it is a positive or negative situation necessitates a value judgment. Random viewing of television shows not necessarily designed for them can, indeed, expose children to ideas and images that may not be considered age-appropriate. Careful parental monitoring, however, can minimize this particular problem, though parents have a legitimate complaint in the dearth of shows they feel are appropriate to young children's entertainment and developmental needs.

Some critics take television to task as a killer of creative fantasy play and as an instigator and reinforcer of an artificial and phoney world in which most problems are presented and solved within 30 or 60 minutes; most people are white and middle-class; and regional variations in speech, dress, and attitude are pureed in a blender that produces a "TV American" who does not, nor ever could, exist. On these points, it is difficult not to appreciate the almost impossible task the networks have set out for themselves; namely, to entertain a vast number of people at any given time with material that is recognizable and acceptable to the audience. It is little wonder that television formats are so repetitive and the temptation to the networks so great to avoid tampering with success. Even in conceding the networks' difficulties, however, it must also be noted that the situation is one of the networks' own design and construction. Their emphasis is necessarily on what will deliver audiences to the advertisers. It is no stretch of facetiousness to argue that the networks approach programming as a series of commercials interrupted by programs.

TV, then, does create a world that is mythic but which appears disarmingly similar to reality. It is easy to suspend reality and recognize fantasy in a show such as "Battleship Galactica"; the lines are not so clearly drawn in "Leave It to Beaver," "The Brady Bunch" or "The Facts of Life." Certainly adults have the ability to discern the differences; the problem for children is a decided lack of perspective and experience, through no fault of their own, against which to measure the images that confront them.

Consider, for example, the syndication of off-network shows that constitutes such a large portion of local station schedules and an increasingly larger percentage of cable offerings. Children of the 1980s are being exposed to shows produced in four very different and distinct decades, shows appropriate for their eras but less so in the here and now. A show such as "I Love Lucy" contains a great number of messages, both blatant and implied, about the role of women in American society. In each episode Lucy has created chaos by trying to get out of her housewife role but is safely returned to the comfort of that role by the end of the show. This message was culturally appropriate to the era in which the series was produced and aired; it is anachronistic today. Adults can watch "I Love Lucy" and appreciate the slapstick comedy while disregarding the outdated social messages; children are unable to filter out this message and soak in all ideas with equal enthusiasm. Ironically, many parents permit and encourage the viewing of these early shows as alternatives to current network fare without pausing to consider that even "Father Knows Best" can have a negative aspect to it.

Perhaps the greatest area of controversy regarding programming concerns the presence of violence, and this concern extends not only to prime time but to cartoons specifically produced for children.

Doctors George Gerbner and Larry Gross of the Annenberg School of Communications at the University of Pennsylvania have, since 1967, issued an annual report titled the "Violence Index," a scale that measures the incidences of violence to which audiences have been exposed through network television viewing for the previous year. A conclusion of this research has consistently been that television cartoons, on a minute-by-minute basis, are six times more violent than the average adult prime-time drama.[3]

In 1972, a special commission directly concerned with the effects of televised violence on children was convened under the auspices of the Surgeon General's office and the National Institute of Mental Health. Controversy surrounded the commission from the beginning, with the selection of an evaluative committee to examine and interpret the research findings. Unfortunately, the commercial TV networks were allowed to exercise veto power over the appointments to the evaluating committee, resulting in a membership heavily weighted toward the bias of commercial TV vendors.[4] The report prepared by this committee stood in stark contrast to the actual research findings. The published report, written by the committee rather than the scientists who had conducted the research, gave the definite impression that the findings linking televised violence with potentially harmful effects on children had been inconclusive. When polled in the aftermath of the report's publication, the researchers involved (regardless of their own personal work or contribution to the study) reflected a far different story: 70 percent felt that viewing TV violence increased aggressiveness; none felt there was no effect; and 30 percent were unwilling to commit themselves.[5] If nothing else, the greater message of this controversy was the discomforting ease with which the commercial TV interests were able to insinuate themselves into the research and reporting process and the alarming coziness of the relationship between the networks and the government sworn to regulate them in the interest of the public good. The power of the networks proved to be more powerful than the power of the government-sponsored committee.

Some attempts were made to respond to groups unsilenced and unconvinced by the blandness and neutrality of the Surgeon General's report. The 1970s became a decade of intensive lobbying by groups concerned with television programming content. The networks launched the ill-fated Family Hour as an industry code change in 1975. It was intended to banish inappropriate sexual and violent content from prime-time shows aired before 9:00 P.M. Meant to be self-regulatory, the Family Hour concept was challenged in the courts as a violation of First Amendment guarantees of freedom of speech and overturned by the courts in the fall of 1976.

The National Association of Broadcasters (NAB), a self-regulatory agency (much like the Hays Office in the early days of commercial movie production), attempted to make significant code changes for its member stations, which included 60 percent of all licensees. These changes, which included the reduction of advertising time allowed on children's programming and the prohibition of product promotion by hosts of children's TV shows, were at least an attempt to curtail the flagrant exploitation of children. However, the current government-backed crush toward deregulation has all but dismantled the need for a self-regulating entity such as the NAB, leaving it largely ineffectual in terms of any programming prohibitions.

The concern over the effects of televised violence on children is not just oriented to a fear that children will become more aggressive as a result of viewing. Equally bothersome is Gerbner's research that indicates that heavy viewers of television (which he defines as those who watch four or more hours per day) often display unrealistic perceptions of the world, heavily influenced by television's unique version of society. Gerbner and Gross have also raised the grim possibility that children might well feel victimized and frightened as a result of viewing televised violence and consequently believe that the world is a far more scary place and their place in it more precarious than is actually true.[6]

Why does violence even exist on television programming aimed at children?

Children are not very different from adults in their attention to excitement and action and to an orientation to television as a source of entertainment. Consequently, it is far easier to attract and hold the easily wandering attention of a child with action-packed programming than with programs that require a more sophisticated level of understanding and synthesis on the part of the audience. Just as comic books, however, hopefully do not provide the sum total of a child's reading experience, so too does television need to be somewhat more diverse in its offerings to children's developing minds. A constant diet of repetitious formats can only lead, ultimately, to mental malnourishment.

Concern over advertising directed toward children has been growing during the past ten years. How appropriate is it to attempt to sell something to an individual who has neither disposable income nor well-developed consumer awareness or judgment? A Federal Trade Commission report, issued in 1978, recommended that legal action be taken to ban all television advertising of any product directed to very young children, ban advertising directed to older children of heavily sugared products that pose a dental health hazard, and require that advertisements directed to older children of other sugared products be balanced by nutritional spots paid for by the manufacturers of sugared products.[7]

Supported by Action for Children's Television (ACT), a national advocate of the placing of children's TV into the realm of noncommercially sponsored public service programming, the FTC and FCC promoted the idea in the late 1970s that children's programming demanded separate attention because of the age and impressionableness of the viewers. An FCC report issued in October of 1979 chastised the networks for their failure to improve children's programming and recommended that the government insist on specific, minimal levels of children's programming on commercial licensees, while also encouraging PBS and cable systems to fill the commercial void.

Just as government pressure was rising for the networks to redress old wrongs, however, the Reagan administration's philosophy of deregulation put an effective halt to the momentum reached before 1980. Under the stewardship of Reagan-appointed FCC Chairman Mark Fowler, the situation has gone from bad to worse. Since 1980, the FCC was exercising a complete hands-off policy in regard to children's TV issues with the to-be-expected dismal results. In an article in *Newsweek*, published in the fall of 1983, critic Harry F. Waters said, "Bluntly stated, American kidvid is a national disgrace. . . . From almost his first day on the job, Fowler sent out a clear message: the quantity and quality of children's TV should be decided by marketplace forces rather than by government pressure."[8] What happened when commercial priorities were allowed to take precedence over other considerations regarding children's television? As Waters pointed out, the results included the abrupt cancellation of shows that held some promise of relief from the standard fare (such as ABC's "Kids Are People Too," NBC's "Project Peacock," and CBS's "30 Minutes") and deluged the audience with shows described by Waters as "little more than 30-minute commercials for games, toys and . . . prime-time series."[9] Citing this as a form of child abuse,

Waters pointed out that the United States "remains the only nation that doesn't officially recognize children as a unique television audience" and provide appropriate guidelines in recognition of that uniqueness.[10]

Within a television system primarily oriented to commercial gain and profit, it is probably unrealistic to anticipate that much will change to broaden the scope of children's programming. In a system that relies on advertisers to support program costs and generate revenues, the very problems already discussed are sure to continue. The dilemma prior to the growth of cable TV was that people who were dissatisfied with network offerings for children had no alternative outlet. Even cable TV offers only a partial solution. The very cost of basic cable service, as well as additional monthly fees for premium channels, potentially excludes the poor from the diversity of children's programming cable has the capacity to deliver. Consequently, station licensees utilizing public airwaves still have responsibility to the viewing public to reexamine their approach to children's TV fare.

The issues pertaining to children's TV have never been clear-cut or easily solved. Television is only one difficult-to-measure factor to which children are exposed as part of their developmental process, but it is a significantly large one. The issue is not even that current children's offerings are wrong or evil, but rather that there seems to be no room for diversity in the network schedules, no allowance for the ability to attempt different formats that might co-exist with the more standard shows. This is not a problem unique to children's TV, but rather a problem that exists for all network TV and all viewer age groups. It may also be the single greatest reason why viewers, when given the opportunity, are switching their allegiances to cable offerings and changing the picture of TV use in the United States.

NOTES

1. Jeff Greenfield, *Television: The First Fifty Years* (New York: Harry N. Abrams, 1977), p. 254.

2. Ibid., p. 255.

3. Evelyn Kaye, *The ACT Guide to Children's Television* (Boston: Beacon Press, 1979), pp. 79–80.

4. H. J. Eysenck and D. K. B. Nias, *Sex, Violence and the Media* (New York: Harper Colophon Books, 1978), pp. 82–83.

5. Ibid., p. 86.

6. Ibid., p. 61.

7. *FTC Report on Television Advertising to Children* (Washington, D.C.: U.S. Government Printing Office, 1978).

8. Harry F. Waters, "KidVid: A National Disgrace," *Newsweek*, October 17, 1983, p. 82.

9. Ibid.

10. Ibid., p. 83.

BIBLIOGRAPHICAL SURVEY

The intensity and diversity of controversies that swirl around children's television programming is perhaps best defined by the large numbers of categories of material in print regarding the subject. The critical analysis of children's programming and its possible effects is an emotionally charged forum where objectivity often takes a back seat to subjective value judgments supported by questionable research results. The issues surrounding children's TV have the power to turn staunch supporters of First Amendment rights of freedom of speech into at least partial proponents of selective censorship of programming directed to the under-ten population.

Books such as Marie Winn's *The Plug-In Drug* (Bantam Books, 1977) imply that television viewing as a process is of greater concern than television programming, that television viewing is an addictive pastime that threatens to damage children's perceptual abilities and overall personality development. Books of this type were popular in the late 1970s, servicing a now-adult baby-boom generation attempting to cope with parental responsibilities.

Perhaps the most helpful book to emerge in the late 1970s was Evelyn Kaye's *The ACT Guide to Children's Television*. Kaye's approach is to provide information to adults and to encourage informed choices regarding television's proper place in each home. Of course there is a recognizable bias present in Kaye's work; the underlying presumption of the book is that television viewing should be monitored and controlled by parents. What is missing, fortunately, is the undercurrent of hysteria so often found in other books aimed at parents. Kaye allows a no-nonsense, informed, and realistic attitude to prevail. Kaye's attitude is, quite naturally, akin to that of Action for Children's Television, an attitude that strives toward finding some kind of middle ground in dealing with the commercial networks and stations. Kaye's book is a highly readable resource guide that attempts to explore both problems and possible solutions to making peace with television in everyday life. This work is not scholarly, but then neither is the audience it is attempting to reach; the book is well documented and contains a helpful bibliography of resource materials.

The books and articles given here cover a number of prime areas of consideration relating to children's television programming, including research on perceptual processes, sex-role learning, corporate ethical responsibility for program content, effects of sexual and violent program content, and alternative uses of television. The works are scholarly and, for the most part, oriented to reporting results of research studies into various issues and viewing phenomena. Several citations represent articles written for a more general audience, attempting to provide a flavor of the multitude of work that exists within the field.

Of all that has been written and researched regarding children and television, perhaps the one truth that emerges most dramatically is the importance of the unknown variable of the individual response, which is difficult to measure and almost impossible to accurately predict. American television does not operate in a vacuum; home environment, innate intellectual ability, family economics and a dozen other demographic factors influence the impact of television. When viewed within this perspective, each particle of research contributes a piece to the complex puzzle that is children and television programming.

BOOKS AND ARTICLES

Anderson, Daniel R. "The Effects of TV Program Comprehensibility on Preschool Children's Visual Attention to Television." *Child Development* 52, no. 1 (March 1981), pp. 151–57.

Barcus, F. Earle, and Rachel Wolkin. *Children's Television: An Analysis of Programming and Advertising*. New York: Praeger Publishers, 1977.

Brown, Mae H., et al. "Young Children's Perception of the Reality of Television." *Contemporary Education* 50, no. 3 (Spring 1979), pp. 129–33.

Cater, Douglass, and Stephen Strickland. *TV Violence and the Child: The Evolution and Fate of the Surgeon General's Report*. New York: Russell Sage Foundation, 1975.

Comstock, George A. *Television Violence: Where the Surgeon General's Study Leads*. Santa Monica, Calif.: Rand Corporation, 1972.

Comstock, George A., and Robin E. Cobbey. "Television and the Children of Ethnic Minorities." *Journal of Communication* 29, no. 1 (Winter 1979), pp. 104–15.

Dorr, Aimee, et al. "Television Literacy for Young Children." *Journal of Communication* 30, no. 3 (Summer 1980), pp. 71–83.

Feshbach, Seymour. "The Role of Fantasy in the Response to Television." *Journal of Social Issues* (Fall 1976), pp. 71–85.

Finn, Peter. "Developing Critical Television Viewing Skills." *Educational Forum* 44, no. 4 (May 1980), pp. 473–82.

Foote, Susan Bartlett, and Robert H. Mnookin. "The KidVid Crusade." *Public Interest* (Fall 1980), pp. 90–105.

Fowles, Barbara R. "Teaching Children to Read: An Argument for Television." *Urban Review*, (Summer 1976), pp. 114–20.

Harmonay, Maureen. "Two for the SeeSaw: Broadcast Responsibility and Children's Rights." *Journal of Current Social Issues* (Summer 1975), pp. 30–35.

Haynes, Richard B. "Children's Perceptions of 'Comic' and 'Authentic' Cartoon Violence." *Journal of Broadcasting* 22, no. 1 (Winter 1978), pp. 63–70.

Kittrell, Ed. "Children and Television: The Electronic Fix." *Children Today* (May-June 1978), p. 20.

Leishman, Katie. "When Is Television Too Scary for Children?" *TV Guide*, January 10, 1981.

Mander, Jerry. "Brainwatching: How TV Advertisers Manipulate the Minds of Children." *New Times*, January 8, 1979.

Mason, Kenneth. "Responsibility for What's on the Tube." *Business Week*, August 13, 1979, p. 14.

Mayes, Sandra L., and K. B. Valentine. "Sex Role Stereotyping in Saturday Morning Cartoon Shows." *Journal of Broadcasting* 23, no. 1 (Winter 1979), pp. 41–50.

Melody, William. *Children's Television: The Economics of Exploitation*. New Haven, Conn.: Yale University Press, 1973.

Nolan, John, et al. "Sex Bias on Children's Television Programs." *Journal of Psychology* (July 1977), pp. 197–204.

Palmer, Edward L., and Cynthia N. McDowell. "Program/Commercial Separators in Children's Television Programming." *Journal of Communication* 29, no. 3 (Summer 1979), pp. 197–201.

Potter, Rosemary Lee. "TV Talk: Life, Essential Skills and TV." *Teacher* 97, no. 3 (November-December 1979), pp. 46–52.

Quarfoth, Joanne M. "Children's Understandiing of the Nature of Television Characters." *Journal of Communication* 29, no. 3 (Summer 1979), pp. 210–18.

Roberts, Donald F., et al. "Developing Discriminating Consumers." *Journal of Communication*, 30, no. 3 (Summer 1980), pp. 94–105.

Sandell, Karin L., and David H. Ostroff. "Political Information Content and Children's Political Socialization." *Journal of Broadcasting* 25, no. 1 (Winter 1981), pp. 49–59.

Sikes, Rhea G. "Programs for Children: Public Television in the 1970s." *Public Telecommunications Review* 8, no. 5 (September 1980), pp. 7–26.

Silverman, L. Theresa, and Joyce N. Sprafkin. "The Effects of 'Sesame Street's' Prosocial Spots on Cooperative Play between Young Children." *Journal of Broadcasting* 24, no. 2 (Spring 1980), pp. 135–47.

Singer, Dorothy, and Jerome Singer. "How Kids Can Get the Most out of TV News." *TV Guide,* March 6, 1982.

———. "Sex on TV: How to Protect Your Child." *TV Guide*, August 7, 1982.

Swerdlow, Joel. "What Is Television Doing to Real People?" *Today's Education* (September-October 1981).

Tegtmeier, Dennis. "VCR's: Key to Taming the TV Monster." *Christianity Today*, January 23, 1981.

Turk, Peter. "Children's Television Advertising: An Ethical Morass for Business and Government." *Journal of Advertising* 8, no. 1 (Winter 1979), pp. 4–8.

"TV and Student Test Scores." *Education Digest* (January, 1981), p. 67.

Webster, James G., and William C. Coscarelli. "The Relative Appeal to Children of Adult Versus Children's Television Programming." *Journal of Broadcasting* 23, no. 4 (Fall 1979), pp. 437–51.

Welch, Renate L., et al. "Subtle Sex-Role Cues in Children's Commercials." *Journal of Communication* v. 29, no. 3 (Summer 1979), pp. 202–9.

"What TV Does to Kids." *Newsweek*, February 21, 1977.

Williams, Tannis MacBeth. "How and What Do Children Learn from Television?" *Human Communication Research*, 7, no. 2 (Winter 1981), pp. 180–92.

VIDEOGRAPHY

"Howdy Doody"
    NBC, Monday-Friday, various times
    Premiere: December 27, 1947
    Host: Buffalo Bob Smith
    Last Program: September 30, 1960

"Kukla, Fran & Ollie"
    NBC, Monday-Friday, 7:00–7:30 P.M.

Premiere: November 29, 1948
Host: Fran Allison
Last Program: August 31, 1957 (ABC)

"Watch Mr. Wizard"
NBC, Saturday, 6:30–7:00 P.M., 1951–1955
Saturday, various morning slots, 1956–1965
Premiere: May 26, 1951
Host: Don Herbert
Last Program: June 27, 1965

"Romper Room"
Syndicated, Monday-Friday, various times
Premiere: 1954 (Baltimore, Maryland)
Host: Sally Claster Gelbard in Baltimore, as well as local hosts in various cities
Last Program: 1983

"Captain Kangaroo"
CBS, Monday-Friday mornings
Premiere: October 3, 1955
Host: Bob Keeshan
Last Program: 1983

"The Flintstones"
ABC, Friday, various prime time slots
Premiere: September 30, 1960
Last Program: September 2, 1966

"Mister Rogers' Neighborhood"
PBS, Monday-Friday, various times
Premiere: May 22, 1967
Host: Fred Rogers

"Sesame Street"
PBS, Monday-Friday, various times
Premiere: November 10, 1969
Host: ensemble

"Electric Company"
PBS, Monday-Friday, various times
Premiere: 1971
Host: ensemble (Bill Cosby, Rita Moreno, and others)

"After School Specials"
ABC, occasional schedule, 4:00–5:00 P.M.
Premiere: 1972

18

Educational and Cultural Programming

FREDERIC A. LEIGH

OVERVIEW

In this chapter, educational and cultural programs are combined within one genre. This combination may be very natural to the viewer as both program types are generally offered by the same outlets. But it also tends to make the boundaries of the genre quite wide. In examining educational programming, one encounters both instructional programs designed for classroom use and public programs designed for general audiences. This chapter will focus on programs designed for general audiences as opposed to the classroom. This does not mean that the programs do not have education as their primary purpose. On the contrary, these programs offer the home viewer an often rich educational experience. But they must do so in competition with an ever-growing diversity of television programming sources available to the contemporary viewer.

Cultural television programming could be considered a genre in itself. Some qualification is necessary in a historical and thematic examination of this area. One might well make the point that *all* television programs offer some cultural content, be it elite or popular culture. In this genre, cultural programming is discussed in the context of elite or high culture generally associated with great works of art or literature. Program content tends to focus on performances, whether they be theatrical, dance, or musical. Within these parameters, the history of educational and cultural television programming can be traced and related issues can be examined.

HISTORICAL DEVELOPMENT

The history of educational broadcasting can be traced back as far as that of commercial broadcasting. The first educational radio station went on the air at the University of Wisconsin at Madison in 1917.[1] WHA radio began as an experiment by the Physics Department and was later licensed as an educational station in 1922. Even today, there are some who argue that WHA was actually the first radio station in the United States. In the early 1920s, a number of educational institutions began experiments with radio stations. Administrators soon realized that a radio station could serve as an extension of educational services to the community. By 1925, there were 171 educational organizations with radio stations on the air.[2] Many of these stations, however, ceased operation eventually due to budgetary problems and frequency reassignments.

The first experiments with educational television may have taken place at the University of Iowa between 1932 and 1939.[3] The Iowa station broadcast a number of programs that featured academic subjects during this period. This experiment was typical of an early concept of educational broadcasting: the use of the broadcast spectrum to extend the traditional classroom. Many educators saw in television the dawn of a new era in education. They realized that if ETV were to have a future, spectrum space must be reserved for their stations. The idea of reserving spectrum space for educational stations was discussed in the congressional debates on the Communications Act of 1934, but it was not until 1945 that the first reservations were actually made.[4] These first reservations were made on the FM band for radio stations. In 1948, the Federal Communications Commission (FCC) initiated its famous freeze on new TV applications, and this gave educators the opportunity to petition for reservations in television assignments.

Unfortunately, educators were not organized in 1948 to make a strong case for educational reservations. There were a number of informal groups of educators who submitted their ideas for reserved channels to the FCC. These groups were not in concert with one another in their proposals; in fact, some even contradicted each other. By 1950, it became obvious that educators must organize on a national scale in order to accomplish their goal. The U.S. Office of Education and the president of the National Association of Educational Broadcasters took the initiative to form the Joint Committee on Educational Television (JCET). The proposal of the JCET to reserve some channels exclusively for educational television was accepted by the FCC. In 1952, when the freeze was lifted, the FCC had reserved 242 channels for educational television.[5] Soon after the freeze was lifted, the first television station devoted entirely to educational programming went on the air at the University of Houston.

While channel reservations had been made and the first ETV station had signed on the air by 1953, there were still few educational organizations willing to fund a television station strictly for education. The cost of building and operating a television station as compared to a radio station was immense. Many educators were still discouraged by the problems they had experienced with their radio stations. Also, by 1950, the commercial networks were firmly committed to television as a profit-making venture. But, by the end of 1960, almost one television station in ten was nonprofit, noncommercial, and locally operated by a university, a school system, a State authority, or a community corporation.[6]

One of the first problems encountered by program directors for new ETV stations was defining "educational television." Some contended that ETV should be an extension of the classroom and offer instructional material for credit. Others argued that ETV should offer more than instructional content; it should broadcast programs designed for the education of the general public. These programs would offer cultural and informational content that would enrich the lives of viewers. Still, most seemed to agree that ETV programming should have a purpose beyond pure entertainment. One educator cited three distinct characteristics of ETV programming: It should be television one watches on purpose; it should expect one to participate; it should encourage one to turn off the set and do what has been suggested—read, paint, discuss.[7]

As more ETV stations came on the air in the 1950s, their program schedules tended to reflect the licensees of the stations. ETV licenses were held by universities, school systems, and community corporations. ETV stations licensed to universities quite naturally used their curricula as the base for television programming. The curriculum for the average university ETV station at that time generally was divided into the "four great areas of knowledge": humanities, fine arts, natural science and social science. ETV stations licensed to community corporations, on the other hand, utilized the resources in their communities such as symphonies, operas, and theaters. Consequently, their schedules included more fine arts or cultural programs than did stations licensed to educational institutions. In a comparison of the different types of ETV stations in 1959, Wilbur Schramm found that school-system stations placed more programming emphasis on the humanities, while university stations concentrated more in the area of natural science.[8] In the comparison, Schramm cited Denver Public School station KRMA, which repeated daytime televised language lessons at night so parents could review the lesson for their children. On the other hand, an example of a prime-time evening program on university station WUNC at the University of North Carolina was "Explorations into Creativity," which featured discussions of creative engineering and design.

These examples of ETV programming at major stations in 1960 are representative of program schedules at the time. It is obvious that the average ETV station was still closer to the classroom than the living room. Educational programming still meant instructional programming in many cases. The concept of educational television programs for general audiences was in the experimental stage. The community stations were the leaders in this area. Community station WQED in Pittsburgh was scheduling programs like "World of Music," "Key to the City," and "Art and Artists."[9] These programs represent some of the first cultural programs aired on ETV stations. The last program cited came from NET, National Educational Television, the beginning of a national network for ETV stations.

NET began as the Educational Television and Radio Center established in Illinois in 1952. It was supported by the Fund for Adult Education as a result of a proposal by the Joint Committee on Educational Television. The center was originally proposed as an exchange center with no production facilities of its own. It was to serve as the central distribution point for programs produced by local ETV stations. A "bicycle" network system was to be used in which kinescopes of programs selected by the center would be circulated to ETV stations around the country. As soon as the first station in the chain finished with the program, it would be mailed to the second station and so forth. This was the beginning of a whole new programming philosophy for ETV; that of the "Fourth Network." By 1959, the center had moved its headquarters to New York City where it became the National Educational Television and Radio Center. By now, ETV executives were visualizing a nationally interconnected network for the distribution of quality ETV programs. They saw two major challenges for ETV as the decade of the 1960s opened. The first was to program enough hours each day to offer a real alternative to commercial television, and the second was to make its programs sufficiently attractive to offer real competition for commercial TV.[10] "Competition" is a key word here, as it represents, for the first time, the concept of a challenge to commercial TV for the general viewer. The stage was now set for the beginning of the transition from educational television to public television.

In the meantime, the commercial networks had been developing their own television programs. While many of these series were video versions of successful comedy and dramatic radio programs, the networks were also experimenting with "teleplays." These plays for television really represent some of the first attempts in cultural programming. The "Kraft Television Theatre" presented its first teleplay, "The Double Door," in 1947.[11] This series was the first among several featuring live television dramas on a weekly basis. The productions ranged from the classics of Shakespeare to the contemporary works of Agatha Christie. The sponsor, Kraft, provided a large budget for the series, which allowed for the best writing and acting talent available at the time as well as large, elaborate sets. The "Kraft Television Theatre" also boasted color programs as early as 1954 on an intermittent basis and regularly by 1956.[12] The series went on to become one of the most successful on early television, running for ten years on NBC. In fact, for two seasons, the series was actually running on two networks simultaneously, NBC and ABC.

Teleplays became a staple of television programming during the 1950s. CBS was experimenting with the "dramatic anthology" in its famous series, "Studio One." This series started on CBS radio in 1947 but switched to television the next year. It went on the air with no sponsor at all, but was picked up by Westinghouse in 1949. The sponsor brought in Betty Furness as spokesperson for the series. As a result, she became one of the most famous commercial spokespersons of all time. The programs featured on "Studio One" were noted for their emphasis on the visual aspect. Producer Worthington Miner was more concerned that his programs have a visual impact than he was with their literary content. His experimentation with camera techniques set a precedent in television production. "Studio One" ran on CBS for ten years and was replaced in 1958 with "Westinghouse Desilu Playhouse."

In the "General Electric Theater," one finds a move toward popular culture. This was another "dramatic anthology" series, but it featured more emphasis on what was then called "diversionary entertainment."[13] Most of the programs were original teleplays ranging from light comedy to heavy drama. The series premiered on CBS in 1953 with no host but within a year had acquired Ronald Reagan as host. It began as a live series but soon went into a filmed format that allowed it to be syndicated later as the "Star Showcase." "General Electric Theater" ran on CBS until 1962.

The series that is often cited as the "most outstanding cultural series in the history of commercial network television" was "Omnibus."[14] The series premiered on CBS in 1953 with host Alistair Cooke. The program featured a variety of segments ranging across the arts from symphonies and operas to plays and adventure films. The premiere of the program included William Saroyan reading an adapation of "The Bad Men," excerpts from "The Mikado," and the teleplay, "The Trial of Anne Boleyn," all in 90 minutes. Even more interesting than the format of the series is the fact that it was aired without a sponsor throughout its history. The series was funded by the Ford Foundation. It ran on CBS until 1956 and then was picked up by ABC until 1957. ABC attempted to revive the series in 1981, but it was not successful.

By the early 1960s, the live studio dramatic production that had been the staple of early cultural television programming had all but disappeared from the commercial networks. Part of the reason for this disappearance was the shift of network television production from the East Coast to the West Coast. In a sense, television experienced a trend away from the theater and toward the Hollywood film. Hollywood film producers had long been making popular films for mass audiences and had developed formulas for their success. These same formulas were soon applied to television drama. In essence, television drama became more realistic, depicting real-life situations to which the average viewer could relate. While stage theater productions (that were once a program source for live television) became more elitist, television drama became more popular. David Boroff points out in an essay on TV drama that "the burden of teaching Americans how to live was assumed by the regular series such as 'The Defenders,' 'Nurses and Doctors,' 'Ben Casey,' etc., which week after week relentlessly tackled the domestic problems that beset Americans."[15]

If we consider cultural programming on television as that which falls into the category of elite culture, the genre is not well represented on commercial network television after 1960. The high art dramatic anthologies presented as regular series in the 1950s became specials in the 1960s. Perhaps the best known of these is the "Hallmark Hall of Fame."

The "Hall of Fame" began on NBC in 1951 and featured dramatic productions five to six times each year. The programs ranged from Shakespearean plays to Broadway shows or original contemporary dramas. When the program presented a production of *Hamlet* in 1953, it was suggested that more people watched a single performance of the play on NBC than saw it in all its stage performances since Elizabethan times.[16] Whether this claim was true or not could not be established, but one can assume that the "Hall of Fame" brought Shakespeare's work to many people that might never have seen it. Hallmark continued its exclusive relationship with NBC until 1978, at which time it was terminated by mutual agreement. The specials had been slipping in the ratings and Hallmark was unhappy with the time slots assigned to them by NBC. Even though the ratings for the specials have often been lower than those for regular series programs, Hallmark has continued to fund them. The "Hallmark Hall of Fame" remains one of the outstanding quality cultural specials on contemporary commercial television.

A good example of an outstanding cultural music series on network television during the 1960s is "The Bell Telephone Hour." This series ran on NBC from 1959 to 1968 and provided a showcase (one of the few) for fine music on commercial network TV. The programs featured music ranging from classical, to popular, to jazz. The early programs in the series placed emphasis on popular and show music, but that changed in 1966, when the focus switched to classical music. Some of the classical highlights include the American TV debuts of Rudolf Nureyev, Joan Sutherland, and Albert Casadesus.[17]

With the demise of the live television anthologies on the commercial networks, there was increased demand on ETV stations for quality cultural programming. Those who criticized the networks for their lack of culture were rallied by the famous speech in 1961 of a new FCC chairman under the Kennedy administration, Newton Minow. Speaking before an annual convention of the National Association of Broadcasters, Minow stated that if commercial broadcasters actually watched a full day of their own programming, they would find a "vast wasteland."[18] ETV administrators took this statement as a cue that the federal government might be sympathetic to a proposal for the establishment of federal funding for educational television. If ETV could seriously offer the quality cultural programming that seemed to be so sorely lacking on the commercial networks, perhaps the government would fund ETV as an alternative to popular television. This was the case as the first legislation authorizing federal funding for educational television was passed the next year. The Educational Facilities Act of 1962 provided matching funds to be used for the construction of new ETV stations across the country.[19]

At the same time, National Educational Television (NET) was building support for the programming component of educational television. In 1963, the Ford Foundation concluded an extensive study of ETV and provided the first of its annual grants to finance the program service of NET. NET now had the financial backing to seriously pursue its ultimate goal: "to create a television program service of substance and quality, to be provided to the American people through the nationwide network of noncommercial ETV stations affiliated with NET."[20] While the thrust of the new NET program service was to be in the area of public affairs, a good part of it would be devoted to cultural programming. According to John F. White, president of NET at the time, the cultural programming included performances in drama, music, and the dance, as well as programs in the arts, humanities, and the sciences. The primary objectives of NET cultural programs, said White, were "to help man know the nature of himself, his world, and his fellow man; to give him a deeper understanding of his own and other cultures; to show him what the past was and what the future may be; to help him think and reason, and to recognize and respond to beauty."[21]

With funding in place, NET began to develop some excellent programming in the educational and cultural genre. One of the best-known drama series was "NET Playhouse," which featured weekly productions of plays, some of which were produced by NET affiliates. Plays were chosen from such playwrights as Ibsen, Chekhov, Williams, and Miller. The series, which began in 1966, was the only regular weekly drama series on television in the United States by 1969.[22] That same year, NET added another dramatic series to its schedule. The BBC had produced a black and white series based on the books of British author John Galsworthy and offered it to the U.S. commercial television networks. All three refused the series, so NET had the opportunity to buy the series at the very attractive price of $140,000. The series, entitled, "The Forsyte Saga," became so popular that one chapter of the series drew the first 3 percent share of the television audience in the history of NET.[23] The "Forsyte Saga" is a good example of a trend toward British dramatic production established early by NET and later continued by the Public Broadcasting Service (PBS).

PBS was established in November of 1969 as a national distribution system for educational or public television programs. This function had been performed by NET until this time, but it was in addition to the function of program producer. PBS was originally created to relieve NET of the responsibility of program distribution so it could concentrate on quality production. NET was then absorbed into television station WNDT, New York, to become WNET, an independent program producer for the national system. That station, along with WGBH, Boston, and several others, remains one of the principal program producers for the contemporary PBS schedule.[24]

With federal funding established by the Public Broadcasting Act of 1967, the foundations were laid for the public television system we have today. Congress had created the Corporation for Public Broadcasting as a private, nonprofit corporation to "foster the growth and development of the nation's noncommercial television and radio stations."[25] CPB would distribute funding to the new network, PBS, and to individual stations across the nation. Programs for the system would be produced independently by the stations and submitted to PBS for distribution. In this way there would be no central monopoly for both the production and distribution of programs as some felt NET had been. Though there has been some conflict between CPB and PBS over program selection and funding, the system has grown significantly over the past decade. PBS was a pioneer in establishing the first national television satellite system in 1978. Most of the programs being distributed on the satellite system are funded and produced by public television stations, but other sources include the Ford, Markle, and

Rockefeller Foundations and the National Endowments for the Arts and Humanities.[26]

PBS has established itself as the premiere source of educational and cultural programming in the United States today. Among its most popular cultural programs are "Masterpiece Theatre" and "Great Performances." These two series represent the longest running performance series in the history of public television. "Masterpiece Theatre" is a current example of the British programming fare that has been so prevalent on PBS. The series began in 1971 with episodes from "First Churchills." Over the years, viewers have enjoyed productions of "Dickens of London," "Duchess of Duke Street," "Anna Karenina," and "I, Claudius." It remains one of the most popular dramatic series on television. *Saturday Review* television critic Karl E. Meyer has written that " 'Masterpiece Theatre' . . . surely owes its long run to its skill at delineating the nuances of caste and class. . . . In a country where birth, private education, and accent count for less, Americans are fascinated by British productions."[27] The program has become a Sunday night addiction for many viewers, some of whom may not watch other PBS programs.

In musical performances, PBS has also been the leading program source in American television. The best known and longest running series in this area is "Great Performances," which began in 1974. The predecessor for the series was "NET Festival," a weekly presentation of performance specials that ran during the late sixties. "Great Performances" is really a generic title for a wide variety of concerts taped live on location. Standard fare is a concert by one of the great orchestras in the country such as the Philadelphia, Chicago, or Los Angeles. The series also has included the mini-series, "Live from Lincoln Center," featuring such memorable performances as the 1978 concert of Luciano Pavarotti. That program was historic in the fact that Pavarotti was the first vocal artist ever to concertize from the Met.[28] "Great Performances" has also been significant because many concerts are simulcast in stereo on FM stations across the country.

While there are many other cultural and educational program series offered by PBS, "Masterpiece Theatre" and "Great Performances" are probably the best representatives of the genre during the last decade. Dramas and musical performances continue to make up the bulk of PBS cultural programming. There have been isolated cultural specials presented by the commercial television networks, but PBS has been the sole source of quality cultural television series. But recently, public television stations have experienced a reduction in federal funding. These cutbacks may have the most drastic effect on the production of new cultural programs for PBS. In addition, the growth of cable television may offer stiff competition for PBS. All three commercial networks have initiated arts performance channels for distribution to cable systems across the country. Because the networks have a much stronger financial base than does PBS, they may be able to lure away the program sources that have traditionally supplied PBS.

THEMES AND ISSUES

From the beginning, the parameters of educational and cultural programming have been difficult to define. The term "educational" was finally replaced by two more definitive terms: "public" and "instructional." Early educational broadcasters were never quite sure of their audiences. The original goal of educational programming was to extend the traditional classroom beyond the educational institution. The first educational TV programs were really instructional in nature, offering the TV viewer specific course materials. But it soon became obvious that educational programmers would have to program more to general audiences. While the viewer of instructional television could be specifically defined, studied, and served, the potential audience for educational programming was considerably more elusive. The appeal of programs for the general audience had to be much broader and, indeed, entertaining. This was one of the major problems of the early educational television programs: a reputation for being boring. While ETV stations considered themselves alternatives to commercial television, they soon discovered that they had to compete with their commercial counterparts for audiences. To compete successfully with commercial TV, they needed much more funding and higher quality programming.

This was the challenge facing educational broadcasting when the Public Broadcasting Act of 1967 was passed. This was the beginning of more than a decade of tremendous growth in a system that came to be known as "public broadcasting." Public broadcasters had learned a great deal from the early years of educational programming. They had learned that television certainly could teach, but the home viewer had to be entertained as well. They also learned that the medium must be utilized to its best advantage. An educational program could not simply be a duplication of the classroom situation; a "talking head." It must incorporate the visual aspect of television to be successful. Perhaps the crowning example of this lesson is the tremendous success of the PBS series "Sesame Street."

"Sesame Street" started in 1966 as an idea in the mind of Lloyd Morrisett, then vice president of the Carnegie Corporation. He had observed the success of commercial television in entertaining children, particularly preschoolers, and wondered whether television could be used to teach them as well. He proposed the idea to Joan Ganz Cooney, a producer for an educational TV station in New York, and she laid the groundwork for a new series. Based on an $8 million grant from the U.S. Office of Education and the Carnegie Corporation, an extensive research project was initiated. In studying preschoolers' television habits and preferences, Cooney discovered that children like the commercials almost as well as the programs. "Television was teaching children whether it intended to or not, and kids went for quality and particularly commercials which are often the costliest items," she said.[29] The research revealed other preschool preferences, such as for animated characters and short segments to match their attention spans. These elements were incorporated into "Sesame Street," although their purpose was not to sell a product but, rather, to teach rudimentary letter and number concepts.

In addition to letters and numbers, "Sesame Street" also deals with social concepts. It attempts to teach social values such as sharing and self-worth. The program even deals with such complicated issues as racial integration and was banned in certain Southern cities for doing so.[30] But the series has grown to be one of the most celebrated and successful educational television series ever produced. The names of the characters have become household words across the country, particularly the names of the "Muppet" puppets featured on the program. "Sesame Street" represents the most renowned example of an effective educational television program. It takes the most successful elements of television and utilizes them to teach classroom concepts. This is educational telelvision at its best.

While "Sesame Street" teaches specific concepts, public television also offers programs that provide a general educational experience for the viewer. In this area, it is difficult to define a program or a series as either educational or cultural. A series such as "The Ascent of Man" might very well be categorized as an educational television series. "Masterpiece Theatre," on the other hand, might be most often called a cultural series. In reality, of course, both series offer the viewer an educational and cultural experience. In comparison to "The Ascent of Man," "Sesame Street" might very well be labeled "instructional." This demonstrates the dilemma ETV, now PTV, stations (and programs) have encountered in building audiences. A program that is described in television listings as "educational" or "cultural" is often ignored by a large part of the viewing audience. And yet, all television programs are educational and cultural to a certain extent. In this genre, one generally finds that educational programs have education (not entertainment) as their primary goal. Cultural programs are generally those that deal with elite rather than popular culture.

Matthew Arnold once defined culture as "being a pursuit of our total perfection by means of getting to know . . . the best which has been thought and said in the world. . . ."[31] The phrase "the best which has been thought and said in the world" is generally applied to great works of art and literature. Television programs that present or examine great works of art, literature, and music are generally categorized as "cultural" programs. More specifically, they are "elite" cultural programs as opposed to "popular" cultural programs. Edward Whetmore suggests that there are two types of culture in America: "Rembrandt represents elite culture, but Norman Rockwell is popular culture. Chamber music is elite, but rock is popular. Medicine is elite, but Marcus Welby is pop."[32] This delineation must be considered when tracing the historical and thematic development in the television genre of cultural programs. It was particularly pronounced in the transition in commercial television from elite dramatic anthologies in the 1950s to the formulaic pop dramatic series of today. The contrast is also quite evident in a comparison of noncommercial and commercial programming.

Ironically, the cultural element of this genre began in commercial television.

In the early days of commercial television, when network programmers were groping for program ideas, it seemed logical to produce great theatrical works on TV. Then, as Hollywood film producers became involved in network productions, television programs began to move away from elite and toward pop culture. This placed the responsibility for elite cultural programming almost totally on noncommercial television. Unfortunately, noncommercial TV has never had the financial base enjoyed by its commercial counterpart. Nevertheless, some of the best cultural series have been produced and broadcast by the Public Broadcasting System. The system has been heavily supported by federal grants that are now being drastically reduced.[33] Public television stations are being forced to rely more on private and listener support. These sources alone probably cannot make up for the reductions in federal funding. In this sense, public broadcasting and the genre itself face a severe crisis.

There are many claims that the future of cultural, if not educational programming, lies in merging technologies. These include cable television, direct broadcast satellite transmissions, and video cassettes. The most promising of these appears to be cable television. All four major television networks, commercial and noncommercial, have explored the potential of cultural networks for cable. Ironically, the one network that has not yet activated such a service is PBS. In 1980, the Carnegie Commission published another study of public broadcasting; this one examining its future in the midst of an explosion of emerging technologies. The primary recommendation of that study was the establishment of a nonprofit cable network for performing arts, culture, and entertainment to be called "PACE."[34] The new cable network was evidently envisioned as public television's key to the emerging technologies of the future. But unfortunately, PACE has not become a reality yet. Perhaps, with the current funding crisis in public broadcasting, PBS is more concerned with just keeping its stations on the air across the country.

Several cable cultural channels have been established by commercial television groups. ABC, in conjunction with the Hearst Corporation, initiated its cultural cable service, ARTS, in 1981. The company described the schedule of ARTS as a "selection of performing and visual arts material from the international repository of acquired and originally produced programming" owned by ABC Video Enterprises.[35] The service premiered with a new production of "Macbeth" and a series of programs on American photographers. ARTS represents one of the first attempts to present cultural cable television programming on an advertiser-supported basis.

Later in 1981, CBS launched its own cultural cable service, CBS Cable. The programming emphasis in this service has been on original production created specifically for CBS Cable. Three-hour programming segments, encompassing classical music, drama, films, jazz, and interviews, were presented four times daily.[36] Program highlights from CBS Cable included a biography of James Joyce and a new production of Gilbert and Sullivan's "The Mikado." Unfortunately, the cable channel lasted only little more than a year. At the end of

1982, CBS Cable went out of business. CBS cited a shortage of advertisers willing to support a specialized cable channel.[37] In the meantime, ARTS and "Bravo," a cultural programming service that offers primarily musical programs to cable systems, continue to survive.

With the demise of CBS Cable, the future of quality cultural television programming again is in jeopardy. While many prognosticators cast doubts on the future of PBS, they point to cable television as the savior of cultural programs. But the cable culture channels have had to deal with the problems that public broadcasters have faced for a long time. The audiences are small, while the programming costs are high. The large question surrounding cultural channels on cable is whether viewer numbers will ever be high enough to seriously interest national advertisers. The failure of CBS Cable may well have confirmed doubts in the minds of many advertising executives about the potential of specialized cultural channels on cable television.

We are certainly in the midst of a period of tremendous growth in communication technologies. The new technologies promise to bring an exciting array of media services and programs. But the educational and cultural programming genre may very well find itself depending on an old friend as its primary outlet in the foreseeable future. That old friend is PBS. As media diversity increases, the role of PBS may change but, hopefully, not diminish in its contribution to quality programming. Noted journalist Bill Moyers has said: "It may be that there'll be a new arrangement. Things will go to cable first, for a narrow audience, then to public broadcasting for a larger audience."[38] But, if public broadcasting is to survive, federal funding must be restored or alternative sources of funding secured. The future of educational and cultural programming may very well depend on it.

NOTES

1. John R. Bittner, *Broadcasting: An Introduction* (Englewood Cliffs, N.J.: Prentice-Hall, 1980), p. 54.

2. Federal Communications Commission Information Bulletin, *Educational Radio* 17 (January 1977).

3. Allen E. Koenig, "The Development of Educational Television," in *The Farther Vision*, ed. Allen E. Koenig and Ruane B. Hill (Madison, Wis.: University of Wisconsin Press, 1967), p. 5.

4. Harrison B. Summers, Robert E. Summers, and John H. Pennybacker, *Broadcasting and the Public* (Belmont, Calif.: Wadsworth Publishing, 1978, p. 280.

5. Koenig, *The Farther Vision*, p. 6.

6. John W. Powell, *Channels of Learning* (Washington, D.C.: Public Affairs Press, 1962), p. 5.

7. Ibid., p. 6.

8. Wilbur Schramm, "The Content of Educational Television," in *The Impact of Educational Television*, ed. Wilbur Schramm (Urbana, Ill.: University of Illinois Press, 1960), p. 12.

9. Ibid., p. 9.

10. Powell, *Channels of Learning*, p. 111.

11. Tim Brooks and Earle Marsh, *The Complete Directory to Prime Time Network TV Shows, 1946–Present*, (N.Y.: Ballantine Books, 1979), p. 410.

12. Ibid.

13. Ibid., p. 279.

14. Ibid., p. 558.

15. David Boroff, "Television and the Problem Play," in *TV as Art*, ed. Patrick D. Hazard (Champaign, Ill.: National Council of Teachers of English, 1966), p. 98.

16. Les Brown, *Encyclopedia of Television* (New York: Zoetrope, 1982), p. 11.

17. Brooks and Marsh, *The Complete Directory to Prime Time Network TV Shows, 1946–Present*, p. 72.

18. Eugene S. Foster, *Understanding Broadcasting* (Reading, Mass.: Addison-Wesley, 1982), p. 400.

19. Koenig, *The Farther Vision*, p. 88.

20. Ibid.

21. Ibid., p. 91.

22. National Educational Television, *NET: The Public Television Network* (pamphlet) (New York, N.Y.: National Educational Television, 1969).

23. Ibid.

24. Public Broadcasting Service, *PBS White Paper* (Washington, D.C.: Public Broadcasting Service, 1975), p. 12.

25. Ibid., p. 10.

26. Ibid., p. 19.

27. Karl E. Meyer, "Television," *Saturday Review*, October 25, 1978, p. 55.

28. Patricia P. Perini, ed., "Highlights on 13," *Vision* (February 1978), p. 22.

29. "TV's Switched-On School," *Newsweek*, June 1, 1970, p. 69.

30. Ibid.

31. Raymond Williams, "Some Versions of Shakespeare on the Screen," in *TV as Art*, ed. Patrick D. Hazard, p. 132.

32. Edward J. Whetmore, *MediAmerica* (Belmont, Calif.: Wadsworth Publishing, 1979), p. 274.

33. "CPB Continues Efforts to Retain Funding," *Broadcasting*, March 21, 1983, p. 62.

34. Sheila Mahony, Nick DeMartino and Robert Stengel, *Keeping PACE with the New Television* (New York: Carnegie Corporation, 1980), p. 4.

35. "Gearing Up for Theme Week at ABC Video," *Broadcasting*, April 6, 1981, p. 131.

36. John J. O'Connor, "CBS Cable's Failure Stresses Need for Public Broadcasting," *Arizona Republic*, December 12, 1982, p. G16.

37. "Sifting through the Fallout of CBS Cable, Disney," *Broadcasting*, September 20, 1982, p. 27.

38. Bill Moyers, "The Quest for Quality TV," *Saturday Review*, February 1982, p. 18.

BIBLIOGRAPHICAL SURVEY

Since the history of the educational and cultural genre is a long one, there have been a number of books written from the historical perspective. These books trace the development of educational radio and television, but one finds little detail on specific programs. There are, of course, a number of good textbooks on broadcasting such as Head's *Broadcasting in America*, Bittner's *Broadcasting*, and Foster's *Understanding Broadcasting*. Each of these offers at least one chapter devoted to educational or public broadcasting.

For more comprehensive examinations of educational television, one can turn to *The Farther Vision*, edited by Allen Koenig and Ruane Hill. This is a good collection of chapters written by various television executives and educators. While dated, it provides a good overview of ETV as it existed in the middle sixties. Two other books that provide a good historical view of educational broadcasting are Powell's *Channels of Learning* and Schramm's *The Impact of Educational Television*. Again, both trace the history to the early sixties.

There are several sources that take ETV history through the development of PBS in the seventies. Probably the most comprehensive of these is *Educational Telecommunications* by Wood and Wylie. Others include Macy's *To Irrigate a Wasteland*, Avery and Pepper's *The Politics of Interconnection*, and Blakely's *To Serve the Public Interest*.

One can gain more insight into educational television in the studies done by the Carnegie Commission in the sixties and seventies. The last of these was published in 1979 and summarized in a book called *Keep PACE with the New Technologies* by Mahony, DeMartino, and Stengel. The book focuses on the Carnegie proposal for a new pay cable network for the performing arts to be operated by public broadcasters. It provides a very good examination of the state of emerging technologies at the time and the role of public broadcasting in the future.

In the area of cultural programming, one does not find a number of books specifically examining the history of the genre. This is probably due, in part, to the difficulty in defining "cultural" in its application to a television series. There are a number of books, however, that do examine television as an art and in its treatment of the arts. *TV as Art*, edited by Patrick Hazard, is an interesting collection of essays written by educators in various disciplines. Subjects include the problem play, Shakespeare on TV, popular culture, television and the culture of the child.

Television as a Cultural Force, edited by Richard Adler and Douglass Cater, provides a more updated collection of essays examining TV and its cultural impact on the viewer. *The Age of Television*, by Martin Esslin, offers a contemporary examination of American TV drama by a British broadcaster. One finds good perspective on the element of drama, a major component of cultural programming, in Esslin's chapters. The author spent nearly 40 years with the BBC, a primary source of cultural programming for PBS.

In addition to books, there are a number of program reviews to be found in various periodicals. Columnist Martin Williams recently published a collection of his columns from the *Village Voice, National Review*, and other periodicals. The collection is entitled *TV—The Casual Art* and provides some interesting reviews and comments on various cultural programs. *Saturday Review* also has a good history of television reviews, many of them on programs in this genre.

BOOKS AND ARTICLES

Adler, Richard, and Douglass Cater, eds. *Television as a Cultural Force*. New York: Praeger Publishers, 1976.

Avery, Robert K., and Robert Pepper. *The Politics of Interconnection: A History of Public Television at the National Level*. Washington, D.C.: National Association of Educational Broadcasters, 1979.

Bittner, John R. *Broadcasting: An Introduction*. Englewood Cliffs, N.J.: Prentice-Hall, 1980.

Blakely, Robert J. *To Serve the Public Interest: Educational Broadcasting in the United States*. Syracuse, N.Y.: Syracuse University Press, 1979.

Broadcasting. "CPB Continues Efforts to Retain Funding," March 21, 1983.

Broadcasting. "Sifting through the Fallout of CBS Cable, Disney," September 20, 1982.

Broadcasting. "Gearing Up for Theme Week at ABC Video," April 6, 1981.

Brooks, Tim, and Earle Marsh. *The Complete Directory to Prime Time Network TV Shows, 1946–Present*. New York: Ballantine Books, 1979.

Brown, Les. *Encyclopedia of Television*. New York: Zoetrope, 1982.

Esslin, Martin. *The Age of Television*. San Francisco, Calif.: W. H. Freeman, 1982.

Federal Communications Commission. *Information Bulletin: Educational Radio*. Washington, D.C.: FCC, 1977.

Foster, Eugene S. *Understanding Broadcasting*. Reading, Mass.: Addison-Wesley, 1982.

Hazard, Patrick D. *TV as Art*. Champaign, Ill.: National Council of Teachers of English, 1966.

Head, Sydney W., and Christopher H. Sterling. *Broadcasting in America*, 4th ed. Boston: Houghton Mifflin, 1982.

Koenig, Allen E., and Ruane B. Hill. *The Farther Vision: ETV Today*. Madison, Wis.: University of Wisconsin Press, 1967.

Macy, John, Jr. *To Irrigate A Wasteland: The Struggle to Shape a Public Television System in the United States*. Berkeley: University of California, 1974.

Mahony, Sheila, Nick DeMartino, and Robert Stengel. *Keeping PACE with the New Television*. New York: Carnegie Corporation, 1980.

Meyer, Karl E. "Television," *Saturday Review*, October 25, 1978.

Moyers, Bill. "The Quest for Quality TV." *Saturday Review*, February 1982.

National Educational Television. *NET: The Public Television Network* (pamphlet). New York: NET, 1969.

O'Connor, John J. "CBS Cable's Failure Stresses Need for Public Broadcasting." *Arizona Republic*, December 12, 1982.

Powell, John W. *Channels of Learning: The Story of Educational Television*. Washington, D.C.: Public Affairs Press, 1962.

Public Broadcasting Service. *PBS White Paper*. Washington, D.C.: PBS, 1975.

Summers, Harrison B., Robert E. Summers, and John H. Pennybacker. *Broadcasting and the Public*. Belmont, Calif.: Wadsworth, 1978.

Schramm, Wilbur, ed. *The Impact of Educational Television*. Urbana, Ill.: University of Illinois Press, 1960.

Williams, Martin. *TV—the Casual Art*. New York: Oxford University Press, 1982.

VIDEOGRAPHY

"Kraft TV Theatre"
  NBC, Wed., 7:30–8:30 P.M. (May-December 1947), and Wed., 9:00–10:00 P.M. (1948–1958).
  Premiere: May 7, 1947, "Double Door" play
  Last Program: October 1, 1958

"Studio One"
  CBS, aired various times, 1948–1958
  Premiere: Nov. 7, 1948, mystery play "The Storm"
  Last Program: September 29, 1958

"Hallmark Hall of Fame" (specials)
  NBC, various times, 1951–1979
  CBS, various times, 1979–present
  Premiere: December 24, 1951, "Amahl and the Night Visitors"

"General Electric Theater"
  CBS, Sundays 9:00–9:30 P.M.
  Premiere: February, 1, 1953
  Host: Ronald Reagan
  Last Program: September 16, 1962

"Omnibus"
  CBS, Sundays, 5:00–6:30 P.M. and 9:00–10:30 P.M., 1953–1957
  Premiere: October 4, 1953
  Host: Alistair Cooke
  Last Program: March 31, 1957

"The Bell Telephone Hour"
  NBC, various times, 1959–1968
  Premiere: October 9, 1959
  Last Program: April 26, 1968

"Masterpiece Theatre"
  PBS, Sundays, 8:00–9:00 P.M., 1971–present
  Premiere: January 10, 1971, "The First Churchills"

"Great Performances"
  PBS, various times, 1973–present
  Premiere: April 15, 1973

19

The Television Church

ROBERT S. ALLEY

OVERVIEW

In pursuing the task of analyzing religious television broadcasting in America it has become increasingly clear that there are two quite recognizable threads. The established Christian churches, Catholic and Protestant, presuming a continuity with their radio past, accepted, generally without competitive motives, responsibility for religious education as a public trust. Religious sects and independents quickly identified TV as a means of proselytizing and fund raising. Until the late seventies these two distinct streams carried on with little friction, but since 1980 the "mainline" churches have found themselves on the defensive as ultra-conservative Christians have created the era of the electronic church, expanding on a tradition that began in the early days of radio and experienced its first television flowering in the fifties.

HISTORICAL DEVELOPMENT

The two divergent religious emphases were evident from the earliest radio broadcasts. "Religious programming started when the U.S. Army Signal Corps broadcast a church service in Washington, D.C., in August 1919. KDKA (Pittsburgh) was probably the first private station to broadcast religious services when, on January 2, 1921, it transmitted an Episcopalian service."[1] In 1924 the "National Radio Pulpit" began as a platform for some of the most prominent Protestant preachers—Harry Emerson Fosdick, Ralph Sockman, Joseph F. Newton. The messages were directed toward ethical values and social responsibility, with little emphasis upon the need for conversion. By the end of the decade Fosdick had established himself as the most popular of the radio preachers, and in 1929 NBC provided him a weekly forum with "National Vespers." In 1930 "The Catholic Hour" appeared, along with "The Lutheran Hour." For the most part these programs were an outreach of the traditional stance of the various denominations. A growing range of such offerings emerged in that decade, and by the close of World War II nearly all the Protestant groups were in the market. One of the most successful programs was that sponsored by the Mormons, which featured the Mormon Tabernacle Choir and a brief homily on Christian living.

Concurrent with these mainline efforts were a series of broadcasts that were designed to proselytize, the most successful of which was the "Old Fashioned Revival Hour" presided over by Charles E. Fuller. His aim was to reach the "unconverted." According to Bill J. Leonard, Fuller wrote to his potential supporters: "You should certainly be interested in reaching fifteen million people in the Western United States and Canada with a ringing Gospel message. It can be done immediately—by radio."[2] Two things are significant about the Fuller experiment that began in 1934. The broadcasts were placed on individual stations rather than through a network, and they were paid for by Fuller in order to place the program in prime hours rather than in the Sunday morning "free" time normally granted by the local stations. These business decisions, coupled with an aggressive evangelizing effort, resulted in a highly lucrative activity for Fuller, one that allowed the formation of Fuller Theological Seminary. Fuller's successes spawned a plethora of imitators that have plied their trade on radio for 50 years.

A bizarre aberration emerged in the CBS program offered by Charles E. Coughlin, a Detroit Roman Catholic priest who used his platform to endorse the candidacy of Franklin Roosevelt. After the election of 1932 Coughlin changed his mind about the new president and began a series of bitter attacks that continued until America entered the War in 1941. A maverick, Coughlin appealed to Catholics and Protestants frightened by the changing world conditions. Of his intentions, Coughlin wrote that while his broadcast was "dedicated primarily to an exposition of Catholic Doctrine and of Christian morality, we have at no time been remiss in discussing both evils and remedies of such topics as Communism-Socialism, which like a red serpent, is slowly insinuating itself into the folds of our national life."[3] By the close of the decade Coughlin had established himself as a strong supporter of German National Socialism and was recognized as anti-Semitic. Writing in 1981, James Hennessey noted, "Coughlin's activities revealed the power of radio preachers to appeal to the darker side of the human condition, feeding racism, prejudice, and bigotry in the name of God."[4]

Protestant preachers abounded in ever more extreme forms as the "suck and blow preaching, a cadence which combined shouts, vocal gymnastics, and unusual breath techniques" gained more and more air time.[5] Along with these came the healers—Oral Roberts and A. A. Allen—who claimed power to cure illnesses in the radio audience. By 1948 radio was a religious zoo. Not only were the preachers proliferating, but sales of religious paraphernalia hawked over powerful transmitters located in Mexico proved rewarding for a group of fundamentalist entrepreneurs in Texas.

The beginning of network television may be dated to 1948, and it is interesting to note that the new medium tended to repeat the experiences of radio. As local stations appeared, church services became a regular part of the public programming required by the FCC. Time offered to churches was on Sunday morning, a financial dead zone until the last few years. There was no immediate transfer of the independent evangelists to the tube because, unlike voice recordings for radio that made syndication feasible, the cost of providing film was prohibitive. A comparable inexpensive means of transcribing visual images did not become available to TV users until the distribution of video tape in the early sixties.

In February of 1952 the DuMont Network introduced Bishop Fulton J. Sheen on Tuesday evenings at 8:00 P.M., and he continued there until April of 1955.[6] In the fall of that year he moved to ABC, first at 8:00 P.M. on Thursday and finally at 9:00 P.M. on Monday. The show ended its run in April of 1957. In 1953 Sheen was an Emmy winner and named the "Most Outstanding Personality" on television for 1952. The award, presented only five times, had gone in previous years to Milton Berle, Ed Wynn, and Groucho Marx. Edward R. Murrow received the last such recognition in 1954.

Bishop Sheen quickly became the "Loretta Young of the sacristy" as he entered into prime-time competition with Milton Berle, prompting a quip by the comedian, "We both work for the same boss, Sky Chief."[7] With a quick wit and a sense of the dramatic, Sheen proved a match for the Madison Avenue crowd. In 1954 he commissioned a statue of the Virgin Mary that he introduced as "Our Lady of Television."[8] While his audience was never large, Sheen was allowed to remain opposite Berle on the schedule for three years. Indeed, he was popular enough to obtain a sponsor in November of 1952, Admiral Corporation, which paid a fee of $1 million to Sheen's organization, Mission Humanity, Inc. In announcing the sponsorship DuMont officials said:

The bishop will open with the usual good evening. Then he will possibly say, "And now a message from our sponsor," and we'll cut away from him to do a one-minute, high-level, institutional commercial. There will be no commercial in the middle of the show and just a little direct sell at the end. When the last commercial is over, the bishop will come back for his goodnight.[9]

The evidence points to the fact that Sheen exercised considerable clout in terms of press coverage. His theological and social outlook was clearly stated and provides interesting reading as one compares his comments with the new breed of TV evangelist.

The world of 1952 was one in which Americans found themselves choosing between the extreme anticommunism of Senator McCarthy and the more reasoned responses of President Truman.

Sheen was particularly strong in his denunciation of communism and perhaps the most notable occasion on which he addressed that topic was in early 1953 when he read the burial scene from *Julius Caesar*, substituting the names of Stalin, Beria, Malenkov, and Vishinsky for Caesar, Cassius, Antony, and Brutus. Stalin, Sheen said, "must one day meet his judgment."[10] A few days later

Stalin was dead of a stroke. While Sheen made no comment on the coincidence, it was reported widely in the press. In this instance, as on many other occasions, Sheen adopted a style of commentary on foreign policy that would become normative for television religious figures in the eighties.

Sheen identified himself with church tradition. In so doing he was a national figure using the airwaves along with his compatriots in local communities, both Catholic and Protestant. There were other figures of prominence during those early days including Norman Vincent Peale, but it was Sheen who mastered the TV technique and propounded his message with effectiveness. As Leonard has noted: "He addressed those moral issues of home and family, nation and patriotism, which Americans were celebrating in the Eisenhower years. His approach influenced a later generation of television preachers of whom Robert Schuller is perhaps the most familiar."[11]

A critique written in 1955 by Everett Parker, David Barry, and Dallas Smythe was less charitable to Sheen, placing him more directly in the vanguard of the later, more aggressive evangels:

He left the impression that universities are suspect because they house agents of Satan. Similarly, references to social reform, when it is concerned with agitation for housing, or security, or labor unions, or the improvement of man's material condition upon this earth, were presented in a negative fashion and with the clear implication that such agitation is a device of communism.[12]

Words and concepts with unfavorable associations included science, ethical reform, sex, Freud, universities, intellegentsia, educated, labor unions, and psychological.[13] The critique went on to state:

The normative belief and behavior sought of the audience is obedience to authority and through established authority to omnipotent God. The individual is expected to reject knowledge or principles that do not come through established authority. There is to be conformity of belief and behavior, which connotes an antilibertarian, antirational, antiliberal, antiintellectual, antinatural attitude as normative. Everyone has an ordained position. There are no shadings of "good" and "bad" either within the pattern of authority or outside of it.[14]

This study of Sheen concludes with words that are apt for many of the modern advocates of religion on television.

It is implicit in the assumptions underlying the Bishop's position that anyone who stands at any distance from the "right" formula for living is virtually as "bad" as the evil forces to which he is thereby exposed. Here is the semantic trap which awaits those who are engaged by sharp bipolarized evaluations. It is parallel to the logic by which a McCarthy assumes that any critic of his perforce must be a "communist"—for obviously a noncommunist would support him.[15]

The importance of this extensive examination of television's first generation of evangelists is quickly recognized when one becomes aware that the study was a project of the National Council of Churches. A quarter of a century later (1980) in a New York meeting jointly sponsored by that same council and the United States Catholic Conference nearly identical language was employed to describe the electronic evangelists. Addressing that group Robert Liebert warned, "Make no mistake about it: nothing less than the definition of Christianity is at stake in this holy war."[16]

The phenomenon of Sheen marked the first and last occasion that prime time was consistently available to a religious figure on a national basis. Sheen did return with a syndicated version of his earlier success, "The Bishop Sheen Program," that lasted from 1961 through 1968, but no longer in the evening and no longer directly competitive with the likes of Berle, Gene Autry, Red Skelton, Bob Cummings, and Groucho Marx.

If Sheen dominated the tube, the reality of politics and power dictated that a Protestant would be the nation's religious symbol in the upper reaches of the government. And, indeed, this was the case, as Billy Graham endeared himself to the White House while Norman Vincent Peale was the resident expert on religion for a growing collection of talk shows and specials. In September of 1954 Peale devoted 30 minutes on CBS "to assuring viewers that an inferiority complex should not prevent financial success."[17] As a *Time* article revealed:

The Peales (husband and wife) told how a friend of theirs, a perennial business failure, utilized his return to the bosom of the church to develop a profitable line of costume jewelry: he featured the "mustard seed of faith" [Matthew 17:20] in charm bracelets, clips and watch fobs. Said Peale: "It helps to have faith in God as well as in yourself."[18]

But it was Billy Graham who emerged as a national religious symbol, friend of presidents, and the dominant religious television personality for twenty years, 1955 to 1975. He, like Sheen, played heavily upon the Communist theme, but his programming technique was different. After early rating successes on radio with his "Hour of Decision," starting in November of 1950, Graham began to select some of his "Crusades," held in various metropolitan areas, to be filmed with the anticipation that they would appear as a kind of mini-series on selected television stations across the nation. Every few months Graham purchased prime time where possible and displaced network offerings for a few days. Due to this particular arrangement, it is virtually impossible to measure the size of Graham's audience or his TV competition.

Graham had already begun, by 1955, to carry his "Crusade" abroad, experiencing notable success in attendance in London. Reflecting upon this American phenomenon, the *Manchester Guardian* reported upon the theology of the growing crop of post-war evangelicals: "Fundamental pietism stands for a pattern of Christianity which should have passed, . . . its revival can in the long run only widen the gulf between organized religion and the estranged millions."[19] The writer continued by stating that it is a symptom of something sick in the mind of Christendom (a sickness both Catholic and Protestant) that has lasted for centuries and in which there is embedded an ugly element of sin, a Christianity that has not dared to love truth at all costs and with complete integrity.

In the summer of 1957 ABC contracted with Graham to broadcast his first "live" evangelical service. The four-week, 61-station presentation was described by *Variety* as a "surefire click" and it proclaimed Billy as "tremendous box-office." Opposite Perry Como and Jackie Gleason, Graham drew an 8 to 1 rating. He was a guest that same month on "Meet the Press" and the "Steve Allen Show."

In the healing genre Oral Roberts first employed television in January of 1954, using a studio. By the following year he was filming in "the world's largest gospel tent." Roberts took this financial gamble and syndicated his service over a collection of stations that very quickly expanded. Along with the increased exposure came the funding, as he made direct pleas for money on each episode. Due to the cost factor, a contemporary, Rex Humbard contented himself with live presentations close to his home base until the availability of videotape in the early sixties.[20]

The approach of Roman Catholics and mainline Protestants, using free air time, was best exemplified in programs such as "This Is Your Life" (Lutheran Church-Missouri Synod) and "Insight" (Roman Catholic-Paulist Fathers). Both programs, dating from the early fifties use drama with a religious message, but without a "hard sell."[21] "Insight" obtained the services of leading television writers and actors who donate their time to support the social messages. The Lutherans also produced an exceptional children's series—"Davey and Goliath."

By 1956 a number of officials within the churches were examining the implications of television for Christianity. They were particularly disturbed by the methods of fund raising over the air. Dr. Clifton E. Moore, director of television for the Los Angeles Presbytery, warned "against the danger of the profiteering electronic evangelist."[22] Moore argued,

The television industry and the respected denominations in your community have this in common—they both have an enemy. This enemy is the fringe or marginal preacher. He makes use of the air lanes for his own monetary gains. The religious exploiter [requests] that you write in for a pamphlet or booklet, with the idea that he has your mailing address for . . . solicitations . . . for money. These religious hucksters do untold damage to the church cause. Some of them make thousands, yes, even hundreds of thousands of dollars' profit with no way of knowing where the money goes.[23]

The 1955 National Council of Churches study already cited made similar points.

The most critical and sensitive spot in the ethics of mass communications, we believe, is on the use of these media for the manipulation of people. . . . The sanction against manipulation, we further suggest, extends specifically to the manipulation of people for what is presumed to be their best interest. . . . There is not as yet on the horizon of religious broadcasting the program that will compare in ''success'' with the mass evangelist of earlier days. The danger is that some creative genius will develop the program that is so ''successful'' by the standards of the commercial users of the media that the fundamental purposes of the Christian church will be ignored or denied.[24]

What was missed by these critics of television religion was the almost single-mindedly devotion of the independent practitioners of revivalism like Graham, Humbard, and Roberts to a theological position defined as premillennialism. Advocates of this persuasion believe that the world is headed for a cataclysmic destruction predicted in the Bible as centering in Armageddon. Every political move in current history is perceived as having been foretold in some biblical passage. The end is inevitable, an awful conflagration in which the powers of evil, led by an anti-Christ, will prevail on earth. The Christian faithful will escape this fate because they will be swept up into heaven to await a time when Jesus will return to earth and establish his kingdom. Any casual listener to Billy Graham in the fifties could have detected this theology.

War, a fallen leader (FDR), an indecisive peace, atomic bombs, and the rise of the Soviet Union to challenge U.S. hegemony seriously eroded the optimism espoused by religious liberals such as Harry Fosdick in their radio broadcasts of the thirties. The inordinate fear of communism that gripped the nation after World War II caused the rapid growth of a patriotism born out of dread and terror. As politicians wrestled with the new nationalist sentiments, premillennial preaching made its debut on television.

As E. Digby Baltzell stated, ''President Eisenhower calmly reigned as representative of a generation still dominated by the Protestant Establishment.''[25] The president retreated to the high road of moralism while Secretary of State John Foster Dulles created a foreign policy. Dulles's brinksmanship, with its emphasis upon America as a fortress, saw this nation as destined by God to save the world with a superior morality. Billy Graham proved a natural ally.

Graham brought to massive television audiences of the fifties an emphasis upon premillennialism, along with a vigorous attack upon those who viewed religion in terms of social reform. With the growth of a cold war mentality and the threat of nuclear war, premillennialism took stock of biblical phrases and found them open to interpretations consistent with apocalyptic thinking. Graham warned of Armageddon, while Sheen stirred TV viewers to a McCarthy-like fever pitch.

A coalition between TV premillennialism and the new, intensified nationalism took shape. Graham used his broadcasts on radio and television to warn of the imminent destruction of America if the population failed to turn to God. Graham's style was traditional, but he learned to control his audiences, avoiding unseemly emotional outbursts. His sermons were filled with the sounds of bombs and missiles, the spectre of total destruction, *unless* America made a decision for Christ. Graham added to Dulles's ''white hat'' policy a litmus test for the nation's prospects of success, defined as a decision for Christ. If America failed the test, did not turn to God, the nation would literally see red. Television became a primary weapon in this holy war. Graham, like his successors on television in the eighties, fashioned a messianic role for the United States. As a natural theological extension of this message, the evangelist identified his detractors as lacking patriotism and having likely leanings toward the left. His preaching became a type of nationalistic ideology.

Graham discovered that there was a great deal of money in television evangelism, and he found there instant celebrity status and power. And this latter, the ability to enter the "power elite" caused Billy Graham to circumscribe his theology with public relations. Conscious that his biblicism was not the majority opinion in America and seemingly intent upon retaining an informal title as the nation's minister, Graham appeared at times to be preaching two gospels, one an uncompromising biblical fundamentalism for the faithful and the other a bland call for some kind of civil religion and piety. It was this dual standard that generated considerable criticism and even ire among the religiously "pure," those literalist premillennialist Christians who felt a sense of God-directed mission, as yet not focused upon domestic and foreign policy. These were persons unwilling to accept a secular state, unwilling to act in cautious ways to achieve some moderate compromise for their god.

By the mid-seventies, some bright, active fundamentalists, recognizing themselves to be the "outs" in American church culture, still smarting from public ridicule dating to the 1925 Scopes Trial, resentful of their confinement to the Sunday morning TV ghetto, and conversant with TV technology (including the significance of cable and satellite), began a religious broadcasting revolution.[26] Their activity was based upon the Graham formula: TV religion means money and celebrity status, leading to power. They, however, added another ingredient—fanaticism.

In the early days of television, these fanatics remained confined to the Sunday morning hours, often selecting other times on radio, particularly Sunday evening. A 1963 survey of public attitudes about television offerings discovered that only 3 percent indicated a desire for more religious programming while no more than 1 percent of viewers were watching religious programs that year.[27] Around the year 1970 the numbers began to increase, and for a period lasting until 1975 the increase continued. Since that year the figures have been flat, with no noticeable change.[28] It was in that growth period that several individuals most clearly identifiable as fundamentalists began a tentative move toward emphasizing social and political issues. The trend was a new one for a group that had traditionally remained aloof from secular entanglements in order to protect their pure doctrine. Indeed, it was this very canon that many felt Graham had violated, although it is a fact that Graham seldom identified himself with particular policies, preferring rather to speak in broad generalities. It was only in the Nixon years that the evangelist actually became a public political partisan.

This new breed of premillennialist, upon entering the political lists, was prepared to indentify the date of the end. In 1983 Jerry Falwell broadcast, "There are 11 signs that prove the Lord is coming very soon. . . . In my opinion, there is no way we can make it to the year 2000. I really believe Jesus is coming first.''[29] Pat Robertson was more definite, claiming that America was mentioned in the Bible (Ezekiel). These men had inherited a coalition that Graham had established with the White House three decades ago. But in the person of Ronald Reagan they had an ideological brother, a true believer, whose public utterances began to reflect a premillennial theology. President Reagan observed in October of 1983:

You know, I turn back to your ancient prophets in the Old Testament and the signs foretelling Armageddon, and I find myself wondering if—we're the generation that is going to see that come about.
    I don't know if you've noted any of those prophecies lately, but, believe me, they certainly describe the times we're going through.[30]

At Harvard, Defense Secretary Casper Weinberger said: ''I have read the Book of Revelation and yes, I believe the world is going to end—by an act of God, I hope—but every day I think that time is running out.''[31]

Christians of the liberal persuasion had never experienced qualms about political and social comment. Fosdick had made this clear in his early broadcasts on radio, and the National Council of Churches was prominent for its public stands on all manner of issues. Martin Luther King, Jr., had exercised the role of biblical prophet as he championed the civil rights causes of the fifties and sixties. Vietnam was a natural focus for Christian protest by the likes of the Berrigans and William Coffin. But the underlying philosophy of this moderate and liberal social comment is in sharp contrast to that espoused by the fundamentalists.

An excellent assessment of the current status of TV religion is found in Charles Swann and Jeffrey Hadden's *Prime Time Preachers*. In their book they identify several types of media ministers: ''The Supersavers''—Billy Graham, Oral Roberts, Rex Humbard, Jerry Falwell; ''The Mainliners''—Robert Schuller; ''The Talkies''—Jim Bakker, Pat Robertson, Paul Crouch; ''The Entertainers''—Jimmy Swaggart, Ross Bagley; ''The Teachers''—Richard DeHaan, Paul Van Gorder; ''The Rising Stars''—James Robison, Kenneth Copeland, Jack Van Impe; and ''The Unconventional''—Ernest Angley.[32] Since the beginning of the decade a new force has been added that allows dozens of lesser known fundamentalists to ply their trade. The Trinity Broadcasting Network (TBN) is now available to most cable subscribers 24 hours a day. In half-hour and hour segments it offers a variety of religious programs heavily weighted with fund raising.

In order to present the current state of the art in TV evangelism a choice has been made to examine two electronic preachers who appear, at this writing, to be the most likely to have historic significance in television terms. In so doing it is clear that the powerful appeal of Swaggart has been manifest in recent extended popularity, that Schuller remains a strong favorite among moderate viewers, that Bakker has many of the characteristics of an Elmer Gantry, and that James Robison is perhaps the most powerful preacher in the group. In addition, the Donahue-like talk show of Richard Hogue, who practices a considered restraint in proclaiming his views, is an excellent illustration of how fundamentalism may be clothed in nonthreatening garments. But for this analysis, Jerry Falwell and Pat Robertson are the "stars."

Jerry Falwell, a native of Lynchburg, Virginia, founded an independent Baptist church, Thomas Road, in that city in 1956. Almost immediately after organizing the congregation Falwell started a radio ministry and six months later began to use a local television channel. He was following the pattern of dozens of similar individuals in communities across the country. However, by the close of the sixties Falwell had come to recognize the potential in radio and TV, and he began to expand his activities, seemingly modelling them on the earlier successes of Charles Fuller. Falwell founded a college and a seminary in Lynchburg and gave every indication of following the long tradition of doctrinal preaching associated with American fundamentalism, but shying away from involvement either in political or social issues. According to Falwell, it was in the year 1973 that he found himself so outraged by the Supreme Court decision concerning abortion that he determined to move his preaching into the social arena.

Armed with an "infallible, inerrant Word of God," the Bible, Falwell heads a vocal band of believers unaccustomed to compromise. They are considered by some to be genuine religious fanatics. Through the careful manipulation of his image and judicious association with the political far right, Falwell had become, by the fall of 1980, a national figure worthy of attention by the major news magazines. Joining with other "evangelical" preachers, he participated in a mass meeting in Texas to mobilize fundamentalists for the fight against immorality.

Answering the call of men like Paul Weyrich and Richard Viguerie, Falwell accepted the leadership of an organization known as "Moral Majority," in June of 1979. He calls the new group "a political organization" necessitated by the "pornographic explosion," the "homosexual revolution," and the "bureaucratic intervention into the ministry."[33] Moving on a wave of national publicity that included a *Newsweek* cover on September 15, 1980, Falwell was bold to support Ronald Reagan through his "Old Time Gospel Hour" as well as in the regional meeting of the National Religious Broadcasters in October. While protesting neutrality, this gathering featured an appearance by candidate Reagan and the far from subtle distribution of bumper stickers at the session on the Liberty Baptist College campus proclaiming "Christians for Reagan."[34] Speaking to a sympathetic audience at lunch on October 2, Falwell stated: "I believe God does not hear the prayers of unredeemed Gentiles or Jews."[35]

Coursing through "Meet the Press," "The Today Show," "Tomorrow," and "Donahue," along with a speech at the National Press Club, Falwell faced no more than a handful of probing questions. On October 12 on "Meet the Press" Falwell was allowed to go unchallenged as he identified Vice President Mondale as a "glossed-over atheist." Alerted to the tactics of the Lynchburg preacher and his fellow fundamentalists, the editor of a Southern Baptist weekly in Virginia commented: "They proceed on the false assumption that a particular political view can be designated 'the Christian view.' Such a position could only result from unbelievable arrogance."[36]

Since the 1980 election Falwell has continued to use his friendship with President Reagan to effect changes in national policy consistent with his goals. Chief among his concerns has been prayer in public schools, a cause he has championed consistently over his TV show and in national appearances. In fact, "The Old Time Gospel Hour" has become, to use Teddy Roosevelt's description of the presidency, a "bully pulpit" for promulgating fundamentalist theology wedded to extreme social conservatism.

"The Old Time Gospel Hour" has a format similar to most Protestant churches of the congregational tradition, with preaching the center of the hour. Falwell adds several ingredients that have allowed him to amass a fortune in gifts. He offers his viewers various articles if they will become "faith partners," and he constantly presses for contributions to Liberty Baptist College. He uses the pulpit to mount attack on what he considers the evils of the nation—abortion, secular humanism, evolution, public schools, liberal Christians, and Norman Lear. An occasional guest such as Charles Stanley or W. A. Criswell allows Falwell to make connections with Southern Baptists with whom he is not affiliated. Statistics suggest that his audience has been somewhat static for several years, but his high visibility, his friendship with Prime Minister Begin and President Reagan, and his backing by wealthy ultra-conservatives retain for him an important place in the public arena. His role as head of Moral Majority has provided an easy platform for public pronouncements beyond the "Gospel Hour" audience. In a perceptive article in *The New Yorker*, Frances FitzGerald indicated that Falwell was moving toward that time when he would have to make a choice as to whether he would move onto the national scene permanently or return to the faithful followers whose theology he champions.[37] By 1984 no such decision was in evidence.

More quietly Pat Robertson of Virginia Beach uses his "700 Club" to spread, on a daily basis, over a large cable and satellite network, the notion that the Christian way requires particular attitudes toward economic policy, foreign affairs, and domestic laws. Less flamboyant and potentially much more powerful than Falwell, Robertson's CBN network, with its flag station WYAH (the first three letters in Yahweh), insinuates itself into the viewer's living room with carefully shaped entertainment-oriented programming. His daily 90-minute talk show, fashioned as a Carson look alike with biblical banter, attracts many entertainment celebrities, and his new soap opera has become quite popular.

Robertson is well educated, the son of a former United States Senator. A Yale Law School graduate, he failed the New York bar exam and went into business in New York City. While living in a charismatic commune in Brooklyn he heard that there was a defunct TV station for sale in Virginia Beach. He managed to raise the money to buy it, and by October 1, 1961, it was on the air. In 1963

Robertson asked for $10 a month from 700 people to support WYAH, the origin of the "700 Club."[38]

The 90-minute talk show with Ben Kinchlow as sidekick is constructed to appeal to a broad range of viewer interest, but the central theme is ever present—the world is coming to an end, Armageddon is upon us. Yet Robertson continues to urge supporters to write congressmen and become politically involved. However, he has retreated from an earlier brush with the total political involvement characteristic of Falwell. Indeed, Robertson withdrew from the Religious Roundtable (an organization founded by Howard Phillips, Jerry Falwell, and Paul Weyrich in September 1979 to educate and publicize the "Christian" perspective on a wide range of public policy issues) in 1980 and has contented himself with being a critic of the political scene from the vantage point of his studio. He espouses an extreme conservatism in economics and domestic social issues and is even more vehement at times than Falwell on matters such as abortion. He views himself as a prophet, anointed by God. In engagements with his foes, "God Himself will fight for me against you—*and He will win.*"

The blush of political victory experienced by the fundamentalist TV evangelists in 1980 has faded. Abortions remain legal, Congress failed to pass the Reagan-sponsored bill on school prayer, evolution has triumphed in Arkansas and Texas. No longer a new, unknown political quantity, the impact of fundamentalist political action on future national elections is likely to be far less dramatic. In 1984 the victory of Senator Jesse Helms could be attributed to vigorous activity by the religious right, but this was an isolated success. Falwell and others have drawn many new voters into the political process and the dust is settling on that accomplishment. In terms of viewers, the electronic church had no more in 1984 than it did in 1980. The top seven ranked evangelists claimed less than 13 million in audience.

Rank	Preacher	Audience
1	Roberts	2,719,250
2	Humbard	2,409,960
3	Schuller	2,069,210
4	Swaggart	1,986,000
5	DeHaan/Gorder	1,519,400
6	Falwell	1,455,720
7	Bakker	668,170

And, relying upon this same 1980 data, the total viewing audience for the entire array of religious broadcasting numbered approximately 20 million.[39] By allowing for duplication of viewers this number shrinks to no more than 10 million. By contrast, a study issued by the Annenberg School of Communication in 1984 estimates that there exists an unduplicated audience of 13.3 million.[40] However, as William Fore and Charles Swann point out, that figure is inflated because it assumes that each household has the maximum 2.6 viewers, the average number of persons presumed to be in each home possessing a television set. A far more realistic estimate would be 1.8, yielding a figure of 9.2 million unduplicated viewers, no real change in the numbers during a four year period.[41] In a related inquiry Gallup found that the most watched religious programs over a seven day period were, in order: Swaggart, Roberts, Robertson, Bakker, Graham, Schuller, Falwell, and Humbard.

The movement of Swaggart and Humbard is significant when compared with the 1980 figures, but the most dramatic change is in Robertson's audience. While the Annenberg study saw no significant impact of cable on its figures, the evidence is otherwise in the case of the "700 Club." Robertson alone of the individuals mentioned has a style of programming that depends upon cable for growth, a live morning talk show. Hence, as the available audience for cable increases, it is reasonable to anticipate Robertson rising to the top, becoming the most influential voice among the TV evangelists.

As for Falwell, his audience has never been particularly large in comparison with his competitors, but his massive national exposure and seeming secure financial base make him the premier TV personality, the heir to Graham and Peale on the interview and talk show circuit. His political sense appears to have ingratiated him to the higher command of the Reagan administration, which will allow Falwell continued access to a far wider public than provided by "The Old Time Gospel Hour."

THEMES AND ISSUES

When all things have been considered, the reason why this collection of TV evangelists is important to the general public lies in its political involvement. This political action has naturally exposed the fundamentalists to severe criticism by those who perceive that these preachers are calling for violations of constitutional principles. And the fundamentalists are guilty of misapplying facts when they argue that their activities are only the conservative version of the type of political action engaged in by the Berrigans, King, and Coffin in the fifties and sixties. The current debate is not a liberal-conservative one, and to construe it thus is to allow this new breed of evangelist too easy an escape from analysis. Men like the Berrigans and King differed with their conservative opponents on the breadth of constitutional guarantees of freedom and justice, not on the values of republican democracy and the Bill of Rights.

The present debate is precisely on this point. Leaders of Moral Majority and Religious Roundtable advocate a form of theocracy; and fully protected by the Bill of Rights, they are utilizing the public airwaves to spread that message. Free expression is not the issue here; Falwell has every right to proclaim his views. The debate should be focused upon the ideological presuppositions advocated. While affirming pluralism, this new brand of Christian political activist seeks to restrict, through constitutional change, the rights of those who differ.

The distinction between human rights and right beliefs is at the heart of this discourse. The American Republic practices a secular morality. Critiques of the social system emanating from preachers like Fosdick have been expansive and inclusive, seeking the broadest application of democracy consistent with constitutional guarantees. Moral Majority, through its use of television, and Pat Robertson, through his entertaining style on the "700 Club," call for Americans to retreat from such a democratic ethic in the name of an exclusive deity.

Further, today's advocates of fundamentalism are striving to influence public policy consistent with an apocalyptic interpretation. Politicians imbued with such philosophy become incapable of serving the commonweal, since they are locked into a deterministic view of history. God and evil are engaged in a cosmic struggle to which mere humans come as spectators. Hence human creativity and imagination count for nothing, a social conscience is meaningless, and freedom is an illusion. Barbara Tuchman has an incisive critique of this mentality: " 'Fate' as a character in legend represents the fulfillment of man's expectations of himself."[42]

Americans are watching a historic engagement. There are those on the one hand who would narrow the American dream, enforce prayer by law, invade individual privacy in the name of morality, and generally seek to impose their own definitions upon us all. Their opponents are the advocates of freedom and diversity, no matter what political or religious label they carry. Television may well turn out to be the means of joining these issues, the theater in which renewed attention may be directed to the words of James Madison: "We must take alarm at the first experiment on our liberties."[43]

NOTES

1. Christopher H. Sterling and John M. Kittross, *Stay Tuned: A Concise History of American Broadcasting* (Belmont, Calif.: Wadsworth Publishing Co., 1978), p. 78.

2. Bill J. Leonard, "The Electric Church: An Interpretive Essay," *The Review and Expositor* 81, no. 1 (Winter 1984), p. 46.

3. Charles Coughlin, *Father Coughlin's Radio Sermons, 1930–31* (New York: Knox and O'Leary, 1931), p. 10.

4. James Hennessey, S.J., *American Catholics* (New York: Oxford University Press, 1981), p. 275.

5. Leonard, "The Electric Church," p. 48.

6. In the year 1954 Sheen was "DuMont's second-highest rated program" only outdrawn by professional football. *Time*, November 15, 1954, p. 89.

7. Erik Barnouw, *Tube of Plenty* (New York: Oxford University Press, 1982). p. 145.

8. *Time*, November 15, 1954, p. 89.

9. *Time*, November 3, 1952, pp. 79–80.

10. Tim Brooks and Earle Marsh, *The Complete Directory to Prime Time Network TV Shows, 1946–Present*, rev. ed. (New York: Ballantine Books, 1981), p. 431.

11. Leonard, "The Electric Church," p. 49.

12. Everett C. Parker, David W. Barry, and Dallas W. Smythe, *The Television-Radio Audience and Religion* (New York: Harper and Brothers, 1955), p. 121.

13. Ibid., p. 123.

14. Ibid., p. 129.

15. Ibid., p. 130.

16. Robert M. Liebert, "The Electronic Church: A Psychological Perspective," paper delivered to Electronic Church Consultation, New York University, February 6–7, 1980.

17. *Time*, September 13, 1954, p. 85.

18. Ibid.

19. "The Bible Says . . . ," *The Manchester Guardian*, June 2, 1955, weekly edition.

20. Jeffrey K. Hadden and Charles E. Swann, *Prime Time Preachers* (Reading, Mass.: Addison Wesley, 1981), p. 26.

21. *Time*, November 4, 1957, p. 55.

22. *Time*, July 30, 1956, p. 43.

23. Ibid.

24. Parker, Barry, and Smythe, *The Television-Radio Audience and Religion*, p. 414.

25. E. Digby Baltzell, *The Protestant Establishment* (New York: Vintage, 1966), p. 296.

26. It is appropriate here to offer a brief definition of fundamentalism. James Barr, in *Fundamentalism* (Westminster Press, 1978, p. 1), offers this description: "The most pronounced characteristics are the following: (a) a very strong emphasis on the inerrancy of the Bible, the absence from it of any sort of error; (b) a strong hostility to modern theology and to the methods, results and implications of modern critical study of the Bible; (c) an assurance that those who do not share their religious viewpoints are not really 'true Christians' at all."

27. Gary A. Steiner, *The People Look at Television* (New York: Alfred Knopf, 1963).

28. Charles Swann, co-author of *Prime Time Preachers*, has verified this observation in a long interview held with him in Richmond, Virginia, in April 1984. Professor Swann was most helpful in contributing his knowledge to this project and I am indebted to him.

29. Jerry Falwell, TV broadcast, "Nuclear War and the Second Coming of Christ, March 25, 1983.

30. Remarks by Reagan to Thomas Dine, executive director of the American-Israel Public Affairs Committee, quoted in an AP story by Donald Rothberg, October 30, 1983. Questioned about this statement by *People* magazine on December 6, Reagan affirmed, "theologians, quite a while ago, were telling me that never before has there been a time when so many prophecies were coming together." It requires little imagination to suggest who those "theologians" were. See also Robert S. Alley, "The Bible as an Engine of American Foreign Policy," *Free Inquiry* (Summer 1984).

31. Ronnie Dugger, "Does Reagan Expect a Nuclear Armageddon?" *Washington Post*, April 8, 1984, p. C4. Barbara Tuchman reminds modern readers that such influence was common enough in past political eras. Commenting on nineteenth century French government she noted: "Ultras held all the ministerial posts, including a religious extremist as Minister of Justice whose political ideas, it was said, were formed by regular reading of the Apocalypse." *The March of Folly* (New York: Alfred Knopf, 1984), p. 24.

32. Hadden and Swann, *Prime Time Preachers*, pp. 20–45.

33. Luncheon speech by Jerry Falwell on October 2, 1980, in Lynchburg, Virginia.

34. These bumper stickers, prominently displaying a cross, carried the notation "Paid

for and Authorized by Reagan-Bush Committee, U.S. Senator Paul Laxalt, Chairman, Bay Buchanan, Treasurer.''

35. Lunch meeting on October 2, 1980, at the Holiday Inn in Lynchburg. Falwell addressed the group, a regional gathering of religious broadcasters. He followed this quote with the remark, ''Yes, I made that statement.''

36. Julian H. Pentecost, ''Christians and Politics,'' *The Religious Herald* 152, no. 38, Oct. 16, 1980, p. 4.

37. Frances FitzGerald, ''A Reporter at Large: A Disciplined, Charging Army,'' *New Yorker*, May 18, 1981, pp. 53–141.

38. Hadden and Swann, *Prime Time Preachers*, pp. 34–37.

39. Ibid., p. 51.

40. *Religion and Television*, A Research Report by the Annenberg School of Communications and the Gallup Organization, 1984.

41. Conversation with Charles Swann on April 18, 1984.

42. Tuchman, *The March of Folly*, p. 49.

43. The Papers of James Madison, vol. 8, edited by Robert A. Rutland (Chicago, University of Chicago Press, 1973), p. 300.

BIBLIOGRAPHICAL SURVEY

The history of the development of the Electronic Church is well presented in Hadden and Swann, *Prime Time Preachers*. It is a thorough examination of the radio tradition as well as the stages of television growth. A highly critical treatment, it should be read in conjunction with Ben Armstrong's *The Electric Church*. A dated, but valuable source, is an analysis of religious broadcasting occurring over New Haven stations in 1955. It was written by Everett Parker, David Barry, and Dallas Symthe under a commission from the National Council of Churches and entitled *The Television-Radio Audience and Religion*.

There are a number of excellent critiques of the modern TV evangelists among which the best are Frances FitzGerald's lengthy examination of Jerry Falwell in *The New Yorker* of May 18, 1981, and a chapter entitled ''Billy Graham: Mass Medium'' in Michael Real's *Mass-Mediated Culture*. In the winter issue, 1984, the Southern Baptist Seminary's *Review and Expositor* presented a series of essays that are largely negative in their assessments of ''The Church and the Media.'' The two best articles in the publication are ''The Electric Church: An Interpretive Essay'' by Bill J. Leonard and ''Wise as Serpents, at Least: The Political and Social Perspectives of the Electronic Church'' by James Dunn. An organization founded in 1980, People for the American Way, has instituted a serious analysis of the electronic evangelists through the monitoring of Falwell and Robertson. Created by Norman Lear, this group is particularly conscious of the power of television. It sought to respond to the religious right with several 30–second spots aired during 1981 and 1982. People for the American Way has produced one film, ''Life & Liberty . . . for All Who Believe,'' narrated by Burt Lancaster, that was shown in 1983 over local stations in some 50 markets.

A conference sponsored by the National Council of Churches and the United

States Catholic Conference, held in New York in February of 1980, produced some excellent papers on the numerous aspects of the burgeoning fundamentalism of TV.

For a study of the history of fundamentalism, George Marsden's *Fundamentalism and American Culture* is excellent, while the theology is treated with scholarly insight by James Barr in *Fundamentalism*.

An examination of the leading figures in the Electronic Church should begin with their own affirmations. See in particular Kenneth Copeland, *Our Convenant with God*; Billy Graham, *World Aflame*; Oral Roberts, *The Call*; Pat Robertson, *Shout It from the Housetops*; Jerry Falwell, *Capturing a Town for Christ*. Each of the evangelists has scores of publications that are regularly offered to viewers, some free, some for a donation. Significant among these are *The Flame*, published by Christian Broadcasting Network; *Abundant Living*, by the Oral Roberts organization; and *Decision,* by the Billy Graham organization. In addition, of course, any research of the subject begins with the viewing of the programs that are the vehicles for these men's preaching.

A recent publication that attempts an analysis of all of the various aspects of religious broadcasting is *Religion and Television*. It is the result of a study conducted jointly by the Annenberg School and Gallup. Published in 1984, this document was funded by numerous seminaries, a religious organization (NCC), and evangelists (Falwell, Robertson). While it appeared too late for thorough examination in this present volume, it is clearly a benchmark for future scholarly inquiry.

BOOKS AND ARTICLES

Alley, Robert S., and Irby B. Brown. "The Moral Monopoly," *EMMY Magazine* 3, no. 1 (Winter, 1981), p. 35.

Armstrong, Ben. *The Electric Church*. Nashville, Tenn.: Thomas Nelson Publishers, 1979.

Ashman, Chuck. *The Gospel According to Billy*. Secaucus, N.J.: Lyle Stuart, 1977.

Baltzell, E. Digby. *The Protestant Establishment*. New York: Vintage, 1966.

Barnouw, Erik. *A Tower of Babel*. New York: Oxford University Press, 1966.

———. *Tube of Plenty*. New York: Oxford University Press, 1982.

Barr, James. *Fundamentalism*. Philadelphia: The Westminster Press, 1978.

Brooks, Tim, and Earle Marsh. *The Complete Directory to Prime Time Network TV Shows, 1946–Present*. Rev. ed. New York: Ballantine Books, 1981.

"The Church and the Media." *Review and Expositor* 51, no. 1 (Winter 1984).

Coughlin, Charles. *Father Coughlin's Radio Sermons, 1930–31*. New York: Knox and O'Leary, 1931.

Crawford, Alan. *Thunder on the Right*. New York: Pantheon Books, 1980.

Electronic Church Consultation. Various papers presented at New York University, February 6–7, 1980.

FitzGerald, Frances. "A Reporter at Large." *The New Yorker*, May 18, 1981, p. 53.

Fore, William F. "The Electronic Church." *Ministry*, January 1979.

Frady, Marshall. *Billy Graham: A Parable of American Righteousness*. Boston: Little, Brown, 1979.

Hadden, Jeffrey, and Charles Swann. *Prime Time Preachers*. Reading, Mass.: Addison-Wesley, 1981.

Hennessey, James. *American Catholics*. New York: Oxford University Press, 1981.

Marsden, George M. *Fundamentalism and American Culture*. New York: Oxford University Press, 1980.

Marty, Martin. *The Improper Opinion: Mass Media and the Christian Faith*: Philadelphia: Westminister Press, 1961.

Noonan, D. P. *The Passion of Fulton Sheen*. New York: Dodd, Mead, 1972.

Parker, Everett C., David W. Barry, and Dallas W. Smythe. *The Television-Radio Audience and Religion*. New York: Harper & Brothers, 1955.

Real, Michael R. *Mass-Mediated Culture*. Englewood Cliffs, N.J.: Prentice-Hall, 1977.

Religion and Television. A Research Report by the Annenberg School of Communications, 1984.

Sterling, Christopher, and John M. Kittross. *Stay Tuned: A Concise History of American Broadcasting*. Belmont, Calif: Wadsworth Publishing, 1978.

Streiker, Lowell D., and Gerald S. Strober. *Religion and the New Morality*. New York: Association Press, 1972.

Steiner, Gary A. *The People Look at Television*. New York: Alfred Knopf, 1963.

Tull, Charles J. *Father Coughlin and the New Deal*. Syracuse, N.Y.: Syracuse University Press, 1965.

VIDEOGRAPHY

"Billy Graham Crusade"
Syndicated, periodic broadcasts, usually three or four nights in a row, pre-empting regular programing in local markets
Premiere: 1951
Host: Billy Graham

"Life Is Worth Living"
DuMont, Tuesday, 8:00–8:30 P.M. ABC-TV, Thursday, 8:00–8:30 P.M. Monday, 9:00–9:30 P.M.
Premiere: February 12, 1952
Host: Bishop Fulton J. Sheen
Last Program: April 8, 1957

"This Is the Life"
Syndicated, usually Sunday morning
Premiere: September, 1952
Host: The Lutheran Church-Missouri Synod

"Rex Humbard"
Syndicated, various times
Premiere: 1953
Host: Rex Humbard

"Oral Roberts and You"
Syndicated, various times

Premiere: January 10, 1954
Host: Oral Roberts

"The Old Time Gospel Hour"
Syndicated, various times, weekly
Premiere: 1956
Host: Jerry Falwell

"The 700 Club"
Live, Monday through Friday, 90 minutes on CBN. Also syndicated, various hours
Premiere: 1965
Host: Pat Robertson

"Day of Discovery"
Syndicated, various times, weekly
Premiere: 1968
Host: Richard De Haan, Paul Van Gorder

"Hour of Power"
Syndicated, various times, weekly
Premiere: 1970
Host: Robert Schuller

"Insight"
Syndicated, various times, usually Sunday morning
Host: Paulist Fathers

"James Robison, Man with a Message"
Syndicated, various times
Premiere: 1970
Host: James Robison

"Jimmy Swaggart, Evangelist"
Syndicated, various times, weekly
Host: Jimmy Swaggart

"The PTL Club"
Syndicated, daily, various times
Premiere: 1974
Host: Jim Bakker

"Kenneth Copeland"
Syndicated, various times
Premiere: 1979
Host: Kenneth Copeland

20

The Television Commercial

DEBORAH FRANKLIN

OVERVIEW

Television has a relatively recent role in advertising history compared to the extensive time line some researchers require to trace the development of advertising communication. In finding the roots of this activity called advertising, some scholars actually go as far back as six centuries B.C., to the days of boatswains crying messages about their ship's cargo for sale.[1] There is consensus that advertising on television is largely as old as the medium itself.

At first, advertisers did not know exactly how to use the television medium effectively. The first commercials were dismal makeovers of radio spots, often with no changes in script. Advertisers needed some time to ascertain ways to exploit the particular visual impact of television. Soon they realized that the "wooden" talking announcer holding a product sample could be replaced with more exciting innovations. Demonstrations became a popular approach, as advertisers gradually discovered they could easily illustrate product benefits for viewers.

Individuals who object to some of the approaches used in television advertising and to the intrusive nature of the medium often are still willing to recognize the contributions television advertising has made to communications development. Television commercials led the medium in innovative use of film, in techniques of animation, in varied creative production techniques, and other areas.

Many of the issues raised in critically analyzing television advertising are concerns common to all of advertising. For example, some scholars argue that advertising makes members of society more materialistic, that it causes them to want things most people cannot realistically expect to have. Another view is that so much of advertising is built on stereotype, as evidenced by commercials that show fathers are incapable of preparing waffles for breakfast, only Italians have the skill to make zesty spaghetti sauce, and today's woman should be able to work at a career all day yet prepare excellent meals for her family when she arrives home in the evening.

It appears these criticisms and many others are more readily identified with television advertising because of the pervasiveness of the medium. Few national campaigns for products or services can succeed if television advertising is excluded. While users of the printed media in some categories appear to be declining, television remains a nearly universal medium of advertising in American culture. So, for many people, television is the primary referent for their views on advertising.

HISTORICAL DEVELOPMENT

Beginning in the late 40s, American television, through its advertisers and their agencies, pursued the perfection of the little one-minute art form known as the TV "commercial." Ensuing years saw the principles and practice of this bit of instantaneous mass marketing raised to undreamed of heights—and profits . . . .

In the late 40s and early 50s, as commercials came to golden flower, American life began to balance on a fulcrum of *things*. Things that could be bought, used, swallowed, or puffed—all sold at a frantic pace day and night by the most accomplished practitioners of the huckster's art.[2]

These two paragraphs come from Lincoln Diamant's introduction to his book *Television's Classic Commercials: The Golden Years*. In a few short sentences, Diamant manages to convey the nearly euphoric state of people in advertising when they gradually realized what a tremendous vehicle for selling and communication was now wide open to them, their financial resources permitting, of course.

There was a brief period of experimentation with television as a popular medium in the years before World War II, but television communication, taking advantage of some of the advances in technology made possible by the war, literally exploded in the late forties.[3] The first television commercials were, at best, uninspired. Live standups were recorded by television show personalities or talent was hired to read the famed "idiot cards." Before completely dismissing such efforts as totally primitive, however, it is important to cite some advantages of these early advertising tactics. Such commercials had an indisputable air of reality to them, errors and all. They established an intimacy with an audience.[4] This atmosphere was enhanced by the presence of former respected radio celebrities such as Arthur Godfrey and Ted Mack, who became part of new live television in 1948.[5] Other stars such as Milton Berle soon followed. These celebrities had a high degree of credibility with audiences, and those feelings translated into trust by viewers of endorsed products.

According to a 1976 article by Roger D. Rice, who was president of the Television Bureau of Advertising at the time, one of the earliest commercials aired in 1944. Hugh Downs sat at a desk piled with Sunoco cans as props and read a commercial as part of a Lowell Thomas news presentation.[6]

Naturally, there was no opportunity to correct mistakes on live commercials. One of the most popular pieces of advertising history trivia illustrates this drawback. Betty Furness was a spokeswoman for Westinghouse, and she often appeared in commercials aired on "Studio One" from 1948 and into the 1950s on CBS.[7] Such live product demonstrations generally were successful until the time a refrigerator door stuck, and Furness was left tugging and pulling in an attempt to open it. So much for live demonstrations, where anything could literally happen, and sometimes still does.

Television initially adopted the same mode of sponsorship that was used by radio. Radio shows had sponsors, such as Oxydol's "Ma Perkins." Television programs in the 1940s were set up in much the same way. Erik Barnouw analyzes this sponsor-supported system and its implications at length in his book, *The Sponsor: Notes on a Modern Potentate*. Some sponsors could point to dramatic sales increases resulting from television advertising. According to Barnouw, Hazel Bishop lipsticks began advertising on television in 1950. Sales increased from $50,000 to $4.5 million in two years.[8] Sponsors wanted to be affiliated with successful programs, and they often tried to have some say in program content.

Early television advertising was low in cost even when compared to radio. "The Texaco Star Theater", as Rice reported, reached 750,000 of the one million homes with television at a weekly charge of $15,000 plus time.[9] With $1 million, a sponsor could buy a one-hour weekly show for about ten months.[10]

By the 1950s, advertisers were also experimenting with a system called alternating sponsorship, with Philco and Goodyear slated for "Television Playhouse" on rotating weeks. Barnouw says each spent in the range of $25,000 to $35,000 per program.[11] His figure does not include straight costs of buying time.

Barnouw credits Sylvester L. Weaver, first a vice president and then president at NBC, with encouraging advertisers to share sponsorship of programs put together by the networks or filmed by independent producers for the networks.[12] This new system, now called a participation show, made more sense as costs of television advertising continued to increase. If it is true that costs of program production and transmission rose as much as 500 percent between 1949 and 1959, then logically advertising time costs were raised commensurately.[13] Even today, the participation show remains the common mode of television advertising. Sometimes a prosperous advertiser who wants to feature multiple products within a show will buy blocks of time and split 60-second spots, for example, between two products. This is a more cost-effective system, as the television advertising budget can then be spread across promotional costs for several products. For the past two decades, sole sponsorship of programs has been the exception rather than the rule, with rare specials carried by a single advertiser, such as the "Hallmark Hall of Fame."[14]

Necessarily, technology limits what the most creative advertiser is able to do. Advertisers in the 1950s used film, and this practice allowed agencies to selectively mail prints to key television stations of their choice. Advertisers were no longer at the mercy of idiosyncratic live talent or poor production quality. The same carefully filmed commercial with the same carefully crafted message could be aired consistently at the advertiser's discretion.[15]

By 1956, there was another technological breakthrough, the use of videotape. Commercials became even easier to produce. There was no "down time" for developing videotape as there was in film. Editing was relatively simple. Sound, recorded simultaneously with video, did not have to be added later. A commercial could be taped and played back immediately to see the results. Adjustments to the set or the script or recommendations to the talent could be made on the spot. Retaping could take place quickly, as producers knew exactly what they had to improve.

Perhaps the 1960s will go down in advertising history for reasons other than technological advances or changes in sponsorship systems. Jonathan Price notes that, in the late 1960s, advertisers began to realize there was not necessarily a correlation between purchasing and the entertainment value of commercials.[16] In earlier periods of advertising development, admen were often dependent on the expertise of creative people in film. These filmmakers were talented individuals, but frequently they did not have the business background necessary for practical resolution of an advertising problem. The conflict between business needs and the entertainment factor of commercials remains even today. In a recent television campaign, an attractive young woman wearing a bikini walks across a beach. She carries a can of a popular diet soft drink. When the commercial was analyzed in audience tests, viewers could not name the product brand in question. Here, then, is a classic example of the entertainment factor in advertising inadvertently taking precedence over the pragmatic business concerns of an advertiser. Maybe this is why, Price points out, the admen began to take more control over the filming of commercials.[17]

By the late 1960s, two schools of thought on the most effective approach for advertising by commercial television emerged. In one camp were the so-called advocates of "light-hearted" commercials, such as the Benson and Hedges spots where people were trying to adjust to longer cigarettes and getting caught in elevator doors and similar predicaments. The goal in such an ad, advocates claimed, was to get across a single idea about a product in a memorable but easy-going fashion.[18] Some executives with a different point of view decided to take tighter controls over creative strategy. Gradually, sophisticated tests were developed to ascertain what products consumers wanted and what advertising techniques translated to profits.[19]

As commercials became more elaborate, production also became more expensive. Costs of straight air time climbed as well. Advertisers responded to this situation by reducing the time allotted for commercial messages. By 1971, the 30-second commercial was used more frequently than the 60-second spot.[20] More than 80 percent of network and nonnetwork commercials are now 30 seconds.[21]

In the late 70s, television's annual billings for advertisers jumped past the

$10 billion mark. The Television Advertising Bureau has predicted an increase to $40 billion by 1990.[22] According to president of the bureau Roger Rice, much of the influx of revenues is due to the realization of local advertisers that television can be a substantial part of their media mix. In a 1979 interview with *Broadcasting* magazine, Rice cited some statistics to validate this point. Among them: airline billings up 40 percent; department stores up 100 percent; food stores up 75 percent.[23] Television advertising has become such an integral part of the economic fabric of the country that, if one business is airing commercials, the competitor frequently has to adjust advertising plans accordingly.

Due to another turn of events in the late 1970s, expanding technology will probably once again impact on traditional advertising media and approaches. Advertising executive Archa O. Knowlton discussed several trends in a recent column. With satellite and cable availability, advertisers can fashion their messages for carefully targeted regional audiences. Interactive cable systems have potential as research vehicles and as "direct marketing tools" of a sort that can more readily identify interested buyers.[24] Some research analysts are predicting there may be as many as a dozen cable networks in less than ten years.[25] Top firms such as J. Walter Thompson are rethinking types of advertising that could be offered via cable. Among the ideas is longer commercials, ranging from ten minutes to full program length.[26] While there are those media experts who express concern that cable will lead to narrowcasting, to programs for limited audiences, others see this development as an opportunity to reach a precisely defined audience, for example, an ethnic group. Spanish International Network is a good example.[27]

Having traced the development of this genre called the television commercial, it seems appropriate to conclude this portion of the chapter with a brief commentary on some of the dramatic devices (or "storytelling techniques" as J. Douglas Johnson labels them) used by advertisers. There is the statement about product attributes as an announcer, on or off camera, does the narration, and a viewer sees the item for sale on the screen. There is also a second device, the demonstration with the product at work. Some advertisers take the demonstration one step further and put their products through torture tests. Football teams use pieces of luggage for practice "balls." Waterproof watches are exposed to inclement weather. Assuming these torture experiments are devised convincingly, such ads have a high degree of credibility. Johnson also discusses a "problem and solution" format. Mrs. Smith's laundry detergent does not perform well. What are her choices for a better product? Ads that engage in direct comparison of competing products delight the Federal Trade Commission and consumer groups who believe this approach makes invaluable information available to buyers, helping them to make informed product decisions. The drama or playlet appears to be a carryover from radio. In this structure, one finds protagonists, antagonists, climaxes, and resolutions of real-life problems, everything from adolescent acne, to bad breath, to household germs. This format is appealing, but it lends itself to exaggeration that is sometimes impossible to take seriously. Commercials of this type may not convince. Finally, Johnson has a category simply called "a chronology." "Events" unfold in a logical scenario. An example is the saga unfolding about wear and tear on a family-room carpet during a given day.[28]

Depending on which advertising scholarship one studies, the list of techniques for presenting the commercial story can be expanded further. Roy Paul Nelson notes the growth of the "song and dance" ad.[29] The popularity of a memorable jingle expands into a carefully choreographed mini-production. Soft drink advertisers led in the development and perfection of this technique. Nelson also isolates special-effects commercials as worthy of scrutiny.[30] The current Saturday morning commercials featuring Ronald McDonald and Rice Krispies cereal ads are examples. These groupings are not necessarily mutually exclusive, but they do create a framework for discussion of devices for shaping the commercial story.

THEMES AND ISSUES

Most of the discussion concerning modern television advertising falls into two categories: impact on cultural norms and values and economic impact. As these issues are outlined, it will become apparent that they are not the sole province of the television medium. Nonetheless, these problems of the medium's impact are applicable to television advertising. More significantly, for many consumers, it is the experience of television advertising that informs their response to and criticisms of current TV practice.

A key ethical issue raised in most discussions of TV advertising is whether it is an exercise in deception. Much of this debate arises from the classic argument about whether advertising should be persuasive or merely informative.[31] Some define "persuasion" as manipulation or coercion rather than as a simple effort to convince. Those who see advertising as coercion usually do not espouse a high level of confidence in consumer decision making.

According to Dunn and Barban, more than 97 percent of the advertisements checked by the Federal Trade Commission each year pass evaluations monitoring deceptive practice.[32] In the case of the other 3 percent, there is often consumer concern about impressions created versus literal interpretation of claims. The local carpet store, for example, may advertise that it offers the most durable indoor-outdoor carpet in town. There are a number of ways to interpret this claim. What is the meaning of "durable"? For how much abuse does this durability allow? Is the brand offered the most durable money can buy, or is this claim based on carpet offered in the local market? How could one ever actually test for the truth of a claim like this? Such superlative assertions do not require substantiation. Consumers can take comfort in knowing that *material* claims must be verifiable.[33] If an automobile manufacturer claims a car uses one gallon of gasoline for 38 miles traveled on highways, there must be evidence from road tests to support that fact. Obviously, any business that deliberately engages in deceptive advertising would certainly be harming its long-range interests.

There are many who raise their objections to advertising on the grounds of poor taste. Such views usually have a number of sources. In some instances, what the consumer is actually viewing is a fundamental problem with the product class itself. Those against drinking alcohol, for example, may prefer to have beer and wine commercials dropped from the airwaves. Avid nutritionists may not be comfortable with the heavy television promotion of snack foods with high sugar content. The debates on such commercials get so involved at times that researchers often forget that a basic disagreement about the legitimacy of the product itself is at issue.

Other assertions about poor taste sometimes rest on the commercial production techniques themselves. Some commercials assault the ears with obnoxious sound effects or inane jingles. Some ads feature pushy hard-sell announcers who are unrelenting in reminding consumers that today is the time to cash in on the latest bargain. Unfortunately, there is a philosophy of advertising, particularly prevalent on the local level, that states that it does not matter how offensive advertising techniques are as long as the consumer remembers the sponsor. Right or wrong, there is some validity to this concept. An advertising agency serving the Baltimore-Washington metropolitan area recently attempted to assess the effectiveness of a series of ads for a local chain of linen stores. The commercials featured boisterous announcers and ridiculous antics. The dialogue moved so fast it was virtually impossible to understand the complete message. The consumers surveyed found the commercials annoying, but they also were highly aware of these stores and were inclined to make purchases there.

Timing of airing of commercials is also a problem in certain instances, contributing to the protestations of poor taste. Commercials on stomachache remedies do not come across well at the dinner hour. Parents often have definite opinions about types of products that should not be advertised during evening family viewing time when children may be watching.[34]

Affiliated with the problem of timing is the issue of repetition. In an evening of television viewing, it is not unusual to see any one commercial three, four, or five times. This practice is called planning a flight of ads. For the advertiser, this method allows saturation of a market within a short period of time and rapid establishment of product identity as well. The average television viewer tends to forget the advertiser's objective to reach as many people as possible at the same time. The advertiser has no way to anticipate the duration of a consumer's television viewing.

In another type of scenario, viewers may find themselves watching a commercial that is simply unappealing or uninteresting to them. It may be that the viewer is simply not part of the demographic group for that commercial and is watching at the "wrong time." The Saturday afternoon commercial on the latest rock music album available at the local store is for the teenager, not for others who may happen to be tuned in at the time. This may also be why people at times feel "talked down to" by commercials. They may not be part of the intended audience.

A key method for understanding complaints about poor taste is to determine whether they arise from a reaction to the nature of the appeal used. Some tactics are fairly easy for most scholars and consumers to accept: appeal to romance; appeal to be part of a group; appeal to a sense of adventure. Research has found that sometimes presenting both sides of an issue will allow more favorable reception of an advertising message.[35] Advertisers appear to be growing in their awareness of this phenomenon. More commercials seem to be presenting lines such as, "Sure, we cost more, but . . . we offer more value."

Problems have the most potential to develop when fear and guilt appeals are used. Fear appeals work when they come from credible sources and deal with salient issues. The difficulties arise when the appeals are trivialized or go to extremes. There is a campaign for a national insurance firm where a mother gently reassures her son that they will be able to keep their home, even if something unfortunate happens to the father, because they have insurance. The consumer can handle the fear here because what is called for is a straightforward, concrete action to deal with the appeal. Buy an insurance policy. Campaigns warning people not to smoke by showing the dread effects of cancer have less potential for success because the fear evoked is so high. People then react by ignoring the message altogether. Too often, fear appeals are trivialized in commercials such as those where people are ostracized due to body odor and bad breath.

Guilt appeals also are prevalent. Again, consumers are bombarded with appeals on such inconsequential problems as whether their laundry is as white as their neighbors'. "Are you doing something wrong?" they are asked. Mothers are the frequent targets of guilt appeals. "Are you feeding your family nutritiously?" commercials ask incessantly. For good or ill, such advertisements sometimes do tap into people's insecurities about themselves and their lives. Does advertising offer products and services to cope with those insecurities or do businesses exploit them? The answer to that question probably depends on one's perspectives on advertising scholarship and on whether one is a proponent or opponent of advertising practice.

Probably the two major objections to television advertising are that it creates stereotypes and perpetuates materialism and conformity.[36] In a sense, the advertiser could well argue that a convenient common understanding can be reached through stereotyping, and such groundwork has to be used to get across the truncated 30-second message. A character has to be quickly placed in a role as a housewife, father, career woman, or farmer, depending on what the commercial requires.

Consumers have differing levels of tolerances for stereotypes. A father struggling to make waffles for breakfast can be humorous, and the commercial can be interpreted lightheartedly. On the other hand, stereotypes can oversimplify or exaggerate. While a mishap in cooking the main dish for dinner is a disappointment, such an incident would probably cause few housewives great distress. Superwomen of television commercial fame, who can fill multiple career and home duties with the greatest ease, seldom exist in reality. Such stereotypes are annoying, perhaps offensive to some members of society. Most advertisers now seem to have a heightened sensitivity to portrayals of the elderly, ethnic groups, and women. Less than a sympathetic view of these segments of the population would probably not be accepted easily by today's consumers.

One of the classic debates in advertising is whether the bombardment of consumers with commercial messages makes them more materialistic and makes them want things they cannot realistically expect to have. Allied with this concern is some people's contention that advertising causes conformity, making all people want the same products, the same lifestyle. It is doubtful this debate will ever be resolved. The outcome rests on one's perceptions about whether advertising acts on society in certain ways or advertising merely reflects society. If advertising did not respond to consumer expectations and demands, chances of success would be questionable. Still, marketing experts discuss something they call the creation of demand. Until air conditioning was made available in automobiles, consumers would not have thought to expect it.

Turning to economic issues related to television advertising, the first factor that comes to mind is the high cost of advertising, particularly on the national level. For major television events, a single spot may cost a quarter of a million dollars. People who look in dismay at the numbers of dollars spent in television advertising sometimes forget to assess the relative cost of the commercial. The cost to deliver that television ad to millions of consumers may actually translate to fractions of a cent per household. Also, rates for local retail are not as prohibitive as they might seem at first. Sixteen 10-second commercials can cost $1,000. A 30-second commercial on a popular syndicated rerun can be as little as $400. Rates charged are highly negotiable and vary tremendously, based on the time of day the commercial is to air, the state of the market, program adjacency, and the current ratings.

Most people who claim television advertising is wasteful are responding in terms of absolute cost, or they are responding to the repetition of commercials. As explained previously, frequent airing of ads is required to reach a maximum portion of the market. Such is the competitive system in which advertisers must work in this country.

Certainly, there is a need to compete in the marketplace. Some scholars have questioned whether heavy advertising allows businesses to acquire a monopoly over a market. Perhaps, in some sense, this is a valid objection. The neighborhood boutique does not have access to the advertising dollars for investment in television that a national clothing store chain has available. Yet, the cost of television advertising to compete on a local level is not prohibitive for all businesses. Even a small local store can win a small market share, although all may not be able to do so through television ads. In the case of manufacturers of similar products, advertising can foster healthy competition among market leaders. For the producer of a product or service, advertising is a good option for breaking into a monopolistic market. Consumers often get the resultant double benefit of product information and competitive pricing.

While it is true that the cost of a product is reflective of necessary production and marketing costs, advertising may create demand for a product, thus lowering individual item cost as production reaches full potential.[37] Conversely, advertising may cause goods to cost more as brand image adds perceived value.[38] People often go into stores seeking specific brands known for quality. In a sense, advertising has raised the value and, therefore, the price of these goods.

Advertising via television will probably continue to arouse discussion far into the future. Members of the television advertising industry report that 90 percent of the top national advertisers invest the bulk of their advertising dollars in television.[39] For all it has contributed to the television art, advertising still has some of the same problems Stockton Helffrich called to the attention of the National Association of Broadcasters 20 years ago. In a 1964 speech, he cited a number of trouble areas: unconvincing clinical data for backup of claims; questionable survey reports in support of claims; demonstrations that do not prove anything; "derogation of the competition"; inappropriate testimonials; and disturbing advocacy of self-diagnosis in drug advertising.[40] The list continued, and much of it would still be appropriate today. While some may have reservations about this phenomenon called the television commercial, Jonathan Price places the genre well:

Commercials represent the pinnacle of our popular culture's artistic expression. More money per second goes into their making, more cash flows from their impact, more business thinking goes into each word than in any movie, opera, stage play, painting or videotape. If commercials are artful, then the art is objective, not subjective; capitalist, not rebellious; part of a social activity rather than a personal search for expression; more like a Roman road than a lyric poem. Their history is economic.[41]

NOTES

1. J. Douglas Johnson, *Advertising Today* (Chicago, Ill.: Science Research Associates, 1978), p. 5.

2. Lincoln Diamant, *Television's Classic Commericals: The Golden Years, 1945–48* (New York: Hastings House, 1971), p. xi.

3. Erik Barnouw, *The Sponsor: Notes on a Modern Potentate* (New York: Oxford University Press, 1978), p. 42.

4. Ibid., p. 7.

5. Elizabeth J. Heighton and Don R. Cunningham, *Advertising in the Broadcast Media* (Belmont, Calif.: Wadsworth Publishing Co., 1976). p. 26.

6. Roger D. Rice, "Baby Medium, Television Grows Up since 1940s," *Advertising Age*, April 19, 1976, p. 111.

7. Heighton and Cunningham, *Advertising in the Broadcast Media*, p. 36.

8. Barnouw, *The Sponsor*, p. 46.

9. Rice, *Advertising Age*, p. 112.

10. Ibid.

11. Barnouw, *The Sponsor*, p. 47.

12. Ibid.

13. Rice, *Advertising Age*, p. 112.

14. Ibid.

15. Ibid., p. 113.

16. Jonathan Price, *The Best Thing on TV: Commercials* (New York: Penguin Books, 1978), p. 5.

17. Ibid., p. 4.

18. Merle Kingman, "13 Creative Heads Laud, Lambaste 1966 Campaigns; See Feuds, Defend Light-Hearted Ads, Young Cubs," *Advertising Age*, January 23, 1967, p. 2.

19. Price, *The Best Thing on TV*, p. 56.

20. Rice, *Advertising Age*, p. 112.

21. Johnson, *Advertising Today*, p. 213.

22. "Television Advertising: The Way Things Were, and May Be," *Broadcasting*, November 12, 1979, p. 36.

23. "Television Is Still the Best Buy," *Broadcasting*, November 12, 1979, p. 39.

24. Archa D. Knowlton, "The Challenges and Opportunities of the 80s," *Broadcasting*, January 7, 1980, p. 14.

25. "2001: Advertising," *Broadcasting*, October 12, 1981, p. 244.

27. Knowlton, "The Challenges and Opportunities," *Broadcasting*, p. 14.

28. Johnson, *Advertising Today*, pp. 216–17.

29. Roy Paul Nelson, *The Design of Advertising*, 4th ed. (Dubuque, Iowa: William C. Brown Co. Publishers, 1981), p. 274.

30. Ibid.

31. John S. Wright, Willis L. Winter, Jr., and Sherilyn L. Zeigler, *Advertising*, 5th ed. (New York: McGraw Hill Book Co., 1982), p. 10.

32. S. Watson Dunn and Arnold M. Barban, *Advertising: Its Role in Modern Marketing* (Hinsdale, Ill.: The Dryden Press, 1978), p. 84.

33. Donald W. Jugenheimer and Gordon E. White, *Basic Advertising* (Columbus, Ohio: Grid Publishing, Inc., 1980), pp. 74–76.

34. Wright, Winter, and Zeigler, *Advertising*, p. 43.

35. Ibid., p. 238.

36. Ibid., p. 47.

37. Dunn and Barban, *Advertising: Its Role*, pp. 10–14.

38. Ibid., p. 75.

39. Wright, Winter, and Zeigler, *Advertising*, p. 146.

40. "TV Ad Content May Trigger Cynicism: Hellfrich to NAB," *Advertising Age*, February 3, 1964, p. 64.

41. Price, *The Best Thing on TV*, p. 2.

BIBLIOGRAPHICAL SURVEY

There have been no comprehensive critical studies of the television commercial as a genre unto itself. The research in scholarly journals often is of an applied nature, reporting on the kinds of appeals that work or assessing demographic or psychographic changes that alter the nature of target markets. Research on dramatic devices is covered sketchily in most basic texts, with techniques discussed in terms of their contribution to marketing results.

Much scholarship on television advertising is included in general works on the history of broadcasting. Erik Barnouw's *Tube of Plenty: A History of Broadcasting in the United States* is probably one of the most detailed commentaries on broadcasting development, along with his examination of the relationship between sponsor and programming practices in *The Sponsor: Notes on a Modern Potentate*.

Two volumes that trace some of the socio-cultural and economic issues related to advertising, although not specific to television, are *Advertising's Role in Society* by John S. Wright and John E. Mertis and *Advertising in Contemporary Society* by Kim B. Rotzall, James E. Haefner, and Charles B. Sandage.

Although not academic in approach, some books focus on the development of television advertising by looking at specific commercials. Two of the top works in this category are Jonathan Price's *The Best Thing on TV* and Lincoln Diamant's *Television's Classic Commercials*. Diamant includes scripts and comments on favorites such as Black Label's "Hey, Mabel," Procter and Gamble's "Meet Mr. Clean," and Old Gold's "Dancing Butts." Price takes a similar approach, but he moves into the later period of the 1960s. His book reproduces a number of storyboards and includes extensive discussion of production problems and techniques. For example, he writes humorously about the struggles of Dancer-Fitzgerald-Sample Advertising in filming commercials for Hamm's Beer. The troublesome "talent" for these spots was a kodiak bear.

For the most complete records on classic commercials, as well as information on buying or renting reels of commercials, interested persons should write the CLIO awards. CLIO awards are given annually in recognition of top performance in broadcast advertising. The organization's offices are located at 30 East Sixtieth Street; New York, New York 10022.

Occasionally, writers offer an insider's look at advertising practice. In *Thirty Seconds* by Michael J. Arlen, the details in making the "Tap Dancing" commercial of the "Reach Out" campaign for AT&T unfold in compelling fashion. Probably the best insider's look at a political advertising campaign is Joe McGinniss's *The Selling of the President, 1968*. The creative strategy and internal management of the Nixon campaign are detailed.

Advertising Age, Adweek, and *Broadcasting*, all trade publications, print most of the current information on campaigns in process. They are frontrunners in identifying trends in broadcasting and new campaigns in progress. *Advertising Age* often features review articles listing the best commercials for the past year or for some designated time. Probably one of the most important of these is Harry W. McMahan's 1964 review of 100 commercials, "The Milestone Commercials Reviewed in Television's First 16 Years: When Baby Medium Becomes a Giant." Among the ads cited are Texaco's "Man with a Star," "Speedy Alka Seltzer," M & M's "Melts in Your Mouth, Not in Your Hand," and Campbell's

"Soup and Sandwich." McMahan compiled a similar survey for the year 1967. Such articles continue to appear regularly. The great value of these publications is their timeliness and long-range view of the future of the field of advertising. The drawback is that they are published by advocates of advertising and for practitioners. True, a self-critical view is often taken, but a proponent's philosophy of advertising underlies their editorial policy.

Probably the most popular textbook on broadcast advertising is Heighton and Cunningham's *Advertising in the Broadcast Media*. Most introductory survey texts include helpful chapters on social, cultural, and economic issues and on practice in television advertising. Among them are *Advertising* by Wright, Winter, and Zeigler; *Advertising: Its Role in Modern Marketing* by Dunn and Barban; and *Basic Advertising* by Jugenheimer and White.

BOOKS AND ARTICLES

"Advertising on Cable TV: It's Working." *Broadcasting*, May 26, 1980.

Arlen, Michael J. *Thirty Seconds*. New York: Farrar, Straus, and Giroux, 1980.

Baker, Samm S. *The Permissible Lie: The Inside Truth about Advertising*. New York: World Publishing Co. 1968.

Baker, Stephen. *Systematic Approach to Advertising Creativity*. New York: McGraw Hill Book Co., 1979.

Baldwin, H. Huntley. *How Television Commercials Are Made*. Evanston, Ill.: Northwestern University, 1970.

Barnouw, Erik. *The Sponsor: Notes on a Modern Potentate*. New York: Oxford University Press, 1978.

————. *Tube of Plenty: A History of Broadcasting in the United States*. New York: Oxford University Press, 1975.

Brozen, Yale, ed. *Advertising and Society*. New York: New York University Press, 1974.

Della Femina, Jerry, and Charles Sopkin, eds. *From Those Wonderful People Who Gave You Pearl Harbor*. New York: Simon and Schuster, 1970.

Diamant, Lincoln. *Television's Classic Commercials: The Golden Years, 1945–48*. New York: Hastings House, 1971.

Dunn, S. Watson, and Arnold M. Barban. *Advertising: Its Role in Modern Marketing*. Hinsdale, Ill.: The Dryden Press, 1978.

Glatzer, Robert. *The New Advertising: The Great Campaigns from Avis to Volkswagen*. New York: Citadel Press, 1970.

Hafer, W. Keith, and Gordon E. White. *Advertising Writing: Putting Creative Strategy to Work*. New York: West Publishing Co., 1982.

Heighton, Elizabeth J., and Don R. Cunningham. *Advertising in the Broadcast Media*. Belmont, Calif.: Wadsworth Publishing Co., 1976.

Johnson, J. Douglas. *Advertising Today*. Chicago, Ill.: Science Research Associates, 1978.

Jugenheimer, Donald W., and Gordon E. White. *Basic Advertising*. Columbus, Ohio: Grid Publishing Inc., 1980.

Kingman, Merle. "13 Creative Heads Laud, Lambaste 1966 Campaigns; See Feuds, Defend Light-Hearted Ads, Young Cubs." *Advertising Age*, January 23, 1967.

Knowlton, Archa O. "The Challenges and Opportunities of the 80s." *Broadcasting*, January 7, 1980.

McGinniss, Joe. *The Selling of the President, 1968*. New York: The Trident Press, 1969.

McMahan, Harry W. "The Milestone Commercials Reviewed in Television's First 16 Years: When Baby Medium Becomes a Giant." *Advertising Age*, December 7, 1964.

———. "The 100 Best Television Commercials of 1966." *Advertising Age*, January 23, 1967.

Nelson, Roy Paul. *The Design of Advertising*. Dubuque, Iowa: William C. Brown Co., Publishers, 1981.

Ogilvy, David. *Confessions of an Advertising Man*. New York: Atheneum Publishers, 1963.

Price, Jonathan. *The Best Thing on TV: Commercials*. New York: Penguin Books, 1978.

"Public's View of TV Ads: Necessary but Annoying." *Advertising Age*, June 25, 1973.

Rice, Roger D. "Baby Medium, Television Grows Up since 1940s." *Advertising Age*, April 19, 1976.

Ross, Wallace A. *Best TV Commercials of the Year*. New York: Hastings House, 1967.

Rotzall, Kim B., James E. Haefner, and Charles H. Sandage. *Advertising in Contemporary Society: Perspectives toward Understanding*. Columbus, Ohio: Grid Publishers, 1976.

Simon, Julian L. *Issues in the Economics of Advertising*. Urbana, Ill.: University of Illinois Press, 1970.

"Television Advertising: The Way Things Were, and May Be." *Broadcasting*, November 12, 1979.

"Television Is Still the Best Buy." *Broadcasting*, November 12, 1979.

"Ten Agencies Control Half the Spending on Network TV." *Advertising Age*, August 20, 1979.

"TV Ad Content May Trigger Cynicism: Hellfrich to NAB." *Advertising Age*, February 3, 1964.

"2001: Advertising." *Broadcasting*, October 12, 1981.

Vadehra, Dave. "Best TV Campaigns." *Advertising Age*, May 25, 1981.

"Why the Criticism of Commercials?" *Broadcasting*, December 4, 1961.

Wright, John S., and John E. Mertes. *Advertising's Role in Society*. New York: West Publishing Co., 1974.

Wright, John S., Willis L. Winter, Jr., and Sherilyn L. Zeigler. *Advertising*. New York: McGraw Hill Book Co., 1982.

Index

About the Editors and Contributors

ROBERT S. ALLEY is Professor of Humanities at the University of Richmond. He is the author of *TV: Ethics for Hire* and co-author with Horace Newcomb of *The Producer's Medium*.

MICHAEL BARSON earned his Ph.D. in American Culture from Bowling Green State University in 1980. He is currently a free-lance writer based in New York City. His writings on popular literature and mass media have appeared in numerous publications.

RAYMOND L. CARROLL is Associate Professor in the Department of Broadcast & Film Communication at the University of Alabama, where he teaches broadcast programming and broadcast news analysis. He received his Ph.D. from the University of Wisconsin-Madison in 1978.

MARY B. CASSATA teaches mass communication courses and is the Director of Project Daytime, an ongoing, comprehensive research program on soap operas, at the State University of New York at Buffalo, where she is a Professor. She is the co-author of *Life on Daytime Television: Tuning-In American Serial Drama*; writes a monthly column for "Soap Opera Digest" called "Ask the Soap Doctor"; and is the co-creator of the soap opera "Getting There."

GARY EDGERTON is Assistant Professor of Radio-Television-Film at Bowling Green State University. He is the author of *American Film Exhibition and an Analysis of the Motion Picture Industry's Market Structure, 1963–1980*, as well as many articles on film and broadcasting in "The Journal of Popular Film and Television," "Journal of Popular Culture," "Quarterly Review of Film Studies," "Journal of the University Film and Video Association," and "Literature/Film Quarterly," among other sources.

DEBORAH FRANKLIN is Assistant Professor in the Department of Communication Arts at the College of Notre Dame of Baltimore, Maryland.

RICHARD GOEDKOOP is Assistant Professor of English and Communication Arts at La Salle University. He earned his Ph.D. in Speech Communication in 1980 from Penn State University. His research interests are in Television Criticism and Political Communication.

THOMAS W. HOFFER is a Professor and filmmaker in the Department of Communication, Florida State University.

FREDERIC A. LEIGH is Assistant Professor of Telecommunications at Arizona State University and manages the campus radio station, KASR. He formerly taught at the University of Nebraska at Omaha and managed public radio station KVNO.

LAWRENCE E. MINTZ is Associate Professor of American Studies at the University of Maryland. His research interests are in the study of American popular culture and American humor; he is the editor of *American Humor: an Interdisciplinary Newsletter*.

ROBERT MUSBURGER is Associate Professor in the Department of Communication, the University of Houston.

RICHARD ALAN NELSON is Associate Professor in the Department of Communication, the University of Houston.

MARTIN F. NORDEN is Associate Professor in the Department of Communication Studies at the University of Massachusetts-Amherst. He is the co-author of *Movies: A Language in Light* and the author of numerous articles on film and television.

DAVID OSTROFF is Assistant Professor and Director of Graduate Studies in the School of Speech Communication, Bowling Green State University. His published research in such periodicals as ''Journal of Broadcasting'' and ''Journalism Quarterly'' has examined policies toward new media technologies, broadcasting history, and political communication.

BROOKS ROBARDS teaches mass communication at Westfield State College in Massachusetts. A former newspaper editor and publisher, she is also a journalist and poet and has just finished writing a novel.

BRIAN G. ROSE is Assistant Professor in the Media Studies Program at Fordham University, College at Lincoln Center. He is the author of *Narrative Structure in Frank Capra's Social Films* and has written articles on television for the ''Journal of Communication'' and the ''Journal of Popular Film & Television.''

TIMOTHY SCHEURER is Chairperson of the Division of Humanities at Franklin University, Columbus, Ohio, where he also teaches courses in writing, the humanities, and popular culture. He has published articles on the film musical, Vietnam and popular culture, and popular music.

MARK SIEGEL is Associate Professor of English at the University of Wyoming, where he teaches Popular Culture, Film, and a variety of genre courses, including one on Science Fiction. He is the author of six books and over thirty articles on these subjects and others.

KAREN STODDARD is the Chairperson of the Department of Communication Arts at the College of Notre Dame of Baltimore, Maryland. She is the author of *Saints and Shrews: Women and Aging in American Popular Film* (Greenwood Press, 1983).

DATE DUE